Money Supply, Money Demand, and Macroeconomic Models

SECOND EDITION

Money Supply, Money Demand, and Macroeconomic Models

SECOND EDITION

Thomas M. Havrilesky
Duke University

John T. Boorman
International Monetary Fund

Harlan Davidson, Inc.
Arlington Heights, Illinois 60004

Library of Congress Cataloging in Publication Data

Havrilesky, Thomas M.
  Money supply, money demand, and macroeconomic models.

  Authors' names in reverse order in 1st ed. 1972.
  Includes index.
  1. Money supply. 2. Demand for money. 3. Monetary
policy. 4. Macroeconomics. I. Boorman, John T.
II. Title.
HG221.H326 1982   332.4'01   81-17423
ISBN 0-88295-408-3 (pbk.)   AACR2

85 McN 9 8 7 6 5 4 3 2

Contents

Preface

In the last decade, one of the most fertile areas of economic controversy has been monetary theory. Relegated to a relatively obscure niche in the mosaic of Keynesian developments of the 1940s and early 1950s, monetary theory surged into prominence in the 1960s. With a vanguard of established economists such as Milton Friedman, James Tobin, Don Patinkin, Karl Brunner, and Allan Meltzer leading a body of enthusiastic younger scholars, and spurred by the failures of stabilization policy, the controversies of monetary theory came into new prominence during the 1970s.

Skirmishes in the continuing struggle between Keynesians and Monetarists are increasingly in the public eye. The issues are numerous and complex: Can the money supply be readily controlled by the Federal Reserve System? Is either the money stock or some other monetary aggregate superior to "the" interest rate as a target for monetary policy? Is fiscal stabilization policy effective? These are only a sampling of the questions facing the policy-makers and their constituency. At the core of much of the controversy there lies a fundamental disagreement among economists about the nature of the supply of and demand for money and their role in macroeconomic theories.

How can the undergraduate economics student taking a course in Money and Banking or Macroeconomic Theory or a beginning graduate student be given a grounding in money supply theory, money demand theory, and their impact on macroeconomic theory sufficient to understand this profound disagreement? Aside from his own teaching skills, the economist-educator has only three tools in his arsenal: the book on money and banking, the book on macroeconomic theory, and the book of readings on monetary economics. When it comes to this task, all of these tools have evident shortcomings.

While steadily improving in theoretical content, books on money and banking traditionally have emphasized historical and institutional material. Macroeconomic theory books usually lack comprehensive study of such vital areas as money supply theory and empirical money demand. One volume books of readings on "monetary economics" often parallel the interesting but broad, descriptive precedent set by the money and banking books. In addition, their treatment of monetary theory, while it occasionally may surpass that of standard money and banking books in interpretive excellence, lacks the unity and comprehensibility of such books.

This book is intended to carry the student of monetary theory from just beyond the principles level to the level of competence expected of well-trained undergraduate economics majors. At Duke University, Rice University, and the University of Maryland, it has been used in manuscript form for specialized study by advanced undergraduates, for review by graduate students, and as a supplement to money and banking and macroeconomic theory books. The chapters are grouped into three subject areas: Part I—*Money Supply*, Part II—*Money Demand* and Part III—*Macroeconomic Models*. Each of the parts of the book is followed by a series of from 3 to 4 readings by outstanding monetary economists. The readings are selected not only because they amplify and extend the basic analysis of the preceding chapters, but also because they carry the student to the threshold of recent theoretical developments. In addition, a few readings provide the seminal insight into contemporary theoretical issues that only a masterwork can offer. Also, one of the authors has prepared his own survey of empirical studies of the demand for money as a reading following Part II.

In order to benefit from this book, the reader needs only some training in algebra and a one semester course in macroeconomic principles; differential calculus would be helpful, but is by no means necessary. Since the book's main audience consists of students, sets of class-tested questions are appended to each chapter in order to allow the student to check his understanding of the material. For further reading and for research purposes, a selected bibliography follows each chapter.

The book is not specifically addressed to monetary policy issues which lie outside the realm of monetary theory. However, most of these topics, such as Federal Reserve independence and bank merger problems, usually receive adequate treatment in standard books on money and banking, or books of readings on monetary economics. This book is not intended as a comprehensive study of all monetary theory; rather it is concerned with money supply, money demand, and their respective effects on macroeconomic models.

We are grateful for the suggestions of Professor Lloyd Atkinson, Professor William Yohe, Professor Edward Kane, and our editor, Sigurd Hermansen, as well as for the reactions of our undergraduate and graduate students at Duke University, Rice University, and the University of Maryland. We should like to thank the authors of the articles used in this book, as well as their publishers, for permission to use copyrighted material.

We are grateful to Paul Holden and Barbara Krimsky for their proofreading of the manuscript and we are especially indebted to Susan Havrilesky for her patience and her helpful comments in proofreading, typing, and retyping the manuscript.

John T. Boorman
Thomas M. Havrilesky

Introduction

A major concern of modern people is their "standard of living." There may be several ways of measuring the prosperity people enjoy, but the most popular is the level of per capita income in an economy. The level and growth of an economy's per capita income are closely related to the degree to which that economy utilizes its productive resources and thereby eliminates underemployment. However, the real value of a dollar of income also depends on the general level of prices for goods and services which that income can buy. If the general price level rises more quickly than nominal income, the real value of income declines. Consequently, modern people are concerned with the general level of prices, as well as the level of their nominal income.

Modern economists are often called upon by business and government to evaluate alternative means of maintaining and increasing human prosperity. To do this, they develop models which explain and predict the level of income, employment, and prices in the economy as a whole. These models focus on the aggregate behavior of economic entities: households, government, and business firms.

Practically all theories about the level of aggregate income, employment, and prices assign an important theoretical role to the supply of and the demand for money. This book proposes to examine theoretical issues about the supply of and the demand for money because they are so intimately related to overall prosperity and well-being in society. **xi**

The term "money" appears regularly when economists theorize about how aggregate household, business, and government behavior affects the level of aggregate income, employment, and prices. Why do economists believe that the supply of and demand for money have a more prominent effect on the level of economic activity than the supply of and demand for, say, used cars?

The answer is that economists believe that money, among all goods, performs unique functions, and because of these functions it affects and is affected by the level of income and prices. First, money functions as a *universally acceptable medium of exchange*. As there is usually a lag between the receipt and disbursement of income, money might be held to facilitate transactions. Economists long have maintained that since money is held between its receipt as income and its disbursement in exchange for goods and services, it can affect the volume of goods and services produced, or their price level, or both. For instance, a primitive theory in economics states that, as the quantity of money supplied increases, proportionately more money is exchanged for goods and services and the prices of these goods and services invariably are bid upward. One inference of this theory is that price inflation can be prevented simply if the money supply is allowed to grow at a slower rate relative to the growth of output of goods and services.

Another function of money is that it may serve as a good *store of value*. Some economists have emphasized the advantages of holding money because it can be easily converted to other asset forms with little cost or inconvenience, i.e., you do not have to "cash it in" in order to acquire another asset. Other economists have emphasized the advantages of holding money because its nominal market value is usually more predictable than that of other assets, and by holding it, individuals avoid the risk of a decline in the market value of their wealth.

Both of these approaches view holding money as an alternative to holding other assets. Therefore, the demand for money as a store of value depends on the benefits from holding other assets (for example, their yields). Since a change in the quantity of money can induce individuals to change their demand for these alternative assets, it thereby affects the prices and yields of other assets. Elementary economic theory teaches that a change in the yields of financial assets (the level of interest rates) affects the level of investment spending, and henceforth the level of income, employment, and prices in the economy.

Other less-important functions or characteristics of money have been adduced, but these two reflect its most relevant aspects in modern macroeconomic theory.

Economists differ in the emphasis they place upon the medium-of-exchange and store-of-value characteristics of money. Some eschew these *a priori* distinctions altogether, believing them to be misleading. As we shall see in chapters 2, 3 and 4, relating to the demand for money, these differences in emphasis lead to dissimilar theoretical explanations of the public's desire to hold money, which, in turn, as we discover in chapters 5, 6, and 7, lead to distinct theories about the manner in which money affects the level of income, employment, and prices.

The aggregate money supply is believed to be important in a modern economy because of its influence on the level of economic activity. Chapter 1 examines the theory of the supply of money. It develops a series of simplified models of the real-world behavior of banks and individuals as they affect the quantity of money supplied. The chapter carries the reader to the threshold of modern money-supply theory.

In elementary microeconomic theory it is learned that supply and demand determine equilibrium prices and quantities in the market. So it is with money: an hypothesis about the determination of the money supply must be combined with an hypothesis about the determination of the demand for money in order to understand how certain market variables (for example, the interest rate and the level of income) are affected. Different hypotheses about the demand for money are presented in Part II (chapters 2, 3 and 4).

When a specific hypothesis about the determination of the demand for money is combined in a more extensive macroeconomic model with specific hypotheses about the determination of: (1) the supply of money, (2) the level of aggregate expenditures, (3) the supply of and demand for labor, and (4) an assumption about the technical conditions of production, differing policy prescriptions emerge. In Part III (chapters 5 through 7), a series of macroeconomic models is developed, showing how different policy implications follow from different demand-for-money hypotheses.

We began this introduction by saying that money is believed to be an important device because it has characteristics that relate it more closely than other specific goods to theories about the determination of the level of aggregate income, employment and prices. Therefore, the seven chapters of this book are addressed primarily to basic theories of the supply of and demand for money and their impact on aggregate economic models.

Yet because theories conflict and have quite different implications for dealing with the problems of inadequate aggregate income, low employment and rapid price inflation, they are continually being challenged, tested, and refined. To capture the quality and direction of the keen intellectual competition among outstanding monetary economists, readings drawn from the professional literature follow Parts I, II, and III. Thus, this book integrates basic monetary theory and closely related readings in one volume.

On the one hand, the theoretical chapters provide the essential knowledge that students of monetary matters must have in order to appreciate fully the contemporary views presented in the readings. On the other hand, the readings really are the foundation of the book, since the controversies they reflect have influenced the authors to develop in their own chapters those aspects of basic theoretical developments that provide maximum insight into recent theoretical conflict and progress.

Introduction to the Second Edition

Since the appearance of the first edition of this book, enormous changes have occured in monetary theory. For example, because of the regulatory reform in the Monetary Control Act of 1980, the theory of money supply determination has changed considerably. Therefore, in Part I the chapter on money supply determination has been rewritten. The focus in the readings which follow the chapter is, as in the first edition, on extensions of the basic theory to interesting, practical applications. One reading examines the new definitions of the money stock which have been necessitated by regulatory reform. Because of the recent focus of the Federal Reserve on monetary aggregates, we incorporated a reading on the derivation of a key monetary aggregate, the monetary base. Finally, as in the other sections of this book, we have included an empirical survey article—in this section an article which examines empirical estimation of the basic money supply relations discussed in the preceding chapter.

The theory of the demand for money discussed in Part II has not changed so drastically as the theory of money supply. Nevertheless, important modifications in the chapters of Part II include consideration of information costs and cost-reducing innovations in the transactions demand for money, inclusion of price (inflation) expectational elements in the quantity theory formulation of the demand for money, and examination of the inflation tax on real money balances. In this section, as in the money supply section, the readings reflect extensions of the basic theory to new horizons. There are articles on portfolio theory involving assets other than money, on the short-term and long-term liquidity nominal income and price expectations effects of money on interest rates, and on the theory of the term structure of interest rates. The section closes with a survey of the empirical literature on the demand for money.

The presentation and synthesis of Keynesian and Neoclassical views of the economy is the objective of Part III. Since the appearance of the first edition it has become possible to present a smoother transition from Keynesian to Neoclassical models. Important additions in these chapters include discussions of the theory of consumption expenditures and the theory of investment expenditures, the review of the very basic Keynesian model as a theoretical starting point, a derivation of short- and long-run Phillips curves from a model of the labor market, and a discussion of the rational expectations hypothesis. In addition, at the end of the last chapter of Part III we apply the aggregate supply–aggregate demand model to a number of contemporary problems, for example, cost-push inflation and the effect of inflation on the nominal rate of interest.

As in Parts I and II the readings serve to expand upon and present extensions of the theories presented in the preceeding chapters. Part III continues this mode. There is a reading on transmission mechanisms in Keynesian and Neoclassical models, a reading on the Phillips curve and the rational-expectations hypothesis, and a reading on the financing constraint in Keynesian models. As in previous sections, there is also an empirical survey article—in this case one which reviews representative Keynesian and Monetarist econometric models of the economy.

PART I
MONEY SUPPLY

ONE
A Framework for the Determination of the Money Supply

Introduction

While it has frequently been assumed in both theoretical and empirical analyses that the money stock is determined unequivocally by the monetary authority, this tradition is being superseded by an alternative approach that views the money supply as an endogenously determined variable. It is now customary to present the determination of the money stock as a process which results from the complex interaction of the behavior of various economic agents rather than as a process dominated solely by an external authority.

To understand the work being done in this field, it is necessary to examine both the behavior of the various groups that influence the money supply and the institutional framework within which this behavior occurs. In this chapter we shall describe this framework and the role of these behavioral patterns. The analysis begins with the derivation of the bank reserve equation from the Federal Reserve balance sheet and the monetary accounts of the Treasury.

Monetary Accounts

The primary business of depositary institutions is to issue deposit liabilities to the public and to acquire income-earning financial assets

3

with the funds created through these deposits. The characteristic that best distinguishes depositary institutions from the other (non-depositary) institutions in our financial system is their ability to issue deposit liabilities that are due on demand, that is, deposit liabilities that may be converted into currency or legal tender money immediately upon request of the depositor or transferred to another person simply by writing a check. No other institutions in our system may issue liabilities with this characteristic.[1] Essentially it is the acceptance by the public of these liabilities as "money" which explains their preeminent role in our economy.

The money supply, narrowly defined, consists of currency in circulation, traveler's checks, and the deposits upon which checks can be drawn for the payment of debts to third parties. This measure of the money supply is labeled M-1B by the Federal Reserve. There are broader measures which include deposits that cannot always be used in making payments.[2] In September 1983, the average total money supply, M-1, in the United States was approximately 516 billion dollars. Over 70 percent of this amount, 305 billion dollars, consisted of "checkable" deposit liabilities of the nation's depositary institutions.

There are several types of depositary institutions. Commercial banks provide demand deposit accounts upon which checks may be drawn but on which no interest is paid. They also offer automatic transfer from savings (ATS) accounts and negotiable orders for withdrawal (NOW and Super-NOW) accounts. Checks may be drawn on both of these and both may pay interest. Noninterest-bearing demand deposits and interest-bearing accounts on which checks may be drawn are also provided by mutual savings banks, savings and loan associations, and credit unions in the form of ATS accounts, NOW accounts, and share draft accounts. At present the bulk of "checkable" deposits in the United States is composed of noninterest-bearing demand deposits in commercial banks. However, the fractions that are provided by nonbank depositary institutions are growing.

As creators of money, depositary institutions are subject to special regulation and supervision. For example, they are required to hold

---

[1]Money which has been declared "legal tender" by the government must be accepted as payment for all debts, public and private. In the United States, Treasury issues and Federal Reserve notes which form the bulk of our "paper money," have been declared "legal tender."

[2]The reading by Neil G. Berkman which follows this chapter defines this monetary aggregate and other related monetary aggregates.

Table 1.1. Consolidated Balance Sheet of the Twelve Federal Reserve Banks

Assets	Liabilities and Net Worth
Gold certificates	Federal Reserve notes outstanding
Special drawing rights certificates	Member reserve deposits
Cash	Deposits due to
Federal Reserve credit	The US Treasury
US government securities	Foreign depositors
Acceptances	Other
Discounts and advances	Other (capital and minor items)
Float	
Other	

some of their assets in a legally approved form specified by the Federal Reserve System. Specifically, for every dollar of deposit liabilities outstanding, depositary institutions must hold some fraction (also set by the monetary authority) in one of the approved asset forms. For example, institutions that are members of the Federal Reserve System are currently permitted to hold their legally required reserves either in the form of deposit balances at a district Federal Reserve bank or as cash in their own vaults.[3] As a result of these requirements, the most important restrictions on the volume of deposit liabilities outstanding at any time are the fractional reserve requirements set by the monetary authority and the stock of legal reserves that are available for these institutions to hold.

In this section we shall examine the accounts of the Federal Reserve banks and the United States Treasury to determine how the stock of these reserve funds is created. We begin with a consolidated balance sheet of the twelve Federal Reserve banks (Table 1.1).

The twelve Federal Reserve district banks, like depositary institutions, issue deposit liabilities (claims against themselves held primarily by member institutions, the US Treasury, and foreign central banks and institutions) and purchase income-earning assets (primarily U.S. government securities and loans to commercial banks).[4] In addition,

---

[3]Both member and nonmember institutions may satisfy their reserve requirements with vault cash or a Federal Reserve account. In addition, nonmember institutions may maintain required reserves with another institution which maintains reserve balances at the Federal Reserve, on a passthrough basis, or at a Federal Home Loan Bank or the National Credit Union Administration's Central Liquidity Facility. In this chapter we shall assume for simplicity that all reserve balances are held at the Federal Reserve.

these banks issue Federal Reserve notes (claims against the district banks which serve as the primary form of paper money used in the United States) and hold gold certificates (claims against the gold stock owned by the Treasury) as well as special drawing rights certificates.[5]

A glance at the consolidated balance sheet in Table 1.1 shows that if the entire currency stock consisted of Federal Reserve notes, the total amount of funds available to be held as reserves would depend upon the willingness of the Federal Reserve to issue certain liabilities (Federal Reserve notes outstanding and reserve deposits of member institutions) and on the distribution of the Federal Reserve notes between these institutions and the public. However, the Treasury also has the power to issue currency, and these coins and notes perform the same functions as Federal Reserve notes. Therefore, if the Treasury increased the volume of its outstanding currency (by making expenditures with newly printed bills, for example) there would be more funds available to be held by the public or by depositary institutions as vault cash. Since vault cash can be counted as reserves by depositary institutions, the issuance of Treasury currency could increase total bank reserves.

We may account for the influence of Treasury currency on reserves by means of the *reserve equation*. Basically, the reserve equation is an accounting statement that lists sources and uses of funds which are potentially available as reserves. This statement is derived by modifying the consolidated balance sheet of the Federal Reserve banks to take account of Treasury influences on the monetary system. The reserve equation is as shown in Table 1.2.

A reconciliation between this statement and the consolidated Federal Reserve bank balance sheet is fairly easy to establish. All the accounts listed under "Federal Reserve credit" and "deposit liabilities

---

[4]Loans to member institutions based on their own promissory notes and a corresponding pledge of collateral are called "advances." Either U.S. government securities or eligible paper may be required as collateral. Eligible paper consists of evidences of debt which have been acquired from customers for short-term operating loans. Loans to member institutions based on eligible paper that is "sold" directly to the Federal Reserve bank (rediscounted) are called "discounts." Of the two forms, advances are the more popular because of the difficulty an institution may have in finding the exact desired quantity of eligible paper for discounting.

[5]Special drawing rights certificates are instruments allocated by the International Monetary Fund to participants in the special drawing account of the Fund. Special drawing rights are generally counted as part of a country's international reserves and may be transferred between central banks in exchange for foreign currencies.

Table 1.2. The Reserve Equation

Sources	
Federal Reserve credit	Currency in circulation outside the Federal
US government securities *largest*	Reserve, the Treasury, and depositary
Acceptances	institutions (i.e., currency in circulation
Discounts and advances	with the public)*
Float	Treasury cash holdings*
Gold stock*	Deposit liabilities of the Federal Reserve
Treasury currency outstanding*	due to:
Special drawing rights	The Treasury
	Foreign depositors
	Others
	Other accounts (net)
	Reserves:
	Member institution reserve deposits plus
	vault cash

*Explained in text.

of the Federal Reserve" appear in the reserve equation exactly as in the Federal Reserve balance sheet. The modifications made in the other accounts are as follows:

Treasury currency outstanding. This account includes all current monetary liabilities of the U.S. Treasury. It appears as a source of reserve funds since any currency issued by the Treasury could find its way into the monetary system and, as vault cash in that system, could serve as reserves. For example, if an employee of the Federal government were to be paid in newly printed paper money issued by the Treasury, he or she would be perfectly free to take this currency to a commercial bank and deposit it in his or her account with that bank. In either case it would increase both deposit liabilities and reserves (in the form of vault cash). When the Treasury first pays out the newly issued currency, according to the reserve equation, a source of funds, namely, Treasury currency outstanding, and a use of funds, namely, currency in circulation with the public, would both increase. When this currency is deposited with a commercial bank, an alternative use of funds, currency in circulation with the public, would decrease, and reserves (vault cash) would increase. Hence the net effect of these transactions would be to increase reserves.

There are two other differences between the Federal Reserve

balance sheet and the reserve equation that involve Treasury currency. One difference is that *cash* in the Federal Reserve balance sheet refers simply to Treasury currency in the vaults of the Federal Reserve banks. In the reserve equation, this item is included under "Treasury currency outstanding." Thus Treasury currency outstanding in the reserve equation refers to the total stock of outstanding currency issued by the Treasury, whether held by the public, depositary institutions, or the Federal Reserve. A second difference is that Federal Reserve notes outstanding appear as a single, explicit item in the Federal Reserve balance sheet, but in the reserve equation these central bank liabilities are divided among several different accounts. Federal Reserve notes held by the public are combined with Treasury currency held by the public under "total currency in circulation." Federal Reserve notes held by the Treasury are included under "Treasury cash holdings." And Federal Reserve notes held by depositary institutions appear together with their holdings of outstanding Treasury currency as "vault cash" under reserves. As a result, the difference between Federal Reserve notes outstanding in the Federal Reserve balance sheet and Federal Reserve notes in circulation with the public, listed under "currency in circulation" in the reserve equation, is that the latter account excludes notes held by the Treasury and notes held by depositary institutions. These modifications provide some insight into currency flows between the public, the depositary institutions, and the Treasury, and their effects on the reserves.

2. **Gold stock.** A further modification made in deriving the reserve equation involves the treatment of the gold stock. Gold certificates, claims against the gold stock that are held by the Treasury, are issued by the Treasury and held by the Federal Reserve banks. The difference between the volume of gold certificates outstanding (all of which are held by Federal Reserve banks) and the total Treasury gold stock is obviously that value of gold against which no certificates have been issued. This is gold held by the Treasury for backing of certain outstanding Treasury currencies and other minor uses. It generally represents a very small portion of the total gold stock and is included within the category of "Treasury cash holdings." Hence the reserve equation includes the entire Treasury gold stock as a source of reserves, and counts under the category of "Treasury cash holdings" (as an alternative use of those funds) that value of the Treasury gold stock which does not have gold certificate claims outstanding against it.

gold stock = Total gold stock - vol of gold certs outstanding

Hence the differences between the Federal Reserve balance sheet and the reserve equation involve only the issuance and holding of currency within the monetary system (specifically, the role of the Treasury in this process) and the treatment of the Treasury gold stock and of special drawing rights.

The reserve equation is written to focus attention on total reserves (either reserve deposits held at Federal Reserve banks or vault cash). A more useful concept that will find frequent application in the following discussion involves the combined measure of total reserves and currency in circulation. This quantity, referred to as the *monetary base* (or high-powered money, or reserve money), can easily be derived from the reserve equation.[6] This derivation is as follows:

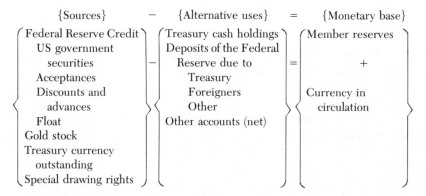

Although the Federal Reserve cannot control all accounts in the monetary base equation, its absolute control over one account, the volume of U.S. government securities that it chooses to hold in its portfolio, gives the Federal Reserve an adequate means to offset or to supplement changes that occur in any of the other accounts in the statement. Therefore, control over its own holdings of government securities provides the Federal Reserve with the necessary power to determine the size of the monetary base. The Federal Reserve can use open market operations not only to offset a decrease in reserve money

[6]For an interesting perspective on this equation, see Leonall C. Andersen, "Three Approaches to Money Stock Determination," *Federal Reserve Bank of St. Louis Review* (October 1967), 6–13. See also Jerry L. Jordan, "Elements of Money Stock Determination," *Review*, Federal Reserve Bank of St. Louis, vol. 51 (October 1969), 10–19 reprinted in Thomas M. Havrilesky and John T Boorman, *Current Issues in Monetary Theory and Policy* (Arlington Heights, IL: AHM Publishing Corporation, 1980).

caused by a small gold outflow or by an increase in Treasury deposits, but also to bring about a substantial net increase in the total monetary base.

In the next section we will analyze the link between the monetary base and the nation's money supply. We then will examine the means by which control over the monetary base allows the Federal Reserve to determine the size of the money stock. In Chapter 7 of this book we will see how various assumptions about the determination of the money stock may be incorporated into aggregate models of the determination of income, employment, and price level.

The Mechanism of Money Supply Expansion

Introduction

The derivation of the monetary base equation represents the first step in the analysis of the monetary system of the United States. The money stock is customarily defined as *currency in circulation* (that is, currency outside depositary institutions, the Federal Reserve, and the Treasury) and *checkable deposits adjusted*. Certain minor difficulties are introduced into the analysis by the fact that checkable deposits adjusted and total deposits are not the same. The differences are caused by the special treatment of the deposits of the U.S. government (the tax and loan accounts), interbank deposits, and other minor items such as deposits "in the process of clearing." These differences are relatively minor, will not affect our results in any substantive manner, and therefore will be ignored in the remainder of this chapter.

A more important consideration which makes this presentation somewhat unrealistic is the fact that not all depositary institutions belong to the Federal Reserve System[7] and that the legal reserve requirement depends on the size of the institution's deposits.[8] In the

---

[7]See footnote 3.

[8]All depositary institutions' demand deposits, NOW accounts, ATS accounts, share drafts, and accounts subject to telephonic transfer or preauthorized transfer are subject to a 3 percent reserve requirement on the first $25 million of such accounts. Such accounts in excess of $25 million are subject to a reserve requirement within a range of 8 to 14 percent; currently this requirement is 12 percent. The $25 million breakpoint will be adjusted every year-(end) by four fifths of the percentage change in such accounts over the year.

Nonpersonal time deposits are time deposits that are transferable or held by a depositor other than a natural person. These consist primarily of large certificates of deposit. They are subject to a reserve requirement of from 0 to 9 percent. Currently that

presentation which follows we shall abstract from these complications. We will assume that the reserve requirement ratios on checkable deposits employed refer to weighted average requirements which take account of these special institutional arrangements and that all depositary institutions hold reserve balances at the Federal Reserve or, on a passthrough basis, at institutions that are Fed members.

This part of the chapter will indicate the way in which the total money supply depends on the size of the monetary base and the allocation of that base between reserves and currency holdings. The discussion proceeds on the basis of extremely restrictive simplifying assumptions concerning the operation of depositary institutions and the public's asset preferences. These assumptions will be successively relaxed in order to produce more realistic models.

Throughout this chapter, static equilibrium models shall be employed to analyze and describe the mechanism of money supply expansion (and contraction). The models will consist of systems of equations with interdependencies among the relevant variables. In the initial formulations of these models, all the equations will be linear in form and will embody either a simplified description of the behavior of some agent important in the determination of the money stock, or an institutional, legal, or definitional relation required to characterize our monetary system. Later, certain nonlinear forms will be introduced. The solution of these systems of equations will yield equilibrium values for the dependent variables. These are values which could be maintained indefinitely in the absence of changes in the behavioral, institutional, or legal characteristics (parameters) of the model. Through the use of these models, the following types of questions shall be addressed: By what amount will the money supply change if legal reserve requirements are raised by one percent? Or, by what amount will the volume of checkable deposit liabilities change if the monetary authority allows the monetary base to increase by one billion dollars?

Model 1.A.   Monetary System with Commercial Banks Issuing Only Demand Deposits

The analysis begins with a set of very restrictive assumptions. First, as a matter of expository simplicity we assume that commercial banks are

---

requirement is 3 percent on all such deposits with maturities of less than 4 years. Such deposits of longer than 4-year maturity and other time and savings deposits are not subject to a reserve requirement.

the only depositary institutions. We, therefore, may use the words "bank" and "depositary institution" interchangeably. Second, these 2 "banks" (depositary institutions) issue only noninterest-bearing demand deposit liabilities and these deposits comprise the total money supply (the nonbank public holds no currency). Third, we assume that banks 3 automatically create as great a volume of demand deposit liabilities as is legally possible with the reserves at their disposal. In short, banks (depositary institutions) desire no reserves in excess of legal requirements.

The symbols which shall be employed in our analysis are defined as follows:

Variables

RT	Total reserves
RR	Reserves legally required against deposit liabilities; $RR_D + RR_C = RR$
RR_D	Reserves legally required against checkable deposit liabilities; $RR_D = r \cdot DD + r \cdot ID$
RR_C	Reserves legally required against certificates of deposit; $RR_C = b \cdot CD$
RE	Excess reserves of depositary institutions
RB	Borrowed reserves
RU	Unborrowed reserves; $RU = RT - RB$
C	Currency holdings of the public, excluding vault cash of depositary institutions
DD	Noninterest-bearing deposits that are transferable by check or wire, e.g., demand deposits
ID	Interest-bearing deposits that are transferable by check or wire, e.g., NOW accounts, ATS accounts, share drafts and accounts subject to telephonic transfer or preauthorized transfer
$DD + ID$	Checkable deposits
TD	Time and savings deposits
CD	Certificates of deposit
B	Monetary base; $B = RT + C$
i_m	A rate of interest on marketable securities
i_{ID}	Interest rate on interest-bearing transferable deposits
i_{CD}	Interest rate on large certificates of deposit
M	Money stock; $M = DD + ID + C$
L	Loans outstanding at depositary institutions

$RT = RR + RE$

Abstracting from all but the most relevant accounts and assuming that net worth is zero, the balance sheet of an individual bank in this system appears as follows:

A Single Commercial Bank in a Multibank System
(millions of dollars)

Assets		Liabilities and Net Worth	
Reserves (reserve deposits with the Federal Reserve plus vault cash)	20	Demand deposits	100
Loans and securities	80		

Under the assumption that the legal reserve requirement on demand deposits is 20 percent ($r = .20$), this depositary institution would be required to hold twenty cents in reserves for each dollar of deposit liabilities. Therefore, it is exactly meeting its legal reserve requirements by holding 20 million dollars in reserves against total deposit liabilities of 100 million dollars.

Assume that, by means of a sale of securities which it currently holds in its asset portfolio, this bank increases its reserves by 10 million dollars to 30 million dollars. For example, the bank may sell these securities to the Federal Reserve in return for an increase in the bank's reserve deposit account of $10 million. In the bank reserve equation, a source of bank reserves, U.S. government security holdings of the Federal Reserve, has increased by $10 million. Since there is no corresponding decrease in any other source of funds and no increase in any alternative use of funds, this transaction increases total bank reserves by $10 million, the amount of the security purchase by the Federal Reserve.[9]

Bank A—Balance Sheet
(millions of dollars)

Assets		Liabilities and Net Worth	
Reserves	30	Demand deposits	100
Loans and securities	70		

[9]This transaction is assumed simply as a starting point for our analysis. It should be noted that such a transaction could generally occur only at the initiative of the Federal Reserve with the cooperation of the bank. In usual circumstances, the Fed buys from government securities dealers. The dealer may or may not be acting as a broker for a commercial bank.

Bank A is now holding $10 million in reserves *in excess* of the amount required against its deposit liabilities.

By what amount can this bank expand its loan and security holdings and its demand deposit liabilities on the basis of these new reserves (that is, what volume of loans and securities can this bank purchase through the creation of demand deposit liabilities)? Let us assume that we are dealing with a small commercial bank in a large multibank system and that the demand deposit created in the process of making the loan will be spent by the borrower. Unless the bank is geographically isolated and has some degree of regional monopoly, it must consider the possibility that the person receiving the check will deposit it at a different bank (call it Bank B). When the check is deposited in the recipient's account at Bank B and cleared against the borrower's account at the lending bank (Bank A), the lending bank will lose reserves to Bank B in an amount equal to the value of the check. Since people usually borrow to facilitate expenditures, it is quite reasonable to assume that checks equal to the total value of the loan will soon be drawn against the new account in the lending bank, therefore causing that bank to lose reserves in the amount of the newly created deposits.[10]

Under these circumstances, the lending bank (Bank A) is in a position to lend only an amount equal to the reserves that it can afford to lose without impairing its legal responsibility to maintain 20 percent of the value of its original deposit liabilities in the form of reserves. In other words, given some original level of deposits, it may lend and hence create new demand deposits in an amount equal to the difference between total reserve holdings RT and reserves required against those original deposits RR, an amount equal to excess reserves RE, that is, $RE = RT - RR$.

The above process is depicted in the following balance sheets:

---

[10]This statement would have to be modified in a situation in which the lending bank requires the borrower to maintain a "compensating balance," that is, a balance equal to some percentage of the loan, on deposit at the lending bank for the duration of the loan contract. This, in effect, lowers the usable value of the loan to the borrower and raises the effective rate of interest. This modification could affect our analysis of the operation of an individual bank, but it would not change our conclusions about the operation of the commercial banking system as a whole in any substantial way. See Joseph E. Burns, "Compensating Balance Requirements: Integral to Bank Lending," *Business Review*, Federal Reserve Bank of Dallas (July 1972), 1–8.

Bank A—Balance Sheet
Before Extension of New Loans
(millions of dollars)

Assets		Liabilities	
Reserves	30	Demand deposits	100
Loans and securities	70		
Addendum: $RT = 30$			
$RR = 20[(.20)(100)]$			
$RE = 10$			

Bank A—Balance Sheet
After Extension of $10 Million in Loans through the Creation of Demand Deposits
(millions of dollars)

Assets		Liabilities	
Reserves	30	Demand deposits	110
Loans and securities	80		

Now if, as assumed, the borrower spends the amount of the loan and this check is deposited in another bank (Bank B), when the check clears, the lending bank (Bank A) will lose deposits and reserves equal to the amount of the new deposit created by the loan:

Bank A—Balance Sheet[11]
(millions of dollars)

Assets		Liabilities	
Reserves	20	Demand deposits	100
Loans and securities	80		

For Bank B, the recipient bank, deposit liabilites and reserves will increase by an equal amount.

[11]Although this balance sheet appears to be exactly the same as the initial balance sheet assumed for Bank A, one important change must be noted. In moving from the initial position to this final equilibrium the bank sold government securities for reserves and then lost the reserves after the expenditure of the deposit which was created in the loan transaction. In effect, government securities have been exchanged for an I.O.U. from a private party, say a corporation. This changes the characteristics of the asset portfolio of Bank A and may have further repercussions on its behavior.

Bank B—Changes in Balance Sheet
(millions of dollars)

Assets		Liabilities	
Reserves	+10	Demand deposits	+10

Note: Only the *changes* in Bank B's balance sheet are shown as it is assumed that prior to this transaction Bank B was exactly meeting its legal reserve requirements.

There are many mechanisms through which the transfer of the demand deposit assumed in this example may be facilitated. For simplicity, assume that both banks maintain their reserves in the form of deposit balances with their district Federal Reserve bank. In this case the check can clear through the Federal Reserve System. The clearance will take place when the Federal Reserve bank decreases Bank A's reserve balances by $10 million, the amount of the check, and increases Bank B's (the recipient bank's) reserve deposit account by an equal amount. There is no change in total reserves in the system, but the check clearing process has lowered the reserves of the lending bank and increased the reserves of the bank of deposit (the recipient bank).

After this transaction is completed, Bank A has $20 million in reserves and $100 million in demand deposit liabilities. With a reserve requirement of 20 percent, it is exactly meeting its legal reserve requirements. If it had loaned out more than $10 million, the amount of its excess reserves, the expenditure of that amount by the borrower would have reduced its reserves below $20 million, resulting in a deficiency of legal reserves. Likewise, if it had loaned less than $10 million, it would have something over $20 million in reserves against its $100 million deposit liabilities, and would still have excess reserves that it did not desire (by assumption) and that could facilitate further expansion. Thus we may conclude that, in a large multibank system in which individual banks are small relative to the system and in which banks do not desire to hold reserves in excess of the legal minimum, *a single bank will lend an amount exactly equal to its excess reserves and no more.*

But what about Bank B? It was assumed that this bank was exactly meeting its reserve requirements before the inflow of reserves took place. After the $10 million increase in both its demand deposit liabilities and its reserve balances (assuming a required reserve ratio of .20 on demand deposits) it must hold an additional $2 million in reserves against these newly acquired deposit liabilities. But since its total reserves have increased by $10 million, it now has $8 million in excess reserves ($RT - RR = RE;$ $10 million $-$ $2 million $=$ $8 million). Bank B will expand its loans by creating $8 million in new demand deposit liabilities. When the borrower spends the newly created demand deposit, in accordance with our previous assumption, these funds will be deposited in another bank, Bank C. The lending bank (Bank B) will lose both reserves and deposit liabilities equal to the amount of the expenditure, $8 million.

Bank B—Changes in Balance Sheet
After Loan Expansion and Check Clearing Process
(millions of dollars)

Assets		Liabilities	
Reserves	+2	Demand deposits	+10
Loans and securities	+8		

Bank C will gain an equal volume of both reserves and deposit liabilities.

Bank C—Changes in Balance Sheet
(millions of dollars)

Assets		Liabilities	
Reserves	+8	Demand deposits	+8

Bank C now has 6.4 million dollars that it can lend out. Its reserves required against newly created deposit liabilities are $1.6 million ($8 million $\times$ .20 = $1.6 million). It has excess reserves of $6.4 million ($8 million $-$ $1.6 million = $6.4 million). This process will continue until all these reserve funds have been absorbed into required reserves at various banks.

The amounts loaned and the deposits created at each stage in this process may be summed to calculate the total loan and deposit expansion for the banking system as a whole. Bank A loaned out an amount x, equal to its excess reserves (in this example, $x = $10 million). This amount cleared against Bank A and became the reserves of Bank B. But

Bank B's demand deposit *liabilities* increased by the same amount x. Consequently, Bank B could loan out only an amount equal to $(x - rx)$, that is, the amount of its new total reserves x in excess of its new requirements rx. This amount cleared against Bank B and became the reserves of Bank C. Bank C, therefore, can loan out an amount equal to its new reserves $(x - rx)$ in excess of new requirements, that is, an amount $(x - rx) - r(x - rx)$. By a continuous process one may add the amounts loaned out at each stage in the expansion process and derive the total expansion of loans, deposits, and the money supply. This process is demonstrated in Table 1-3.

Since the expansion at each step in this sequence may be represented as the expansion in the previous step times some constant factor $(1 - r)$, the process may be represented by a geometric series; the total expansion of demand deposits and loans may be expressed as follows:

$$\Delta DD = x + (x - rx) + [(x - rx) - r(x - rx)] + \cdots$$
$$= x + x(1 - r) + x(1 - r)^2 + \cdots + x(1 - r)^n.$$

Thus, as the sum of a geometric progression, total expansion is equal to[12]

$$\Delta DD = \frac{x - x(1 - r)^{n+1}}{1 - (1 - r)} . \qquad (1.1)$$

But as n, the number of stages in the expansion process, becomes large, this expression simplifies greatly; for if $r < 1$, which it always will be,

$$\lim_{n \to \infty} \frac{x - x(1 - r)^{n+1}}{1 - (1 - r)} = \frac{1}{r^x} = \frac{1}{r} \Delta B \qquad (1.2)$$

where r is the reserve requirement on demand deposits and x is the initial injection of excess reserves (the change in the monetary base, ΔB). Thus the total expansion of loans and deposits in the entire multibank system in our example will be $(1/.20)$ ($10 million) = (5) ($10 million) = $50 million.

---

[12]Let $k = x + x(1 - r) + x(1 - r)^2 + \cdots + x(1 - r)^n$. Then $(1 - r)k = x(1 - r) + x(1 - r)^2 + \cdots + x(1 - r)^n + x(1 - r)^{n+1}$. Subtracting, $k - (1 - r)k = x - x(1 - r)^{n+1}$. Factoring the left-hand side and dividing.

$$k = \frac{x - x(1 - r)^{n+1}}{1 - (1 - r)} .$$

Table 1.3. Banking System Expansion on the Basis of New Reserves (millions of dollars)

	Deposits Received in Check Clearing Process	Reserves Required against Received Deposits	Reserves in Excess of Legal Requirements	Demand Deposits Created in the Loan Process	Reserves and Deposits Lost in Check Clearing Process
Bank A	—	—	10	10	10
Bank B	$10 = x$	2	8	$x - rx = 8$	8
Bank C	$8 = x - rx$	1.6	6.4	$x(1 - r)^2 = 6.4$	6.4
Bank D	$6.4 = x(1 - r)^2$	1.28	5.12	$x(1 - r)^3 = 5.12$	5.12
Bank E	$5.12 = x(1 - r)^3$	1.024	4.096	$x(1 - r)^4 = 4.096$	4.096
Bank F	$4.096 = x(1 - r)^4$	.819	3.277	$x(1 - r)^5 = 3.277$	3.277
Bank G	$3.277 = x(1 - r)^5$	.655	2.622	$x(1 - r)^6 = 2.622$	2.622
Bank H	$2.622 = x(1 - r)^6$				
⋮		⋮		⋮	
Total	50.0	10.0		50.0	

An Alternative Approach

The multiple expansion of the loans and demand deposit liabilities of depositary institutions may be demonstrated much more succinctly with the aid of a model that assumes a few simple relationships between the monetary base, reserves, and demand deposits. By the assumption of no currency in circulation, the first of these basic relations is

$$B = RT \tag{1.3}$$

That is, in the absence of currency holdings by the nonbank public, the entire monetary base would consist of reserves. Furthermore, by assuming that banks wish to hold no reserves in excess of the legal requirements, total reserves would be employed solely as reserves required against demand deposit liabilities. This relationship would be implied by a model that assumed that profit maximization was the goal of bank management, and that bank portfolio managers had perfect knowledge (certainty) about the safety, risk, and liquidity characteristics of both their assets and their liabilities. Under these conditions bankers would always prefer interest yielding loans and securities to noninterest yielding reserve balances, and the presence of excess reserves would immediately generate an expansion of deposits as banks attempted to replace reserve balances with earning assets.

Therefore, equilibrium—the absence of any current forces for change—would prevail only when, for each individual bank and for the banking system as a whole, total reserves were employed solely as required reserves against demand deposit liabilities:

$$RT = RR_D \tag{1.4}$$

$$RR_D = r \cdot DD = RT. \tag{1.5}$$

Substitution of Equation (1.5) into Equation (1.3) yields

$$B = r \cdot DD$$

$$DD = (1/r)B \tag{1.6}$$

or, in terms of changes in the levels of the variables,

$$\Delta DD = (1/r) \, (\Delta B). \tag{1.7}$$

The term $1/r$ is referred to as the demand deposit expansion coefficient since it defines the relation between a given change in the size of the monetary base and the expansion of demand deposits which that change will bring about. This expression is identical to Equation (1.2) derived above. The emphasis in that derivation, however, was on the logic of $1/r$ as the outcome of an explicit behavioral process.

The assumptions required to derive the conclusion stated in Equation (1.7) include the following:

(1) Banks issue only noninterest-bearing demand deposit liabilities.

(2) There is no currency in the system.

(3) Banks desire to hold no reserves in excess of legal requirements, that is, banks are assumed to be profit maximizers in a regime of perfect knowledge.

(4) Individual banks suffer a loss of reserves in the expenditure and check clearing process equal to the amount of loans they extend.

Note: the fourth assumption was made for convenience and is not necessary for the result presented above.

In the discussion which follows we relax some of these simplifying assumptions. We examine more realistic models of loan and deposit expansion by successively adding currency, interest-bearing deposits, and time deposit holdings of the public and desired holdings of excess legal reserves and borrowings of depositary institutions. In this process only the monetary base equation is considered. We leave it to the reader to derive the manner in which the geometric expansion of demand deposits takes place under these new assumptions through the flow of reserve funds among individual banks.

Model 1.B.   A Monetary System that Includes Both Currency Holdings and Demand Deposits

Let us now introduce currency holdings into the system. We continue, for expository simplicity, to use the words "bank" and "depositary institution" interchangeably. We continue to assume that there are no interest-bearing deposits and that banks wish to hold no excess legal reserves. Under these assumptions the monetary base is defined as the sum of total reserves plus currency in circulation:

$$B = RT + C \tag{1.8}$$

So long as we continue to assume that banks issue no interest-bearing deposits and that desired reserves in excess of legal requirements are zero, banks will be in equilibrium (in the sense of desiring no expansion or contraction of loans and deposits) only when all reserves are required against their demand deposit liabilities. Thus,

$$RR_D = r \cdot DD \tag{1.9}$$

$$RT = RR_D = r \cdot DD \tag{1.10}$$

Substitution of Equation (1.9) or (1.10) into (1.8) yields

$$B = r \cdot DD + C. \tag{1.11}$$

Within this model the nonbank public determines the *relative* amounts of currency and demand deposits it holds. Although the size of the total money stock (or the monetary base) may actively be controlled by the monetary authorities, the composition of that stock is determined by the public's own preferences. However, from Equation (1.8) it can be seen that the greater the public's currency holdings, the smaller the stock of funds available out of a given monetary base to serve as reserves against demand deposit liabilities. Therefore, the total level of deposit liabilities and loans outstanding at commercial banks will depend on the public's relative preferences for the different forms in which they may hold their monetary assets.

Rewriting Equation (1.11), we derive the following basic relation:

$$DD = (1/r)(B - C). \tag{1.12}$$

Writing this relation in a form that expresses the change in the stock of deposits with respect to a change in the base,

$$\Delta DD = (1/r)(\Delta B - \Delta C). \tag{1.13}$$

If the monetary base changes, but currency holdings of the public remain constant ($\Delta C = 0$), then $\Delta DD = (1/r)(\Delta B)$, which is identical to Equation (1.2). Thus if we include currency holdings within our model but assume that those holdings remain constant, the expansion mechanism of the commercial banking system is seen to operate exactly as in a model that assumes that no currency is held by the public. However, rather than assuming that currency holdings remain constant, it may be more realistic to assume that the public desires to hold the components of its total monetary wealth ($DD + C$) in fixed proportions.

Assume, for example, that the public wishes to maintain a 4:1 ratio between its holdings of demand deposits and currency, that is, for each dollar held in checking accounts, individuals wish to hold twenty-five cents in currency. This may be expressed as follows:

$$C = s \cdot DD = .25 \cdot DD \tag{1.14}$$

and for changes in the levels of these variables,

$$\Delta C = s \cdot \Delta DD = .25 \cdot \Delta DD. \tag{1.15}$$

Substitute this expression into the bank reserve Equation (1.11) as follows:

$$\begin{aligned}
\Delta B &= r \cdot \Delta DD + \Delta C \\
&= r \cdot \Delta DD + s \cdot \Delta DD \\
&= \Delta DD(r + s)
\end{aligned}$$

$$\Delta DD = \frac{1}{r + s} (\Delta B). \tag{1.16}$$

Assume, as before, that $r = .20$, $s = .25$, and bank reserves increase by $10 million, $\Delta B = \$10$ million,

$$\Delta DD = \frac{1}{r + s} (\Delta B) = \frac{1}{.20 + .25} (\$10 \text{ million}) = \frac{1}{.45} (\$10 \text{ million})$$

$$= (2.22)(\$10 \text{ million}) = \$22.22 \text{ million}.$$

Thus an increase in the monetary base of $10 million (which supplies undesired excess reserves to the banking system and thereby disrupts the initial equilibrium and stimulates expansion) will bring about an increase in demand deposits outstanding of $22.22 million.

When we assumed that there were no currency holdings, an increase in the monetary base of $10 million increased demand deposit liabilities by $50 million; but with currency holdings introduced, the same expansion in the base increases deposit liabilities by only $22.22 million. In the first model, every new dollar of funds supplied by the increase in the monetary base was available to serve as reserve backing for newly created demand deposits. In the second model, *for every dollar of demand deposits created, an additional twenty-five cents is withdrawn from the banking system by the public to be held in the form of currency.* Currency drains represent a decrease in the amount of funds remaining within the banking system available to be held as reserves against deposit liabilities. Therefore, with an assumed currency drain, the given increase in the base supports a smaller increase in the volume of deposit liabilities than would occur in the absence of such a drain.

By how much will currency holdings increase in this process? This figure may be derived from the actual change that occurred in demand deposits:

$$\Delta C = s \cdot \Delta DD$$
$$= (.25)\ (\$22.22\ \text{million}) = \$5.56\ \text{million}$$

or by substitution,

$$\Delta C = s \cdot \Delta DD = s[1/(r + s)](\Delta B) = [s/(r + s)]\Delta B \qquad (1.17)$$
$$= \frac{.25}{.20 + .25}\ (\$10\ \text{million}) = (5/9)(\$10\ \text{million}) = \$5.56\ \text{million}$$

where $s/(r + s)$ is referred to as the currency expansion coefficient. To double check our computations we can calculate the total amount of funds that flow out of the banks in the form of currency plus the amount which remains in the banks to support the newly created demand deposit liabilities. This total must exhaust the increase in the monetary base:

$$\Delta B = \Delta RT + \Delta C = \Delta RR_D + \Delta C$$
$$= (.20)\ (\$22.22\ \text{million}) + (\$5.56\ \text{million})$$
$$= (\$4.44\ \text{million}) + (\$5.56\ \text{million})$$
$$= \$10\ \text{million}$$

Remember our assumption of an initial increase in excess reserves with no initial change in deposits (the result of an open market purchase). For the banking system as a whole, loans outstanding, not including securities given up in the open market purchase, have increased by an amount equal to the total expansion of currency *and* demand deposits. For example, given an injection of $10 million in excess reserves, a single bank will create new deposits and expand its loans by exactly that amount. As the $10 million in newly created demand deposits is spent and the checks which transfer these deposits clear, an amount of currency equal to $2 million will be withdrawn from the banking system and only $8 million will be deposited. The joint expansion of demand deposits and currency by $8 million and $2 million, respectively, maintains the 4:1 ratio between these two forms of monetary wealth that the nonbank public is assumed to want to maintain. In addition, we see that the sum of the new currency holdings of the public and the new deposit liabilities at the second bank is equal to the volume of loans created at the first bank.

The second bank in this process will expand its loans by an amount equal to its inflow of excess reserves [$8 million − (.2) ($8 million) = $6.4 million]. Of this amount, $1.28 million will be withdrawn as currency and $5.12 million will be redeposited in the third bank. At each stage of the expansion, the outflow of currency from the system enables the nonbank public to maintain the desired ratio between the components of its monetary wealth, but at the same time reduces the volume of reserves that flow to the next bank in the expansion process. Loans created at each stage of the process equal the outflow of currency at that stage plus the value of demand deposits which flow to the bank at the next stage of the expansion process. The process continues in this fashion throughout the banking system.

Therefore we may calculate the total volume of loan expansion (not including the reduction in securities caused by the initial open market purchase) as follows:

$$\Delta L = \Delta DD + \Delta C = \$22.22 \text{ million} + 5.56 \text{ million}$$
$$= \$27.78 \text{ million}. \qquad (1.18)$$

The measure ΔL represents the total change in loans that occurs as a result of the existence of excess reserves in the banking system. By our assumption this process began with an open market sale of securities to the Federal Reserve by a bank. Consequently, those excess reserves were a concomitant of the equivalent decrease in that bank's holdings of securities. To reflect this, one may wish to define the net increase in loans and securities which takes place as a result of the entire chain of events (open market sale to the Federal Reserve and bank loan expansion). In this case, that *net* increase would be

$$\Delta L_{net} = \Delta L - \Delta B$$

where ΔB represents the initial sale of securities to the Federal Reserve and the initial generation of excess reserves in the commercial bank's portfolio. Since it is assumed that banks desire no excess reserves, the change in the base must ultimately be absorbed as required reserves or currency:

$$\Delta B = r \cdot \Delta DD + \Delta C.$$

Therefore,

$$\Delta L_{net} = \Delta L - \Delta B = \Delta DD + \Delta C - (r \cdot \Delta DD + \Delta C)$$
$$(1 - r)\Delta DD = \$22.22 \text{ million} - (.2) (\$22.22 \text{ million})$$
$$= \$17.78 \text{ million}$$

which agrees with the balance sheet identity,

Δloans + Δsecurities + Δreserves = Δdeposits
$$= \$27.78 \text{ million} - \$10.0 \text{ million} + \$4.44 \text{ million}$$
$$= \$22.22 \text{ million.}[13]$$

Using the definition of the money supply, we can show that the money stock expansion coefficient equals $(1 + s) / (r + s)$:

$$M = DD + C$$
$$\Delta M = \Delta DD + \Delta C. \tag{1.19}$$

Substituting Equation (1.16) for ΔDD and Equation (1.17) for ΔC into Equation (1.19),

$$\Delta M = \left(\frac{1}{r + s} \right) \Delta B + \left(\frac{s}{r + s} \right) \Delta B = \left(\frac{1 + s}{r + s} \right) \Delta B. \tag{1.20}$$

In the present example,

$$\Delta M = \frac{1 + .25}{.20 + .25} (\$10 \text{ million}) = (2.778)(\$10 \text{ million}) = \$27.78 \text{ million,}$$

by coincidence equal to the gross expansion of loans.[14]

Model 1.C.   A Monetary System that Includes Interest-Bearing Deposit Liabilities

We continue to assume that depositary institutions want no excess legal reserves and therefore will expand or contract their outstanding loans and securities any time that total reserves differ from required reserves. In addition, we assume that depositary institutions may issue interest-bearing deposits as well as noninterest-bearing deposits.

Interest-bearing deposits consist of interest-bearing deposits that are transferable by check or wire (ID) and large certificates of deposit (CD) and time and savings deposits (TD) that are not so transferable. For the time being we assume that time and savings deposits are zero. We assume that there is a uniform reserve requirement against all checkable deposits $(ID + DD)$.

---

[13]Note that the change in reserves in the final balance sheet is not equal to the initial change in the monetary base because of the leakage of currency into circulation.

[14]As seen subsequently, the equality between the expansion of the money supply and the expansion of loans outstanding is *not* a necessary result.

$$RR_D = r(DD + ID) \tag{1.21}$$

where r will still be assumed to be .20 against checkable deposits.[15] In addition we assume a legal reserve requirement against certificates of deposit:

$$RR_C = b \cdot CD \tag{1.22}$$

where $b = .10$.

Therefore, total required reserves are

$$RT = RR_D + RR_C = rDD + rID + bCD \tag{1.23}$$

Substituting Equation (1.23) into the monetary base, Equation (1.8), yields

$$B = r \cdot DD + r \cdot ID + b \cdot CD + C \tag{1.24}$$

or, in terms of change in the levels of the variables:

$$\Delta B = r \cdot \Delta DD + r \cdot \Delta ID + b \cdot \Delta CD + \Delta C. \tag{1.25}$$

By what amount will checkable deposits $(DD + ID)$ expand in response to a given increase in the monetary base? As in the case of currency holdings, rather than assuming a constant stock of a monetary asset, we assume that the public maintains fixed proportions between interest-bearing and noninterest-bearing deposits:

$$ID = m \cdot DD \tag{1.26}$$

$$CD = n \cdot DD \tag{1.27}$$

Specifically, we assume that for every dollar of noninterest-bearing deposits the public wishes to hold eighty cents of interest-bearing transferable deposits (ID) and fifty cents of certificates of deposits:

$$ID = m \cdot DD = .80DD \tag{1.26}$$

$$CD = n \cdot DD = .50DD \tag{1.27}$$

We continue to assume the desired 4:1 ratio between noninterest-bearing demand deposits and currency holdings and sub-

---

[15]At this point, time deposits (TD) could be introduced to the model also. However, as time deposits have no legal reserve requirement, the amount of reserves that a depositary institution would hold against them is strictly volitional. Some reserves, nevertheless, would be held and the money supply and loan expansion process would be modified in a manner very similar to the way it is altered when we add certificates of deposits to the analysis.

stitute Equations (1.14), (1.26), and (1.27) into Equation (1.24), expressing the result in terms of changes in the levels of the variables,

$$\Delta B = r\Delta DD + r\cdot\Delta ID + b\Delta CD + \Delta C$$

$$= r\Delta DD + r\cdot m\cdot\Delta DD + b\cdot n\cdot\Delta DD + s\cdot\Delta DD$$

$$= \Delta DD\cdot(r + rm + bn + s)$$

$$\Delta DD = \left(\frac{1}{r + rm + bn + s}\right)\Delta B$$

$$\Delta DD + \Delta ID = \left(\frac{1 + m}{r + rm + bn + s}\right)\Delta B \tag{1.28}$$

Returning to our example, if the base is increased by \$10 million, noninterest-bearing demand deposits will increase by \$15.15 million.

$$\Delta DD = \frac{1}{.20 + (.20)(.80) + (.10)(.50) + (.25)}(\$10 \text{ million})$$

$$= \frac{1}{.66}(\$10 \text{ million}) = \$15.15 \text{ million}$$

In this case the expansion of demand deposits on the basis of the \$10 million increase in the monetary base is smaller than in either of the two previous models. The reason for this should be obvious. In the first model, the entire increase in the monetary base was available to serve as reserves required against newly created noninterest-bearing demand deposits. In the second model the increase in the monetary base ultimately served two functions, increased currency holdings by the public and increased required reserves against noninterest-bearing demand deposits issued by commercial banks. In the third model, however, in addition to the drain into currency holdings, there is a further drain into reserves required against newly created interest-bearing deposits. Notice again that it makes no difference how the initial increase in the base comes about nor in what form the banks prefer to expand their liabilities. The final result will be the same since the public, through its asset preferences, decides how the new funds shall be allocated.

In this model, interest-bearing deposits that are transferable by check or wire will expand by

$$\Delta ID = m\cdot\Delta DD = \frac{m}{r + rm + bn + s}\Delta B$$

$$= \frac{.8}{.66}(\$10 \text{ million}) = \$12.12 \text{ million}$$

and checkable deposits will expand by

$$\Delta DD + \Delta ID = \Delta DD + m \cdot \Delta DD = \frac{1 + m}{r + rm + bn + s} \Delta B$$

$$= \left(\frac{1.8}{.66} \right) (\$10 \text{ million}) = \$27.27 \text{ million.}$$

certificates of deposit will expand by

$$\Delta CD = n \cdot \Delta DD = n \frac{1}{r + rm + bn + s} \cdot \Delta B = \frac{n}{r + rm + bn + s} \cdot \Delta B$$

$$= (.50/.66)(\$10 \text{ million}) = \$7.58 \text{ million}$$

where $n/(r + rm + bn + s)$ is the certificate of deposit expansion coefficient. Currency holdings will increase by

$$\Delta C = s \cdot \Delta DD = s \frac{1}{r + rm + bn + s} \cdot \Delta B = \frac{s}{r + rm + bn + s} \cdot \Delta B$$

$$= (.25/.66)(\$10 \text{ million}) = \$3.78 \text{ million}$$

where $s/(r + rm + bn + s)$ is the currency expansion coefficient. These increases exhaust the increase in the monetary base:

$$\Delta B = r \cdot \Delta DD + r \cdot \Delta ID + b \cdot \Delta CD + \Delta C$$
$$= (.20) (\$15.15 \text{ million}) + (.20) (\$12.12 \text{ million}) + (.10) (\$7.58 \text{ million}) +$$
$$3.78 \text{ million}$$
$$= \$10 \text{ million.}$$

The money supply (M1) expansion in this case is

$$\Delta M = \Delta DD + \Delta ID + \Delta C$$

$$= \frac{1}{r + rm + bn + s} \Delta B + \frac{m}{r + rm + bn + s} \Delta B + \frac{s}{r + rm + bn + s}$$

$$\Delta B = \frac{1 + m + s}{r + rm + bn + s} \Delta B = \$31.05 \text{ million.}$$

Finally, total loans outstanding increase by the sum of the expansion of currency, checkable deposits and certificates of deposit:

$$\Delta L = \Delta DD + \Delta ID + \Delta CD + \Delta C = \$15.15 \text{ million} + \$12.12 \text{ million} +$$
$$\$7.58 \text{ million} + \$3.78 \text{ million}$$
$$= \$38.63 \text{ million}$$

but loans *net* of the initial decrease in securities brought about by the open market sale of securities to the Federal Reserve will have expanded by only $28.64 million:

$$
\begin{aligned}
L_{net} &= \Delta L - \Delta B \\
&= \Delta DD + \Delta ID + \Delta CD - (r \cdot \Delta DD + r \cdot \Delta ID + b \cdot \Delta CD) \\
&= \Delta DD + \Delta ID + \Delta CD - r \cdot \Delta DD - r \cdot \Delta ID - b \cdot \Delta CD = (1 - r)\Delta DD + \\
&\quad (1 - r)\Delta ID + (1 - b)\Delta CD \\
&= \$15.15 \text{ million} + \$12.12 \text{ million} + \$7.58 \text{ million} - (.2)\$15.15 \text{ million} \\
&\quad - (.2) \$12.12 \text{ million} - (.1) (\$7.58 \text{ million}) \\
&= \$28.64 \text{ million}
\end{aligned}
$$

which agrees with the balance sheet identity,

$$\Delta \text{loans} + \Delta \text{securities} + \Delta \text{reserves} = \Delta \text{deposits}$$
$$\$38.63 \text{ million} - \$10 \text{ million} + \$6.22 \text{ million} = \$34.85 \text{ million}.$$

Note that in this case total loan expansion is greater than the expansion in the money stock. If the reader investigates what would have happened had we defined "money" to include time deposits or CDs, he or she will see why this is so.

Model 1.D.   A Model with Desired Excess Legal Reserves

It is quite reasonable (and historically accurate) to assume that depositary institutions may not act like the "automatic dispensers of credit" pictured above. On the contrary, they may quite possibly wish to hold reserves in excess of legal requirements, even though these reserves yield no explicit monetary income. That is, banks may choose not to expand loans and deposit liabilities to the full extent permitted by law. For various reasons they may wish to maintain a positive level of excess reserves as a contingency against unusually large adverse clearing balances, unusually large withdrawals of currency, or as a speculative balance. This assumption is completely consistent with our assumed goal of profit maximization by the bank management. In the face of uncertainty, an individual bank must weigh the cost of holding reserves in excess of legal requirements with the cost of falling below the required reserve minimum if unexpected cash withdrawals or adverse clearing balances occur at a time when the bank is just meeting its reserve requirements. The former cost may be represented by the income foregone on earning assets which could have been acquired with excess reserves. The latter cost may be represented by the cost of borrowing from the Federal Reserve or in the Federal funds market to correct a reserve deficient position. When the cost of a reserve deficiency is greater than zero and there is some finite probability attached to the risk of such a deficiency, it is perfectly reasonable for a profit maximizing bank to hold reserves in excess of those required by law.

This extra complication is easily integrated into the analysis. We may assume that banks wish to maintain a fixed proportional relation between their holdings of excess reserves (RE) and their demand deposit liabilities, that is,

$$RE = w \cdot DD \tag{1.29}$$

The rationale for this assumption is that the larger the demand deposit liabilities, the greater is the risk of a deposit loss of a given size and the greater the demand for excess reserves to protect the bank from this risk. We must modify the monetary base equation to allow for these holdings of excess legal reserves:

$$B = RT + C \tag{1.8}$$

but

$$RT = RR_D + RR_C + RE$$
$$= r \cdot DD + r \cdot ID + b \cdot CD + RE.$$

Thus,

$$B = r \cdot DD + r \cdot ID + b \cdot CD + RE + C.$$

Employing the proportionality relations assumed previously,

$$C = s \cdot DD \tag{1.14}$$

$$ID = m \cdot DD \tag{1.26}$$

$$CD = n \cdot DD \tag{1.27}$$

$$RE = w \cdot DD \tag{1.29}$$

and making the appropriate substitutions,

$$B = r \cdot DD + r(m \cdot DD) + b(n \cdot DD) + w \cdot DD + s \cdot DD$$

$$= DD(r + rm + bn + s + w)$$

$$DD = \left(\frac{1}{r + rm + bn + s + w} \right) B \tag{1.30}$$

or in terms of changes in the levels of the variables,

$$\Delta DD = \frac{1}{r + rm + bn + s + w} \cdot \Delta B. \tag{1.31}$$

Substituting back into Equations (1.14), (1.26), (1.27) and (1.29) and employing changes in the levels of the variables,

$$\Delta ID = m \cdot DD = \left(\frac{m}{r + rm + bn + s + w} \right) \Delta B \tag{1.32}$$

$$\Delta C = s \cdot \Delta DD = \left(\frac{s}{r + rm + bn + s + w} \right) \Delta B \tag{1.33}$$

$$\Delta CD = n \cdot \Delta DD = \left(\frac{n}{r + rm + bn + s + w} \right) \Delta B \tag{1.34}$$

$$\Delta RE = w \cdot \Delta DD = \left(\frac{w}{r + rm + bn + s + w} \right) \Delta B. \tag{1.35}$$

Likewise, since $\Delta M = \Delta DD + \Delta ID + \Delta C$,

$$\Delta M = \frac{1 + m + s}{r + rm + bn + s + w} \cdot \Delta B. \tag{1.36}$$

Equations (1.31) through (1.36) represent a rather general model for monetary expansion and contraction caused by increases or decreases in the monetary base. The multiplicative terms in these equations are asset expansion coefficients.

Continuing with our example (assuming all parameter values as before, $r = .20$, $b = .10$, $m = .80$, $n = .50$, $\Delta B = \$10$ million, and assuming further that $w = .10$),

$$\Delta DD = \frac{1}{(.20) + (.20)(.80) + (.10)(.50) + (.25) + (.10)} (\$10 \text{ million})$$

$$= \frac{1}{(.76)} (\$10 \text{ million}) = (1.317)(\$10 \text{ million}) = \$13.17 \text{ million}$$

$$\Delta C = s \cdot \Delta DD = (.25)(\$13.17 \text{ million}) = \$3.29 \text{ million}$$

$$\Delta ID = m \cdot DD$$

$$= (.80)\$13.17 \text{ million}$$

$$= \$10.54 \text{ million}$$

$$\Delta CD = n \cdot \Delta DD = (.50)(\$13.17 \text{ million}) = \$6.59 \text{ million}$$

$$\Delta RE = w \cdot \Delta DD = (.10)(\$13.17 \text{ million}) = 1.32 \text{ million}$$

$$\Delta M = \Delta DD + \Delta ID + \Delta C = \$13.17 \text{ million} + \$10.54 \text{ million}$$
$$+ \$3.29 \text{ million} = \$26.87 \text{ million}$$

$$\Delta L = \Delta C + \Delta ID + \Delta DD + \Delta CD = \$3.29 \text{ million} + \$10.54 \text{ million}$$
$$+ \$13.17 \text{ million} + \$6.59 \text{ million} = \$33.46 \text{ million}.$$

Check:

$$\Delta B = r \cdot \Delta DD + r \cdot \Delta ID + n \Delta CD + \Delta RE + \Delta C$$
$$= (.20)(\$13.17 \text{ million}) + (.20)(\$10.54 \text{ million}) + (.10)(\$6.59 \text{ million}) +$$
$$(\$1.32 \text{ million}) + (\$3.29 \text{ million}) = \$10 \text{ million}.$$

In accord with the balance sheet identity

$$\Delta \text{loans} + \Delta \text{securities} + \Delta \text{reserves} = \Delta \text{deposits}$$
$$\$33.46 \text{ million} - \$10.0 \text{ million} + \$6.84 \text{ million} = \$30.30 \text{ million}.$$

Model 1.3. Interest Rates and Other Variables in the Behavioral Relations

In reality, perhaps only quite complicated functions may accurately describe the true relationships that determine the public's asset holdings.[16] This may involve the introduction of new variables into our model. Let us suppose, for example, that we found a proportional currency demand function to be satisfactory explanation of the "true" relationship between the public's holdings of demand deposits and currency, and we also found a proportional relationship to be a sufficient explanation of actual bank holdings in excess legal reserves. However, what if neither of these functional forms satisfactorily explains the interest-bearing deposit holdings of the public? We must search for an explanation through other functional forms which might include new variables.

The fact certain deposit balances yield an interest return to their

[16]See Frank de Leeuw and Edward Gramlich, "The Channels of Monetary Policy: A Further Report on the Federal Reserve–MIT Model," *Journal of Finance*, vol. 24, no. 2 (May 1969), 265–290.

holders while others do not ought to influence the public's decisions as to how to allocate their monetary assets. For example, the higher the rate of interest on time deposits, *ceteris paribus*, the more costly it would be in terms of foregone income to hold a dollar in the form of noninterest-bearing deposits or currency. Therefore the level of the interest rate on these deposit balances as well as the size of overall deposit balances (as a proxy for wealth) may influence desired deposit holdings. One might postulate, for example, that interest-bearing deposit holdings are a linear function of both the stock of noninterest-bearing deposit balances and the rate of interest on deposits, that is,

$$ID = e + f \cdot DD + j \cdot i_{ID} \tag{1.37}$$

$$CD = g + h \cdot DD + l \cdot i_{CD} \tag{1.38}$$

These modifications would affect all expansion coefficients derived earlier. Replacing equations (1.26) and (1.27) in the previous model with Equations (1.37) and (1.35),

$$B = r \cdot DD + r \cdot (e + f \cdot DD + j \cdot i_{ID}) + b(g + h \cdot DD + l \cdot i_{CD}) + RE + C$$

$$RE = w \cdot DD \tag{1.29}$$

$$C = s \cdot DD \tag{1.14}$$

Substituting:

$$\begin{aligned} B &= r \cdot DD + r(e + f \cdot DD + j \cdot i_{ID}) + b(g + h \cdot DD + l \cdot i_{CD}) \\ &\quad + w \cdot DD + s \cdot DD \\ &= DD(r + rf + bh + w + s) + r \cdot j \cdot i_{ID} + b \cdot l \cdot i_{CD} \\ &\quad + re + bg \end{aligned}$$

$$DD = \left(\frac{B - re - bg - r \cdot j \cdot i_{ID} - b \cdot l \cdot i_{CD}}{r + rf + bh + w + s} \right).$$

By substituting the behavioral relations representing the public's and the bank's asset holding behavior into the definition of the monetary base, we derive a "reduced form" equation[17] that specifies the equilibrium volume of demand deposits consistent with given values of the monetary base B, the interest rate on deposits (i_{ID} and i_{CD}), and the legal (r and b) and behavioral ($w, a, c, d, f, g, h, j, l$) parameters of

---

[17]A reduced form equation specifies the equilibrium value of an endogenous variable—a variable whose value is determined within the framework of the model, such as demand deposits—as a function of the parameters and exogenous variables that appear in the structural equations (asset preference equations and definitions) of our model.

the monetary system. Since the legal parameters and the monetary base are under the control of the monetary authority if we could estimate the behavioral parameters of the system (say, by regression techniques), a knowledge of the current level of the interest rate on time deposits would enable us to predict the equilibrium level of demand deposit balances.

As one further example, let us suppose that the preferred asset holdings of the banks and the public are dependent on some market interest rates.[18] For example, the public may consider very short-term U.S. government securities as an alternative to their holdings of currency and checkable deposits.[19] The greater the rate on these securities with all other interest rates unchanged, the greater the opportunity cost of holding currency and checkable deposits. Likewise, commercial banks may be influenced by the rate on these securities when determining their desired level of excess legal reserves. The greater the market rate, the more costly it is to hold nonearning excess reserves. In this instance the asset demand functions may be written as linear equations:

$$ID = e + f \cdot DD + g \cdot i_m \qquad (1.39)$$

$$C = a + d \cdot DD + c \cdot i_m \qquad (1.40)$$

$$RE = v + w \cdot DD + h \cdot i_m \qquad (1.41)$$

In order to simplify the analyses we shall ignore certificates of deposit in the present model.

In each case desired asset holdings depend upon both the volume of noninterest-bearing demand deposit liabilities and the market rate of interest i_m relative to deposit rates. We assume that when the rate of interest on marketable securities changes, all other rates, including the rate paid on checkable deposits, i_{ID}, are unchanged.

This assumption squares with reality. Under the Monetary Control Act of 1980, there are legal ceilings on rates of interest paid on NOW accounts (which are part of checkable deposits). These ceilings together with ceilings on interest rates paid on time deposits and

---

[18]Though very many individual interest rates exist on the market at any moment, let us assume that one of those rates or some composite of those rates is the most important rate in determining the asset preferences specified in the model. This would represent a formidable problem if we were to try to estimate the model empirically.

[19]The empirical importance of the role of the interest rate in the determination of the supply for money (whether or not we consider time deposits in our definition of the money stock) is discussed in the reading by Robert Rasche which follows this chapter.

smaller denomination nonnegotiable certificates of deposit are being phased out over a period of years ending in 1988. Therefore, the relation between the asset holdings in Equations 1.39, 1.40, and 1.41 and the market rate will be inverse; that is, the signs attached to g, c, and h will be negative. Thus, when the interest rate on short-term securities or some other market instrument rises, the public will desire a smaller volume of currency and checkable deposits and the banks will desire fewer excess legal reserves.

Incorporating these relations into our basic framework,

$$B = rDD + rID + C + RE$$
$$B = rDD + r(e + f \cdot DD + g \cdot i_m) + a + d \cdot DD + c \cdot i_m$$
$$+ v + w \cdot DD + h \cdot i_m \cdot \tag{1.42}$$

$$= r \cdot DD + rf \cdot DD + d \cdot DD + w \cdot DD + re + a + v + rg \cdot i_m$$
$$+ c \cdot i_m + h \cdot i_m$$

$$= DD(r + rf + d + w) + (re + a + v) + (rg + c + h)i_m$$

$$DD = \frac{B - (re + a + v) + (rg + c + h)i_m}{(r + rf + d + w)} \cdot$$

Let

$$\zeta = (re + a + v)$$
$$\gamma = (rg + c + h).$$

Then

$$DD = \frac{B - \zeta - \gamma \cdot i_m}{r + rf + d + w} = \frac{1}{r + rf + d + w} \cdot (B - \zeta - \gamma \cdot i_m). \tag{1.43}$$

Equation (1.43) is a "reduced form" equation. In this expression, $\gamma \cdot i_m$ represents the total influence of the short-term market interest rate on the volume of demand deposit liabilities through its effects on the preferred asset holdings of the public and the banks. Since the parameters g, c, and h above are negative and r is positive, γ is also negative. Since (negative) γ is preceded by a minus sign in Equation (1.43), as the market rate increases, the equilibrium quantity of demand deposits increases. This relation is depicted graphically in Figure 1.1.

An examination of the intercept term

$$\frac{B - \zeta}{r + rf + d + w}$$

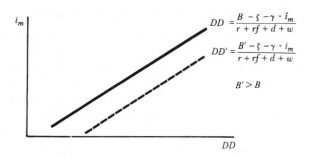

$$DD = \frac{B - \varsigma - \gamma \cdot i_m}{r + rf + d + w}$$

$$DD' = \frac{B' - \varsigma - \gamma \cdot i_m}{r + rf + d + w}$$

$$B' > B$$

Figure 1.1. Reduced form DD relation.

reveals that an increase in the monetary base B will cause the curve to shift to the right, increasing the quantity of demand deposits supplied at all levels of the interest rate as shown in Figure 1.1. Similarly, the curve will shift out to the right if any one of the parameters in the denominator of the intercept term is decreased. For example, a reduction in the reserve requirement ratio on bank demand deposits will increase the supply of deposits at all interest rates. A function similar to this one will be employed in Chapter 7 when the money supply relationship is included as one of the behavioral equations in a model of the determination of aggregate income.

This discussion shows that there could be numerous money multipliers or expansion coefficients, and that the money supply could be influenced by several different interest rates. The form of the expansion coefficients and the choice of interest rate variables that affect the money supply, as demonstrated, depend directly on the form of behavioral relations employed to explain the asset holdings of the banks and the public. These equations could be expanded to include additional variables such as income, wealth, expectations, and the many other factors that may be important in the determination of the public's and the banks' asset preferences. The "best" money supply model will be the one that explains the actual data (actual past values of these variables) and predicts future values better than any of the other models tested.[20]

[20]For a survey of empirical estimation of money supply models, see Robert H. Rasche, "A Review of Empirical Studies of the Money Supply Mechanism," *Review*, Federal Reserve Bank of St. Louis (July 1972), 11–19. Reprinted at the end of this chapter.

A Nonlinear Model of the Money Supply Relation[21]

In previous models, desired holdings of currency, certificates of deposit, time deposits and excess reserves were treated in a very simple fashion. We assumed that the demand for each of these assets was proportional to the level of demand deposits. Earlier this strict proportionality assumption was relaxed, but it was still assumed that the size of these desired holdings would vary in a linear fashion with the level of demand deposits. Finally, in the preceding section we introduced the market rate of interest into the demand relations. Nevertheless, strict linearity was still assumed.

A more general, somewhat more sophisticated and realistic approach is to express the desired ratios of currency, certificates of deposits, and excess reserves to checkable deposits, not as constants as in Equations (1.14), (1.27) and (1.32), but as functions of other variables.[22] (We will now use the notation DD to stand for checkable deposits.) As in Equations (1.39), (1.40) and (1.41) of the previous model, the market rate of interest will have an influence on asset-holding behavior. In this case, however, the interest rate together with the level of income shall determine these desired ratios.[23] Thus the proportions of currency, certificates of deposit, and excess reserves to checkable deposits will vary with the market rate of interest i_m and the level of aggregate income Y as follows:[24]

[21]Much of the material in this section is derived from Albert E. Burger, *The Money Supply Process* (Belmont, CA: Wadsworth, 1972).

[22]For example, studies by George Kaufman and Phillip Cagan have suggested that the desired currency ratio varies inversely with the level of income, because as income increases, proportionately more transactions are handled by check. In addition, the desired interest-bearing deposit ratio may vary directly with income, if time deposits are a luxury good. See Phillip Cagan, *Determinants and Effects of Changes in the Stock of Money 1875–1960* (New York: Columbia University Press, 1965), and George G. Kaufman, "The Demand for Currency," Staff Economic Study, Board of Governors of the Federal Reserve System (1967).

[23]In Chapters 2–4 the demand for currency plus checkable deposits is expressed as being dependent on the level of permanent income, wealth, expected price level increases, and other variables. These other variables could enter the relations below but would clutter the analysis without adding much to our understanding at this point. Many of the relationships postulated in the present chapter to exist between interest rates and income as explanatory variables and the demand for currency, checkable deposits, and time deposits as dependent variables have been empirically estimated. See the reading by Robert Rasche which follows this chapter.

[24]The notation F_i, F_Y, etc., means $\delta(C/DD)\delta i$, $\delta(C/DD)/\delta Y$, etc. In other words, F_i, F_Y, etc., are partial derivatives of the desired ratios on the left-hand side of Equations (1.44), (1.45), and (1.46) with respect to the rate of interest and the level of income. In short, this notation signifies the expected magnitude (less than or greater

$$\text{directly} \quad \frac{C}{DD} = F(i_m, Y), \ F_{i_m} > 0, \ F_Y < 0 \tag{1.44}$$

$$\text{dir} \quad +\frac{CD}{-DD} = G(i_m, Y), \ G_{i_m} > 0, \ G_Y > 0 \tag{1.45}$$

$$\text{inv} \quad - \ \frac{RE}{DD} = H(i_m), \ H_{i_m} < 0. \tag{1.46}$$

Equation (1.44) indicates that the desired ratio of currency to checkable deposits is assumed to vary directly with the market rate of interest, that is $F_{i_m} > 0$. The reason for this is that, because interest is not paid on currency holdings and because interest paid on checkable deposits is subject to a legal ceiling, both the demand for currency and the demand for checkable deposits vary inversely with the market rate.[25] Since checkable deposits may reasonably be assumed to be closer substitutes for interest-bearing securities, the demand for checkable deposits is assumed to be more sensitive to changes in the market rate of interest than is the demand for currency.

Equation (1.45) indicates that the desired ratio of certificates of deposit to checkable deposits is assumed to vary directly with the market rate of interest, that is $G_{i_m} > 0$. The reason for this is that the demand for checkable deposits varies inversely with market rate of interest and, since the rate paid on CDs moves with the market rate of interest, the demand for CDs does not vary inversely with the market rate.

By similar reasoning, the desired ratio of excess reserves to checkable deposits in Equation (1.46) is assumed to vary inversely with the market rate of interest. That is, $H_{i_m} < 0$. This occurs because the interest rate is the opportunity cost of holding excess reserves. As a result, a higher market rate of interest causes institutions to reduce excess reserves relative to checkable deposits.[26]

Equation (1.44) indicates that the desired ratio of currency to checkable deposits varies inversely with the level of income, that is, $F_Y < 0$. While both the demand for currency and the demand for

than zero) of the change in the desired ratios when either the market rate of interest or the level of income change by a small amount while all other variables are assumed to remain constant.

[25]According to the Monetary Control Act of 1980, the legal ceiling on rates of interest paid on checkable deposits is scheduled to be removed gradually by 1988.

[26]The behavior of banks has considerable influence on the determination of the money supply. Here we focus on only one aspect of bank behavior. In the next section of this chapter bank borrowing (of reserves) is introduced.

checkable deposits vary directly with the level of income, checkable deposits may reasonably be assumed to be superior goods relative to currency. Moreover, there are likely to be greater economies of scale in the demand for currency than in the demand for checkable deposits.[27] As the level of an individual's income rises, that person generally makes more use of checking account services, and therefore carries, on average, a larger checking account balance. In turn, certificates of deposit are assumed to be superior goods relative to checkable deposits. As income rises asset holders may reasonably be assumed to add proportionately more to these accounts than they add to their checking accounts. Therefore, in Equation (1.45) the desired ratio of CDs to checkable deposits varies directly with the level of income, $G_Y > 0$.

In the linear money supply relation of earlier models a money supply expansion factor or "multiplier" was explicitly derived that was a constant regardless of the level of income or the interest rate. In the models where currency, CDs, and excess reserve demands were strictly proportional to demand deposits, the money stock varied in direct proportion to the monetary base, and changes in the interest rate or level of income had no effect. In models where these demands varied inversely with the market rate of interest, increases in currency, interest-bearing deposits, and excess reserve holdings brought about by decreases in the market rate were viewed as causing a reduction in the level of reserves available for money supply expansion, but as having no effect on the expansion coefficient itself. For example, in Equation (1.42), with the level of income and interest rates paid on interest-bearing deposits assumed unchanged as the market rate of interest declined: the desired level of currency holdings rose and the level of total reserves decreased; the desired level of deposits increased and reserves available to support deposit expansion fell; and the desired level of excess reserve holdings rose and reserves available to support deposits declined. Consequently, as the market rate declined,

---

[27]See Cagan, *op. cit.*, and Kaufman, *op. cit.* Stephen Goldfeld and William Hosek indicate, in contrast, that the desired currency ratio may vary directly with the level of income. See Stephen M. Goldfeld, *Commercial Bank Behavior and Economic Activity* (Amsterdam: North Holland, 1966); William Hosek, "Determinants of the Money Multiplier," *Quarterly Review of Economics and Business* (Summer 1970), 37–46. Alan Hess contends that the desired currency ratio may vary either inversely or directly with income, depending on the stage of the business cycle. See Alan C. Hess, "An Explanation of Short-Run Fluctuations in the Ratio of Currency to Demand Deposits," *Journal of Money, Credit and Banking* (August 1971), 92–97.

the level of deposits fell, even though the expansion coefficient itself, $1/(r + rf + d + w)$, was unaffected.

In the present model changes in the market rate of interest and the level of income are viewed as actually affecting the money multiplier itself. Thus we express the money supply relation in general form as

$$M_s = \phi \left(\frac{RR}{DD}, \frac{RR}{CD}, \frac{C}{DD}, \frac{CD}{DD}, \frac{RE}{DD} \right) \cdot B \qquad (1.47)$$

where $\phi(\ )$ is the expansion factor by which the monetary base is multiplied to determine the equilibrium stock of money. Unlike all previous models this multiplier is no longer a constant. Instead it depends upon five basic ratios: the ratio of required reserves to checkable deposits, RR/DD, the ratio of required reserves to certificates of deposit RR/CD, the desired ratio (by the public) of currency to checkable deposits C/DD, the desired ratio (by the public) of CDs to checkable deposits CD/DD, and the desired ratio (by banks) of excess reserves to checkable deposits RE/DD.

The first two of these ratios are our old friends, the legal reserve requirements against checkable deposits and CDs and may be treated as constant terms r and b, respectively. We have already seen that the multiplier varies inversely with each of these legal reserve requirement ratios, that is, $\phi_r < 0$ and $\phi_b < 0$.

The latter three ratios also affect the multiplier. As we have seen from our earlier, linear models, an increase in any of the three ratios will cause the multiplier to decrease, that is, $\phi_{C/DD}, \phi_{CD/DD},$ and $\phi_{RE/DD} < 0$.

These three desired ratios are also the dependent variables in Equations 1.44, 1.45, and 1.46. As such, each ratio is now viewed as a function of the market rate of interest and the level of income. This allows us to rewrite the money supply relation as

$$M = \phi[r, b, F(i_m,Y), G(i_m,Y), H(i_m)] \cdot B \qquad (1.48)$$

where $\phi_r, \phi_b, \phi_F, \phi_G, \phi_H < 0$ and from Equations (1.44)–(1.46) F_{im}, $G_{i_m}, G_Y > 0$ and $F_Y, H_{i_m} < 0$.

The multiplier $\phi[\ ]$ is now a function of the variables i_m and Y. Because we are multiplying variables (i_m and Y) by a variable (B, the monetary base) to determine the money stock, the expression is nonlinear. Therefore we can simplify the previous relation as follows:

$$M = \eta(r, b, i_m, Y) \cdot B \tag{1.49}$$

where η_r, η_b, <0 but η_{i_m} and η_Y are ambiguous.

The word "ambiguous" means that without further information we cannot deduce the effect of a change in income or the interest rate on the magnitude of the money multiplier. An increase in either of the legal reserve requirement ratios will always cause the money multiplier to decrease, that is, η_r and $\eta_b < 0$, but the effect of an increase in the market rate of interest and the level of income is not so clear. For example, if the market rate of interest rises, the desired ratios of currency to checkable deposits and CDs to checkable deposits will rise ($F_{i_m} > 0$, $G_{i_m} > 0$). This will *reduce* the money multiplier ($\phi_{C/DD} < 0$, $\phi_{CD/DD} < 0$). However, the desired ratio of excess reserves to checkable deposits will *fall* if the interest rate rises ($H_{i_m} < 0$). This change will *increase* the money multiplier ($\phi_{RR/DD} < 0$). This is what is meant when we say η_{i_m} is *ambiguous*. The final effect depends on the relative sizes of these partial influences. However, empirical observation may help to resolve the ambiguity.

Certificates of deposit movements are quantitatively an important element in our financial system. In recent years they have become quite interest sensitive. It is likely therefore that the effect of a change in the market interest rate on the money multiplier (working through the desired CD ratio and the desired currency ratio) outweighs the effect of change in the market interest rate on the money multiplier (working through the desired excess reserves). Consequently, the "net" effect of an increase in the market rate of interest on the multiplier for the money stock (M-1) may be reasonably assumed to be negative, that is $\eta_{i_m} < 0$.

The effect of an increase in the level of income on the money multiplier is also ambiguous. For example, if the level of income rises, the desired ratio of currency to checkable deposits will fall ($F_Y < 0$). This will increase the money multiplier ($\phi_{C/DD} < 0$). However, the desired ratio of certificates of deposit to checkable deposits will rise ($G_Y > 0$). This will *reduce* the money multiplier ($\phi_{C/DD} < 0$). Once again, because CDs are quantitatively such an important element in our financial system, it is likely that the effect of changes in the level of income, working through the desired ratio of CDs to checkable deposits, outweighs the effect of changes in the level of income working through the desired currency ratio. Consequently, the net effect of an increase in the level of income on the money multiplier is likely to be negative ($\eta_Y < 0$).

So far this chapter has revealed the sensitivity of the form of the money supply mechanism to the specific behavioral assumptions that underlie the model. Modifications in the behavioral relations have considerable effect on the reduced form equations for demand deposits and the money supply. It has also been shown that, given the monetary base, the currency and deposit demands of the public and the demand for excess legal reserves by banks could reasonably be assumed to respond to changes in various interest rates and the level of income. Therefore, the equilibrium quantities of demand deposits and money may also be so regarded.

The Monetary Base and Member Borrowed Reserves

Quite often it is assumed that the monetary base B is exogenously determined by the monetary authority. Let us investigate this assumption and its implications more closely. All factors which either supply or divert to alternative uses funds that are potentially available to serve as currency or reserves are listed in the monetary base equation. Therefore, to determine which factors influence the size of the monetary base B, we must examine the determinants of the items in that statement.[28]

The only item in the statement of the sources and uses of reserves over which the monetary authority, the Federal Reserve, has absolute control, is "United States government securities" held by the Federal Reserve, listed under "Federal Reserve credit." This account represents the largest single source of funds in the monetary base equation. Other items listed as sources and all alternative uses of funds are not under the control of the Federal Reserve. For example, variations in the level of the gold stock are determined primarily by the decisions of the U.S. Treasury and of official international organizations. Foreign deposits at the Federal Reserve and deposits other than those of member institutions are varied at the discretion of the holder. "Float,"[29] a technical item that arises in the check clearing process, can

---

[28]A fairly complete exposition of the monetary base equation appears in the reading by Balbach and Burger which follows this chapter.

[29]Federal Reserve "float" is the difference between "cash items in process of collection" and "deferred availability cash items" in the consolidated balance sheet of the

be affected by strikes, by the weather, and by many other factors that can delay the delivery of checks.

From the point of view of the monetary authority, however, control over just one item in the source of the monetary base equation, particularly an item as important and flexible as government security holdings, may be as good as control over all accounts. If the Federal Reserve can predict the changes that will occur in the items which it does not directly control, it can take appropriate measures to offset the effects of these changes by adjusting its holdings of United States government securities through open market operations.[30] Even if the monetary authority cannot predict these changes before they occur, the director of the System's Open Market Account can move fairly rapidly to take corrective measures to offset the effects of any change that comes to his attention. For example, suppose there is a decrease in Treasury deposits at the Federal Reserve. As an alternative use of funds in the monetary base equation, this would lead to an increase in reserves (assuming other accounts remain constant). However, if the Treasury notifies the Federal Reserve of impending changes in the level of its deposits, the Federal Reserve can sell securities on the open market, thereby decreasing the size of their security portfolio and offsetting the effects of the Treasury action on reserves. As another example, suppose there is an outflow of Treasury gold to a foreign country. By itself, this movement would decrease the Treasury's gold stock, a source of the monetary base. However, this result could be negated by a purchase of securities by the Federal Reserve. Thus it would appear that through defensive (offsetting) open market operations, the monetary authorities can control the level of the monetary base. However, there is an item in the source base that is varied primarily at the discretion of depository institutions. This is borrowing from the Federal Reserve, included under "discounts and advances" in the monetary base equation. When a depository institution finds itself temporarily short of reserves for whatever reason, it has the privilege of borrowing reserves from its

---

Federal Reserve banks. Float results from the practice of crediting a member reserve account for checks deposited in Federal Reserve banks before the checks are actually collected from another bank. Consequently, strikes and bad weather that interfere with the check collection process can cause an increase in float and, thereby, an increase in the monetary base.

[30]For a related discussion of aspects of trying to achieve control of the money supply, see Alan R. Holmes. "Operational Constraints on the Stabilization of Money Supply Growth." *Controlling Monetary Aggregates* (Boston: Federal Reserve Bank of Boston, 1969), 65–78.

district Federal Reserve bank. These funds are borrowed on a very short-term basis (under conditions set by the Federal Reserve Board) to restore its reserves to the level required by law.

By itself, an increase in borrowing from the Federal Reserve increases the total reserves. If there is no change in the other accounts in the monetary base equation, this borrowing causes an increase in the monetary base and will support a multiple expansion of loans and deposits just as an increase in reserves from any other source would; yet many observers believe that the Federal Reserve generally (though perhaps only partially) offsets changes in the borrowing of depository institutions through open market operations. For example, when depository institutions borrow, the monetary authority could sell an equal volume of securities on the open market. The net effect of these two actions would be to maintain the monetary base at a constant level determined by the monetary authority.

Whether the Federal Reserve actually offsets every change in the level of borrowing or simply lets such borrowing change the monetary base is an empirical question (with very important policy implications).[31] Regardless of its actual policy, we may assume that the monetary authority finds it useful to be able to predict borrowing. Let us view the role of these borrowed reserves within the linear money supply framework. This modification in our linear model may be demonstrated rather simply.

We may view the total reserve stock available to depository institutions composed of two separate elements:

(1) All reserve funds supplied by the Federal Reserve other than through the borrowing mechanism. This component is called unborrowed reserves, RU.

(2) Those reserves created through borrowing from the Federal Reserve, RB.

---

[31]For example, the impact of monetary policy on income is estimated to be relatively weak if the unborrowed base is used as an exogenous measure of monetary policy. See Michael J. Hamburger, "The Lag in the Effect of Monetary Policy: A Survey of Recent Literature," *Monetary Aggregates and Monetary Policy* (New York: Federal Reserve Bank of New York, 1974), 104–111.

The procyclical variation of elements of the source base, such as borrowing, is the foundation of the "reverse causation" controversy. If the base varies procyclically, then estimates of a strong positive relationship between it, as a purported explanatory variable, and income, as a dependent variable, do not reflect one-way causality. Raymond Lombra and Raymond Torto have suggested a resolution of this problem in "Measuring the Impact of Monetary and Fiscal Actions: A New Look at the Specification Problem." *Review of Economics and Statistics.* vol. 56, no. 1 (February 1974), 23–27.

Therefore, we write the following definition:

$$RT = RU + RB. \tag{1.50}$$

If the Federal Reserve does not offset every movement in reserve borrowing by changes in the level of unborrowed reserves (RU) borrowing will affect the total stock of reserves in the system.

How will this new element introduced into the analysis modify the money multipliers and expansion coefficients derived in the previous chapter? Let us assume that the sum of the unborrowed reserves and currency components of the monetary base are determined by the Federal Reserve. This does not deny the possibility that the monetary authority could in fact offset borrowing through variations in RU, but it does provide a convenient framework to relate borrowed reserves to our money expansion model.

Recall the two definitions of aggregate bank reserves:

$$RT = RR + RE$$
$$RT = RU + RB.$$

By substitution,[32]

$$RU = RR + RE - RB. \tag{1.51}$$

Define a new measure, the unborrowed monetary base $\overline{B}$:

$$\overline{B} = B - RB$$
$$\overline{B} = RT - RB + C = RU + C. \tag{1.52}$$

Therefore, by substituting Equation (1.51) into (1.52), we get

$$\overline{B} = RR + RE - RB + C.$$

Using the definition of required reserves given in Equation (1.23) yields

$$\overline{B} = r \cdot DD + b \cdot CD + RE - RB + C. \tag{1.53}$$

---

[32]We may define another measure called "free reserves," equal to excess reserves less borrowing of $RF = RE - RB$. Some analysts have chosen to focus on this measure as the behavioral variable in studying behavior of depository institutions and in relating that behavior to the money supply process. For several very good reasons presented elsewhere, we choose not to focus our attention on this combined measure, but rather to investigate each of the components separately. See A. J. Meigs, *Free Reserves and Money Supply* (Chicago: University of Chicago Press, 1962), and Karl Brunner and Allan H. Meltzer, "The Federal Reserve's Attachment to Free Reserves: Testimony before the Subcommittee on Domestic Finance of the House Committee on Banking and Currency, 88th Congress, 2nd Session (May 7, 1964), 1–27.

To derive the money multipliers and expansion coefficients we need only to specify behavioral relations for each of the variables in the equation and to substitute these relations in the equation for the unborrowed monetary base and solve. For example, we may once again assume the familiar proportionality relations for CDs, currency and interest-bearing deposits:

$$C = s \cdot DD \tag{1.14}$$

$$CD = n \cdot DD. \tag{1.27}$$

$$ID = m \cdot DD \tag{1.26}$$

What can we assume about the demand for excess reserves and the demand for borrowed reserves?

At the present, in anticipation of the results of that discussion, assume that the demand for excess reserves is a linear function of some market interest rates and the volume of demand deposit liabilities,

$$RE = v + w \cdot DD + h \cdot i_m. \tag{1.54}$$

The discount rate is the explicit cost of borrowed reserves. Assume that borrowing depends on the relationship between this rate and a market interest rate (the return to be earned from acquiring earning assets with the borrowed funds). Assume also that the instability or volatility of deposits will influence borrowing behavior. Let this latter factor remain unspecified but be represented by the symbol λ. Then postulate that the level of borrowing is a linear function of the stability factor λ and the algebraic difference between the market interest rate i_m and the discount rate i_D:

$$RB = a + d(i_m - i_D) + z(\lambda). \tag{1.55}$$

Substituting these behavioral relations into our basic relation, Equation (1.53), yields the reduced form equation for demand deposits:

$$\begin{aligned}
\bar{B} &= r \cdot DD + rm \cdot DD + bn \cdot DD + s \cdot DD + v + w \cdot DD + h \cdot i_m - a \\
&\quad - d(i_m - i_D) - z(\lambda) \\
&= DD[r + rm + bn + s + w] + [v - a] + h \cdot i_m - d(i_m - i_D) - z(\lambda)
\end{aligned}$$

$$DD = \frac{\bar{B} - h \cdot i_m + d(i_m - i_D) + z(\lambda) - (v - a)}{r + rm + bn + s + w}. \tag{1.56}$$

Since the money supply has been defined as checkable deposits plus currency in circulation, we may write

$$M = DD + ID + C = DD + m \cdot DD + s \cdot DD = (1 + s + m)DD$$

$$M = \frac{1 + s + m}{r + rm + bn + s + w} \; [\bar{B} - h \cdot i_m + d(i_m - i_D) + z(\lambda) - (v - a)]. \quad (1.57)$$

This result represents a reduced form equation relating equilibrium values of the money stock to the legal and behavioral parameters and exogenous variables of our model. Suppose, for example, that the reserve requirement ratios b and r, the parameters of the behavioral equations (n,m,s,v,w,h,a,d,z), λ, and the market interest rate all remain constant, but that the Federal Reserve increases the discount rate. What effect will this action have on the money supply? Since all factors but i_D remain constant and the coefficient d is likely to be positive, an increase in i_D will lower $(i_m - i_D)$ and thereby lower the money supply.

Estimates of the parameters of the behavioral equations and information on the usefulness of our assumed functional forms can be derived through the use of statistical methods—primarily regression analysis. Work has been done on this problem over the past several years. Some of this work has been inspired by the "new view" that the behavior of the public and the depositary institutions (as influenced by factors such as the rate of interest, the level of income, and other economic conditions) so dominates the money supply determination process that there is no close predictable relationship between the money supply and the variables controlled by the monetary authority.[33] Although only limited confidence can be attached to the estimates derived through econometric analysis, they can provide some guidance to the monetary authority on problems such as this.

Summary and Conclusion

In this chapter we have attempted to describe a framework within which to analyze the process through which the money stock is determined. We included the derivation of the reserve equation from the Federal Reserve banks' consolidated balance sheet and certain United States Treasury accounts, a demonstration of the role and operation of the individual depositary-institution system and the influence of the behavior of the depositary institutions and the public on the equilibrium money stock. Our objective was not to present the money sup-

---

[33]See the reading by Robert Rasche which follows this chapter.

ply process in a completely precise and empirically relevant manner. We have indicated, however, the outlines of several models of money supply determination and the role of assumed behavioral relations in such models. In later chapters some of the forms derived from these models will be used in the development of macroeconomic models.

QUESTIONS

1. Assume that the public and commercial banks are in "equilibrium," that is, that the public is holding its preferred relative amounts of currency, demand deposits, and certificates of deposits and banks are holding their desired level of excess reserves. Given the data below, use the kind of proportionality relations we employed in the early models of this chapter to answer the following questions.
   Current required reserve ratio on demand deposits = .15
   Current required reserve ratio on certificates of deposits = .10
   Currency outstanding = $50 billion
   DD liabilities of commercial banks = $200 billion
   CD liabilities of commercial banks = $100 billion
   Total reserves held by banks = $50 billion
   a. What is the value of the demand deposit expansion coefficient?
   b. By how much will demand deposits increase if the Fed increases bank reserves by $5 billion (by a direct purchase of government securities from banks, for example)?
   c. By how much will the injection of reserves in (b) increase the money supply?
   d. What volume of excess reserves will the banks hold after the above deposit expansion has been completed?
   e. What volume of new loans will be generated by the banking system through this process.
2. The currency needs of the public are strongly influenced by "seasonal" factors. For example, the traveling, shopping, and gift giving traditions associated with Christmas greatly increase the public's need for cash. Describe the problems which this seasonal variation in currency demand might cause for the monetary authorities. How would such variations affect their ability to control the money stock?
3. What relationship is generally hypothesized between the market rate of interest and
   a. The demand for currency as a percentage of demand deposits
   b. The demand for CDs as a percentage of demand deposits
   c. The demand for excess reserves

  d. The quantity of money supplied (Be sure you can explain this one by using a, b, and c above).
4. In the linear money supply model the rate of interest did not influence the expansion coefficient but it did influence the quantity of money supplied. Explain.
5. In the nonlinear model the rate of interest influenced the expansion coefficient. Explain.
6. What is the unborrowed base? How would one reasonably assume borrowed reserves would vary with the discount rate? with the market rate of interest?
7. Why is the relationship between the level of income and the expansion coefficient in the nonlinear model regarded as "ambiguous"?

BIBLIOGRAPHY

ASCHEIM, JOSEPH, "Commercial Banks and Financial Intermediaries: Fallacies and Policy Implications," *Journal of Political Economy*, vol. 67 (February 1959), 59–71.

BLACK, ROBERT P., "The Impact of Member Bank Reserves upon the Money Supply," *Southern Economic Journal*, vol. 29 (January 1963), 199–210.

BRUNNER, KARL, and ALLAN H. MELTZER, "The Federal Reserve's Attachment to Free Reserves," Testimony before the Subcommittee on Domestic Finance of the House Committee on Banking and Currency, 88th Congress, 2nd Session (May 7, 1964), 1–27.

BURGER, ALBERT E., *The Money Supply Process* (Belmont, CA: Wadsworth, 1972).

BURNS, ARTHUR, "The Role of the Money Supply in the Conduct of Monetary Policy," *Monthly Review*, Federal Reserve Bank of Richmond (December 1973), 2–8.

CAGAN, PHILLIP, *Determinants and Effects of Changes in the Stock of Money 1875–1960* (New York: Columbia University Press, 1965).

DE LEEUW, FRANK, and EDWARD GRAMLICH, "The Channels of Monetary Policy: A Further Report on the Federal Reserve MIT Model," *Journal of Finance*, vol. 24, no. 2 (May 1969), 265–290.

FAND, DAVID I., "Some Implications of Money Supply Analysis," *The American Economic Review*, vol. 57 (May 1967), 380–400.

———, "Some Issues in Monetary Economics: Can the Federal Reserve Control the Money Stock," *Review*, Federal Reserve Bank of St. Louis, vol. 52 (January 1970), 10–27.

FRIEDMAN, MILTON, "Letter on Monetary Policy," *Monthly Review*, Federal Reserve Bank of Richmond (May–June 1974), 20–23.

FRIEDMAN, MILTON, and ANNA SCHWARTZ, *A Monetary History of the U.S. 1867–1960* (Princeton, NJ: Princeon University Press, 1963), app. B.

GOLDFELD, STEPHEN M., *Commercial Bank Behavior and Economic Activity* (Amsterdam: North Holland, 1966).

GURLEY, JOHN G., and EDWARD S. SHAW, *Money in a Theory of Finance* (Washington: The Brookings Institution, 1960).

GUTTENTAG, JACK M., and ROBERT LINDSAY, "The Uniqueness of Commercial Banks," *Journal of Political Economy*, vol. 67 (October 1968), 991–1014.

HAMBURGER, MICHAEL J., "The Lag in the Effect of Monetary Policy: A Survey of Recent Literature," in *Monetary Aggregates and Monetary Policy* (New York: Federal Reserve Bank of New York, 1974), 104–111.

HESS, ALAN C., "An Explanation of Short-Run Fluctuations in the Ratio of Currency to Demand Deposits," *Journal of Money, Credit and Banking*, (August 1971).

HOLMES, ALAN R., "Operational Constraints on the Stabilization of Money Supply Growth," in *Controlling Monetary Aggregates* (Boston: Federal Reserve Bank of Boston, 1969), 65–78.

HOSEK, WILLIAM, "Determinants of the Money Multiplier," *Quarterly Review of Economics and Business* (Summer 1970), 37–46.

KAUFMAN, GEORGE, "The Demand for Currency," Staff Economic Study, Board of Governors of the Federal Reserve System.

LOMBRA, RAYMOND, and RAYMOND TORTO, "Measuring the Impact of Monetary and Fiscal Actions: A New Look at the Specification Problem," *Review of Economics and Statistics*, vol. 56, no. 1 (February 1974), 23–27.

MAYER, THOMAS, "Statement in Monetary Policy Oversight," Hearings, Committee on Banking, Housing and Urban Affairs, U.S. Senate, 94th Congress, 1st Session (1975), 179–186.

MEIGS, A. J., *Free Reserves and the Money Supply* (Chicago: University of Chicago Press, 1962).

NEWLYN, W. T., "The Supply of Money and Its Control," *Economic Journal*, vol. 74 (June 1964), 327–346.

ORR, DANIEL, and W. G. MELLON, "Stochastic Reserve Losses and Expansion of Bank Credit," *American Economic Review*, vol. 51, no. 4 (September 1961), 614–623.

PHILLIPS, C. A., *Bank Credit* (New York: Macmillan 1926).

RASCHE, ROBERT H., "A Review of Empirical Studies of the Money Supply Mechanism," *Review*, Federal Reserve Bank of St. Louis (July 1972), 11–19.

SAMUELSON, PAUL, and MILTON FRIEDMAN, "Statement on the Conduct of Monetary Policy," Hearings, Committee on Banking, Housing and Urban Affairs, 94th Congress, 1st Session (November 1975).

SMITH, PAUL F., "Concepts of Money and Commercial Banks," *Journal of Finance*, vol. 21 (December 1966), 635–648.

SMITH, WARREN, "Financial Intermediaries and the Effectiveness of Monetary Controls," *Quarterly Journal of Economics*, vol. 73 (November 1959), 533–553.

TEIGEN, RONALD, "Demand and Supply Functions for Money in the United States: Some Structural Estimates," *Econometrica*, vol. 32, no. 4 (October 1964), 476–509.

TOBIN, JAMES, "Commercial Banks as Creators of 'Money,'" in *Banking and Monetary Studies*, Deane Carson, ed. (Homewood, IL: Richard D. Irwin, 1963), 408–419.

Introduction to Readings / Part I

In the preceding chapter we specified an analytical framework to examine the behavior of the public, depository institutions and the monetary authority, as this behavior relates to the determination of the money stock. The readings in this section will focus on three of the most controversial subjects surrounding the determination of the money stock.

The first article, by Anatol Balbach and Albert Burger, explains the derivation of the monetary base—the set of assets held by depository institutions and the public that constrains the money supply. Because, as indicated in the preceding chapter, the stock of money depends also on other variables, is not immediately controllable by the central bank, and is sensitive to regulatory and institutional changes. The monetary base, being much more controllable and stable than various measures of the money stock, has gained importance in recent years.

In the preceding chapter mention was made of alternative measures of the money stock—measures that include assets other than M-1B, deposits that may be transferred by check or wire and currency in circulation. Because of ever changing institutional and regulatory developments the Federal Reserve recently announced redefinition of the various measures of the money stock. The second article in this section, by Neil G. Berkman describes these new measures and compares them to older measures. This reading also surveys some technical issues involved in these measurements.

As we have pointed out, the money stock, however it is measured, is not strictly controllable by the monetary authorities. In other words, it may be affected by the state of the economy, particularly the level of interest rates and the level of aggregate income. The preceding chapter examined the reasons why these variables might influence the money stock. The final article in this section, by Robert Rasche, provides statistical estimates of the magnitude of these influences. Rasche's work provides some empirical underpinning for the theoretical work presented in the preceding chapter.

Derivation of the Monetary Base

Anatol B. Balbach
Albert E. Burger

Although the monetary base has been a key concept in monetary analysis for two decades, its use has been primarily restricted to the monetary systems of industrial nations.[1] Specifically, the base as constructed and measured in the United States has tended to be applied with some modifications to other economies. This article is an attempt to establish a general definition of a monetary base applicable to all relevant institutional structures and to provide guidelines for the identification and measurement of the base.

Given a set of institutional arrangements and predictable behavior on the part of market participants, changes in the monetary base produce predictable changes in the money stock. Under these conditions the base can be used as a predictor of the money stock and as a variable whose control implies the control of changes in the quantity of money. Thus the practical use of the base encompasses only those institutional structures where the money stock cannot be predicted and controlled *directly* by monetary authorities, but where the base can be measured and affected.

Where it is the case that every unit of the money stock can be directly created or destroyed by monetary authorities, or that economic forces or policy actions affect the base and the money stock by exactly the same magnitudes, there is no reason to resort to the use of the base concept. Alternatively, if the constraint on money creation consists solely of a single money-creator's decisions as to how much money to create in order to have it acceptable as money to all users, the

Reprinted from *Review*, November 1976, 2–8, by permission of the Federal Reserve Bank of St. Louis and the author.

[1]For further discussion of the concepts of monetary base and high-powered money, see Karl Brunner and Allan H. Meltzer, "An Alternative Approach to the Monetary Mechanism," U.S. Congress, House of Representatives, Committee on Banking and Currency, Subcommittee on Domestic Finance, 88th Cong., 2nd Sess., August 17, 1964, 9–20; Milton Friedman and Anna Jacobson Schwartz, *A Monetary History of the United States 1867–1960* (Princeton: Princeton University Press, 1963); Phillip Cagan, *Determinants and Effects of Changes in the Stock of Money 1875–1960* (New York: National Bureau of Economic Research, 1965). Also see Leonall C. Andersen and Jerry L. Jordan, "The Monetary Base—Explanation and Analytical Use," Federal Reserve Bank of St. Louis, *Review*, August 1968, 7–11.

base, while it exists in principle, is not obectively measurable and cannot be used either as a predictor or as a control variable. This leaves the monetary base as a useful concept in monetary systems which are characterized by the existence of fiat money, more than one money-creating institution, and fractional reserve banking.

The Concept

In a system which exhibits these features, the money stock in the hands of the public will potentially consist of commodity money (such as gold and silver coins), liabilities of monetary authorities (currency) and liabilities of private institutions (bank notes and/or bank deposits). These assets of the nonbanking public will be used as money only if transactions costs associated with other assets are higher. In other words, since the productivity of any asset used as money lies in its ability to facilitate transactions, it must be an instrument which minimizes the costs of conducting transactions. Apart from such features as divisibility, convenience and safety it must also reasonably maintain its purchasing power vis-à-vis other assets. Any asset that is convenient in every respect but whose purchasing power fluctuates widely and unpredictably will impose high risks on its holders and, in effect, high transaction costs.

The stability of purchasing power, as used here, refers to its exchange value against the bundle of all other available assets, goods, and services. One of the main requisites of this stability is a relatively stable supply of this asset called money. If money is created without restraint or if its production fluctuates widely, its purchasing power will fluctuate accordingly, and the costs imposed on its holders will encourage them to use some other asset to facilitate transactions. Thus, for any asset to function as money, its users must be convinced that its supply is constrained either by some institution they trust or by some set of other assets that are deemed to be relatively fixed in quantity or adequately controlled by market or institutional forces. The monetary base is this set of assets that constrains the growth of the money stock.

Commodity money is accepted because of the belief that market forces are such as to assure a relatively stable supply. Government liabilities—currency—are accepted so long as it is believed that the monetary authorities will maintain a relatively stable growth of these liabilities. But what induces the nonbanking public to accept liabilities of private, profit-making institutions such as banks? Obviously, it is because something limits the growth of these deposits and hence insures that there will remain a fairly stable rate of exchange of these deposits for other assets.

In a banking system where there exists more than one bank and where the money stock is comprised solely of bank liabilities (deposits, currency, and coin issued by the banks), the users of these liabilities will frequently deposit liabilities of one bank at another bank. If the banks were to use assets which were each others' liabilities as a basis for issuing new money, there would be no effective constraint on the expansion of money and, consequently, banks could find that their liabilities cease to be accepted as money. Knowing this, they will not accept each others' liabilities without being able to convert them into some asset which is not dominated by actions of banks themselves. The asset that will emerge will also have the lowest transactions cost. This asset, whatever it is, will then constitute part of the monetary base.

Each bank, knowing that its liabilities will be presented to it by other banks for conversion into this acceptable asset, will have to hold a stock of this asset as a reserve for conversion. In the absence of legal constraints, the size of this cushion or reserve, relative to the amount of monetary liabilities it creates, will depend upon the probability with which the bank's monetary liabilities are deposited at other banks. Thus, the total amount of this reserve asset will constrain the amount of money that can be produced by the system.

If the money stock includes commodity money or currency issued by monetary authorities in addition to private bank liabilities, then the banks will have to be ready to convert their monetary liabilities into forms acceptable not only to other banks but also to the nonbanking public. Thus they will have to hold a reserve of those assets that may be demanded by both. The monetary base will then consist not only of those assets that banks use to settle monetary liabilities among themselves but also those assets that are used to satisfy the conversion demands of the public. This does not preclude the possibility that the interbank settlement asset is the same as the one that is used in settling with the public.

To sum up, in a system where the money stock consists of commodity money, governmental liabilities, and bank liabilities, the base will consist of commodity money, governmental monetary liabilities, and whatever assets the banks use to settle interbank debts. The assets that constrain the growth of money stock (the monetary base) can therefore be identified in any monetary system by ascertaining and summing the following:

1. those assets which the consolidated banking sector uses to settle interbank debt;[2] and
2. those items, aside from bank liabilities, which are used as money.

Measurement and Control

Once the monetary base is identified and measured, and the behavior of the banks and the public described and estimated, changes in the base can be used to predict changes in the money stock. What remains is the task of finding what causes the base to change and how to control these changes, since control of the size of the base, given the behavior of banks and the public, implies the control of the money stock.

If the base were to consist solely of commodity money or real assets, then one would have to analyze the forces which affect the supply of these assets; attempts at control of these forces would constitute the exercise of monetary policy. For example, if gold coin were the sole constituent of the base, then the control of production and importation of gold coin would allow for the control of the money stock. Under such circumstances, factors affecting the supply of gold coin could be identified and measured in the balance sheets of domestic gold producers and in the balance of payments.

Suppose that the base consists of currency issued by the government. If we were to assume that government maintains a complete balance sheet and that its creation of currency depends upon changes in the configuration of its assets and liabilities, then the factors affecting the monetary base would be found in and could be analyzed from the balance sheet of the government. It is usually the case, however, that governments cannot and do not maintain complete balance sheets. Furthermore, the issuance of currency may be based on arbitrary or political decisions that cannot be quantified. Under such circumstances the base or its currency component has to be taken as given at any time

---

[2]We look at the assets of the consolidated banking sector in order to eliminate correspondent balances which are used as instruments of settlement among respondent banks. These deposits are acceptable to respondent banks only because they represent a claim on the reserves of correspondent banks. Thus, the constraint is still exercised by the availability of assets which are not dominated by actions of individual banks.

and the control of the base rests solely with governmental authorities who, in their desire to have their liabilities acceptable as money, will presumably limit currency growth.

When, in addition to the above-mentioned components, the banking system uses central bank liabilities as reserves necessary for conversion of their own monetary liabilities, the factors affecting changes in this component of the base are summarized in the balance sheet of the central bank. Central banks do maintain balance sheets and any changes in their "reserve liabilities" reflect changes in their assets and/or other liabilities. By definition, a balance sheet implies that any subset of liabilities must equal the algebraic sum of all assets and remaining liabilities and capital in that balance sheet. Thus the central bank component of the base can be alternatively measured as the algebraic sum of all entries in the central balance sheet other than its reserve liabilities. This measure is frequently referred to as the "sources of the monetary base." Since factors supplying the central bank component of the base are represented in the sources, the analysis, prediction, and control of the monetary base must begin with the identification and measurement of its sources.

At present, in virtually all modern monetary systems the base consists of either central bank liabilities, government liabilities, or both. These items are the ones used to settle interbank debt and some circulate as money. Government liabilities must be taken as given since decisions as to their supply are determined by factors which cannot be quantified. In the case of central bank liabilities, it is necessary to derive the sources of the base component, which consist of the algebraic sum of all other assets and liabilities in the central bank balance sheet. These sources permit the identification of causes of changes in the monetary base and, consequently, of policy actions which control these changes.

Examples of Derivation and Usefulness of the Sources of Monetary Base

Case 1.   Base Consists Solely of Central Bank Liabilities

Suppose there exists a monetary system where the money stock consists of the public's deposits at banks and currency issued by the central bank and held by the public. Suppose that we observe further that the asset of the consolidated banking sector which is used to settle interbank debts consists of deposits at the central bank. Conversion of monetary liabilities of banks to the public is in the form of currency. This implies that the monetary base consists of banks' deposits at the central bank and currency issued by the central bank, which is thus the sole producer of the base. Since all changes in the base result in corresponding changes in all other entries of the central bank balance sheet, the sources of the base can be identified.

A hypothetical balance sheet of the central bank is given below.

Central Bank

Assets	Liabilities
Gold (G)	Demand Deposits of Banks (DB)
Foreign Assets (FA)	Currency Held by Banks (CB)
Government Securities (BC)	Currency Held by Public (CP)
Loans and Discounts (LD)	Demand Deposits of Treasury (DT)
Other Assets (OA)	Demand Deposits of Foreign Central Banks (DF)
	Currency Held by Treasury (CT)
	Other Liabilities and Capital (OL)

The monetary base is comprised of demand deposits of banks at the central bank (DB) and currency, issued by the central bank, that is held by banks (CB) and by the public (CP). Thus the sources of the base, as derived from the central bank's balance sheet, are the algebraic sum of all other balance sheet entries:

$$G + FA + BC + LD + OA - OL - DT - DF - CT$$

Measures of these items are readily available from central bank accounts and can be used to trace the impact of any transaction in the economy on the monetary base.

The process is simple—one must merely ascertain whether a transaction affects any of the items in the sources of the base and sum the effects. Suppose that the Treasury collects taxes and deposits the proceeds in its account at the central bank. The transactions involved are:

	Central Bank		*Banks*	
	DB − 100	DB − 100	DP − 100
	DT + 100		

The only entry that appears in the sources statement of the base and is affected is demand deposits of the Treasury (DT), which is a negative item and rises by 100. Thus, the base declines by 100. It is immediately apparent what has happened with the base and what has caused the change.

Another example could be a central bank purchase of government securities from banks (BB).

Central Bank		Banks	
BC + 100	DB + 100	DB + 100	
		BB − 100	

Again, the only entry affected in the sources statement is government securities held by the central bank, an item which affects the base positively. It has risen by 100; thus the base has increased by 100.

Suppose this country engages in attempts to peg the exchange rate. A deficit in its international balance of payments will cause the central bank to enter the exchange market as a seller of foreign currencies (its holdings of these currencies are represented by the item foreign assets). A representative net transaction would be as follows:

Central		Banks	
FA − 100	DB − 100	DB − 100	DP − 100

Foreign assets (FA) is the only item in the sources statement that has been affected. Its decline of 100 implies the same change in the base.

Case II.   Base Consists of Central Bank and Government Liabilities

Another type of monetary system has a money stock that is made up of the public's deposits at private banks, currency issued by the government or by both the government and the central bank. If central bank deposit liabilities function as an instrument of interbank settlement and the public periodically converts some of its deposits into currency, the monetary base includes bank deposits at the central bank and currency issued by the central bank and by the Treasury.

In principle, this would mean that the sources statement of the base would have to be derived from the consolidation of Treasury and central bank balance sheets. But, as was discussed earlier, complete Treasury balance sheets are universally unavailable. In this case, the base and its sources must be modified by simply adding Treasury currency in the hands of banks and the public to both the base and the sources of the base. The monetary base would then become demand deposits of banks at the central bank (DB) plus central bank currency held by banks (CB) plus Treasury currency held by banks (TCB) plus central bank currency held by the public (CP) plus Treasury currency held by the public (TCP). And the sources statement is:

$$G + FA + BC + LD + OA + TCB + TCP$$
$$- OL - DT - DF - CT$$

The analysis uses the new statement in exactly the same way that previous transaction examples used the preceding one. Suppose that the Treasury prints and sells new currency to commercial banks and deposits the receipts in the central bank.

Treasury		Central Bank		Banks	
DT + 100	TCB + 100	DB − 100	TCB + 100		
		DT + 100	DB − 100		

Treasury currency held by the banks increases and so do Treasury deposits at the central bank. Since they enter into the sources statement with opposite signs, there is no change in the monetary base. Commercial banks have simply changed the form of their reserves without changing the total amount.

Another illustrative transaction is the sale of Treasury currency to the central bank.

Treasury		Central Bank	
DT + 100	TCC + 100	OA + 100	DT + 100

Since Treasury currency at the central bank has not been specifically included in the central bank balance sheet, it must appear in other assets of the central bank (OA), which rises by 100 together with deposits of the Treasury at the central bank (DT). Since these items enter the sources statement with opposite signs there is, again, no change in the monetary base.

But if the Treasury prints new currency and buys services from the public, the transaction is recorded as follows:

	Treasury		Central Bank	
Services + 100	TCP + 100		No Change	No Change

	Banks		Public
No Change	No Change	TCP + 100 Services − 100	

While the central bank balance sheet is unaffected, the sources statement indicates that the base rises by 100 because TCP has increased.

While the vast majority of relevant monetary systems are represented by the two cases discussed above, there are occasionally some institutional or market arrangements which require additional refinements.

It may be that the consolidated banking system, due perhaps to regulations imposed upon it, uses government securities as well as central bank deposits to settle interbank liabilities. As is the case with Treasury currency, there is no government balance sheet which allows us to identify the sources of this base component; therefore, holdings of government securities by banks and the public must be added to the base and its sources as derived from the central bank balance sheet. Similarly, if any other asset is used for interbank clearing or as part of the money stock, it must be accounted for in the sources of the monetary base. The general rule for inclusion is as follows:

1. If the asset is the liability of an entity that maintains a balance sheet, the balance sheets of that entity and the central bank are to be consolidated and the sources of the base derived in a similar manner as in Case I.
2. If the asset is a liability of an entity which does not have a balance sheet, or is a real asset, then the quantities of that asset that are held by commercial banks and the public must be added to the sources and the monetary base which were constructed from the central bank balance sheet.

Obviously, analysis and control are enhanced by the ability to identify as many factors as possible that may affect monetary base. Consequently, when balance sheets are available, they should be used in the derivation of base statements. The simple addition of other assets included in the base to the sources statement assumes that these assets are predetermined and not subject to control by the central bank.

Summary

In most general terms the monetary base is that set of assets held by the banks and the public which constrains the money stock. The items that constitute the base in any country can be identified by determining those assets which the consolidated banking sector uses to settle interbank debt, and those items, aside from bank liabilities, which are used as money. The factors that cause the amount of base to change can be determined by consolidating the balance sheets of the producers of the base. In the case where the central bank is the sole producer of base, this process can proceed from the balance sheet of the central bank. Any change in the base will appear as a change in one or more other entries in the central bank's balance sheet. When there are other producers of base, such as the Treasury, this article showed how the base could be constructed to take this into account.

The sources statement of the base is most important to the monetary authorities. This statement serves as a scheme for analyzing how actions taken by the monetary authorities, such as purchases or sales of securities, or lending to banks, influences the base and, hence, the money stock. It also permits them to analyze how other factors influence the base and, consequently, permits them to identify the type of offsetting actions that must be taken to counter these outside influences.

Appendix

The purpose of this Appendix is to demonstrate how the principles of monetary base construction can be applied to the US monetary system and to show how a base construct can be reconciled with data which is regularly published in the Federal Reserve *Bulletin*.

The US monetary system is characterized by the existence of three sets of money-creating institutions: (1) the US Treasury which issues coin and which has some Treasury notes and silver certificates outstanding, (2) the Federal Reserve System, which issues Federal Reserve notes and demand deposits, and (3) commercial banks which issue demand deposits. Commercial banks, which constitute the private money-creating sector, can use as instruments of settlement currency (Federal Reserve notes and Treasury currency and coin) and demand deposits at the Federal Reserve Banks. Therefore, the base consists of monetary assets of the consolidated domestic private sector (currency and coin held by banks and the public, and demand deposits of member banks at Federal Reserve Banks). These are the monetary liabilities of the government sector to the private domestic sector. Consequently, the base and the sources of the base, as derived from the Federal Reserve balance sheet, must be supplemented by the addition of Treasury currency and coin held by commercial banks and the public.

It should also be noted that certain monetary relationships between the central bank and the government are unique to US monetary institutions. For example, gold is held by the Treasury, which issues gold certificates to the Federal Reserve System, and coin is issued by the Treasury while almost all of the currency is issued by the Federal Reserve Banks. These unique features, however, present no difficulty in the development of base statements and perhaps demonstrate even more forcefully that such construction is applicable to all institutional arrangements.

A simplified balance sheet for the Federal Reserve System is given below:

Federal Reserve System

Assets	Liabilities
Gold Certificates (GC)	FR Notes Held by:
Special Drawing Rights (SDR)	Treasury (CT)
Coin Held by the FR (TCC)	Commercial Banks (CB)
Loans and Discounts (LD)	Public (CP)
Government Securities Held	Demand Deposits:
by FR (BC)	Treasury (DT)
Other Assets (OA)	Commercial Banks (DB)
	Foreign (DF)
	Other Liabilities and Capital of the FR (OL)

The base, as defined and identified in the Federal Reserve's balance sheet, consists of demand deposits of banks at the Federal Reserve Banks (DB), Federal Reserve notes held by banks and the public (CB + CP) and Treasury currency held by banks (TCB) and the public (TCP):

$$DB + CB + CP + TCB + TCP \qquad (1)$$

The sources statement consists of the algebraic sum of all the remaining assets and liabilities in the Federal Reserve balance sheet plus monetary liabilities of the Treasury held by banks and the public (TCB + TCP). Therefore, the sources of the base consist of the following balance sheet entries:

$$LD + BC + OA + GC + SDR + TCC - CT$$
$$- DT - DF - OL + TCB + TCP \qquad (2)$$

Data for derivation of sources of the base is published monthly in the Federal Reserve *Bulletin* in a table entitled "Member Bank Reserves, Reserve Bank Credit, and Related Items." This table is divided into two parts:

Factors supplying reserve funds:
Reserve Bank Credit Outstanding (RBC)
Gold Stock (G)
Special Drawing Rights (SDR)
Treasury Currency Outstanding (TCO), and

Factors absorbing reserve funds:
Currency in Circulation (CC)
Treasury Cash Holdings (TK)
Deposits, other than Member Bank Reserves with FR (d)
Other Federal Reserve Liabilities and Capital (OL)
Member Bank Reserves with FR Banks (DB)
Currency and Coin held by Member Banks (CMB)

In terms of this statement, the base consists of member bank deposits at Federal Reserve Banks (DB) plus currency and coin in circulation issued by the Federal Reserve Banks (CB + CP) and issued by the Treasury (TCB + TCP). Thus, in terms of our balance sheet notation, it consists of DB + CB + CP + TCB + TCP which is identical to Statement 1 from the balance sheet of the Federal Reserve.

For the sources statement we have to define the published entities in terms of balance sheet notation.

RBC = LD + BC + OA (where Federal Reserve float[1] is included in OA)
G   = Gold

---

[3]Federal Reserve float is computed from the balance sheets and is cash items in process of collection minus deferred availability cash items. See Federal Reserve Bank of New York, Glossary: "Factors Affecting Bank Reserves," Weekly Federal Reserve Statements (October 1975), 17–18.

SDR = Special Drawing Rights
TCO = TCB + TCP + TCC + TCT (where TCT refers to Treasury
            currency held by the Treasury)
TK   = (G − GC) + TCT + CT
d   = DT + DF
OL   = Other Liabilities

The sources statement, which is derivable from factors supplying and absorbing reserve funds, is:

$$RBC + G + SDR + TCO − TK − d − OL. \tag{3}$$

When balance sheet notation is substituted for published notation, and addition and subtraction are completed, statement (3) becomes,

$$LD + BC + OA + GC + SDR + TCC − CT$$
$$− DT − DF − OL + TCB + TCP \tag{4}$$

This statement is an identical statement to (2) which implies that the data published in the form of factors supplying and absorbing reserve funds is consistent with the sources statement as derived from the Federal Reserve balance sheet.

As an example of this procedure the following numerical example is presented. The balance sheet for the Federal Reserve System is for September 29, 1976, as reported on page A10 of the October 1976 Federal Reserve *Bulletin.*

Consolidated Statement of Condition of All Federal Reserve Banks
(Millions of Dollars)

Assets		Liabilities	
Gold Certificates	$ 11,598	FR Notes	$ 79,802
SDR	700	Demand Deposits:	
Cash Held by FR	365	Treasury	12,212
Loans and Discounts	324	Member Bank	
Government Securities		Reserves	29,807
Held by FR	99,224	Foreign	245
Other Assets	19,694	Other Liabilities	
		and Capital	9,839
	$131,905		$131,905

---

[4]Includes $920 million of other deposits.

In the notation used in this appendix, the base consists of demand deposits of commercial banks held at Federal Reserve Banks (DB) which equal $29,807 plus currency held by commercial banks and the public (CP + CB + TCP + TCB). This currency consists of FR notes ($79,802) plus Treasury currency outstanding ($10,757) which comes from the Treasury accounts, less the currency and coin held by Treasury ($425), called "Treasury cash," less Federal Reserve holdings of coin, called "cash held by FR" ($365).[5] The total currency component of the base consists of $89,769 million. Therefore, the base amounts to $29,807 plus $89,769, and equals $119,576.

The sources of the base consist of Treasury currency and coin held by commercial banks and the public, and all the items in the Federal Reserve's balance sheet except the two entries demand deposits of commercial banks (member bank reserves) and Federal Reserve notes. In other words, if one consolidates all the entries in the Federal Reserve balance sheet for the week of September 29, 1976, excluding Federal Reserve notes ($79,802) and demand deposits of member banks ($29,807), the total amount is $109,609 million. As was shown previously the amount of Treasury currency and coin held by commercial banks and the public was $9,967 million for the same date.[6] Hence, the total base is $109,609 plus $9,967 equals $119,576 million.

Using the notation presented in this appendix, the sources of the base may also be constructed from the entries that appear in the table "Member Bank Reserves, Federal Reserve Bank Credit, and Related Items" that appears on pages A2–A3 of the October 1976 Federal Reserve *Bulletin*. For September 29, 1976, the data are as follows:

Reserve Bank Credit (RBC) .... $113,972 million
Gold (G) 11,598
SDR 700
Treasury Currency Outstanding (TCO) 10,757
Treasury Cash (TK)........................ 425
Demand Deposits of Treasury (DT) 12,212
Foreign Demand Deposits (DF).............. 245
Other Liabilities[5] (OL)..................... 4,569

[5]FR notes held by FR banks are excluded from the entry. "FR notes" in the consolidated balance sheet.

[6]Treasury currency and coin held by banks and the public is the sum of silver certificates, United States notes and total coin. These amounts are available for the end of the month in Table MS-1, "Currency and Coin in Circulation," U.S. Department of the Treasury, Treasury *Bulletin*.

[7]Includes $920 million of other deposits.

Using the previous formula for the sources of the base given in Equation 3:

$$RBC + G + SDRs + TCO - TK - DT - DF - OL$$

we find that the summation of the sources stated in this manner, and applying the appropriate sign, equals $119,576 which is exactly equal to the base as derived from the Federal Reserve's balance sheet with the addition of Treasury currency held by commercial banks and the public.

Some Comments on the New Monetary Aggregates

*By Neil G. Berkman**

The past few years have been a period of rapid innovation in the nation's financial markets. Negotiable order of withdrawal (NOW) accounts, money market mutual funds, automatic transfer service (ATS) accounts, repurchase agreements, and other new short-term interest-paying investments have developed and grown rapidly in the fertile environment of high interest and inflation rates since the mid-1970s. Ongoing changes in bank regulation and legislation have blurred the distinctions between commercial banks and thrift institutions and between the types of deposits offered by these institutions (see the table on p. 72). The proliferation of "near-monies" and alteration in the characteristics of conventional "monies" are a source of concern for the Federal Reserve because of the difficulties they create for the implementation of monetary policy and the interpretation of the monetary aggregates.

The new financial instruments are close substitutes for the bank liabilities traditionally identified as money, mainly checking and savings deposits variously combined, so a persuasive argument can be made for their inclusion in at least one of the conventional measures of the money stock. Changes in the characteristics of the traditional com-

*Senior Economist, Federal Reserve Bank of Boston. The author thanks Stephen Blough for his research assistance.

Reprinted from *New England Economic Review*, Federal Reserve Bank of Boston, pp. 45–63, by permission of the publisher and author.

ponents of the aggregates may also have rendered the conventional definitions obsolete. Support for this position is provided by the observation that formerly reliable statistical associations between interest rates, GNP, and the monetary aggregates as conventionally defined have apparently broken down, a finding that emphasizes the policy dilemma created by the dramatic changes in the financial environment which have occurred in recent years.[1] In recognition of these problems the Fed began officially to review the definitions of the monetary aggregates in the mid-1970s.[2] A set of new aggregates was adopted early this year.[3] This paper describes these new monetary statistics, reviews the empirical evidence presented in their support, and offers some comments about how their behavior is likely to differ from the behavior of the old aggregates they were designed to replace.[4]

I. The New Monetary Aggregates

The new definitions of the monetary aggregates are presented in Table 1. The table also shows the old definitions for purposes of comparison. Examination of the table reveals the two most significant changes that distinguish the new from the old definitions. The first change is the explicit incorporation of the important new, highly liquid financial instruments into the monetary statistics. The second is the reclassification of conventional savings and time deposits in the new aggregates to acknowledge the growing similarities among the liabilities of all depositary institutions. These plus other more subtle changes will be discussed below.

M-1A: The first of the new definitions—M-1A, the most basic measure of the quantity of transactions balances—is quite similar to old M-1. The difference between these two money stock measures is that demand deposits in U.S. commercial banks held by foreign commercial

---

[1]See Stephen M. Goldfeld, "The Case of the Missing Money," *Brookings Papers on Economic Activity*, 3 (1976), 683–740. For a contrary view see R. W. Hafer and Scott E. Hein, "Evidence on the Temporal Stability of the Demand for Money Relationship in the United States," *Review*, Federal Reserve Bank of St. Louis, December 1979.

[2]See *Improving the Monetary Aggregates: Report of the Advisory Committee on Monetary Statistics.* Board of Governors of the Federal Reserve System, 1976.

[3]See Thomas D. Simpson, "The Redefined Monetary Aggregates," Federal Reserve *Bulletin*, Feburary 1980, 97–114.

[4]For a more technical discussion of these issues, see Neil G. Berkman, "The New Monetary Aggregates: A Critical Appraisal," *Journal of Money, Credit, and Banking*, May 1980.

Table 1. New and Old Monetary Aggregate Definitions

The New Monetary Aggregates	Amount in billions of dollars, November 1979	The Old Monetary Aggregates	Amount in billions of dollars, November 1979
M-1A Currency	106.6	M-1 Currency	106.6
Demand Deposits[1]	265.5	Demand Deposits[2]	276.0
M-1B M-1A	372.2		
NOW and ATS account balances, credit union share draft balances, demand deposits at mutual savings banks	115.7		
M-2 M-1B	387.9	M-2 M-1	382.6
Overnight RPs issued by commercial banks[3]	20.3	Savings deposits at commercial banks	210.6
Overnight Eurodollar deposits at Caribbean branches of US banks held by US nonbank residents	3.2	Time deposits at commercial banks[4]	352.1
Money market mutual fund shares	40.4		
Savings deposits at all depositary institutions	420.0		
Small time deposits at all depositary institutions[5]	640.8		
M-2 consolidation component[6]	-2.7		
M-2	1510.0	M-3 M-2	945.3
Large time deposits at all depositary institutions[7]	219.5	Savings and time deposits at thrift institutions	664.2
M-3 Term RPs issued by commercial banks	21.5		

Term RPs issued by savings and
loan associations   8.2

	M-4	M-2	
			1609.5
		Large negotiable time deposits at all depositary institutions	945.3
			95.9
	M-5	M-3	1041.2
			1609.5
		Large negotiable deposits at all depositary institutions	95.9
			1705.4

L	M-3	1759.1
	Other Eurodollars of US nonbank residents	34.5
	Bankers acceptances	27.6
	Commercial paper	97.1
	Savings Bonds	80.0
	Liquid Treasury obligations[8]	125.4
		2123.8

---

[1] Equals demand deposits at all commercial banks other than those due to domestic commercial banks and the U.S. government, less cash items in the process of collection and Federal Reserve float, less demand deposits due to foreign commercial banks and official institutions.

[2] Equals demand deposits at all commercial banks other than those due to domestic commercial banks and the U.S. government, less cash items in the process of collection and Federal Reserve float, plus foreign demand balances at Federal Reserve Banks.

[3] Estimated at 51 percent of all commercial bank RPs with the nonbank public and net of RPs held by money market mutual funds.

[4] Time certificates of deposit other than negotiable time certificates issued in denominations of $100,000 or more.

[5] Time deposits issued in denominations of less than $100,000.

[6] Consists of demand deposits included in M-1B that are held by thrift institutions and are estimated to be used for servicing their savings and small time deposits included in the new M-2 measure.

[7] Negotiable and nonnegotiable time certificates of deposit issued in denominations of $100,000 or more.

[8] Consists of Treasury bills with an original maturity of one year or less plus Treasury notes and bonds which mature within 18 months.

Selected Developments Affecting the Nature of the Monetary Aggregates

Development	Date First Introduced	Deposit Liability	New Monetary Aggregate Containing Deposit Liability
Preauthorized transfers	9/70	Savings balances at S&Ls and commercial banks	M-2
NOW accounts	6/72	Savings balances at MSBs, S&Ls, and commercial banks	M-1B
2½ year, 4-year, 6-year, and 8-year time deposits	1/70, 7/73 12/74, 6/78, respectively	Time deposits at MSBs, S&Ls, and commercial banks	M-2, M-3
Substantial penalty on early withdrawal of time deposits	7/73	Time deposits at commercial banks, S&Ls, and MSBs	M-2, M-3
Point-of-sale terminals (POS) permitting remote withdrawals of deposits from savings	1/74	Savings balances at S&Ls	M-2
Credit union share drafts	10/74	Regular share accounts at federal credit unions	M-1B
Savings accounts from domestic governments and businesses	11/74, 11/75, respectively	Savings balances at commercial banks	M-2
Telephone transfers	4/75	Savings balances at commercial banks	M-2
Demand deposits at thrifts	5/76	Deposits of MSBs and S&Ls	M-1B
6-month money market certificates	6/78	Time deposits at S&Ls, MSBs and commercial banks	M-2
Automatic transfer services (ATS)	11/78	Savings balances at commercial banks and thrifts having transactions balances	M-1B

Source: "A Proposal for Redefining the Monetary Aggregates," Federal Reserve Bulletin, January 1979, p. 15.

banks and official institutions are netted out of the demand deposit component of M-1A but are included in the demand deposit component of old M-1. These deposits are not believed to be held to finance goods and services transactions within the United States; rather, the evidence indicates that they serve primarily as clearing balances for financial transactions between banks operating in the Eurodollar and foreign exchange markets.[5] Since the monetary aggregates are designed to measure the value of balances that enter directly or indirectly into the *domestic* income-generating process, these deposits, which amounted to about $12 billion in 1979, were excluded from the new definitions.

M-1B: M-1B is defined as M-1A plus the major new forms of interest-paying *checkable* deposits issued by banks and thrift institutions as well as demand deposits issued by mutual savings banks. By including, in addition to currency held by the public, all of the types of deposits that are currently widely used to effect direct payment for goods and services, M-1B is a more comprehensive measure of transactions balances than either old M-1 or M-1A.

The importance of NOW and ATS accounts, credit union share draft balances, and demand deposits at mutual savings banks in M-1B is indicated in Figure 1. As late as 1975, these new checkable deposits accounted for less than 0.5 percent of M-1B; by the end of 1978 they represented only 2.3 percent; by December 1979 they totaled $16.2 billion and contributed 4 percent. By contrast, the currency component averaged just over 25 percent of M-1B during this period. Thus, despite their rapid growth the new checkable deposits have yet to capture a substantial share of total transactions balances. But their obvious usefulness for transactions purposes in competition with conventional noninterest-paying demand deposits and the high likelihood of their continued growth in the future clearly warrant their inclusion in the transactions balance measure of the money stock at the present time.

New M-2:   In addition to the "means-of-payment" balances included in M-1B, new M-2 includes those deposits which, while not currently

---

[5]See Helen T. Farr, Lance Girton, Henry S. Terrell, and Thomas H. Turner, "Foreign Demand Deposits at Commercial Banks in the United States," *Improving the Monetary Aggregates: Staff Papers*, Board of Governors of the Federal Reserve System, 1978, 35–54.

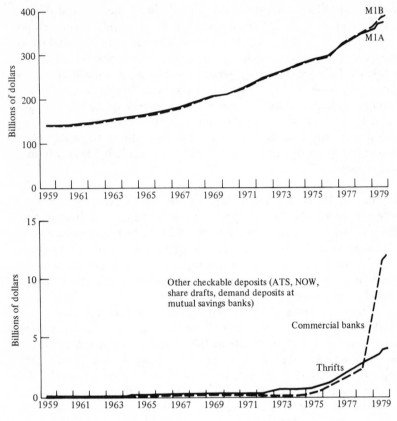

Figure 1. New M-1 Measures and Selected Components.
Source: Board of Governors of the Federal Reserve System.

accepted in payment for goods and services (with the exception of checks written against money market mutual fund shares), serve as temporary stores of purchasing power readily and inexpensively convertible into direct transactions-type balances.

Some of the components of new M-2 were included in either old M-2 or old M-3, and some appear in the aggregate definitions for the first time. In the former category are savings and small time deposit balances (under $100,000) issued by commercial banks and thrift institutions. As shown in Table 1, the old aggregates distinguished between these deposits on the basis of the institution by which they were issued:

old M-2 was defined to include only savings and time deposits issued by commercial banks; old M-3 added savings and time deposits (other than large negotiable time deposits) issued by thrift institutions to old M-2. One justification for this procedure was the observation that savings and time deposits at thrift institutions were less liquid and therefore less than perfectly substitutable with comparable deposits at commercial banks because deposits at thrifts could be converted to checkable form only after the expenditure of the time and trouble necessary to transfer them to a demand deposit account at a commercial bank. Legislative authorization for thrift institutions nationwide to issue checkable deposits is currently under consideration, however, so this argument for the continued segregation of savings and time deposits by type of institution is mitigated. Hence, new M-2 includes savings and time deposits (including money market certificates—MMCs) issued by all institutions.

Among the components of new M-2 that appear in the monetary aggregates for the first time is money market mutual fund shares (MMS). Their contribution to new M-2 is indicated in Figure 2. Unlike the conventional components of the aggregates, MMS are not issued by banks or thrift institutions. They are nevertheless included in new M-2 because they share most of the characteristics of those bank liabilities traditionally included in the broader definitions of money. Specifically, MMS can be converted into currency or demand deposits quickly and at low cost and, except under exceptional circumstances, their nominal value does not change with every change in open market interest rates.[6]

Since many money market mutual funds offer check-writing privileges, these accounts also can serve in principle as transactions balances. This would appear to make them eligible for inclusion in M-1B. The reason they were not included in this aggregate is that money market fund balances are in fact infrequently used for transactions purposes. Whether because of the high minimum check size required by most funds or because of other implicit or explicit costs associated with writing checks against fund balances, the rate of share redemptions over the past few years of rapid growth in the total value of shares outstanding has been extremely low—these balances have turned over at about the same rate as savings accounts and at about

---

[6]Although the yield on MMS changes as market interest rates change, in general the funds are organized so that the value of each share remains very close to $1.

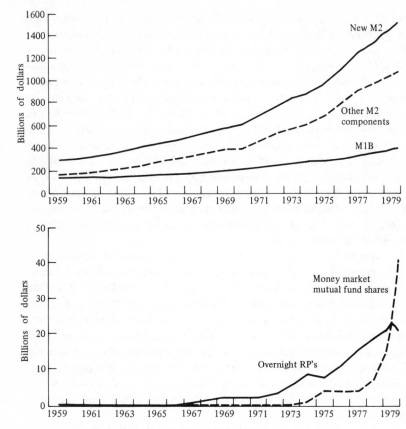

Figure 2. New M-2 and Selected Components.
Source: Board of Governors of the Federal Reserve System.

one-fiftieth the rate of demand deposits.[7] Despite the check-writing feature, MMS evidently compete predominately with savings and other "store of value" deposits rather than with the transactions balances included in M-1B.

Overnight repurchase agreements (RPs) and overnight Eurodollar

[7]In April 1979, the turnover rate—total debits or redemptions divided by the average level of deposits or shares outstanding—for demand deposits was 156.8, for savings deposits 3.2, and for MMS 3.1. See Timothy Q. Cook and Jeremy G. Duffield, "Money Market Mutual Funds: A Reaction to Government Regulations or A Lasting Financial Innovation?" *Economic Review*, Federal Reserve Bank of Richmond, July/ August 1979.

deposits at Caribbean branches of US banks are the two additional deposit components of new M-2. Both of these financial instruments have come into wide use recently in conjunction with the development of modern cash management techniques.[8] The prohibition of explicit interest payments on demand deposits under Federal Reserve Regulation Q creates an incentive for firms to minimize their checking account balances. One way firms can do this is by purchasing Treasury securities from their bank with funds known today not to be needed until some time in the future, perhaps for only a day or two. The bank agrees to repurchase the securities at a slightly higher price on this agreed-upon day. The firm benefits by earning a positive return on its temporarily idle cash balances. The bank benefits in two ways: first, by having use of the funds gained in exchange for its Treasury bills to make new loans; second, by lowering its required reserve burden. This second benefit occurs because reserve requirements on RPs are lower than reserve requirements on demand deposits. When a firm pays for the Treasury bills with its excess demand deposit balance, reservable deposits on the bank's books are reduced.

Another way for firms and banks to generate these benefits is through Eurodollar deposits. A firm can arrange to have its excess demand deposit balances transferred to a dollar-denominated time deposit at an offshore branch of a US bank—a Eurodollar deposit—near the end of a business day and repatriated on a convenient day in the future. Since the branch bank is in a foreign country neither regulation Q deposit rate ceilings nor Federal Reserve reserve requirements apply to the Eurodollar balances created in this way.[9] Both RPs and Eurodollar deposits at Caribbean banks have proven very popular. By the end of last year Caribbean Eurodollar deposits reached $3.5 billion, up from virtually zero in 1975, and total commercial bank RPs (overnight plus term) exceeded $40 billion, up from less than $15 billion in 1975.

Although RPs and Eurodollar deposits at Caribbean branches of US banks are highly liquid and carry only minimal capital risk, they are not checkable and so are not included in M-1B. The more difficult

[8]For a description of these techniques, see Ralph C. Kimball, "The Federal Reserve Wire Transfer System and the Demand for Money," elsewhere in this *Review*, and Thomas D. Simpson, "The Market for Federal Funds and Repurchase Agreements," Staff Studies 106, Board of Governors of the Federal Reserve System, 1979.

[9]However, such deposits are indirectly subject to a 10 percent marginal reserve requirement if they return to the parent bank in the form of borrowing from the branch bank.

problem is to decide in which higher order aggregate they properly belong. New M-2 is intended to measure the stock of transactions balances plus close substitutes for transactions balances held by the public. Since RPs and Eurodollar deposits may be viewed analytically either as an alternative to demand deposits not subject to Regulation Q interest ceilings or as an alternative to money market investments such as Treasury bills, bank certificates of deposit (CDs), or corporate commercial paper, only that proportion of these instruments that are held for the former purpose should be included in new M-2.[10] In the absence of direct evidence on the distribution of RP and Eurodollar accounts between "transactions balance substitute" and "longer term investment," a somewhat arbitrary classification is used in the aggregate definitions: only those RP and Eurodollar deposits with an original maturity of one day are included in new M-2; longer term RPs issued by commercial banks and thrift institutions are included in new M-3; longer term Eurodollar deposits are included in the broadest aggregate "L."[11]

Beginning in 1980, the weekly RP data being collected distinguish overnight from term deposits. Prior to 1980, however, the overnight component was estimated as 51 percent of total RPs. This estimate came from a survey that also indicated a substantial regional variance of the maturity distribution of total RPs across banks. Moreover, the maturity distribution may have varied systematically over the course of the interest rate cycle. Changes in the maturity distribution of RPs due to deposit shifts among banks or movements in market interest rates may therefore cause an unpredictable measurement error to be introduced into historical data for new M-2 as long as the 51 percent estimate is maintained.

The final component of new M-2 is the consolidation component. The aggregates measure various concepts of the money stock held by the public; as more components are added into each higher order

---

[10]This view is described in detail in Peter A. Tinsley and Bonnie Barnett, with Monica E. Friar, "The Measurement of Money Demand," Board of Governors of the Federal Reserve System, 1978, processed, and John Wenninger and Charles Sivesind, "Changing the M-1 Definition: An Empirical Investigation," Federal Reserve Bank of New York, 1979, processed. For an intriguing alternative view, see Richard D. Porter, Thomas D. Simpson, and Eileen Mauskopf, "Financial Innovation and the Monetary Aggregates," *Brookings Papers on Economic Activity* 1, 1979, 213–229.

[11]Eurodollar data are currently available with a long lag. If the data were available on a more timely basis, long-term Eurodollar deposits would be treated in the same way as long-term RPs and included in new M-3.

aggregate, the composition of the public itself changes. In M-1A, for example, the public is implicitly defined to include private firms and individuals as well as all depositary institutions other than the Federal Reserve and commercial banks. Demand deposits held by commercial banks at other commercial banks are therefore netted out of the demand deposit component of M-1A but demand deposits owned by other depositary institutions are included in the demand deposit component of this aggregate.

Certain of the liabilities of thrift institutions and money market mutual funds are added to those of the Federal Reserve and commercial banks in the definition of new M-2. Thus, these two groups are no longer part of the public in the new M-2 definition. For this reason, demand deposits held by thrift institutions and money market mutual funds to facilitate customers' withdrawals from savings and time deposits and redemptions of mutual fund shares should be removed from the demand deposit component of new M-2. The new M-2 consolidation component performs this function, at least partially. Although the lack of data on the demand deposit holdings of money market mutual funds prevents their inclusion in the consolidation component (survey data indicate that these holdings are small, however, and overnight RPs held by the funds are netted out of the RP component), it includes an estimate of demand deposits held by thrift institutions to service the savings and small time deposits included in new M-2 and therefore reduces the potential for double counting associated with these deposits.

New M-3:   New M-3 is constructed by adding to new M-2 longer term RPs and large denomination time deposits (over $100,000, including large CDs) issued by all depositary institutions. The dollar amounts involved in these components are substantial. Term RPs at commercial banks and thrifts totaled nearly $30 billion—60 percent of total outstanding RPs—and large time deposits exceeded $210 billion—12 percent of new M-3—by the end of 1979. New M-3 and its components are shown in Figure 3.

The long-term and hence relatively illiquid RPs and large *negotiable* and hence relatively risky CDs included in new M-3 move this aggregate a step further from the pure transactions balance concept underlying M-1A and B and the broader near-money concept underlying new M-2. While the conceptual differences between these money stock measures and their individual components are clear, the practical differences between them often are not. For example, since the small

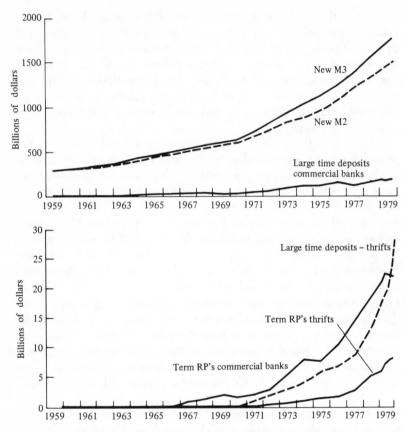

Figure 3.   New M-3 and Selected Components.
Source: Board of Governors of the Federal Reserve System.

time deposits included in new M-2 are subject to substantial early withdrawal penalties and are for this reason less liquid than savings deposits, MMS, or overnight RPs, they could have been included in new M-3 instead. Alternatively, only the money market certificates (MMCs) now included in the small time deposit component could have been added to new M-3 rather than to new M-2 on the grounds that except for the difference in scale between MMCs and CDs ($10,000 for MMCs, $100,000 for CDs), similar economic considerations determine the demand for both of them.

Since it is arbitrary to assume that overnight RPs always serve as transactions balance substitutes and that term RPs never do, another close "judgment call" was required to distribute these instruments between new M-2 and M-3. For that matter, it is not obvious that overnight RPs belong in new M-2 rather than M-1B. Until more is known about the behavior of the new near-monies, whether new M-2 or new M-3 is the most suitable broad aggregate definition—and in conjunction with M-1A or B the most appropriate target of monetary policy—is a matter of intuition and informed judgment as well as objective economic analysis.[12]

L: The aggregate L—liquid assets—is constructed by adding longer term Eurodollars held by U.S. nonbank residents, bankers acceptances, commercial paper, savings bonds, and liquid Treasury obligations to new M-3. Liquid Treasury obligations include all bills with an original maturity of less than one year and all Treasury notes and bonds scheduled to mature within 18 months. As in the case of the other aggregates, each component of L is recorded net of holdings by banks and other institutions whose liabilities appear elsewhere in the money measures.

L is a broad aggregate indeed, totaling over $2.1 trillion in November 1979. At $2.5 trillion nominal GNP in the fourth quarter of last year exceeded this figure by only 15 percent! The aggregates traditionally have included only instruments issued by banking institutions. While the introduction of MMS in new M-2 bends this tradition slightly, the inclusion of such items as Treasury securities and commercial paper in L breaks it completely. Since variation in the quantity of these components reflects the overall portfolio and financing decisions of private nonbank corporations and the Treasury as well as of banks, thrift institutions, and the Federal Reserve, L is more naturally interpreted as a measure of total short-term credit or liquidity in the economy than as a broad measure of the stock of money in the sense of new M-3.

II. Empirical Evidence

Following the trend of policy over the previous several years, the Federal Open Market Committee (FOMC) shifted the emphasis of its short-run operating strategy from money market conditions to rates of

---

[12]Another problem—which aggregate is most easily controllable by the Federal Reserve—will be explored in a subsequent article.

growth of the monetary aggregates in the early 1970s. Explicit growth rate ranges for the old aggregates were introduced in 1974, a practice given formal congressional endorsement with the promulgation of House Concurrent Resolution 133 in 1975 and the Humphrey-Hawkins Act in 1978. These initiatives focused public attention on the money growth target ranges announced periodically by the FOMC. They also focused the attention of the FOMC on the problem of selecting (and achieving) appropriate money growth objectives.

Among the analytical devices applied by the Federal Reserve Board Staff to the aggregate growth target selection problem are "money demand" equations estimated with historical data relating the demand for the various monetary aggregates to interest rates and GNP. Using these statistical relationships suggested by economic theory together with other analytical tools, the implications of alternative aggregate growth paths for the likely future course of interest rates, GNP and other important macroeconomic variables may be analyzed and monetary policy recommendations formulated. But the confidence that can be placed in the results of such simulation exercises depends on the reliability of the underlying statistical equations. Unfortunately, in recent years these relationships have not performed well—at least when specified in terms of the old aggregates. For example, relative to actual levels, simulations of standard money demand equations produced a cumulative *overprediction* of old M-1 of 15.5 percent and old M-2 of 10 percent between 1974 and 1979.[13] The resulting uncertainty about which rates of growth of the old aggregates were consistent with the FOMC's outlook for the economy created undesirable ambiguities in the specification of the monetary aggregate growth ranges and required the FOMC occasionally to adjust its targets in a relatively *ad hoc* fashion.[14]

Economists speculated that the money demand overpredictions were due to the public's substitution of the new near-money instru-

[13]Not all money demand equations behaved so badly. While still generating overpredictions, the disaggregated and more elaborately specified equations in the Federal Reserve Board model performed somewhat better than the standard equations during this period. See Richard D. Porter, Thomas D. Simpson, and Eileen Mauskopf, "Financial Innovation and the Monetary Aggregates."

[14]The October 6, 1979, Directive to the Manager of the Open Market Account illustrates the problem: "The range for M-1 had been established on the basis of an assumption that expansion of ATS and NOW accounts would dampen growth by about 3 percentage points over the year. It now appears that expansion of such accounts will dampen growth by about 1½ percentage points over the year..." Record of Policy Actions of the FOMC, Federal Reserve *Bulletin*, December 1979, 976.

ments that began to grow rapidly in the mid-1970s for those included in the old aggregates. This reduced the demand for the components of the old aggregates for given values of GNP and interest rates below what was expected from statistical analysis of historical data. This suspicion accelerated the search both inside and outside the Fed for the new aggregate definitions adopted in February 1980. It also established as one empirical test of the new definitions their ability to get the money demand equations back "on track."

The new aggregates generally perform satisfactorily in this first empirical test.[15] Although the demand equation for M-1B fit to data through 1974:II consistently overpredicts actual M-1B when stimulated over the 1974:III–1979:II period, the average overprediction (mean forecast error) is about 10 percent smaller than is that for old M-1. Moreover, the individual quarterly forecast errors (root mean square error) in the out-of-sample simulations are slightly smaller for new than for old M-1. Apparently the substitution of new checkable deposits for conventional demand deposits partially explains the downward "drift" in the demand for old M-1.

Generalizations about the relative performance of the money demand equations for the new and the old higher order aggregates are more difficult to formulate. The reason is that because of the substantial changes in the definitions of new M-2 and M-3, it is not obvious which old aggregates most closely correspond to the new ones. Since new M-2 includes savings and time deposits and most of their natural substitutes, this aggregate should probably be compared to old M-2 and M-3. Similarly, since new M-3 includes large denomination CDs and one of their natural substitutes—term RPs—this aggregate should be compared to old M-4 and M-5.

The average error from a simulation of the new M-2 demand equation over the 1974–79 period is small: new M-2 is *underpredicted* by an average of only $0.1 billion, compared to average overpredictions of $40.2 and $71.1 billion for old M-2 and M-3, respectively. Moreover, the individual quarterly forecast errors for new M-2 are significantly smaller than those for old M-2 and M-3. On the other hand, the average overprediction from the new M-3 demand equation is slightly

---

[15]The results described in this section are from David J. Bennett, Flint Brayton, Eileen Mauskopf, Edward K. Offenbacher and Richard D. Porter, "Econometric Properties of the Redefined Monetary Aggregates," Board of Governors of the Federal Reserve System, 1980, processed, and various other Board staff technical papers on the new monetary aggregates.

larger than the average overpredictions from the demand equations for old M-4 and M-5, and the individual quarterly forecast errors for this new aggregate are also larger than are those for the old aggregates M-4 and M-5.

The money demand results for the new aggregates thus present a mixed but basically favorable picture. The demand relationship for new M-2 appears to be reliable in the sense that it tracks the general trend of actual money growth without the large bias recently exhibited by the demand relationships for old M-2 and M-3. But on a quarter-to-quarter basis the equation for M-1B and new M-3 generated forecast errors (both over- and underpredictions) of a similar order of magnitude to those experienced with the old definitions.

Two other empirical tests of the new monetary statistics yield ambiguous results. One test examines the importance of the new relative to the old aggregates in equations relating the rate of growth of nominal GNP to current and past monetary growth and to a measure of current and past fiscal policy. These relationships are often interpreted as a measure of the relative *causal* significance of monetary and fiscal policy in influencing the economy.[16] The relative reduction in mean forecast errors and root mean square forecast errors from these equations for outside-of-sample simulations over the 1974–79 period is greatest in the case of new M-2, compared to old M-2 and M-3, although both M-1B and new M-3 do a marginally better job "explaining" GNP than old M-1 or old M-4 and M-5, respectively.

A second, closely related test analyzes the value of the new aggregates as *indicators* of GNP by measuring the correlation between the quarterly rate of growth of GNP and the contemporaneous rate of growth of each aggregate.[17] Because data on current growth of the monetary aggregates are available sooner than data on current growth of GNP, the aggregates may provide policy-makers with useful information about the state of the economy whether or not they "cause" GNP and whether or not they also function as intermediate policy targets in their own right. The results of this analysis do not indicate that the new definitions are clearly superior to the old ones. Although both L and M-1B have a slightly higher correlation with current GNP growth than any of the old aggregates, old M-1 marginally outperforms

[16]See Leonall C. Anderson and Jerry L. Jordan, "Monetary and Fiscal Actions: A Test of Their Relative Importance," *Review*, Federal Reserve Bank of St. Louis, November 1968.

[17]See Peter A. Tinsley and Paul A. Spindt, with Monica E. Friar, "Indicator and Filter Attributes of Monetary Aggregates: A Nit-Picking Case for Disaggregation," Board of Governors of the Federal Reserve System, 1978, processed.

both new M-2 and M-3, and old M-2 marginally outperforms new M-2 as an indicator of the state of the economy.

Overall, the empirical evidence in support of the new monetary aggregates is favorable but far from overwhelming. This may reflect the relative youthfulness of many of the components of the new aggregates and the alteration of the characteristics of some of the traditional components by new legislation, so that too few observations are available now to support clear-cut statistical conclusions on the usefulness of the new definitions. It may also reflect weaknesses in the statistical procedures themselves. One lesson of the redefinition exercise is that currently available empirical techniques are not sharp enough to reveal economically meaningful distinctions among alternative but closely related aggregates with the data at hand. Dramatic improvement in statistical performance should probably not have been expected in the first place. Then too, the ambiguous empirical results may simply reflect hidden weaknesses in the new definitions, or some combination of this plus the other two factors.

Despite these caveats, the immediate problem of tracking money demand faced by the FOMC is ameliorated (if only for the time being) by the new definitions, so they have this much to recommend them. Another point in their favor is that the new definitions incorporate present realities in the nation's payments mechanism in an intuitively (if not necessarily empirically) appropriate way. Such *a priori* considerations must be taken into account in judging the new monetary statistics, especially when the empirical results suggest that the specific component combinations are less important than the presence of the new components *somewhere* in the aggregates if money demand overpredictions are to be avoided.

In view of these considerations, perhaps a more sympathetic interpretation of the empirical evidence is warranted. The new aggregates solve one problem and in addition generally perform slightly better than the old aggregates in standard empirical applications. Unless and until a subsequent round of financial innovation renders them obsolete, the new monetary statistics are a worthwhile improvement on the old ones.

III. Cyclical Behavior

The new aggregate definitions alter the estimated magnitude of the money stock substantially. As of December 1979, for example, new M-2 averaged slightly more than $1,500 billion while old M-2 averaged only about $950 billion. This difference in *levels* simply reflects the broader coverage of the new definitions and in itself has no economic significance. More important are the implications of the broader coverage for the behavior of rates of growth and velocities of circulation (the ratio of GNP to money) of the new monetary statistics over the course of the business cycle. This section offers some comments about how the definitional changes are likely to affect the cyclical behavior of the monetary aggregates.

Table 2 reports the average growth rates and the standard deviation of growth rates (one measure of growth rate stability) of the new and the old aggregates and their velocities of circulation for the period 1960–1979 and for two subperiods. Table 3 shows the rates of monetary and velocity growth of both sets of aggregates measured from the peak to the trough and from the trough to the peak of the three business cycles that have occurred since 1960.

Comparing first old M-1 to M-1A, the tables reveal little difference in trend growth rates or stability of growth rates over the past 20 years, nor in the pattern of money and velocity growth during cyclical upswings and downswings. Since these two aggregates were essentially the same during this period, these observations are hardly surprising.

Until recently, M-1B behaved in the same manner as M-1A and old M-1. But as the "other checkable deposits" included in M-1B grew rapidly in the last half of the 1970s, the similarities gradually disappeared. The trend rate of M-1B growth accelerated from 3.8 percent in the decade of the 1960s to 6.6 percent in the last decade, while old M-1 and M-1A growth accelerated 3.8 percent in the first to 6.1 percent in the second of these subperiods. Note also that M-1B grew at over 7 percent in the most recent cyclical upswing, compared to M-1A and old M-1 growth during the same period of about 6.2 percent. Prior to this episode, the cyclical pattern of M-1B growth was virtually identical to that of the other two transactions balance aggregates.

This emerging disparity in the cyclical behavior of M-1A and M-1B reflects the public's substitution of interest-bearing checkable deposits for conventional demand deposits. To a more limited extent it may also reflect substitution of interest-bearing checkable deposits for passbook savings accounts.[18] The former process tends to reduce the

[18]Evidence from the New England NOW account experience indicates that this chain of substitution has not been very important. See Ralph C. Kimball, "Recent Developments in the NOW Account Experiment in New England," *New England Economic Review,* November/December 1976.

Table 2. Monetary and Velocity Growth Rates of the Old and the New Monetary Aggregates

Period	New Monetary Aggregates										Old Monetary Aggregates									
	M-1A		M-1B		M-2		M-3		L		M-1		M-2		M-3		M-4		M-5	
	μ	σ	μ	σ	μ	σ	μ	σ	μ	σ	μ	σ	μ	σ	μ	σ	μ	σ	μ	σ
Rate of Monetary Growth[1]																				
1960–69	3.8	1.9	3.8	1.9	7.1	1.7	7.5	2.6	6.9	1.9	3.8	2.0	6.4	2.2	7.2	1.9	6.7	3.1	7.4	2.6
1970–79	6.1	1.3	6.6	1.5	10.0	3.0	11.1	2.1	10.8	1.9	6.2	1.3	9.1	1.5	10.3	2.4	10.0	2.1	10.6	2.2
1960–79	5.0	2.0	5.2	2.2	8.5	2.8	9.3	3.0	8.8	2.7	5.0	2.1	7.8	2.3	8.7	2.6	8.4	3.1	9.0	2.9
Rate of Velocity Growth[2]																				
1960–69	2.9	1.8	2.9	1.8	-0.2	2.1	0.02	2.8	-0.1	1.8	2.9	1.8	0.4	1.8	-0.3	2.2	0.1	2.7	-0.5	2.8
1970–79	3.6	1.7	3.2	1.6	0.03	2.6	-1.0	2.0	-0.8	0.9	3.5	1.7	0.7	2.0	-0.3	2.2	0.2	2.9	-0.6	2.3
1960–79	3.3	1.8	3.0	1.7	-0.1	2.4	-0.5	2.5	-0.4	1.5	3.2	1.8	0.6	1.9	-0.3	2.2	0.2	2.8	-0.6	2.5

Note: μ = mean annual growth rate; σ = standard deviation of annual growth rate. Annual data for L are available only through 1978.

[1]Annualized growth rates based on seasonally adjusted annual data.

[2]Velocity is defined as nominal GNP divided by the money stock; annualized growth rates based on seasonally adjusted annual data.

Source: computed from annual data on the new and old monetary aggregates supplied by the Board of Governors of the Federal Reserve System.

Table 3. Cyclical Behavior of Monetary and Velocity Growth Rates of the Old and the New Monetary Aggregates

	New Monetary Aggregates				Old Monetary Aggregates				
	M-1A	M-1B	M-2	M-3	M-1	M-2	M-3	M-4	M-5
Rate of Monetary Growth									
Peak to trough[1]									
1960:2–1961:1	1.9	1.9	6.5	7.0	1.9	5.6	7.1	5.7	7.2
1969:4–1970:4	4.8	4.8	5.7	8.7	4.8	7.1	7.2	9.8	8.9
1973:4–1975:1	4.2	4.3	6.2	8.2	4.4	7.3	7.3	9.7	8.8
Trough to peak[2]									
1961:1–1969:4	4.2	4.2	7.2	7.5	4.2	6.7	7.3	7.0	7.5
1970:4–1973:4	6.8	6.8	10.8	12.9	6.9	10.1	11.4	11.8	12.5
1975:1–1979:4	6.2	7.1	10.6	10.6	6.3	9.1	10.3	8.1	9.7
Rate of Velocity Growth									
Peak to trough									
1960:2–1961:1	-1.7	-1.7	-6.3	-6.7	-1.7	-5.3	-6.8	-5.5	-6.9
1969:4–1970:4	-0.3	-0.3	-1.2	-4.1	-0.3	-2.6	-2.5	-5.2	-4.3
1973:4–1975:1	1.5	1.4	-0.5	-2.4	1.3	-1.5	-1.4	-3.9	-3.0
Trough to peak									
1961:1–1969:4	3.1	3.1	0.1	-0.2	3.1	0.6	0.0	0.3	-0.2
1970:4–1973:4	3.6	3.5	-0.4	-2.4	3.5	0.3	-1.0	-1.4	-2.0
1975:1–1979:4	4.9	4.1	0.6	0.6	4.9	2.1	0.9	3.0	1.5

[1]Averages of annualized quarterly rates of growth from quarter following peak to trough. Dates are NBER reference cycle dates.
[2]Averages of annualized quarterly rates of growth from quarter following trough to peak.

Source: Thomas D. Simpson, "The Redefined Monetary Aggregates," Federal Reserve *Bulletin*, February 1980, pp. 103, 105.

rate of growth of M-1A relative to M-1B, and hence to raise the velocity of circulation of M-1A relative to M-1B, for given levels of GNP and interest rates, while the latter process tends to raise the rate of growth of M-1B relative to M-1A and to old and new M-2. M-1B growth will therefore continue to exceed M-1A growth in every phase of the business cycle until adjustment to the new checkable deposits is complete.

Of the "other checkable deposits" included in M-1B, credit union share draft balances, demand deposits at mutual savings banks, and ATS accounts at commercial banks have been available nationwide for more than a year but NOW accounts are issued currently only by banks and thrift institutions in the Northeast and Atlantic seaboard states. Should legislation authorizing nationwide NOW accounts be passed by Congress, M-1B growth is likely to continue to exceed M-1A growth for another year or two at least. Should interest-paying checkable deposits supplant conventional demand deposits completely as the public's preferred transactions balance medium, the divergence in M-1A and M-1B growth rates may continue much longer.

Table 2 shows that the trend rate of growth of new M-2 fell between the trend rates of old M-2 and M-3 growth throughout the 1960–1979 period, while the trend rate of new M-3 growth consistently exceeded the trend growth rates of old M-4 and M-5. But reflecting the rich menu of financial instruments included in the new definitions, the pattern of relative growth rates of these two sets of aggregates over the course of the business cycle shown in Table 3 is different from the pattern described by old and new M-1. In particular, while M-1B and old M-1 growth rates tended to be within a tenth of a percentage point or so of each other during expansions and contractions until "other checkable deposit" growth accelerated in 1975, new M-2 has generally tended to grow significantly slower than old M-2 and M-3 during contractions and significantly faster than old M-2 during expansions. Similarly new M-3 has generally tended to grow significantly slower than old M-4 and M-5 during contractions and significantly faster than old M-4 during expansions.

The explanation for this difference in the cyclical behavior of the old and the new higher order aggregates lies in the changing distribution of the flow of funds among their various components as the economy expands and contracts. The distribution of financial flows depends in the first instance on the level of savings, a variable in turn dependent on disposable income. As illustrated in Figure 4, household accumulation of financial assets as a percentage of disposable income tends to rise in the early stages of a cyclical expansion, the phase of the business cycle when income rises most rapidly, and to decline as the economy slows and a larger share of income must be used to maintain the accustomed rate of growth of consumption.

The financial assets accumulated by households include corporate equities, corporate and government bonds, and life insurance and pension fund reserves as well as currency, demand and savings deposits, and the other components of the monetary statistics. The distribution of household saving flows among these alternative instruments is not constant, however, but varies as relative yields vary with changing business conditions. For example, when interest rates rise during an expansion, low-yielding savings and time deposits become less attractive than Treasury bills or money market fund shares, so funds tend to flow out of banks and thrifts into open market assets. The subsequent decline in open market rates during the contraction tends to reverse this flow (see Figure 5). Thus, cyclical fluctuations in income and interest rates lead to fluctuations in the share of particular instruments in total financial asset accumulation by households and hence in the rate of growth of any aggregate that includes them among its components.

Figure 6 illustrates this process for the case of new and old M-2. In addition to currency and demand deposits, old M-2 includes only savings and time deposits at commercial banks. New M-2 includes these plus a broad range of other components, many whose yields vary directly with open market yields. Because of its broader coverage, new

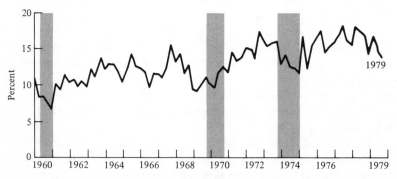

Figure 4.   Household Net Acquisition of Financial Assets (Percent of Disposable Income).

Source: U.S. Dept. of Commerce, Bureau of Economic Analysis; Board of Governors of the Federal Reserve System. Source data are seasonally adjusted. Shading indicates recessions.

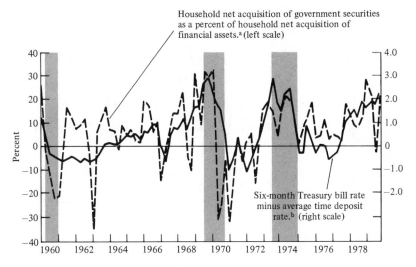

Household net acquisition of government securities as a percent of household net acquisition of financial assets.[a] (left scale)

Figure 5.

a. Source: Board of Governors of the Federal Reserve System.
b. Source: See N. Berkman, "Mortgage Finance and the Housing Cycle," *New England Economic Review,* September/October 1979, 76. Seasonally adjusted data.

M-2 captures a larger share of total financial asset acquisition than old M-2. During cyclical upswings, rising income and interest rates both work to cause new M-2 to grow faster than old M-2: rising income increases total financial asset accumulation; rising interest rates increase the share going to high-yielding assets included in new M-2 but not in old M-2.[19] During cyclical downswings, this process works "in reverse" to cause new M-2 to grow slower than old M-2: declining income growth reduces the rate of asset accumulation; declining interest rates reduce the share going to assets included in new M-2 but not in old M-2.

Cyclical variations in the distribution of the flow of funds among alternative financial assets will continue in the future. Because the pattern of these financial flows depends on the unique pattern of in-

[19]Factors working on the "supply side" reinforce the effect of shifting household savings flows on relative aggregate growth rates. For example, commercial banks are likely to market large nonnegotiable time deposits less aggressively in the early stages of a cyclical upswing since lower yielding small time deposits normally grow rapidly during this phase of the business cycle. Large time deposits are included in old M-2 but not in new M-2; thus, banks' supply-side behavior will cause the rate of growth of old M-2 to fall relative to the rate of growth of new M-2.

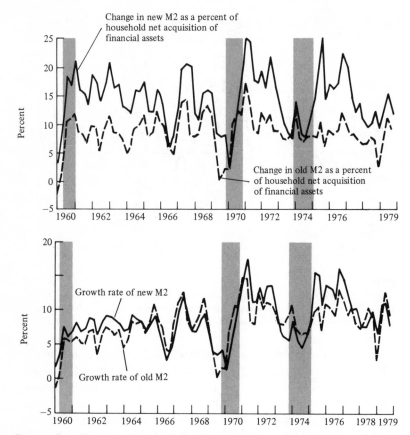

Figure 6.   Change in New M-2 as a Percent of Household Net Acquisition of Financial Assets.

Shaded periods are recessions.
All source data from the Board of Governors of the Federal Reserve System.
All source data seasonally adjusted at annual rates.
Growth rates are compound annual rates.

come growth and interest rate differentials that occur in each cycle, the behavior of the new relative to the old aggregates, and of the new aggregates relative to each other, cannot be predicted with certainty. What can be said is that the new higher order aggregates (and probably M-1B as well) will not grow at the same rate as the old ones for given paths of GNP and interest rates. Until analysts become familiar with the characteristics of the new components of the money stock measures, this may complicate the task of interpreting movements in the aggregates. The additional effort is warranted, however, since it was the emergence of their new components as well as the changes in the characteristics of traditional components that created the need for new aggregate definitions in the first place.

IV. Conclusion

Professional opinion has traditionally been divided on the issue of the appropriate definition of "money," a subject vigorously debated from time to time over the past several hundred years.[20] The new aggregate definitions described in this paper mark the conclusion of the second postwar incarnation of this controversy, the first having ended in 1970 with the adoption by the Federal Reserve of the old definitions M-1 through M-5.[21] As was often the case in previous episodes, the latest debate was ignited by the appearance of new financial instruments that could be used as substitutes for the existing means of payment and stores of value included in the aggregates, and hence to disrupt efforts by the central bank to influence the economy by encouraging or discouraging the expansion of conventional measures of money and credit.

Because the new monetary aggregates reflect the current payments mechanism in the United States more accurately than the old ones, their future growth is likely to provide more useful information about the state of the economy than the aggregates they replace. The new aggregates also correct some technical problems that were complicating the process of monetary control. However, the broader coverage of the new monetary statistics will cause their cyclical behavior to differ from the behavior of the old statistics to which observers had grown accustomed. The ultimate benefits to be derived from the new aggregates once people have become accustomed to analyzing variations in the broad range of financial assets incorporated in them thus may have to be purchased at the cost of some uncertainty about the significance of their movements in the near future.

[20]Prominent examples include the bullionist controversies of the seventeenth and eighteenth centuries and the banking school-currency school debates of the nineteenth century. See Joseph A. Schumpeter, *History of Economic Analysis.* New York: Oxford University Press, 1954, esp. 289–299 and 729–731.

[21]See Milton Friedman and Anna Schwartz, *Monetary Statistics of the United States*, National Bureau of Economic Research, New York, 1970.

A Review of Empirical Studies of the Money Supply Mechanism

Robert H. Rasche

In recent years there has been considerable discussion concerning techniques for conducting monetary policy. The traditional practitioners of the art of policymaking have argued for the use of operating procedures which focus on "money market conditions." At various times this has been construed to mean free reserves, the Treasury bill rate, the Federal funds rate, or a combination of these.[1] Alternatively, it has been argued that the target of monetary policy actions should be a monetary aggregate and that this target can be achieved by control of some reserve aggregate concept such as the monetary base.[2]

This article surveys the accumulated empirical evidence on the interest sensitivity of some reserve multipliers. If these multipliers are highly sensitive to interest rate changes, then it may be difficult to implement monetary control through the control of reserve aggregates. The available evidence consistently indicates, however, that the interest sensitivity of various multiplier concepts is extremely low. This suggests that control of monetary aggregates through reserve control should not be very difficult to implement.[3]

Conditions Inhibiting Control of the Money Stock

The issue examined here is the feasibility of control of a monetary aggregate such as the narrowly defined money stock (M_1), given con-

Reprinted from the Federal Reserve Bank of St. Louis, *Review* (July, 1972), 11–19, by permission of the publisher and the author.

[1]Stephen H. Axilrod, "The FOMC Directive as Structured in the Late 1960's: Theory and Appraisal," in *Open Market Policies and Operating Procedures—Staff Studies* (Washington, D.C.: Board of Governors of the Federal Reserve System, 1971), 1–36.

[2]For example, see Albert E. Burger, Lionel Kalish III, and Christopher T. Babb, "Money Stock Control and Its Implications for Monetary Policy," this *Review* (October 1971), 6–22.

[3]If, however, these multipliers *are* highly sensitive to interest rate changes, then accurate monetary control through a reserve control procedure requires a precise estimate of the impact of reserve changes on interest rates, in addition to a precise estimate of the interest elasticity of the reserve multiplier.

trol of some reserve aggregate concept. The problem can be illustrated by the equation

$$M = mR$$

where M is the money stock, R is some reserve aggregate concept, and m is the appropriate reserve multiplier.[4] Two sources of difficulty can arise in such a control procedure.

First, there can be systematic feedbacks on m through market forces which tend to offset the expected effect of a change in the reserve aggregate on the money stock. This influence of the behavior of reserves on the value of the multiplier can be stated as

$$m = f(R).$$

The sources of feedback from changes in R to changes in m will vary depending on the choice of a reserve aggregate concept. If the net source concept is used for R, the associated multiplier (m) is

$$m = \frac{1 + k}{(r - b)(1 + t + d) + k}$$

where r and b are the ratios of bank reserves and member bank borrowings to commercial bank deposits, respectively, t, k, and d, respectively, are the ratios of time deposits, currency held by the public, and US Government deposits at commercial banks to the demand deposit component of the money supply. Therefore, the important behavioral relationships influencing the stability of the multiplier in the presence of reserve changes are the public's demand for currency and time deposits, banks' demand for excess reserves and borrowings, and the supply of time deposits.[5]

An example of a feedback effect on m would be where there exists a sizable short-run interest elasticity of demand for excess reserves by

[4]A number of candidates have been proposed for R including the monetary base, unborrowed reserves plus currency, total reserves, unborrowed reserves, and reserves available to support private deposits. For a discussion of the relative virtues of many of these, see Richard Davis, "Short-Run Targets for Open Market Operations," in *Open Market Policies and Operating Procedures—Staff Studies* (Washington, D.C.: Board of Governors of the Federal Reserve System, 1971), 37–45.

[5]For a detailed discussion of the functional relationship of the multiplier expression to asset holdings of the nonbank public, the banking system, and the Treasury, see Albert E. Burger, *The Money Supply Process* (Belmont, California: Wadsworth, 1971), especially chs. 4–5, and Karl Brunner and Allan H. Meltzer, "Liquidity Traps for Money, Bank Credit, and Interest Rates, *Journal of Political Economy* (January/February 1968), 1–37.

commercial banks. In order to force additional reserves into the banking system to expand the money stock, the Federal Reserve would have to buy Government securities, thus pushing short-term interest rates down. If the amount of excess reserves demanded by banks is very sensitive to changes in short-term interest rates, this interest rate movement would induce banks to hold larger quantities of excess reserves. This portfolio shift then offsets the policy to increase the money stock.

The existence of strong feedback effects on the reserve multiplier does not mean that monetary control through reserve aggregates is impossible. The stronger the feedback, the larger the necessary magnitude of the open market operation required to achieve a given change in the money stock and the larger the associated variance in short-term interest rates.

The second source of difficulty in this type of monetary control procedure is that the relationship between the reserve aggregate and the money stock is subject to random fluctuation. Specifically, we can write

$$m_t = f(R_t) + \epsilon_t$$

where ϵ_t is an unknown random disturbance to m_t. If such fluctuations are truly random, then in the long run policymakers should be able to hit the desired average stock of money quite closely. If this random component is large, then in a short time period, such as one or two months, the average m could deviate considerably from the forecast m and cause a large average error around the desired path of the money stock.

It can be shown that for a given variance of ϵ_t, under a control procedure such as that recently proposed by Burger, Kalish, and Babb, the variance of the actual path of the money stock around the desired path will depend on the sensitivity of the reserve multiplier (m) to changes in the reserve aggregate.[6] The smaller the sensitivity of the multiplier, the smaller will be the variance of the actual money stock around the desired money stock.

The Nature of Available Evidence on Multiplier Sensitivity

Over the past decade there has been considerable empirical research directed at measuring the relationship between the money stock and

---

[6]Burger, Kalish, and Babb, "Money Stock Control."

various reserve aggregates. This work has evolved primarily from attempts to construct econometric models of basic financial relationships in the US economy. As a byproduct, these studies provide information on the interest elasticities of the behavioral parameters of the reserve multiplier, the existence of which cause feedbacks against policy actions as discussed above.

Most of the more detailed studies have worked with quarterly data, which may be too highly aggregated in time to provide information that policymakers desire if the reactions of the banking system and the public are distributed over time. However, studies using shorter time horizons do exist for some components of the money supply mechanism, and these can be used to obtain information on how the estimated elasticities are likely to change as the horizon becomes shorter.

There are several potential sources of feedback which will offset the expected impact of a change in reserve aggregates on the change in the money stock. Some of the feedback, such as a change in the demand for currency and time deposits by the nonbank public as a result of increased economic activity, has been shown to occur only slowly, and does not cause difficulties for short-run control.[7]

The troublesome source of changes in the multiplier relationship is the impact of changes in interest rates on the behavioral parameters in the multiplier. Changes in market interest rates and changes in reserves available to the banking system cannot be controlled simultaneously by the Federal Reserve System. When the Federal Reserve follows a reserve aggregate operating procedure, interest rates are affected by changes in reserves. Under a money market conditions operating strategy, changes in reserve aggregates come about as a result of the attempt to achieve certain levels of interest rates. Hence, if the goal is to control money through changes in reserve aggregates, the major issue is the interest elasticity of the relationship between the money stock and reserve aggregates.

It will be necessary to distinguish between short-run, or impact, elasticities of the reserve multiplier and long-run, or equilibrium, elasticities. The former include only the impact which comes from the adjustment of economic units to a change in interest rates within one period of time. Many studies, however, have indicated that economic units respond to such changes with a distributed lag; that is, part of the

---

[7]See David I. Fand, "Some Implications of Money Supply Analysis," *American Economic Review* (May 1967), 380–400.

response takes place in the same period, and the remainder of the response takes place over several periods following a change in interest rates. The impact, or short-run, interest elasticity is the percentage change in the reserve multiplier with respect to a percentage change in interest rates within the time period in which the interest rate changes. The equilibrium, or long-run, elasticity is the total response of the reserve multiplier after economic units have had sufficient time to adjust to a new portfolio equilibrium.[8]

In the studies below, estimates have been obtained for the interest elasticity of the money stock for given values of various reserve aggregates. Thus, the money stock elasticities computed are the interest elasticities of the reserve multiplier.

Interest Elasticity Estimates from Data Prior to 1965

Teigen 1

An early econometric investigation of the money supply relationship was that of Ronald Teigen.[9] His study does not develop the detailed specifications which are characteristic of more recent studies. In particular, the stocks of currency in the hands of the public and demand deposits at nonmember banks are assumed exogenous.[10] In addition,

---

[8]For a discussion of impact versus long-run responses, see Arthur S. Goldberger, *Impact Multipliers and Dynamic Properties of the Klein-Goldberger Model* (Amsterdam: North-Holland, 1959).

[9]Ronald L. Teigen, "Demand and Supply Functions for Money in the United States: Some Structural Estimates," *Econometrica* (October 1964), 476–509.

[10]It is necessary to distinguish here between the construction of the model from historical data and the use of the model to determine interest elasticities. In the construction of the model, the ratio of currency to demand deposits at member banks and the ratio of demand deposits at nonmember banks to those at member banks are, in fact, exogenous variables which vary from one observation to the next. In determining the value of the elasticity of the relationship, these exogenous variables are kept fixed at some point, conventionally their mean value for the sample period. Hence, the computations implicitly assume positive interest rate responses for the public's currency demand and the supply of demand deposits by nonmember banks, which are equal to the interest rate response of demand deposits supplied by member banks. For nonmember banks, the assumption probably does not seriously affect the analysis. On the other hand, the public's currency demand is usually found to have a zero, or slightly negative, interest elasticity, at least in the long run. If the true interest elasticity of currency demand is zero, then the bias introduced by the constant ratio of currency to money stock is indeterminate. On the one hand, the *direct* effect of increased currency in the hands of the public as demand deposits supplied by banks increase biases the interest elasticity of the money supply upward. On the other hand, the *indirect* effect that the assumed

Teigen takes the quantity of time deposits at member banks and government deposits at member banks as exogenous variables.[11]

Teigen tests the hypothesis that the banking system takes more than one period to respond to changes in interest rates, but this hypothesis is rejected for the post-war data. Thus his impact and equilibrium interest elasticities of the money supply relationship are equal. His estimated coefficients of elasticity are .1950 for the commercial paper rate and −.1695 for the discount rate.[12]

De Leeuw I

Frank de Leeuw attempted to obtain more detailed numerical estimates of behavior in important financial markets than did Teigen.[13] In particular, de Leeuw separates bank borrowing and excess reserve behavior, and explicitly estimates functions for currency demand and time deposit demand at commercial banks by the nonbank public.

The interest elasticity estimates from this study are summarized in Table 1. In all cases the absolute value of the long-run elasticities are less than one, and the short-run elasticities never exceed .2 in absolute value. The available data do not permit reconstruction of the interest elasticities of excess reserves. However, de Leeuw did publish the results of a computation of the implicit interest elasticities of the money-reserve relationship derived from the estimated borrowings and excess reserves functions. In this computation, he takes the ratios of currency, time deposits, U.S. Government deposits, and nonmember bank demand deposits to money stock as constant. Thus the biases which were introduced into Teigen's computations are again present here. De Leeuw's reserve aggregate is nonborrowed reserves plus currency in the hands of the public. His estimated long-run elas-

increase in currency withdraws reserves from the banking system causes the model to understate the desired amount of deposit expansion. Since the magnitudes involved are small, the net bias should not be substantial.

[11]These variables do not explicitly appear in his model. However, the reserve aggregate which he uses is unborrowed reserves available to support private demand deposits. Later studies use more broadly defined aggregates such as unborrowed reserves, or unborrowed reserves plus currency. To make the studies comparable, the model must be reformulated with time deposits at member banks and government deposits at member banks explicitly appearing as exogenous variables.

[12]Teigen, "Demand and Supply Functions," 502.

[13]Frank de Leeuw, "A Model of Financial Behavior," in *The Brookings Quarterly Econometric Model of the United States*, ed. James S. Duesenberry et al. (Chicago: Rand McNally, 1965). ch. 13.

Table 1. Interest Elasticities of Various Functions in de Leeuw's Original Brookings Model

Specification	Impact*	Equilibrium*
Currency Demand		
Private Securities Rate	− 0.032	− 0.364
Time Deposit Rate	− 0.012	− 0.136
Time Deposit Demand		
Treasury Bill Rate	− 0.038	− 0.374
Time Deposit Rate	0.070	0.683
Bank Borrowings		
Treasury Bill Rate	0.134	0.50
Discount Rate	− 0.186	− 0.70
Excess Reserves		
Treasury Bill Rate	n.a.	n.a.
Discount Rate	n.a.	n.a.

*Impact elasticities are calculated by using the respective equilibrium elasticities and regression coefficients of the lagged dependent variables from various tables in the source cited below.

Source: Frank de Leeuw, "A Model of Financial Behavior," in *The Brookings Quarterly Econometric Model of the United States,* ed. James S. Duesenberry et al. (Chicago: Rand McNally, 1965), ch. 13.

ticities, valued at the sample means, are .172 and −.214 for the Treasury bill rate and the discount rate, respectively. When valued in 1962 (the end of his sample period) these elasticities are .245 and −.348, respectively.[14]

These numbers seem quite compatible with those obtained by Teigen for approximately the same sample period. However, de Leeuw finds that the entire adjustment of banks to portfolio changes takes place only gradually over time, and his impact elasticities for borrowings are only about one-fourth of the equilibrium values. This suggests that if the data were available to compute the short-run elasticity for the money supply relationship, the estimates over a one-quarter period would be considerably lower than those obtained by Teigen.

The currency and time deposit demand equations which de Leeuw incorporates into the above computations are almost com-

[14]*Ibid.,* 518.

pletely insensitive to interest rate changes over a one-quarter horizon. This implies that over a one-quarter horizon changes in reserves available to support private demand deposits, which are caused by interest induced changes in currency and time deposit demand, are negligible. Thus, it is highly probable that the assumptions of constant currency/ money stock or time deposit/money stock ratios result in a net upward bias in the computed interest elasticity of the money supply relationship.

De Leeuw II

In a subsequent study for the Brookings model de Leeuw produced a condensed model of financial behavior in which the excess reserve and borrowings equations were aggregated into a single function to explain free reserves.[15] In that study estimates of the interest elasticity of the money supply relationship are not provided. However, using the free reserve-interest rate coefficient estimates and information given in the earlier study it is possible to replicate the computations of the larger model.[16]

The estimated impact elasticities at the sample means are .037 for the Treasury bill rate, and −.046 for the discount rate.[17] The corresponding long-run elasticities are .096 and −.118, respectively. The absolute values are lower by a factor of almost fifty percent from the values obtained in the earlier study, even though the data and the sample period have remained essentially unchanged.

It is likely that some downward bias has been introduced into these estimates by aggregating excess reserves and borrowings into free reserves in the estimation of the model. From the information presented in the first study, it is not possible to aggregate the interest elasticities of these two components. However, the early work suggests that the response of banks to a disequilibrium in borrowings from the Federal Reserve is much faster than the response to a similar situation with respect to excess reserves.

[15]Frank de Leeuw, "A Condensed Model of Financial Behavior," in *The Brookings Model: Some Further Results*, ed. James S. Duesenberry et al. (Chicago: Rand McNally, 1969), 270–315.

[16]De Leeuw, "A Model of Financial Behavior."

[17]Unless otherwise stated, data cited have been computed by this author.

Goldfeld

The most detailed study of financial markets is found in the work of Stephen Goldfeld.[18] In this study, equations are specified for both the demand for excess reserves and the demand for borrowings from the Federal Reserve System. Separate equations are estimated for country banks and city banks.

The Goldfeld results suggest very large (in absolute value) interest elasticities for the borrowings equations relative to those found by de Leeuw. There do not appear to be large differences in the impact elasticities of borrowings across the bank classes, but the speed of adjustment to interest rate changes is much slower for borrowings by country banks than for city banks. This is reflected in the lower impact elasticities and the higher equilibrium elasticities for the country banks than the corresponding numbers for the city banks.

The excess reserve interest elasticities reported by Goldfeld are negligible, particularly when compared with the borrowings elasticities. In addition, he finds that banks respond quite quickly to disequilibrium in excess reserve holdings. Thus, the long-run elasticities for excess reserve demand are not much different from the impact elasticities, particularly for city banks. This result is similar to that of the Teigen study where no evidence of a distributed lag in bank response was found.

Goldfeld reports interest elasticities of a money supply relationship comparable to that derived by both Teigen and de Leeuw. The impact elasticities, with respect to the Treasury bill rate and the discount rate in this function, .042 and −.029, respectively, are derived from the elasticities reported in Table 2. The corresponding long-run elasticities are .222 and −.076.[19] These results are quite close to the values reported by both Teigen and de Leeuw for the Treasury bill rate, but considerably below the estimates for the discount rate in the other studies.

The sources of the differences are fairly conspicuous. In Teigen's study, where there is no disaggregation of excess reserves from borrowings, the Treasury bill rate and the discount rate appear only as the differential between the two rates. Hence the regression coefficient of

[18]Stephen M. Goldfeld, *Commercial Bank Behavior and Economic Activity* (Amsterdam: North-Holland, 1966).
[19]*Ibid.*, 191.

Table 2. Interest Elasticities of Various Functions in the Goldfeld Model

Specification	Impact*	Equilibrium*
Currency Demand		
Treasury Bill Rate	− 0.008	− 0.07
Time Deposit Rate	− 0.015	− 0.14
Time Deposit Demand		
Time Deposit Rate	0.028	0.37
Long-Term Government Rate	− 0.125	− 1.62
Bank Borrowings		
City Banks		
Discount Rate	− 0.98	− 2.382
Treasury Bill Rate	0.88	2.134
Country Banks		
Discount Rate	− 0.88	− 2.926
Treasury Bill Rate	0.79	2.625
Excess Reserves		
City Banks		
Treasury Bill Rate	− 0.38	− 0.35
Country Banks		
Treasury Bill Rate	− 0.15	− 0.25

*The equilibrium elasticities for currency and time deposit demand are found on p. 160 of the source cited below. The corresponding impact elasticities are calculated by using the equilibrium elasticities and regression coefficients of the lagged dependent variables from Tables 5.7 and 5.9, respectively. Both equilibrium and impact elasticities for bank borrowings and excess reserves are found on pp. 150 and 149, respectively.

Source: Stephen M. Goldfeld, *Commercial Bank Behavior and Economic Activity* (Amsterdam: North-Holland, 1966).

the discount rate is constrained to have the same absolute value, but with the opposite sign from that of the bill rate. Since the mean of the discount rate for the sample period is slightly larger than that of the bill rate, the computed coefficient of elasticity of the discount rate is, in effect, constrained to be slightly smaller in absolute value than that of the bill rate. De Leeuw constrains this excess reserve specification to include only the differential between the bill rate and the discount rate. With the constraints that are imposed in the estimation of the Teigen and de Leeuw studies, it would seem reasonable to conclude that the Goldfeld estimate of the response of the money supply relationship to discount rate changes is more reliable for this period.

There seem to be no major discrepancies in the estimated long-run responsiveness of the money supply to changes in the bill rate, but considerable variance exists among the short-run elasticity estimates. The most uncertain issue, on the basis of the evidence reviewed so far, is the source of the interest elasticity. Goldfeld suggests that the source is bank borrowing behavior, de Leeuw suggests that it is bank behavior with respect to excess reserves, and Teigen does not attempt to discriminate between the two.

Goldfeld and Kane

There exists an additional study by Goldfeld and Kane which provides some independent information on the question of the interest elasticity of bank borrowings from the Federal Reserve.[20] This study is based on weekly data from the period July 1953 to December 1963 and disaggregates banks into four classes—New York City, Chicago, Other Reserve City, and Country banks. They find that the estimated short-run (one week) Treasury bill rate elasticities range from a high of .56 for New York City banks to a low of .08 for Chicago banks. When aggregated over all classes of banks, the short-run interest elasticity for the banking system as a whole is found to be .21. Their reported long-run interest elasticities of borrowings range from 2.8 to 3.9.[21]

These estimates seem consistent with the results of the quarterly study by Goldfeld and tend to add to the uncertainty of the high excess reserve and low borrowings elasticities reported by de Leeuw. The only difficulty in reconciling the weekly estimates with the quarterly work of Goldfeld is the implied definition of long run. In the quarterly study, the long run is achieved only after several quarters have elapsed. In the weekly study, the implied long run is a period of several weeks. The possibility remains that long run in the two studies has two different meanings. However, it seems safe to conclude that borrowing behavior of banks is an important source of interest elasticity of the money supply relationship when the Treasury bill rate changes and the discount rate remains constant.

[20]Stephen M. Goldfeld and Edward J. Kane, "The Determinants of Member-Bank Borrowing: An Econometric Study," *Journal of Finance* (September 1966), 499–514, and Stephen M. Goldfeld, "An Extension of the Monetary Sector," in *The Brookings Model: Some Further Results*, ed. James S. Duesenberry et al. (Chicago: Rand McNally, 1969), 317–360.

[21]Goldfeld and Kane, "The Determinants of Member-Bank Borrowing: An Econometric Study," 512.

Teigen II

A quarterly study which deals with the period of the 1950s through the early 1960s is that of Teigen.[22] The study contains supply elasticities only for the demand deposit component of the money supply. The results for the elasticity of the discount rate are not very different from those reported by Goldfeld, but the elasticity of the Treasury bill rate is considerably lower than the results obtained by Goldfeld, de Leeuw, and Teigen's earlier results.

Brunner and Meltzer

Karl Brunner and Allan Meltzer have estimated the interest elasticity of the money supply relationship using annual data over a sample period including the interwar and postwar periods.[23] In the two-stage least-squares estimates of their "nonlinear" money supply hypothesis, they find that the elasticity of the money supply function with respect to the adjusted monetary base is insignificantly different from one. Therefore, the interest elasticities of this function can be interpreted as interest elasticities of the reserve multiplier. Their estimate of the Treasury bill rate elasticity is 0.66 and the estimate of the discount rate elasticity is $-.31$.[24] Since there are no lagged variables in the equation, these estimates can be compared with the equilibrium elasticities derived from the studies which used shorter time intervals. Both elasticities appear to differ from the implied equilibrium values of the quarterly studies by a factor of over two. Given the many difficulties in estimating distributed lag effects from time series data, such inconsistencies are not surprising.

Estimates from Data Including Post-1965 Period

The shortcoming of the studies discussed so far is that they are based on data generated in the 1950s and early 1960s. During the 1960s there were many changes in the environment in which the banking system operated which could have significantly altered (and presumably in-

---

[22]Ronald L. Teigen, "An Aggregated Quarterly Model of the U.S. Monetary Sector, 1953-1964," in *Targets and Indicators of Monetary Policy*, ed. Karl Brunner (San Francisco: Chandler Publishing Company, 1969), 175-218.

[23]Karl Brunner and Allan H. Meltzer, "Some Further Investigations of Demand and Supply Functions for Money," *Journal of Finance* (May 1964), 240-283.

[24]*Ibid.*, 277.

creased) the interest elasticity of the money supply relationship. These changes included the evolution of an active market for large negotiable certificates of deposit, the involvement of large banks in the Eurodollar market through borrowings from (or lending to) their foreign subsidiaries, and the entrance of banks into the commercial paper market through parent one-bank holding companies.

Unfortunately, it is difficult to obtain empirical evidence on many of these innovations since they were effectively legislated out of existence before enough data were generated to assess their effects. The impact of the CD market can be assessed, along with the responsiveness of the banking system in terms of free reserves in the 1960s, through the quarterly financial model in the MPS model.[25] In addition, estimates of the interest elasticity of the money supply-reserve relationship on a monthly basis can be obtained from a financial market model developed by Thomas Thomson and James Pierce.[26]

Evaluation of Quarterly Money Supply Elasticities

The quarterly MPS model contains a financial sector which includes detail specifications of the commercial loan market and the mortgage market, as well as specifications dealing with bank and nonbank behavior with respect to holdings of currency, time deposits and free reserves. The estimated elasticities for the latter set of functions are tabulated in Table 3. Both the CD demand and supply functions, which did not exist in the earlier studies, assume that the full response to an interest rate change takes place within one quarter. Thus the impact and equilibrium elasticities are equal.

The CD demand function, in particular, indicates a highly sensitive response to interest rate changes, which is consistent with casual impressions of the nature of the CD market. However, these estimates are drawn from a considerably smaller sample than that for the rest of the specifications, and therefore there is less certainty about the stability of the functions over time.

The estimates for the currency demand equation and the demand equation for non-CD time deposits tend to confirm the de Leeuw and

[25]This model is the publicly available version which developed out of the Federal Reserve–MIT–Pennsylvania econometric model project.

[26]Thomas D. Thomson and James L. Pierce, "A Monthly Econometric Model of the Financial Sector" (a paper presented at the May 1971 meeting of the Federal Reserve System Committee on Financial Analysis).

Table 3. Interest Elasticities of Various Functions in the MPS Model

Specification	Impact Elasticity	Equilibrium Elasticity
Currency Demand		
Treasury Bill Rate	0.0037	0.026
Non-CD Time Deposit Demand		
Time Deposit Rate	0.3	2.9
S&L—Mut. Sav. Bk. Rate	− 0.2	− 2.0
Treasury Bill Rate	− 0.15	− 1.4
CD Demand [1969 Values]		
Treasury Bill Rate	− 6.14	− 6.14
Commercial Paper Rate	− 4.28	− 4.28
CD Rate	11.46	11.46
Free Reserves		
Treasury Bill Rate		
1965 Values	− 2.99	− 6.42
1969 Values	− 3.95	− 8.47
Discount Rate		
1965 Values	3.23	6.93
1969 Values	3.48	7.46
Supply of CDs by Banks [1969 Values]		
CD Rate	− 1.06	− 1.06
Treasury Bill Rate	0.98	0.98

Goldfeld results of extremely low impact elasticities. The time deposit function does suggest higher long-run elasticities than had been previously estimated. This appears attributable, in part, to the evolution of special forms of time deposit accounts, such as small consumer-type CDs, during the late 1960s.[27]

The MPS model does not distinguish between excess reserves and borrowings of member banks, but does estimate a relationship between the Treasury bill rate, the discount rate, and free reserves. No constraints are applied to the coefficients of the two rates. In Table 3 both the impact and the equilibrium elasticities of this function are considerably higher than those estimated in the earlier studies. This is partially due to the fact that the estimated function is linear and therefore the value of the elasticity coefficient is not constant at all points

[27]The estimated function allows for a change in structure during the early 1960s, which indicates that the interest elasticities in the latter part of the sample period are about fifty percent higher than those estimated for the first part of the sample period.

along the function. Evaluation of the elasticity coefficient at the very high values of interest rates in 1969 gives estimates of the impact and equilibrium Treasury bill rate elasticities which are 50 and 25 percent higher, respectively, than the values at 1965 interest rate levels. Even after accounting for the higher levels of interest rates in the late 1960s, it appears that differences in specifications and/or differences in sample periods have produced higher interest rate elasticity estimates for the free reserve relationship than had previously been found.

Simulation experiments were performed with the MPS model which permitted relaxation of restrictions under which interest elasticities of the money supply relationship were computed in the studies discussed above. First, in addition to the impact elasticities, the pattern of response of the money stock over time to a maintained change in the Treasury bill rate was computed. The simulations were continued for eight quarters, after which the computed elasticities settled down at close to the equilibrium values.

Second, the response of the demand for currency and the demand for time deposits to the changes in interest rates can be included or excluded from the computation of the elasticities. Time deposit demand is split into large negotiable certificates of deposit and other time deposits. The inclusion of the currency and time deposit responses in the simulation is analogous to a controlled experiment in which the nonbank private sector demand for bank demand deposits is shifted once and maintained in its new position. This shift is allowed to occur without any effect on the demand functions for time deposits or currency. This shift generates an initial change in interest rates. The changes in the money stock, which are observed over time, are the result of the interest rate induced portfolio shifts by banks and the nonbank public, and they trace out the interest elasticity of the money supply relationship over various time intervals. Finally, elasticities are computed for both demand deposits and the M-1 money stock concept.

The estimated elasticities from three sets of simulations are presented in Table 4. These computations are generated under the assumption that the Federal Reserve would not impose a Regulation Q constraint which would prevent banks from offering new CDs at competitive rates.

If such constraints were effective, increases in the Treasury bill rate would cause a shift in the demand for CDs. At the constrained new issue rate for CDs the public would not renew outstanding certificates as they matured. Over time the stock of CDs would decline, and there

Table 4. Money Supply Elasticity Computations—MPS Model

A. Currency, Time Deposits, and CDs Included

Quarter	Demand Deposits	M_1
1	0.106	0.083
2	0.175	0.137
3	0.214	0.167
4	0.240	0.188
First-Year Average	0.184	0.144
5	0.279	0.218
6	0.309	0.240
7	0.317	0.247
8	0.337	0.250
Second-Year Average	0.311	0.239

B. Currency, CDs Included; Time Deposits Excluded

Quarter	Demand Deposits	M_1
1	0.099	0.078
2	0.157	0.123
3	0.185	0.145
4	0.204	0.159
First-Year Average	0.161	0.126
5	0.233	0.181
6	0.254	0.196
7	0.256	0.198
8	0.259	0.200
Second-Year Average	0.251	0.194

C. CDs Included; Time Deposits, Currency Excluded

Quarter	Demand Deposits	M_1
1	0.094	0.074
2	0.149	0.118
3	0.173	0.136
4	0.186	0.147
First-Year Average	0.151	0.119
5	0.202	0.159
6	0.211	0.166
7	0.220	0.173
8	0.226	0.177
Second-Year Average	0.215	0.169

could be a sizable reduction in the ratio of time deposits to demand deposits. The change in this ratio would, in turn, cause a fluctuation in the reserve multiplier. The observed result would also be highly sensitive to the initial conditions of the Treasury bill rate relative to the Regulation Q ceiling, and the historical pattern of Regulation Q restraint.

In the first section of Table 4, the interest elasticities include the interest rate induced reactions in the public's demand for currency, large certificates of deposit as well as other time deposits, and the interest elasticity of the commercial banking sector's supply function for large certificates of deposit. The interest elasticity of M-1 is consistently smaller than the interest elasticity of the demand deposit component. This is because the model indicates a small negative response of the demand for currency to changes in interest rates. Hence, as interest rates increase and the amount of bank deposits available to the economy expands, there is an offsetting movement in currency balances outstanding.

The exclusion of the nonbank private sector's demand for currency and time deposits other than large certificates of deposit lowers the interest elasticity of the money supply relationship.[28] This is because a rise (fall) in interest rates decreases (increases) the quantity demanded of both of these assets. This relationship is straightforward in the case of currency. For time deposits the expected equilibrium response would be for a large quantity of time deposits to be demanded with higher levels of all interest rates. The model postulates, however, that the rate which banks offer on non-CD time deposits responds quite sluggishly to changes in market interest rates. Thus the short-run effect is for disintermediation away from commercial bank time deposits. If the elasticity patterns were computed over a longer time horizon, the elasticities in the first experiment would eventually become smaller than those for the second experiment. In all cases the impact elasticities are essentially the same size.

These results can be compared with those from earlier empirical studies which do not include the CD market. It appears from section C of Table 4 that when the CD market is operating freely, the estimated interest elasticity of the money supply relationship differs little from the results drawn from studies of earlier periods. If anything, the elas-

---

[28]This exclusion of currency and time deposit demand allows these demand functions to shift in such a way that the quantity demanded at the new Treasury bill rate is exactly equal to the quantity demanded at the original level of the Treasury bill rate.

ticities reported in this section of the table are generally lower than those discussed above. On the other hand, sections A and B of Table 4 suggest that the net bias involved in computing the interest elasticities with a constant currency/deposit ratio and a constant level of time deposits tends toward zero. That is, the estimates obtained under these assumptions give estimates of elasticities which are too low.

Evaluation of Monthly Money Supply Elasticities

The same type of analysis of the money stock-reserve relationship as that performed with the MPS quarterly econometric model can be carried out on a monthly basis using the financial market model of Pierce and Thompson. The results over an eighteen month period are presented in Table 5. In this model, demand for currency by the public is specified to be completely interest inelastic, so the assumptions

Table 5. Money Supply Elasticity Computations
(Monthly Financial Market Model)

Month	Time Deposits Included	Time Deposits Excluded
1	0.138	0.137
2	0.195	0.192
3	0.231	0.226
4	0.250	0.243
5	0.252	0.244
6	0.250	0.243
First 6-Month Average	0.219	0.214
7	0.266	0.256
8	0.272	0.262
9	0.275	0.262
10	0.279	0.269
11	0.284	0.272
12	0.292	0.281
Second 6-Month Average	0.278	0.267
13	0.303	0.290
14	0.311	0.296
15	0.236	0.222
16	0.220	0.202
17	0.233	0.216
18	0.246	0.230
Third 6-Month Average	0.258	0.243

underlying the calculations of sections B and C of Table 4 are identical to the assumptions made for the right-hand column of Table 5. The analogy to section A of Table 4 is presented in the left-hand column of Table 5.

The implication of the monthly model is that the money stock-reserve relationship is slightly more elastic in the short run than the various quarterly estimates imply. The implied impact elasticity (over a one-month period in this case) is about .15. The average elasticity over this first twelve months is estimated at about .25, or about one-third more than the estimate over the corresponding four-quarter horizon from the MPS model. After eighteen months have elapsed the elasticity values reflect the long-run, or equilibrium, values. This horizon agrees reasonably well with the horizon of the MPS model.

Conclusions

It is difficult to draw a finely defined set of conclusions from the set of studies which have been examined. There exists a range of elasticity estimates among these studies which cannot be reconciled with the information which is readily available at the present time.

However, while a single point cannot be established as the most probable value for the interest elasticity of the money supply, it appears that the studies do provide information which can be of value in policy discussions concerning the control of the money stock. A broad, but valuable conclusion is that the interest elasticity of the money supply during the sample period of these studies appears to be extremely low. It seems appropriate to conclude with almost complete certainty that the long-run elasticity during this period was less than .5 and that the impact elasticity (one quarter) was probably no greater than .10 to .15. All these elasticities are relevant for policy actions which result in changes in the Treasury bill rate, while leaving the discount rate unchanged.

For the class of policy actions which simultaneously alters the Treasury bill rate and the discount rate by the same amount from an initial position where the two are approximately equal, it is the sum of the interest elasticities of the money supply which is relevant. Two of the studies suggest that the elasticity with respect to the discount rate is slightly smaller than that with respect to the bill rate. The estimation of these relationships involves constraints on parameters, and hence, is not a valid test of the hypothesis that the two elasticities are significantly different. In the Goldfeld study, where there are no constraints imposed on the estimated parameters, the estimated coefficient of elasticity for the discount rate is considerably smaller in absolute value than that of the bill rate. Therefore, it would appear that while the interest elasticity of the money supply relationship is likely to be smaller when both rates are changed simultaneously, it is almost certain that the coefficient of elasticity will remain positive. Furthermore, the elasticity under such a policy probably does not exceed one-half to two-thirds of the interest elasticity under a policy of keeping the discount rate fixed.

The available evidence suggests quite conclusively that the short-run feedbacks through interest rate changes, which would be generated by policy changes in reserve aggregates, are very weak and should cause little, if any, difficulty for the implementation of policy actions aimed at controlling the money stock through the control of a reserve aggregate. Of course, the size of random fluctuations in the reserve multiplier remains a major factor in determining the size of deviations of the money stock from its targeted value. An issue which remains to be investigated is the size of the variance of the multipliers associated with various reserve concepts.

PART II
MONEY DEMAND

TWO
The Transactions Demand for Money

Introduction

In the previous chapter we examined some alternative specifications of the asset-holding behavior of the public and the banks and the effects of this behavior on the supply of money. Only recently have economists done much research on the money supply relation despite the importance of the money stock in most hypotheses about aggregate economic behavior. In contrast, the *demand* for money has been more thoroughly studied, largely because the implications and predictions that follow from alternative demand-for-money hypotheses have been recognized to generate widely contrasting prescriptions for economic policy.

There are various theoretical approaches to the demand for money. The present chapter focuses on the view that money, as the generally acceptable medium of exchange, is held in the interval between the receipt and disbursement of income primarily because there is some *cost* associated with both the purchase of interest-earning assets out of income and the subsequent sale of these assets to make disbursements. This chapter begins with a review of the basic determinants of the transactions demand for money, examines William Baumol's inventory-theoretic treatment of the subject (1952), and then expands the conception of cost in examining the role of information cost in the transactions demand for money.

117

Chapter 3 will suggest that an individual also holds money, as one of several financial assets in his wealth portfolio, because he may thereby avoid losses from decreases in the market value of other, income-earning, assets. It describes John Maynard Keynes' original liquidity preference theory (1936) and then develops James Tobin's approach to the subject (1958). A reading following Chapter 4 examines general portfolio theory of which the theory of the demand for money is a subset.

Chapter 4 will consider the classical demand for money together with its modern (neoclassical) reformulation.[1] The classical demand for money inspired Keynes' work and is an important antecedent of the modern neoclassical reconsideration of money demand. The latter stresses neither the role of money in facilitating transactions nor its usefulness as a hedge against the risk of loss from holding other assets, but rather treats the demand for money as part of the general theory of demand.

While, in principle, these approaches are not always incompatible with one another, they will generate different models of the demand for money and different prescriptions for economic policy.[2] In the survey of empirical tests of various demand-for-money hypotheses following Chapter 4 we shall see how well the factors suggested by each hypothesis explain variations in the demand for money.

The Transactions Motive for Holding Money

Most modern economists believe that money is demanded, like any asset, because of the flow of services it renders. With most assets the value of this flow of services is approximated by a dollar yield. With money, however, the income stream is usually not measurable by a simple nominal dollar return; by law commercial bank demand deposits, for instance, may yield no interest return yet they provide a valuable flow of services to their owners. Economists have found it useful to associate this flow of services with the functions that money

---

[1] Throughout this book we use the rubrics *classical* and *neoclassical* in a manner common to many monetary economists but perhaps disconcerting to historians of economic thought. We mean by the classical-neoclassical distinction not the difference between the labor-theory-of-value and marginalist schools but rather the historical hiatus between the pre- and post-Keynesian proponents of the quanity theory of money.

[2] See, for instance, the implications that different demand-for-money functions have for monetary and fiscal policy, discussed in Chapters 6 and 7.

performs. The functions of money are commonly said to include those of a medium of exchange, a store of value and a unit of account.[3]

As a medium of exchange, money is held between the receipt and disbursement of income because of the costs (brokerage fees, inconvenience, etc.) of converting into and out of other, earning assets which themselves are not generally acceptable as media of exchange. The amount of money demanded to finance expenditures, in principle, thus depends on these conversion *costs* as well as on the *size* of the expenditures and how far in the future they will be made. Most economists, nevertheless, have emphasized the size of expenditures as the primary constraint affecting the demand for money as a medium of exchange. In fact, the transactions demand for money, associated with its use as a medium of exchange, is usually depicted as varying in direct proportion with the level of expenditures. Following this tradition, where

M_j/P_T = the average quantity of real transactions balances demanded by the jth individual[4]

T_j = the level of the jth individual's total real expenditures over a period of time

k_j = a proportionality factor for the jth individual with a magnitude $0 < k_j < 1$ for long periods of time, such as a month,

the individual's transactions demand function is

$$M_j/P_T = k_j T_j. \qquad (2.1)$$

The order of magnitude of k_j relates the size of the average money stock needed to finance a flow of expenditures to the size of that total flow. For instance, suppose an individual is paid a monthly income of $300 on the first day of each month. Assume further that that person spends this income at a uniform rate of $10 per day for 30 days until paid again on the first day of the next month. The average transactions balance will be $150; that is, since the person's holdings are $300 on

---

[3]The services associated with the store of value function of money are discussed in the next chapter. The unit of account function of money simply means that money is commonly used as a denominator or *numeraire* in which the prices of all other goods or services are reckoned. We devote no further discussion to the unit of account function of money.

[4]The concept of real expenditures, real income, real money balances, etc., is one that abstracts from price changes and measures what the dollar totals would be if prices remained constant. Real measures may be expressed by dividing ("deflating") a nominal measure by a price index; in the present case we deflate the nominal money stock by P_T, an index of the average price level of all goods and services exchanged in the economy over a given period of time.

the first day of the month and zero on the last day and since these balances decline uniformly over the course of the 30-day month, the average value of the transactions balances is the mean of these two figures:

$$\frac{\$300 + 0}{2} = \$150.$$

Therefore,

$$k_j = \frac{M_j/P_T}{T_j} = \frac{\$150}{\$300/\text{month}} = \frac{1}{2} \text{ month.}$$

This individual holds an average of one-half of the monthly income *flow* in the form of a *stock* of money balances.

If we were to measure this individual's total expenditures on a yearly basis but continue to assume the person is paid once each month and spends the income uniformly over the course of each month,

$$k_j = \frac{\$150}{\$3600/\text{year}} = \frac{1}{24} \text{ year} = \frac{1}{2} \text{ month.}$$

Therefore, we may view k_j as either the average period of time over which the jth individual holds a unit of money or, more usefully, as the average proportion of his total expenditures which an individual holds in the form of transactions balances.

This example can be used to illustrate the effect of a change in the frequency of receipts (for example, a change in the length of the pay period) or the effect of a change in the frequency of cash disbursements on the average size of transactions balances. Consider first a change in the frequency of receipts. Continue to assume that this individual *earns* $300 per month and spends income at a rate of $10 per day. However, now assume that he or she is *paid* every fifteen days rather than once a month. The person will receive $150 on the first and sixteenth days of each month. The average transactions balance will be

$$\frac{\$150 + 0}{2} = \$75$$

and k_j will equal ¼:

$$k_j = \frac{\$75}{\$300/\text{month}} = \frac{1}{4} \text{ month.}$$

Thus an increase in the frequency of receipts reduces the average amount of money which individuals must hold as a proportion k_j of a given volume of expenditures T_j.

Now consider an example of the effect of a change in the frequency of disbursements. Assume the above individual is again being paid $300 on the first day of each month, but now assume that he or she makes lump sum disbursements of $100 every 10 days. The transactions balances will be $300 for the first 10 days, $200 for the next 10 days, and $100 for the last 10 days of the month. His average money holdings will be

$$\frac{(\$300 \times 10 \text{ days}) + (\$200 \times 10 \text{ days}) + (\$100 \times 10 \text{ days})}{30 \text{ days}} = \$200$$

and k_j will equal $\frac{2}{3}$:

$$k_j = \frac{\$200}{\$300/\text{month}} = \frac{2}{3} \text{ month.}$$

In this particular case the decrease in the frequency of disbursements increases the average amount of money which individuals must hold in order to facilitate a given volume of expenditures and therefore k_j rises.

Finally, if the individual could make *all* monthly purchases on credit and make one lump sum payment on the first of the next month, the average transactions balance would be

$$\frac{29 \times \$0 + 1 \times \$300}{30} = \$10$$

and k_j will equal $1/30$:

$$k_j = \frac{\$10}{\$300} = \frac{1}{30} \text{ month.}$$

In this case the use of credit leads to a rather dramatic reduction in k_j.

Other aspects of individual payments and spending habits, such as different coincidences of receipts and disbursements, nonuniform rates of disbursement and the desire to maintain idle balances, influence the size of k_j. The role of individual payments and spending habits is discussed again later in this chapter and in Chapter 4. For the moment let us simply posit that k_j will always be a positive fraction of the flow of total expenditures measured over periods of time as long as a month.

Since our major concern in later chapters will be the analysis of aggregate economic behavior, we must aggregate over all individuals in the economy and show what determines the value of k for the economy as a whole. The fraction that measures the individual's average transactions balance for a given flow of total expenditures over a period of time can be expressed by dividing each side of Equation (2.1) by T_j:

$$k_j = \frac{M_j/P_T}{T_j} \ . \tag{2.2}$$

For the economy as a whole let the average aggregate transactions balance for a given flow of aggregate total expenditures be

$$k_T = \frac{M/P_T}{T} \ . \tag{2.3}$$

Now to show the relationship between the individual k_j and the aggregate k_T we first sum over individual holdings of real money balances where there are n individuals in the economy:

$$\frac{M}{P_T} = \sum_{j=1}^{n} \frac{M_j}{P_T} \ . \tag{2.4}$$

Summing Equation (2.1) over j and substituting Equation (2.4) into the result yields

$$\frac{M}{P_T} = \sum_{j=1}^{n} k_j T_j. \tag{2.5}$$

Substituting this result into Equation (2.3) gives

$$k_T = \sum_{j=1}^{n} k_j \frac{T_j}{T} \ .$$

The value of k_T for the entire economy is the summation of the individual k_j, each weighted by that individual's share of aggregate total expenditures for a given period of time.

At the outset of the book we noted that theories about the demand for money are considered important because money is widely believed to affect the level of production and employment. Therefore it will be useful to reformulate the demand for transactions balances as a function of the level of output of newly produced goods and services (real income) rather than the level of total expenditures. In any economy total expenditures exceed expenditures on the aggregate output of newly produced goods and services, since total expenditures include expenditures on everything exchanged in the economy, including transactions involving financial assets (for example, stock market transactions) and second-hand physical assets, as well as intermediate transactions between business firms which do not directly add to the level of aggregate output.

Define k_o as the ratio of real aggregate transactions balances to the level of aggregate output,

$$k_o = \frac{M/P_o}{O} \ . \tag{2.6}$$

This can be rewritten as

$$k_o = \frac{M/P_T}{T} \cdot \frac{T}{O} \cdot \frac{P_T}{P_o} \ .$$

Using Equation (2.5) gives

$$k_o = \sum_{j=1}^{n} k_j \frac{T_j}{T} \cdot \frac{T}{O} \cdot \frac{P_T}{P_o} \ . \tag{2.7}$$

We can now see how k_o, a term which is used extensively as just k in later chapters, depends on the ratio of individuals' money holdings to their total real expenditures (as discussed above, the k_j reflect habits of payment and disbursement in the economy), the individuals' shares of aggregate total expenditures T_j/T, the ratio of aggregate total expenditures to aggregate real income T/O, and the ratio of the price index for total expenditures to the price index for newly produced goods and services P_T/P_o. Since none of these ratios is expected to change systematically as the level of aggregate real income changes, k_o is usually treated as a constant, and the demand for transactions balances is viewed as varying in direct proportion with the level of real income.[5] This relation is depicted in Figure 2.1 as a straight line through the origin with a slope of k_o.

[5]We shall assume that the ratio of aggregate total expenditures T to aggregate income O does not change systematically with real income in the short run, even though in the long run such things as the vertical integration of business firms and increased specialization (both of which alter the level of intermediate transactions in the economy) will change this ratio. We shall also assume that, even though changes in various price indices are, in reality, seldom uniform, the ratio of the index of prices of goods and services comprising aggregate expenditures, P_T, to the index of prices of goods and services comprising aggregate output, P_o, does not change systematically with real income in the short run.

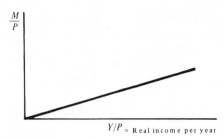

Figure 2.1. Aggregate transactions demand for money as a function of the level of aggregate real income, $0 < k_o < 1$.

The Interest Rate and the Transactions Demand for Money

While many earlier economists, including Fisher and Keynes, pointed out that income was not the only variable affecting the transactions demand for money, it took some time for economists to develop rigorously a rather sophisticated hypothesis of how conversion costs might affect transactions demand. Simply conceived, as the interest rate on other financial assets rises, the *net* cost of converting into and out of money balances for a given period of time is reduced and individuals will reduce their demand for transactions balances.

Consider our earlier example. Assume a bank raises its interest rate on time deposits from 2 percent to 6 percent per annum, payable on the 20th of each month. The individual who formerly held all $300 in transactions balances on the first day of the month, may now be induced to put $100 in the bank as a time deposit for the first 20 days of the month. He or she would do so because the interest income on $100 for 20 days rose from 11 cents to 33⅓ cents, assumed to be enough to compensate for the cost (inconvenience) of two monthly trips to the bank. The average transactions balance is $100 for the first 20 days and $50 for the last 10 days of the month, or $83.33 for the entire period.

In a similar fashion, Keynes in *The General Theory of Employment, Interest and Money* (1936),[6] Hansen in *Monetary Theory and Fiscal Policy* (1949),[7] and others rationalized that a relatively high yield on liquid nonmoney assets could effect an economization in the

---

[6]John Maynard Keynes, *The General Theory of Employment, Interest and Money* (London: Harcourt Brace and World, 1936).

[7]Alvin H. Hansen, *Monetary Theory and Fiscal Policy* (New York: McGraw-Hill, 1949).

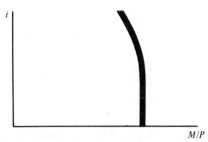

Figure 2.2. Aggregate transactions demand for real money balances as a function of the yield on liquid nonmoney assets.

demand for transaction balances. Therefore we write the aggregate transactions demand for real money balances as:[8]

$$(M/P)_d = f(O,i). \tag{2.8}$$

In this expression $(M/P)_d$ is postulated to vary *directly* with the level output O, as discussed above, and *inversely* with the market rate of interest i. It is possible, however, that the latter relationship may hold only at "very high" interest rate levels.

The relation between aggregate real transactions balances demanded and the rate of interest is shown in Figure 2.2 where the level

[8]*Nominal*, as opposed to *real*, income is defined as being equal to the general price of nominal money balances demanded as a function of the level of nominal income and level of newly produced goods and services times the level of output, $Y \equiv P \cdot O$; the level of nominal money balances demanded as a function of the level of nominal income and the rate of interest i may be written as

$$M_d = f(Y,i).$$

While we use the demand for *real* money balances in the rest of this book, Equation (2.8) is not the original Keynesian version. Keynes was rightfully accused of having a "money illusion" in his total money demand function which added together the transactions plus precautionary demands L_1 and the speculative demand L_2. Keynes wrote the total demand for money as

$$M_d = L_1(P \cdot O) + L_2(i).$$

In the above formulation a rise in the general price level could not affect the demand for money for speculative purposes. Hence if P and M increase proportionately at a constant i, individuals have the "illusion" that they are "better off" even though their *real* money balances are unchanged.

It would be proper to include an expression for total wealth in this demand function since, as we shall see in Chapter 3, Keynesians view the speculative demand for money in terms of the proportion of total financial wealth individuals will hold in the form of money. In addition, in the reading by John Boorman which follows Chapter 4, wealth (or some measure of permanent income) is shown to explain more of the variation in money demand than current income.

of aggregate real income and other variables which could affect the transactions demand are assumed constant. The function is drawn as it traditionally appears in money and banking and macroeconomic theory textbooks and is premised on the idea that some minimum interest rate is necessary to cover the minimum possible transactions cost in economizing on transactions balances.

Baumol's Approach to the Transactions Demand for Money

While the earlier work of Keynes, Hansen, and others is important, it was William Baumol who most precisely and systematically introduced the interest rate into the demand for transactions balances.[9] Baumol proceeds from the assumption that the stock of real cash balances is the jth individual's inventory of the medium of exchange and that the rational individual will attempt to minimize the cost of holding this inventory by holding the proper proportions of money and bonds. He assumes that transactions are perfectly foreseen and occur in a steady stream over a given time period. Real income per period is T_j dollars, and, by assumption, the individual pays out all of his T_j dollars per period at a constant rate. Thus, as the period progresses, he will be holding an ever-diminishing stock of assets.

In what form will these assets be held, bonds or money? If the individual holds money, he or she will lose the interest income he or she could have earned on bonds. If the individual holds bonds, it will cost something every time he or she "cashes" one in.

The jth individual is to begin the period holding all of his or her income in bonds. He or she is assumed to withdraw (disinvest) the money from bonds in lot-sized units of C_j dollars evenly spaced. For example, if an individual's T_j is $600 per month, his C_j might be $600 every 30 days, $300 every 15 days, $150 every 7½ days, or $20 per day. Whatever the value of C_j there will be T_j/C_j withdrawals made during the period. For each withdrawal he must pay a unit real transactions cost of b_j dollars. The expression $b_j \cdot T_j/C_j$ is a kind of "inventory replenishment cost" which includes not only the explicit costs (broker-

[9]William Baumol, "The Transactions Demand for Cash: An Inventory Theoretic Approach," *Quarterly Journal of Economics*, vol. 66 (November 1952), 545–556. For a somewhat more difficult but equally important treatment, *see* James Tobin, "The Interest Elasticity of the Transactions Demand for Cash," *Review of Economics and Statistics*, vol. 38 (August 1956), 241–247.

age fees, transfer taxes, etc.) of selling assets to get cash but also the implicit cost (the inconvenience) of doing so.

On the assumption that the withdrawal of C_j dollars is expended at a constant rate, the individual's average cash balance is $C_j/2$, the amount of C_j dollars he holds halfway through the interval from one withdrawal to another. The cost of holding cash is equal to the return i foregone by holding part of his portfolio in the form of an asset that does not bear a monetary yield.

The expression $i \cdot C_j/2$ represents the "interest opportunity cost" from holding transactions balances in the form of cash. The total cost of holding the inventory of cash is, therefore,

$$X_j = b_j \cdot \frac{T_j}{C_j} + i \cdot \frac{C_j}{2} \, . \tag{2.9}$$

The problem then becomes one of picking the value of the disinvestment lot size C_j which minimizes the total cost (transactions costs plus interest foregone) of holding the inventory of cash. At one extreme a single massive withdrawal (or disinvestment) from bonds at the outset of the period means a high interest opportunity cost; at the other extreme numerous small withdrawals mean a high inventory replenishment cost. At some point between these extremes, the *increase* in interest opportunity cost from slightly increasing C_j is just equal to the *decrease* in inventory replenishment cost from slightly increasing C_j, that is, the increment to total cost is zero. This (first-order) condition is satisfied where $dX_j/dC_j = 0$. At this point we can say that total cost is at a minimum. Solving the resulting expression for optimal C_j, that is, the value of C_j at which $dX_j/dC_j = 0$, gives[10]

$$C_j = \sqrt{(2b_j T_j)/i} \tag{2.10}$$

which seems to indicate that a rational individual, acting to minimize the cost of holding transactions balances, will demand cash in proportion to the square root of the value of the transactions.

---

[10]The derivative is $dX_j/dC_j = - \dfrac{bT_j}{C_j^2} + \dfrac{i}{2} = 0.$

This is rearranged to get Equation (2.10). The second-order condition for a minimum is likewise met:

$$d^2X_j/dC_j^2 = \frac{2b_j T_j}{C_j^3} > 0.$$

Since the optimal average balance was said to be $C_j/2$,

$$C_j/2 = (\tfrac{1}{2})\sqrt{(2b_j T_j)/i}. \tag{2.11}$$

Now let $k_j = (\tfrac{1}{2})\sqrt{2b_j}$ and let P_T be the general price level introduced to convert the expression into a demand for nominal balances. The above expression may be rewritten

$$M_j = k_j T_j^{1/2} i^{-1/2} P_T. \tag{2.12}$$

The result shows that (1) the jth individual's demand for transactions money balances does not generally vary in proportion to the level of total expenditures T_j, instead, there should be economies of scale in the management of cash balances,[11] (2) the quantity of transactions balances $C_j/2$ varies inversely with the interest rate i,[12] and (3) because of the transactions cost of exchanging cash for bonds ($b_j > 0$) it generally pays to hold cash, that is, in a perfectly frictionless world where purchases and sales of assets are costless, $b_j = 0$, there is *no* transactions demand for cash because it costs absolutely nothing to switch from bonds to cash when expenditures must be made.[13]

---

[11]From Equation (2.12) it can be seen that

$$\partial M_j/\ \partial T_j = (\tfrac{1}{2})k_j T_j^{-1/2} i^{-1/2} P_T \neq k,$$

$$\partial^2 M_j/\ \partial T_j^2 = -\ (\tfrac{1}{4})k_j T_j^{-3/2} i^{-1/2} P_T < 0.$$

and the elasticity is $\tfrac{1}{2}$.

Notice that when T_j increases the demand for money does *not* increase by the factor of proportionality, k_j. This result (falsified by empirical work reported in the reading by John Boorman which follows Chapter 4) would indicate a lack of proportionality between the demand for money and the level of income.

[12]Taking the transactions demand for money

$$M_j = k_j T_j^{1/2} i^{-1/2} P_T,$$

the inverse relationship is shown by

$$\partial M_j/\ \partial i = -\ (\tfrac{1}{2})k_j T_j^{1/2} i^{-3/2} P_T < 0,$$

and the elasticity is $-\tfrac{1}{2}$.

[13]Keynes also postulated a demand for money to be held as a reserve against future contingencies such as personal emergencies or unforeseen expenditures. Here again the existence of conversion costs explains why money is held to satisfy these needs even though it pays no dollar return. In this book, as in much of the professional literature, this precautionary demand for money is included with the transactions demand and is viewed as varying directly with the size of income and inversely with the market rate of interest.

The inventory-theoretic approach can typically be modified to incorporate an expression for the demand for precautionary balances. The only new element would be to multiply the first term of the total cost Equation (2.9) by some measure of statistical dispersion reflecting the probability of an unexpected cash drain. This measure of risk

Baumol's model is extremely suggestive and has implications for the macroeconomic models that are developed in Chapters 5–7. Two implications are of foremost concern. First, the demand for money can, in principle, depend upon the interest rate (as well as the level of income) without considering the speculative demand for money. The interest rate, as it affects the demand for money and, therefore, is affected by changes in the supply of money, is of crucial import for policy-makers who may control that supply. For instance, the model in Chapter 6 suggests that if monetary policy cannot influence the interest rate, it is less powerful.

Second, if the demand for money varies less than in proportion to the level of income, a given change in the money supply will, *ceteris paribus*, require a relatively large change in income to increase the quantity of money balances demanded and bring the money market into equilibrium. The Baumol model lends credence to the belief that monetary policy is a potent way to influence the level of income.

Given the theoretical possibility of an important role for the interest rate, is the appropriate interest rate in the money demand relation a long-term or a short-term rate? Based on the inventory-theoretic model one might reasonably assume that it would be the rate on the closest money substitutes, presumably a short-term rate. In this case changes in the supply of money would directly affect this rate, and longer term interest rates would respond only after a time lag. For example, given an increase in the supply of money, the short-term rate would decline; asset holders would then shift their portfolios out of short-term assets to higher yielding longer term ones, and this would, in turn, cause longer term interest rates to decline. In this case the process of interest rate adjustment to the initial increase in the money supply might take a considerable period of time.[14]

---

would therefore appear in the numerator of the square root formulas in Equations (2.10) and (2.11). An increase in the variability of cash flows would increase the demand for cash. See E. L. Whalen, "An Extension of the Baumol–Tobin Approach to the Transactions Demand for Cash," *Journal of Finance*, vol. 23 (March 1968), 113–134; and S. C. Tsiang, "The Precautionary Demand for Money: An Inventory Theoretical Analysis," *Journal of Political Economy*, vol. 77 (January–February 1969), 99–117.

[14]In a number of econometric models monetary impulses are transmitted from short-term rates to longer term rates to expenditures. See, for example, the reading by Yung Chul Park which follows Chapter 7.

Tests of hypotheses regarding which interest rate and which measure of income, if any, best explain variations in the demand for money are also surveyed in this article.

A discussion of time lags in the effect of money on expenditures as well as an

Information Costs and the Transactions Demand for Money

In the preceding section the focus was on the *cost* of holding transactions balances. In that section the only cost explicitly avoided by an individual who held transactions balances was a brokerage cost.[15] In the real world, if this were the only productive service from the holding of transactions balances, it would seem unlikely that any more than an absolute minimum quantity would be held during periods of a very high interest opportunity cost of holding money. Surely there are benefits from holding money other than the convenience of avoiding trips or calls to the "broker." Let us reconsider some of these benefits.

Earlier in this chapter we said that under the assumption that transactions costs were not zero, transactions balances would be held in the *interval between receipts and expenditures*. Careful reflection will suggest that under certain circumstances a transactions balance can be avoided even if receipts and disbursements are not perfectly synchronized. For example, picture an economy where the differences in timing between receipts and expenditures are adjusted by costlessly enforced verbal promises to exchange goods later. In the interim between receipts and expenditures individuals can hold interest-earning bonds. Without further investigation of the exchange process, there would seem to be no need to hold transactions money balances at all.

An examination of the reason transactions money balances are held shall require a closer look at the process of exchange. In an hypothetical barter economy an individual is typically viewed by economists as entering the market with an initial endowment of commodities. This initial bundle of commodities may differ from the combination of commodities the individual would prefer. Once he or she learns what the relative prices of all commodities actually are, money is

---

examination of why changes in money might have only small discernible effects on observed interest rates is found in Yung Chul Park, "Some Current Issues on the Transmission Process of Monetary Policy," *Staff Papers*, International Monetary Fund (March 1972), 1–45. Joseph Crews, "Econometric Models: The Monetarist and Non-Monetarist Views Compared," Federal Reserve Bank of Richmond *Monthly Review* (February 1973), 3–12. This article is reprinted in the readings which follow Chapter 7.

[15]Our emphasis on transactions in this chapter should not be interpreted to mean that only media of exchange should be included in the definition of money. The appropriate definition of money would seem rather to depend on the particular problem being addressed by the economic analyst. See the reading by John Boorman which follows Chapter 4 for further discussion of this problem.

typically seen as making less costly the transformation of an endowed bundle to a preferred bundle.[16]

More specifically, an important way in which money is seen as reducing the cost of exchange is through its effect on saving resources that would otherwise have to be used in the search for market information. Without money the individual's search for information regarding market opportunities would be more costly. By carrying out exchange with a medium of exchange, the number of market prices to be learned is reduced because all prices can be quoted in terms of the medium of exchange; this saves on resources used to acquire, process, and store market information.[17]

In addition, without money, before an individual arrived at his or her preferred bundle, he or she would have to engage in a sequence of barter transactions. These exchanges too would be costly in *time* if not in income. By using a medium of exchange the individual can save resources by not having to carry out so many exchanges before he obtains his desired bundle.

It should, therefore, be clear that one of the resources saved by the holding of transactions balances is time.[18] The saving of *exchange time* through the use of transactions balances then suggests that the demand-for-money decision be viewed as a concomitant of the allocation-of-time decision. The use of money increases the amount of leisure in society. This could generate a *leisure-time valuation effect* in the demand for transactions balances.[19] Since the opportunity cost of leisure is the wage rate, this indicates that an increase in the wage rate increases the value of transactions time. This leads, in turn, to an increase in the demand for money in order to economize on that time.

This analysis suggests that an empirically observed income elasticity of unity in the demand for money need not necessarily falsify the Baumol economies-of-scale hypothesis. An observed unitary elasticity

[16]For example, see Jurg Niehans, "Money in a Static Theory of Optimal Payment Arrangements," *Journal of Money Credit and Banking*, vol. 1 (November 1969), 706–726.

[17]Karl Brunner and Allan H. Meltzer, "The Uses of Money: Money in the Theory of an Exchange Economy," *American Economic Review* (December 1971), 784–805.

[18]Thomas R. Saving, "Transactions Costs and the Demand for Money," *American Economic Review*, vol. 51 (June 1971), 407–420.

[19]See Dean S. Dutton and Warren P. Gramm, "Transactions Costs, the Wage Rate and the Demand for Money," *American Economic Review*, vol. 53 (September 1973), 652–665.

could hypothetically represent the sum of a less-than-unitary income elasticity and a less-than-unitary leisure-time valuation elasticity.[20]

The preceding analysis implies that in a world of imperfect market information the holding of inventories of transactions balances will be a means of reducing the cost of carrying out exchanges. This, in turn, implies that by bringing about lower costs of acquiring information and transacting, the "invention" of money speeded the development of the market system and freed productive resources for other uses. This suggests that a society or group within a society will never settle forever on a single monetary asset. It is, indeed, more likely that there will be a fairly continual exploration for different means of lowering transactions and information costs and that this will result in the development of new media of exchange.[21]

Finally, the preceding analysis also implies that in a world of great uncertainty regarding market opportunities, the demand for money will increase because the marginal productivity of money as a means of economizing on information search costs is higher. This may help to explain the hypothetical appearance of a strong preference for liquidity (a more interest sensitive demand for money) during periods of economic instability such as a recession.

Economizing on Transactions Balances

The theoretical possibility that the variables which determine the value of an individual's time, such as the wage rate and the level of income,

[20]Assume, for example, that the level of b, the inventory disinvestment cost, in Equation (2.11) in the previous section varies directly and proportionately with the level of the jth individual's income. This simply would reflect the high correlation between an individual's income and the value of his time. Under this condition the observed income elasticity of that individual's demand for transactions balances would be unity.

[21]The pace of monetary innovation will not be constant but, like other types of innovation, will depend on the degree of uncertainty in the economic environment and also on the degree of price flexibility within the market system. For example, in a hypothetical world where exchange rates between different exchange media were flexible, in the long run a money that is stable in value would drive out an undependable one. Conversely, in the real world where exchange rates between different types of money are fixed, bad (unstable) money drives out good (stable) money. The absence of price (exchange rate) flexibility has impeded monetary innovation. Producers of unstable money (such as government) thereby have had an incentive to fix exchange rates by having their money labeled "legal tender." See Benjamin Klein, "The Competitive Supply of Money," *Journal of Money, Credit and Banking* (November 1974), 423–454. See Chapter 6 for a discussion of the "invisible" taxation associated with the anticipated inflation arising from the issuance of government ("outside") money that is legal tender.

could influence the demand for money suggests that in a high-wage, high-income economy there will be a strong demand for transactions balances. Earlier in this chapter we saw that in a high-interest-rate economy there will be considerable attempts to economize on the holding of transactions balances.

Many innovations in financial markets in recent years do, in fact, reflect attempts to economize on transactions balances. In the preceding section it was pointed out that if differences in the timing of receipts and expenditures could be adjusted by promises to pay at a later date, the demand for transactions balances would be significantly reduced. In other words, the development of credit markets is one way of economizing on transactions balances. A simple numerical example at the beginning of this chapter indicated how the use of credit could reduce the average level of transactions balances. In recent years the expanded use of credit cards, including bank credit cards, is a good example of how the development of credit markets economizes on the demand for transactions balances.[22] An additional mechanism for economizing on transactions balances is the use of trade credit. *Trade credit* is the exchange of a promise to pay the vendor later for currently received goods and services. This appears to reduce the quantity of money balances immediately necessary to finance current transactions. Some economists view unused but available trade credit as so close a substitute for transactions balances as to include it in their definition of money.[23]

The existence of a large volume of trade credit belies a serious problem of inefficiency in capital markets. If capital markets were competitively structured, specialists at credit extension (financial intermediaries) would be able to satisfy such credit demands through routine means, such as short-term loans and bank credit cards. Ven-

---

[22]With reference to the Baumol model, this could be reflected by subtracting from total transactions T_j the amount of one's purchases that are charged z_j. By replacing T_j with $T_j - z_j$ in Equation (2.12), one's average transactions balance would fall. The level of credit purchases would vary inversely with annual credit charges. As a consequence, where credit charges vary directly with the market rate of interest, the overall interest elasticity of the demand for transactions balances will fall in absolute magnitude. See A. S. Rama Sastry, "The Effect of Credit on the Transactions Demand for Cash," *Journal of Finance*, vol. 25 (September 1970), 777–782.

For some empirical estimates which do not falsify this hypothesis see Kenneth J. White, "The Effect of Bank Credit Cards on the Households Transactions Demand for Money," *Journal of Money, Credit and Banking* (February 1976), 51–61.

[23]Arthur B. Laffer, "Trade Credit and the Money Market," *Journal of Political Economy*, vol. 78 (March/April 1970), 239–267.

dors would not normally be able to compete with financial intermediaries. In addition to inefficiency in capital markets the existence of a significant volume of trade credit may also reflect an inefficiently large demand for money balances.[24]

Aside from innovations in credit markets, there have been several other developments in recent years that have reduced the transactions demand for money, where money is defined as checkable deposits plus currency in circulation. A most important area of innovations has involved reductions in the cost of disinvesting in interest-earning assets, that is, reductions in the "brokerage" cost term b of Baumol's inventory theoretic model. As discussed in Chapter 1 and the readings which follow Chapter 1, in recent years the spread of negotiable order of withdrawal (NOW and Super-NOW) accounts has been an important innovation in the payments mechanism. A NOW account is basically a deposit upon which a form of check can be written. Thereby, with such an account one need not make a trip to the commercial bank, savings bank or savings and loan association in order to transfer funds. This innovation has reduced the transactions cost of disinvesting in interest-earning accounts in order to make expenditures. As pointed out in Chapter 1 it has also caused a redefinition of the money stock.

Another innovation involves the use of point-of-sale terminals. Under this system electronic terminals are placed in stores. In payment for a purchase, funds can be transferred electronically out of one's bank account into the vendor's account. This saves time in writing checks and withdrawing funds for cash purchases.[25] It also reduces the volume of outstanding checks (float) in the banking system.[26]

[24]Capital market imperfections are not unrelated to the government franchise given to depositary institutions to do a checking account business. These franchises are hard to obtain. Depositary institutions, therefore, have a degree of monopoly power in both deposit and local loan markets. Because of the "customer relationship" that follows from this monopoly power and because of legal ceilings on explicit interest payments on deposits, depositary institutions may grant favorable credit terms only to big depositors. This leads to an inefficient allocation of credit because big depositors are not necessarily the most credit worthy. It also causes depositors to carry an inefficiently large quantity of demand deposit balances in order to qualify for favorable credit terms. Moreover, by making credit available to smaller depositors only at a higher cost from nonspecialists, it causes them to carry larger transactions balances than they would if credit markets were more competitively structured. The feasibility of making banking and credit markets more competitive is investigated by a number of authors in Havrilesky and Boorman, *Current Perspectives in Banking, op. cit.*

[25]With reference to the Baumol model, modified to reflect a demand for "precautionary" balances (footnote 13), there also occurs a decrease in the variability of cash flows, particularly for business firms because float is reduced and more orders are paid

Concluding Comment

The incentive for financial innovations can be better appreciated if one has an understanding of the interest rate as an opportunity cost of holding total money balances, not just transactions balances. In the next chapter we explore theories regarding the demand for speculative money balances. In Chapter 4 we view the demand for money from the perspective of the neoclassical quantity theory of money. A good understanding of the demand for money will be helpful in the later study of macroeconomic models.

QUESTIONS

1. "Keynes did not allow uncertainty to enter his transactions demand for money, reserving its effects entirely for his liquidity preference hypothesis." Evaluate this statement. How could uncertainty enter into the Baumol model?
2. Explain the effects which the development of an extensive credit card system would have on the transactions demand for money.
3. What are some of the ways in which a corporate treasurer could conserve on his transactions balances in order to minimize the opportunity cost of holding such balances?
4. Explain the role of the interest rate in Baumol's "inventory theoretic" hypothesis of the demand for money.
5. "As income becomes more equitably distributed in our economy, Baumol's square root rule suggests that monetary policy will be more effective." Evaluate.

---

for immediately. This also reduces the demand for cash. See Mark J. Flannery and Dwight M. Jaffee, *The Economic Implications of an Electronic Money Transfer System* (Lexington: D. C. Heath, 1973). See also Robert E. Knight, "The Changing Payments Mechanism: Electronic Funds Transfer," *Monthly Review*, Federal Reserve Bank of Kansas City (July–August 1974), 10–20, reprinted in Havrilesky and Boorman, *Current Perspectives in Banking, op. cit.*

Flannery and Jaffee point out that lower costs of running the nation's payments mechanism might enable financial intermediaries to reduce the service charges on demand deposits, thereby reducing the interest opportunity cost of holding cash and *increasing* the quantity of transactions balances demanded.

[26]Other innovations which may be viewed as reducing the magnitude of Baumol's *b* include telephone transfers from savings to checking accounts, the ability to write checks on money market mutual funds, and changes in laws allowing state and local governments to hold savings deposits. Several economists have claimed that these innovations have led in recent years to a downward shift in the demand for money. The stability of the demand-for-money function is examined in the reading by John Boorman which follows Chapter 4.

6. Prove that the interest elasticity of the demand for money in the Baumol model is equal to $-\frac{1}{2}$.
7. "Trade credit reduces the demand for money." Evaluate.

BIBLIOGRAPHY

BAUMOL, WILLIAM J., "The Transactions Demand for Cash: An Inventory Theoretic Approach," *Quarterly Journal of Economics*, vol. 66 (November 1952), 545–556.

BRUNNER, KARL, and ALLAN H. MELTZER, "Economies of Scale in Cash Balances Reconsidered," *Quarterly Journal of Economics*, vol. 81 (August 1967).

———, "The Uses of Money: Money in the Theory of an Exchange Economy," *American Economic Review* (December 1971), 784–805.

DE LEEUW, FRANK, and EDWARD M. GRAMLICH, "The Channels of Monetary Policy: A Further Report on the Federal Reserve–MIT Model," *Journal of Finance*, vol. 24, no. 2 (May 1969), 265–290.*

DUTTON, DEAN S., and WARREN P. GRAMM, "Transactions Costs, the Wage Rate and the Demand for Money," *American Economic Review*, vol. 53 (September 1973), 652–665.

FLANNERY, MARK J., and DWIGHT M. JAFFEE, *The Economic Implications of an Electronic Money Transfer System* (Lexington: D. C. Heath, 1973).

HAMBURGER, MICHAEL J., "The Lag in the Effect of Monetary Policy: A Survey of Recent Literature," *Monetary Aggregates and Monetary Policy* (New York: Federal Reserve Bank, 1974), 104–111.*

HANSEN, ALVIN H., *Monetary Theory and Fiscal Policy* (New York: McGraw-Hill, 1949).

JOHNSON, HARRY G., "Notes on the Theory of the Transactions Demand for Cash," *Indian Journal of Economics*, vol. 44 (July 1963), 1–11.

———, "A Note on the Theory of Transactions Demand for Cash," *Journal of Money, Credit and Banking*, vol. 3 (August 1970), 383–384.

KEYNES, JOHN MAYNARD, *The General Theory of Employment, Interest and Money* (London: Harcourt Brace and World, 1936).

KLEIN, BENJAMIN, "The Competitive Supply of Money," *Journal of Money, Credit and Banking* (November 1974), 423–454.

KNIGHT, ROBERT E., "The Changing Payments Mechanism: Electronic Funds Transfer," *Monthly Review*, Federal Reserve Bank of Kansas City (July–August 1974), pp. 10–20.†

---

*Reprinted in Thomas M. Havrilesky and John T. Boorman, *Current Issues in Monetary Theory and Policy* (Arlington Heights, IL: AHM Publishing, 1980).

†Reprinted in Thomas M. Havrilesky and John T. Boorman, *Current Perspectives in Banking* (Arlington Heights, IL: AHM Publishing Corporation, 1980).

LAFFER, ARTHUR B., "Trade Credit and the Money Market," *Journal of Political Economy*, vol. 78 (March–April 1970), 239–267.

MILLER, H. LAWRENCE, "On Liquidity and Transactions Costs," *Southern Economic Journal*, vol. 32 (1965), 43–48.

NIEHANS, JURG, "Money in a Static Theory of Optimal Payment Arrangements," *Journal of Money, Credit and Banking*, vol. 1 (November 1969), 706–726.

PARK, YUNG CHUL, "Some Current Issues on the Transmission Process Of Monetary Policy," *Staff Papers*, International Monetary Fund (March 1972), 1–45.*

SASTRY, A. S. RAMA, "The Effect of Credit on the Transactions Demand for Cash," *Journal of Finance*, vol. 25 (September 1970), 777–782.

SAVING, THOMAS R., "Transactions Costs and the Demand for Money," *American Economic Review*, vol. 51 (June 1971), 407–420.

SMITH, P. E., "Probabilistic Demand for Cash Balances and (s,S) Inventory Policies," *Weltwirtschaft. Archiv*, vol. 93 (March 1961), 72–83.

SPRENKLE, CASE, "The Usefulness of Transactions Demand Models," *Journal of Finance*, vol. 24 (December 1969).

TOBIN, JAMES, "The Interest Elasticity of Transactions Demand for Cash," *Review of Economics and Statistics*, vol. 38 (August 1956), 241–247.

TSIANG, S. C., "The Precautionary Demand for Money: An Inventory Theoretical Analysis," *Journal of Political Economy*, vol. 77 (January–February 1969), 99–117.

WHALEN, E. L., "An Extension of the Baumol–Tobin Approach to the Transactions Demand for Cash," *Journal of Finance*, vol. 23 (March 1968), 113–134.

WHITE, KENNETH J., "The Effect of Bank Credit Cards on the Households' Transactions Demand for Money," *Journal of Money, Credit and Banking* (February 1976), 51–61.

THREE
The Keynesian Speculative Demand for Money

Introduction

In the previous chapter we examined the transactions demand for money. In a world where the costs of buying and selling interest-earning assets (to be held in the interval between the receipt and disbursement of income) are not negligible, money, the generally accepted medium of exchange, will be held.

In this chapter we show that money is also held because it functions as a liquid store of wealth whose market value may be less variable than other wealth forms. (Individuals may demand money merely to hold it "idle.")[1]

At first blush it seems irrational to hold financial wealth in a nonearning form. Yet, as discussed more fully in the next chapter, the earlier Cambridge economists indicated that an individual's uncertainty about future market prices of earning assets, among other things, could induce him to forego these earnings and to hold money. The market value of money may be less variable. Keynes articulated this in his liquidity preference theory, one subject of this chapter.[2]

---

[1]Thus, total money demand M_d may consist of transactions (plus precautionary) balances M_1 and speculative balances M_2.

[2]What we develop here is a contemporary interpretation of the liquidity preference theory of John Maynard Keynes' *The General Theory of Employment, Interest and Money* (London: Harcourt Brace and World, 1936).

As discussed in this chapter, Keynes asserted that the lower the market rate of interest relative to an expected future rate, the greater the expected decline in the prices of earning assets. Therefore, at low rates of interest liquid money balances are a preferable hedge against the expected capital loss of holding earning assets. In a subsequent section of this chapter James Tobin's version of this hypothesis is considered. Tobin indicated that even if the expected capital loss is zero, some risk of capital loss is always present. He further stated that the lower the rate of interest, the less the individual's preference to hold earning assets and assume this risk, and the greater his preference for liquidity (money balances).

Because of these Keynesian contributions and Baumol's inventory-theoretic approach to transactions demand, economists are inclined to concede, in principle, that the total demand for money depends on the rates of interest (yields) on financial assets as well as on the level of income and/or wealth. However, the extent to which any of these variables explain variations in the demand for money is largely an empirical question. In the reading by John Boorman which follows Chapter 4 we shall present a survey of empirical work on this question.

The Relationship between Interest Rates and Bond Prices

Before we begin our analysis, it is necessary to explain the relationship between interest rates and the prices of existing debt instruments which promise to pay the holder certain periodic interest payments and to repay the principal value at maturity.

When we speak of the *yield* on debt instruments such as bonds we shall mean the "yield to maturity." One measure of the yield of an obligation may be calculated simply by dividing the dollar amount of the interest paid per year by the current market price of the instrument. However, this is not a completely satisfactory measure, for it fails to consider the capital gain or loss to be incurred if that obligation is held to maturity. For example, the *current yield* on an obligation selling for $950 and paying $50.00 per year is $50/$950 = .0526 or 5.26%. But if the face value of this bond is $1000, it will return an additional $50 above purchase price to the owner upon redemption at maturity. Thus if the bond is held to maturity the owner will realize a capital gain of $50 on his investment in addition to the yearly interest return. This capital gain must be included in the complete return when calculating the total yield to maturity on the security.

Yield to maturity may be calculated by means of a formula for computing the present value of a future stream of returns. If we wish to calculate the present value of a single $50 payment to be made one year from today, we "discount" that $50 according to the simple formula:

$$\text{present value} = P = \frac{50}{1 + i}$$

where i is the interest (or discount) rate. For example, the present value of $50 discounted at 2% for one year is

$$P = \frac{\$50}{1 + .02} = \frac{\$50}{1.02} = \$49.02.$$

In other words, $49.02 invested for 1 year at 2% yields $50. In general, a single payment of Y dollars to be received 2 years in the future is currently valued at

$$P = \frac{Y}{(1 + i)^2} \cdot$$

At 2%, then, the present value of this *single* $50 payment to be made 2 years from today is

$$P = \frac{\$50}{(1 + i)^2} = \frac{\$50}{(1 + .02)^2} = \frac{\$50}{(1.0404)} = \$48.06.$$

If we generalize this formula, the present value of any payment Y_n to be made n years from now is

$$P = \frac{Y_n}{(1 + i)^n} \cdot \tag{3.1}$$

Therefore, if a debt instrument carries an obligation to pay $50 *per year* for the next 5 years and a final repayment of principal of $1000.00 at the end of the 5 year period, the present value of that stream of returns discounted at a rate of $100i\%$ per year is

$$P = \frac{Y_1}{(1 + i)} + \frac{Y_2}{(1 + i)^2} + \frac{Y_3}{(1 + i)^3} + \frac{Y_4}{(1 + i)^4} + \frac{Y_5}{(1 + i)^5} + \frac{\text{principal}}{(1 + i)^5} \tag{3.2}$$

where $Y_1 = Y_2 = Y_3 = Y_4 = Y_5 = \$50$.

For example, if the return demanded by the lender is 6 percent per year, he would be willing to pay $957.87 for a bond with these characteristics:

$$P = \frac{\$50}{(1.06)} + \frac{\$50}{(1.06)^2} + \frac{\$50}{(1.06)^3} + \frac{\$50}{(1.06)^4} + \frac{\$50}{(1.06)^5} + \frac{\$1000}{(1.06)^5}$$

$$= \$47.17 + \$44.50 + \$41.98 + \$39.60 + \$37.36 + \$747.26$$

$$= \$957.87.$$

Alternatively, knowing the current market price of the instrument, we may use the formula to calculate its yield to maturity. For example, if the obligation is currently selling for $950.00, the yield is given by the formula

$$\$950 = \frac{\$50}{(1 + i)} + \frac{\$50}{(1 + i)^2} + \frac{\$50}{(1 + i)^3} + \frac{\$50}{(1 + i)^4} + \frac{\$50}{(1 + i)^5} + \frac{\$1000}{(1 + i)^5}$$

$$i = .0619 \qquad 100i = 6.19\%.$$

It is clear from the formula that the higher the (interest) rate at which future expected returns are discounted (in the denominators), the lower will be the present value of that income (the market value of the obligation); conversely, the lower the rate of discount, the higher will be the present value.

It is through variations in the market price of outstanding securities (with fixed payments and a fixed face value) that the yield on those instruments is adjusted to current market conditions.

The formula suggests that when the market rate or current yield in the denominator is equal to the 5% *coupon rate* (the $50 annual interest payment divided by the $1000 principal), the bond sells in the market at "par," that is, its market price is equal to its principal value. When the market rate is greater than the coupon rate, the bond sells below par or at a discount, and when the market rate is less than the coupon rate, the bond sells above par or at a premium.

This shows how bond prices adjust, in the market where bonds are traded, to bring a bond's yield to maturity into line with the market rate of interest. It indicates that bond prices vary inversely with the market rate of interest.

Finally, the formula indicates that the market prices of longer term debt instruments will fluctuate more widely for a given change in the market rate than the prices of shorter term debt instruments, since instruments with a longer term to maturity contain larger powers of $(1 + i)$ in the formula. This is important because it means longer term bonds are more subject to capital gains and losses than shorter term bonds.

In the remainder of this chapter we shall deal exclusively with *consol bonds* because the relationship between the market price of a consol bond and the market rate of interest can be reduced to a very convenient expression. A consol continues to pay interest indefinitely but does not repay principal. Therefore, the general present value formula, Equation (3.2), is written without the final term for the repayment of principal:

$$P = \frac{Y_1}{(1 + i)^1} + \frac{Y_2}{(1 + i)^2} + \frac{Y_3}{(1 + i)^3} + \cdots + \frac{Y_n}{(1 + i)^n} \tag{3.3}$$

Now multiply both sides of this equation by $1/(1 + i)$:

$$\frac{1}{1 + i} P = \frac{Y_1}{(1 + i)^2} + \frac{Y_2}{(1 + i)^3} + + \cdots + \frac{Y_n}{(1 + i)^{n+2}} . \tag{3.4}$$

Assume that $Y_1 = Y_2 = Y_3 = \cdots = Y_n$ and subtract Equation (3.4) from Equation (3.3):

$$P \left[1 - \frac{1}{1 + i} \right] = \frac{Y}{1 + i} - \frac{Y}{(1 + i)^{n+1}} .$$

Multiply both sides by $(1 + i)$ and rearrange terms:

$$P = \frac{Y}{i} \left[1 - \frac{1}{(1 + i)^n} \right] . \tag{3.5}$$

This is a general expression for the present value of a continuous stream of future interest payments. If we add an expression for repayment of principal, it is often a convenient way to reformulate the present value formula, Equation (3.2).

To derive the expression for the present value of a consol simply let the maturity of the bond n become infinite, so that the expression $(1 + i)^n$ becomes infinitely large and the term $1/(1 + i)^n$ becomes zero as n approaches infinity. This gives

$$P = \frac{Y}{i} \tag{3.6}$$

which says that the present value of a consol is inversely proportional to the rate of interest.

Now we are ready to begin our analysis of the speculative demand for money. If we ignore physical assets and equities (which have roughly similar portfolio properties as physical assets),[3] an individual may hold his wealth in two forms, debt instruments and money. As discussed earlier, money has the advantage of being generally acceptable as a medium of exchange. In addition, the market value of money may be subject to less volatile swings than the market value of debt instruments. Economists traditionally have said that the confluence of these two properties make money a unique, most "liquid" financial asset.

The Early Keynesian Approach to Liquidity Preference

In *The General Theory of Employment, Interest and Money*,[4] Keynes assumes that all individuals wish to avoid losses and that the gains or losses they anticipate from holding debt instruments (bonds) depend solely on the rate of interest i_e which they are certain will occur at some uncertain date within the forthcoming time period t.[5]

Capital losses would be expected if the current rate of interest i were less than the expected rate i_e because, as discussed above, as bond yields rise, bond prices fall. If the current rate i were sufficiently lower than the expected rate i_e, it would be unprofitable for the individual firm or household to hold bonds now. Rather, if capital losses were greater than interest income, the individual would hold money balances until the rate i rises toward its expected level (and bond prices fall). At some point, as the interest rate rises and bond prices fall, he would buy bonds. Conversely, if the rate of capital loss were

[3]Both debt and money differ from physical assets and equities in that their values do not fluctuate with the price level and in that they are unattractive investments when the price level is expected to rise. In Chapters 2 and 7 the effect of price expectations on the demand for money and debt is examined as part of a discussion of the relation between nominal and real rates of interest. For the present our analysis abstracts from changes in the general price level.

[4]John Maynard Keynes, *op. cit.*

[5]The expected rate is forecasted by the individual. For analytical simplicity we overlook the behavior that generates the rate expected to occur within the forthcoming time period. We assume it occurs independently of the level of the current rate, that is, we assume perfectly inelastic interest rate expectations. Keynes had in mind inelastic, but not perfectly inelastic, interest rate expectations (Keynes, *op. cit.*, p. 202). They were tied to his concept of the "normal" rates. The "normal" rate of interest, according to Keynes, is the level toward which the expected rate gravitates over time. *The further the current rate diverges from normal, the more it would be expected to bounce back in the forthcoming time period.* This notion of "regressive expectations" in Keynes' theory is not confined to his money demand hypothesis. It permeates his entire theory.

less than the current interest rate i (or if capital gains were expected), the individual would hold bonds now.[6] Thus the individual's financial wealth will consist of either all bonds or all money in Keynes' model.

Keynes proposed that the economy's speculative demand for money slopes downward because, as the current rate falls, increasingly more individuals become convinced that the rate of capital loss outweighs the interest rate; that is, as the current rate falls, more and more individuals feel that the current rate is sufficiently below their expected rate to warrant holding all of their speculative financial wealth in the form of money balances.

expect rate to ↑

Mathematically the sufficient condition for the financial investor to hold all his speculative portfolio as money is

$$i + g < 0 \tag{3.7}$$

where $g < 0$. Let P_e = expected bond price and P = current bond price. The definition of the rate of capital loss is

$$g = \frac{P_e - P}{P} \tag{3.8}$$

where $P_e < P$. Substituting Equation (3.8) into (3.7),

$$i + \frac{P_e - P}{P} < 0$$

or

$$i + \frac{P_e}{P} - 1 < 0.$$

Assume for purposes of analytical convenience that all bonds are *consols* (bonds paying a fixed income in perpetuity). This makes bond prices and bond yields inversely proportional, as shown in Equation (3.6), so that the last expression may be rewritten as

$$i + \frac{i}{i_e} - 1 < 0.$$

[6]Contrast this analysis, where the *expected value* of the capital gain or loss is nonzero and known with certainty, to Tobin's approach where the *expected value* of the capital gain and loss in a probability distribution is zero, and yet the individual will still be wary of holding bonds because there is a "risk" in holding bonds. "Risk," in Tobin's analysis, is measured by the spread or *dispersion* of possible capital losses and gains about this zero *expected value*.

Multiplying through by i_e, we get

$$i \cdot i_e + i - i_e < 0.$$

The condition for holding all financial wealth as money is then

$$i \cdot i_e + i < i_e$$

As an example, assume a consol paying $50 a year is currently priced at $1000, so that $i = .05$. But it is expected to attain a market price of $950 sometime within the forthcoming period; by Equation (3.6) the expected rate i_e is .0526. At this rate it follows that $i \cdot i_e + i = i_e$ and the individual is indifferent between bonds or money. If the expected rate i_e were higher, he or she would hold all money; if it were lower, he or she would hold all bonds. The reader may calculate that where the income per year is $40 on the same bond, the current rate is .04 and the critical expected rate is .0417. A convenient (though slightly inaccurate) rule of thumb is that the expected rate which would induce an individual to hold all money must be greater than the current rate i plus its square i^2, that is, if $i + i^2 < i_e$, one would hold all money, and if $i + i^2 > i_e$, one would hold all bonds.

Now if Keynes' hypothesis is considered, the individual demand for real speculative money balances[7] M_2 may be depicted as the discontinuous function shown in Figure 3.1. When the market rate of interest i is sufficiently below the expected rate i_e as discussed, the individual holds all his or her speculative portfolio in the form of real money balance. Otherwise he or she holds all the speculative portfolio in the form of bonds.[8]

To derive the demand curve for speculative balances for the entire economy, we simply sum across all individual demand curves. A necessary condition for the smooth downward sloping of this aggregate

[7]In future chapters we refer, as did Keynes, to transactions balances as M_1 and speculative balances as M_2. It must be pointed out now, as we do in detail in Chapter 4, that the usefulness of the concept of separable money demand components is challenged by many economists.

[8]Where future rates are not assumed to be expected with certainty, the individual may actually mix his or her bond–money holdings. The more the current rate departs from the "normal" rate, the greater the probability with which the individual expects the rate to move back to its "normal" level. In this case the greater the rise in the current rate, the greater the proportion of financial wealth held in the form of bonds and the greater the decline in the current rate, the greater the proportion held in the form of money. Unlike the Tobin approach this variation of Keynes' analysis still ties *risk* to the expected rate.

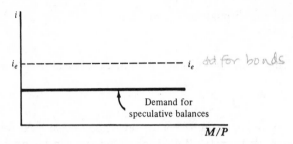

Figure 3.1 The individual's demand for speculative money balances.

curve, as depicted in Figure 3.2,[9] is that as the market rate i falls, successively greater numbers of individuals feel that this rate is sufficiently below their expected rate to warrant holding all of their speculative portfolio in the form of real money balances.

This analysis carries several crucial implications. First, Keynes suggested that at some low interest rate practically everyone will feel the current rate is sufficiently below their expected rate to warrant holding their portfolio in the form of money balances. At this point the economy's demand-for-money function approaches an infinite interest elasticity as shown in Figure 3.2. No matter how large the increase in the money supply, only a very, very small decrease in the interest rate is sufficient to convince individuals to hold all of their portfolio in the form of money balances. As discussed in detail in Chapter 7, if the economy is in this "liquidity trap," it may make monetary policy completely ineffective.

Notice that Keynes did not introduce earning assets of very short maturity into his analysis. In the *real* world these assets *might* be held until bond prices fell and then would be liquidated, the funds being used for the purchase of low-priced bonds. The financial investor need not hold money which bears no explicit yield. Nevertheless Keynes' purposeful omission of such "money substitutes" does not vitiate his hypothesis that the rate of interest affects the demand for money, because, as discussed in Chapter 2, earning assets have explicit and implicit conversion costs as they are purchased and liquidated; therefore, the rational individual will generally hold some of his speculative wealth in the form of money balances.[10] Also, as Keynes assumes that

[9]Again, as in Chapter 2 to avoid Keynes' specification of money illusion, we depict the demand for *real* money balances.

[10]This line of reasoning suggests that the rate of interest on close money substitutes might be the most relevant one for the demand-for-money relation. For further discussion, see footnote 14 in Chapter 2 and footnote 20 in this chapter.

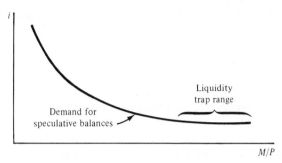

Figure 3.2.   Demand for speculative balances in the economy.

the exact date of the bond price decline is not known with certainty, an individual holding even short-term assets would surely incur some (albeit a small) capital loss. Therefore, money substitutes may not be a profitable hedge against the expected loss from holding long-term bonds.

Over the years Keynes' liquidity preference hypothesis has drawn critical fire. Specifically, to the extent that the expected rate were subject to change, as Keynes suggested, the demand for money would be statistically unstable. In contrast (as reported in the survey of empirical work on the demand for money which follows Chapter 4), the function actually appears to be quite stable statistically. One might then attempt to preserve Keynes' hypothesis, in light of this evidence, by assuming that the expected rate is relatively constant. There has been considerable criticism of this assumption's lack of realism. In fact, in a world where all individuals have learned to expect the same or very similar "normal" rates,[11] the speculative demand schedule would have a nearly angular (convex) shape. This shape is not revealed by statistical tests reported in the survey which follows Chapter 4.

It has been argued that the primary weakness of Keynes' original liquidity preference hypothesis is its assumption of a *certain* expected rate.[12] In order to get the stable money demand function revealed by statistical tests, this rate must be relatively fixed by the individual. At the same time, in order to obtain the typical smooth aggregate money demand function (shown in Figure 3.2) that seems to fit the actual

[11]The role of the normal rate in Keynes' analysis is discussed in footnote 5 at the beginning of this section.

[12]Axel Leijonhufvud defends this formulation of Keynes as being completely consistent with his world view. See Axel Leijonhufvud, *On Keynesian Economics and the Economics of Keynes* (New York: Oxford, 1968).

data,[13] the expected rate would have to differ between individuals, and each individual's holdings would have to be small relative to the total for the economy. This clearly imposes severe restrictions on an already barely tenable assumption.

The Tobin Approach to Liquidity Preference

A major advance in monetary theory was the explanation of the inverse relationship between the rate of interest and the quantity of money demanded, without the restrictive rate-forecasting assumption of Keynes. We shall now present an abbreviated, simplified version of James Tobin's hypothesis.[14]

Definitions Assume a two-asset economy where portfolios are comprised of money and/or consol bonds with an annual market rate of interest of i percent; also assume that each financial investor is *uncertain* about the value of the market rate in the next period. Each investor believes that the probability that the market rate will fall by x percent is equal to the probability that it will rise by x percent, and no rate is any riskier, in and of itself, than any other. (Notice how these two assumptions differ from Keynes' original necessary assumption of a *certain* expected rate that differs between individuals and results in their portfolios consisting of either bonds *or* money.)

   Let

   A_1 = the fraction of total assets which the investor holds as money, where $0 \leqslant A_1 \leqslant 1$
   A_2 = the fraction of total assets which the investor holds as consols, where $0 \leqslant A_2 \leqslant 1$
   $A_1 + A_2 = 1$ by the assumption of a two-asset economy
   E = the expected percentage increase in the value of the portfolio during a year (which by the assumption above excludes probable capital gains or losses),[15] that is,

---

[13]As reported in the survey of empirical work, which follows Chapter 4, most statistical tests do not indicate the presence of the liquidity trap.

[14]For all points requiring further detail, see James Tobin, "Liquidity Preference as Behavior towards Risk," *Review of Economic Studies*, vol. 25 (February 1958), 65–86.

[15]For the reader with some knowledge of elementary mathematical statistics, the individual assesses the *expected value* of probable capital gains and losses as zero and therefore the expected value of holding a bond is just its interest yield.

$$E = A_2 \cdot i \tag{3.9}$$

R = the risk associated with holding consols, measured as a percentage, that is,

$$R = A_2 \cdot s \tag{3.10}$$

where $s(0 \leqslant s \leqslant 1)$ is a fixed coefficient measuring the risk of capital loss from holding a bond and is subjectively determined by each investor.[16]

Note that, unlike Keynes' original hypothesis, the capital loss from holding a bond is assumed to be independent of the *level* of the interest rate.

Utility Now the individual's problem is this: each bond held increases expected earnings, but it also increases the risk (possible fluctuation of value) of the portfolio. Earnings, viewed here as additions to wealth, are "good" since they add to utility; risk is "bad" since it subtracts from utility. What combination of expected earnings and risk will make the individual "happiest"? To answer this question we turn to a tool of elementary economic theory, the *indifference curve*.

Assume that every combination of expected increases in the value of the portfolio E and risk R gives the financial investor a certain amount of expected utility or "satisfaction," I. Further assume that there are numerous sets of possible combinations of E and R that give the investor *equal* amounts of expected utility, $I_1, I_2, I_3, \ldots, I_n$. In Figure 3.3 expected utility is constant along each line, I.

Assume that for every level of risk R, the associated value of expected earnings E along I_2 is greater than the corresponding E along I_1. Hence I_2 represents a greater amount of expected utility than does I_1; therefore I_2 and I_1 cannot intersect in the graph. As we move from the lower right to the upper left in Figure 3.3 we go to higher and higher levels of expected total utility.

Now let us engage in an experiment. Assume that the individual in

[16]Again, for the reader with some knowledge of mathematical statistics, the risk from holding bonds is not the *expected value* of the capital gain or loss (which is assumed to be zero) but rather the standard deviation of the probability distribution of expected future bond prices. Thus, $s = \sigma$.

Other measures of risk have been used in models of portfolio behavior. An important treatise on portfolio theory shows the Tobin model presented here to be a special case of a more general theory of asset choice. See Bernell K. Stone, *Risk, Return and Equilibrium* (Cambridge: M.I.T. Press, 1970). A survey of modern portfolio theory appears in the readings which follow Chapter 4.

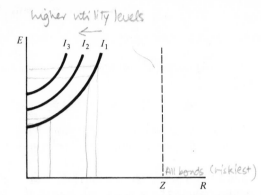

Figure 3.3. An indifference map in risk-expected return space.

Figure 3.3 remains at a constant level of expected utility, that is, he stays on a given indifference curve. If this individual receives a small increment of risk R, in order to stay at the same level of total expected utility (to stay on the same indifference curve), he or she must be compensated with an increase in expected earnings E. This must occur because risk is "bad" and subtracts from utility, while expected earnings are "good" and add to expected utility. Therefore, the tradeoff between risk R and expected earnings E along a given indifference curve is positive, and the indifference curve slopes upward in (E, R) space, that is, dE/dR is positive.

Next consider a series of small, equal, successive increments of risk while total expected utility remains at a constant level in Figure 3.3. Consecutive *equal* increments of risk (a "bad") can preserve a constant level of total expected utility only if they are compensated for by consecutively *larger* increments of expected earnings (a "good") because of diminishing marginal expected utility of expected return. Thus the indifference curve in Figure 3.3 is convex to the origin. In Figure 3.3 it is seen that along any indifference curve as E increases, dR/dE decreases. An investor whose indifference curves reflect this pattern is said to be "risk averse."[17]

Note also that total risk R has a limiting value Z, which is reached when A_2 equals unity, that is, when the entire portfolio is held as bonds. The portfolio can become no riskier.

[17]The mathematics of this analysis is given in one of the readings which follow Chapter 4. Tobin mapped out the behavior of "risk lovers" and "plungers" as well. The tradeoff between risk and earnings is quite different for these individuals. However, the concept of the "risk averter" will suffice in developing the conventional speculative demand for money.

Constraints We have now mapped out lines of equal expected utility, called indifference curves. The individual is indifferent between any combinations of E and R along any one curve but prefers combinations along a higher curve to those along a lower one. The problem faced by the financial investor is to maximize his expected utility by finding, among all points available to him, the combination of E and R that gives him the greatest level of expected utility. Each financial investor would like to be at the highest possible level of total expected utility. There are, however, two factors that constrain this process, the market rate of interest i and the risk coefficient s.

The market rate of interest i measures the expected percentage increase in portfolio value E that the investor can realize by increasing A_2 [that is, Equation (3.9), $E = A_2 \cdot i$]. The risk coefficient s measures the increase in risk R that is a concomitant of the increase in A_2 [that is, Equation (3.10) $R = A_2 \cdot s$] and not, as in Keynes' hypothesis, a concomitant of the level of i.

Solving Equations (3.9) and (3.10) for A_2 equating the results, and solving for E we find

$$E = \frac{i}{s} \cdot R \qquad (3.11)$$

This expression denotes what the market *allows* the investor to do. (What he would *desire* to do is shown by his indifference map.) The market allows the investor to obtain a higher (or lower) expected return E only by accepting a greater (or lesser) degree of risk R. The first derivative of Equation (3.11) with respect to R is

$$\frac{dE}{dR} = \frac{i}{s} . \qquad (3.12)$$

This shows that the successive amounts of additional E that can be obtained by accepting greater R are constant and equal to i/s.

Maximization. The investor must reconcile his or her desire as expressed by the indifference or equal expected utility curves, I_1, $I_2, \ldots , I_n$, to the objective limitations (constraints) imposed by the market. He or she must choose the desired combinations of E and R that provide maximum total expected utility subject to the known values of i and s. This may be demonstrated by plotting Equation (3.11) on the same diagram as the indifference map (Figure 3.4). As can be seen from Equation (3.11), the slope of the constraint OC is the ratio

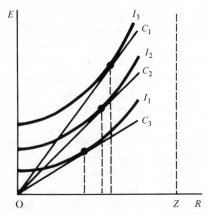

Figure 3.4.   Maximization of expected utility.

i/s. Every time the market rate i falls, the OC constraint will pivot downward (more additional risk must be assumed for a given increment to earnings).

Tangency between a constraint and an indifference curve depicts the first-order condition for a maximization of expected utility.[18] Each indifference curve (I_1, I_2, I_3) shows how the individual *desires* to exchange E for R. Each constraint (OC_1, OC_2, OC_3) shows how the market *permits* the individual to exchange E for R. A financial investor maximizes expected utility when the desired increase in expected return E relative to the desired increase in risk R along I is equal to the tradeoff between E and R permitted by the market OC. In short, the investor increases the proportion of consols in his or her portfolio by successive increments until it is no longer possible to gain more expected utility from increased expected earnings than the expected utility lost from increased risk. The individual moves along the given constraint OC until he or she reaches the highest possible level of total expected utility. This is the point where the constraint is tangent to the indifference curve.[19]

---

[18]Second-order conditions are satisfied by the convexity of the indifference curve.

[19]This may be expressed mathematically. Let the expected utility function in general notation be

$$U = U(E,R).$$

To specify movement along an indifference curve, take the total differential of this function and set it equal to zero:

$$dU = (\partial U/\partial E)dE + (\partial U/\partial R)dR = 0.$$

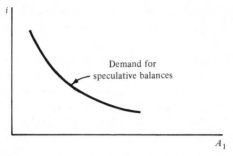

Figure 3.5. The risk averse individual's speculative demand for money.

The demand for idle money balances. As the market rate i falls and the risk coefficient of the investor s remains constant, the OC constraint pivots downward, and risk R may either rise or fall, depending on how the financial investor desires to exchange E for R. If, as shown in Figure 3.4, the preferences of the investor are such that the equilibrium value of R falls, from Equation (3.10) it can be seen that the equilibrium value of the fraction of the investor's wealth held as consols A_2 also falls, and hence (as $1 = A_1 + A_2$), the fraction of the investor's wealth held in the form of money balances A_1 rises. Therefore, if less risk R is acceptable at a lower market rate i, the quantity of money demanded as a proportion of total speculative wealth varies inversely with the rate of interest as shown in Figure 3.5.

Does R fall as i falls? In this analysis, as with the usual indifference analysis, there are an income and substitution effects associated with a shift in the constraint.

The "tradeoff" or marginal rate of substitution is derived by rearranging this expression to get

$$\frac{dE}{dR} = - \frac{\partial U/\partial R}{\partial U/\partial E} \ .$$

Set this equal to the constraint imposed by the market [Equation (3.12)] and the first-order condition for a maximum is satisfied,

$$\frac{i}{s} = - \frac{\partial U/\partial R}{\partial U/\partial E} \ .$$

The second-order condition is satisfied by the convexity of the indifference curve. If the expected utility function were more fully specified, the demand for money could be directly derived. More detail on investor indifference curves is provided in the reading on portfolio theory which follows Chapter 4.

First consider the substitution effect. Given an increase in i (a fall in bond prices), risk R becomes less expensive to acquire and the investor can increase his expected earnings E by reducing A_1, his proportionate holdings of money. An increase in the rate of interest is an incentive to take more risk; in terms of the substitution effect, it reflects a substitution of earnings for safety. Conversely given a fall in i, risk R becomes more expensive and the investor can reduce R (and E) by increasing A_1. This reflects a substitution of safety for earnings—a substitution of less risk A_1 for more risk A_2 as the relative "price" of risk rises.

Now consider the income effect. As the price of any commodity falls, the individual may buy more of all commodities (that is, he or she will experience an "income effect") because he is "better off." Keynesian models often assume an income elasticity of the demand for money of unity. Under this assumption a rise in the interest rate raises expected earnings and, because of the income effect, the individual desires to hold more money and more bonds but to continue to hold them in the same proportion. Thus, the income effect would not counteract the substitution effect. The latter will always ensure that as the interest rate rises, the quantity of money demanded as a proportion of speculative wealth decreases.

Now relax this usual assumption and assume the risk R is an inferior good. In this case, because an individual is "better off," he or she will buy less of an "inferior" good as his income rises. Suppose there is a rise in i (a fall in the price of risk). Clearly, by Equation (3.9) expected earnings increase. In this case, the income effect will dictate that the individual hold less risk. Equation (3.10) shows that he can only do this by reducing A_2 and increasing A_1. If risk is an "inferior" good, the income effect will require that the investor hold proportionately fewer bonds as he or she is "better off."

Conversely, if there is a decrease in i (a decrease in expected earnings), the income effect will require that an individual hold more of the inferior good. In order to acquire more risk, the proportion A_2 must increase. In a sense, as i falls, the individual is increasing his or her proportionate bond holdings A_2 and reducing his proportionate money holdings A_1 in order to maintain his income level.

If the equilibrium value of R increases as i decreases (and vice versa), the income effect (in this special case) dominates the substitution effect. If R decreases as i decreases (and vice versa), the substitution effect dominates the income effect. To obtain an inverse relation between the market rate of interest and the fraction of the financial investor's wealth held in the form of money balances under the assumption that risk is an inferior good, the substitution effect must dominate.

Summary

Keynes asserted that the quantity of speculative balances demanded would vary inversely with the market interest rate. For the individual, the lower the market rate relative to his or her expected rate, the greater his or her expected capital loss (the greater his *risk* of holding earning assets). At some level a decline in the market rate would induce the rational individual to switch from holding all of his or her speculative wealth in the form of bonds to holding it in the form of money balances.

Statistical findings impose two severely restrictive conditions on Keynes' hypothesis regarding the demand for money. A smooth, downward-sloping speculative demand function, as revealed by most statistical tests, requires the condition that individuals have different expected rates. Statistical tests that show the money demand function to be stable require the condition that these rates be relatively fixed.

James Tobin's more sophisticated liquidity preference hypothesis is a vast improvement because it disposes of Keynes' assumption of a certain, expected rate and the corresponding restrictions that it be fixed by the individual and differ between individuals.[20] Tobin shows that even if the expected capital loss is independent of the current interest rate an inverse relation between the interest rate and the demand for speculative balances will prevail as long as individuals are less willing to accept risk as the market rate declines.

QUESTIONS

1. In a world of numerous money substitutes, individuals will never hold speculative balances. True or false?

[20]The Tobin analysis is important also because it is a precursor of the portfolio balance approach to monetary theory. The portfolio balance approach introduces as many financial assets and as many interest rates as there are imperfect substitutes among these assets. Statistical tests showing which are the most relevant interest rates in the money demand relation are surveyed following Chapter 4. For a review of the portfolio balance approach see Yung Chul Park, "Some Current Issues on the Transmission Process of Monetary Policy," *Staff Papers*, International Monetary Fund (March 1972), 1–45; and Roger W. Spencer, "Channels of Monetary Influence," *Review*, Federal Reserve Bank of St. Louis (January 1970), 16–21. The Park reading follows Chapter 7.

2. Either Keynes' speculative demand is unstable or else it must be perfectly convex to the origin (L-shaped). Evaluate.
3. What shape would the speculative demand for money take if individuals felt that the risk were an inferior good and if the income effect outweighed the substitution effect?
4. Explain why the market prices of long-term bonds are more influenced by interest rate changes than are the prices of short-term bonds.
5. "If the income elasticity of the demand for money is constrained to unity, the proportion of speculative wealth held in the form of money balances will always vary inversely with the interest rate." Evaluate.
6. Explain the relation between the market rate and the coupon rate when a bond sells "above par."

BIBLIOGRAPHY

CHOW, GREGORY C., "On the Long-Run and Short-Run Demand for Money," *Journal of Political Economy*, vol. 74 (April 1966), 111–131.

DUESENBERRY, JAMES S., "The Portfolio Approach to the Demand for Money and Other Assets," *Review of Economics and Statistics*, vol. 45 (February 1963), supplement, pp. 9–24.

KEYNES, JOHN MAYNARD, *The General Theory of Employment, Interest and Money* (London: Harcourt Brace and World, 1936).

KONSTAS, PANOS, and MOHAMAD W. KHOUJA, "The Keynesian Demand-for-Money Function," *Journal of Money, Credit and Banking*, vol. 1 (November 1969), 765–775.

LAIDLER, D. A., "The Rate of Interest and the Demand for Money—Some Empirical Evidence," *Journal of Political Economy*, vol. 74 (December 1966), 543–555.

LATANÉ, HENRY A., "Income Velocity and Interest Rates: A Pragmatic Approach," *Review of Economics and Statistics*, vol. 42 (November 1953), 445–449.

LEE, T. H., "Alternative Interest Rates and the Demand for Money: The Empirical Evidence," *American Economic Review*, vol. 57 (December 1967), 1168–1181.

LEIJONHUFVUD, AXEL, *On Keynesian Economics and the Economics of Keynes* (New York: Oxford, 1968).

LINTNER, JOHN, "Security Prices, Risk and Maximal Gains from Diversification," *Journal of Finance* (December 1965).

MARKOWITZ, HARRY, *Portfolio Selection*, Cowles Foundation Monograph 16 (New York: Wiley, 1959).

MAYER, THOMAS, and MARTIN BRONFENBRENNER, "Liquidity Functions in the American Economy," *Econometrica*, vol. 28 (October 1960), 810–834.

MELTZER, ALLAN H., "The Demand for Money: The Evidence from the Time Series," *Journal of Political Economy*, vol. 71 (June 1963), 219–246, 768–783.

MOSSIN, JAN, "Equilibrium in a Capital Asset Market," *Econometrica* (October 1966), 768–783.

PARK, YUNG CHUL, "Some Current Issues on the Transmission Process of Monetary Policy," *Staff Papers*, International Monetary Fund (March 1972), 1–45.*

SHARPE, WILLIAM F., "A Simplified Model for Portfolio Analysis," *Management Science* (January 1963), 277–293.

——, "Capital Asset Prices: A Theory of Market Equilibrium under Conditions of Risk," *Journal of Finance* (September 1964), 425–442.

SPENCER, ROGER W., "Channels of Monetary Influence," *Review*, Federal Reserve Bank of St. Louis (January 1970), 16–21.*

STARLEAF, D. R., and R. REIMER, "The Keynesian Demand Function for Money: Some Statistical Tests," *Journal of Finance*, vol. 22 (March 1967), 71–76.

STEDREY, ANDREW C., "A Note on Interest Rates and the Demand for Money," *Review of Economics and Statistics*, vol. 41 (August 1959), 303–307.

STONE, BERNELL K., *Risk, Return and Equilibrium* (Cambridge: M.I.T. Press, 1970).

TOBIN, JAMES, "Liquidity Preference as Behavior Towards Risk," *Review of Economic Studies*, vol. 25 (February 1958), 65–86.

——, "Money, Capital, and Other Stores of Value," *American Economic Review, Papers and Proceedings*, vol. 51 (May 1961), 26–37.

——, "The Theory of Portfolio Selection," in *The Theory of Interest Rates*, F. H. Hahn and F. P. Brechling, eds. (New York: St. Martin's Press, 1965).

*Reprinted in Thomas M. Havrilesky and John T. Boorman, *Current Issues in Monetary Theory and Policy* (Arlington Heights, IL: AHM Publishing, 1980).

FOUR
The Quantity Theory of Money

Introduction

In Chapters 2 and 3 we examined several theories of the demand for money. Chapter 2 presented the basic analysis of the transactions demand for money, using both the traditional Keynesian approach as well as the somewhat more complex inventory-theoretic analysis of William Baumol. Two variants of the asset demand for money were described in Chapter 3: the *liquidity preference theory* of J. M. Keynes and the *risk aversion theory* of James Tobin.

In this chapter the classical view of the demand for money is surveyed. We shall present the major outlines of the theories of Irving Fisher, A. C. Pigou, Alfred Marshall, and J. M. Keynes. The analytic approach taken by these writers in the works cited is generally referred to as the *quantity theory of money*. We shall also describe the modern reformulation of the quantity theory by Milton Friedman and relate his conclusions to those implicit in the older presentations of this doctrine.

In the following chapters we shall see that the classical approach to the demand for money[1] results in a model of the aggregate economy which contrasts markedly with the more familiar Keynesian model.[2] In

[1] It must be emphasized that dissimilarity in money demand functions is not the *only* distinction between the classical and the Keynesian models.

[2] The Keynesian model referred to in this context is the familiar textbook model that derives originally from Keynes' major theoretical work, *The General Theory of*

particular, very different policy prescriptions are derived from these alternative forms.

Traditional Formulations of the Quantity Theory of Money

It may safely be said that the quantity theory was the theory of the value of money held by virtually all classical economists.[3] This theory is believed by many to have had its origin in the sixteenth century in the writings of Jean Bodin, an official of the French court and a philosopher as well. The impetus for his work was the great rise in prices which took place in France and in most of Western Europe during the latter part of the sixteenth century. Though Bodin recognized several possible causes for these price increases, he laid greatest stress on the rising "stocks of coin" to be found in the country as a result of the huge inflows of "precious" monetary metals from the newly settled colonies in America. His statement was far from a complete analysis of all the forces at work influencing the determination of the absolute price level (a task which has still not been completed by economists), but it did represent the first clear analysis of the relationship between *variations in the price level and changes in the stock of money.*

Though many writers, notably John Locke, David Hume, David Ricardo, and John Stuart Mill, contributed to the development of the quantity theory during the 18th and 19th centuries, it reached an acme of sophistication in the works of Irving Fisher, Alfred Marshall, A. C. Pigou, and J. M. Keynes in the early part of this century.

Irving Fisher's Equation of Exchange

Fisher's formulation of the quantity theory of money is summarized in his "equation of exchange." In this equation Fisher relates the circulation of the money stock to the amount of money expended in the economy during a given period of time. If p_i is the average price of a

Employment, Interest and Money (London: Harcourt Brace and World, 1936). This model is discussed in Chapter 6 and elaborated upon in Chapter 7. Keynes' earlier work, as represented in his other major works, *A Tract on Monetary Reform* (London: Harcourt Brace and World, 1923) and *A Treatise on Money* (London: Harcourt Brace and World, 1930), is more squarely in the tradition of the classical quantity theory of money.

[3]By "the value of money" we mean the exchange value or the purchasing power of a unit of the monetary stock, the quantity of real goods and services commanded by one unit of "money," however defined.

particular commodity (the ith commodity) and q_i is the total quantity of that commodity sold, $p_i \cdot q_i$ is the total money value spent on that commodity during that time period. For all n commodities in the economy, then,

$$p_1 q_1 + p_2 q_2 + \cdots + p_n q_n = \sum_{i=1}^{n} p_i q_i = P \cdot T$$

where P is an index of prices (a weighted average price of all goods exchanged in the economy) and T is an index of the quantity of goods traded. The product $P \cdot T$ will be a measure of total monetary expenditures on all goods sold in the economy. If we divide this total level of expenditures $P \cdot T$ by the average quantity of money in the economy during the period in which those expenditures took place, the quotient, $(P \cdot T)/M$, will be the average rate of turnover of money in the exchange of those goods. Fisher terms this average rate of turnover the velocity of circulation of money V. Therefore,

$$V = (P \cdot T)/M \quad \text{or} \quad M \cdot V = P \cdot T. \tag{4.1}$$

The velocity of circulation represents the number of times an average dollar in the total money stock must change hands (during the period in which the flow of goods is measured) for that money stock to finance a given level of transactions. For example, if a money stock of 400 billion dollars serves to facilitate the transfer of 1600 billion dollars in goods and services during a given period of time such as a year, the velocity of circulation of that money stock is 4:

$$V = (P \cdot T)/M = \frac{1600 \text{ billion dollars/year}}{400 \text{ billion dollars}} = 4 \text{ times per year.}$$

Though the relation embodied in the equation of exchange must always hold true if V is viewed as a residual term defined to ensure equality between the two sides of the equation $[V = (P \cdot T)/M]$, this truism is not meaningless. Rather, the equation represents an algebraic statement of the proximate influences on the value of money " . . . through which all others (influences) whatsoever must operate."[4] (parentheses added) In addition, where V is not defined residually but is instead a variable determined by forces at work in the economy, the equation of exchange may be viewed as an equilibrium condition,

[4]Irving Fisher, *The Purchasing Power of Money* (New York: Macmillan, 1911), p. 150.

summarizing the primary factors which influence the determination of the absolute price level P, that is, $P = (M \cdot V)/T$.

Within the framework provided by this equation, Fisher examined the quantity theory of money. His analysis of the factors specified within the equation led him to conclude that since an increase in the quantity of money M would generally not be expected, of itself, to change either the velocity of circulation V or the volume of transactions in the economy T, we could expect that the price level P would vary directly with the quantity of money in circulation. As he stated it, ". . . the normal effect of an increase in the quantity of money is an exactly proportional increase in the general level of prices."[5] This result, to Fisher, was the basis of the quantity theory:

> . . . we find then that, under the conditions assumed, the price level varies (1) directly as the quantity of money in circulation (M), (2) directly as the velocity of its circulation (V), (3) inversely as the volume of trade done by it. . . . The first of these three relations is worth emphasis. It constitutes the "quantity theory of money."[6]

It is clear from his own writings that Fisher did not mean to imply that V and T would never change. He viewed V, the velocity of circulation, as an institutionally determined factor influenced primarily by such things as the public's payment habits, the extent of the use of credit, the speed of transportation and communication as it influences the time required to make a payment, and other technical factors that ". . . bear no discoverable relation to the quantity of money in circulation."[7] Likewise, the volume of trade T was determined by factors other than the quantity of money, factors such as the supply of natural resources and the technical conditions of production and distribution.[8] Thus as any of these secondary influences changed, V and T could indeed change, and this could affect the general level of prices. For

---

[5]Irving Fisher, *op. cit.*, p. 157.

[6]Irving Fisher, *op. cit.*, p. 29.

[7]Irving Fisher, *op. cit.*, p. 152. See also the discussion in the second section of Chapter 2.

[8]More specifically, the level of real income was assumed to be determined outside the system of equations represented by the equation of exchange. The body of economic theory summarized in Walrasian equations of general equilibrium is held to explain the determination of the level of output. See Milton Friedman, "A Theoretical Framework for Monetary Analysis," *Journal of Political Economy*, vol. 78 (March/April 1970), 193–238. The determination of the level of real income in a neoclassical model is featured in Chapter 7.

example, if T, the volume of trade generated in the economy, were to change significantly while the money stock M and the velocity of circulation V remained relatively constant, the price level P would have to adjust to ensure the equality embodied in the equation of exchange.

History provides us with many examples of this phenomenon. For instance, during the latter part of the 19th century in this country the secular expansion of trade T outpaced the growth of the money stock M. With T increasing faster than M and with a relatively stable V, there was a continual decline in the average price level, arrested only by the discovery of new gold deposits and the rapid expansion in the use of the checking account toward the end of the century.

But Fisher was mainly interested in the results of a particular change in the stock of money at a particular time. His conclusion on this point was that such a change would cause a proportionate change in the equilibrium price level P, *not* because V and T never change, but rather because there is no reason to believe that the equilibrium values of those variables would change *in response to* the given change in M. Thus the directly predictable result of a doubling, say, of the money stock, would be unchanged values of V and T and doubled P.

Although the equation of exchange, by itself, is a somewhat mechanical formulation of the factors involved in the determination of the absolute price level, in the hands of a theorist as skilled as Irving Fisher, who emphasized the myriad of secondary factors influencing the level of the variables explicitly displayed in this equation, it was a useful analytical tool. In the hands of the less skillful and more dogmatic analyst, who did not appreciate the subtleties of the complete Fisherian model, however, V and sometimes even T degenerated into constants and the equation of exchange became a rigid tool which purported a *necessary* proportionality between M and P.

Fisher's view of the role of the equation of exchange as an analytical device was stated clearly in *The Purchasing Power of Money*.

One of the objectors to the quantity theory attempts to dispose of the equation of exchange . . . by calling it a mere truism. While the equation of exchange is, if we choose, a mere "truism," based on the equivalence, in all purchases, of the money or check expended, on the one hand, and what they buy, on the other, . . . this equation is a means of demonstrating the fact that normally the P's (price levels) vary directly as M, that is, demonstrating the quantity theory. "Truisms" should never be neglected. The greatest generalizations of physical science, such as that forces are proportional to mass and acceleration, are truisms, but, when duly supplemented by specific data, these truisms are the most fruitful sources of useful mechanical knowledge.[9]

The flexibility of Fisher's use of the equation of exchange is evidenced by two of his most important contributions to the development of the quantity theory: his discussion of the events that occur during a "transition period" which follows a monetary change[10] and his detailed statistical investigations of the determinants and behavior of the velocity of circulation. On the former point he notes

> . . . that a sudden change in the quantity of money and deposits will temporarily affect their velocities of circulation and the volume of trade. . . . Therefore, the "quantity theory" will not hold true strictly and absolutely during transition periods.[11]

Thus the quantity theory conclusions refer only to the effects on the equilibrium values of the variables in the model that occur in response to a monetary change.[12] Fisher's emphasis on this point was lost on many analysts. On the latter point, the data presented in *The Purchasing Power of Money* show clearly, however, that Fisher himself was under no illusion about the variability of the velocity of circulation.

The emphasis in Fisher's model of the quantity theory of money is on the *supply of money* and on the institutional and technical factors that influence the level of production and the value of the velocity of circulation. He had little to say about the psychological factors that influence the "individual habits" that determine an individual's (and society's) velocity of money. He viewed money as a commodity that yields *no utility* to the holder and is held simply to facilitate exchange. He notes that

[9]Irving Fisher, *op. cit.*, p. 157.

[10]The "transition period" analysis that Fisher presents is basically a discussion of the dynamics of moving from one monetary equilibrium to another. He recognized, for example, that although a doubling of the money supply may be expected to double the price level, this result will not occur immediately or automatically. The economy will go through a transition period during which the price level increases to its new value. During that period other variables in the economy (such as the rate of interest and the level of real income) may very well be affected.

[11]Irving Fisher, *op. cit.*, p. 161.

[12]This point is discussed in greater detail in Chapter 7.

The quantity theory of money rests, ultimately, upon the fundamental peculiarity which money alone of all goods possesses,—the fact that it has *no power to satisfy* human wants except a power *to purchase* things which do have such power.[13]

A. C. Pigou and the Cambridge Equation

An alternative conception of the functions performed by money was advanced by Alfred Marshall, A. C. Pigou, and other economists associated with Cambridge University in England. In this view, which is now generally accepted by most economists, *money is capable of yielding utility or satisfaction in and of itself,* since it satisfies two particular needs for the person who possesses it. The first is the provision of convenience and the second, the provision of security. As Pigou notes:

... everybody is anxious to hold enough of his resources in the form of titles to legal tender (money) both to enable him to effect the ordinary transactions of life without trouble, and to secure him against unexpected demands, due to a sudden need, or to a rise in the price of something he cannot easily dispense with.[14]

The major motivation for holding money in the Cambridge version of the quantity theory remains the use it provides to the holder in facilitating transactions. If all receipts and expenditures could be perfectly synchronized as they could be in a perfectly static, timeless model, there would be no need for anyone to hold positive money balances. Even when a disparity does exist between receipts (income flows) and expenditures, in the absence of transactions costs—costs such as brokers' fees and transfer taxes incurred in switching from money to interest-yielding assets—there may still be no net demand for money balances. The absence of transactions costs would allow a person to channel his money income into interest bearing assets immediately upon receipt, and convert those assets into money only at the exact moment the money was required in exchange. In this instance, average money balances held by individuals would be zero.

[13]Irving Fisher, *op. cit.,* p. 32.
[14]A. C. Pigou, "The Value of Money," *The Quarterly Journal of Economics,* vol. 32 (November 1917), 41.

However, when finite transactions costs are introduced into the analysis, it becomes evident that although one could earn interest by purchasing income producing assets and divesting oneself of money balances, the cost involved in purchasing and selling these assets may well exceed the short-term return from the investment. In such a case, money balances actually yield a higher rate of return net of transactions costs then the interest yielding security. Consequently, the randomness of the timing of receipts and expenditures and the possibility of unforeseen contingencies, together with the finite transactions and information costs incurred in switching between money and earning assets, lead individuals to hold money rather than to convert all cash balances into income earning assets upon receipt of those balances.[15]

In the Cambridge formulation, the quantity of money demanded for these purposes was postulated to vary proportionately with the volume of final transactions or the level of money income, that is,

$$M_d = k \cdot Y = k \cdot P \cdot O \tag{4.2}$$

where M_d = the quantity of money demanded
  Y = the level of money income, $= P \cdot O$
  P = an index of the general price level for newly produced goods and services
  O = the level of real output in the economy
  K = a factor of proportionality, the Cambridge k.

Since, in equilibrium, the quantity of money demanded must equal the quantity supplied, we may equate this formula for the demand for money with the given money supply M_s, determined exogenously by the authorities. This substitution yields the famous Cambridge equation:

$$M = k \cdot Y. \tag{4.3}$$

This formulation can be reconciled with Fisher's equation of exchange quite simply. Let O be the level of output of newly produced goods and services in the economy (real GNP) rather than a measure of *total* transactions (which include exchanges involving used goods, financial assets, etc.). This latter measure was represented by T in Fisher's model. Therefore $O < T$. Also, call V' the *income velocity of*

---

[15]For a more complete discussion of the role of transactions and information costs in determining the demand for money, see Chapter 2.

circulation of money. Then we may write the equation of exchange to refer only to transactions in final, newly produced goods and services.[16]

$$M \cdot V' = P \cdot O. \tag{4.4}$$

In the Cambridge version

and $$M = k \cdot Y = k \cdot P \cdot O$$

$V = 1/k$ $$M(1/k) = P \cdot O. \tag{4.5}$$

Therefore, the reciprocal of k, the proportionality factor, is equal to V', the income velocity of circulation or the "rate of turnover" of money in the purchase of currently produced goods and services. Thus, while Fisher was concerned with the length of time an average unit of the money stock would be held, Pigou focused on the proportion of income (or expenditures) which would, on average over that length of time, be held in the form of money. Just as V, the velocity of circulation of money, may be viewed either as a residual measure defined to ensure the equality expressed in Fisher's equation of exchange, or as a measure of the velocity of circulation of money balances *desired* by the public, that is, as a volitional measure of the public's demand for money, so too, k, the ratio of money balances to income, may be viewed either as an ". . . observed ratio so calculated as to make equation (4.3) an identity, or as the 'desired' ratio so that M is the 'desired' amount of money . . ."[17] Equilibrium in the money market then requires an equality between the desired and observed magnitudes in each of these models so as to equate the supply of and the demand for real money balances.

Pigou has commented on the relation between his own analysis and that which centers on the velocity of circulation of money. As he notes,

> . . . there is no conflict between my formula and that embodied in the quantity theory. But it does not follow that there is nothing to choose between them . . . . The claim that I make on behalf of mine is that it is a somewhat more effective engine of analysis. It focusses attention on the proportion of their resources that people choose to hold in the form of

[16]We assume that the prices of all goods in the economy change in the same proportion as the price index. In this way, we need not distinguish between the price index of all goods (in Fisher's equation of exchange) and the index of currently produced goods (in the Cambridge equation). For a reconciliation of these two approaches see Chapter 2.

[17]Milton Friedman, "A Theoretical Framework . . . ," *op. cit.*, 200.

legal tender instead of focussing it on "velocity of circulation." This fact gives it, as I think, a real advantage, because it brings us at once into relation with volition—an ultimate cause of demand—instead of with something that seems at first sight accidental and arbitrary.[18]

Thus the Cambridge contribution involves much more than the renaming of variables. First of all, whereas the emphasis in the Fisherian version is on changes in the *supply of money* and on a (primarily) institutionally determined "rate of turnover" of that money stock, attention in the Cambridge version is placed equally on *money supply* and *money demand*. Second, the volitional element on the demand side of the market is more obvious in the Cambridge equation and leads one to consider the specific motivations involved in an individual's demand for money balances. Given the institutional framework outlined by Fisher, the size of k depends on the strength of the public's motivations for holding money.

This orientation led the Cambridge economists to formulate a fresh line of monetary inquiry from which emanate many of the modern developments in monetary economics. By emphasizing the individual's demand for money and the utility which money balances may yield, Cambridge economists were led to examine choices facing the individual. For example, with Pigou the individual determined the size of his desired money balances by equating the marginal returns from holding those money balances with the marginal returns from the alternative use of his resources, capital investment.

The more recent manifestation of this tradition views money as simply one among many assets, both physical and financial, that an individual may hold. As a result, the determination of desired money balances involves equating the marginal returns from all these assets in the individual's portfolio. We shall return to this development later in this chapter.

Let us consider more thoroughly the determinants of k, the proportion of money income people desire to hold in the form of money balances. The historical and institutional factors that influenced Fisher's V may be viewed as characteristics of the same socio-economic framework within which the Cambridge economists studied the behavioral determinants of k.[19] These relatively objective institutional

---

[18] A. C. Pigou, *op. cit.*, 54.

[19] In Chapter 2, there is considerable discussion of the effect of these factors on the order of magnitude of k.

factors include (1) the length of the period between wage and salary payments, (2) the degree of sophistication of the population in the use of credit, and (3) the degree of vertical integration of business firms. The more subjective behavioral determinants of the size of k which were emphasized by the Cambridge economists include (1) the public's degree of preference for present consumption over future consumption, (2) their expectations concerning the future return from investment in "industrial activity," and (3) their expectations about price movements. On the last point, for example, Pigou notes that ". . . any expectation that general prices are going to fall increases people's desire to hold (money); and any expectation that they are going to rise has the contrary effect."[20]

In short, the Cambridge theory recognized the same institutional factors that Fisher discussed as determinants of V, but added to them a pronounced emphasis on individual psychological factors such as preferences and expectations. In the Cambridge version, $M = k \cdot Y$, just as in the Fisherian version, $M \cdot V' = P \cdot O$; if it is assumed that a change in the stock of money has no direct effect upon any of the factors except P, the price level, both versions arrive at the familiar quantity theory conclusion that the price level will vary in direct proportion to the size of the money stock. However, the emphasis on the volatile volitional determinants of k in the Cambridge formulation left no doubt that this result would be somewhat less than certain, for a change in the public's preferences and expectations could easily nullify the simple quantity theory result.

Consequently, the less obvious forces in Fisher's model, which are introduced only in his discussion of "transition periods," are brought to the fore in the Cambridge theory and made an integral part of the analysis. Though the conclusions of the models often appeared identical and indeed were thought identical by their architects, it is far more obvious in the Cambridge version that the price level or the level of money income merely *tends* to follow the size of the money stock and that strict proportionality between these variables is highly unlikely.

[20]A. C. Pigou, *op. cit.*, 48. Fisher also placed great emphasis on the role of price expectations in the determination of velocity, particularly in his analysis of the transition period. The Cambridge formulation of the quantity theory is better suited to the explicit inclusion of this factor into the analysis, however. For an examination of the price expectations effect and its role in the determination of the level of interest rates, see Milton Friedman, "Factors Affecting the Level of Interest Rates," *Savings and Residential Financing*, 1968 Conference Proceedings, United States Savings and Loan League (May 1968). Reprinted with the readings following this chapter.

The flexible Cambridge formulation of the quantity theory, as the foundation of much modern monetary theory, has proven more viable than the Fisherian version. However, this was not its major contribution. The most important result of the work of the Cambridge economists (and one that has not yet been completely exploited) was the fact that it provided a more promising line of inquiry than the model of Irving Fisher. It led economists to consider a utility analysis of the demand for money balances and to view money as simply one asset in a multi-asset portfolio. In this way the analysis of the demand for money came to be perceived simply as the application of the general theory of demand to a specific problem. The results of this orientation were the development of Keynes' liquidity preference theory as reviewed in Chapter 3 and the reformulation of the Fisherian model by Milton Friedman.

The Neoclassical Reformulation

Very few economists today proffer either the Cambridge or the Fisherian quantity theories in their original form. In fact, the liquidity preference theory as presented in Chapter 3 and its role in the general equilibrium macroeconomic models to be presented in Chapters 5-7 represents today's most widely accepted theoretical paradigm. However, the quantity theory approach is also an important analytical tool in the work of a growing number of influential theorists, most notably Milton Friedman of the University of Chicago.[21]

Friedman's quantity theory[22] is more sophisticated than the theories of Fisher and the Cambridge economists, yet it remains in their tradition. Like the earlier quantity theorists, he maintains the hypothesis that the demand for money function is the most stable macroeconomic relation economists have discovered, and he promotes it as the most reliable basis for aggregate economic analysis and policy decisions. In contrast to those who favor the familiar Keynesian ana-

[21]Friedman's major works in this field include: "The Quantity Theory of Money—A Restatement," in *Studies in the Quantity Theory of Money*, Milton Friedman, ed. (Chicago: University of Chicago Press, 1956), 1-21; "The Demand for Money: Some Theoretical and Empirical Results," *Journal of Political Economy*, vol. 67 (August 1959), 327-351; and "Money and Business Cycles," with Anna J. Schwartz, *Review of Economics and Statistics*, vol. 45 (Supplement) (February 1963). These works and an essay entitled, "The Optimum Quantity of Money" are reprinted in Milton Friedman, *The Optimum Quantity of Money and Other Essays* (Chicago: Aldine Publishing, 1969).

[22]The classification of Friedman's work as part of the "quantity theory tradition" has been challenged by Don Patinkin. See "The Chicago Tradition, the Quantity Theory, and Friedman," *Journal of Money, Credit and Banking*, vol. 1 (February 1969), 46-70.

lytic framework, he explicitly rejects the idea that the Keynesian consumption function (more specifically, multipliers derived from models based on the Keynesian consumption function) represents a more stable and reliable function. The theoretical money demand function which Friedman postulates appears quite different from the simple equation of exchange of Irving Fisher. Nevertheless, the final empirical form of this function, which incorporates the conclusions of his statistical analysis, supports the major conclusions of the classical quantity theory.[23]

In his analysis of the demand for money Friedman does not separate the individual's money stock into analytically distinct components, such as "active" and "idle" balances, as is a common practice in some versions of the liquidity preference theory. Rather, he views money as one kind of asset in which a wealth-owning unit may hold a part of its wealth or as a capital good that yields productive services that a business enterprise can combine with the services of other productive assets or with labor to produce an output. Money, therefore, is seen as a commodity that yields utility to its holder according to the functions it performs. As Friedman notes: ". . . the most fruitful approach is to regard money as one of a sequence of assets, on a par with bonds, equities, houses, consumer durable goods, and the like."[24]

Friedman's procedure, then, is to develop a theory of the demand for money on the basis of an examination of the services that money performs for wealth-owning units and business enterprises. He is not primarily concerned with the motives that lead people to hold money. Rather, it is taken as given that money is held by households and business firms and the principles of traditional demand theory are applied to determine the factors that may influence the size of the money balances that these groups desire. As he notes, "To the ultimate wealth-owning units in the economy, money is one kind of asset, one way of holding wealth. To the productive enterprise, money is a capital good, a source of productive services that are combined with other productive services to yield the products that the enterprise sells."[25]

[23]For a more complete discussion of the differences between the pre-Keynesian quantity theory and its post-Keynesian reformulation, and the relationship of these theories to Keynesian liquidity preference, see David Fand, "Keynesian Monetary Theories, Stabilization Policy and the Recent Inflation," *Journal of Money, Credit and Banking*, vol. 1 (August 1969), 561–565.

[24]Milton Friedman, "The Demand for Money: Some Theoretical and Empirical Results," *op. cit.*, 349.

[25]Friedman, "The Quantity Theory of Money—A Restatement," *Studies on the Quantity Theory of Money, op. cit.*, 4.

Friedman's analysis of the demand for money by the ultimate wealth-owning unit is based on the theory of the demand for a consumption service. The major factors adduced by this theory as important in the determination of money demand include: the total wealth of the unit; the division of wealth between human and nonhuman forms; the relative returns on alternative wealth forms, including money; and the tastes and preferences of individuals. For the business enterprise, the theory of the demand for the services of productive resources suggests that the demand for money is determined by the cost of services yielded by money balances, that is, the cost of raising funds by borrowing or by other means, the cost of substitute productive services, and the contribution of money as a productive factor to the value of the output of the production process.

In his restatement of the quantity theory, Friedman writes the following (approximate) demand for money function:[26]

$$\frac{M_d}{P} = f\left(i_m, i_b, i_e, \frac{1}{P}\frac{dP}{dt}, W, n \right) \tag{4.6}$$

where M_d/P = the *real* quantity of money demanded
$\quad\quad i_m$ = the rate of return on money
$\quad\quad i_b$ = the rate of return on bonds
$\quad\quad i_e$ = the rate of return on equities (stocks)
$\quad\quad P$ = an index of the general price level of newly produced goods and services
$\dfrac{1}{P}\dfrac{dP}{dt}$ = the rate of change of the price index P over time
$\quad\quad W$ = wealth
$\quad\quad n$ = the ratio of nonhuman to human wealth.

The presence of the terms i_m, i_e, i_b and $(1/P)(dP/dt)$ reflects the influence of the rates of return on alternative wealth forms in the determination of the desired level of money balances. For example, i_e measures the nominal return on equities and $(1/P)(dP/dt)$ measures (in

---

[26]A velocity function can be derived from a demand-for-money function by setting nominal money demand equal to nominal money supply, inverting the functions and multiplying by income:

$$M_s = M_d = f\left(i_m, i_b, i_e, \frac{1}{P}\frac{dP}{dt}, W, n \right)$$

$$Y/M_s = Y/f\left(i_m, i_b, i_e, \frac{1}{P}\frac{dP}{dt}, W, n \right).$$

part) the change in the real value of that return as the general price level changes. The term W is a measure of wealth and reflects the constraint imposed on an asset holder by the size of his portfolio. This variable plays a role analogous to that of the income constraint in the traditional theory of the demand for consumer goods.

The final term n is a measure of the "human wealth" component in an individual's total wealth. Since wealth is simply the discounted present value of a future stream of returns (or income) to be received from a certain stock of capital, Friedman recognizes that an individual can increase this flow of income (and his wealth) by "investing" in education or by other activities which increase the value of his labor power. To account for the human factor in the total wealth stock, Friedman includes the ratio of nonhuman to human wealth in his money demand function. We may expect that the larger the "human" component of an individual's total stock of wealth, the greater will be his or her demand for money, since holding a larger stock of money balances is one means of balancing the illiquidity or nonmarketability of human wealth.

The demand for money by business firms can be explained, as Friedman suggests, by the same variables that explain the demand for money by other wealth-owning units. Consequently, the demand-for-money function—or velocity function—for the entire economy will have the same form as Equation (4.6) and will include interest rate terms, wealth measures, and price factors as explanatory variables. Friedman indicates that the influence of both the interest rate variables and price variations on the volume of money balances demanded will be negative, while the relation between wealth and money demand is positive.

Few economists could disagree with Friedman on the general lines of his formal analysis or even his abstract formulation of the money demand (velocity) function. Nonetheless, when his theory suggests that it is some measure of *wealth* rather than *current income* that is the basic constraint on the public's desired money holdings, it contrasts with the money demand theories discussed in the previous chapters and the earlier sections of this chapter.[27] Friedman notes that "the emphasis on income as a surrogate for wealth, rather than as a measure of the 'work' to be done by money, is conceptually perhaps

[27]However, Keynesian-type models of recent vintage do often incorporate a wealth constraint.

the basic difference between more recent work and the earlier versions of the quantity theory."[28]

Friedman's theory gives little indication of the relative importance of the variables included in the money demand function. Consequently, critical appraisal of Friedman's quantity theory of money must rest on empirical analysis of the public's money holding behavior; it is on this point (the interpretation of empirical evidence) that most of the disagreements surrounding Friedman's theories arise.

The most important questions which empirical analysis can help to answer concern:

1. the actual importance of the various interest rates in the money demand function,
2. the relative explanatory power of income and wealth in such a function, and
3. the stability of the function over time.[29]

Friedman himself has presented evidence relevant to these questions.[30] However, other investigators have often disagreed both with his methods and with his conclusions. Specifically, though his reformulated quantity theory explicitly recognizes several interest rates as independent variables, Friedman concludes from his empirical studies that no statistical significance can be attached to them.[31] In other words, though *economic theory* would lead one to expect that interest rates influence the public's desired money balances, Friedman claims that the *empirical evidence* he presents shows that this influence, if present at all, is of minor importance. As he states it, he was unable ". . . to find any close connection between changes in velocity (or desired money balances) from cycle to cycle and any of a number of interest rates."[32] (parentheses added)

Of much more importance, according to Friedman's interpretation of the available evidence, is the response of the volume of real money balances demanded to changes in the level of "permanent in-

[28]Milton Friedman, "A Theoretical Framework . . . ," *op. cit.*, 203.

[29]These questions are dealt with in detail in the survey of the empirical work done in this field which appears in the reading by John Boorman which follows this chapter.

[30]Milton Friedman, "The Demand for Money: Some Theoretical and Empirical Results," *op. cit.*

[31]Statistical significance means that the relationships discussed have been subjected to empirical tests and have been found "significant" or "nonsignificant" by the usual 95% interval tests applied to the coefficients in regression analysis.

[32]Milton Friedman, "The Demand for Money . . . ," *op. cit.*, 349.

come." Permanent income is a concept he developed in connection with a study of the consumption function.[33] It is a measure of a long-run income concept thought to be the most important factor relevant to consumer spending decisions.[34] Empirically, this figure is constructed as a weighted average of past values of "measured" income (net national product, for example).[35]

Friedman's empirical analysis leads him to conclude that a satisfactory explanation of money demand behavior can be achieved through the application of the following equation to aggregate data:

$$\frac{M_d}{NP} = \gamma \left(\frac{Y_p}{NP} \right)^\delta$$

where M_d and P are as defined above and N = population, Y_p = permanent income, and γ and δ are behavioral parameters.

This equation indicates that real per capita money balances demanded are an exponential function of real per capita permanent income. Thus the interest rate and the price change terms have been dropped from the empirical function as explanatory variables. As Friedman notes, "In our experiments, the rate of interest had an effect in the direction to be expected from theoretical considerations but too small to be statistically significant. We have not as yet been able to isolate by correlation techniques any effect of the rate of change of prices, though a historical analysis persuades us that such an effect is present."[36] Consequently only the permanent income variable, employed as a proxy measure for the theoretically more relevant concept of wealth, remains in the final form of the equation, and it assumes a form similar to Fisher's equation of exchange.

---

[33]Milton Friedman, *A Theory of the Consumption Function* (Princeton, NJ: Princeton University Press, 1957).

[34]The role of permanent income in the demand for money is discussed in the reading by John Boorman which follows this chapter.

[35]Friedman's use of this concept is partly the result of inadequate data on alternative wealth measures. As he notes,

In practice, estimates of total wealth are seldom available. Instead, income may serve as an index of wealth. However, it should be recognized that income as measured by statisticians may be a defective index of wealth because it is subject to erratic year-to-year fluctuations, and a longer term concept, like the concept of permanent income . . . , may be useful.

Friedman, "A Theoretical Framework . . . ," *op. cit.*, 203.

[36]Milton Friedman, "The Demand for Money . . . ," *op. cit.*, 329.

Money Demand, the Interest Rate, and Price Expectations

Although many variables are included in his theoretical money demand function, Friedman concludes that a single measure of income (a wealth proxy) is sufficient to explain most changes in the demand for money.[37] This conclusion is disputed in much of the recent empirical literature on the demand for money.[38] Most analysts find that when the empirical money demand function includes some interest rate measure, the explanatory power and predictive capability of that equation is significantly improved. However, the presence of a statistically significant interest rate term in the money demand function is not sufficient cause, by itself, to reject the quantity theorists' formulation of the demand for money or their analysis of the aggregate economy.

Quantity theorists have long recognized that the demand for money may be influenced by interest rates. Nonetheless, in static quantity theory models of the aggregate economy, although the interest rate may enter the money demand function, adjustments in the monetary sector (changes in the supply of money, for example) do not in turn influence the equilibrium level of real interest rates.[39] They merely exert *temporary effects* on interest rates during what Fisher referred to as "transition periods." As seen in Chapter 7, the equilibrium real interest rate in static, neoclassical aggregate models is determined solely by "real" factors in the economy—productivity (investment) and thrift (saving).

Despite their independence in *static* models, in *dynamic* models there is quite an important relationship between the growth rate of the money supply, changes in the average level of prices in the economy over time, and changes in the level of nominal interest rates. While the equilibrium level of real interest rates is determined by "real"

---

[37]Some of the doubts concerning the meaning of Friedman's empirical results center on his use of the permanent income measure. His critics contend that this empirical measure ". . . combines wealth, interest rates, population, and lagged income in a single variable and thus combines their separate effects." Allan H. Meltzer, "The Demand for Money: The Evidence from the Times Series," *Journal of Political Economy* (June 1963), 221.

[38]See the survey of the empirical literature on the demand for money by John Boorman which follows this chapter.

[39]See Chapter 7 for a complete discussion of the assumptions which must be incorporated into the static, neoclassical model of the aggregate economy to generate these results.

phenomena in static models, in a dynamic context there are means whereby price level changes caused by monetary disturbances may influence nominal market interest rates.

Friedman's analysis begins with a discussion of the three effects that a monetary change ultimately may have on the level of interest rates. These are (1) the liquidity effect, (2) the nominal income effect, and (3) the price expectations effect. The *liquidity effect* refers to the initial short-run influence which a change in the money stock (or the rate of change of the money stock in a dynamic framework) will have on interest rates. It is recognized, for example, that an increase in the money stock, since it disturbs the equilibrium of the public's asset portfolio, will induce individuals who find themselves holding excess cash to readjust their portfolios by purchasing securities. This action will bid up security prices and temporarily decrease interest rates. This response is similar to that described in the Keynesian literature on liquidity preference. Quantity theorists emphasize, however, that this is only a transitory "first-round" effect and that the lower interest rates which may follow an increase in the money stock do not represent the final adjustment to a new equilibrium. This change is simply a manifestation of the transition period. For, generally, as interest rates fall, there will be an increase in expenditures and nominal income.[40] This, in turn, will increase the demand for loanable funds and for transactions balances, reversing the fall in interest rates and pushing them back up to their previous level. This is referred to as *the nominal income effect*.

The *price inflation expectations effect* may actually drive interest rates beyond their previous level.[41] This reaction is suggested in the work of Irving Fisher. Fisher distinguished sharply between two components in observed (nominal) interest rates: ". . . the 'real' rate of interest, to which real saving and investment respond, and a premium based on expected changes in the price level."[42] During periods of rising prices, for example, the premium component reflects an attempt on the part of lenders to recoup through an interest return an amount equal to the loss of real purchasing power which they expect to suffer from the

[40]For a more complete explanation of this mechanism see Chapter 7. Also see William E. Gibson, "Interest Rates and Monetary Policy," *Journal of Political Economy*, vol. 78 (May/June 1970), 431–455.

[41]Milton Friedman, "Factors Affecting the Level of Interest Rates," which appears as a reading following this chapter.

[42]William P. Yohe and Denis Karnosky, "Interest Rates and Price Level Changes, 1952–1969," *Review*, Federal Reserve Bank of St. Louis (December 1969), 18.

deterioration of the real principal value of their assets. During periods of a stable price level, when no change is anticipated in future prices, there would be no premium and the real rate and the nominal rate would be the same. However, during periods of rapidly changing prices, the nominal rate could diverge sharply from the real rate even for a long period of time.

Thus, it is this *price inflation expectations premium* that is likely to push nominal market interest rates beyond their previous level. As the initial increase in the money supply temporarily lowers interest rates and induces a rise in spending and nominal income, it also may induce an increase in prices. If a new rate of money supply growth persists over time after prices have been rising for some time, individuals will eventually come to anticipate that prices will continue to rise. In these circumstances, lenders ". . . would hedge against changes in the real value of their loan principal by adding the (expected) percentage change in prices over the life of the loan to the interest charge" (parenthesis added by authors), and borrowers, ". . . expecting money income to change in proportion to prices, would readily accept the higher rate."[43]

A study by William Yohe and Denis Karnosky indicates that just such a price inflation expectations effect may be the critical element in the explanation of the rise in nominal interest rates which occurred in the late 1960s (1952–1969). In particular, they conclude that ". . . price level changes since 1952 have evidently come to have a prompt and substantial effect on price expectations and nominal interest rates. . . . Most significant is the finding that price level changes, rather than (changes in) 'real' rates, account for nearly all the variation in nominal interest rates since 1961."[44]

The Tax on Real Balances from Anticipated Inflation

The foregoing analysis suggests that any fully anticipated inflation will impose a loss on holders of real money balances because money earns no interest. A principal gainer from inflation will be issuer of money— government. Let us examine this process more carefully.

Figure 4.1 shows the aggregate demand curve for real money balances as a decreasing function of the nominal rate of interest. Be-

[43]William P. Yohe and Denis Karnosky, *op cit.*, 19.
[44]William P. Yohe and Denis Karnosky, *op. cit.*, 35–36.

cause real money balances earn no interest, the nominal rate of interest represents the number of cents an individual must give up per time period for every dollar of real money balances held. If the fully antici-pated rate of inflation is $\dot{P}_e$, individuals are anticipating that govern-ment will, in the future, be increasing the nominal supply of money at a rate that will produce an inflation rate of $\dot{P}_e$. This generates the nominal rate i_M in Figure 4.1. Assuming that output is constant, the quantity of real money balances demanded at an interest rate i_M is $(M/P)_M$. In this situation, in order to *maintain* real money balances at $(M/P)_M$ individuals must sacrifice consumption, be forced to save, in order to add to their nominal money balances at a rate $\dot{M}$ equal to the anticipated rate of inflation $\dot{P}_e$. Thus $\dot{P}_e$ is tantamount to a "tax" (rate), a tax on real money balances. In short, individuals must give up con-sumption every period to acquire additional *nominal* money balances from government at a rate equal to the anticipated rate of inflation. Only in this fashion can they keep their *real* money balances at the desired level $(M/P)_M$.

If we assume for simplicity a zero real rate of interest, then the expected growth rate of money itself determines the nominal rate of interest because it determines the anticipated rate of inflation. Under this assumption, in Figure 4.1 the inflation tax rate is OB and the tax proceeds to government from inflation is the area $O-B-A-(M/P)_M$. If government would choose not to tax by inflation, then the (optimal) quantity of real money balances demanded would be $(M/P)_c$. There would be a (welfare) gain to the private sector from a zero-inflation policy of area $(M/P)_M - A - (M/P)_c$ in Figure 4.1.[45]

This discussion indicates the scope of the work currently being done by writers in the quantity theory tradition and its immediate relevance to the inflationary environment of the 1980s.[46] The quantity theory of money in its modern reformulation is not simply a static theory of the demand for money. Rather, building on the path-breaking work of Irving Fisher, the neoclassical quantity theory represents a theory of money income based on an analysis of money

[45]It can be seen that the government revenue maximizing rate of inflation is where the rectangle under the curve is largest. Another name for the proceeds to government from its right to issue money is *seigniorage*. For further discussion, see Martin J. Bailey, "The Welfare Costs of Inflationary Finance," *Journal of Political Economy* (June 1956).

[46]In chapter 7 this view of the relationship between money, inflation, and interest rates is discussed in the context of the macroeconomic model developed in later chap-ters. That analysis provides a useful explanation of the link between inflation, interest rates, and monetary policy over the business cycle.

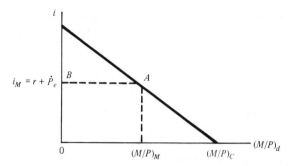

Figure 4.1.   Tax from a fully anticipated rate of inflation.

demand. It is a theory that incorporates Fisher's detailed analysis of the determinants of the velocity of circulation, the Cambridge analysis of the psychological factors influencing the public's desire for money balances, and the dynamic analysis that begins with Fisher's discussion of the "transition period."

Concluding Remarks

We have presented a review of the major theoretical formulations of the quantity theory of money as developed by Fisher, Pigou, Friedman, and others. Though seemingly diverse, each begins from the same focal point in analyzing the aggregate economy. Furthermore, they each come to similar conclusions about the role of money in the economy and the relative efficiency of monetary and fiscal policy for control of the economy. Friedman has provided the best description of what it means to be a "quantity theorist." As he states it:

> The quantity theorist accepts the empirical hypothesis that the demand for money is highly stable—more stable than functions such as the consumption function that are offered as alternative key relations. . . . The quantity theorist not only regards the demand for money function as stable; he also regards it as playing a vital role in determining variables that he regards as of great importance for the analysis of the economy as a whole, such as the level of money income or of prices. . . . The quantity theorist also holds that there are important factors affecting the supply of money that do not affect the demand for money.[47]

[47]Milton Friedman, "The Quantity Theory of Money—A Restatement," in *Studies in the Quantity Theory of Money, op. cit.*, 16.

This last point is crucial, since "a stable demand function is useful precisely in order to trace out the effects of changes in supply, which means that it is useful only if supply is affected by at least some factors other than those regarded as affecting demand."[48]

This chapter has been limited almost exclusively to an examination of the demand for money function (the equation of exchange or the velocity function, in alternative formulations) as developed in the literature on the quantity theory of money. We have not discussed at length the contributions made by the writers in this tradition to the broader aspects of macroeconomic analysis. Specifically, our brief discussion of the dynamic adjustment process incorporated in the quantity theorists' analysis of the aggregate economy is extended in Fisher's discussion of the "transition period" and in Friedman's discussion of the factors determining the level of interest rates.

In later chapters we shall incorporate the quantity theorists' contribution to the theory of the demand for money into a general equilibrium model of the aggregate economy.

QUESTIONS

1. a. What is the equation of exchange? Define each variable that appears in this equation. What does it mean to say that the equation of exchange may be viewed as an "identity"?
   b. "To say that $MV = PT$ is to espouse the quantity theory." True or false? Explain.
2. What two assumptions are necessary to make the Fisher and/or Cambridge versions strict quantity theories of money?
3. a. Why does the Cambridge formulation of the quantity theory represent more than a simple renaming of the variables of the Fisherian equation of exchange?
   b. "Unmistakably Keynes' monetary theory bore the Cambridge imprint!" Do you agree or disagree?
4. List the basic institutional factors which determine V, the velocity of circulation of money. What additional influences were stressed by the Cambridge economists in discussing the determinants of k, the proportionality factor in the money demand equation?
5. How does Milton Friedman's analysis of the factors affecting the demand for money differ from the Keynesian liquidity preference analysis?
6. Explain the rationale by which Friedman includes an interest rate term in

---

[48]Milton Friedman, "The Quantity Theory of Money—A Restatement," in *Studies in the Quantity Theory of Money, op. cit.*, 16–17.

his theoretical demand-for-money function. What is his empirical finding about this factor as a determinant of money demand?

7. By persistently attempting to maintain interest rates that are lower than their real equilibrium levels, the monetary authority will cause nominal interest rates to rise. Explain.

BIBLIOGRAPHY

ALLAIS, MAURICE, "A Restatement of the Quantity Theory of Money," *American Economic Review*, vol. 56 (December 1966), 1123–1157.

CHOW, GREGORY C., "On the Long-Run and Short-Run Demand for Money," *Journal of Political Economy*, vol. 74 (April 1966), 111–113.

FAND, DAVID, "Keynesian Monetary Theories, Stabilization Policy and the Recent Inflation," *Journal of Money, Credit and Banking*, vol. 1 (August 1969), 561–565.

————, "A Monetarist Model of the Monetary Process," *Journal of Finance*, vol. 25 (May 1970), 275–289.

FISHER, IRVING, *The Purchasing Power of Money* (New York: Augustus M. Kelley, Bookseller, 1963), reprint of new and revised edition, 1922.

FRIEDMAN, MILTON, "The Quantity Theory of Money—A Restatement," in *Studies in the Quantity Theory of Money*, Milton Friedman, ed. Chicago: University of Chicago Press, 1956, 1–21.

————, *A Theory of the Consumption Function* (Princeton, N.J.: Princeton University Press, 1957).

————, "The Supply of Money and Changes in Prices and Output," *The Relationship of Prices to Economic Stability and Growth: Compendium of Papers Submitted to the Joint Economic Committee*, 85th Congress, 2nd Session (March 31, 1958) (Washington: Government Printing Office, 1958).

————, "The Demand for Money: Some Theoretical and Empirical Results," *Journal of Political Economy*, vol. 67 (August 1959), 327–351.

————, "The Demand for Money," *American Philosophical Society Proceedings*, vol. 105 (June 1961), 259–264.

————, "Postwar Trends in Monetary Theory and Policy," *National Banking Review*, vol. 2 (September 1964), 1–10.

————, "Interest Rates and the Demand for Money," *Journal of Law and Economics*, vol. 9 (October 1966), 71–85.

————, "Factors Affecting the Level of Interest Rates," *Savings and Residential Financing*, 1968 Conference Proceedings, United States Savings and Loan League (May 1968).*

*Reprinted in Thomas M. Havrilesky and John T. Boorman, *Current Issues in Monetary Theory and Policy* (Arlington Heights, IL: AHM Publishing, 1980).

————, *The Optimum Quantity of Money and Other Essays* (Chicago: Aldine Publishing, 1969).

————, "A Theoretical Framework for Monetary Analysis," *Journal of Political Economy*, vol. 78 (March/April 1970), 193-238.

————, and ANNA SCHWARTZ, "Money and Business Cycles," *Review of Economics and Statistics*, vol. 45 (Supplement) (February 1963).

————, "Comment on Tobin," *Quarterly Journal of Economics*, vol. 84 (May 1970), 318-327.

GIBSON, W. E., "Interest Rates and Monetary Policy," *Journal of Political Economy*, vol. 78 (May/June 1970), 431-455.

————, "The Lag in the Effect of Monetary Policy on Income and Interest Rates," *Quarterly Journal of Economics*, vol. 84 (May 1970), 288-300.

————, "Price-Expectations Effects on Interest Rates," *Journal of Finance*, vol. 25 (March 1970), 19-34.

JOHNSON, HARRY G., "A Quantity Theorist's Monetary History of the U.S.," *Economic Journal*, vol. 75 (June 1965), 388-396.

KEYNES, JOHN MAYNARD, *The General Theory of Employment, Interest and Money* (London: Harcourt Brace and World, 1936).

————, *A Tract on Monetary Reform* (London: Harcourt Brace and World, 1923).

————, *A Treatise on Money* (London: Harcourt Brace and World, 1930).

MELTZER, ALAN H., "The Demand for Money: The Evidence from the Time Series," *Journal of Political Economy* (June 1963), 221.

————, "Irving Fisher and the Quantity Theory of Money," *Orbis* (March 1967), 32-38.

PATINKIN, DON, "The Chicago Tradition, the Quantity Theory, and Friedman," *Journal of Money, Credit and Banking*, vol. 1 (February 1969), 46-70.

PIGOU, A. C., "The Value of Money," *The Quarterly Journal of Economics*, vol. 32 (November 1917), 41.

SAMUELSON, PAUL, "What Classical and Neoclassical Monetary Theory Really Was," *Canadian Journal of Economics*, vol. 1 (February 1968).

SARGENT, THOMAS J., "Commodity Price Expectations and the Interest Rate," *Quarterly Journal of Economics*, vol. 83 (February 1969), 127-140.

TOBIN, JAMES, "Money and Income: Post Hoc Ergo Propter Hoc?" *Quarterly Journal of Economics*, vol. 84 (May 1970), 301-317.

YOHE, WILLIAM P., and DENIS S. KARNOSKY, "Interest Rates and Price Level Changes, 1952-1969," *Review*, Federal Reserve Bank of St. Louis (December 1969), 18.

Introduction to Readings / Part II

The three chapters in this section were concerned with theories of the demand for money. We have examined several models formulated to explain the behavior of the public in holding money balances. In the next part of the text we shall relate the implications of those models to the broader questions of the determination—of the level of real income, the interest rate, and the price level.

The implications of the Keynesian theory of the demand for money were presented in Chapter 3, a portfolio approach to the theory. Yet only two assets, money and bonds, were considered. In reality there is a broad spectrum of assets available that vary in terms of yield, risk, and other characteristics. The first article in this section is a general, more advanced, extension of the portfolio theory of Chapter 3 to cover a wider selection of assets. It has obvious relevance for the reader with an interest in finance, portfolio management, and the application of theory to the real world.

The implications of the quantity theory formulation of the theory of the demand for money are explored in greater detail in the next article by Milton Friedman. The work rests firmly on Irving Fisher's distinction between real and nominal rates of interest and his careful discussion of liquidity, nominal income, and price inflation expectational effects of a change in the money stock on interest rates. It is an invaluable aid to predicting the effects of variations in money supply growth on interest rates in the shorter- and longer-runs. This piece also should be of considerable interest to those who would apply monetary theory to real world forecasting.

Another important and practical extension of the effect of monetary, supply and demand, and expectational factors on interest rates is the theory of the term-to-maturity structure of interest rates as exposited by Burton Malkiel. Instead of discussing "the" interest rate as an average of all rates, the focus here is on the relationship among interest rates on securities with various terms-to-maturity. Like the other readings in this book, Malkiel's treatment provides an extension of the basic theory presented in the preceding chapters to the real world of a multiplicity of interest rates.

We conclude this section with a survey of the empirical literature on the demand for money. In this article, John Boorman surveys several formulations of the money demand functions and compares the results of alternative tests of these relations. Like the Rasche article on empirical tests of the money supply theory presented in Part I, Boorman offers some empirical underpinning for the theories discussed in the chapters of Part II.

Portfolio Theory

Thomas M. Havrilesky
John T. Boorman

... The basic premise in all portfolio theory is that the return or yield from an asset (or liability) in a portfolio cannot be known in advance with certainty. The best one can expect is that various possible outcomes from holding specific assets can be delineated and that a likelihood or probability can be associated with each of these outcomes. This, again, is simply to say that the yield cannot be predicted with certainty. Rather the yield itself is a random variable and the outcome of the investment process can be described only in terms of probability distributions.

One can gain considerable insight into empirical and theoretical work in portfolio analysis with knowledge of only a few fundamental concepts. Basically these are the statistical properties of a distribution of random outcomes: (1) the expected return of the portfolio and its components, (2) the variability of the expected return of a portfolio—an indicator of risk, and (3) the extent to which the expected returns to the component assets of a portfolio move together. A minimum knowledge of these concepts is necessary for further work in this area. Three standard statistical measures are used extensively to reflect these concepts. These are (1) the arithmetic mean or *expected value*, (2) the *variance* or the square root of the variance, the standard deviation, and (3) the *covariance* and the *coefficient of correlation* between two series. Let us begin by defining these concepts more precisely.

Reprinted, with deletions, from *Monetary Macroeconomics* (Arlington Heights, Ill.: AHM Publishing Corp., 1978), 129-145, by permission of the publisher.

When an experiment is performed in which the result, represented by a numerical quantity, will depend upon chance, the experiment may be referred to as a *random* experiment and the result a random quantity. The throwing of a six-sided die is an obvious example of such an experiment. A *random variable* may then be defined as a function which relates some numerical quantity to each possible event or outcome that could occur in a random experiment. In the case of investment in a financial asset in which the possible outcomes of the investment experiment (holding the asset for a particular period of time) are themselves numerical (percentage yields or dollar returns) the random variable may be viewed as the listing of all possible numerical outcomes of that experiment.

The random variable may by its very nature assume many different values. However, for investment purposes we often need to compare the potential results of holding different assets, each of whose yield is random. Consequently, we need some means of comparing random variables. We can do this through the associated *probability distributions*. The (probability) distribution of a random variable is simply a listing of all possible values that the random variable may assume and the associated probability of each of the outcomes which generate those values in the performance of the random experiment.[1] For example, in the die throwing experiment cited above, each of the integer values from 1 to 6 associated with the outcome of the experiment may have a probability of 1/6 associated with it.

In order to compare random variables, it is useful to be able to compare the properties of their probability distributions, most importantly, the means and variances of those distributions.

The *expected* (or *mean*) *value* of a (discrete) probability distribution is the sum of all values the random variable may assume, each weighted by its associated probability. If X is a random variable which can assume the values $x_1, x_2, \ldots, x_n$, each with an associated probability of $P(x_1), P(x_2), \ldots, P(x_n)$, then the expected value of X is

$$E(X) = \sum_{i=1}^{n} x_i \cdot P(x_i). \qquad (1)$$

[1]This definition is modified in the case of a continuous random variable which may theoretically assume any one of an infinite number of values. We assume here that the random variables describing the outcome of an investment "experiment" are discrete random variables, that is, random variables that may assume only a finite number of values.

While the expected value is a useful measure and serves, in one sense, to locate the "center" of a probability distribution, it tells us nothing about the spread of the values which the random variable may assume around that center. For example, if the age of a person picked at random from a "group" is the random variable, the expected value of the probability distribution of that random variable may be 20 years. However, the spread of the probability distribution or the variance of the values which may occur from picking a person at random will be very much different if we are picking from a "group" comprised of the entire population of the United States or from a group comprised solely of university students. The smaller the spread of a probability distribution around its central tendency or expected value, the more confident one can be that, in the performance of a random experiment characterized by that probability distribution, the result will, in some sense, be "close to" that central tendency. In the case of financial investment, for example, if the probability distribution of the holding period yield on an asset has a relatively small dispersion, one can predict with greater confidence that the actual yield will differ from the expected yield by less than some given amount than he could in the case of an asset whose random yield had a larger dispersion. For this reason, some measure of the spread or dispersion of the probability distribution of asset yields has been used extensively as a measure of risk.

The most commonly used measure of dispersion is the variance. The *variance* σ^2 of a probability distribution is measured as the sum of the squared deviation between each value the random variable may assume and the mean of that random variable weighted by the associated probability of that value; that is,

$$\sigma^2 = \sum_{i=1}^{n} (x_i - E(X))^2 \cdot P(x_i). \tag{2}$$

An additional useful measure is the square root of the variance, referred to as the standard deviation.

Probability distributions, such as those characterizing the return on investment in specific assets, may be compared by use of the expected value and the variance. However, the relation between the outcome of two random experiments may also be of interest. For example, an expected acceleration in the rate of inflation which would cause the outcome of the holding of a particular asset, such as land, to be relatively high may also lead to a relatively high yield on some other asset, such as agricultural commodities. In such a case, repeated experiments over time may indicate that *relatively* high (above expected value) values of one random variable tend to occur at the same time as *relatively* high values of some other random variable. In this case, the random variables would be said to be positively correlated or to have a positive covariance. The *covariance* between two random variables may be defined as the sum of the products of the deviation of each possible outcome of each of the random variables from their respective means, weighted by the (joint) probability of each pair of those values occurring together; that is, where x and y are random variables:

$$\text{cov}(X,\ Y) = \sum_{i=1}^{n} \sum_{j=1}^{n} [x_i - (Ex)][y_j - (Ey)] \cdot P(x_i y_j). \tag{3}$$

The *coefficient of correlation* is a related measure of similarity or dissimilarity in the behavior of two random variables,

$$\rho_{xy} = \frac{\text{cov}_{xy}}{\sigma_x \sigma_y}. \tag{4}$$

This measures the covariance between two random variables, not as an absolute value but relative to the product of the standard deviations of the individual variables.

These concepts can be illustrated graphically. Assume that there are two random variables X and Y. Their (probability) distributions are shown in Figure 1.[2] When the distribution is bell-shaped, as in Figure 1, it is often referred to as a *normal distribution*. This means, among other things, that the expected value and variance of the random variable are mathematically sufficient to completely specify the distribution. Assuming that X and Y are measured in the same units and that the same scale is depicted on the horizontal axes, in Figure 1 the expected value of X, $E(X)$, is greater than the expected value of Y, $E(Y)$. At the same time, the variance of X is considerably greater than the variance of Y. Finally, if it happens that relatively high values of X tend to be associated with relatively high (above mean) values of Y and relatively low values of X are associated with relatively low (below mean) values of Y, they are said to be positively correlated.

If one is working with *normal distributions*, then expected return and variance are the only statistical measures one need deal with.

---

[2]These random variables are pictured as having continuous distributions for simplicity's sake.

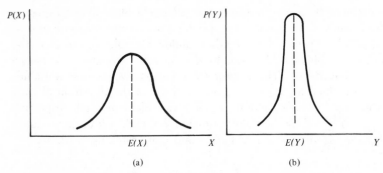

Figure 1.   Probability distributions of random variables X and Y

Unfortunately, few random variables in monetary and financial economics are going to have the smooth symmetry of the curves in Figure 1; today's sophisticated portfolio analysis does indeed consider abnormal distributions and their associated statistical measures.[3] However, the starting point of all work in portfolio theory confines the analysis to expected value as a measure of return and variance as a measure of risk.

The Expected Risk-Return Locus

One is generally concerned not solely with the return on any one particular asset, but rather with the return, and the variability of that return, on an entire portfolio consisting of more than one asset. The return on the portfolio will be denoted as the weighted sum of the returns on individual assets. The expected return on a portfolio consisting of two assets is[4]

$$E = x_i E_1 + x_2 E_2 = x_1 E_1 + (1 - x_1)E_2 \tag{5}$$

where x_1 is the (nonrandom) proportion of one's financial wealth held in the form of asset 1; x_2 is the (nonrandom) proportion of one's financial wealth held in the form of asset 2; and $x_1 + x_2 = 1$. E_1 is the expected return from asset 1 and E_2 is the expected return from asset 2. E_1 and E_2 are expressed as percentages.

---

[3]See, for example, Bernell L. Stone, *Risk, Return and Equilibrium* (Cambridge: M.I.T. Press, 1970).

[4]This result derives from the fact that the expected value of a random variable (the return on the portfolio) defined as the sum of two or more random variables (the returns on individual assets) is equal to the sum of the expected values of those random variables.

The formula for the variance of the return on the portfolio is given as follows:[5]

$$\text{var } E = x_1^2 \text{ var } E_1 + 2x_1x_2 \text{ cov}(E_1, E_2) + x_2^2 \text{ var } E_2$$
$$\sigma^2 = x_1^2\sigma_1^2 + 2x_1x_2 \rho_{12}\sigma_1\sigma_2 + x_2^2\sigma_2^2$$
$$= x_1^2\sigma_1^2 + 2x_1(1 - x_1) \rho_{12}\sigma_1\sigma_2 + (1 - x_1)^2\sigma_2^2 \tag{6}$$

where σ_1^2 is the variance of the return on asset 1 and σ_2^2 is the variance of the return on asset 2. The covariance must be included to reflect how variations in the return to asset 1 are offset or accentuated by variations in the return to asset 2 and vice versa. Equation 4 is substituted for $\text{cov}(E_1, E_2)$ in Equation 6.

Now in the case where the coefficient of correlation between the two returns is unity, $\rho_{12} = 1$, Equation 6 yields

$$\sigma^2 = x_1^2\sigma_1^2 + 2x_1(1 - x_1)\sigma_1\sigma_2 + (1 - x_1)^2\sigma_2^2$$
$$= [x_1\sigma_1 + (1 - x_1)\sigma_2]^2. \tag{7}$$

The square root of Equation 7 gives the standard deviation of the return on the portfolio:

$$\sigma = x_1\sigma_1 + \sigma_2 - x_1\sigma_2$$
$$= \sigma_2 + x_1(\sigma_1 - \sigma_2). \tag{8}$$

Solving Equation 8 for x_1,

$$x_1 = \frac{\sigma - \sigma_2}{\sigma_1 - \sigma_2}$$

and substituting the result into Equation 5 yields

$$E = \left(\frac{\sigma - \sigma_2}{\sigma_1 - \sigma_2} \right) E_1 + E_2 - \left(\frac{\sigma - \sigma_2}{\sigma_1 - \sigma_2} \right) E_2$$
$$= E_2 - \sigma_2 \left(\frac{E_1 - E_2}{\sigma_1 - \sigma_2} \right) + \left(\frac{E_1 - E_2}{\sigma_1 - \sigma_2} \right) \sigma, \tag{9}$$

a linear function in (E, σ) space with constant term

$$E_2 - \sigma_2 \left(\frac{E_1 - E_2}{\sigma_1 - \sigma_2} \right)$$

and slope $\left(\dfrac{E_1 - E_2}{\sigma_1 - \sigma_2} \right)$.

[5]If a random variable is defined as a linear combination of two other random variables, for example, $Z = aX + bY$, where X and Y are random variables and a and b are constants, the variance of that random variable is given by the following:

$$\text{var } Z = a^2 \text{ var } X + b^2 \text{ var } Y + 2ab \text{ cov } (X, Y).$$

The risk-expected return locus for this case is graphed in Figure 2. In common-sense terms, this line describes the tradeoff between risk and expected return when the expected returns on the two assets being considered always vary together in the same direction such that the correlation coefficient between them is positive and equal to unity. That is, whenever asset 1's return is below its average by a given number of standard deviations, the return on asset 2 is below its average by the same number of standard deviations; and whenever asset 1's return is above its average by a given number of standard deviations, the return on asset 2 is above its average by the same number of standard deviations.

If $\sigma_1 < \sigma_2$, it is seen from Equation 8 that minimum risk can be established where $x_1 = 1$ at point W. At this point by Equation 5 total expected return consists entirely of the expected return on asset 1, E_1, that is, if $x_1 = 1$, then $E = E_1 + E_2 - E_2 = E_1$. Total risk in Equation 8 consists entirely of the variation in the return of that asset, σ_1 (that is, if $x_1 = 1$, then $\sigma = \sigma_2 + \sigma_1 - \sigma_2 = \sigma_1$). (The extreme case of the least risky asset having a zero expected return and a zero risk is graphed in Figure 4.) As one diversifies the portfolio, that is, holds less of the less risky asset 1, the overall expected return rises because the more risky asset 2 will have a higher expected return in the market than the less risky one. At point Z the portfolio can become no riskier as it is exclusively devoted to the riskier asset 2, $x_2 = 1$.

$$E = 0 \cdot E_1 + E_2 - 0 \cdot E_1 = E_2 \text{ and } \sigma = \sigma_2 + 0 \cdot (\sigma_1 - \sigma_2) = \sigma_2.$$

The preceding analysis may be clarified by an example of two assets with highly positively correlated returns. Two such assets might be

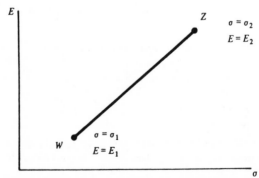

Figure 2. Risk-return locus where two assets are perfectly correlated.

long-term U.S. Treasury bonds and the long-term bonds of a typical highly rated industrial corporation. Their actual returns may move together (positively) very closely; the long-term government bond, however, has less risk, a lower variance, and, consequently, a lower expected return. If an investor confined his choice set to these two assets, a risk minimum could be realized by holding all financial wealth in long-term government bonds. A desire for higher expected return would require holding a larger proportion of riskier long-term industrial bonds.

This analysis suggests that if there existed a perfectly riskless asset that has a positive expected return (such as in FDIC-insured savings account), abstracting from the various transactions and information costs . . . an investor would never hold money, narrowly defined: The risk-return locus for that asset and another risky asset with which its return was positively correlated would be a positively sloped straight line with a positive intercept. Even if the investor were completely risk averse, he or she could always attain zero risk and still have an expected return by holding all of his or her wealth in the insured savings account.

In the case where the correlation between the two returns is negative unity, $\rho_{12} = -1$, Equation 4 can be substituted into Equation 6 to yield

$$\sigma^2 = x_1^2\sigma_1^2 - 2x_1(1 - x_1)\sigma_1\sigma_2 + (1 - x_1)^2\sigma_2^2$$
$$= [x_1\sigma_2 - (1 - x_1)\sigma_2]^2. \tag{10}$$

The square root of Equation 10 gives the standard deviation of the portfolio

$$\sigma = x_1\sigma_1 - \sigma_2 + x_1\sigma_2$$
$$= \sigma_2(-1 + x_1) + x_1\sigma_1. \tag{11}$$

In order to represent the risk-expected return locus graphically using Equations 11 and 5, let us now let x_1 vary over the range $0 < x_1 < 1$ to find the ordered triples (x_1, σ, E) where we assign the following values: $E_1 = 30\%$, $E_2 = 60\%$, $\sigma_1 = 10$, and $\sigma_2 = 15$. The results are given in Table 1. These values will satisfy Equations 11 and 5 and are graphed in Figure 3 as the (dashed) locus AZ. However, σ can never be negative and an absolute value restriction must be imposed on Equation 11, $\sigma \geq 0$. This restriction yields the (solid) discontinuous locus ABC in Figure 3.

In commonsense terms Figure 3 describes the tradeoff that is

Table 1. Relation between the Proportion Invested in Asset 1 and the Risk and Return of the Portfolio

Proportion of Portfolio Invested in Asset 1 x_1	Risk σ	Expected Return (in Percentages) E
1.0	10.0	30
.9	7.5	33
.8	5.0	36
.7	2.5	39
.6	0.0	42
.5	(−)2.5	45
.4	(−)5.0	48
.3	(−)7.5	51
.2	(−)10.0	54
.1	(−)12.5	57
0	(−)15.0	60

possible between risk and expected return when the expected returns on the two assets always vary together in opposite directions. Whenever asset 1's return is above its average, the return on asset 2 is *below* its average by the same number of standard deviations; whenever the return on asset 1 is *below* its average, the return on asset 2 is *above* its average by the same number of standard deviations.

Table 1 and Equation 11 show that if the portfolio is devoted to the less risky asset ($x_1 = 1$), portfolio risk consists entirely of the risk associated with that asset, $\sigma = -\sigma_2 + \sigma_2 + \sigma_1 = 10$. At this point (point A in Figure 3), Table 1 and Equation 5 indicate that the overall

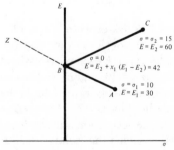

Figure 3. Risk-return locus for a two-asset portfolio with perfectly negatively correlated returns.

expected return for the portfolio consists entirely of the expected return on the less risky asset, $E = E_2 + E_1 - E_2 = 30$.

Nevertheless, even though asset 1 is the less risky asset, by decreasing the proportion of the portfolio held in asset 1, that is, by diversifying the portfolio, we can, up to a point, actually *reduce* risk and *increase* expected return. This may be seen from Table 1 and Equation 11. Upward and to the left of A, as x_1 is reduced from unity, total risk declines because the negative term $\sigma_2(-1 + x_1)$ increasingly offsets the positive term $x_1\sigma_1$.

Because the less risky asset has the lower expected return, as we hold less of it and more of the riskier asset with the higher return, total expected return increases. Equation 11 indicates that this offsetting can proceed to the point where risk can be completely eradicated. This occurs where x_1 is set equal to $\sigma_2/(\sigma_1 + \sigma_2)$, because at that point

$$\sigma = 0 = \sigma_2(-1 + x) + x_1\sigma_1 = -\sigma_2 + x_1\sigma_2 + x_1\sigma_1$$

$$= -\sigma_2\left(\frac{\sigma_1 + \sigma_2}{\sigma_1 + \sigma_2}\right) + \sigma_2\left(\frac{\sigma_2}{\sigma_1 + \sigma_2}\right) + \sigma_1\left(\frac{\sigma_2}{\sigma_1 + \sigma_1}\right)$$

$$= \frac{-\sigma_2^2 - \sigma_1\sigma_2 + \sigma_1\sigma_2 + \sigma_2^2}{\sigma_1 + \sigma_2} = 0. \tag{12}$$

Substituting $x = \sigma_2/(\sigma_1 + \sigma_2)$ into Equation (5) gives a total expected return at that point of

$$E = x_1E_1 + (1 - x_1)E_2$$

$$= \frac{\sigma_2}{\sigma_1 + \sigma_2} E_1 + \left(1 - \frac{\sigma_2}{\sigma_1 + \sigma_2}\right) E_2$$

$$= E_2 + \left(\frac{E_1 - E_2}{\sigma_1 + \sigma_2}\right) \sigma_2$$

$$= E_2 + (E_1 - E_2)\left(\frac{\sigma_2}{\sigma_1 + \sigma_2}\right) > E_1.$$

Since $E_2 > E_1$, the second term will be negative and equal to the difference between E_1 and E_2 but weighted by $\sigma_2/(\sigma_1 + \sigma_2)$ which is less than 1. Therefore, the second term reduces total return, but not as much as the difference between E_1 and E_2. As a result, the total return at point B in Figure 3 exceeds the total expected return at point A.

In summary, because of the negative correlation between returns, it is possible to reduce overall risk by holding some of the riskier asset. At the same time, because the riskier asset has a higher expected return, such *diversification* actually increases the overall expected return. Thus the rational investor would never consider a portfolio on the locus AB when he could always find a higher expected return for the same level of risk on the locus BC. Being on AB is inefficient; being on BC is efficient.

Upward from B in Figure 3, as x_1 is further decreased, the negative term in Equation 11, $\sigma_2(-1 + x_1)$, is increasingly less offset by the positive term, $x_1\sigma_1$. Algebraically σ becomes negative. However, because Equation 11 is subject to an absolute value restriction, total portfolio risk actually increases from zero upward and to the right of B. As portfolio risk increases, total portfolio return also increases. At point C in Figure 3 the entire portfolio is fully invested in asset 2, $x_2 = 1$. Here risk and expected return consist entirely of the risk and expected return associated with the riskier asset, $\sigma = -\sigma_2$ and $E = E_2$. For example, by Equation 11, $\sigma = -\sigma_2 + 0 \cdot \sigma_2 + 0 \cdot \sigma_1$ subject to $\sigma > 0$, and by Equation 5 $E = E_2 + 0 \cdot E_1 - 0 \cdot E_1$.

This analysis may also be illuminated by an example from the real world. Consider a portfolio consisting of two very highly, but not perfectly, negatively correlated assets. Such a situation may exist, for example, during certain stages of the business cycle. For instance, imagine a period in which the investor anticipates an acceleration of the rate of inflation. During such a period, if he or she were to purchase commodities to sell in the future at prices expected to prevail then, he or she would anticipate a higher return. During the same period, if he or she were to purchase long-term government bonds, he or she would expect a lower return. This occurs because if price inflation accelerates as expected, as long as the acceleration had not been fully anticipated by other participants in the government bond market, the nominal yield on government bonds must rise (bond prices must fall) as other investors come to require higher yields to match the rate of inflation. The expected drop in bond prices would produce a capital loss for the bondholder.

The opposite of this pattern would occur during periods when the investor anticipates a deceleration of inflation ahead of other investors. Holding commodities would incur a lower return. Holding long-term bonds would result in a higher return because of likely capital gains to bondholders. Thus the expected returns on these two assets move in opposite directions.

Now let us assume that the rate of price inflation is never steady; it is either accelerating or decelerating. Let us further assume that commodities over the entire business or inflation cycle have higher risk but offer a higher return than long-term bonds.

If the investor confined his or her choice set to these two assets, he or she could never realize a risk minimum by holding all of his or her wealth in the form of bonds. Because returns always move in opposite directions, he or she could reduce risk *and* increase overall return by holding some proportion of his or her wealth in commodities.

Now in the real world expected returns are neither perfectly negatively nor perfectly positively correlated. In general the risk-return locus will fall between these two extreme cases. In fact, if we solved Equation 5 for x_1 and substituted the result into Equation 6, the risk-return locus would be a hyperbola such as that shown in Figure 4.

The riskiest portfolio, and the one with the highest expected return, is found at point C'. The least risky portfolio is found at the leftmost point, B'. However, without perfect negative correlation the locus will not reach the vertical axis; there will be no completely riskless portfolio. The closer the correlation coefficient is to $+1$, the more it will resemble the locus in Figure 2; the closer the correlation coefficient is to -1, the more it will resemble the locus in Figure 3.

Finally, as in the preceding analysis, we can always find a frontier of efficient combinations of risk and expected return, $B'C'$, with no rational investor choosing to stay on the inefficient locus $A'B'$.

Investor Indifference Curves

... Our purpose now will be to present a... general formulation of investor attitudes toward risk and return. By making explicit the expected utility function, attitudes toward risk other than risk aversion

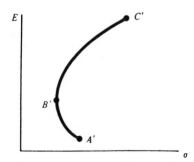

Figure 4.   Portfolio with intermediate correlation of returns.

can be shown. In addition, we can easily show that risk aversion reflects diminishing marginal utility of income.

Assume that an individual's total utility from income y is measurable. In a quadratic utility function

$$U = ay + by^2$$

where $a > 0$, marginal utility will be positive over a range of income beginning at zero, $dU/dy = a + 2by$. The range of b will indicate whether there is decreasing or increasing marginal utility of income; $d^2U/dy^2 = 2b < 0$ if $b < 0$, and $d^2U/dy^2 > 0$ if $b > 0$.

If we consider y a random variable, we should not talk about utility but must refer to *expected* utility. The assumption of a quadratic expected utility function is a convenient way of introducing a risk measure into the analysis. At the same time the assumption of a quadratic expected utility function has the advantage of limiting our approach to consideration of only two parameters, risk and expected return.[6]

In other words, where y is randomly, but not necessarily normally, distributed, the expected utility function

$$E(U) = \overline{E\,ay)} + E(by^2) \tag{13}$$

may be written

$$E(U) = aEy + b(Ey)^2 + b\sigma^2{}_y. \tag{14}$$

This follows because the expected value of a random variable times a constant is equal to the constant times the expected value of the random variable.[7] In addition, the expected value of a random variable squared is equal to the variance of that random variable plus the square of its expected value.[8]

---

[6]Earlier we mentioned that the assumption of a normally distributed random variable would *also* allow us to limit analysis to these two parameters.

[7]Assuming y is a discrete random variable,

$$E(ay) = \frac{1}{n} \sum_i ay_i = a \cdot \frac{1}{n} \sum_i y_i = a \cdot Ey.$$

[8]$$\begin{aligned}
Ey^2 &= \sigma^2{}_y + (Ey)^2 \\
&= E(y - Ey)^2 + (Ey)^2 \\
&= E[(y^2 - 2y \cdot Ey + (Ey)^2] + (Ey)^2 \\
&= Ey^2 - 2Ey \cdot Ey + (Ey)^2 + (Ey)^2 \\
&= Ey^2 - 2(Ey)^2 + 2(EY)^2 \\
&= Ey^2
\end{aligned}$$

Now in order to derive the indifference curve, we must take the total differential of Equation 14 and set it equal to zero:

$$dE(U) = \frac{\partial E(U)}{\partial(Ey)} \, d(Ey) + \frac{\partial E(U)}{\partial \sigma_y} \, d\sigma_y = 0$$

$$= (a + 2bEy)dEy + (2b\sigma_y)d\sigma_y = 0. \tag{15}$$

The marginal rate of substitution,

$$\frac{dEy}{d\sigma_y} = \frac{-2b\sigma_y}{a + 2bEy}, \tag{16}$$

is positive where the marginal expected utility of expected return is positive,

$$\frac{\partial E(U)}{\partial Ey} = a + 2bEy > 0 \tag{17}$$

and where $b < 0$. Where the marginal rate of substitution is positive, it can easily be shown that there will be an *increasing* marginal rate of substitution. The upward-sloping indifference curve will be *convex* to the origin if the marginal expected utility of expected return is decreasing (that is, if b in Equation 16 is negative).[9] These properties generate the risk averse behavior depicted in Figure 5A. An intuitive explanation of why the risk averter's indifference curve is upward sloping and convex to the origin is simply that risk is a "bad" and return is a "good" and that consecutive *equal* increments of risk can preserve a constant level of expected utility only if they are compensated for it by consecutive *larger* increments of expected earnings because of the diminishing marginal expected utility of expected returns.

The marginal rate of substitution, Equation 16, is negative where the marginal expected utility of expected return and b have the same signs. If b is positive, the marginal expected utility of expected return is positive and increasing. There will be a decreasing marginal rate of substitution and the indifference curves will be concave to the origin. This depicts "risk loving" behavior. The indifference curves for a risk lover are drawn in Figure 5B.

For the risk lover, risk is not a "bad." Therefore, in order to stay at the same level of expected utility as an increment to risk is acquired,

[9] $\dfrac{d^2Ey}{d\sigma_y{}^2} = \dfrac{d}{d\sigma_y} \left(\dfrac{-2b\sigma_y}{a + 2bEy} \right) = -2b \left[\dfrac{a + 2bEy - \sigma_y \left(2b \dfrac{dEy}{d\sigma} \right)}{(a + 2bEy)^2} \right] > 0$, if $b < 0$.

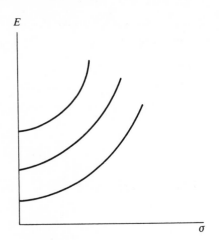

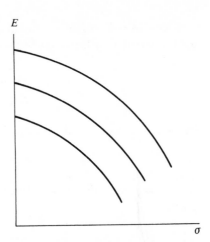

Figure 5A.   Indifference curves of a
risk averter

Figure 5B.   Indifference curves of a
risk lover

there must be a decrease in expected return. Thus the risk lover's
indifference curves are downward sloping. Moreover, consecutive
equal increments to risk, a "good," can preserve a constant level of
total expected utility only if they are compensated for by consecutive
increasing reductions in expected return, because of an increasing
marginal expected utility of expected return.

Risk Aversion, Risk Loving, and the
Efficient Risk-Return Locus

Combining the notion of an efficient risk-return locus and two classes of
behavior toward risk, we see in Figure 6 contrasting modes of behavior.
The risk averter chooses a point of tangency X between the risk-return
locus and his or her indifference map. It generally pays to diversify. An
increase in the rate of expected return on an asset will result in an
increase in the proportion of the portfolio devoted to that asset if that
asset is a normal good. . . .

The optimal position for the risk lover in Figure 6 will always be
the upper end of the risk-return locus, C. The indifference curves can
never be tangent to the efficient (upward sloping) part of the risk-
return locus. The risk lover simply devotes his or her entire portfolio to
the riskiest asset. Diversification has no advantage for the risk lover.

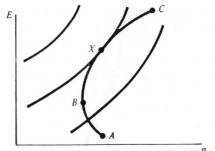

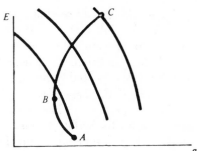

Figure 6A. Risk averter's equilibrium

Figure 6B. Risk lover's equilibrium

However, in the real world even risk lovers may diversify; they may carry an inventory of a less risky asset, in order to save on transactions and information costs. . . .

More than Two Assets

Figure 7 shows the risk-return locus for a portfolio of more than two assets. In a world of three assets, there will be an additional risk-return locus in (σ, E) space representing some fixed proportion of asset 1 and asset 2 (D on the AC locus in Figure 7) and a third asset. The locus DF in Figure 7 represents combinations of the fixed proportion of asset 1 and asset 2 with asset 3. At point D all of the portfolio is in the fixed 2-asset combination; at point F all of the portfolio is in the third asset.

In general, every point on the AC locus represents the starting

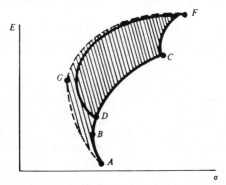

Figure 7.   Risk return locus for the three-asset portfolio

point of a three-asset portfolio. The shaded area in Figure 7 represents the domain of all such loci. The external boundary AF is the relevant risk-return locus in a three-asset world. As was the case in the 2-asset world, GF represents the efficient part of this locus. One can always obtain more expected return for any given level of risk in the 3-asset world than in the 2-asset world. The efficient GF locus is everywhere upward from the BC locus. The 3-asset portfolio presents the risk averter with the ability to move to a higher level of total expected utility. There are obvious gains here to the risk averter from further diversification as long as transaction costs are ignored.

The pure risk lover will never hold more than one asset, the riskiest one. In Figure 7 he or she, too, will be at a higher level of total expected utility at endpoint F than at C, his or her optimum in the 2-asset case. This analysis can easily be extended to more than three assets.[10]

Factors Affecting the Level of Interest Rates

Milton Friedman   Relation between qty of money (M⁴) and interest rates.

There is a problem in terminology that is worth commenting on at the outset. In all sorts of monetary discussions, there is a tendency to use the word "money" in three different senses. We speak of a person making money when we mean that he or she is earning income. We speak of a person borrowing money when we mean that he or she is engaging in a credit transaction. Similarly, we speak of the money

[10]Obviously, in the real world of many assets an enormous number of computations would be required to identify the efficient locus because of the number of covariances involved for each pair of assets. To expedite security analysis, computational programs must be devised. The professional finance literature in this area considers a number of ways to perform the necessary calculations. See, for example, Harry Markowitz, *Portfolio Selection*, Cowles Foundation Monograph 16 (New York: Wiley, 1959). By relating return to an overall index of the performance of many assets, the burden of calculation can be reduced considerably. This line of reasoning led to the development and widespread use of the *beta* coefficient which relates the fluctuations in the price of a security to the fluctuations in the Dow-Jones Industrial Average. See William F. Sharpe, "A Simplified Model for Portfolio Analysis," *Management Science*, January 1963, 277–293.

Reprinted from the *Proceedings* of the 1968 Conference on Savings and Residential Financing, sponsored by the United States Savings and Loan League (Chicago: The League, 1969), 11–27, by permission of the publisher and the author.

market in the sense of a credit market. Finally, we talk about money when we mean those green pieces of paper we carry in our pocket or the deposits to our credit at banks.

Confusion of Credit with Money

Much of the misunderstanding about the relationship between money and interest rates comes from a failure to keep those three senses of the term "money" distinct, in particular to keep "credit" distinct from "quantity of money." In discussing credit, it is natural and correct to say that the interest rate is the price of credit. General price theory tells us that the price of anything will be lowered by an increase in supply and will be raised by a reduction in supply. Therefore, it is natural to say that an increase in credit will reduce the rate of interest. That is correct. A shift to the right of the supply curve of loanable funds—that is, an increase in the supply of loanable funds at each interest rate—will, other things being the same, tend to reduce the interest rate. A decrease in supply will tend to raise it.

The tendency to confuse credit with money leads to the further belief that an increase in the quantity of money will tend to reduce interest rates and a reduction in the quantity of money will tend to increase interest rates.

Because of this confusion, there is also a tendency to regard the term "monetary ease" as unambiguous, as meaning either a more rapid increase in the quantity of money or lower interest rates and, similarly, monetary tightness as meaning either a reduction in the quantity of money or higher interest rates.

Interest Rate Price of Credit, Not Money

My main thesis is that this is wrong, that the relation between the quantity of money and the level and movement of interest is much more complicated than the relation that is suggested by the identification of money with credit. It is more complicated because the interest rate is not the price of money. The interest rate is the price of credit. The price level or the inverse of the price level is the price of money. What is to be expected from general price theory is what the quantity theory says, namely, that a rapid increase in the quantity of money means an increase in prices of goods and services, and that a decrease in the quantity of money means a decrease in the price of goods and services. Therefore, to see what effect changes in the quantity of money have on interest rates, it is necessary to look more deeply beneath the surface.

Before going into the detailed analysis, let me prepare the groundwork by discussing some facts. If you ask most economists, or most noneconomists for that matter, certainly if you ask most people at savings and loan institutions or in banks, whether an increased quantity of money will mean higher or lower interest rates, everybody will say lower interest rates; but looking at broad facts shows the reverse.

If I ask in what countries in the world are interest rates high, there will be widespread agreement that they are high in Brazil, Argentina, and Chile. If I say, "I take it that in those countries there are very low rates of increase in the quantity of money and that interest rates are high because money has been tight," you will laugh at me. Those are countries which have had very rapid increase in the quantity of money and inflation.

If I ask in what countries of the world are interest rates low, you will tell me in countries like Switzerland. On the usual view, this would imply that they have been having rapid increases in the quantity of money. Yet we all know that the situation is precisely the reverse. Switzerland is a country which has held down the quantity of money.

Let us turn to the United States. Suppose I said, "What is the period in the United States when interest rates fell most rapidly?" There is not the slightest doubt when that was. It was the period from about 1929 to the mid-1930s. Would you then say, "That must have been the period when the quantity of money was increasing." Obviously not. We all know that it is the opposite. From 1929 to 1933, the quantity of money fell by one-third and, as I shall proceed later to say, therefore interest rates fell, although in terms of the usual presumptions that economists have and which are enshrined in our elementary textbooks, one would say precisely the opposite.

Similarly, interest rates are high now in the United States in nominal terms. Nominal interest rates are far higher than they were in the mid-'30s, far higher than they were just after the war. Yet, in the past 5 or 6 years, the quantity of money has been increasing relatively rapidly.

The point of this crude and rough survey of experience is to bring home that the broadest factual evidence runs precisely contrary to what most of us teach our students and what is accepted almost without question by the Federal Reserve System, by bankers, by the savings and loan business.

So far I have mentioned one set of broad facts, namely, the relation between the level of interest rates and the rate of change in the quantity of money. When the quantity of money has been increasing very rapidly, there is a tendency to have high interest rates; when it has been decreasing very rapidly or increasing slowly, there is a tendency to have low interest rates.

Gibson Paradox: Prices, Interest Rates Move Together

Another empirical regularity, which was pointed out many years ago, exists not between money and interest rates but between prices and interest rates. The Gibson paradox is the observed empirical tendency for prices and interest rates to move together. When prices are rising, interest rates tend to be rising; when prices are falling, interest rates tend to be falling.

This was regarded as a paradox because of the orthodox view I have been questioning. Ordinarily, prices would be expected to be rising because the quantity of money is increasing. If the quantity of money is increasing, the orthodox view is that interest rates should be falling. Yet we find that when prices are rising, interest rates are rising, and when prices are falling, interest rates are falling.

That is another piece of empirical evidence which needs to be interpreted by any theory which tries to explain the relationship between the changes in the quantity of money, on the one hand, and the level or direction of movement in interest rates, on the other hand.

Let me turn from this background to a theoretical analysis of the relationship between money and interest rates. This analysis is one which has been developed over the past few years, and in that period three different empirical pieces of work have been done which I am going to summarize for you. To the best of my knowledge, none is yet published.

The first is some work that Anna Schwartz and I have done in studying the relationships between longer term movements in the quantity of money and in interest rates. The second is some work that Phillip Cagan has done at the National Bureau on shorter term movements in interest rates within the cycle. Schwartz's and my work uses as the basic unit a half-circle, so it has to do with the intercycle movement. Phil Cagan's work has to do with the intracycle movement.

The third is a doctoral dissertation just recently completed at the University of Chicago by William Gibson, who is now at the University of California in Los Angeles, which also deals with the shorter period relationships between money and interest rates.

The new work in this area is an interesting phenomenon because it reflects a very long cycle. Irving Fisher worked on this problem back in the '20s and '30s. What the three of us have done is to redo Fisher and find that he was right after all. While there has been considerable work done in these past three years, it owes a great deal to the much earlier work done by Fisher. This is particularly true of the analysis of the Gibson paradox.

Analysis of Changes in Money, Interest Rates

I should like to present to you what seems to me now to be the correct theoretical analysis of the relationship between changes in the quantity of money and interest rates. I shall argue that there are three sets of effects which have to be distinguished. The first is the liquidity effect. The second is what I shall call the income effect. The third is the price anticipations effect. I shall argue that, of these three effects, the first one works in the direction which has been generally expected, but the second and the third work in the opposite direction. If the effect of monetary change on interest rates is to be understood, all three have to be taken into account.

The liquidity effect in its simplest form is the usual textbook relationship between the quantity of money and the interest rate which says that the larger the quantity of money, the lower the interest rate will have to be to induce people to hold it. I have drawn it in that form in Figure 1, but no one who is careful writes it in that form and this is one of the slips in the analysis. What really should be measured on the horizontal axis is not M, the nominal quantity of money, but M/P, the real quantity of money.

Part of the story of tracing the effect of a change in money is going from a change in the nominal quantity of money to what happens to the real quantity of money. For the moment, however, let us waive that. We shall come back to it because it is in the second set of effects—the income effect or income-and-price effect. Let us stay here for the moment with the liquidity effect.

Consider now Figure 2, in which time is measured on the horizontal axis. Let us suppose that up to some moment of time, t_o, there has been a constant rate of increase in the quantity of money, say 3 percent per year. At a certain time it suddenly starts increasing at 5 percent a

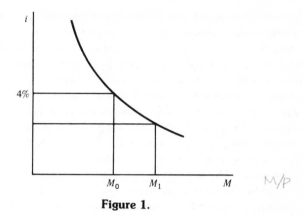

Figure 1.

year. Let us suppose that interest rates prior to t_0 have been 4 percent, as shown on Figure 2. What should we expect to be the pattern of behavior of interest rates as a result of this one-shot change in monetary growth as it works itself out through time? That is the central theoretical problem.

The first tendency of any economist, in terms of our present literature, is to stress the fact that in order to get people to hold the large quantity of money, interest rates will have to go down. As shown in Figure 1, people were willing to hold M_0 at a rate of interest of 4 percent. To get them to hold more, there will have to be a movement along the curve to lower interest rates. There is an implicit assumption in that analysis that needs to be brought to the surface. The implicit assumption is that prices are not in the first instance affected by the change in the quantity of money.

Let us suppose that prior to this time, prices were stable. Let us

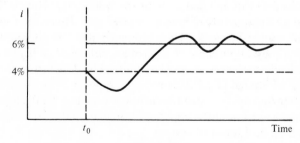

Figure 2.

suppose for a moment that 3 percent corresponds to the rate of output increase in the economy and that velocity is constant, just to keep matters simple. None of these assumptions really affects the essence of what I am saying. If, when the quantity of money started increasing at 5 percent per year instead of 3 percent, prices suddenly started increasing at 2 percent per year, you would stay exactly in the same place on the curve in Figure 1 (if the horizontal axis is interpreted as M/P), and there would be no tendency for interest rates to go down. The implicit assumption that, in the first instance, the effect is not likely to be on prices, is consistent with much empirical evidence. I should qualify this statement. The implicit assumption seems correct if this jump from 3 percent to 5 percent is an unanticipated jump. If it were announced that the jump was going to occur, it would be more plausible that it would have an immediate effect on prices.

Liquidity Effect: Price of Securities Up, Interest Rate Down

If this is an unanticipated jump in the rate of monetary increase, it is reasonable to suppose that its first impact will be that people will find the composition of their portfolios disturbed. Holders of cash will find that they have more cash than they planned to have. Their first impulse will be to attempt to readjust the portfolios by replacing cash with other securities. This will bid up the price of other securities and lower the rate of interest. This would be the liquidity effect.

This is the effect which explains why academic economists, in general, will say offhand that an increase in the quantity of money will lower interest rates. In economic terminology, we would call this an effect through stocks. The financial economist or Federal Reserve economist will argue a little differently. He or she would expect an immediate effect through flows. He or she would say, "How is the rate of increase in the quantity of money stepped up?" He or she would say that in our kind of financial system ordinarily it will be stepped up by an increased rate of purchase of securities by the central banks, which in turn will add to the reserves of commercial banks which will expand by making additional loans. This person would say that the very process of stepping up the quantity of money in our kind of financial system operates to raise the supply of loanable funds. That is entirely true of our kind of financial system.

It is interesting to note that discussions of the problem in earlier literature, for example, in John Stuart Mill's *Principles of Political Economy*, written over a century ago, very clearly stated that the first-round effect which was to be expected from a change in the quantity of money would be different as it occurred through the credit market or as it occurred through a change in gold production. It was argued that if it occurred through gold production, its first-order effect would be not on interest rates but on the wages of gold miners and the prices of commodities they bought and that it would spread from there. On the other hand, if the increase in the quantity of money occurred through the credit market, its first-round effect would be on interest rates.

These two factors—the effect on stocks and the effect through flows—would work in the same direction. However, the title "liquidity effect" under which I have included both is not an entirely descriptive term. Both factors tend to make for an initial decline in the rate of interest—the stock effect because of a movement along the liquidity curve and the flow effect because of a movement to the right in the supply of loanable funds. There is a difference. The flow effect would produce a decline in the interest rate which might be expected to happen immediately. As long as prices do not react, the effect through stocks will exert a continuing downward pressure on the interest rate. So it is not clear whether the liquidity effect would produce simply a sudden drop to a new level or a period during which interest rates fall, as I have shown it on Figure 2. That is the first effect—a liquidity effect.

Income-and-Price Level Effect

The next effect is the income-and-price level effect. As cash balances are built up, people's attempts to acquire other assets raise the prices of assets and drive down the interest rate. That will tend to produce an increase in spending. Along standard income and expenditure lines, it will tend to increase business investment. Alternatively, to look at it more broadly, the prices of sources of services will be raised relative to the prices of the service flows themselves. This leads to an increase in spending on the service flow and, therefore, to an increase in current income. In addition, it leads to an increase in spending on producing sources of services in response to the higher price which can now be obtained for them.

The existence and character of this effect does not depend on any doctrinal position about the way in which monetary forces affect the economy. Whether monetary forces are considered as affecting the economy through the interest rate and thence through investment spending or whether, as I believe, reported interest rates are only a few of a large set of rates of interest and the effect of monetary change is exerted much more broadly, in either case the effect of the more rapid rate of monetary growth will tend to be a rise in nominal income.

For the moment, let us hold prices constant and suppose that the rise in nominal income is entirely a result of rising output. What effect will that have? It will raise the demand curve for loanable funds. A business expansion is in process and the increasing level of income will raise the demand for loanable funds. This will exert a force tending to raise interest rates, or at least to counteract the downward pressure from the increasing stock of money. In addition, the rising incomes will tend to shift to the right the liquidity preference curve of Figure 1, since the higher the income, the larger the quantity of money demanded at each interest rate. (Strictly speaking, under our assumptions that the initial position was one of a 3 percent per year rate of growth in real income, the effect will be a still more rapid shift of the liquidity preference curve. Alternatively, we can interpret Figure 1 as representing a trend-corrected curve.)

Suppose the expansion in income takes the form in part of rising prices. This will not alter the tendency for the demand for loanable funds, expressed in nominal terms, to rise. But, if we measure the real quantity of money (M/P) on the horizontal axis of Figure 1, this tendency will affect that figure. Suppose prices go up as rapidly as the increased rate of monetary growth, in our assumed case, 2 percent. The real quantity of money will remain constant. If prices go up more rapidly than that, you will tend to move back along the curve. As income rises, whether or not prices rise, interest rates will turn around and go up, as a result of the rising demand for loanable funds, the shift of the liquidity preference curve, and the possible movement along it.

There are many reasons to believe that this rise in interest rates will go too far. It will overshoot. I cannot cover this point in full here, but let me suggest some reasons to expect even this short-run effect to overshoot.

In the first place, we started out by saying that prices will be slow to react and that the initial effect is the disturbance of portfolios. That means that there is some catching up to do. We can see what is involved most readily by looking at the ultimate long-run position.

If the rate of monetary growth stayed at 5 percent, the long-run equilibrium position would involve nominal income rising at 2 percent per year more than it did prior to the increase in the monetary growth rate. In Figure 3, Line C is a continuation of the original trend of rising income, let us say, at 3 percent a year. Line B shows a trend linked to the initial trend but with a rate of rise of 5 percent. If at first income proceeds along C but ultimately has to proceed along B, then for some period income will have risen more rapidly in order to catch up. That is one reason for a tendency to overshoot.

A second reason is a little more complicated. The true long-run equilibrium position of income will not be Line B but a higher line, say Line A. It will be a higher line because the amount of real balances that people want to hold will be smaller when prices are rising at 2 percent per year than when they are stable.

Price Anticipation Effect

This brings us to our third effect, the price anticipation effect. When prices are rising at 2 percent a year and people come to anticipate that they will continue to, this raises the cost of holding cash. Consequently, they will want to hold smaller balances relative to income. This is clearly the case and has been well-documented for hyperinflation and substantial inflation. Phil Cagan's study on hyperinflation, which is by now a classic, documents very clearly that in such episodes, the higher the rate of change of prices, the higher is monetary velocity or the lower are real balances.

Studies for countries like Argentina and Brazil and Chile, countries that have had very substantial inflation, show the same phenome-

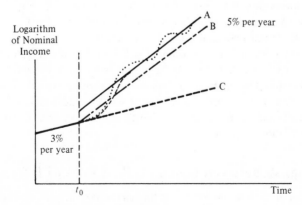

Figure 3.

non. For the United States, it has been much harder to pin down that phenomenon because our price movements have been mild.

In the study I did with Anna Schwartz, using averages for half-cycles, referred to earlier, we have been able for the first time to extract from the American data the same kind of response to the rate of change in prices as had been extracted for the more extreme inflationary episodes.

As a theoretical matter, the higher the rate of change of prices, the higher the velocity expected. This shows up as an empirical phenomenon. This is why the long period equilibrium will be a path like A in Figure 3 rather than like B. Therefore, even if there were no lag in the initial adjustment, at some time or other income or prices have to rise faster than the ultimate equilibrium rate of 2 percent per year in order to get up to this higher level. To digress for a moment, the phenomenon I have been describing is, in my opinion, the fundamental reason why a shift in the quantity of money tends to produce cyclical reaction patterns and not smooth movements. The dotted lines show two possible paths, one involving damped oscillations, the other a direct approach to equilibrium. But note that even the latter involves a cyclical reaction in the rate of change of income.

The price anticipation effect is the one that is most closely linked to Irving Fisher, that he investigated statistically, and that he introduced to explain the Gibson paradox.

If I may go back a moment, I am sliding over one point that I ought to make explicit. For simplicity, I have been talking as if the initial position we started from was one where there was reasonably full employment, so that while in the interim there can be a period with income increasing and prices stable, sooner or later the higher rate of rise in income will be translated into a higher rate of price increase. That really is not essential for my story at all.

It may be that part of the effect will be taken up in output rather than in prices. All that is essential is that there be some tendency for prices to rise somewhat more than they otherwise would, although I may say that, as an empirical matter, I would expect a shift from one fairly steady rate of monetary growth to another to be reflected fully, sooner or later, in prices.

Distinguish between Nominal, Real Rate of Interest

As long as there is some tendency for part of the increase in the rate of growth of the quantity of money to end up in a higher rate of price rise, sooner or later people will come to anticipate it. As people come to anticipate it, we introduce a distinction that I have so far kept out of the picture, namely, the distinction between the nominal rate of interest and the real rate of interest.

We are all very much aware of the distinction right now. It is also a distinction that goes back in our literature, at least to Irving Fisher who analyzed it most exhaustively. If the nominal interest rate is 4 percent per year and if prices over any period rise at the rate of 2 percent per year, then the realized real yield will be 2 percent, not 4 percent.

However, what matters for the market is not the *ex post* yield which is realized after the event but what people anticipate in advance. People today are buying bonds or other securities or making loans for the long-term future on the basis of what they anticipate will happen.

Let us designate the nominal interest rate by R_B (the B for bonds) and the real rate by R_E (E for equity). Now $1\ dP/P\ dt$ is the percentage rate at which prices are changing at time t. Let an asterisk attached to it stand for an anticipated rate, so $(1\ dP/Pdt)^*$ is the anticipated rate of change in prices. Then, the relation Fisher developed is $R_B = R_E + (1\ dP/P\ dt)^*$. In other words, the nominal rate of interest in the market will be equal to the real rate of interest plus the anticipated rate of price change. Therefore, if R_E stays the same but the anticipated rate of price change goes up, the nominal interest rate will also go up. That is the third effect.

Returning to Figure 2, we see that if the whole of this 2 percent higher rate of monetary growth goes into prices, and if the initial equilibrium interest rate was 4 percent, then the new long-run equilibrium rate will be 6 percent. The interest rate pattern then will be something like that shown in Figure 2 and will ultimately get up to 6 percent.

What Theoretical Analysis Determines

That is the whole of the theoretical analysis that leads to tracing out a path of reaction in interest rates. I have exaggerated somewhat what can be traced out from the theoretical analysis alone since the fluctuations I have put in are not well determined. What is really determined by the theoretical analysis is an initial decline, a subsequent rise, and an ultimate attainment of a level about 2 percent higher than the initial one.

Let me give this theoretical analysis some empirical content. How long are these periods? What is their duration? Of the three studies that I have described, the one that Anna and I have done traces out the time pattern at the end, while Cagan's and Gibson's studies trace out the time pattern at the beginning. So far we have a missing link in between. The empirical work all three of us have done is entirely consistent with the pattern traced out in Figure 2. Empirically, there is a tendency for a rapid rate of monetary growth to be followed by a decline in interest rates and, after a lag, by a rise and then a final ultimate movement to a level higher than the starting point. The major patterns are recorded in the empirical evidence and do come out very clearly.

I have been talking about an increase in the rate of monetary expansion. Obviously, everything is reversed for a decrease, and our empirical studies, of course, cover both increases and decreases.

It turns out that the initial decline in interest rates after an acceleration of monetary growth lasts about 6 months. Clearly, there is variation but the average period is about 6 months. The time it takes to get back to the initial level is something like 18 months.

Long Period to Final Equilibrium Level

The period it takes to get to the final equilibrium level is very long. Fisher came out with a period of something like 20 years. He did a number of different studies which gave him estimates of 20 or 30 years. Our own estimates are about the same. They make a distinction which Fisher's did not. They suggest that the period is different for short rates than it is for long rates. Fisher did his studies for long rates and did not make that distinction.

As a purely theoretical matter, one would expect that it would take longer for long rates than for short rates. When you are buying a security with a short life, you are really interested in extrapolating price movements over a shorter future period of time than when you are buying a very long-term security. It seems not unreasonable that if you are extrapolating for a short period, you will look back for a shorter period than when you are extrapolating for a longer period.

I regard it as very strong empirical confirmation of this interpretation of the evidence that it does turn out that the period it takes to get full adjustment tends to be much longer for long rates than it does for short rates.

In Figure 2, the time it takes to get to the final equilibrium level depends on how long it takes for a change in the rate of monetary change to produce general anticipation of further price rises. That implicitly means that it depends on how far back people look in forming their anticipations. The mean period of price anticipation turns out to be something like 10 years for short rates and 20 years for long rates. Since these are the average periods, they imply that people take an even longer period of past history into account. These results are wholly consistent with Fisher's.

One more interesting point—and here I am much more tentative—such evidence as I have seen suggests what is to be expected, namely, that the period it takes is much longer in a country which has experienced mild price movements than in a country which has experienced rapid price movements. In one of the South American countries where prices have moved much more rapidly, the period it takes appears to be much shorter. That is what is to be expected in a more variable world where anticipations would be formed over a briefer period of time.

Relationship between Analysis and Gibson Paradox

Let me tie this in to the Gibson paradox and show how this analysis is related to that. The explanation that Fisher offered for the Gibson paradox was the same as what I have called the third effect, but it hinges very much on how long it takes for people to form their anticipations. If price change were perfectly anticipated, if people instantaneously anticipated what was actually going to happen, high interest rates would be associated with rapid rates of price rise and low interest rates would be associated with low rates of price rise or with price declines, but there would be no reason to expect a connection between rising prices and rising interest rates.

Let me see if I can make this clear. Suppose that the historical record of prices was like that plotted in Figure 4, where the ordinate is the logarithm of the price, so that straight lines correspond to constant rates of price increase or decrease. If people fully anticipated this, the result would be that for periods a and c the interest rate would be high, for periods b and d the interest rate would be low—as shown by the dashed steps. There is no reason why rising prices should be associated with rising interest rates. Rising prices would be associated with high interest rates; falling prices with low interest rates. Yet the Gibson paradox is that rising prices are associated with rising interest rates and falling prices with falling interest rates.

In order to explain the Gibson paradox on this basis, Fisher says

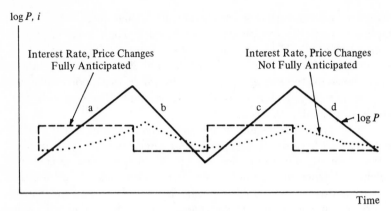

Figure 4.

that if prices start to rise, people do not really believe it. It takes a long time before they accept the idea that prices are rising. Therefore, if we plot on Figure 4 not what the actual rate of change of prices is but what the anticipated rate of change of prices is, we find that it behaves like the wavy dotted line; the anticipated rate of change of prices starts being low, and only gradually rises, and keeps on rising for a time after actual prices start declining. Only after a lag will it start to decline, and then it will decline only gradually.

So, said Fisher, let prices start to rise when those prices have been stable. As prices rise, people gradually come to anticipate the rise. Only after prices have been rising for a long time will people take full account of the actual rate of rise.

Price Swings and Anticipation Time

In order for this delayed formation of anticipations to explain Gibson's paradox empirically, it is clear that there has to be a particular relation between the length of the period that it takes for people to form their anticipations and the actual long swings in prices. If people formed their anticipations very rapidly—much more rapidly than the length of a price rise or fall—then interest rates would rise for only a short period along with prices and soon would be high but constant. When prices started declining, interest rates would be low but constant. They would look more like the steps in Figure 4 than like the wavy dotted line. In order to have a close correlation between rising prices and rising interest rates, there must be a particular relation among the periods. It must be that the period of the long swings in prices is roughly comparable to the period of time which it takes for people to form anticipations.

That is what Fisher found. Indeed, that is the way in which he estimates the period it takes to form anticipations, and it is the way we have done it as well.

Fisher's conclusions as he presented them in the 1920s tended to be disregarded by almost all economists. Very few people paid any attention to him. The explanation is simple. People said, "That's silly theory, why should it take people 20 to 30 years to form anticipations about price changes? Surely, a theory which requires such a long period must be wrong."

What Schwartz and I did was to recalculate the correlations for an additional 40 years or so beyond the period for which Fisher had data. The correlations are just as good for the additional 40 years as they were for the period before. This is a rare event in applied economics. All of us have had problems with spurious results. We try a dozen different correlations and finally get one that is satisfactory. How do we know it will hold for the future? It usually does not. But in this case, it so happens that Fisher studied this up through the '20s and we have about 40 more years of experience. Nobody since has paid any attention to this particular aspect of the data. Yet they show exactly the same thing for the period since then that they showed before, namely, a high correlation between the rate of change of prices and the rate of change of interest rates. The correlation is higher than the correlation between the level of interest rates and the rate of change of prices. That is to say, it is not the step relation in Figure 4 that dominates but the wavy one.

It is interesting to ask the question, "Why is it that it should take people so long to form anticipations?" I think another feature of the work that Schwartz and I did gives a very important clue to the answer and has importance beyond this particular problem. You will recall that I mentioned the repeated failure in former work to find a relationship between the rate of price change and velocity in the United States. In the study we made, we found it for the first time. The reason we did, I believe, is that we used as our unit of analysis the half-cycle. Ordinarily, in most such work when we introduce lags we tend to introduce constant chronological lags—1 year, 2 years, 3 years.

When we started to work on this problem, we found ourselves introducing variable lags without intending to do so because if economic series are averaged over half-cycles, some half-cycles are short, some are long. Consequently, when we related velocity today to price change in a prior cycle phase, we implicitly had a lag that was long when the cycle phases were long and short when the cycle phases were short.

Distinction between Psychological, Chronological Time

What led me to continue along this line was the work that Maurice Allais described in his "A Restatement of the Quantity Theory of Money," recently published in the *American Economic Review* and in which he made a very basic and important distinction between psychological time and chronological time.

Let me translate this idea without going into Allais' particular way of putting it—though I believe his paper is one of the most important and original that has been written for a long time, not particularly because of its treatment of the demand for money but for its consideration of the problem of the formation of expectations.

People who are trying to form anticipations have some understanding of the nature of the society. They know that the economy goes in cycles and has its ups and downs. Suppose you are trying to form an anticipation about what is going to happen to prices. You will say, "I had better average out over these cycles. I had better look back to what was happening in a corresponding phase of the last cycle." If you are examining past history with the idea that there is some kind of cyclical pattern, it is perfectly reasonable for you to go back a roughly fixed number of cycles, not years.

That is exactly what our results suggested. Better results were obtained by taking as a unit of measurement the cycle and not the year. Let us apply this idea to the present problem. Let us say that you are going to buy a 40- or 50-year bond. You want to make a prediction for a long period on the basis of the past. It is reasonable for you to form your anticipation not on the basis of short-period data of the last few years but of a period that will encompass, as it were, full economic episodes.

Because of limitations of time, I am proceeding very dogmatically and sketchily, but this establishes a theoretical reason why it is not surprising to find that the period over which the anticipation is formed bears a relationship to the observed period of long swings in prices.

Correlation between Anticipation Period, Fluctuations

You might say that Fisher's result is a pure coincidence. His result depends on the periods of formation of anticipations being roughly as long as the periods of sustained price movements. Why should they be? If people are intelligently forming anticipations about the future on the basis of an analysis of the past, it is not a foolish thing for them to behave that way. That is why I believe that you will find that this period of anticipation is shorter in those countries which have sharper and more rapid fluctuations than in those which have slower and longer fluctuations.

I was very much struck with this point the other day when I was in New York acting as a representative of many of you at a College Retirement Equity Fund lunch. Some financial people started talking about the difference between the behavior of young people today and of their own behavior with respect to borrowing on credit. These people's behavior today was being very much influenced by what had happened in the 1930's. This was over a 30-year lag in their behavior.

Now of course the actual lag for the society is an average over all age classes and this is the longest lag, but once you start to look at it in that way, it does not seem to me too surprising that the lag should be so long.

Let me give you another empirical illustration. There is little doubt in my mind that the widespread expectation that prevailed in the United States after World War II that there would be a price fall involved using data going back roughly 150 years.

You ask yourself, "How shall I form an anticipation about what happens after a major war?" There is no use looking at what happened during peace time. It is better to look at what happened after earlier major wars. People who were forming these anticipations after World War II looked back at what happened after World War I, what happened after the Civil War, what happened after the War of 1812, and they found that in each of these cases, within about 10 or 15 years after the end of the war, prices were half what they had been at the end of the war. So it was not at all absurd for people to form their anticipations on the basis of a period stretching back over 100 years.

Recent Experience Illustrates Analysis

Let me conclude simply by applying this analysis to recent experience because it applies beautifully. When I say this analysis, I really am talking mostly about the short-period analysis, not Fisher's long period analysis. Consider what happened in 1966 and 1967 because it was almost a perfect representation of the relationship I have shown in Figure 2.

There was a rapid rate of growth in money until April 1966. (The exact rate depends on whether you use a narrow or a broad definition of money but nothing I say will be affected by that because the patterns of behavior of the different rates are the same although the quantitative rates of change are different.) From April 1966 to about December 1966 there was a brief but sharp decline in the rate of monetary change.

From December 1966 or January 1967 through most of 1967, to something like October or November of 1967, there was an even more rapid rate of increase than before April 1966. Since about November 1967 there has been a tapering off in the rate of growth.

Delayed Impact of Earlier Monetary Growth

What happened to interest rates during that period? Prior to April 1966 interest rates were rising. Why were they rising? This was the delayed impact of the earlier high rate of monetary growth.

Suddenly there was a tightening of money—a sharp decrease in the rate of growth of the quantity of money. What does our theory say? Turn Figure 2 upside down. It says a rapid increase in interest rates would be expected because the delayed effect of earlier monetary ease is reinforced by the impact effect of monetary tightness. That, of course, is what happened. There was a very sharp rise in interest rates culminating in the so-called credit crunch.

The interesting thing is when did that culminate? In September or October 1966, several months before the reversal in monetary growth. That is exactly what our analysis would lead you to expect—a turnaround about 6 months after the shift in monetary growth.

At this point the tight money was having a depressing effect on interest rates. The liquidity effect had shot its bolt; the income effect was beginning to take over. That income effect resulted in a slowdown in the economy in the first half of 1967 which reduced the demand for loanable funds and so interest rates fell.

Then what happened? After monetary growth accelerated in January 1967, the short-term effects of easy money reinforced the delayed effect of the tighter money and so interest rates continued to fall.

But this time the short-term effect was abnormally short—less than 6 months. Interest rates turned around some time in March or April that year and started to go up. These delayed effects of easy money were then reinforced in November 1967 by the tapering off of monetary growth.

Many Factors Affect Interest Rates

Obviously, I am not trying to say for a moment that monetary change is the only thing that affects interest rates. Do not misunderstand me. I am trying to isolate that part of the interest rate movement which is determined by monetary change. Many, many other things affect interest rates.

In particular, I have no reason to doubt that the sharp increase in the federal government's deficit, which meant an increase in the demand for borrowing by the federal government, was a factor which was raising interest rates through most of 1967. It may be that is why there was an abnormally short delay before the initial impact of easy money was reversed.

I should have made this qualification about other factors earlier. Our squared correlations are perhaps on the order of about .5 which means they account for half of the fluctuations in nominal interest rates. I do not for a moment want to suggest that if you understand the effect of monetary change on interest rates, you therefore have a theory of interest rates. In the first place, there are other forces which will change real interest rates. In the second place, there are undoubtedly other forces changing nominal interest rates, but it so happens that the major movements of nominal interest rates in 1966 and 1967 seem to have been dominated by the monetary effects so they serve to bring out very clearly the relations I have described.

One more word about the longer term relations. If this analysis is right, our present interest rates of 6 percent or 6.5 percent are still on the way up because they are still reflecting the building up of anticipations of price increases. Our present interest rates are extremely low—if you subtract the rate of price change, you have very low real interest rates. Therefore, if this analysis is right, the long-term trend of interest rates ought still to be up.

The Term Structure of Interest Rates: Theory, Empirical Evidence, and Applications

Burton G. Malkiel

Market rates of interest for the various types of debt securities differ for a variety of reasons. Perhaps the major cause of differences is the credit risk of the instruments, that is, the risk of default of the promised interest and principal payments. In addition, significant differences result from differences in the provisions of various sorts of bonds: whether they are tax-exempt, whether they can be converted into common stocks, whether they can be redeemed at the option of the company, and so forth. Indeed, the major reasons for differences in bond yields may be unrelated to the maturity of the securities involved. Nevertheless, one of the most intriguing differences among market interest rates concerns the relationship among the yields of high-grade securities that differ *only* in their term to maturity, that is, in the length of time until the principal amount of the loan becomes due and payable. This relationship is called the "term structure of interest rates," or, more popularly, "the shape of the yield curve."

In this essay, we shall first explain the algebra of bond yields and the method of construction of the yield curve, and then review the patterns that have occurred in the past. Next will be a discussion of three alternative explanations of the shape of the yield curve and of the empirical evidence that has been marshaled in their support. Then the implications of the analysis for monetary policy will be presented. Finally, we shall consider how investors interested in improving bond-portfolio performance and corporate issuers interested in minimizing borrowing costs may benefit from an understanding of the determinants of the shape of the yield curve and a study of its historical patterns.

The Algebra of Bond Yields and Bond Prices

The market value of a bond is determined by four factors: (1) the face value of the bond, i.e., the principal amount to be paid at maturity,

Reprinted from Malkiel, Burton G., *The Term Structure of Interest Rates: Theory, Empirical Evidence, and Applications* (1970). Reprinted by permission of Silver Burdett Company.

which we denote by F; (2) the coupon or interest paid periodically to the bondholder, denoted by C; (3) the effective interest rate per period, R, which is referred to as the bond's yield to maturity or, more simply, the yield of the security; and (4) N, the number of years to maturity. The market price, P, is simply the sum of the present values of all the coupons to be received as interest and the principal amount to be paid at maturity.[1]

$$P = \frac{C}{(1 + R)} + \frac{C}{(1 + R)^2} + \cdots + \frac{C}{(1 + R)^N} + \frac{F}{(1 + R)^N} . \tag{1}$$

Given the values of the promised coupon interest payments, face value, and length of time to maturity we may solve Equation (1) for R, the annual yield of the bond.[2]

An Illustration of the Bond-Pricing Equation

To illustrate the use of the bond-pricing equation, suppose a bond has a market price of $104, an annual coupon of $9, a term to maturity of five years, and a face value of $100. In fact, most bond prices are stated in terms of $100 of face or par value.[3] We may then calculate the annual yield to maturity from the bond-pricing formula:

$$104 = \frac{9}{1 + R} + \frac{9}{(1 + R)^2} + \frac{9}{(1 + R)^3} + \frac{9}{(1 + R)^4} + \frac{9}{(1 + R)^5} + \frac{100}{(1 + R)^5} . \tag{1a}$$

[1]The present value of an amount S_1 to be paid one year from now, is defined as a present amount P, which when invested now at a given interest rate, R, will accumulate to the amount S_1 next year. Since a present amount invested at rate R will accumulate to an amount $S_1 = P(1 + R)$ next year, the present value, P, of that future amount S_1, is given by the expression $P = S_1/(1 + R)$. If the present amount P is left to accumulate at interest for two years, the relevant future amount $S_2 = P(1 + R)(1 + R) = P(1 + R)^2$. Hence the present value of S_2 is simply $S_2/(1 + R)^2$. In general, the present value of a future amount to be paid N years from now is $S_N/(1 + R)^N$.

[2]R is also referred to as the bond's internal rate of return. C, the periodic interest to be paid, is referred to as the bond's coupon because, in fact, coupons are usually attached to each bond indicating the amount of interest due at each payment date. These coupons may be "clipped" from the bond and surrendered for cash on the appropriate payment dates. In this study we shall use the words "interest rate" and "bond yield" interchangeably.

[3]Nevertheless, it is not possible to buy a $100 government or corporate bond. A single bond has traditionally consisted of $1,000 of face, or par, value. When we speak of buying ten bonds, we mean a purchase of bonds with a face value of $10,000. The coupon on a bond is of course adjusted for the particular face value. Thus, in our example above of a $9 coupon (per $100 of face value), the actual coupon on a $1,000 bond would be $90, or $45 semiannually.

Equation 1a may be solved for R, which turns out to be 8 percent.

We have assumed that coupon interest payments are made once a year. In fact, interest payments are typically made semiannually, with half the annual coupon paid each 6 months. This requires only a small change in the pricing formula:

$$P = \frac{C/2}{(1 + R/2)} + \frac{C/2}{(1 + R/2)^2} + \frac{C/2}{(1 + R/2)^3} + \cdots + \frac{C/2}{(1 + R/2)^{2N}} + \frac{F}{(1 + R/2)^{2N}} \cdot$$
(2)

For example, suppose a bond has an annual coupon of $6, a term of maturity of twenty years, and sells at a market price of 85½. The yield to maturity (expressed as an annual rate) may be calculated as follows:

$$85.50 = \frac{3}{(1 + R/2)} + \frac{3}{(1 + R/2)^2} + \cdots + \frac{3}{(1 + R/2)^{40}} + \frac{100}{(1 + R/2)^{40}} \cdot$$
(2a)

The yield to maturity, R, is 7.40 percent. The present value of the stream of $3 coupons to be recieved each 6 months and of the $100 face value to be paid at maturity is $85.50 when discounted at a 7.40 percent rate.[4]

The Use of Bond Tables

Fortunately, there are handy books of tables, called "bond tables," that make laborious calculations unnecessary. Bond tables are available to cover most of the coupons and maturities that arise in practice. The tables show, for a given market price, coupon rate, and maturity, the appropriate yield to maturity. A sample page from a book of bond

---

[4]A simplified rule of thumb for the calculation of bond yields may aid in the interpretation of the concept. The yield to maturity is approximately equal to the average annual interest payment and capital-gain return expressed as a percentage of the investor's average investment. Looking at the return side first, we see that the purchaser of a twenty-year $100 bond at $85.50 will receive $6 annual interest and an average annual capital gain of $.725 (i.e., $1/20$ of $14.50, the difference between the $100 maturity value of the bond and the $85.50 current market price). Thus the average annual overall return is $6.725 per bond. The average investment over the life of the bond may be approximated by averaging the current value $85.50 and the maturity value $100, to obtain $92.75. On this approach

$$\text{Yield to maturity} \approx \frac{\text{average yearly returns}}{\text{average investment}} = \frac{6.725}{92.75} = 7.25\%$$

which is not too far from the correct yield of 7.40 percent.

tables is shown in Table 1. Term to maturity is designated along the columns, yield to maturity is listed down the rows, while the numbers within the table are bond prices. The coupon, expressed as a percentage of the face value, is shown on the top right-hand corner. With this table we can see how easy it is to solve for R in a case such as that given in Equation (2a). By reading down the twenty-year column until we come to a bond price of 85½ (three rows up from the bottom) we find the corresponding yield in the left-hand column. For prices (or maturities) between those listed in the table, the appropriate yields can be found by interpolation.

Bond Yields and Bond Prices

Economists have typically formulated theories of the structure of interest rates in terms of bond yields rather than bond prices. Bonds are traded in terms of price, however, not yield. They are bought and sold by speculators, long-term investors, and financial institutions who are vitally concerned with price movements. An examination of the connection between bond yields and bond prices will be very helpful in understanding the actual structure of yields in the bond markets.

First, it should be noted from Equation (1) that an increase in yield, R, implies a lower present value and thus a lower bond price. Moreover, for a given change in yield the corresponding change in bond prices is greater the longer the term to maturity. For example, if the yields of bonds of all maturities rose from 6 percent to 7 percent, the prices of long-term bonds would fall more than short-term issues. In Table 2, the greater price volatility of long-term issues, for a given change in interest rates, is illustrated. Bond prices are calculated for cases where yields for all maturities either rise to 7 percent or fall to 5 percent. The table assumes that initially all bonds are selling at face value (100) and have $6 coupons.[5]

The Yield Curve: Method of Construction and Historical Patterns

The yield curve is the most widely used graphic device for examining the relationship between yield and term to maturity of comparable debt securities. It refers simply to a chart depicting the general shape

[5]By the formula shown in Equation (1), it will be seen that for $P = F = 100$ and $C = 6$, the initial yield to maturity, R, of each bond must be 6 percent.

Table 1. Sample Page from a Book of Bond Tables

6%

Mat. Yield	19Y	19½Y	20Y	20½Y	21Y	21½Y	22Y
4.40	120.46	120.80	121.14	121.45	121.78	122.10	122.41
4.45	119.74	120.07	120.39	120.70	121.01	121.31	121.60
4.50	119.02	119.34	119.65	119.95	120.24	120.53	120.81
4.55	118.31	118.61	118.91	119.20	119.48	119.75	120.02
4.60	117.61	117.90	118.18	118.45	118.72	118.99	119.24
4.65	116.91	117.19	117.45	117.72	117.98	118.23	118.47
4.70	116.22	116.48	116.74	116.99	117.23	117.47	117.71
4.75	115.53	115.78	116.02	116.26	116.50	116.72	116.95
4.80	114.85	115.09	115.32	115.55	115.77	115.98	116.19
4.85	114.17	114.40	114.62	114.83	115.04	115.25	115.45
4.90	113.50	113.71	113.92	114.13	114.33	114.52	114.71
4.95	112.83	113.04	113.23	113.43	113.62	113.80	113.98
5.00	112.17	112.37	112.55	112.73	112.91	113.08	113.25
5.05	111.52	111.70	111.87	112.04	112.21	112.37	112.53
5.10	110.87	111.04	111.20	111.36	111.52	111.67	111.82
5.15	110.22	110.38	110.54	110.69	110.83	110.97	111.11
5.20	109.58	109.73	109.87	110.01	110.15	110.28	110.41
5.25	108.95	109.09	109.22	109.35	109.47	109.60	109.72
5.30	108.32	108.45	108.57	108.69	108.80	108.92	109.03
5.35	107.69	107.81	107.92	108.03	108.14	108.24	108.35
5.40	107.07	107.18	107.28	107.38	107.48	107.58	107.67
5.45	106.46	106.56	106.65	106.74	106.83	106.92	107.00
5.50	105.85	105.94	106.02	106.10	106.18	106.26	106.34
5.55	105.24	105.32	105.40	105.47	105.54	105.61	105.68
5.60	104.64	104.71	104.78	104.84	104.91	104.96	105.02
5.65	104.05	104.10	104.16	104.22	104.27	104.32	104.38
5.70	103.45	103.50	103.55	103.60	103.65	103.69	103.73
5.75	102.87	102.91	102.95	102.99	103.03	103.06	103.10
5.80	102.28	102.32	102.35	102.38	102.41	102.44	102.47
5.85	101.71	101.73	101.75	101.78	101.80	101.82	101.84
5.90	101.13	101.15	101.17	101.18	101.20	101.21	101.22
5.95	100.56	100.57	100.58	100.59	100.60	100.60	100.61
6.00	100.00	100.00	100.00	100.00	100.00	100.00	100.00
6.05	99.44	99.43	99.42	99.42	99.41	99.40	99.40
6.10	98.88	98.87	98.85	98.84	98.82	98.81	98.80
6.15	98.33	98.31	98.29	98.27	98.24	98.22	98.20
6.20	97.79	97.75	97.73	97.70	97.67	97.64	97.62
6.25	97.24	97.20	97.17	97.13	97.10	97.07	97.03
6.30	96.70	96.66	96.62	96.57	96.53	96.49	96.45
6.35	96.17	96.12	96.07	96.02	95.97	95.93	95.88
6.40	95.64	95.58	95.52	95.47	95.41	95.36	95.31
6.45	95.11	95.05	94.98	94.92	94.86	94.81	94.75
6.50	94.59	94.52	94.45	94.38	94.32	94.25	94.19
6.55	94.07	93.99	93.92	93.84	93.77	93.70	93.64
6.60	93.56	93.47	93.39	93.31	93.23	93.16	93.09
6.65	93.05	92.96	92.87	92.78	92.70	92.62	92.54
6.70	92.54	92.44	92.35	92.26	92.17	92.09	92.00
6.75	92.04	91.93	91.83	91.74	91.65	91.56	91.47
6.80	91.54	91.43	91.32	91.22	91.12	91.03	90.94
6.85	91.04	90.93	90.82	90.71	90.61	90.51	90.41
6.90	90.55	90.43	90.32	90.20	90.09	89.99	89.89
6.95	90.06	89.94	89.82	89.70	89.59	89.48	89.37
7.00	89.58	89.45	89.32	89.20	89.08	88.97	88.86
7.10	88.62	88.48	88.35	88.21	88.09	87.96	87.85
7.20	87.68	87.53	87.38	87.24	87.11	86.98	86.85
7.25	87.21	87.06	86.91	86.76	86.62	86.49	86.36
7.30	86.75	86.59	86.44	86.29	86.14	86.00	85.87
7.40	85.84	85.67	85.50	85.35	85.19	85.05	84.91
7.50	84.94	84.76	84.59	84.42	84.26	84.11	83.96
8.00	80.63	80.42	80.21	80.01	79.81	79.63	79.45

1369

Source: *Comprehensive Bond Values Tables* (Financial Publishing, 1958).

Table 2. Relationships between Bond-Price Movements and Yield Changes[a]

Years to Maturity (N)	Price (P) to Yield 7% (R) to Maturity	Loss Incurred If Market Yields Rise from 6% to 7%	Price (P) to Yield 5% (R) to Maturity	Gain Realized If Market Yields Fall from 6% to 5%
1	99.05	0.95	100.96	0.96
2	98.16	1.84	101.88	1.88
3	97.34	2.66	102.75	2.75
4	96.56	3.44	103.59	3.59
5	95.84	4.16	104.38	4.38
10	92.89	7.11	107.79	7.79
20	89.32	10.68	112.55	12.55
30	87.53	12.47	115.45	15.45
Consol (Perpetual Bond)	85.71	14.29	120.00	20.00

[a] All examples assume semiannual compounding.

of the relationship among bond yields of varying maturities. Along the horizontal scale is measured years to maturity and along the vertical axis, yield to maturity. A point is plotted on the chart for each security whose yield is to be used in constructing the curve. Then a relatively smooth curve is drawn, which describes the indicated relationship. Only issues similar in all characteristics should be plotted together, since, as was indicated above, special features of particular issues may alter their yields significantly. It is important, for example, to avoid plotting low- and high-coupon issues together, since low-coupon issues give more of their total yield in favorably taxed capital gains and hence tend to sell at relatively low yields.

Illustration of the Construction of a Yield Curve

The construction of a yield curve may be illustrated by using the actual yields of U.S. Treasury bonds on a specific date. Table 3 presents the actual price and yield quotations for selected Treasury bonds as of March 31, 1970. Reading across the last row of the table we find first the description of the bond. "3½s, 1998 Nov." refers to the U.S. Treasury bonds maturing in November 1998 and carrying a 3½ percent coupon. Next we find the bid price, 68⁸/₃₂, the price at which government-bond dealers stood ready to buy these bonds from sellers, and then the asked price, 68²⁴/₃₂, the price at which dealers were willing to sell bonds to buyers. The next column shows that the bid price of a bond fell ⁴/₃₂ from the previous day's quotation. Finally, the yield to maturity (based on the asked price) is calculated. The term to maturity of the bond is simply the number of years from the date of the quotation to the maturity date of the bond, or slightly more than 28½ years.

In Figure 1, the yields of the bonds quoted in Table 3 and their corresponding maturities are indicated on the chart. In addition, the yields of a few additional Treasury issues (not listed in the table) were plotted to help fill in some of the maturity gaps.[6] Then a relatively smooth freehand curve was fitted by eye to the scatter of points to present the general relationship between yields and term to maturity. Care was taken in fitting the yield curve to avoid using those issues whose yields were significantly affected by special features. Three

---

[6]In selecting these additional issues care was taken to avoid using Treasury securities with very low coupons (e.g., 1½ percent) or very high coupons (e.g., 8 percent) for the reasons mentioned in the text.

Table 3.   Prices of Selected Treasury Bonds*a*

Government, Agency and Miscellaneous Securities

Tuesday, March 31, 1970
Over-the-Counter Quotations: Source on request.
Decimals in bid-and-asked and bid change represent
32nds (101.1 means 101 1-32).

Treasury Bonds			Bid	Asked	Bid Chg.	Yld
4s,	1970	Aug.	99.0	99.4	....	6.37
2½s,	1966-71	Mar.	96.8	96.12	....	6.49
4s,	1971	Aug.	96.4	96.12	+ .2	6.81
3⅞s,	1971	Nov.	95.8	95.16	....	6.86
4s,	1972	Feb.	94.19	94.27	+ .1	6.98
2½s,	1967-72	June	91.2	91.10	....	6.81
4s,	1972	Aug.	93.14	93.22	....	6.93
2½s,	1967-72	Sept.	90.2	90.10	....	6.86
2½s,	1967-72	Dec.	89.3	89.11	....	6.88
4s,	1973	Aug.	90.16	90.24	— .2	7.13
4⅛s,	1973	Nov.	90.6	90.14	....	7.17
4⅛s,	1974	Feb.	89.16	89.24	....	7.20
4¼s,	1974	May	89.16	89.24	....	7.17
3⅞s,	1974	Nov.	86.28	87.4	— .2	7.20
4s,	1980	Feb.	78.24	79.8	— .8	6.94
3½s,	1980	Nov.	73.24	74.8	— .8	6.97
3¼s,	1978-83	June	69.4	69.20	— .2	6.76
3¼s,	1985	May	68.14	68.30	— .2	6.57
4¼s,	1975-85	May	74.14	74.30	— .6	6.95
3½s,	1990	Feb.	68.8	68.24	— .4	6.27
4¼s,	1987-92	Aug.	72.8	72.24	— .4	6.59
4s,	1988-93	Feb.	70.2	70.18	....	6.48
4⅛s,	1989-94	May	70.8	70.24	— .4	6.56
3s,	1995	Feb.	68.10	68.26	— .2	5.26
3½s,	1998	Nov.	68.8	68.24	— .4	5.74

---

a Bonds for which a range of maturity dates are given (such as the 4s, 1988–93 Feb.) mature on the final date listed, February 1993, but may be redeemed as early as February 1988 at the option of the government. The yield to maturity has been calculated on the basis of the final maturity date, since the government is unlikely to wish to exercise its early call privilege when the general level of market yields is higher than the coupons on existing bonds. If the general level of market yields were lower than existing coupons, however, the yield to maturity would have been figured to the earliest call date (February 1988).

Source: *The Wall Street Journal*, April 1, 1970.

Treasury securities so affected by extraneous factors are indicated by a triangle in the figure.[7] These three issues, when part of the estate of a decedent, are redeemable at par (100) in payment of estate taxes. Since these issues were selling at just over 68, the potential tax benefit for certain investors was substantial. Consequently, we would expect that these securities should sell at considerably lower yields than would

[7]The issues are the 3½s of 1990, the 3s of 1995, and the 3½s of 1998.

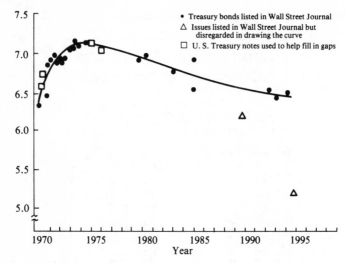

Figure 1. Yield Curve for U.S. Treasury Securities, March 31, 1970.

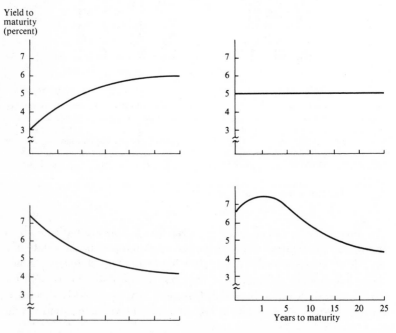

Figure 2. Alternating shapes of the Yield Curve.

issues of the same maturity similar in all respects except for the estate-tax advantage. It would be highly misleading to use such issues in the construction of the yield curve.

Historical Yield-Curve Patterns

Generally, the yield curve approximates one of four shapes illustrated in Figure 2. The curve may display the lowest yields on short-term issues and then rise at a diminishing rate until it becomes relatively flat in the longest maturities, thus forming an ascending curve. Alternatively, but somewhat less frequently, yields may be highest on short-term securities and then decrease at a diminishing rate until they level out, thus forming a descending (or reverse) yield curve. Still less frequently, yields are the same for all maturities, thus forming a flat yield curve. Finally, yields may rise in the early maturities, reach a peak, and then decline until they finally level out in the later maturities, as they did on March 31, 1970.

Figure 3 depicts yield curves for the highest-quality US corporate bonds (free from all extraneous influences) during the twentieth century in three dimensions.[8] It will be noted that short-term yields have been considerably more volatile than long-term yields. In periods of restricted credit conditions short rates tend to rise more than long rates, while in periods of easy money they fall farther. Furthermore, the data indicate that descending yield curves (or curves with descending segments) are apt to occur when both long- and short-term rates are relatively high. Conversely, ascending yield curves have always been formed when relatively low rates prevailed for all maturities. On average, however, over the present century short rates have been considerably lower than long rates. . . . It is worth noting that conspicuously humped yield curves existed through many months of 1957, 1959,

[8]These yield curves were estimated by David Durand from 1900 through 1958. Yields for the period 1959 through 1970 were estimated by methods similar to those employed by Durand. Yields until 1942 were estimated from averages of yields recorded during the first three months of the year; yields after 1942 were calculated using January and February prices; and since 1951 yields have been based on February 15 prices. Since Durand was attempting to estimate the yields of the highest-quality corporate bonds outstanding, his curves were fitted to the lowest yields plotted. Also, it should be noted that Durand limited himself to fitting only the top three of the basic yield-curve shapes depicted in Figure 2. Finally, the freehand curves were smoothed to make successive differences between maturities sufficiently regular. I am grateful to Sidney Homer of the investment firm of Salomon Bros. & Hutzler for making the yield curves since 1958 available to me.

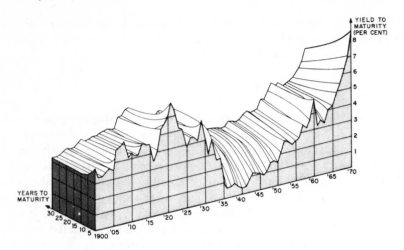

Figure 3. Yield Curves for prime U.S. corporate bonds.

1960, and 1966 through 1970,[9] when relatively high interest rates prevailed. For selected dates, some representative yield curves are displayed in Figure 4. As was true in the case of the corporate securities,
the "average" yield curve for US Treasury securities is an ascending
one. Similar yield-curve patterns have been observed for Canadian and
British securities, as well as for the securities of those few other nations
whose capital markets are sufficiently developed to generate data covering a wide range of securities.

Usefulness of the Yield Curve

Before turning to an explanation of the various yield-curve patterns we
observe in the market, it is possible to point out immediately one
potential benefit that bond investors can derive from the construction
of a yield curve. Once the individual yields are plotted and the yield
curve is drawn, one can immediately identify those particular issues
that are "out of line" with comparable bonds of the same maturity.
Such a procedure may aid the investor in bond selection. Bonds whose
yields are substantially lower than other securities of comparable

---

[9]The method employed by Durand for estimating the yields of corporate bonds
precludes the identification of humped yield curves for these securities.

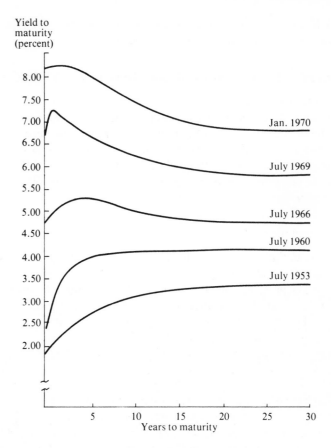

Figure 4. Selected Yield Curves for U.S. Treasury Securities.

maturity may be regarded as "overpriced" and should not be purchased. On the other hand, issues whose yields are well above the
average for that maturity, as indicated by the yield curve, may be
regarded as "underpriced" and may offer particularly good value, given
the investor's circumstances. For example, it is quite clear that unless
an investor can use the particular potential estate-tax advantage offered
by the 3s of February 1995, this issue should be avoided. Similarly,
from time to time issues may offer very good value. This might occur,
for example, at a time when a large new issue is being "digested" by
the market. The very construction of the curve may be useful in isolat-

ing such temporary pricing anomalies or market imperfections that may be exploited for profit by bond investors.[10]

Alternative Explanations of the Slope of the Yield Curve

What determines the slope of the yield curve? Why are short-term rates of interest sometimes higher and at other times lower than long-term yields? Despite the considerable study that has been devoted to these questions, much controversy remains. Among economists, three competing theories have attracted the widest attention. These are known as the expectations, liquidity-preference, and institutional or hedging-pressure theories of yield curve.

The Expectations Theory

According to the expectations theory, the shape of the yield curve can be explained by investors' expectations of future interest rates. Suppose, for example, investors believe that the prevailing level of bond yields is unusually high relative to historical precedent and that lower rates in the future are more probable than higher ones. In fact, a survey [see Kane and Malkiel, 1967] of interest-rate expectations (of the major institutional investors in the United States) during 1966 revealed that just such expectations were held then. Under such circumstances, long-term bonds will appear to many investors relatively more attractive than short-term ones if both maturities sell at equal yields. This is so for two reasons: First, long-term bonds will afford an investor an option of earning a high rate relative to the historical level of rates for a longer time period than will shorter issues. Investors who buy short-term bonds will subject themselves to the risk of having to reinvest their funds later at the lower yields that are expected. Second, if investors sell prior to maturity, the longer the maturity of the bond

[10]Of course, some bonds may offer particularly high yields because they have relatively large coupons and thus their returns tend to be taxed at ordinary income tax rates. On the other hand, deep-discount bonds with low coupons may offer relatively low yields because they tend to give a substantial part of their return in favorably taxed capital gains. Whether or not the higher-yielding bond with the larger coupon is in fact a good buy depends on the tax bracket of the investor. Clearly, for tax-exempt investors, only the yield to maturity matters. For an investor who pays taxes, the yields to maturity of the various bonds available for purchase may be calculated on an after-tax basis in order to isolate particularly good values for that particular investor. Depending on the investor's tax bracket, different issues will better suit his objectives.

they buy, the larger will be the potential capital appreciation they gain should their expectations prove correct. For example, the magnitude of the differential gains from a fall in all yields from 6 to 5 percent was illustrated in Table 2.

If investors act in accordance with these expectations, they will tend to bid up the prices (force down the yields) of long-term bonds and sell off short-term securities, causing their prices to fall (yields to rise). These operations will produce a descending yield curve with short-term issues yielding more than long-term bonds. . . .

In a similar manner, the expectations theory predicts that the yield curve will be upward sloping at a time when investors expect interest rates to rise. If yields were the same on all securities, investors would sell intermediate- and long-term bonds (where possibilities of substantial capital loss exist) and buy short-term securities. Such purchases and sales would tend to raise long rates relative to short rates.

The relationship of long and short rates under the expectations theory The expectations theory implies a formal relationship between long- and short-term rates of interest. Specifically, the analysis leads to the conclusion that the long rate is an average of current and expected short-term rates. To see why this is so, consider the following very simple example. Let us suppose that there are only two securities, a 1-year bond and a 2-year bond, and that all investors have funds at their disposal for either 1 or 2 years. Assume further that the current 1-year market rate of interest is 7 percent, today's actual 2-year rate is 7½ percent, and the 1-year rate expected next year is 8 percent. The standard (but, unfortunately, necessarily complicated) notation, which can serve as a reference for the rest of the study, uses the following conventions:

- Let capital Rs stand for actual market rates (yields).
- Let lower-case rs stand for expected rates.
- The pre-subscript represents the time period for which the rates are applicable.
- The post-subscript stands for the maturity of the bonds.

For example, in the expression $_tR_5$
pre-subscript t = period for which rate is applicable
capital R = actual rate
post-subscript 5 = maturity of bond for which rate applies.

Specifically, $_tR_5$ stands for the actual 5-year market rate of interest (the yield to maturity on a 5-year bond) today, i.e., in period t.

$_{t+1}r_5$ stands for the *expected* 5-year market rate of interest that investors anticipate for the next year (period $t + 1$).

$_{t-2}r_1$ indicates the one-year rate of interest that investors anticipate will prevail in the market 2 years from now, i.e., in period $t + 2$.

Thus, in our simple example above, $_tR_1 = 7$ percent, $_tR_2 = 7\frac{1}{2}$ percent, and $_{t+1}r_1 = 8$ percent.

Under the assumptions of the pure expectations theory, there are no transactions costs and all investors make identical forecasts of future interest rates. Moreover, there is perfect certainty and accurate forecasting. If investors are profit maximizers, it follows that each investor will choose that security (or combination of securities) that maximizes his or her return for the period during which the funds are available.

Let us consider the alternatives open to the investor who has funds at his or her disposal for 2 years. He or she may buy a 2-year bond from which he or she obtains an annual yield of 7½ percent. Alternatively, he or she may buy a 1-year bond, from which he or she receives a 7 percent return, and next year he or she may reinvest the proceeds in another 1-year bond expected to yield 8 percent. In either case the average annual return is (approximately) 7½ percent.

The comparison is only slightly more complicated in the case of the investor with funds at his or her disposal for 1 year. If he or she buys a 1-year bond, the return over his or her investment period (i.e., holding-period yield) is 7 percent. Why can't he or she do better by buying a 2-year bond yielding 7½ percent and then selling it after holding it for 1 year? The answer is that if 1-year rates do indeed rise to 8 percent next year, the 2-year security will suffer a half-point capital loss.[11] Thus, the realized return from the 2-year bond over his investment period will be only 7 percent, as is shown below:

[11]Assume that the 2-year security bears a 7½ percent coupon and is currently selling at par (100). The price next year may be found by the bond-pricing formula, Equation (1).

$$\text{Price} = \frac{\text{coupon payment + face value at maturity}}{1 + \text{yield}}$$

In our example, next year's price $= (7\frac{1}{2} + 100)/108 \approx 99\frac{1}{2}$, so the investor has a half-point capital loss.

Return over investment period =

$$\frac{\text{coupon payment} + \text{capital gain (loss)}}{\text{purchase price}} = \frac{7\frac{1}{2} - \frac{1}{2}}{100} = 7\%. \tag{3}$$

Correspondingly, we find that the investor with funds available for 1 year also receives the same return whichever maturity he or she buys. Again the holding-period return is the same on both maturities.

From this simple example, the determination of an equilibrium rate structure can be made clear. Suppose that expected returns on 1-year and 2-year securities were *not* equal. For example, let the 2-year rate be 8 percent rather than 7½ percent, but let the future rate on 1-year securities still be expected to equal 8 percent next year. It would turn out that all investors would prefer to hold the 2-year security because it would promise a larger holding-period yield irrespective of the investment period of the buyer.[12] Consequently, investors would tend to sell 1-year securities and buy 2-year bonds. This process would continue until any differential in expected returns over the two investment periods was eliminated. On the assumptions of the theory, the long rate must turn out to be an average of present and future short-term rates of interest. Only when this is true can the pattern of short and long rates in the market be sustained. The long-term investor, for example, must expect to earn through successive investment in short-term securities the same return over his investment period that he would earn by holding a long-term bond to maturity.

The equilibrium relationship between long and short rates may be shown formally as follows. The 2-year investor will have no incentive to move from one bond to another when he or she can make the same investment return from buying a combination of short issues or holding one long issue to maturity. If such an investor invests one dollar in a 1-year security and then reinvests the proceeds at maturity [i.e., $(1 + {}_tR_1)$] in a 1-year issue next year, the total capital will grow to $(1 + {}_tR_1)(1 + {}_{t+1}r_1)$ at the end of the 2-year period.[13] Alternatively, if

---

[12]The 2-year investor would earn an 8 percent annual yield by buying the longer security, whereas an average yield of only 7½ percent would be earned by buying 1-year bonds now yielding 7 percent and reinvesting the proceeds in 8 percent issues next year. Similarly, the 1-year investor would earn 8 percent by buying 2-year bonds and selling them after 1 year, whereas only 7 percent would be earned by holding 1-year bonds to maturity.

[13]For example, if an investor invested $1.00 in an investment that paid interest at the rate of 5 percent, paid annually, he or she would have at the end of the year the

he or she invests his dollar in a 2-year issue (and leaves all interest to be reinvested until the final maturity date in 2 years) he or she will have a maturity $(1 + {}_tR_2)^2$. In equilibrium, where the investor has no incentive to switch from security to security, the two alternatives must offer the same overall yield, i.e.,

$$(1 + {}_tR_2)^2 = (1 + {}_tR_1)(1 + {}_{t+1}r_1). \tag{4}$$

Thus, the 2-year rate can be expressed as a geometric average involving today's one-year rate and the 1-year rate of interest anticipated next year.

$$(1 + {}_tR_2) = \sqrt{(1 + {}_tR_1)(1 + {}_{t+1}r_1)}. \tag{5}$$

In similar fashion, the rate on longer-term issues can be expressed in terms of a whole series of expected short rates. In general,

$$(1 + {}_tR_N) = [(1 + {}_tR_1)(1 + {}_{t+1}R_1) \ldots (1 + {}_{t+N-1}r_1)]^{1/N}. \tag{6}$$

How the theory accounts for the different shapes of the yield curve
The expectations theory can account for every sort of yield curve. If short-term rates are expected to be lower in the future, then the long rate, which we have seen must be an average of those rates and the current short rate, will lie below the short rate. Similarly, long rates will exceed the current short if rates are expected to be higher in the future. It is even possible to account for humped yield curves (of the type that existed in the United States during many periods of the 1960s) by assuming that investors expect rates first to rise and then to fall later to much lower levels.

A simple numerical example will be useful both to clarify the averaging mechanism and to show the conditions under which a humped yield curve may be generated. Suppose the current 1-year rate, ${}_tR_1$, is 7 percent. Further assume that the market expects next year's 1-year rate, ${}_{t+1}r_1$, to be 8 percent, and that future anticipated (1-year) rates are as listed in the right-hand side of the table on the following page:

---

original investment of $1.00 plus interest of .05 × 1.00 or $.05, for a total of $1.05 = $1.00 (1.05). If he or she then reinvested the proceeds of $1.05 at a 6 percent interest rate, he or she would have at the end of the next year $1.05 (1.06) = $1.113 = $1.00(1.05)(1.06).

Actual Market Rates	Anticipated Market Rates
$_tR_1 = 7\%$	
$_tR_2 =$	$_{t+1}r_1 = 8\%$
$_tR_3 =$	$_{t+2}r_1 = 6\%$
$_tR_4 =$	$_{t+3}r_1 = 5\%$

Using the averaging formula in Equation (5), we find that the equilibrium 2-year rate, $_tR_2$, is, according to the expectations theory, approximately 7½ percent.[14] The 3-year rate, $_tR_3$, is an average of the 1-year rate, $_tR_1$, 7 percent; the 1-year rate expected next year, $_{t+1}r_1$, 8 percent; and the 1-year rate expected 2 years from now, $_{t+2}r_1$, 6 percent. The equilibrium 3-year rate is then approximately 7 percent. The reader may verify that the equilibrium 4-year rate is approximately 6½ percent. Notice that the yield curve, which can be plotted from the market rates for the different maturities, will first rise and then fall to lower levels, giving a humped appearance.

In all this analysis, relative supplies of securities of different maturities have not even been mentioned. The previous argument shows that, in the model of the expectations theory, changes in the maturity composition of the total outstanding debt are irrelevant for the determination of the rate structure. Unless they alter expectations, changes in relative supplies can have no long-run effect on the term structure, which is determined fully by expectations of future short-term interest rates in the manner shown by Equation (6). The reason is that in equilibrium all investors (no matter how long their investment period) are indifferent concerning which maturities they hold. The investor with funds for 1 year, for example, will earn the same return over his or her investment period whether he or she holds 1-year bonds and lets them mature or long-term issues, which are sold after 1 year. Consequently, if the maturity distribution of the outstanding debt changes so that the relative supply of 1-year issues decreases while the relative supply of long-term bonds increases, investors will be happy to rearrange their portfolios with no change in the relative yields of short- and long-term issues.

Notice that the expectations theory is consistent with the historical

[14]For simplicity, one can use arithmetic rather than geometric averaging to get an approximate answer. Thus, Equation (5) becomes

$$_tR_2 = \frac{_tR_1 + _{t+1}r_1}{2} . \tag{5a}$$

patterns of yield curves depicted in Figures 3 and 4. When the general level of rates was low relative to the historical "normal" level, so that investors may plausibly have expected a rise in rates, we can see that ascending curves were the rule. On the other hand, yield curves (or segments of curves) that descend have been recorded when the general level of rates was very high relative to historical precedent. Thus, the expectations theory can explain the shape of the yield curve in a manner consistent with the historical evidence under an assumption of "return-to-normality" forecasting of interest rates. As will be indicated below, formal statistical tests confirm this finding.

Expected interest rates and the rate of inflation   Before leaving our discussion of the expectations theory it will be helpful to examine the relationship between the yield curve and expected rates of inflation. Inflation influences the yield curve through its effect on expected interest rates. Irving Fisher argued that the stated (nominal) rate of interest in the market may be decomposed into two constituent parts: first, a "real rate of interest" paid to investors as a reward for foregoing present consumption, and second, a compensation for the expected loss of purchasing power the investors will suffer from inflation. Thus, if the stated interest rate is, say, 8 percent, perhaps 5 percent represents the real rate of interest with the remaining 3 percent a compensation for the anticipated rate of inflation.

Suppose we know that the real rate of interest for both the current year and expected for next year is 5 percent and that a 3 percent inflation is expected this year while a 4 percent inflation is anticipated next year. In such a case the current stated one-year rate ($_tR_1$) will be 8 percent (equal to the sum of the real rate plus the compensation for inflation), while the expected market rate next year ($_{t+1}r_1$) will rise to 9 percent because of the increase in the anticipated rate of inflation. Thus, the 2-year market rate, $_tR_2$, will be 8½ percent, higher than the 1-year rate because the market expects an increase in the rate of inflation. Other things being the same, an increase in the expected rate of inflation in the future will tend to raise long rates relative to short ones, while a decrease in the expected rate of inflation will have the opposite effect.

Summary   We may now summarize our discussion by noting that the expectations theory explains the shape of the yield curve by investors' anticipations about future interest rates. If the market expects higher rates in the future, the yield curve will tend to be upward sloping. Bond investors would favor short-term over longer securities if both sold at the same yield. Short-term issues will soon be paid off at face value, allowing investors to reinvest the proceeds at the coming higher interest rates. On the other hand, long-term bonds will decline in value if interest rates do indeed rise as forecast. The result is that the prices of short issues would be bid up (their yields would fall) and long-term bonds would fall in price (their yields would rise). Similar sorts of incentives exist for would-be borrowers as well. At a time when the general level of rates was expected to rise, borrowers in need of funds over a long period would be particularly anxious to convert short-term indebtedness into long-term bonds. Such switches would insure that long-run needs of the firm can be financed at the current advantageously low rates. Of course, the simultaneous retirement of short-term debt and issuance of long-term bonds will also tend to raise long rates relative to short ones. The larger the rise in rates that is expected, the steeper will be the slope of the yield curve. The theory explains the shapes of other types of yield curves with the same logic.

The Liquidity-Preference Theory

An important line of criticism against the expectations theory has been directed at the naive extension of the perfect-certainty variant of the theory (where forecasting is presumed to be accurate) to a world of uncertainty (where forecasting errors will be the rule rather than the exception). It is argued that in a world of uncertainty short-term issues are more desirable than longer securities because the former are more "liquid." By the liquidity of an asset we generally refer to the characteristic of its convertibility into cash on short notice without appreciable loss of principal value. The basic argument can best be understood in the context of a situation where short rates were expected to remain unchanged in the future. In such a case, liquidity theorists would argue, the long-term bonds ought to yield more than shorts by the amount of a risk premium. The holder of a long-term bond must be given a yield in excess of that obtainable on short-term issues in order to compensate him for assuming the risks of greater potential price fluctuations, should there be an unexpected change in the level of rates. As was indicated in Table 2, if the general level of rates does change, long-term bonds can be expected to fluctuate in price to a far greater extent than short-term issues. The expectations theory, on the other hand, holds that short- and long-term bonds ought to sell at equal yields whenever no change is expected in future rates. This is so because neglecting transactions costs, the investor's expected return from buying longs or shorts will be the same no matter how long he or she has funds to invest.

A numerical example will help clarify the disagreement between the two theories. Suppose that the current short (1-year) rate is 6 percent and that the short rate for the following year and for all succeeding years is also expected to be 6 percent. The expectations theory holds there should be a flat yield curve and that a 1-year investment will earn 6 percent whether a security maturing in 1, 2, or 20 years is bought.

According to the liquidity theory, however, an investor with short-term funds for investment will prefer the shorter security. If interest rates do not stay at the 6 percent level as expected, but instead unexpectedly rise to 7 percent, an investor who bought the 1-year security will be unaffected by the change—the security will mature and be paid off at par. Indeed, even if he or she has to sell his or her bond prior to maturity he or she will be little affected by the change in rates since the prices of short-term issues are relatively unresponsive to changes in market interest rates. Consequently, investors in short-term bonds takes little or no risk—they are assured of earning their 6 percent for the year they have funds available for investment. On the other hand, the investors who buy the 20-year, 6 percent coupon bond in the expectation of selling it at par the next year will find that its price has fallen to approximately 89½ with the change in interest rates. Thus, instead of receiving a 6 percent return, they will lose 4½ percent (equal to 6 percent interest minus 10½ percent capital loss) on their investments. The longer the security they buy, the larger will be their risk of price decline should the general level of interest rates rise unexpectedly. This is so because long-term bonds fluctuate more in price than shorts, for a given change in rates.

Of course, if all interest rates fall, the prices of long-term bonds will rise more than the price of shorter issues, as we showed in Table 2.[15] Nevertheless, if an investor has funds to invest for only a short

---

[15]In practice, long yields do not usually change by as much as short yields and therefore Table 2 overstates the probable extra volatility of longer-term issues. As was mentioned earlier, long yields are conceived as being a complicated geometric average of current and future short-term rates of interest. Even if investors raise their forecasts of short-term rates for a few periods ahead, long-term rates need not rise by the same

time and does not wish to take a chance of losing some of his or her principal, he or she will prefer to invest in short-term issues and will accept a somewhat lower yield thereon as the price of gaining added safety.

The crux of the liquidity-preference theory is that long-term bonds, because of their greater potential price volatility, ought to offer the investor a larger return than short-term securities. If no premium were offered for holding long-term bonds, it is argued, most individuals and institutions would prefer to hold short-term issues to minimize the variability of the money value of their portfolios.[16] On the borrowing side, however, there is assumed to be an opposite propensity. Borrowers can be expected to prefer to borrow at long term to assure themselves of a steady source of funds. This leaves an imbalance in the pattern of supply and demand for the different maturities—one which speculators might be expected to offset. Hence, the final step in the argument is the assertion that speculators are also averse to risk and must be paid a liquidity premium to induce them to hold long-term securities. Thus, even if interest rates are expected to remain unchanged, the yield curve should be upward sloping, since the yields of long-term bonds will be augmented by risk premiums necessary to induce investors to hold them. While it is conceivable that short rates could exceed long rates if investors thought that rates would fall sharply in the future, the "normal relationship" is assumed to be an ascending yield curve. This is consistent with the historical evidence reported above that, on average, long-term rates have exceeded short rates over the present century.

Formally, the liquidity premium is typically expressed as an amount that is to be added to the expected future rate in arriving at the equilibrium-yield relationships described in Equations (4) through (6). If we let L_2 stand for the liquidity premium that should be added to next year's forecasted 1-year rate, we have

$$(1 + {_tR_2})^2 = (1 + {_tR_1})(1 + {_{t+1}r_1} + L_2), \tag{7}$$

---

amount if the forecasted short ranges many years in the future remain unchanged. Nevertheless, empirical evidence indicates that when expectations are revised in an uncertain world, investors usually change a whole series of expected short-term rates and not just those rates for the years immediately ahead. Thus, long rates do tend to be quite volatile and investors in long-term bonds subject themselves to considerably more price variability than to purchasers of shorter issues.

[16]For an alternative explanation of liquidity premiums, see Stiglitz.

and

$$(1 + {}_tR_2) = \sqrt{(1 + {}_tR_1)(1 + {}_{t+1}r_1 + L_2)}. \tag{8}$$

Thus, if L_2 is positive (i.e., if there is a liquidity premium), the 2-year rate will be greater than the 1-year rate even when no change in rates is expected. It has also been customary to assume that L_3, the premium to be added to the 1-year rate forecasted for 2 years hence (i.e., for period $t + 2$) is even greater than L_2, so that the 3-year rate will exceed the 2-year rate when no change is expected in short-term rates over the next 3 years. In general, the liquidity-premium model may be written as

$$(1 + {}_tR_N) = [(1 + {}_tR_1)(1 + {}_{t+1}r_1 + L_2)(1 + {}_{t+N-1}r_1 + L_N)^{1/N}. \tag{9}$$

Assuming that $L_N > L_{N-1} > \cdots > L_2 > 0$, the yield curve will be positively sloped even when no changes in rates are anticipated.

Mkt Segmentation
The Institutional or Hedging-Pressure Theory

Another group of critics of the expectations theory argues that liquidity considerations are far from the only additional influence on bond investors. While liquidity may be a critical consideration for a commerical banker looking for an investment outlet for a temporary influx of deposits, it is not important for a life insurance company seeking to invest an influx of funds from the sale of annuity contracts. Indeed, if the life insurance company wants to hedge against the risk of interest-rate fluctuations, it will prefer long maturities. This is because an annuity contract, in essence, guarantees to the annuitant a specified earnings rate over a long period. Therefore, the risk-averting insurance company will base its contracts on currently available long-term yields to maturity and immediately invest the proceeds from the sale of such contracts in the long market. Such long-term investments will guarantee the insurance company a profit regardless of what happens to interest rates over the life of the contract.

Many pension funds and retirement savers find themselves in a wholly analogous situation. While investment in short-term issues insures that the principal of the fund will be kept intact, such investments leave uncertain the fund's future income. Since such investors are concerned with guaranteeing themselves *certainty of income* (rather than *certainty of principal*) over the long run, risk aversion on their part should lead to a preference for long-term rather than short-term securities.

The institutional critics freely admit that other financial institutions such as commerical banks and corporate investors are interested primarily in liquidity and hedge against risk by the purchase of short-term issues. But that is precisely the thrust of the hedging-pressure argument. The institutionalists believe that different groups of investors have different maturity needs that lead them to confine their security purchases to restricted segments of the maturity spectrum. Similarly, many bond issuers are believed to tailor the maturity of their offerings to the type of asset to be financed or the length of time over which they need the funds. Thus, there are severe impediments to substitutability over maturity ranges of the yield curve for the various participants on both sides of the market. Under an extreme form of this argument, the short and long markets are effectively segmented. Financial institutions are presumed to select a maturity structure of assets suited to their needs and hold to that structure regardless of expected future interest-rate changes. The prices and yields in the short and long sectors of the market are set solely by the particular supply-and-demand relationships existing within it, since allegedly neither borrowers nor lenders shift between markets in response to rate differentials.

An institutional view of the determination of the term structure has been advanced by economists such as Culbertson but has perhaps been most vigorously argued by some market practitioners. For example, Homer and Johannesen (members of a large Wall Street firm specializing in bonds) do not regard short- and long-term issues as two ends of the same mustache, but rather ". . . as different from each other as stocks are from bonds, or more so . . . the [yield] curve should not be expected to behave traditionally or logically, as though the rates were linked together by a mathematical formula."

An important implication of the institutional theory is that the relative supplies of debt instruments play a central role in the determination of the equilibrium-yield structure. If, for example, the government retired $10 billion of short-term debt and increased the supply of long-term issues by the same amount, institutionalists would expect such an operation to raise the long rate relative to the short. In contrast, according to the expectations theory, such changes in the maturity composition of the outstanding bonds should, by themselves, have no effect on market-yield relationships.

Summary Comments

To summarize the discussion to this point, three theories have been advanced to explain the shape of the yield curve. The expectations theory argues that the term structure of interest rates can be fully explained by the market's anticipations regarding the course of future interest rates. According to this theory, an upward-sloping yield curve is formed when the market expects rates to rise in the future; a descending curve is formed when rates are expected to fall. The liquidity-preference theory, while not denying the importance of expectations, insists that an important additional factor must be considered. Specifically, liquidity theorists have argued that a yield premium must be offered to the buyers of long-term bonds to compensate bondholders for greater potential price volatility of such issues compared with short-term securities. Consequently, even when no change in future rates is expected, long-term bonds ought to yield more than shorts by the amount of risk (or illiquidity) premium. The institutional or hedging-pressure theory recognizes the risk-aversion argument advanced by the liquidity theorists and agrees that it is a good description of the behavior of many investors with fairly short horizons, such as commercial banks. Nevertheless, for certain investors with long-term obligations such as insurance companies, hedging behavior would indicate a preference for long-term bonds, which promise certainty of income payments over a long period, rather than short issues. Thus, different types of institutions have different maturity preferences. In the extreme form of the argument, the maturity preferences of different investors and borrowers are so strong that they never purchase securities outside their preferred maturity ranges to take advantage of yield differentials. As a result, it is argued that the short and long markets are effectively segmented and yields are determined by supply and demand in each market. . . .

Summary of Empirical Work

Empirical studies . . . have found considerable evidence concerning the importance of expectational elements in determining the shape of the yield curve. Unfortunately, little evidence is available on the actual expectations held by investors at different periods in the past. Nevertheless, empirical investigators have developed indirect methods of estimating how expectations might have been formed that have enabled us to make reasonable judgments that expectations play a central role in the determination of the rate structure. The shapes of actual yield curves have consistently been related to these fabricated expectations in precisely the manner suggested by the expectations theory.

There is also evidence, however, that expectations are not the unique determinant of the term structure. It would appear that the yield curve has an upward bias. For example, the normal average yield curve, calculated over long periods of bond-market history, has been an ascending one. This evidence is consistent with the liquidity-preference view that investors in long-term bonds must be paid a yield in excess of that obtainable on short-term securities for accepting the risks of greater potential price fluctuations. The institutional or hedging-pressure theory has generally been tested by examining a major implication of the theory—that nonexpectations-induced changes in the maturity structure of the outstanding debt should alter the shape of the yield curve. Various problems associated with these tests suggest, however, that the evidence assembled thus far is inconclusive. . . .

We have seen that it is possible to marshal strong empirical evidence in support of both the expectations and the liquidity-preference theories of the yield curve. Evidence supporting the importance of institutional factors is rather weak, but, as noted above, the tests performed suffer from several drawbacks. In any case, all three theories should really be viewed as complementary rather than competitive. For example, the liquidity-preference explanation does not deny the importance of expectations; it only suggests that expectations *alone* are insufficient to determine the shape of the yield curve. Thus, those two theories together may be viewed as offering a more complete explanation of the term structure of interest rates than either theory alone. . . .

BIBLIOGRAPHY

ALMON, SHIRLEY. "The Distributed Lag between Capital Appropriations and Expenditures." *Econometrica* 33 (January 1965), 78–96.

BAUMOL, WILLIAM J., BURTON G. MALKIEL, and RICHARD E. QUANDT. "The Valuation of Convertible Securities." *Quarterly Journal of Economics* 80 (February 1966), 48–59.

BIERWAG, G. O., and M. A. GROVE. "A Model of the Term Structure of Interest Rates." *Review of Economics and Statistics* 49 (February 1967), 60–62.

Buse, A. "Interest Rates, the Meiselman Model and Random Numbers." *Journal of Political Economy* 75 (February 1967), 49–62.

Cagan, Phillip. "A Study of Liquidity Premiums on Federal and Municipal Government Securities." In Jack M. Guttentag and Phillip Cagan, eds. *Essays on Interest Rates.* Columbia University Press for the National Bureau of Economic Research, 1969.

Conard, Joseph W. *The Behavior of Interest Rates.* (New York: Columbia University Press for the National Bureau of Economic Research), 1966.

Culbertson, John M. "The Term Structure of Interest Rates." *Quarterly Journal of Economics* 71 (November 1957), 485–517.

De Leeuw, Frank. "A Model of Financial Behavior." In James Duesenberry et al., eds. *The Brookings Quarterly Econometric Model of the United States.* (Chicago: Rand McNally), 1965.

Diller, Stanley. "Expectations in the Term Structure of Interest Rates." In Jacob Mincer, ed. *Economic Forecasts and Expectations.* (New York: Columbia University Press for the National Bureau of Economic Research), 1967.

Durand, David. *Basic Yields of Corporate Bonds, 1900–1942.* Technical Paper 3, National Bureau of Economic Research, 1942.

Fair, Ray C., and Burton G. Malkiel. *The Determination of Yield Differentials between Debt Instruments of the Same Maturity.* Research Memorandum No. 5, Financial Research Center, 1970.

Fisher, Lawrence. "Determinants of Risk Premiums on Corporate Bonds." *Journal of Political Economy* 67 (June 1959), 217–237.

Grant, J. A. G. "Meiselman on the Structure of Interest Rates: A British Test." *Economica* 31 (February 1964), 51–71.

Hickman, W. Braddock. "The Interest Structure and War Financing." Unpublished manuscript. National Bureau of Economic Research, 1943.

Homer, Sidney, and Richard I. Johannesen. *The Price of Money, 1946 to 1969.* (New Brunswick, NJ; Rutgers University Press), 1969.

Kane, Edward J. "The Term Structure of Interest Rates: An Attempt to Reconcile Teaching with Practice." *Journal of Finance* 25 (May 1970), 361–374.

Kane, Edward J., and Burton G. Malkiel. "The Term Structure of Interest Rates: An Analysis of a Survey of Interest-Rate Expectations." *Review of Economics and Statistics* 49 (August 1967), 343–355.

Kessel, Reuben A. *The Cyclical Behavior of the Term Structure of Interest Rates.* Occasional Paper 91, National Bureau of Economic Research, 1965.

Macaulay, Frederick R. *The Movements of Interest Rates, Bond Yields, and Stock Prices in the United States since 1856.* National Bureau of Economic Research, 1938.

MALKIEL, BURTON G. *The Term Structure of Interest Rates: Expectations and Behavior Patterns.* (Princeton, NJ: Princeton University Press), 1966.
_____. "How Yield Curve Analysis Can Help Bond Portfolio Managers." *The Institutional Investor,* 1 May 1967.
_____, and EDWARD J. KANE. "Expectations and Interest Rates: A Cross-Sectional Test of the Error-Learning Hypothesis." *Journal of Political Economy* 76 (July–August 1968), 453–470.
MEISELMAN, DAVID. *The Term Structure of Interest Rates.* Prentice-Hall, 1962.
MODIGLIANI, FRANCO, and RICHARD SUTCH. "Innovations in Interest Rate Policy." *American Economic Review: Papers and Proceedings* 56 (May 1966), 178–197.
_____. "Debt Management and the Term Structure of Interest Rates: An Empirical Analysis." *Journal of Political Economy* 75 (August 1967), 569–589.
_____. "The Term Structure of Interest Rates: A Reexamination of the Evidence." *Journal of Money, Credit and Banking* 1 (February 1969), 112–120.
NELSON, C. R. "Time Series Methods for Testing a Model of the Term Structure of Interest Rates." Unpublished manuscript, 1969.
ROSS, MYRON H. "'Operation Twist': A Mistaken Policy?" *Journal of Political Economy* 74 (April 1966), 195–199.
SLOANE, PETER E. "Determinants of Bond Yield Differentials." *Yale Economic Essays* 3 (Spring 1963), 3–55.
STIGLITZ, JOSEPH E. "The Term Structure of Interest Rates and Portfolio Management." Unpublished manuscript, 1968.
TELSER, LESTER G. "A Critique of Some Recent Empirical Research on the Explanation of the Term Structure of Interest Rates." *Journal of Political Economy* 75 (August 1967), 546–561.
THEIL, HENRI. *Economic Forecasts and Policy,* 2nd ed. (Amsterdam: North Holland), 1961.
VAN HORNE, JAMES. "Interest Rate Risk and the Term Structure of Interest Rates." *Journal of Political Economy* 73 (August 1965), 344–351.
WALLACE, NEIL. "Buse on Meiselman—A Comment." *Journal of Political Economy* 71 (July–August 1969), 524–527.
WHITE, WILLIAM H. "The Structure of the Bond Market and the Cyclical Variability of Interest Rates." *International Monetary Fund Staff Papers,* March 1962.
WOOD, JOHN H. "Expectations, Errors, and the Term Structure of Interest Rates." *Journal of Political Economy* 31 (April 1963), 160–171.

The Evidence on the Demand for Money: Theoretical Formulations and Empirical Results *

John T. Boorman

Introduction

Numerous theories have been proposed to explain the public's demand for money. Though the range of hypotheses implicit in these theories is extremely broad, there are certain important elements common to all of them. Most significantly, almost all of these theories can be generalized into a proposition about the existence of a stable relationship between a few important economic variables and the stock of money demanded.

While diverse theories often posit similar variables to explain the demand for money, they frequently differ in the specific role assigned to each. For example, in the simplest version of the transactions theory of the demand for money, the stock of money demanded is hypothesized to be strictly proportional to a single variable—the volume of transactions to be facilitated by that money stock. In comparison, the inventory theoretic view, which recognizes the interest rate as an opportunity cost of holding money balances and introduces brokerage fees and other charges as explicit costs of switching wealth between interest-bearing assets and money, denies this proportionality between money and income. In this model the minimization of the total cost of managing money balances leads to a solution that suggests the possibility of substantial economies of scale in the demand for money.

As another example, in the liquidity preference theories of John Maynard Keynes and James Tobin the role of money as an asset is stressed and the motives for holding money examined. An analysis of the costs (income foregone) and benefits (risks avoided) of holding wealth in the form of money balances suggests a hypothesis in which income and the interest rate on alternative financial assets are suggested as the primary determinants of desired money balances. In comparison, Milton Friedman's "Restatement" of the quantity theory

---

*The author thanks Thomas Havrilesky for helpful comments and assistance in preparation of this article.

eschews a specific focus on the "roles" of money or on the "motives" of individuals in holding money balances.[1] Instead, Friedman emphasizes the services yielded by money in individual and business portfolios. In this view money is simply one among the many assets—including physical and human assets—held by the public. This leads to the hypothesis that all of the alternatives available to the wealth holder may influence his desired money balances.

These examples of alternative money demand hypotheses suggest some of the major questions that have been the focus of empirical investigation. A more complete list would include the following specific problems:

1. What empirical measure should be used to represent the theoretical concept of "money"?

2. How are empirically testable money demand functions conventionally specified? In this connection it is useful to examine some of the more common formulations that have included either a role for expectations in the determination of desired money balances or a distinction between the long-run equilibrium level and the short-run adjustment pattern by which equilibrium is approached.

3. What is the role of the interest rate in the money demand function? This issue raises several related questions:

   a. If the interest rate is statistically important in the determination of the demand for money, what is the interest elasticity of money balances?

   b. Which one of the alternative interest rate measures available is most relevant to the determination of the demand for money?

   c. Given that the interest rate is important in the money demand function, has evidence been presented that would support the existence (historical or potential) of a "liquidity trap"?

4. What is the relative significance of income, wealth, and other economic variables that have been suggested along with the interest rate as determinants of the demand for money?

---

[1]M. Friedman, "The Quantity Theory of Money, A Restatement," in Milton Friedman (ed.), *Studies in the Quantity Theory of Money* (Chicago: Aldine, 1956). See D. Patinkin, "The Chicago Tradition, The Quantity Theory and Friedman Journal of Money Credit and Banking (February, 1969), 16–70.

5. Do money demand functions that include the essential arguments suggested by alternative theories appear to be stable
over the postwar period?

These are the major issues raised in the empirical literature on the
demand for money. Each of these will be considered in turn.[2]

The Empirical Definition of Money

What assets ought to be included in our measure of "the money stock"?
If we focus on those theories that emphasize the transactions motive for
holding money, the proper definition of the money stock is not a profound problem. Money should be defined to consist only of those assets
that serve as generally acceptable media of exchange. It is widely agreed
that only commercial bank demand deposits and currency in circulation
provide this service. However, if the public's demand for money is viewed
as arising from a speculative motive, the list of assets in the definition of
money may be expanded to include at least some assets that are stable
in nominal value, i.e., fixed dollar assets whose value is independent of
variations in the interest rate. Finally, if the demand for money is
approached as part of the general theory of demand, all assets that are
close substitutes for the media of exchange (and respond to the same
yields in the demand function) should be included in the definition.
This approach clearly indicates that the proper definition of the money
stock is largely an empirical question.

Allan H. Meltzer has enunciated one possible criterion for selecting the appropriate definition of money.

> The problem is one of defining money so that a stable demand function
> can be shown to have existed under differing institutional arrangements,
> changes in social and political environment, and changes in economic
> conditions, or to explain the effects of such changes on the function.[3]

This criterion focuses on the implications of the definition of the money
stock for the degree of control that the monetary authority has over crucial macroeconomic variables.[4] The money stock and interest rates are

[2]More general issues, particularly those dealing with econometric problems in the
estimation of money demand functions, will be discussed—often in footnotes—at various
points of the text.
[3]A. H. Meltzer, "The Demand for Money: The Evidence from the Time Series,"
Journal of Political Economy, 71 (June 1963), 222.
[4]There are, of course, additional criteria by which to define a measure of the
money stock. George Kaufman, following Milton Friedman and David Meiselman, de-

thought to have a strong effect upon aggregate demand, employment, and the price level in the economy. If the demand for money is unstable (shifts unpredictably), the effect of monetary policy actions on the equilibrium money stock and interest rates will be uncertain. In short, stability of the money demand function and a capability on the part of the monetary authority to influence closely the stock of assets corresponding to the theoretical concept of money employed in that function would seem to be necessary conditions for the successful implementation of monetary policy.[5] These conditions will allow the authorities to exert a predictable influence over the equilibrium stock of money, the interest rate, and other variables in the money demand equation.

Economists traditionally have defined the money stock in the "narrow" sense as the sum of demand deposit liabilities of commercial banks and currency held by the public. However, a number of analysts include time deposits at commercial banks within their measure of the money stock. Milton Friedman, for example, views time deposits as "a temporary abode of purchasing power" and includes them in the "broad" measure of money that he employs in his empirical work. A few researchers go beyond even this "broad" concept to include such things as savings and loan shares, mutual savings bank deposits, and claims

---

fines money according to its correlation with income (taking into consideration the possible lead-lag relationship between money and income). In selecting the set of financial assets to be included in the money supply, he employs two criteria originally specified by Friedman and Meiselman: choose that set that (1) has the highest correlation with income and (2) has a higher correlation with income than any of the components separately. This alternative operational approach, unlike the Meltzer criterion, derives from the proposition that the equilibrium nominal money stock can be controlled by the monetary authority and suggests a rather specific theoretical model on which to base monetary policy. The Meltzer criterion is preferred here since it is compatible with a more broadly defined set of money demand functions. See G. G. Kaufman, "More on an Empirical Definition of Money," *American Economic Review*, 59 (March 1969), 78–87. M. Friedman and D. Meiselman, "Relative Stability of Monetary Velocity and the Investment Multiplier in the United States 1897–1957," Commission on Money and Credit, *Stabilization Policies* (Englewood Cliffs, N.J. 1963).

Frederick C. Schadrack, in "An Empirical Approach to the Definition of Money," *Monetary Aggregates and Monetary Policy*, Federal Reserve Bank of New York (1974) 28–34 extends these empirical criteria to include goodness of fit, stability over time and predictive accuracy in regression equations with GNP as a dependent variable and six different monetary aggregates as alternative explanatory variables.

[5]See S. J. Maisel, "Controlling Monetary Aggregates," in *Controlling Monetary Aggregates: Proceedings of the Monetary Conference of the Federal Reserve Bank of Boston* (June 1969), 152–174, and M. J. Hamburger, "The Demand for Money in 1971: Was There a Shift? A Comment," *Journal of Money, Credit and Banking*, 5 (May 1973), 720–725.

against other financial intermediaries in their measure of "money." Conceptually, of course, it is possible to go even further and include still other financial assets (or even some measure of credit availability, such as commercial bank "lines of credit") in a measure of money.[6] In this survey, evidence on the question of the best definition of money must be satisfied in accord with the Meltzer criterion. David Laidler has suggested an explicit set of conditions by which to evaluate the relative stability of alternative empirical functions. As he expresses it:

> A "more stable demand for money function" may be taken to be one that requires knowledge of fewer variables and their parameters in order to predict the demand for money with a given degree of accuracy or, which amounts to the same thing, one that yields parameter estimates that are less subject to variation when the same arguments are included in the function and hence enable more accurate prediction of the demand for money to be made.[7]

In an empirical study Laidler (40) contends that the most stable money demand function he has been able to isolate is one employing Friedman's broad definition of money (M-2). This contrasts with earlier results presented by Karl Brunner and Allan Meltzer (5), in which they found that the narrow measure (M-1)—demand deposits plus currency—yielded the most satisfactory money demand relation.

What accounts for these contrasting conclusions? First, these two studies specify different explanatory variables in their money demand equations. Second, they use data from different time periods to estimate the parameters of these relations. Finally, they employ different procedures to test their hypotehses. Since the relative performance of alternative measures of the money stock in empirical money demand functions is likely to be highly sensitive to all of these considerations, it is impossible to choose the better measure of money on the basis of these studies alone.

However, an alternative empirical approach is available. The stability of the money demand function is closely linked to the degree of substitutability that exists between money, as it is defined in that function, and other financial assets. For example, if the secular and

---

[6]See A. B. Laffer, "Trade Credit and the Money Market," *Journal of Political Economy*, 78 (March/April 1970), 239–267.

[7]D. Laidler, "The Definition of Money: Theoretical and Empirical Problems," *The Journal of Money, Credit and Banking* 1 (August 1968), 516.

cyclical changes in the competitive position of financial intermediaries make available substitutes for currency in circulation and demand deposits held by the nonbank public (the narrowly defined money stock), the demand for money, so defined, may shift as these substitutes appear. In such a case a demand function for some broader measure of money, one that includes these close substitutes, would be more stable, i.e., would shift less over time, than a function defined on a narrow money measure.[8] Under these conditions monetary policy actions that concentrate on the narrower measure of money would be focusing on an unstable, shifting target. Policy actions that focus on broader measures of money would be more appropriate.

A substantial body of evidence has now been presented on this issue. Specifically, the question that has been addressed is the following: Are assets such as commercial bank time deposits, savings and loan shares, mutual savings bank deposits, and others that have been suggested for inclusion in a measure of "money" sufficiently close substitutes for commercial bank demand deposits to warrant treating them in a single measure?

In a study on the demand for liquid assets by the public, Edgar Feige (15) measured the cross elasticities of demand between various assets.[9] Using data on the volume of liquid assets held by households in

---

[8]Gurley and Shaw, for example, emphasize the substitutability between claims on certain financial intermediaries and demand deposits at commercial banks, and they argue that "money" must be defined so as to include these substitutes. Evidence supporting this position is presented below. See J. G. Gurley and E. S. Shaw, *Money in a Theory of Finance* (Washington, D.C., 1960).

This view is also embodied in the report of the Radcliffe Committee, which views "liquidity" and "the stock of liquid assets" held by the public as the relevant concept on which to focus in monetary theory and policy. In this view only policy actions that change the *total liquidity* of the public—and not simply the composition of the public's stock of liquid assets—are likely to lead to predictable results. This is so because of the high degree of substitutability that exists between the narrowly defined money stock and near-monies. See *The Radcliffe Report*, Committee on the Working of the Monetary System (London, 1959).

[9]The cross elasticity of demand is the most frequently used measure of substitutability. If we consider two assets X and Y, and the returns on each, i_x and i_y, the cross elasticity of X with respect to Y equals the percentage change in the quantity of X demanded, divided by the percentage change in the return of Y.

$$\eta_{x \cdot y} = \frac{\Delta x / x}{\Delta i_y / i_y}$$

If an increase in the return on asset Y (Δi_y positive) causes a switch in holdings from X to Y, Δx will be negative and the cross elasticity will be negative. In this case the assets X and Y are said to be "substitutes." If η_{xy} is positive, indicating a *direct* relationship between the return on Y and holdings of asset X, these assets are said to be "complements."

each state of the United States for each year during the period from 1949 to 1959, Feige found that the yields on nonbank intermediary liabilities (savings and loan shares, etc.) did not affect the demand for money. Ownership of each of these assets was found to be highly sensitive only to its "own rate" of interest. In Feige's results there appears to be little substitutability between demand deposits, time deposits, savings and loan shares, or mutual savings bank deposits. In fact, demand deposits were found to be mildly *complementary* with savings and loan shares and mutual savings bank deposits; demand and time deposits at commercial banks were only very weak substitutes for each other. From this and other evidence Feige concludes that the narrow definition of money is the preferred definition when estimating money demand functions and that analysts need not concern themselves with the effects of the activities of other intermediaries on the public's demand for money.[10]

Feige's conclusions are disputed by T. H. Lee (46) and V. K. Chetty (10). Lee's work will be described in detail in connection with our survey of the relevance of alternative interest rate measures in the money demand function. Briefly, Lee suggests that the liabilities of financial intermediaries, particularly savings and loan shares, are indeed very good substitutes for money. Rather than supporting Friedman's "broad" definition of money, however, he claims that the definition should be extended to encompass an even broader collection of assets, including as a minimum, shares in savings and loan associations.

Chetty makes a similar proposal. In his work a technique originally developed in production theory to measure the substitutability between capital and labor in the production process is employed to measure the substitutability among assets in the consumer's utility function.[11] Chetty assumes that consumers attempt to maximize their utility (subject to the budget constraint) by combining money (demand deposits plus currency in circulation), time deposits, and other assets

[10]Feige's methods in deriving these results are subject to several criticisms. First, there are serious questions as to whether the way in which he measures the rate of return on commercial bank demand deposits reflects the relevant return considered by asset holders in allocating their portfolios. Second, his data measure the assets owned in a state by residents of all states when, in fact, the relevant measure for his purposes should have been the assets owned by the residents of each state. His data probably require the inclusion of rates on out-of-state assets in order to capture the effects of ownership that crosses state lines. These problems detract from Feige's results.

[11]See K. J. Arrow, H. B. Chenery, B. S. Minhas, and R. M. Solow, "Capital Labor Substitution and Economic Efficiency," *Review of Economics and Statistics* 63 (August 1961), 225–250.

to produce desired levels of liquidity at the lowest cost. By combining the conditions required for utility maximization with the budget constraint, he derives an equation that contains parameters that, when estimated, yield measures of the partial elasticities of substitution between money and other assets.

On the basis of his estimates, Chetty concludes that while savings and loan shares and mutual savings bank deposits are rather good substitutes for money, time deposits appear to be virtually perfect substitutes. This last finding supports Friedman's use of the "broad" definition of money. Nevertheless, as did Lee, Chetty suggests that an even broader measure of money may be more appropriate and shows how such a measure may be calculated. Employing weights that measure the "moneyness' of assets as implied by their substitutability with demand deposits and currency, he constructs a weighted average of demand deposits and currency (with weights constrained to unity), time deposits (TD), saving and loan shares (SL), and mutual savings bank deposits (MS). The final form of the equation defining this average "money" stock is

$$M_a = DD + C + TD + .615SL + .88\ MS.$$

Note that the coefficient (unity) on the time deposit variable reflects Chetty's conclusion of perfect substitutability between these deposits and narrowly defined money.[12]

While these findings by Lee and Chetty clearly favor a broader measure of money, an important recent study by Stephen Goldfeld (24), which provides consistent and comparable data on several of the questions addressed in this survey, contains persuasive evidence that focusing on narrow measures of money will yield demand functions with significantly superior predictive capabilities to those that define money in some broader fashion. Goldfeld does not concentrate explicitly on the substitutability of various potential components of "money." Rather, his procedure is to confront various hypotheses with the same set of data and very closely related functional specifications. This has the advantage of limiting the number of factors that can be introduced to explain differing statistical results—the major problem in making

[12]This evidence also lends support to the broad measure of money used by Lydall in his empirical study of the demand for money in Britain and increases the importance of Lydall's conclusions on the issues discussed below. See H. Evdall, "Income, Assets, and the Demand for Money," *Review of Economics and Statistics*, 40 (February 1958), 1-14.

comparative judgments on the diverse evidence presented by the authors cited above.

Goldfeld begins by noting that the inclusion of time deposits in the definition of money seems questionable on theoretical grounds "since it constrains the specification . . . of M-1 (narrow money) and time deposits to be the same" and potentially distorts the influence of interest rates on the component measures. However, he recognizes that these weaknesses could be offset if an empirically more stable demand function resulted from this formulation. His results, however, suggest that this "is definitely not the case."[13]

The alternative equations Goldfeld estimated with broad money include a lagged dependent variable, income, and interest rates as arguments. His estimates are such as to make one suspicious of the use of the broad money measure as the dependent variable. First, the time deposit rate appears to have a negligible influence on holdings of broad money. This may be an empirical reflection of the offsetting effects of this rate on demand deposits and time deposits and the loss of information involved in aggregating over those components. Second, the long-run elasticity of broad money is extremely high, exceeding the elasticities estimated separately for each of the components. Both of these results suggest serious problems with a function specified on the broad money measure. Goldfeld's additional statistical tests strengthen the initial suspicion engendered by those results. While the traditional criterion statistics—R^2 and the standard error of the estimate—provide little help choosing between the broad money or narrow money formulation, dynamic simulations and stability tests provide persuasive evidence of the superiority of the narrow money form. The broad money equation yields "ludicrously" large errors in long-run forecasting tests and is easily rejected on the basis of formal stability tests.[14]

---

[13]S. M. Goldfeld, "The Demand for Money Revisited," *Brookings Papers on Economic Activity* (3:1973), 593.

[14]Goldfeld's primary test consists of dynamically simulating his estimated equations. This involves forecasting both within-sample and out-of-sample values for the dependent variable and evaluating the quality of those forecasts by a measure such as the root mean square error. His tests take two general forms: (1) four quarter ex post forecasts made by taking sequentially longer subperiods within the sample from which to derive coefficient estimates and evaluating forecasts for four quarters beyond each successive estimating period and (2) splitting the sample period in half, deriving estimates from the first half data and evaluating the long-run forecasting ability of the equation over the second half of the sample period. In both cases the broad money equation performed substantially worse than the narrow money form. These results were formerly confirmed through the use of the Chow test of stability. See Goldfeld, *op. cit.*, 592–595.

Additional tests on the forecasting performance and stability of equations estimated for each of the components of M-2 (broad money), suggest his general conclusion that

> the simple specification used for M-1 will not work for time deposits, and . . . even given the questionable time deposit equation, the ex post forecasts of M-2 obtained from the aggregate equation are inferior to those obtained from adding together the separate component forecasts, thus suggesting that *aggregation is inflicting some positive harm*[15] (emphasis added).

In short, Goldfeld's results suggest that in model building and other work *more* rather than *less* disaggregation of the money demand equation seems to be desirable.[16]

Because of these conflicting results, many economists feel that this issue is still unresolved, and further evidence is sought. In the remainder of this survey, therefore, whenever we are reporting on empirical work, we shall cite the specific definition of money used by a particular author. In several instances, work reported on in connection with other issues will have direct implications for the appropriate empirical definition of money. Let us now turn to an examination of the general form of the money demand functions specified in empirical work and to a review of the evidence on the role of the interest rate in determining the public's demand for money. This latter issue has critical implications for national economic policy.

Conventional Formulations of the Demand for Money Function

In most formulations of the money demand function real money balances are related to "the" interest rate on relevant substitute assets and some scale variable related to economic activity, such as income or wealth. The equation specified is sometimes linear but more often exponential in form. These alternative forms may be specified as follows:

[15]*Ibid.*, 595.

[16]Dickson and Starleaf suggest a similar conclusion. Their estimates of various functions that include distributed lags on all arguments suggest that "the Demand Functions for $M1$ and TD (time deposits) appear to be so different as to dictate their separate, rather than combined analysis." H. D. Dickson and D. R. Starleaf, "Polynomial Distributed Lag Structures in the Demand Function for Money" *Journal of Finance*, 27 (December 1972), 1042.

$$\frac{M_d}{P} = m_d = a_1 + a_2 i + a_3 X \tag{1}$$

$$\frac{M_d}{P} = m_d = \alpha i^{\beta_1} X^{\beta_2} \tag{2}$$

where M_d/P is the stock of real money balances demanded, i is an interest rate, and X represents other variables such as wealth, permanent income, or current income.[17] When equation (2) is employed, a logarithmic transformation is made so that the equation is *linear* in the logarithms of the variables and, more importantly, linear in the parameters to be estimated. Taking natural logs of both sides of the equation;

[17]Money demand functions are generally cast in real terms on the assumption that the price elasticity of nominal money balances is unity. The implication of this assumption is that price-level changes alone will cause no change in the demand for *real* money balances or, alternatively, that the demand for nominal balances is proportional to the price level. This assumption implies that the public is free of money illusion in its demand for real money balances. Let us examine this assumption further. Let X in equation (2) above be a measure of real wealth, W. Then:

$$\frac{M_d}{P} = \alpha \times i^{\beta_1} \cdot w^{\beta_2}.$$

If *nominal* money balances were specified as a function of *nominal* wealth, this equation would be

$$M_d = \alpha \times i^{\beta_1} \times (P \cdot W)^{\beta_2}.$$

But these two equations are quite different. The first equation implies that the price-level elasticity is unity—the exponent of P equals one—and β_2 is the wealth elasticity of *real* money balances. But in the latter form β_2' is some *average* of the price level and wealth elasticities of nominal money balances. Consequently, if the price level elasticity is really unity, but the true wealth elasticity is not equal to one, β_2' will be *biased* toward that value and will not be a good estimate of the true wealth elasticity. To avoid that bias, investigators have generally chosen to work with functions cast in real terms.

The validity of this procedure is supported by evidence presented by Allan Meltzer (49). His work indicates that when the price variable is included as a separate argument in a log-linear equation, its coefficient is very close to unity. Furthermore, if nominal wealth is employed in an equation with nominal balances specified as the dependent variable, the wealth elasticity is closer to unity than if these measures are cast in real terms.

Additional evidence on this point has been presented by Harold D. Dickson and Dennis R. Starleaf (13). Employing an equation similar in form to (3) but with distributed lag functions defined on the independent variables, including GNP, they found that the estimated price elasticity of the narrowly defined money stock, $M1$, was not significantly different from unity. On this evidence they concluded that the demand for real money balances is homogenous of degree zero in the price level; therefore, the demand for money is free of money illusion. On this and other evidence the assumed proportionality of nominal money balances to the price level would appear to have a firm basis in empirical analysis.

$$\ln \frac{M_d}{P} = \ln m_d = \ln \alpha + \beta_1 \ln i + \beta_2 \ln X. \quad [18] \qquad (3)$$

These simple linear (in the coefficients) models may be fitted to empirical observations of variables if, and only if, two additional assumptions are made. First, we must assume that the money market is always in equilibrium so that desired money balances, M_d, equal the actual money stock reported in the statistical series, M. Second, we must assume that there exist exact empirical counterparts to the theoretical variables specified; for example, the average of daily rates quoted by the New York Federal Reserve Bank on U.S. Treasury Bills may be chosen as the empirical measure of "the interest rate." With data on each of the variables specified in the equation, multiple regression methods may be employed to derive estimates of the coefficients in these single equation models. [19]

Several modifications can be made to this basic equation to introduce significant additional flexibility into the hypotheses. One of the

---

[18]In this form the coefficients β_1, and β_2 can be directly estimated by linear regression techniques, and those coefficients will be elasticities. This may be shown as follows: Let $\eta_{m \cdot i}$ denote the interest elasticity of money demand (let m in this instance represent real money balances demanded); then,

$$\eta_{m \cdot i} = \frac{\partial m / m}{\partial i / i} = \frac{\partial m}{\partial i} \cdot \frac{i}{m} \ ;$$

but, from equation (2),

$$\partial M / \partial i = \beta_1 \ (\alpha X^{\beta_2}) \cdot i^{(\beta_1 - 1)};$$

therefore,

$$\eta_{M \cdot i} = \beta_1 \ (\alpha X^{\beta_2}) \cdot i^{(\beta_1 - 1)} \cdot \frac{i}{\alpha X^{\beta_2} \cdot i^{\beta_1}} = \frac{\beta_1 \cdot i^{\beta_1}}{i^{\beta_1}} = \beta_1.$$

Consequently, elasticities may be estimated directly by employing the log-linear form of equation (2) in the regression procedure.

[19]Least-squares regression analysis may be defined as a procedure whereby an hypothesized relationship may be confronted with actual data in order to derive numerical estimates of the parameters specified in that relationship. Under specified conditions concerning the nature of the hypothesized relationship and the characteristics of the data employed, these techniques will yield estimates with certain desirable statistical properties. In the models above, for example, data on the size of the money stock, the value of the interest rate, and, say, national wealth may be employed in regression analysis to derive estimates of β_1, the interest elasticity of money demand, and β_2, the wealth elasticity of money demand. For a discussion of the mechanics of least-squares regression and the properties of least-squares estimators, see S. Hymans, *Probability Theory* (Englewood Cliffs, N.J., 1966), Chapter 8, and J. Kmenta, *Elements of Econometrics* (New York, 1971), Chapters 7 and 10.

most important of these is the introduction of the concept of "desired," as opposed to "actual," money balances and the specification of a "partial adjustment" mechanism by which actual holdings adjust to desired levels.

For example, desired real money balances, m_T^*, may be postulated to depend upon the same variables specified in Equation (3)

$$\ln m_T^* = \ln \alpha + \beta_1 \ln i_T + \beta_2 \ln X_T \tag{4}$$

and the adjustment process of actual to desired levels of money demand may be specified as follows:

$$(\ln m_T - \ln m_{T-1}) = \lambda (\ln m_T^* - \ln m_{T-1}). \tag{5}$$

In this form λ, the adjustment coefficient, measures the rate at which adjustments are made to bring *actual* money holdings in line with the current *desired* level. Generally, λ is specified to be between zero and one, indicating that any such process of adjustment is only partially successful during one period. (The magnitude of λ will often be explained in empirical literature as reflecting the cost of adjusting portfolios relative to the cost of not adjusting them.)

While m_T^*, the current desired level of real money holdings, is not directly observable or measurable, postulation of the above adjustment process allows derivation of an estimating equation with solely observable quantities. Substituting Equation (4) into the adjustment Equation (5) and rearranging yields

$$\ln m_T = \lambda \ln \alpha + \lambda \beta_1 \ln i_T + \lambda \beta_2 \ln X_T + (1 - \lambda) \ln m_{T-1}. \tag{6}$$

In this form λ can be calculated from the coefficient estimate of the lagged dependent variable, m_{T-1}, and α, β_1, and β_2 can be calculated from this value and the coefficients estimated for the other terms. If, for example, a coefficient of .60 is estimated on the lagged term, then $\lambda = (1 - .60) = .40$, suggesting that in each period 40 percent of the gap between actual and desired money balances will be closed by the public's actions.[20]

[20]In this formulation, the long run interest and income (or wealth) elasticities are β_1 and β_2, respectively. The short run elasticities are given by $\lambda \beta_1$ and $\lambda \beta_2$. For example, in steady-state equilibrium, $M_T = M_{T-1} = M_{T-2} \ldots$
Then, from Equation (6),

$$\ln M_T - (1 - \lambda) \ln M_{T-1} = \lambda \ln \alpha + \lambda \beta_1 \ln i_T + \lambda \beta_2 \ln X_T$$
$$\ln M_T[1 - 1 + \lambda] = \lambda \ln \alpha + \lambda \beta_1 \ln i_T + \lambda \beta_2 \ln X_T$$
$$\ln M_T = \ln \alpha + \beta_1 \ln i_T + \beta_2 \ln X_T$$

as in Equation (4). Because of the assumed constraint on λ, short run elasticities will be smaller (in absolute terms) than longer run elasticities.

While this form has proved useful in many applications, it has the unfortunate characteristic of restricting the adjustment pattern in the dependent variable to be the same regardless of the source of the initial disturbance. Whether an interest rate change or an income (or wealth) change disturbs the initial (long-run) equilibrium, the adjustment path to a new equilibrium must be the same. There are several plausible theoretical reasons why this is not likely to be the case. In addition, empirical results often suggest implausibly long lags for the adjustment process. These long lags are difficult to explain on the basis of probable costs involved in adjusting financial portfolios.

An alternative, and perhaps superior, rationale for the presence of a significant lagged term in the money demand function derives from the "adaptive expectations" model. In this formulation it is assumed that the public is actually holding its desired level of money balances but that level itself is assumed to depend upon expected values of one or more of the independent variables rather than on current actual values. Thus,

$$\ln m_T = \ln \alpha + \beta_1 \ln i_T + \beta_2 \ln X_T^e, \tag{7}$$

where X_T^e is the value of X expected to prevail in period t. Since X_T^e is not observable some hypothesis must be specified on how expectations are formulated. It may be postulated, for example, that current expectations are formed by modifying previous expectations in the light of current experience. For example:

$$\ln X_T^e - \ln X_{T-1}^e = (1 - \lambda)(\ln X_T - \ln X_{T-1}^e) \tag{8}$$

or equivalently,

$$\ln X_T^e = (1 - \lambda) \ln X_T + \lambda \ln X_{T-1}^e \quad 0 \leqslant \lambda < 1.$$

This formulation depends upon knowledge of X_T in period t. An alternative formulation, which avoids this implicit assumption that X_T be known in advance of formulating the expectation, makes the revision of expectations dependent upon the most recent error in expectations, assuming data on current period values are not available, i.e.,

$$\ln X_T^e - \ln X_{T-1}^e = (1 - \lambda)(\ln X_{T-1} - \ln X_{T-1}^e). \tag{9}$$

In this form expectations are revised by some fraction of the discrepancy between last period's expectations and the actual value of X_{T-1}.

Either of these forms can be employed to derive an estimating equation specified solely in terms of observable values. For example, substituting the basic demand relation Equation (4) into the first of the adaptive expectations models specified above Equation (8) and applying a Koyck transformation yields,[21]

$$\ln m_T = (1 - \lambda) \ln \alpha + (1 - \lambda) \beta_1 \ln X_T + \\ (1 - \lambda) \beta_2 \ln i_T + \lambda \ln m_{T-1}. \qquad (10)$$

In this formulation the adaptive expectations model is formally the same as the partial adjustment model although the interpretation of the estimated coefficient on the lagged dependent variable and other variables is very different in the two equations. The adaptive expectations model, however, is the starting point for a whole family of models that allow the introduction of a great many alternative hypotheses into the basic structure. In particular, different expectational patterns may be specified for each of the independent variables in the equation or expectations on one or more of the variables may be allowed to adjust in different proportions to two or more of the previous expectations (forecasting) errors.[22] For example,

$$\ln X_T^e - \ln X_{T-1}^e = (1 - \lambda_1) (\ln X_T - \ln X_T^e) + \\ (1 - \lambda_2) (\ln X_{T-1} - \ln X_{T-1}^e). \qquad (11)$$

where λ_1 is not restricted to equal λ_2. In addition, the adaptive expectations model may be combined with the partial adjustment model to capture the potential lagged effects generated by each. An example of this will be seen below.

Unfortunately, the capacity to specify new and richer lag structures rather quickly surpasses the econometric ability to derive useful statistical estimates of the included parameters.[23] Because of this limitation, a far more general lag model has gained wide popularity. The Almon distributed lag technique allows estimation of a rather general lag pattern that can be rationalized in any number of ways. Only the length of the lag and the degree of the polynominal along which the weights lie must be specified in advance.[24] Perhaps the major advantage of this form over the models specified above is the elimination of the somewhat restrictive assumption that the weights describing the assumed adjustment path lie along a monotonically declining simple

[21]See Kmenta, *op. cit.*, pp. 474 ff.

[22]See Goldfeld, *op. cit.*, p. 600.

[23]See Z. Griliches, "Distributed Lags: A Survey," *Econometrica*, 35 (January 1967).

[24]See S. Almon, "The Distributed Lag Between Capital Appropriations and Expenditures," *Econometrica*, 33 (January 1965).

geometric lag structure. On the other hand, the method requires less care in the formulation of detailed hypotheses to rationalize the introduction of any lag structure.

Some form of one of the basic models specified above underlies most of the empirical work on the money demand function. We shall now turn to an examination of the results of that work for one of the most important issues in this area—the importance of the interest rate in determining the public's money demand.

The Role of Interest Rate in the Money Demand Function

Single-Equation Estimates

The stimulus for much of the econometric work on the demand for money and for the primary focus of that work on the importance of the interest rate as an argument in the money demand function derives from Keynes' presentation of the liquidity preference theory in *The General Theory of Employment, Interest, and Money* (1936). Although Pigou as early as 1917 had suggested that the interest rate was a potentially important factor determining the public's money holding behavior, it was Keynes' full explication of the "speculative" motive for holding "idle" money balances that provided the major impetus for testing this hypothesis. Research has been further encouraged by the work of Milton Friedman (19). Contrary to the findings of most other investigators, he finds little basis for assigning a significant role for the interest rate in determining the demand for money.

One of the earliest studies to address this issue was done by Henry Latané (45). Latané specified and tested three alternative models of the demand for money. In his first test he proposed a constant ratio of total money balances to nominal national income, $M/Y = k$. This hypothesis represented a crude form of the quantity theory. By showing graphically that this ratio was highly variable, fluctuating between a low of .26 to a high of .50 in the period from 1919 to 1952, Latané rejected this hypothesis.

In his second test Latané proposed a Keynesian-type money demand function, in which the total demand for money balances was specified to be the sum of a transactions component dependent on the level of income and an asset or speculative component dependent on the rate of interest:

$$M = a \left(\frac{1}{i} \right) + bY + c. \tag{12}$$

Latané showed that this form implies a continually declining ratio of money balances to income as income increases (and the interest rate remains constant).[25] Since empirical evidence indicated that this was not the case, Latané also rejected this form.

Latané's last model proposed that the ratio of nominal money balances to (nominal) aggregate income was dependent upon the rate of interest:

$$\frac{M}{Y} = f(i). \tag{13}$$

In testing this model, he specified a simple linear form, and derived the following regression estimates:

$$\frac{M}{Y} = .0074 \left(\frac{1}{i} \right) + .1088.$$

This equation was then used to predict values of the dependent variable for dates not included in the original data. The success of these predictions prompted Latané to conclude that he had identified a stable behavioral relation between cash balances, income, and the long-term rate of interest. Specifically, "In the past 30 years, each 1.0 percent change in $(1/i)$ has tended to be associated with a change of .8 percent in gross national product held as currency and demand deposits."[26]

One characteristic of Latané's last model, shared by the money demand functions tested by several other authors, should be mentioned. The equation form chosen by Latané to test the interest sensitivity of the cash balance ratio constrains the income elasticity of the

[25]This may be seen by dividing both sides of Equation (12) by Y:

$$\frac{M}{Y} = \frac{a}{i \cdot Y} + b + \frac{c}{Y}$$

If Y increases, a/Y and c/Y will decline. Thus, with the interest rate constant, the proportion of income held in the form of money balances would decline as income increased.

[26]H. A. Latané, "Cash Balances and the Interest Rate—A Pragmatic Approach," *Review of Economics and Statistics*, 36 (November 1954), 460.

demand for money to equal unity.[27] The effects of this arbitrary restriction on the value of the income elasticity of money balances can only be judged by comparing the results of this model with those derived from models that are not so constrained.

Several investigators, in testing the liquidity preference theory, have attempted to isolate the "asset" or "idle" balance component of the public's total money holdings from money balances held strictly for transactions purposes and to estimate the influence of the interest rate on the former component alone. James Tobin (64), in an early study, and Martin Bronfenbrenner and Thomas Mayer (4), in subsequent work, employed this approach.

In calculating the idle balance component of total money balances, Tobin (like Latané) assumed that desired *transactions* balances are

[27]This may be shown as follows: Let $\eta_{M \cdot Y}$ denote the income elasticity of money balances. Then,

$$\eta_{M \cdot Y} = \frac{\Delta M/M}{\Delta Y/Y} = \frac{\Delta M}{\Delta Y} \cdot \frac{Y}{M}.$$

But from Latané's basic model, Equation (13), we may write

$$\Delta M = f(i) \cdot \Delta Y.$$

Therefore,

$$\eta_{M \cdot Y} = f(i) \cdot \frac{Y}{M} = \frac{f(i) \cdot Y}{f(i) \cdot Y} = 1.$$

One alternative but equally restrictive approach to the demand for transactions balances is represented by the inventory theoretic model of the Baumol-Tobin type. In this model the demand for money is shown to conform to the familiar "square root law" of inventory analysis, i.e.,

$$M_d = \frac{1}{2} \sqrt{\frac{2bT}{i}} = \frac{1}{2} \cdot \sqrt{2b} \cdot T^{1/2} \cdot i^{-1/2}$$

where T is the volume of expenditures financed in a given period, b is the cost of switching between income earning assets and money, and i is the interest rate. In this case

$$\eta_{M \cdot T} = \frac{\partial M}{\partial T} \cdot \frac{T}{M} = \frac{\frac{1}{2} \cdot \frac{1}{2} \cdot \sqrt{2b} \cdot T^{-1/2} i^{-1/2}}{1} \cdot \frac{T}{\frac{1}{2} \cdot \sqrt{2b} \cdot T^{1/2} \cdot i^{-1/2}} = \frac{1}{2}$$

i.e., the transactions (or income) elasticity of the demand for money balances is one half. In this framework one would expect to find substantial economies of scale in the holding of money balances. These are ruled out in Latané's formulation as they are in the crude form of the quantity theory. See W. Baumol "The Transactions Demand for Cash: An Inventory Theoretic Approach," *Quarterly Journal of Economics*, 66 (November 1952).

proportional to the level of income. To determine the exact factor of proportionality between transaction balances and income, Tobin further assumed that during periods of very high interest rates and high economic activity, when the ratio of total money holdings to income is at its lowest level, idle balances are zero and the total money stock is held solely for transactions purposes. The minimum value for this ratio was found to occur in 1929. Therefore, Tobin asserted that his 1929 ratio actually measures the constant factor of proportionality between transactions balances and income. This may be seen symbolically. Let

$$M_{\text{total}} = M_{\text{idle}} + M_{\text{trans}} = f(i) + kY,$$

where

$$M_{\text{idle}} = f(i) \text{ and } M_{\text{trans}} = kY.$$

If $M_{\text{idle}} = f(i) = 0$, as Tobin asserts for 1929, then in 1929

$$M_{\text{total}} = kY \text{ and } \frac{M_{\text{total}}}{Y} = k$$

Since k (the reciprocal of the transactions velocity of circulation of money, V_t) was assumed to be a constant, this allowed a calculation of idle balances for other years as

$$(M_{\text{idle}})_t = (M_{\text{total}})_t - (M_{\text{trans}})_t = (M_{\text{total}})_t - k_{1929}(Y_t)$$

Tobin plotted idle balances calculated in this manner for each year against interest rates. For the period ending in 1945 he obtained excellent representations of what appeared to be Keynesian liquidity preference functions—the roughly hyperbolic functions generally depicted in the discussion of Keynesian theory. Although the scatter diagrams did not appear to yield such well-behaved relations for subsequent years, it did appear that Tobin had isolated a statistical liquidity preference function.

In their work Bronfenbrenner and Mayer (4) estimated regression coefficients in equations that contained a wealth measure and lagged money balances as explanatory variables, in addition to the interest rate. As the dependent variable, they alternately used total money balances and a measure of idle balances, similar to the one originally defined by Tobin. The equation they estimated in log-linear form was

$$\log (M/P)_t = \alpha_1 + \alpha_2 \log i + \alpha_3 \log W + \alpha_4 \log (M/P)_{t-1}. \tag{14}$$

This is virtually identical to the basic form derived in the previous section. In the equations employing idle balances as well as in those specifying total money balances as the dependent variable, the coefficient of the interest rate had a negative sign attached to it and was statistically significantly different from zero at the 1 percent level.[28]

In further tests based on equations similar to the one above Bronfenbrenner and Mayer concluded that the liquidity preference hypothesis did a better job of predicting the movement of money balances from year to year than did a "naive" model that assumed that there would be no relation (or a random relation) between movements in the interest rate and money balances. This again appeared as evidence favorable to the liquidity preference hypothesis.

Virtually all work presented since the Bronfenbrenner and Mayer study has wisely avoided the arbitrary classification of money balances into active and idle components. Even earlier authors, such as Latané, felt that such a distinction did not allow for the possible effect of the interest rate on "active balances."[29] Many economists believe that such a dichotomy is unreasonable since total money balances are simply one of many assets held for the services they provide and cannot be separated into unique components.[30]

Among studies specifying total money balances as the dependent variable are those by Meltzer (49), Brunner and Meltzer (5, 6), Laidler (40, 41), Heller (30), Chow (11) and Goldfeld (24). These studies use different time periods to test their basic hypotheses; they include variables other than the interest rate in the money demand equation; and often they differ in the empirical measure chosen to represent "the interest rate," some specifying the rate on U.S. Treasury Bills or short-term commercial paper, while others employ the rate on long-term government bonds or corporate securities. Yet, in spite of these many differences, these studies, like the ones above, show that the interest rate measure is an important factor in explaining variations in

---

[28]To say that a coefficient is "statistically significantly different from zero at the 1 percent level is to imply that there is less than one chance in a hundred that the estimated coefficient differs from zero solely because of random (chance) factors affecting the data from which the estimate was derived. If we cannot judge a coefficient to be significantly different from zero at the 1 percent level or 5 percent level of significance, we generally have little confidence in the hypothesized relation which that coefficient represents.

[29]Latané, *op. cit.*, pp. 456–457.

[30]M. Friedman, "The Demand for Money: Some Theoretical and Empirical Results," *Journal of Political Economy*, 67 (June 1959), 327–351.

the demand for money. Some of the more important characteristics of these studies are summarized in Table 1.

In addition to the unanimous conclusion that the interest rate is an important determinant of the demand for money, these studies demonstrate a strong consistency in their estimates of the interest elasticity of money balances. (As discussed below, such consistency over different periods of time suggests a rather stable demand for money function.) Those studies employing a long-term rate of interest report elasticities in the range of $-.4$ to $-.9$. However, the estimates in the lower half of this range occur only when money is defined in a "broad" sense (inclusive of commercial bank time deposits). Considering only those studies that use the narrow measure of money we find that the range of elasticity estimates narrows to $-.7$ to $-.9$.

When the short-term rate of interest is employed, the estimated elasticities range from $-.07$ to $-.50$. However, the estimates in the upper part of this range derive from those studies that specify "idle" balances as the dependent variable. If we exclude these results and consider only total money balances as the dependent variable, the elasticity of money balances with respect to the short-term interest rate lies in the range from $-.07$ to $-.20$. This result holds whether money is defined in the "narrow" or "broad" sense. The difference between the long-rate and the short-rate elasticities may be an indication of the different rates of adjustment by the public to what they consider to be temporary versus long-term movements in financial variables. Statistically, it also reflects the fact that the long-term rate fluctuates far less than the short-term rate. We shall consider this point again below.

Simultaneous-Equation Models

All of the studies reported in Table 1 have one basic characteristic in common: the estimates of interest elasticities are derived from single-equation models. Elementary statistics teaches that in order for estimated coefficients derived by least-squares regression methods to have certain desirable characteristics (unbiasedness, efficiency, etc.), there must be a one-way causation from the independent to the dependent variable, with no direct feedback. Thus, in the single-equation models specified above, the interest rate and other explanatory variables must be assumed to influence the stock of money, the dependent variable, but the stock of money must not, in turn, influence these variables.

In contrast, if the conventional aggregate economic model is con-

Table 1. The Demand for Money in Single-Equation Studies

Study	Interest Rate Elasticity of M		Interest Rate Measure Employed	Other Variables in M_D Function	Data and Time Period
1. Latané (45)	a) −0.3		R_B	GNP	1919–1952 (A)
2. Bronfenbrenner and Mayer (4)	a) −	−0.5 (M_{idle})	R_{4-6}	GNP, Wealth	1919–1956 (A)
	b) approx. −0.1	(M1)	R_{4-6}	GNP, Wealth	1919–1956 (A)
3. Meltzer (49)	a) −0.7	−0.9 (M1)	$R_{20\,yr}$	Net Nonhuman Wealth	1900–1958 (A)
	b) −0.5	−0.6 (M2)	$R_{20\,yr}$	Net Nonhuman Wealth	1900–1958 (A)
	c)	−0.4 (M3)	$R_{20\,yr}$	Net Nonhuman Wealth	1900–1949 (A)
4. Heller (30)	a)	−0.1 (M1)	R_{60-80}	GNP	1947–1958 (Q)
	b)	−0.1 (M2)	R_{60-80}	Private Nonhuman Wealth	1947–1958 (Q)
5. Laidler (40)	a) not available	(M1)	R_{4-6}	Permanent Income	1920–1960 (A)
	b) not available	(M2)	R_{4-6}	Permanent Income	1892–1960 (A)
6. Laidler (41)	a) −0.18	−0.20 (M1)	R_{4-6}	Permanent Income	1919–1960 and subperiods (A)
	b) −0.5	−0.8 (M1)	$R_{20\,yr}$	Permanent Income	1919–1960 and subperiods (A)
	c) approx. −0.15	(M2)	R_{4-6}	Permanent Income	1892–1960 and subperiods (A)
	d) −0.3	−0.5 (M2)	$R_{20\,yr}$	Permanent Income	1892–1960 and subperiods (A)
7. Chow (11)	a) approx. −0.75	(M1)	$R_{20\,yr}$	Permanent Income	1897–1958 (excl. war years) (A)
	b) approx. −0.79	(M1)	$R_{20\,yr}$	Current Income and Lagged Money Stock	1897–1958 (excl. war years) (A)
8. Goldfeld (25)	a)	−0.07 (M1)	R_{4-6}	GNP	1952–1972 (Q)
		−0.16	R_{TD}		
	b)	−0.07 (M1)	R_{4-6}	GNP	1952–1972 (Q)
		−0.15	R_{TD}	(Almon lags)	

Notes: $M1 = DD + C$; $M2 = M1 + TD$; $M3 = M2 +$ Deposits at Mutual Savings Banks and the Postal Savings System; $R_B =$ interest rate on high-grade corporate bonds; $R_{20\,yr} =$ rate on 20-year corporate bonds; $R_{4-6} =$ rate on 4–6 month prime commercial paper; $R_{60-80} =$ rate on 60–80 day commercial paper; $R_{TD} =$ commercial bank time deposit rate; $A =$ annual; $Q =$ quarterly.

sidered, it is obvious that the causation between interest rates, real factors, and the money stock is not unidirectional. There are simultaneous interrelations between both the supply of and demand for money as well as between monetary and real factors. This leads to what is commonly referred to as an "identification" problem.[31]

[31]The source and nature of "simultaneous-equation bias" may be illustrated as follows. Consider the usual supply-demand relationship as drawn in Figure A.

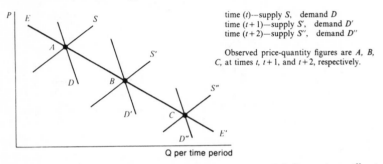

time (t)—supply S,   demand D
time ($t+1$)—supply S',   demand D'
time ($t+2$)—supply S'',   demand D''

Observed price-quantity figures are A, B, C, at times t, $t+1$, and $t+2$, respectively.

Q per time period

An attempt to fit a statistical demand or supply curve to empirical observations will not, in fact, yield the desired relationship except in very special circumstances. The usual time series observations of price (P) and quantity (Q) do not correspond to either any one demand curve or any one supply curve. Rather, they are intersection points of various supply and demand curves that are almost continuously shifting either randomly or systematically due to the influence of outside factors.

Attempts to derive single-equation estimates of these curves on the basis of observed data will result in a statistical construct that is neither a supply curve nor a demand curve. For example, the least-squares regression line that could be fit to the data in Figure A would be EE'. This line would have a negative slope in the situation drawn here only because of the tendency for the supply curve to shift relatively more than the demand curve. Yet a statistical study of the data involved could easily be misunderstood by the unwary to represent the true demand relation. This would lead one to accept a meaningless estimate of the slope and, thus, of the elasticity of the demand curve.

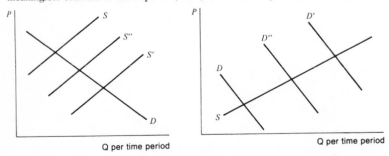

Q per time period   Q per time period

The only way in which such time series data could readily yield true structural estimates of the parameters of either the supply curve or the demand curve would be in

Fortunately, a substantial body of empirical work does assume simultaneity either between money supply and money demand or, more generally, between the monetary and the (real) expenditure sectors of the economy. These studies employ statistical techniques designed to correct for the interaction among "dependent" and "independent" variables specified within a single equation and to derive estimates which have certain desirable statistical properties. In these studies the money demand function is estimated as one element in a multiequation model. Some examples of the results of these studies are presented in Table 2.[32]

The results derived from simultaneous-equation models generally confirm the single-equation results reported above. Those studies employing a short-term market rate of interest in the money or demand deposit demand equation, report elasticities in the range of −.08 to −.18. This compares with the −.7 to −.2 range reported in the single equation studies in Table 1. The elasticity estimates with respect to the rate on commercial bank time deposits is generally −.17 or −.18.[33] The elasticity measures based on long-term rates are again substantially higher than the short-term rate elasticities. They range from −.35 in de Leeuw's work to −.75 in Brunner and Meltzer's model. Since de Leeuw's measure is a weighted average of rates on private securities of different maturities, and not a long-term rate comparable to the corporate bond yields used in the other studies, these results are not inconsistent with the evidence presented in Table 1.

Most of the equations reported in Table 2 are estimated within an explicitly specified structural model either of the monetary sector or of the monetary and expenditures sectors combined. Several authors, interested primarily in the money demand relation outside the framework of a fully specified multiequation model but cognizant of the

---

the very special circumstances where one of the curves is stable and the shifting of the other curve traces out points along the desired curve. This is pictured in Figure B. To get around this problem, the true interaction of supply-demand relations in determining price-quantity figures must be considered. This may be done by specifying a simultaneous-equation model including both a supply equation and a demand equation and by taking care to observe well defined rules for "identification." See G. Tintner, *Econometrics* (New York, 1962), Chapter 6.

[32]All of the studies reported in Table 2 employ two-stage least squares in the estimating process. For a discussion of the mechanics of this technique and the characteristics of the estimates derived from it, see J. Johnston, *Econometric Methods* (New York, 1963), Chapter 9, or Kmenta, *op. cit.*, Chapter 13.

[33]This is virtually identical to the result obtained by Goldfeld in his single-equation study. See Table 1.

Table 2. Money and Deposit Demand in Simultaneous-Equation Models

Study	Representative Equation (seasonal dummies omitted where appropriate)	Interest Elasticity	Interest Rate Measure	Data
1. Brunner and Meltzer (6)	$M1 = -18.994\, r^* + 0.201\, W/Pa - 54.72\, Y/Y_p + 0.347 P_y$ W/Pa = real public wealth P_y = price index Y/Y_p = ratio of current to permanent income	-0.75	r = bond yield	1930–1959 (A)
	$M2 = -16.806\, r^* + 0.340\, W/Pa - 44.81\, Y/Y_p + 0.290 P_y$	-0.42	r = bond yield	1930–1959 (A)
2. Teigen (62)	$\Delta D = 3.101 + 0.0719 Y^* - 0.0018 r_b^* Y^* - 0.0066 r_p Y^* - 0.1895\, D_{T-1}$ D = demand deposits adjusted at commercial banks Y = gross national product	-0.10 -0.43	r_b = Treas. bill rate r_p = rate on bank time deposits	1953–1964 (Q)
3. de Leeuw (47)	$\dfrac{\Delta D}{W} = 0.0067 - 0.158\left(\dfrac{D}{W}\right)_{r-1} - 0.00355\, r_s^*$ $-0.0451 r_p^* - 0.140\, \dfrac{Inv}{W_{r-1}} + $ other terms W = wealth measure $Inv.$ = bus. investment	-0.35 -0.17	r_s = yield on private securities r_p = rate on bank time deposits	1948–1962 (Q)
4. Goldfeld (24)	$\Delta D = -0.270 - 0.127 D_{T-1} + 0.140 Y^*$ $-0.0066 r_b^* Y^* - 0.012 r_p Y^*$ Y = gross national product	-0.11 -0.18	r_b = Treas. bill rate r_p = rate on bank time deposits	1950–1962 (Q)
5. Dickson and Starleaf (13)	$M1 = \ln a_0 + 0.660 \ln Y^* - 0.077 \ln R_{4-6}^* - 0.182 \ln R_{TD}^*$ $+ 1.037 \ln P^*$	-0.08 -0.18	R_{4-6} = comm. paper rate R_{TD} = comm. bank time deposit rate	1952–1969 (Q)

Where * indicates weighted average of current and past values; estimated using Almon distributed lags.

*An asterisk is used to denote an independent variable used in the money (or D) demand function, which is treated as endogenously determined within the multiequation model as a whole. A = annual; Q = quarterly.

potential estimation problems implicit in the single-equation approach, have employed the method of instrumental variables in deriving their estimates of the parameters in the money demand equation. Essentially, this method allows a person to act as if he or she is operating within a fully specified structural model by postulating the exogenous variables that would appear in the model were it to be fully defined. In this way those exogenous variables can be employed as "instruments" in the first stage of a two-stage least-squares estimation process with the predicted values of the "endogenous" or jointly dependent variables from this first-stage estimation being employed in the money demand function in the second stage.

One interesting example of this approach is contained in a recent paper by Harold D. Dickson and Dennis R. Starleaf (13). Their work is all the more interesting because it applies this technique to an equation that contains Almon-estimated distributed lag terms on each of the independent variables—income, the interest rate and the price level. Their results, reported in Table 2, are broadly consistent both with the results of simultaneous-equation models and with the single-equation results presented by Goldfeld, which employ a similar equation form. Using quarterly data for 1952-I through 1969-IV, they obtain estimated interest elasticities of $-.077$ and $-.182$ for the 4–6 month commercial paper rate and the rate on commercial bank time deposit, respectively.

In summary, it should be emphasized that both those studies based on single-equation models as well as those that employ multiequation estimation techniques appear to support the hypothesis that the interest rate is an important determinant of the demand for money. Furthermore, since the multiequation estimates are less likely to be biased because they take explicit consideration of the simultaneous nature of the relations involved, the similarity of results from those studies with those in single-equation work lends strong support to the single-equation estimates and indicates that, in this case, the identification problem may not be particularly serious.

Alternative Interest Rate Measures in the Money Demand Function

The studies cited in the previous section contain virtually overwhelming evidence that some interest rate should appear in the demand for money function. However, there is still disagreement as to which empirical measure should be used to represent the theoretical argument.

Much of the available evidence that attempts to determine which rate best explains the demand for money is inconsistent. Furthermore, tests by different analysts often employ data from different time periods, specify different dependent variables, and include dissimilar constraints within the function, making comparisons among these empirical studies rather tenuous.

The problem may stem partly from the fact that theory provides little guidance on this issue. Some writers, like Brunner and Meltzer, argue that the demand for money should be treated within the broad theory of portfolio selection and suggest that this demand depends on the yield on equities as well as that on bonds. Others, like Bronfenbrenner and Mayer (4), Laidler (40, 41), and Heller (30), argue that some short-term interest rate is the more relevant argument since it measures the opportunity cost of holding money as the rate of return on what they consider to be money's closest substitutes. Still others, including Gurley and Shaw (26) emphasize the liquidity of money and the minimal risks associated with changes in its nominal value. They argue that the closest substitutes for money are assets with similar characteristics, such as the liabilities of financial intermediaries (e.g., savings and loan associations), and that it is the rates on these assets that are most relevant to the money demand function.[34]

One attempt to present direct evidence on this issue was made by Heller in 1965. In alternative money demand equations Heller compared the performance of the long-term rate of interest as measured by the rate on U.S. government bonds with that of a short-term rate, measured as the yield on 60–90-day commercial paper. Regression coefficients were estimated for equations in log-linear form using quarterly observations for the period 1947–1958. Both M-1 and M-2 were tried as dependent variables with the interest rate and current income or nonhuman wealth specified as alternative constraints. In these regressions the long-term rate of interest never appeared as a statistically important explanatory variable,[35] while the short-term rate was important in all equations but one. Consequently, Heller concluded,

> The short-term rate is of greater importance (than the long-term rate) in the money function. The closest substitute for money available, a 60 to 90 day commercial paper, is most influential in deciding whether to hold

[34]See the first section of this survey for some implications of this view.

[35]The long-term rate was never significant at the 5 percent level, and in some of the equations it appeared with the wrong sign.

assets in the form of money or not. Long-term interest rates do not influence the quantity of money demanded. . . .[36]

Results presented by Laidler (41) generally support Heller's conclusions. Laidler examines evidence derived from equations fit to annual data for the period 1892–1960 and for subperiods therein. He bases his analysis on the following proposition:

> Given that the interest rate is an important variable in the demand for money, and that movements of various interest rates are related to one another, one would expect almost any rate chosen at random to show some relationship to cash balances . . . however, though all interest rates are interrelated, there is no reason to suppose that the nature of their interrelationship remains unchanged for all time. Thus, if the demand function for money is stable, one would expect the "right" interest rate to show the same relationship to the demand for money in different time periods while the "wrong" one need not.[37]

Laidler uses the rate on 4–6 month commercial paper and the yield on 20-year bonds as his alternative interest rate measures. His equations are in log-linear form and include only permanent income as an additional explanatory variable. When his dependent variable is M-2, he claims that "there is little question of the superior explanatory power of the shorter interest rate."[38] When the dependent variable is specified as M-1 his results are somewhat contradictory. When he employs levels of the logarithms of the variables, the long-term rate explains more of the variation in M-1 for most periods than does the short rate. Nonetheless, he maintains his original conclusion that a short-term rate is the relevant rate measure in the money demand function arguing that "the contradictory conclusions obtained with the narrower definition reflect only the fact that that definition is an unsatisfactory one."[39] The basis for his conclusion on this matter is to be found in our comments on his previous work (40), reported in the first section of this survey.

The conclusions derived from this work by Heller and Laidler are challenged by Michael Hamburger. In his study of the demand for money by households Hamburger (27) concludes that long-term inter-

---

[36]H. R. Heller, "The Demand for Money—The Evidence from the Short-Run Data," *Quarterly Journal of Economics*, 79 (May 1965), 297.

[37]D. Laidler, "The Rate of Interest and the Demand for Money—Some Empirical Evidence," *Journal of Political Economy*, 74 (December 1966), 547.

[38]*Ibid.*, p. 547.

[39]*Ibid.*, p. 553.

est rates are the relevant determinants of the demand for money. Employing a model that includes distributed lags to measure the rate of adjustment of households to changed market conditions, he finds that in the household demand for money function "for short-run analysis . . . , it is useful to include two yields—one on debts and one on equities—and that the elasticities of the demand for money are approximately the same with respect to both of these rates."[40] His findings show that government bills (short-term securities) may be poorer substitutes for money for the household sector than longer-term securities. Commenting on previous work, Hamburger claims that Heller's conclusions depend on the choice of time period. During the period 1947–1951 the Federal Reserve pegged interest rates distorting more normal market relationships. When Hamburger reruns Heller's regressions excluding these years, he finds that the long-term rate and the short-term rate appear equally important.

Additional evidence has been reported by T. H. Lee (46). Lee criticizes the previous work done by the cited authors because they restrict their comparisons to only two alternative rate measures. Furthermore, he argues that the *differentials* between interest rates and the yield on money, rather than simply interest rate *levels*, are the relevant measures that should appear in money demand functions.

Like Laidler, Lee specifies a Friedman-type permanent income money demand model as the basic framework for his tests. He tries both M-1 and M-2 as dependent variables and, in addition to his alternative interest rate measures, either permanent income or permanent income and lagged money balances as explanatory variables. His regression estimates show that "the yield on nonbank intermediary liabilities is the most significant interest rate variable in affirming the demand for money." Specifically, "the yield on savings and loan shares performs the best in terms of R^2 among respective regressions of static or dynamic formulations."[41]

With the exception of Lee's work, the interest rate measure included in the other money demand functions cited was the absolute level of the rate on some asset alternative to money.[42] One implication

[40]The rates Hamburger used were Moody's Aaa rate on long-term corporate bonds and Moody's dividend yield. M. J. Hamburger, "The Demand for Money by Households. . . ." *Journal of Political Economy*, 74 (December 1966), 608.

[41]T. H. Lee, "Alternative Interest Rates and the Demand for Money: The Empirical Evidence," *American Economic Review*, 57 (December 1967), 1171.

[42]Hamburger later criticized Lee's evidence because his "findings depend critically on the use of interest rate differentials. Once this procedure is abandoned and the yield on money is introduced as a separate variable, there is little evidence that S + L

of this formulation is that the (marginal) rate of return on money is assumed to be zero. Robert S. Barro and Anthony M. Santomero (2) have argued that "at least one component of (narrowly defined) money, demand deposits, bears a form of interest which should be taken into account in determining the opportunity cost of holding money."[43] Their argument rests on the assumption that the provision of services or the remission of charges by banks in accordance with the size of a customer's deposit balance represents an effective interest return on those deposits.

To test this proposition, Barro and Santomero surveyed the largest one hundred commercial banks in the United States to determine "the rates at which they have remitted service charges as a function of demand deposit balances."[44] From the survey results an annual series measuring the imputed marginal rate of return on demand deposits was constructed for 1950–1968. This measure was then employed within the framework of a Baumol-Tobin inventory theoretic model of the demand for money by households.[45] Relating real per capita money balances, (M/PN), real per capita consumption expenditure, (Y/PN), and the differential between the rate on an alternative asset—the dividend rate on savings and loan shares—and the imputed demand deposit rate, the following estimates are derived:

$$\log \left(\frac{M}{PN} \right)_T = -3.96 + 1.044 \log \left(\frac{Y}{PN} \right)_T - 0.549 \log (r_S - r_D)_T.$$

These results support the basic hypothesis: There is a substantial interest elasticity of household money demand with respect to the rate differential $(r_s - r_D)$.

---

shares are closer substitutes for money (narrowly defined) than other assets. In addition, the demand for money appears to adjust more slowly to changes in yields on S + L shares than to changes in other rates." Hamburger, "Alternative Interest Rates . . . ," op. cit., 407.

[43]R. J. Barro and A. M. Santomero, "Household Money Holdings and the Demand Deposit Rate," Journal of Money, Credit and Banking, 4 (May 1972), 397.

[44]Ibid., p. 399.

[45]An interesting implication of their formulation of the inventory model is that the income elasticity need not be less than one. This contradicts the conventional view that inventory models are necessarily associated with economies of scale. As they argue: "The key element which is typically neglected is transactions costs. As transaction volume increases, economies of scale are realized only to the extent that transactions costs rise less than transactions volume. Since transaction costs depend largely on value of time, and since value of time may increase even faster than transactions volume, diseconomies of scale (money being a "luxury") is quite compatible with the inventory approach." Barro and Santomero, op. cit., 408.

It is important to note that the estimated interest elasticity applies solely to the rate differential. Since that differential (as measured by Barro and Santomero) has been fairly constant over the postwar period, the elasticity with respect to the level of rates may be quite small. The coefficient of real per capita expenditure indicates the expenditure elasticity of money demand is close to unity, suggesting an absence of economies of scale in household demand for money.

The highly tentative nature of these results should now be evident. While Heller and Laidler argue that the short-term rate is the relevant measure in the money demand function, this conclusion is challenged by both Hamburger and Lee. Lee's results further indicate that it may be the differential between the yield on money and the yield on the liabilities of some financial intermediary rather than a market interest rate that is the most appropriate constraint on desired money balances. But this contention is disputed by Hamburger. Barro and Santomero's results suggest the addition of some measure of the return on demand deposits to the equation. Additional work in which a serious attempt is made to make new results comparable to the results of previous investigators will be required before any firm conclusions are possible on this critical empirical issue.

Interest Elasticity and the Liquidity Trap

The evidence reviewed above clearly supports the Keynesian notion of an interest sensitive demand for money or liquidity preference function.[46] However, Keynes went further than merely to posit the interest rate as a determinant of the public's demand for money. In *The General Theory* he also speculated briefly about the shape of the liquidity preference function. Specifically, he noted,

> There is the possibility . . . , that, after the rate of interest has fallen to a certain level, liquidity preference may become virtually absolute in the sense that almost everyone prefers cash to holding a debt which yields so low a rate of interest. In this event the monetary authority would have lost effective control over the rate of interest. But while this limiting case

[46]All of the studies cited above employ data from the United States. The evidence employing data from the United Kingdom is somewhat less conclusive on this issue. See, for example, A. A. Walters, "The Radcliffe Report—Ten Years After: A Survey of Empirical Evidence," in O. R. Croome and H. G. Johnson (eds.), *Money in Britain 1959–1969* (Oxford, 1969).

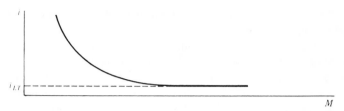

Figure 1

might become practically important in the future, I know of no examples of it hitherto.[47]

In spite of Keynes' disclaimer, his suggestion that the liquidity preference curve may become perfectly interest elastic at some low level of the interest rate attracted much attention and stimulated a substantial amount of "searching" for this phenomenon. His suggestion is responsible for the shape given the liquidity preference curve in most texts (as shown in Figure 1).

The implication of this hypothesis is that the interest elasticity of the liquidity preference function should increase as the interest rate declines. This proposition has been tested by Bronfenbrenner and Mayer (4), by Meltzer (49), by Laidler (41), by Konstas and Khouja (38) and by others.

Bronfenbrenner and Mayer, after examining the relation between the short-term interest rate and the Cambridge k, (M/Y), tested to see if the elasticity of their estimated liquidity functions increased as the interest rate fell. Specifically, they calculated the "rank" correlation coefficient between elasticities and the level of interest rates. This involves ordering the level of interest rates from highest to lowest and comparing the ordering of the elasticities associated with those rates. If the highest rate were associated with the lowest elasticity, the lowest rate with the highest elasticity, and so on for all rates in between, there would be perfect negative rank correlation between these two measures. However, Bronfenbrenner and Mayer calculate a rank correlation coefficient of $+.16$, which not only is not statistically significant, but is of the wrong sign. They concluded that "the absence of a negative correlation in a period when interest rates were at times quite low,

[47]J. M. Keynes, *The General Theory of Employment, Interest, and Money* (London and New York, 1936), 207.

casts doubt on, if not the truth, then at least the relevance of the liquidity trap proposition. . . ."[48]

Other investigators have supported these conclusions. In 1963 Allan Meltzer (49) fit velocity functions for the six decades from 1900 to 1958. As he interprets his results, "The data deny that the interest elasticity of the demand for money or velocity became exceptionally large during that decade (the 1930s). Indeed, the interest elasticity of V_1 was slightly below the average for the (entire) fifty-nine years."[49] This evidence of a lower than average interest elasticity during periods of low interest rates is consistent with Bronfenbrenner and Mayer's positive rank-correlation coefficient.

Meltzer's work with Karl Brunner (5) adds additional support to this position. Using estimates derived from data for the 1930s, they were able to predict the velocity of circulation for the 1950s with sufficiently small mean errors to conclude that the velocity function remained highly stable over these periods of differing interest rate levels. They conclude that "the liquidity trap proposition is denied by the evidence."[50]

David Laidler (41) has reported evidence from a test somewhat similar to Bronfenbrenner and Mayer's. Employing both the narrow (M1) and the broad (M2) definitions of money and testing both the long-rate and the short-rate of interest in separate regressions, Laidler divided the observations for the period 1892–1960 into two subsets: those years in which the relevant interest rate was above the mean and those in which it was below the mean. The general equation tested was

$$\ln M = a + b_1 \ln Y_p + b_2 \ln i$$

where Y_p is permanent income. Laidler's results, using both logarithms and first differences of logarithms of the variables defined above, demonstrated very little tendency for the interest elasticity (b_2) to be higher (in absolute value) for the low interest rate observations than it was in the equations fitted to the high interest rate observations. As he notes, "the elasticity with respect to the short rate seems to fall a

---

[48]M. Bronfenbrenner and T. Mayer, "Liquidity Functions in the American Economy," *Econometrica*, 28 (October 1960), 831.

[49]For the purpose of these tests, Meltzer defines income as the return on wealth, i.e., the interest rate or rate of return, r, times the wealth stock, W. The wealth measure used to calculate income in this formula is net nonhuman wealth of the public—the same variable employed in his money demand functions. The measure of money he employs is narrow money ($DD + C$). Meltzer, *op. cit.*, 243.

[50]Brunner and Meltzer, *op. cit.*, 350.

little at low rates of interest, though the elasticity with respect to the long rate rises slightly at low interest rates. . . . Thus, the hypothesis of the liquidity trap, as it is usually presented, appears to be refuted."[51]

An interesting article by Konstas and Khouja reports on statistical tests relevant to this issue. In their study the authors attempt to specify a functional form for the demand for money relation which accurately portrays the characteristics originally suggested by Keynes. In their model,

> In regard to the speculative part of the demand for money. . . . the function which is consistent with Keynesian requirements must be stated in the following manner:

$$M - 2 = \frac{\beta}{r - \alpha} \; ; \beta > 0, \, \alpha > 0.[52]$$

This formulation quite accurately reflects the properties of the function shown in Figure 1. It allows for a minimum interest rate level, α, and for increasing interest elasticity of money balances as interest rates decline toward α. The authors estimate the parameters of this model using annual observations for the period 1919–1965. In general, the data seem to fit this relationship rather closely.

Konstas and Khouja use their estimated relation to examine the claim that the United States economy was in a liquidity trap in the 1930s. Specifically, they calculate an estimate of the speculative component of total money balances by subtracting estimated transactions balances from (actual) total money balances for each of the years 1919–1965. The pattern indicated in the relation between the long-term interest rate and calculated idle balances fails to confirm the claim that monetary policy was impotent in the 1930's because of the very high interest elasticity of the demand for money. They conclude that their test "does not seem to offer much evidence in support of this claim."[53] These results add to the weight of the evidence reported above.

[51]Laidler, "The Rate of Interest. . .", *op. cit.*, 550.

[52]Konstas and Khouja, *op. cit.*, 767. For another study that claims to formulate and test Keynes' original liquidity preference hypothesis more accurately than is done in some of the literature cited above, see D. R. Starleaf and R. Reimer, "The Keynesian Demand Function for Money: Some Statistical Tests." *Journal of Finance*, 22 (March 1967), 71–76. Their work relates primarily to the Keynesian proposition that it is not necessarily the absolute level of the rate of interest that is important in determining the demand for money but the relationship of that current rate to a conceptual "normal" rate. Starleaf and Reimer found no evidence to suggest that the normal rate, as they calculated it, was an important variable in the demand for money.

[53]Konstas and Khouja, *op. cit.*, 774.

Most of the individual tests cited in this section approach the question of the liquidity trap indirectly. Furthermore, some of the results of Laidler's tests with the long-term rate of interest could be taken as very weak support for the existence of the low level trap. However, the weight of all these studies together seems sufficient to allow a rather firm judgment against the historical existence of the liquidity trap. In addition, work by Brunner and Meltzer has shown that the necessary and sufficient conditions for the occurrence of a liquidity trap in the demand function for money are extremely restrictive.[54] Consequently, the conclusion on the absence of a liquidity trap would seem warranted by the lack of any falsifying evidence.

An Alternative View: Interest Rates, Permanent Income and Variations in Velocity

One implication of the work surveyed above is that cyclical variations in interest rates are important determinants of the evident cyclical variations in the demand for money and the velocity of circulation of money. This view has been disputed by at least one important analyst, Milton Friedman. Although in his "Restatement" of the quantity theory of money Friedman develops a theoretical money demand function that includes several interest rate terms as explanatory variables, his statistical work leads him to question the empirical significance of the interest rate in determining actual money holdings.

Friedman's empirical work begins with an observation on the behavior of the income velocity of money. He notes that from 1870 to 1954, over long periods of time, the income velocity of circulation (Y/M) moved in a direction opposite to that of real income, but over shorter periods of time, during business cycles, these variables moved in the same direction.[55] He attempts to reconcile these observations by explaining the public's behavior regarding the demand for real money balances.

Friedman argues that the *nominal* stock of money in the economy is determined in the first instance on the supply side of the market by

[54]K. Brunner and A. H. Meltzer, "Liquidity Traps for Money, Bank Credit, and Interest Rates," *Journal of Political Economy*, 76 (February 1968), 1–37.

[55]The inverse long-term relation between income and velocity implies more than simply a direct relation between income and money. It implies that as income increases, money increases more than proportionately, so that money may be viewed as a "luxury" good. This long-term relationship has not prevailed in the postwar period, however, as velocity has trended upward rather strongly.

the monetary authorities and that "holders of money cannot alter this amount directly." In contrast, however, the holders of money "can make the *real* amount of money anything in the aggregate they want to."[56] For, if individuals find themselves holding too large a stock of nominal money balances, their attempt to decrease these balances by increasing expenditures will reduce the real quantity of money to the desired level by raising money income and prices. Conversely, lowering expenditures to increase money holdings will lower money income and prices, thereby raising the real quantity of money to the desired equilibrium level.

This analysis suggests that since the *nominal* stock of money is predetermined by the monetary authorities, an explanation of the observed behavior of the *real* volume of money balances and the income velocity of money requires an examination of the demand for money.[57] It may be possible to explain the patterns exhibited by velocity through an analysis of the historical behavior of the explanatory variables that enter a stable demand for money function. However, Friedman's attempt to find variables in addition to income that enter the money demand function and that "exert an influence opposite to that of income... sufficiently potent to dominate the [cyclical] movement of velocity"[58] is unsuccessful. As he reports,

> ... the other variables that come first to mind are interest rates, and these display cyclical patterns that seem most unlikely to account for the sizable, highly consistent, and roughly synchronous cyclical pattern in velocity.[59]

As an alternative approach, suggested by his work on the consumption function, Friedman employs the concept of permanent income in the money demand function to reconcile the cyclical and secular behavior of velocity. This attempt starts by viewing "the statistical magnitude called 'real income' as corresponding to a different theoretical construct in the cyclical than in the secular analysis."[60] This reconciliation de-

---

[56]M. Friedman, "The Demand for Money...," *op. cit.*, 330.

[57]Following Fisher in employing the equation of exchange, Friedman often couches his analytical discussion in terms of the velocity of circulation of money rather than the demand function for money balances. But since $V = (Y/M)$, an increase in the demand for nominal balances relative to nominal income will be reflected in a decrease in the income velocity of circulation of money and, conversely, a decrease in the demand for money will be reflected as an increase in velocity.

[58]Friedman, "The Demand for Money...," *op. cit.*, 332.

[59]*Ibid.*

[60]*Ibid.*

pends on the relation between measured and permanent income. If permanent income rises less than measured income during cyclical expansions and falls less than measured income in contractions, and if money balances are adapted to permanent income, "they might rise and fall more than in proportion to permanent income, as is required by our secular results, yet less than in proportion to measured income, as is required by our cyclical results."[61]

On the basis of this theoretical reconciliation of the conflicting behavior of observed velocity, Friedman turns to an empirical examination of this phenomenon. As he notes, "An interpretation in terms of interest rates can also rationalize the qualitative results; [but] we reject it because it appears likely to be contradicted on a more detailed quantitative level."[62]

In his empirical tests Friedman measures both money balances and permanent income in real (i.e., deflated) per capita form and specifies the following exponential money demand function:

$$\frac{M}{NP} = \alpha \left(\frac{Y_p}{NP} \right)^{\delta}$$

or, in logarithmic form,

$$\ln \frac{M}{NP} = \ln \alpha + \delta \ln \left(\frac{Y_p}{NP} \right) \tag{15}$$

where P is an index of (permanent) prices, N is population, and Y_p is permanent income.[63]

Friedman fits this function to cycle-average data for the period 1869–1957. His estimate of δ, the permanent income elasticity of real money balances, is 1.8. Using this relationship, he calculates annual within-cycle projections of the velocity of circulation of money and finds that his formulation predicts actual velocity figures fairly well. Most importantly, however, he also finds that *the errors that are evident in these predictions are almost completely unrelated to the level of interest rates.* Thus, he concludes that there is little role for the interest

[61]*Ibid.*, p. 334.
[62]*Ibid.*, p. 335.
[63]Friedman originally derived his permanent income concept in connection with his studies on the consumption function. Permanent income is calculated as a weighted average of past income levels with the weights attached to the income levels of the more distant past declining geometrically. See M. Friedman, *A Theory of the Consumption Function* (Princeton, N.J., 1957), 142–147.

rate, in addition to permanent income, in explaining variations in the velocity of circulation of money or the variation in money balances.[64]

Friedman achieves these results by using some statistical techniques not generally used by other investigators. His use of cycle-average data,[65] for example, contrasts with the more common practice of using chronologically determined, annual or quarterly data in regression studies. Also, his use of the broad definition of money is claimed by many to bias his results against finding any role for the interest rate in the determination of money demand.[66] This latter contention may be explained as follows: if demand deposit balances are negatively related to interest rates, but time deposits are positively related to the rate paid on such deposits, a general increase in interest rates will decrease the demand for demand deposits and increase the demand for time deposits. If these two assets are added together in a single measure, these movements will tend to cancel out and the sum, $DD + TD$, may appear to be completely interest-insensitive.

In addition, Laidler (41) has pointed out that over the period covered by Friedman's study there was a slight downward trend in interest rates and that by omitting an interest rate term from his regression equation some of the (trend) influence of the interest rate on money balances was attributed to the trend in the permanent income

[64]Friedman's conclusion would seem to be supported for the postwar period in evidence presented by Sam Peltzman. Challenging the conventional conclusion, Peltzman argues that his "results do imply strongly that interest rate movements cannot explain the postwar rise in velocity" (p. 134). In Peltzman's work this increase is associated with a secular trend in (unspecified) factors other than income and interest rates. See S. Peltzman, "The Structure of the Money-Expenditure Relationship," *American Economic Review*, 59 (March 1969), 129–137. For a critique of Peltzman's methodology, see D. M. Jaffee, "The Structure of the Money Expenditure Relationship: Comment," *American Economic Review*, 60 (March 1970), 216–219. In view of the serious econometric problems that arise in interpreting Peltzman's use of second differences and Jaffee's use of first differences, the uncertainty surrounding Peltzman's assumption about the public's behavior as regards the formulation of expectations about changes in the money stock, and the fact that Jaffee found some role for the interest rate in Peltzman's "reformulated" model, the overwhelming evidence on this issue from other sources would seem to stand.

[65]An annual time series of observations on a given variable, X, represents a list of values for that variable for each year over a specified period of time. Cycle-average data on the other hand rely not on calendar years to generate observations, but rather on the cyclical swings in economic activity as defined by the National Bureau of Economic Research. Those who use cycle-average data argue that such a choice of values is economically more meaningful than the arbitrary designation of the calendar (or fiscal) year as the standard measure of time used to generate statistical data.

[66]See the discussion of this problem in connection with some results reported by Goldfeld (25).

variable. Since the decline in rates over this period would be expected to cause a relative increase in money balances, the absence of an interest rate term in the equation may help to explain the rather high (1.8) income elasticity estimated in Friedman's tests.

Friedman's results have been even more seriously challenged in the work of other analysts. Several of the studies reported in Table 1 include interest rates along with Friedman's measure of permanent income in log linear money demand functions. For example, Meltzer (49) showed that the long-term rate of interest generally appears as a highly significant variable in his regressions. He suggests that Friedman's use of the permanent income measure combines the influence of income, wealth, and interest rates into a single measure and obscures the separate impact of each on money demand. In addition to demonstrating the significant role of the interest rate when explicitly included in the function, Meltzer derives an estimate of the (permanent) income elasticity that is closer to unity than to Friedman's estimate of 1.8. This would appear to confirm Laidler's contention mentioned above.

Other works by Brunner and Meltzer (5) and by Chow (11) confirm the important role of the interest rate in alternative money demand or velocity functions. However, one important point with respect to these studies must be mentioned in defense of Friedman. These studies employ annual time series data, and these data are not strictly comparable to Friedman's (perhaps more subtle) cycle-average data. Consequently, their results do not represent a satisfactory refutation of his findings. However, Laidler (41), employing cycle-average data for the period 1891–1957, refitted Friedman's original equation and compared the results with those obtained when an interest rate term was included in the equation. His results are as follows:

$$\log \frac{M}{NP} = -2.017 + 1.618 \log \left(\frac{Y_p}{NP} \right)$$

$$\log \frac{M}{NP} = -1.403 + 1.430 \log \left(\frac{Y_p}{NP} \right) - 0.158 \log i_e$$

where i_e is the rate on 4–6-month commercial paper.

Laidler used these estimates to predict annual levels of per capita real money balances—a procedure very similar to Friedman's use of his equation to predict annual within-cycle values for the velocity of circulation of money. The mean error of prediction[67] for the equation that includes the interest rate is less than half that for the equation that contains only permanent income. Since the interest rate equation explains the data significantly better than Friedman's original equation, Laidler concludes that "the difference in the intercept and coefficient of the logarithm of permanent income that results from the omission of the interest rate is sufficient to produce misleading results (about the relation between prediction errors and the level of the rate of interest)." It appears that there was indeed "some secular (long-term) correlation between permanent income and [the] interest rate which caused permanent income to pick up part of the effect of interest rates in the regression from which the latter variable was omitted."[68]

As Laidler points out, then, the evidence coming from so many different sources is so persuasive that "it is probably safe to conclude that the rate of interest must be included in the demand function for money."[69] Friedman's results may be attributed in large part to his rather special statistical techniques.

The Scale Factor in Money Demand Functions: Current Income, Permanent Income, or Wealth

The results surveyed above suggest that the performance of any given interest rate measure in an empirical money demand function depends both on the way in which the dependent variable is defined and on the choice of other explanatory variables included in the equation. As already indicated, the other factors most commonly specified as determinants of the demand for money are income and wealth. The use of income—or some other measure of the volume of transactions—as a constraint on the level of money demand is generally related to the role of money as a medium of exchange. This is stated explicitly in Keynesian demand function, $M_d = L_1(Y) + L_2(i)$, in the Cambridge equation, $M = k \cdot Y$, and in the inventory theoretic model of money demand, $M_d = 1/2 \sqrt{2bT/i}$, where Y is the level of income and T is a measure of the volume of transactions.

---

[67]The mean error of prediction is the arithmetic average of the absolute value of the difference between the actual and predicted values of a given variable for all points for which a prediction is obtained.

[68]D. Laidler, "The Rate of Interest . . . ," *op. cit.*, 546.

[69]*Ibid.*

On the other hand, when the role of money as a productive asset or a durable consumer good is stressed, a wealth measure is generally proposed as the relevant explanatory variable in the demand for money function. Attention is focused on "the equilibrium of the balance sheet, the allocation of assets, and the services that money provides." In this view "effecting a volume of transactions is but one of these services."[70]

In statistical work three measures have most frequently been employed as empirical counterparts to these theoretical constraints: current income, proposed as a proxy for the volume of transactions to be effected by the money stock; nonhuman wealth, measured as consolidated net worth in the balance sheet of the public; and Friedman's "permanent income," proposed as a proxy for a wealth concept that includes the present value of future labor income as well as the value of real physical assets. This last measure includes the value of both human and nonhuman wealth.[71]

Meltzer (49) tests all three of these variables in log-linear equations that specify both M-1 and M-2 as dependent variables and which include the yield on corporate bonds as the measure of the interest rate. Meltzer's basic model proposes nonhuman wealth (W) as the relevant constraint on money demand. He finds the elasticity of "narrow" money (M-1) with respect to this measure of wealth to be close to unity. This contrasts with Friedman's finding (reported above) of an elasticity of "broad" money balances with respect to permanent income ("total" wealth) of 1.8.

Meltzer attempts to reconcile these results. His findings, which are confirmed by those of Laidler, suggest that Friedman's use of "broad" money as the dependent variable in his equation and the absence of an interest rate term from that equation are responsible for his very high estimate of this parameter. Meltzer contends that it is time deposits which are highly elastic with respect to wealth and that by including these deposits in his measure of "money" Friedman has overstated the wealth elasticity of money defined as $(DD + C)$. More importantly, Meltzer claims that his measure of nonhuman wealth pro-

---

[70]Meltzer, op. cit., 232.

[71]Permanent income may be interpreted as "reflecting the effect of those factors that the unit regards as determining its capital value or wealth: the nonhuman wealth it owns; the personal attributes of the earners in the unit, such as their training, ability, personality; the attributes of the economic activity of the earners, such as the occupation followed, the location of the economic activity, and so on. It is analogous to the "expected" value of a probability distribution." M. Friedman, A Theory of the Consumption Function, op. cit., 21.

duces an empirical money demand function which explains a slightly higher proportion of the variance of money balances defined either as M-1 or M-2 than does Friedman's permanent income measure.[72]

Meltzer also finds his wealth measure "superior" to current income in the empirical demand for money function; for when both wealth and income are included in the equation, the income variable appears to play no significant role in explaining the variation in money balances, whereas the wealth variable maintains approximately the same size coefficient (and significance) in all tests. Thus, Meltzer concludes that a nonhuman wealth measure is slightly superior to Friedman's permanent income variable and far more important than current, measured income in explaining variations in the demand for money.

These results are supported in further tests carried out by Brunner and Meltzer (5). Their experiments involved comparisons of the predictions of measured velocity made from various formulations of the money demand function. In their words,

> ... the tests sharply discriminate between the effects of income and wealth on the demand for money.... income appears to play a much smaller role than wealth as a determinant of desired money balances. The evidence from a number of Keynesian-type equations that take income as a constraint and ignore the effect of wealth suggests that, in general, such equations will not predict velocity or desired money balances as well as a "naive" model.[73]

Their tests on human versus nonhuman wealth measures as explanatory variables in the money demand function yield less certain results. They conclude that the relative importance of these two measures remains an "open question" in their work.

Further evidence has been put forward by Heller (30), Laidler (40), Chow (11), and Goldfeld (24). Employing quarterly data for the postwar period, Heller calculates regression coefficients for six alternative relations. Both M-1 and M-2 are specified as dependent variables

---

[72]Meltzer's basic "wealth" definition includes "total wealth" as estimated by Goldsmith, adjusted to exclude government securities, inventories, public land, and the monetary gold and silver stock and to include the monetary and nonmonetary debt of state, local, and federal governments. R. W. Goldsmith, *A Study of Savings in the United States* (Princeton, N.J., 1956).

[73]Brunner and Meltzer, *op. cit.*, 350. The "naive" model referred to by the authors is a model that assumes that velocity in any one year will be the same as actual velocity in the previous period.

in equations that include income and the short-term rate of interest, wealth and the short-term rate, or both income and wealth and the short-term rate as explanatory variables. The coefficients of both GNP and wealth are statistically significant in all equations in which only one of these variables appears with the short-term interest rate. However, when both of these constraints are included in the same equation, only one of them retains its significance: GNP in the M-1 equation and wealth in the M-2 equation.

Heller attributes this result to the fact that time deposits (included in the M-2 measure) are related positively to wealth and negatively to income. A negative income coefficient results when time deposits are regressed against both income and wealth in a single equation. This indicates a substitution effect between time deposits and demand deposits: i.e., with wealth constant an increase in GNP will cause a fall in the volume of time deposits and a rise in the quantity of currency and demand deposits. Heller interprets this evidence as showing that time deposits and demand deposits are demanded for different reasons: "the transactions motives for cash and demand deposits and the speculative or precautionary motive for time deposits."[74]

The results of tests such as those conducted by Heller appear to be quite sensitive to the quarterly time frame in which the data are measured. Sharply contrasting results are derived from annual data. For example, Laidler set out to compare the explanatory power of four alternative money demand hypotheses. These include (1) the textbook equation with current income and an interest rate as constraints, (2) a Friedman-type permanent income formulation, (3) a model that includes permanent income as a proxy for the volume of transactions and a measure of accumulated transitory income and negative transitory consumption to account for the allocation of funds from these sources to money balances, and (4) a model that includes the last factor specified above and a nonhuman wealth measure defined as accumulated savings out of permanent income.

Implicit in Laidler's tests of these hypotheses is a comparison of the explanatory power of current income, permanent income, and his indirect measure of nonhuman wealth (accumulated savings out of Y_p) as explanatory variables in the money demand function. From his regressions, which employ first differences of annual observations, Laidler finds that "though the results are not absolutely decisive, they strongly suggest that permanent income provides a better theory of the

[74]Heller, op. cit., 300.

demand for money than does either nonhuman wealth or any other set of variables tested."[75]

Laidler's third hypothesis, which includes a measure of transitory income in the money demand equation, performs the least satisfactorily over the period covered by his data. Although both the nonhuman wealth (4) and the permanent income (2) hypotheses explain the variation in the dependent variable quite satisfactorily, Laidler judges the results with permanent income to be marginally superior. More importantly, both wealth and permanent income explain more of the variation in the dependent variable than does current income (1) hypothesis. Furthermore, this last finding obtains regardless of the definition of money employed. Thus, using annual data rather than quarterly figures, Laidler challenges Heller's assertion that current income is the relevant constraint on narrow money balances.

An interesting set of experiments performed by Gregory Chow may shed some light on the apparent inconsistencies in these results. Chow attempts to isolate two different sets of factors influencing money holdings: those that determine the long-run equilibrium demand for money and those that influence the rate at which people will make short-run adjustments to restore equilibrium. These adjustments take place when a discrepancy exists between the long-run desired level of money balances and actual money holdings.

Chow reasons that money may be treated as a consumer durable good. He applies to the analysis of the demand for money a model originally developed to explain the demand for automobiles. In this model the long-run demand for money is posited to depend on some measure of the individual's total assets (a wealth measure) and the opportunity cost of holding those balances, the interest rate. The short-run demand for money, however, will depend on the rate at which individuals try to adjust their actual money balances to this long-run desired level. This speed of adjustment in turn depends on the actual size of any discrepancy between actual and desired balances and the rate of change of the individual's total assets (or the rate of savings)—the source from which money balances may be accumulated. Chow summarizes these factors as follows:

> Three sets of factors govern the demand for money. The first set is derived from considering the demand for services from holding money in the long-run. The second is due to time lags in the adjustment of demand

---

[75]D. Laidler, "Some Evidence on the Demand for Money," *Journal of Political Economy*, 74 (February 1966), 63.

to equilibrium. The third is from treating the change in the money stock as a part of saving.[76]

This model reflects both the expectational factors and partial adjustment mechanism described in the second section of this survey.

Like Laidler, Chow tests his hypothesis on annual data. The period covered is 1897–1958. In the long-run equilibrium demand function permanent income always performs far better than current income but, as in Laidler's work, only marginally better than a wealth measure.[77] However, in the short-run functions that attempt to measure the speed of adjustment to equilibrium current income is preferable to either wealth or permanent income.

A word of caution is in order in interpreting these estimates. The use of permanent income as the constraint variable determining the long-run desired level of money balances muddies the results. Permanent income is calculated as a weighted average of past levels of measured income. Consequently, the long-run demand for money function that employs this variable may be written as follows (ignoring interest rates):

$$\left(\frac{M_d}{P} \right)_T = f(Y_p) = b(Y_p)_T = b[\beta_0\, Y_T + \beta_1\, Y_{T-1} \ldots \beta_n\, Y_{T-n}].$$

Assuming the weights, β_i, follow a geometrically declining lag function (following Friedman), we may write

$$\left(\frac{M_d}{P} \right)_T = b[\beta_0\, Y_T + \beta_0\, (1 - \beta_0)\, Y_{T-1}$$
$$+ \beta_0\, (1 - \beta_0)^2\, Y_{T-2} \ldots \beta_0\, (1 - \beta_0)^n\, Y_{T-n}).$$

But if $(1 - \beta_0)^j \to 0$ as $j \to n$, by a Koyck transformation,[78] this can be shown equivalent to

$$\left(\frac{M_d}{P} \right)_T = (1 - \beta_0) \left(\frac{M_d}{P} \right)_{T-1} + b\beta_0 Y_T. \tag{16}$$

---

[76]Gregory Chow, "On the Short-Run and Long-Run Demand for Money," *Journal of Political Economy*, 74 (April 1966), 115.

[77]Chow uses the same measure of net nonhuman wealth as was employed by Meltzer.

[78]The third section of this article explains the Koyck transformation. See also R. J. Wonnacott and T. H. Wonnacott, *Econometrics* (New York; 1970), 145–146.

On the other hand, if the public only partially adjusts its current money holdings to the long-run desired level and this desired level depends on *current measured income*, the following may be specified to describe this behavior:

$$\left(\frac{M}{P}\right)_T - \left(\frac{M}{P}\right)_{T-1} = \lambda \left(\frac{M}{P}\right) - \left(\frac{M}{P}\right)_{T-1}$$

where $(M/P)_i^*$ is the desired level of money balances and

$$\left(\frac{M}{P}\right)_{T^*} = a\, Y_r$$

Substituting:

$$\left(\frac{M}{P}\right)_T - \left(\frac{M}{P}\right)_{T-1} = \lambda \left[a\, Y_T - \left(\frac{M}{P}\right)_{T-1} \right]$$

$$\left(\frac{M}{P}\right)_T = (1 - \lambda) \left(\frac{M}{P}\right)_{T-1} + \lambda a\, Y_T. \tag{17}$$

But this form (17), derived from a partial adjustment model in which desired money balances depend on current measured income, is indistinguishable from equation (16), which postulates that the demand for money depends on permanent income.

These relationships make unique interpretation of Chow's results impossible. They suggest that in his short-run adjustment relation, from which he concludes that current income is the appropriate explanatory variable in the demand for money function, he may simply have been measuring an equilibrium relation between desired money balances and permanent income. In short, this test is not sufficient to distinguish between a permanent income hypothesis and the hypothesis that the demand for money balances depends on current measured income but that the public is slow to adjust to its long-run desired level.

However, if there is any validity to Chow's results, they suggest a possible reconciliation of the conflict between those obtained by Heller using quarterly data and those presented by Laidler based on annual data. Heller's method may have picked up the influence of short-run adjustment factors which dominate the quarterly figures, but are less important in the longer-run annual observations.

Additional evidence using quarterly data is presented by Goldfeld (25). Within the framework of his basic log-linear model—which includes a lagged dependent variable (derived from a partial adjustment hypothesis) and both the commercial paper rate and the rate on bank time deposits—he compares the relative power of income, net worth, and changes in net worth in explaining holdings of narrow money. His results show that the absence of an income variable reduces the estimated speed of adjustment to an unreasonably low figure. When income and wealth are both included, the latter is insignificant while the former remains important. When the change in wealth is added as a third constraint, "the level effect of net worth is obliterated."[79]

The comparative predictive ability of Goldfeld's wealth equation in dynamic simulations is far inferior to that of his original income-only equation. In addition, though the inclusion of the change in net worth variable "improves the explanatory power of the equation, [it] slightly worsens its predictive ability."[80]

In summary, the bulk of the evidence available from studies employing annual data indicates rather clearly that some measure of wealth rather than measured income is the most relevant constraint on the equilibrium level of the demand for money balances. Whether this constraint is best represented by a permanent income measure that purports to include a human wealth component or by a nonhuman wealth measure, such as those employed by Chow or Meltzer, is much less apparent. At the same time, other evidence certainly suggests that current income may be related to the demand for money through short-run adjustments made to bring *actual* money balances in line with *desired* money holdings. Unfortunately, measurement difficulties with quarterly wealth data make the results of tests employing these measures difficult to interpret. However, this in turn suggests that for pragmatic policy purposes one may wish to choose that variable that performs best when the criteria chosen is predictive and forecasting accuracy. On these grounds, current income, as suggested by Goldfeld's results, is probably the most useful scale factor to employ in short-run money demand functions.

The Stability of the Money Demand Function

Harry Johnson, in his 1962 survey of monetary theory (32), listed three unsettled issues related to the demand for money. These issues included

[79]Goldfeld, *op. cit.*, 614.
[80]*Ibid.*, 615.

the appropriate empirical definition of the money stock, the choice of arguments to be included in the money demand function, and the stability of the empirical relationship between those arguments and the monetary aggregate. These are not, of course, separable issues. The stability of any empirical function will depend upon the variables included in that function. Likewise, the criteria for choosing the appropriate definition of the money stock has most often been defined in terms of the stability of the demand function for that monetary measure. However, for heuristic purposes, we have attempted to separate these issues in the empirical literature. It is hoped that by this point in the survey the major areas of agreement and of continuing contention on the first two issues have become evident.

It should be clear, however, that there has been an underlying assumption throughout this discussion that we were in fact dealing with stable relationships. While the diversity of functional forms and data periods employed by the various authors cited has made more difficult the task of reconciling divergent results, the similarity of elasticity estimates over these wide ranging studies would seem to support the essential validity of this assumption. It is worthwhile, however, briefly to consider this stability issue more explicitly.

One serious attack on the apparent stability of postwar money demand functions was presented by William Poole (54). Employing a log-linear money demand function similar to equation (3) above, Poole estimated interest elasticities of real money balances by constraining the values of the income elasticities within a range .5 to 3.0. Employing quarterly data for 1947–1969, his results demonstrate a *direct* relation between the constrained income elasticity and the estimated interest elasticity. More importantly, he finds that "the goodness of fit is practically unchanged over an extremely wide range of income elasticities," implying that there is insufficient information in the statistics to permit a choice among these results. On this evidence he makes the very strong assertion that "using postwar data alone, it is impossible to obtain a satisfactory estimate of the demand for money function."[81]

Goldfeld (24) has taken up this issue and persuasively countered Poole's critique. Employing an equation similar to the one specified by Poole but including a lagged dependent variable, he finds that "the

[81]W. Poole, "Whither Money Demand?" *Brookings Papers on Economic Activity* (3: 1970), 489. Poole's final conclusion is not that we must give up on money demand functions, but rather that since postwar data are unreliable, additional weight must be given to long-run estimates.

interest elasticities display a clear tendency to increase with [the constrained income elasticity] but the rise is not nearly as pronounced as Poole found."[82] While Goldfeld also finds uniformly high R^2's for the various forms of the equations, he claims that this is misleading and convincingly demonstrates this by additional testing on these equations.

Though the R^2's are uniformly high for all equations, they tend to rise slightly with the constrained value of the income elasticity. However, this statistic is not strictly comparable across equations and cannot be used alone as a selection criterion. Goldfeld demonstrates this by constraining the income elasticity to the value first derived in an unconstrained form of the same equation. The constrained form reproduces the results of the unconstrained form except for the R^2, indicating the noncomparability of the R^2's resulting from the use of different dependent variables.[83]

However, there may still be a statistical means by which to choose among these equations. Goldfeld first examines the standard error of the regression and finds it lowest, as it must be, for the value derived from the unconstrained form. He then evaluates the equations by examining the root mean-square error derived from two different types of dynamic simulations on the estimated equations. As he notes, this is a more stringent test of the estimation results and is likely to be more relevant from a forecasting point of view. His results show clearly that the root mean-square errors deteriorate even more rapidly than the standard error of the regression as elasticity values diverge further from the value estimated in the unconstrained equation. He concludes, then, that Poole's rejection of estimates derived from postwar data is unwarranted and that the "income elasticity can be pinned down within a reasonable range of accuracy."[84] The estimate that he derives is .68, significantly less than unity and consistent with the proposition that there are economics of scale in holding money balances.

Additional dynamic simulations on his basic equation convince Goldfeld that the relationship underlying his empirical estimates has remained rather stable in the postwar period. Both short-term (out of sample) forecasts four quarters ahead of various defined subsamples of

---

[82]Goldfeld, *op. cit.*, 585.
[83]The dependent variable is $(ln\ M_T - e\ /n\ Y_T)$ where e is the constrained income elasticity. This variable will differ, of course, for each assumed value of the elasticity constant.
[84]Goldfeld, *op. cit.*, 589.

the data period and longer-term simulations over a later part of the sample period based on estimates for an earlier subperiod, suggest reasonable stability. A formal Chow test of stability, carried out by splitting the data sample into two subperiods suggested by the major institutional change brought about by the introduction of certificates of deposits (CDs) in 1961, also fails to deliver evidence upon which to reject the hypothesis of stability.[85]

The evidence on the postwar stability of the money demand relation generally conforms to the results of work that has examined the issue over longer periods with annual data. The work by Brunner and Meltzer (9), Meltzer (49), Laidler (44), and other authors cited directly supports this long-run stability. Recent work by Moshin S. Khan, using a new and more flexible technique to determine whether a regression estimate is stable over a full sample period, adds to the weight of evidence in favor of this conclusion. Using either current income or permanent income along with a long-term rate of interest, his tests over the period 1901–1965 fail to offer any support for the hypothesis that there were significant structural shifts in the money demand relations over that period.[86]

One final piece of evidence is worth citing on this issue. In 1971, both within and outside of the Federal Reserve, it was fairly widely held that, regardless of the historical stability of the money demand function, a substantial shift had occurred in the early part of that year. Even the Council of Economic Advisers in the *Economic Report to the President* in 1972 expressed this view: "In the first half of 1971, the public apparently wanted to hold more money balances at the prevailing level of interest rates and income than past relations among income, interest rates, and money balances suggested."[87]

Hamburger (29) has examined this view in the light of more recent evidence. Fortunately for the conclusions reached in the studies cited

[85]For an alternative view of the effect of the creation of the CD market see M. B. Slovin and M. E. Sushka, "*A Financial Market Approach to the Demand for Money and the Implications for Monetary Policy*," Board of Governors of the Federal Reserve System (1972), manuscript.

[86]Kahn's tests with the short-term rate suggest some instability in the relationship around 1948. This instability appears whether money is defined narrowly or broadly. In this respect Kahn's results conflict with Laidler's conclusion that the most stable demand function is one that includes the short-term rate as an explanatory variable. See M. S. Khan, "The Stability of the Demand for Money Function in the United States, 1901–1965," International Monetary Fund (July 1974).

[87]Council of Economic Advisers, *Economic Report to the President* (January 1972), 58.

above, but unfortunately for our judgment on the ability of monetary economists to recognize short-run fluctuations in money demand, this recent evidence fails to confirm the instability widely assumed over that period.

In the second quarter of 1971 in the face of an increase in interest rates and a decline in the rate of growth of income, contrary to what conventional theory would predict, there was a sharp *increase* in the growth of the narrow money stock. But there is a certain weakness in conventional theory in its simplest form in that it fails to consider delayed reactions ("adjustments") to previous income and interest rate changes. Hamburger suggests that within the framework of the FRB–MIT–Penn Model, once allowance is made for such lagged adjustments even "the evidence that was available in 1971 provided only marginal support for the hypothesis that there was an upward shift in the demand for money" at that time.[88] On the basis of results obtained with more recent versions of the model that incorporate the influence of inflation on money demand, even that marginal support disappears. Perhaps more disturbing, equations developed since that time to explain month-to-month changes in M-1 have no difficulty "explaining the rapid growth of M-1 during the second quarter of 1971 *with relationships derived from earlier periods*" (emphasis added).[89]

This episode is reviewed here to point out a continuing dilemma facing policy makers. While it can be shown that the existence of a stable demand for money function is necessary for the conduct of effective monetary policy and while it is widely accepted, on the basis of the evidence surveyed here, that this condition has been met over a long period in the United States, it is another matter entirely for policy makers and their advisers "to make reasonably accurate on-the-spot judgments as to whether changes in the demand for money are occurring at particular points in time."[90] At this point the science of the economist becomes partner to the artistry of the policy maker.

Concluding Comment

The first and most important result of this survey is that the evidence supporting the existence of a reasonably stable demand for money function would seem to be overwhelming. This is true both of long-

---

[88]M. J. Hamburger, "The Demand for Money in 1971 . . . ," *op. cit.*, 721.
[89]*Ibid.*, 723.
[90]*Ibid.*, 724.

term evidence covering the last seventy years or so and of the evidence from the postwar period. Second, and perhaps next in importance for the conduct of monetary policy, the vast majority of this same evidence supports the hypothesis that the interest rate plays a significant role in the determination of the public's desired money holdings. Furthermore, the range of estimates for the interest elasticity of money balances has been fairly narrowly circumscribed, with the best results suggesting an elasticity of about −.2 for the short rate and approximately −.7 for the long rate. Unfortunately, it is not yet possible to state confidently which particular interest rate measure yields the most stable money demand relationship. Moreover, this question is so intimately connected with the problem of the "correct" definition of money that judgment must be suspended on this issue pending additional work, including work on the term structure of interest rates.

Third, there appears to be almost no support for the liquidity-trap hypothesis.

Finally, the best evidence to date suggests that, in addition to an interest rate measure, some measure of wealth—either a direct balance sheet measure or a proxy variable such as permanent income—would seem to be most relevant to the public's long-run decision to hold money balances. However, there is a growing body of evidence that short-run movements in money balances, determined by the speed at which people adjust their actual money holdings to a long-run equilibrium level, may be dependent upon the flow of income in this period and in the recent past.

These conclusions rest primarily on the evidence cited in this study. Other important works, many of which are included in the References, could also have been used to support some of these conclusions. The studies reviewed were selected because of their historical importance in the debate on the issues to which we have directed our attention or because they represent the best starting point for students of these problems. In short, no claim is made that this survey, in spite of its length, represents an exhaustive review of all of the literature in this field.

REFERENCES

1. BARRO, ROBERT J., "Inflation, the Payments Period, and the Demand for Money," *Journal of Political Economy*, 78 (November/December 1970), 1228–1263.

2. _____, and ANTHONY M. SANTOMERO, "Household Money Holdings and the Demand Deposit Rate," *Journal of Money, Credit, and Banking*, 4 (May 1972), 397–413.

3. BAUMOL, W., "The Transactions Demand for Cash: An Inventory Theoretic Approach," *Quarterly Journal of Economics*, 66 (November 1952), 545–556.

4. BRONFENBRENNER, MARTIN, and THOMAS MAYER, "Liquidity Functions in the American Economy," *Econometrica*, 28 (October 1960), 810–834.

5. BRUNNER, KARL, and ALLAN H. MELTZER, "Predicting Velocity: Implications for Theory and Policy," *Journal of Finance*, 18 (May 1963), 319–354.

6. _____, "Some Further Evidence on Supply and Demand Functions for Money," *Journal of Finance*, 19 (May 1964), 240–283.

7. _____, "Economics of Scale in Cash Balances Reconsidered," *Quarterly Journal of Economics*, 81 (August 1967), 422–436.

8. _____, "Liquidity Traps for Money, Bank Credit, and Interest Rates," *Journal of Political Economy*, 76 (February 1968), 1–37.

9. _____, "Comment on the Long-Run and Short-Run Demand for Money," *Journal of Political Economy*, 76 (November/December 1968), 1234–1239.

10. CHETTY, V. K., "On Measuring the Nearness of Near-Moneys," *American Economic Review*, 59 (June 1969), 270–281.

11. CHOW, GREGORY, "On the Short-Run and Long-Run Demand for Money," *Journal of Political Economy*, 74 (April 1966), 111–131.

12. _____, "Long-Run and Short-Run Demand for Money: Reply and Further Notes," *Journal of Political Economy*, 76 (November/December 1968), 1240–1243.

13. DICKSON, HAROLD D., and DENNIS R. STARLEAF, "Polynomial Distributed Lag Structures in the Demand Function for Money," *Journal of Finance*, 27 (December 1972), 1035–1043.

14. EISNER, ROBERT, "Another Look at Liquidity Preference," *Econometrica*, 31 (July 1963), 531–538.

15. FEIGE, EDGAR, *The Demand for Liquid Assets: A Temporal Cross Section Analysis.* Englewood Cliffs Company, 1964.

16. _____, "Expectations and Adjustments in the Monetary Sector," *American Economic Review*, 57 (May 1967), 462–473.

17. FRIEDMAN, MILTON, *A Theory of the Consumption Function.* (Princeton: Princeton University Press), 1957.

18. _____, "The Quantity Theory of Money, A Restatement," in Milton Friedman (ed.), *Studies in the Quantity Theory of Money.* (Chicago: University of Chicago Press), 1956.

19. _____, "The Demand for Money—Some Theoretical and Empirical Results," *Journal of Political Economy*, 67 (June 1959), 327–351.

20. _____, and ANNA J. SCHWARTZ, *A Monetary History of the United States, 1867–1960*. Princeton: National Bureau of Economic Research, 1963.

21. _____, and DAVID MEISELMAN, "Relative Stability of Monetary Velocity and the Investment Multiplier in the United States 1897–1957," in Commission on Money and Credit, *Stabilization Policies* (Englewood Cliffs, N.J., Prentice-Hall), 1963.

22. GALPER, HARVEY, "Alternative Interest Rates and the Demand for Money: Comment," *American Economic Review*, 59 (June 1969), 401–407.

23. GOLDFELD, STEPHEN, *Commercial Bank Behavior and Economic Activity*. (Amsterdam: North-Holland), 1966.

24. _____, "The Demand for Money Revisited," *Brookings Papers on Economic Activity* (3:1973), 577–638.

25. GRILICHES, ZVI., "Distributed Lags: A Survey," *Econometrica*, 35 (January 1967), 16–49.

26. GURLEY, JOHN G., and EDWARD S. SHAW, *Money in a Theory Finance*. Washington, D.C.: The Brookings Institution, 1960.

27. HAMBURGER, MICHAEL J., "The Demand for Money by Households, Money Substitutes, and Monetary Policy," *Journal of Political Economy*, 74 (December 1966), 600–623.

28. _____, "Alternative Interest Rates and the Demand for Money: Comment," *American Economic Review*, 59 (June 1969), 407–412.

29. _____, "The Demand for Money in 1971: Was There a Shift? A Comment," *Journal of Money, Credit, and Banking*, 5 (May 1973), 720–725.

30. HELLER, H. R., "The Demand for Money—The Evidence from the Short-Run Data," *Quarterly Journal of Economics*, 79 (June 1965), 291–303.

31. JAFFEE, DWIGHT M., "The Structure of the Money-Expenditure Relationship: Comment," *American Economic Review*, 60 (March 1970), 216–219.

32. JOHNSON, HARRY G., "Monetary Theory and Policy," *American Economic Review*, 52 (June 1962), 335–384.

33. JONES, DAVID, "The Demand for Money: A Review of the Empirical Literature," Staff Economic Studies of the Federal Reserve System, paper presented to the Federal Reserve System Committee on Financial Analysis in St. Louis (October 1965).

34. KAMINOW, I. P., "The Household Demand for Money," *Journal of Finance*, 24 (September 1969), 679–696.

35. KARNI, EDI, "The Value of Time and the Demand for Money," *Journal of Money, Credit, and Banking*, 6 (February 1974), 45–64.

36. KAUFMAN, GEORGE G., "More on an Empirical Definition of Money," *American Economic Review*, 59 (March 1969), 78–87.

37. KEYNES, JOHN MAYNARD, *The General Theory of Employment, Interest, and Money*. (London: Harcourt, Brace and World), 1936.

38. KONSTAS, PANOS, and MOHAMAD W. KHOUJA, "The Keynesian Demand-for-Money Function: Another Look and Some Additional Evidence," *Journal of Money, Credit and Banking*, 1 (November 1969), 765–777.

39. LAFFER, ARTHUR B., "Trade Credit and the Money Market," *Journal of Political Economy*, 78 (March/April 1970), 239–267.

40. LAIDLER, DAVID, "Some Evidence on the Demand for Money," *Journal of Political Economy*, 74 (February 1966), 55–68.

41. _____, "The Rate of Interest and the Demand for Money—Some Empirical Evidence," *Journal of Political Economy*, 74 (December 1966), 545–555.

42. _____, *The Demand for Money: Theories and Evidence*. Scranton: International Textbook Company, 1969.

43. _____, "The Definition of Money: Theoretical and Empirical Problems," *Journal of Money, Credit and Banking*, 1 (August 1969), 509–525.

44. _____, "A Survey of Some Current Problems," in G. Clayton, J. C. Gilbert, and R. Sidgewick (eds.), *Monetary Theory and Monetary Policy in the 1970's*. (New York: Oxford University Press), 1971.

45. LATANÉ, HENRY A., "Cash Balances and the Interest Rate—A Pragmatic Approach," *Review of Economics and Statistics*, 36 (November 1954), 456–460.

46. LEE, T. H., "Alternative Interest Rates and the Demand for Money: The Empirical Evidence," *American Economic Review*, 57 (December 1967), 1168–1181.

47. DE LEEUW, FRANK, "A Model of Financial Behavior," in James Duesenberry, Gary Fromm, Lawrence Klein, and Edwin Kuh (eds.), *The Brookings Quarterly Econometric Model of the United States*. (Chicago: Rand McNally and Company), 1965, 464–530.

48. LYDALL, HAROLD, "Income, Assets, and the Demand for Money," *Review of Economics and Statistics*, 40 (February 1958), 1–14.

49. MELTZER, ALLAN H., "The Demand for Money: The Evidence from the Time Series," *Journal of Political Economy*, 71 (June 1963), 219–246.

50. _____, "The Demand for Money: A Cross Section Study of Business Firms," *Quarterly Journal of Economics*, 77 (August 1963), 405–422.

51. OCHS, J., "The Transaction Demand for Money and Choices Involving Risk," *Journal of Political Economy*, 76 (March/April 1968), 289–291.

52. PATINKIN, DON, "The Chicago Tradition, The Quantity Theory and

Friedman," *Journal of Money, Credit and Banking*, 1 (February 1969), 46–70.

53. PELTZMAN, SAM, "The Structure of the Money Expenditure Relationship," *American Economic Review*, 59 (March 1969), 129–137.

54. POOLE, WILLIAM, "Whither Money Demand?" *Brookings Papers on Economic Activity* (3:1970), 485–500.

55. SANTOMERO, ANTHONY M., "A Model of the Demand for Money by Households," *Journal of Finance*, 29 (March 1974), 89–102.

56. SCHADRACK, FREDERICK C., "An Empirical Approach to the Definition of Money," *Monetary Aggregates and Monetary Policy*, Federal Reserve Bank of New York (1974), 28–34.

57. SHAPIRO, A. A., "Inflation, Lags, and the Demand for Money," *International Economic Review*, 16 (February 1975), 81–96.

58. SHAPIRO, HAROLD, "Distributed Lags. Interest Rate Expectations and the Impact of Monetary Policy: An Econometric Analysis of a Canadian Experience," *American Economic Review*, 57 (May 1967), 444–461.

59. SLOVIN, M. B., and M. E. SUSHKA, "A Financial Market Approach to the Demand for Money and the Implications for Monetary Policy," Board of Governors, Federal Reserve (1972), manuscript.

60. STARLEAF, DENNIS R., and RICHARD REIMER, "The Keynesian Demand Function for Money: Some Statistical Tests," *Journal of Finance*, 22 (March 1967), 71–76.

61. TEIGEN, RONALD, "Demand and Supply Functions for Money in the United States, Some Structural Estimates," *Econometrica*, 32 (October 1964), 477–509.

62. ———, "An Aggregated Quarterly Model of the U.S. Monetary Sector, 1953–64," unpublished manuscript presented to the Conference on Targets and Indicators of Monetary Policy, University of California at Los Angeles (April 1966).

63. TOBIN, JAMES, "Liquidity Preference and Monetary Policy," *Reveiw of Economics and Statistics*, 29 (May 1947), 124–131.

64. ———, "The Interest Elasticity of Transaction Demand for Cash," *Review of Economics and Statistics*, 38 (August 1956), 241–247.

65. ———, "Liquidity Preference as Behavior Towards Risk," *Review of Economic Studies*, 25 (February 1958), 65–86.

66. TAYLOR, L. D., and J. P. NEWHOUSE, "On the Long-Run and Short-Run Demand for Money: A Comment," *Journal of Political Economy*, 77 (September/October 1969), 851–856.

67. TSIANG, S. C., "The Precautionary Demand for Money: An Inventory Theoretical Analysis," *Journal of Political Economy*, 77 (January/February 1969), 99–117.

68. TURNOVSKY, STEPHEN J., "The Demand for Money and the Determina-

tion of the Rate of Interest Under Uncertainty," *Journal of Money, Credit, and Banking*, 3 (May 1971), 183–204.

69. WALTERS ALAN A., "The Demand for Money–The Dynamic Properties of the Multiplier," *Journal of Political Economy*, 75 (June 1967), 293–298.

70. WHALEN, EDWARD L., "A Cross-Section Study of Business Demand for Cash," *Journal of Finance*, 20 (September 1965), 423–443.

71. ZAREMBKA, P., "Functional Form in the Demand for Money," *Journal of the American Statistical Association*, 63 (June 1968), 502–511.

PART III
MACROECONOMIC MODELS

FIVE
Some Fundamentals of Macroeconomic Theory

In the very basic model of income and expenditures determination with which we begin, several very strong and unrealistic assumptions are made about the economy. For example, the price level is assumed constant at all levels of income and expenditures. This implies that whenever a dollar magnitude, such as consumption expenditures, investment expenditures, government expenditures, income, or wealth, is mentioned, that measure is viewed in real or purchasing power terms. It means that all behavioral entities are concerned only with the real values of the variables influencing their decisions to consume, invest, and produce.

Together with the assumption of given prices, the level of nominal wages is also assumed given. This implies that we shall postpone until later chapters a detailed analysis of the decisions of firms to hire labor, produce output, and adjust the price of that output, and the decisions of laborers to sell their services or engage in leisure activities. In this chapter we shall not inquire as to the effect of changes in production on employment, nominal wages, and the price level.

Finally, in addition to assuming that nominal wages and price levels are constant, we also assume that the market rate of interest is given and is not affected by any of the activities described in this chapter. Thus when aggregate expenditures change in our model, there is no pressure on interest rates, and hence, no feedback from interest rates to **307** aggregate expenditures. Later in the chapter when the interest rate (and wealth) are explicitly introduced as determinants of consumption, saving, and investment behavior, we shall simply assume that the rate is given by forces outside our model.

These are very unrealistic assumptions. They are made in order to allow one to get an uncluttered grasp of key expenditures decisions. The implications derived from models in which these assumptions are maintained should probably be regarded with great caution. In subsequent chapters, as these assumptions are gradually relaxed, we may gain a more realistic view of the economy.

Consumption: The Keynesian Theory

Consumption was defined in the previous chapter as total current expenditures of households on newly produced goods and services. Keynes' "fundamental psychological law," promulgated in his *General Theory of Employment, Interest and Money*, is that consumption expenditures depend positively on current income and that an increase in current income will result in an induced increase in consumption expenditures which is somewhat smaller than the increase in income. Thus the "marginal propensity to consume," in a linear relation the *slope* of the consumption function, is greater than zero but less than unity, $0 < \Delta C/\Delta Y < 1$.

Keynes further stated that at all levels of income the marginal propensity to consume, the change in consumption with respect to the change in income $\Delta C/\Delta Y$, is less than the average propensity to consume, the ratio of the level of total consumption to the level of total income C/Y. Therefore, Keynes' theory may be represented by the following equation:

$$C = a + bY \qquad (5.1)$$

where $a > 0$, $0 < b < 1$ and

C = consumption expenditures
Y = current income
a = *autonomous* consumption expenditures (that level of consumption which is autonomous of, that is, "independent" of, the level of income)[1]
b = the marginal propensity to consume, $\Delta C/\Delta Y$

---

[1]Whether or not a and b are constants or are proxies for other variables is examined later in this chapter.

and where bY is *induced* consumption expenditures (that level of consumption expenditures which depends on the level of income). Equation (5.1) is graphed in Figure 5.1. The intercept term represents autonomous consumption expenditures a. The slope term is the marginal propensity to consume b.

Equation (5.1) embodies Keynes' notion that the average propensity to consume, the ratio of consumption to income, will always be greater than the marginal propensity to consume. Dividing Equation (5.1) by Y yields

$$\frac{C}{Y} = \frac{a}{Y} + b \tag{5.2}$$

since $a/Y > 0$, $a/Y + b > b$; this is reflected graphically in Figure 5.1. The slope of any ray from the origin to any point on the function, reflecting the ratio C/Y, will always exceed the magnitude of the slope of the function b.

Consider now the aggregate budget identity which indicates that all income must be consumed (C), saved (S), or transferred away as taxation (T).

$$Y \equiv C + S + T. \tag{5.3}$$

Substituting Equation (5.1) into (5.3) and assuming initially that taxation T is zero, yields the saving function

$$S = -a + (1 - b)Y = -a + sY. \tag{5.4}$$

Here S = saving

    $-a$ = autonomous (dis)saving (the negative of autonomous consumption)

    s = the marginal propensity to save

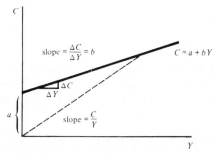

Figure 5.1. Short-run Keynesian consumption function.

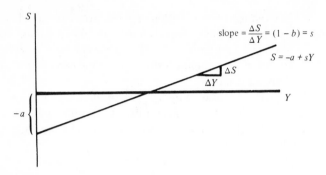

Figure 5.2.   Keynesian saving function.

where $a > 0$ and $0 < s = (1 - b) < 1$.

Substituting Equations (5.1) and (5.4) back into (5.3) and assuming $T = 0$ gives

$$Y \equiv a + bY - a + sY \equiv (b + s)Y$$

indicating that $b + s \equiv 1$, that is, the marginal propensity to save plus the marginal propensity to consume equal unity. In other words, if taxation is zero, all income must either be consumed or saved.

In Figure 5.2 Equation (5.4) is graphed. The intercept term represents autonomous dissaving $-a$. The slope term is the marginal propensity to save s.

Where taxation is included, more sophisticated and realistic versions of the saving or consumption relations are sometimes specified as follows:

$$C = a + bY_d \tag{5.5}$$

and

$$S = -a + sY_d \tag{5.6}$$

where

$$Y_d \equiv Y - T \tag{5.7}$$

is the definition of disposable income. Here both saving and consumption vary positively with disposable income Y_d, defined as aggregate income Y less the taxation, net of transfer payments, paid to government T.[2]

[2]Using the budget identity and defining T as a constant T_a, we can still demonstrate that the marginal propensity to save plus the marginal propensity to consume out

A traditional problem in macroeconomic theory centers on the determination of the equilibrium level of aggregate income. The condition for equilibrium in the income-expenditures sector of the economy was said to be the equality of aggregate income to aggregate demand,

$$Y = C + I + G \tag{5.8}$$

Using the budget identity (5.3), and substituting into (5.8), the equilibrium condition can also be expressed as

$$S + T = I + G \tag{5.9}$$

which says that "leakages" from the spending stream $(S + T)$ are equal to "injections" into the spending stream $(I + G)$.

Assuming that investment, taxation and government expenditures are autonomous (i.e., independent of any other variable in the model) we may write:

$$I = I_a \tag{5.10}$$

$$T = T_a \tag{5.11}$$

$$G = G_a \tag{5.12}$$

Having written relations for all the components of aggregate demand, we may now develop a simple model of income determination.

Substituting autonomous taxation (5.11) into the definition of disposable income (5.7) and the result into the consumption function (5.5) yields

$$C = a + bY - bT_a. \tag{5.13}$$

Substituting this result together with autonomous government expenditures, Equation (5.12), and autonomous investment, Equation (5.10), into the expression for total aggregate demand yields

$$C + I + G = a - bT_a + I_a + G_a + bY. \tag{5.14}$$

---

of disposable income equals unity. Substituting Equation (5.7) into (5.5) and (5.6), and the results into (5.3),

$$Y \equiv a + bY - bT_a - a + sY - sT_a + T_a$$
$$\equiv (b + s)Y - (b + s)T_a + T_a.$$

Therefore, $Y - T_a \equiv Y_d \equiv (b + s)Y_d$ and $b + s = 1$. This shows the importance of the budget identity in developing income-expenditures models.

Substituting this relation into the equilibrium condition (5.8) and rearranging terms provides the solution for the equilibrium level of income,[3]

$$Y_e = \frac{a + I_a + G_a - bT_a}{1 - b} \ . \tag{5.15}$$

The model can be graphed to show this same result.

In Figure 5.3 the consumption function, Equation (5.13), is graphed to show an intercept consisting of autonomous consumption a less autonomous taxation times the marginal propensity to consume $-bT_a$. Each subsequent line adds to total consumption at every level of income a constant level of autonomous expenditures by an additional sector. The top line represents the sum of autonomous aggregate demand $(a - bT_a + I_a + G_a)$ and induced aggregate demand bY. The equilibrium condition is graphed as a 45° line from the origin. At any point along this line directed distances measured horizontally equal directed distances measured vertically. Therefore, at every point along this line aggregate income and aggregate expenditures are equal. The intersection of the aggregate demand function and the 45° line yields the equilibrium level of aggregate income [Equation (5.15)].

One of the most politically relevant implications of all monetary and macroeconomic theory is the Keynesian autonomous expenditures multiplier. In the present model the Keynesian autonomous expenditures multiplier is simply $1/(1 - b)$. Any change in the equilibrium level of aggregate income is the product of a change in any element of autonomous aggregate demand and the multiplier. This may easily be seen algebraically. The original equilibrium level of income was

$$Y_e = \frac{a + I_a + G_a - bT_a}{1 - b} \ . \tag{5.15}$$

After allowing one of the components of autonomous aggregate demand to change (ΔG_a), we get a new equilibrium level of income:

$$Y'_e = \frac{a + I_a + G_a - bT_a + \Delta G_a}{1 - b} \ . \tag{5.16}$$

---

[3]Alternatively, use the saving function (5.6) instead of the consumption function (5.5). Then use the leakages = injections definition of equilibrium (5.9) instead of the aggregate demand = aggregate income definition (5.8). This approach yields the same solution as Equation (5.15).

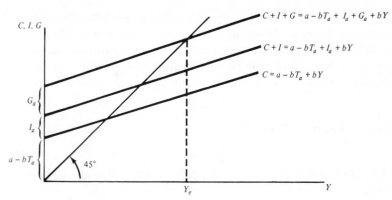

Figure 5.3. Solution for the equilibrium level of aggregate income.

The change in income is the difference between Equation (5.16) and (5.15):

$$\Delta Y = Y'_e - Y_e = \frac{a + I_a + G_a - bT_a + \Delta G_a}{1 - b} - \frac{a + I_a + G_a - bT_a}{1 - b}$$

$$= \left(\frac{1}{1 - b} \right) \Delta G_a. \tag{5.17}$$

Therefore the autonomous expenditures multiplier in this model is

$$\frac{\Delta Y}{\Delta G} = \left(\frac{1}{1 - b} \right). \tag{5.18}$$

The same multiplier would obtain for changes either in autonomous consumption a or in autonomous investment expenditures I_a.

There are a number of alternative perspectives on the autonomous expenditures multiplier. One is to use the alternative way of expressing income–expenditures equilibrium,

$$S + T = I + G. \tag{5.9}$$

Assuming that taxation T is constant, any change in government expenditures G with investment expenditures I unchanged must be matched by an equal change in saving S. Similarly, any change in investment expenditures I with government expenditures G unchanged must also be matched by an equal change in saving S. Otherwise the equilibrium condition would not be satisfied. According to the saving relation (5.4), saving will change if and only if income Y changes in the same direction.

Therefore, assuming a change in autonomous investment expenditures ΔI, with taxation T and government expenditures G unchanged, in order to sustain equilibrium in income and expenditures,

$$\Delta S = \Delta I. \tag{5.19}$$

Since by Equation (5.4)

$$\Delta S = s\Delta Y, \tag{5.20}$$

substitution of Equation (5.20) into (5.19) and rearranging yields

$$\frac{\Delta Y}{\Delta I} = \frac{1}{s} = \frac{1}{1 - b} \tag{5.21}$$

which is the autonomous expenditures multiplier. The greater the value of the marginal propensity to consume b, the smaller the value of the marginal propensity to save s, and the larger the change in income ΔY that is necessary to generate the necessary change in saving ΔS to match the initial change in autonomous investment expenditures ΔI.

The autonomous expenditures multiplier process may also be shown graphically. In Figure 5.4 the change in aggregate income is a "multiple" of the change in autonomous aggregate demand. It can be seen that given any change in autonomous expenditures, the greater the slope of the aggregate demand relation (the greater the marginal

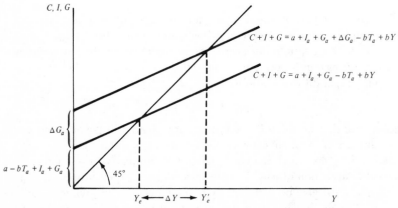

Figure 5.4. The autonomous expenditures multiplier in a simple model of income determination.

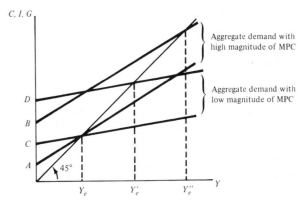

Figure 5.5.   Demonstration of the relationship between the size of the multiplier and the magnitude of the MPC.

propensity to consume), the greater the change in income from one equilibrium position to the other. This can be seen in Figure 5.5. Here two alternative aggregate demand functions are drawn to produce the same equilibrium level of income at Y_e. Then both aggregate demand relations shift upward by the same amount ($AB = CD$) as a result of an increase in autonomous aggregate demand. For the aggregate demand function with the smaller slope or the lower marginal propensity to consume (MPC), the new equilibrium level of income is Y_e'. For the aggregate demand function with the larger slope or the greater marginal propensity to consume, the new equilibrium level of income is Y_e''. This demonstrates graphically that the magnitude of the autonomous expenditures multiplier varies directly with the magnitude of the marginal propensity to consume. It explains that the degree to which an initial increase in the level of income generates further increases in income is the core of the multiplier principle.

The multiplier process can also be explained intuitively. We have seen that, in equilibrium aggregate income equals aggregate expenditures. Any shock to equilibrium in the way of an increase in autonomous expenditures creates a situation of disequilibrium. Equilibrium can only be restored if aggregate income rises once again to equal aggregate demand. If the MPC is quite small (positive but near zero in magnitude), a relatively small rise in aggregate income can restore equilibrium. In fact, where b is very small, income need rise only by an amount equal to the increase in autonomous aggregate demand [by Equation (5.18) as $b \rightarrow 0$, $1/(1 - b) \rightarrow 1$]. If, on the other hand, the

MPC is quite large, only a relatively large increase in aggregate income can restore equilibrium. This obtains because as income rises with a relatively large MPC, more aggregate (consumption) expenditures are induced by the rise in income. In fact, where b is large but still less than unity, the size of the autonomous expenditures multiplier approaches infinity [by Equation (5.18) as $b \to 1$, $1/(1 - b) \to \infty$].

This simple model can also be manipulated to yield multipliers premised on changes in the other components of autonomous aggregate demand. For example, changing autonomous taxation T_a in Equation (5.15) and working through an algebraic process similar to Equations (5.16) and (5.17) yields an autonomous taxation multiplier:

$$\frac{\Delta Y}{\Delta T_a} = \frac{-b}{1 - b} . \tag{5.22}$$

The autonomous taxation multiplier is negative and smaller in absolute magnitude than the autonomous expenditures multiplier. This occurs because any change in autonomous taxation affects autonomous aggregate demand through its effect on autonomous consumption.

For example, a lump sum tax increase of ΔT_a does not reduce autonomous aggregate demand by ΔT_a, but rather through the consumption function,

$$C = a + bY - bT_a \tag{5.13}$$

it reduces autonomous aggregate demand by $-b$ times the tax increase or $(-b)(\Delta T_a)$. Thus, the effect on aggregate income is the decrease in aggregate demand induced by the tax increase times the autonomous expenditures multiplier or

$$\Delta Y = (-b)(\Delta T_a) \cdot \frac{1}{1 - b}$$

which after rearranging yields

$$\frac{\Delta Y}{\Delta T_a} = \frac{-b}{1 - b} \tag{5.22}$$

the autonomous taxation multiplier.

A particularly celebrated concept is the balanced budget multiplier. The balanced budget multiplier specifies the change in income that will result from any change in autonomous government expenditures that is matched by an equal change in autonomous taxation so that there is no change in the deficit or a surplus that is run in the government budget. Thus, the condition for an incrementally balanced budget is

$$\Delta G_a = \Delta T_a. \tag{5.23}$$

Assume that our initial equilibrium is described by

$$Y_e = \frac{a + I_a + G_a - bT_a}{1 - b} \tag{5.15}$$

and that the increase in autonomous government expenditures alone would cause income to rise to

$$Y'_e = \frac{a + I_a + G_a - bT_a + \Delta G_a}{1 - b} \tag{5.16}$$

as described above. However, under the condition of Equation (5.23) the increase in autonomous government expenditures is matched by an equal increase in autonomous taxation. Therefore the new equilibrium level of income will be

$$Y''_e = \frac{a + I_a + G_a - bT_a + \Delta G_a - b\Delta T_a}{1 - b} \tag{5.24}$$

and the change in income is the difference between Equations (5.24) and (5.15):

$$\Delta Y = Y''_e - Y_e = \frac{a + I_a + G_a - bT_a + \Delta G_a - b\Delta T_a}{1 - b} -$$

$$\frac{a + I_a + G_a - bT_a}{1 - b}. \tag{5.25}$$

Substituting Equation (5.23) into (5.25) and simplifying yields

$$\Delta Y = \left(\frac{1 - b}{1 - b} \right) \Delta G$$

Therefore, the balanced budget multiplier in the present model is unity:

$$\frac{\Delta Y}{\Delta G} = \left(\frac{1 - b}{1 - b} \right) = 1. \tag{5.26}$$

This can be seen in Figure 5.6. Here the increase in income, resulting solely from the increase in autonomous government expenditures which is not subject to the incrementally balanced budget condi-

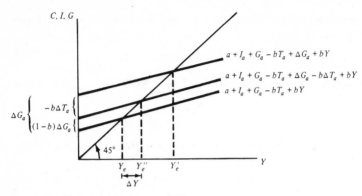

Figure 5.6.   Balanced budget multiplier.

tion of Equation (5.23), would have been identical to the increase shown in Figure 5.5,

$$Y'_e - Y_e = \Delta G_a \left(\frac{1}{1 - b} \right) .$$

However, because the budget must be incrementally balanced, the aggregate demand function has a "net" upward shift of only $\Delta G_a - b\Delta T_a$, or the net result of shifting upwards by ΔG_a (the effect of the increase in autonomous government expenditures) *and* shifting downwards by $-b\Delta T_a$ (the effect of the increase in lump sum taxation on autonomous consumption). Since $\Delta G = \Delta T_a$ by the assumption of an incrementally balanced budget (5.23), this "net" increase in autonomous aggregate demand is $\Delta G(1 - b)$, as shown in Figure 5.6. As expressed earlier, the increase in income is equal to the autonomous expenditures multiplier times this "net" change in autonomous expenditures, or

$$\Delta Y = \Delta G(1 - b) \left(\frac{1}{1 - b} \right) .$$

Collecting terms gives the balanced budget multiplier

$$\frac{\Delta Y}{\Delta G} = \left(\frac{1 - b}{1 - b} \right) = 1. \tag{5.26}$$

The foregoing analysis adds a few complications to the simple model of income determination. A number of textbooks add even more. However, because the model is predicated on several extremely unrealistic assumptions, it is more important to modify these assumptions than to continue to manipulate the model and its multipliers.

The preceding analysis has made it clear that the magnitude of the various multipliers varies directly with the magnitude of the marginal propensity to consume b and inversely with the magnitude of the marginal propensity to save $(1 - b)$. We have shown that Keynes' "fundamental psychological law," his consumption relation, is indeed fundamental to his "multiplier principle." Nevertheless, lying behind the multiplier principle are two salient aspects of a crude Keynesian view of the economy which should be made explicit.

The first is that when aggregate demand changes, prices do not change but only quantities produced do. Thus in the very basic Keynesian model the price level and the interest rate are assumed constant. These assumptions are retained throughout the present chapter. In the next chapter the assumption of a fixed interest rate will be relaxed and it will be shown, in a more sophisticated model, that a much smaller autonomous expenditures multiplier may result. Under this more realistic assumption it will be seen that as the level of income increases, there may occur a rise in the rate of interest which serves to choke off investment expenditures and reduce the magnitude of the multiplier. In Chapter 7 it will be seen that as the assumption of a fixed price level is relaxed, the autonomous expenditures multiplier grows even smaller until, in a world of assumed perfect price flexibility, it is zero. Thus, the crude Keynesian assumptions of a fixed interest rate, a fixed price level and a variable level of output production are essential to the results presented in this chapter.

The second key element to the Keynesian model is the assumption that consumption is constrained predominantly by current income. If, in contrast, because of borrowing, current consumption can be carried out even if current cash income is low, then consumption depends only weakly on current income and the multiplier loses some theoretical power. Consequently, an examination of alternative theories of consumption is of theoretical importance for the development of improved theories of aggregate economic activity.

Consumption: The Neoclassical Theory

We begin the analysis with a household that has a two-period planning horizon. Assume that the household begins and ends each period with the same stocks of assets (there is no running down of assets), and that the household expects with certainty an income of Y_1 in period 1 and an income of Y_2 in period 2. Assume further that the rate of interest paid by borrowers is the same as the rate earned by lenders. The household begins at point B in Figure 5.7. In Figure 5.7 the maximum amount of consumption in year 1 can be realized by consuming *all* of year 1's income ($\$Y_1$) and consuming nothing in year 2, thereby borrowing against *all* of year two's income $\$Y_2$. At a market rate of i_0, this borrowing would yield additional resources of $\$Y_2/(1 + i_0)$ in year one. Therefore, the maximum consumption in year 1 is $C_{1\,max} = Y_1 + Y_2/(1 + i_0)$. In contrast, in year 2 maximum consumption is obtained by consuming all of year 2's income in that year and by spending nothing in year 1 (saving) and lending it at the market rate until year 2. This would yield maximum consumption of $C_{2\,max} = Y_2 + Y_1(1 + i_0)$.

By saving the amount $(Y_1 - C_1)$ in year 1 and lending it at a rate of interest i_0 the household can increase consumption in year 2 by $(1 + i_0)$ $(Y_1 - C_1)$. Conversely, in order to dissave the amount $(C_2 - Y_2)$ in year 2, the household must decrease consumption by $(C_2 - Y_2)/(1 + i_0)$ in year 1. In short, the market allows the household to consume anywhere along (or below) a locus connecting maximum consumption in year 1 with maximum consumption in year 2. This locus, the budget line, has a slope of $-(1 + i_0)$.

The amounts the household will actually choose to consume and save will depend on its utility from consumption in each year. Assume that there exists a family of intertemporal indifference or equal-utility curves (in Figure 5.8, I_0, I_1, and I_2). Because total utility is the same at all points along each equal-utility curve, and because consumption in

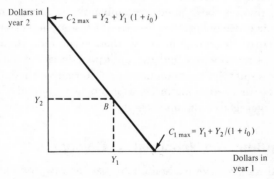

Figure 5.7. Budget constraint.

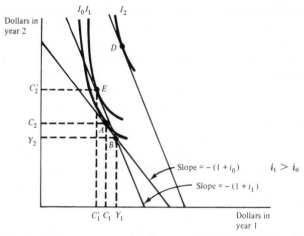

Figure 5.8. Indifference curves and changes in the budget constraint.

each year generates positive utility (that is, consumption in each year is "good"), as consumption in one year is increased, consumption in the other year must decrease (that is, the indifference or equal-utility curves must have a negative slope). Moreover, if we assume diminishing marginal utility of consumption in each year, as consumption in one year is increased in consecutive units of one dollar, consumption in the other year must decrease by consecutively smaller absolute amounts (that is, the indifference or equal-utility curves are convex to the origin). Total utility can be maximized, given the budget constraint, at a point where the set of consumption allocations allowed by the market (the budget line) reaches (is tangent to) the highest possible level of utility. This occurs at point A in Figure 5.8; point B represents the assumed initial income stream.

In Figure 5.8 at an interest rate of i_0 the individual chooses to save $Y_1 - C_1$ in year 1 and dissaves $Y_2 - C_2$ in year 2. As the interest rate rises to i_1, one dollar saved in year 1 will yield $(1 + i_1)$ dollars in year 2, and one dollar not saved in year 2 will require sacrifice of $[1/(1 + i_1)$ dollars of consumption in year one. The budget line becomes steeper but, as initial income is unchanged, it must still go through point B. In other words, one dollar saved in year 1 will yield a larger return in year 2 when the interest rate is i_1 than when it is i_0. As the rate rises to i_1, and the reward to saving increases, the household depicted in Figure 5.8

maximizes its utility at point E; it chooses to increase its saving in year 1 from $(Y_1 - C_1)$ to $(Y_1 - C_1')$. This allows the household to increase its consumption in year 2 by $(C_2' - C_2)$.

At work here are both a substitution effect and an income effect. As the interest rate rises, the "price" of present consumption relative to future consumption rises, that is, it costs a household more to consume in the present year because for each dollar of goods consumed presently more future goods are being sacrificed. A rational household would substitute the cheaper good, future consumption, for the more expensive one, present consumption, under these circumstances. The substitution effect applies unambiguously to all households—lenders (present savers who will save more at higher rates) such as the one pictured in Figure 5.8, as well as borrowers (present dissavers who will borrow less at higher rates).

An income effect is also at work. As the interest rate rises for lenders (savers in year 1), such as the household in Figure 5.8, the level of real income from dollars saved in the present year rises. Therefore, if consumption goods in each year are not "inferior goods," lenders will increase consumption in both years. For borrowers (dissavers in year 1) as the interest rate rises, the level of their real income in the present year declines. Therefore if consumption goods are not inferior, borrowers will reduce consumption in both years.

For the household depicted in Figure 5.8 (a lender) the substitution effect of an increase in the rate of interest in reducing present consumption outweighs the income effect of an increase in the interest rate in increasing present consumption. The combined (substitution plus income) effect of an increase in the interest rate on consumption is negative; present consumption declines. (For other individual lenders it would, of course, be possible for the income effect to outweigh the substitution effect.)

For the economy as a whole an increase in the interest rate will generate a substitution effect which will cause both present savers (lenders) and present dissavers (borrowers) to consume less. For the economy as a whole an increase in the interest rate will have an income effect that will cause present savers to consume more and present dissavers to consume less. If, for the economy as a whole, a change in the market rate of interest cannot create any new resources, then it cannot raise the level of real income. There will then be no more resources available after the interest rate change than there were before the change. Under this condition, for the economy as a whole there can only be a substitution effect as long as the marginal propensity to consume of savers equals the marginal propensity to consume of dissavers. A rise in the rate of interest has a positive income effect on the consumption of present savers (lenders), but this is assumed to be exactly offset by its negative income effect on the consumption of present dissavers (borrowers). Since the substitution effect is unambiguous for lenders and borrowers, we may specify that current aggregate consumption varies inversely with the market rate of interest

$$C = f(i) \qquad f_i < 0. \qquad (5.27)$$

Using the household budget identity,

$$Y \equiv C + S + T \qquad (5.3)$$

where current income is unchanged, assuming transfer payments are not affected by interest rates, the effect of an interest rate change on consumption must be exactly offset by an equal and opposite effect on saving. Therefore, for the economy as a whole saving varies positively with the market rate of interest.

$$S = g(i) \qquad g_i > 0. \qquad (5.28)$$

Let us return once more to the individual household. If a household's income should increase in year 2, the present (year 1) value of its income stream will increase. Likewise, if year 1 income should increase, the future (year 2) value of its income will increase; this is evident from Figure 5.7. At point B the budget line has coordinates Y_1, Y_2. If either Y_1 or Y_2 rises, point B would move horizontally or vertically. Thus an increase in income in any year would move the budget line out without changing its slope. This will allow the household to reach a new higher level of utility. If consumption in any period is not an inferior good, an increase in one year's income should increase consumption expenditures in both years. This is the case in Figure 5.8. When the budget line shifts out, consumption expenditures are seen to increase in both years to point D.

The relation between the present value of an income stream PV and current consumption expenditures can be generalized by looking at income beyond two periods:

$$C = k(PV) = k \sum_{t=0}^{n} \left[\frac{Y_t}{(1 + i)^t} \right], \qquad 0 < k \leqslant 1 \qquad (5.29)$$

where t is the number of years in the future in which a particular household's income is received. This says that a household's consumption in time t varies positively with the present time t value of all future income.[4]

The right-hand side of Equation (5.29) is the present discounted value of an income stream. The income stream includes current income as well as all future income. For the time being, let us define wealth as the present discounted value of all future income *excluding current income*. (This dichotomy is related to the Modigliani-Ando treatment below.) Therefore, the present value of an income stream is, under this definition of wealth, the sum of current income and wealth:

$$Y_0 + \sum_{t=1}^{n} \frac{Y_t}{(1 + i)^t} = \sum_{t=0}^{n} \frac{Y_t}{(1 + i)^t} . \tag{5.30}$$

Equation (5.29) can be written out to show the effect of current income and the present value of all future income, that is, wealth, on current consumption:

$$C = k \left(Y_0 + \frac{Y_1}{(1 + i)} + \frac{Y_2}{(1 + i)^2} + \cdots + \frac{Y_n}{(1 + i)^n} \right) . \tag{5.31}$$

The parameter k, being positive but less than unity, indicates that current consumption varies directly with the level of current income as well as with the level of wealth.

The effect of current income and wealth on current saving can now be derived by using the budget identity

$$Y = C + S + T. \tag{5.3}$$

For analytical simplicity we shall assume that T (current taxation) is constant. Substituting Equation (5.31) into (5.3) and rearranging yields

$$S = Y_0 - kY_0 - k \frac{Y_1}{(1 + i)} - k \frac{Y_2}{(1 + i)^2} - \cdots - k \frac{Y_n}{(1 + i)^n} - T$$

$$= (1 - k)Y_0 - k \sum_{t=1}^{n} \frac{Y_t}{(1 + i)^t} - T. \tag{5.32}$$

---

[4]The condition $k \leq 1$ follows from the constraint that the present value of future consumption cannot exceed the present value of future income. Therefore, one can currently consume no more than the present value of one's future income. Negative consumption in any period is ruled out as being unreasonable.

Thus current saving varies positively with current income but inversely with the level of wealth as defined above. This indicates that, as long as current income is unchanged, when wealth, so defined, increases current saving will decline.[5]

Equation (5.29) also indicates that the longer the planning horizon of the household, the smaller the effect of a change in any one year's income (including the current year) on current consumption. Thus the effect of current income on current consumption in the neoclassical theory could be quite small. Focusing on current income as but one component of the present value of an income stream could considerably reduce the theoretical magnitude of the marginal propensity to consume. As a consequence, neoclassical theories of the relationship between current consumption and current income, wealth, and the rate of interest, will generally modify in a downward direction the expected magnitude of the autonomous expenditures multiplier.

A Reconciliation of Keynesian and Neoclassical Theories of Consumption: Albert Ando and Franco Modigliani

The foregoing should not suggest that the consumption theory of Keynes is inconsistent with neoclassical consumption theories. To the contrary, Albert Ando and Franco Modigliani have reconciled the Keynesian and neoclassical theories by breaking up the income stream into labor income (Y_{Lt}) and property income (Y_{Pt}) components. Property income has a present market value and is referred to as a household's net nonhuman wealth a. Wealth is therefore defined to include both human and nonhuman wealth. As in Equation (5.29), Ando and Modigliani begin with the relation between current consumption and the present value of an income stream,

$$C = k(PV) = k \sum_{t=0}^{n} \left[\frac{Y_t}{(1 + i)^t} \right], \qquad 0 < k \leq 1 \qquad (5.29)$$

where present value now is broken up into human and nonhuman components:

$$(PV) = Y_{L_0} + \sum_{1}^{n} \frac{Y_{L_t}}{(1 + i)^t} + a. \qquad (5.33)$$

[5]Once again, the budget identity allows us to show that the partial effects of a change in wealth on consumption, saving, and transfer payments must sum to zero as long as current income is unchanged.

The first two terms measure the human component. The last term, the nonhuman component, may be defined as

$$a = \sum_{0}^{m} \frac{Y_{P_t}}{(1 + i)^t} \; . \tag{5.34}$$

On the assumption that current labor income is a multiple of the present value of future labor income,

$$\lambda Y_{L_0} = \sum_{1}^{n} \frac{Y_{L_t}}{(1 + i)^t} \tag{5.35}$$

present value is expressed as

$$PV = Y_{L_0} + \lambda Y_{L_0} + a. \tag{5.36}$$

By substituting Equation (5.36) into (5.29), Ando and Modigliani derive a consumption function that looks remarkably Keynesian:

$$C = k(1 + \lambda)Y_{L_0} + k \cdot a \tag{5.37}$$

where $k(1 + \lambda)$ is the marginal propensity to consume out of current labor income (estimated to be .7) and k is the marginal propensity to consume out of nonhuman wealth (estimated to be .06).[6]

A Reconciliation of Keynesian and Neoclassical Theories of Consumption: Milton Friedman

Milton Friedman's theory of consumption behavior also uses a wealth approach. However, rather than separating current income from wealth, Friedman works entirely within the concept of wealth, defined to include current as well as future income from human and nonhuman sources.

Because wealth is not easily measured, Friedman develops a new

---

[6]See Albert Ando and Franco Modigliani, "The 'Life Cycle' Hypothesis of Saving: Aggregate Implications and Tests," *American Economic Review* (March 1963). Where the assets comprising the nonhuman wealth term a are defined to include bonds and equities, monetary policy that lowers interest rates effects capital gains for households. The money-equities link has proven important in several econometric studies. See, for example, Frank de Leeuw and Edward M. Gramlich, "The Channels of Monetary Policy," *Federal Reserve Bulletin*, no. 55 (1969). For a survey of possible wealth effects on aggregate demand, see Roger W. Spencer, "Channels of Monetary Influence: A Survey," *Review*, Federal Reserve Bank of St. Louis (November 1974). Both of the last two studies are included in Harvrilesky and Boorman, *Current Issues in Monetary Theory and Policy.*

concept called permanent income,[7] which theoretically is the product of wealth and a rate of interest. Friedman contends that a household forms expectations about its permanent income, and hence its wealth, from past experience:

$$Y_{pt} = \beta Y_t + \beta(1 - \beta)Y_{t-1} + \beta(1 - \beta)^2 Y_{t-2} + \cdots + \beta(1 - \beta)^n Y_{t-n} \quad (5.38)$$

where Y_{pt} is permanent income in period t, β is the factor which determines the weights attached to prior years' incomes, and Y_{t-j} is income as measured j years earlier. The term β is assumed to have a range between zero and unity, $0 < \beta < 1$, so that the further back one looks, the smaller the weight attached to that year's income. That is, if β is .5, the weights on the right-hand side of Equation (5.38) decline in a geometric pattern as follows: .5, .25, .125, etc.

The equation for last year's permanent income is

$$Y_{pt-1} = \beta Y_{t-1} + \beta(1 - \beta)Y_{t-2} + \cdots + \beta(1 - \beta)^{n-1}Y_{t-n} + \beta(1 - \beta)^n Y_{t-(n+1)}. \quad (5.39)$$

Rewriting in this fashion allows substantial simplification as every term in Equation (5.38) after βY_t is equal to $(1 - \beta)$ times every term in Equation (5.39) except the last term. Because that last term is very small, it follows approximately that

$$Y_{pt} \cong \beta Y_t + (1 - \beta)Y_{pt-1} \quad (5.40)$$

which says that permanent income is a weighted average of current income and the previous period's permanent income. If current income is equal to last period's permanent income, then $Y_{pt} = Y_t$. If current income is different from last period's permanent income, this period's permanent income will change, but by less than the difference.

The permanent income hypothesis is that current consumption is proportional to permanent income:

$$C_t = aY_{pt} \quad (5.41)$$

where $0 < \alpha < 1$. Substituting Equation (5.40) into (5.41) yields

$$C_t = \alpha \beta Y_t + \alpha(1 - \beta)Y_{pt-1}. \quad (5.42)$$

If $\alpha(1 - \beta)Y_{pt-1}$ is treated as a constant, this equation may be regarded as an individual household's short-run consumption function with

[7]Milton Friedman, *A Theory of the Consumption Function* (Princeton, NJ: Princeton University Press, 1957).

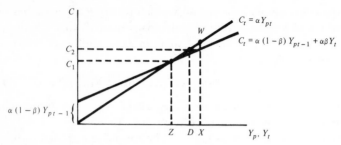

Figure 5.9.   The permanent income hypothesis.

intercept $\alpha(1 - \beta)Y_{pt-1}$ and slope $\alpha\beta$. This function is graphed in Figure 5.9.

Where current income OZ equals permanent income, the household is on both its permanent and its short-run consumption functions. If current income increases from Z to X, consumption rises from C_1 to C_2. Equation (5.40) indicates that permanent income will then rise by a fraction (β) of ZX or by ZD. Thus is *appears* that the increase in consumption was caused by the rise in current income ZX, when in fact it was caused by the rise in *permanent* income ZD. If current income remains at X, Equation (5.39) indicates that eventually current income will equal last year's permanent income Y_{pt-1}, and the intercept of Equation (5.42) in Figure 5.9 would increase until both functions intersect above X at W.

Empirical Studies of Consumption Behavior

Many empirical studies of short-run consumption behavior have estimated a relationship between the current consumption of different households and their current income.[8] These cross section estimates tend to show that households spend a declining percentage of current income on consumption goods and services as current income increases. A number of economists have argued that if C/Y declines as an individual household's income rises, then C/Y should decline as the aggregate of all households' incomes rises. Additional empirical esti-

---

[8]Empirical studies of the consumption function are surveyed in most macroeconomics texts. See, for example, William Branson, *Macroeconomic Theory and Policy* (New York: Harper and Row, 1972); Michael K. Evans, *Macroeconomic Activity, Theory, Forecasting and Control* (New York: Harper and Row, 1967); and David J. Ott, Attiat F. Ott, and Jang H. Yoo, *Macroeconomic Theory* (New York: McGraw-Hill, 1975).

mates using short-run (quarterly) time series data on aggregate current income and aggregate current consumption show that C/Y does indeed decline as aggregate income rises. Thus the cross section and short-run time series empirical estimates seem to be consistent with the aggregate short-run Keynesian consumption relations, given in Equations (5.1) and (5.2) at the beginning of this chapter. They would also appear to be consistent with the Ando–Modigliani consumption function [Equation (5.37)].

Friedman would argue that the empirical studies which use cross section data are merely reflecting the illusion discussed above. Individual household consumption *appears* to respond to current income when it really is responding to permanent income. The short-run time series estimates may be similarly interpreted. Aggregate consumption, reflecting the behavior of individual households, *appears* to be responding to aggregate current income when it is really responding to permanent income.

Other empirical studies using long-run time series data estimate that aggregate consumption is a relatively constant percentage of income at all levels of aggregate income. These results imply that the long-run aggregate consumption function is a straight line through the origin implying that C/Y is constant, that is, $C = \gamma \cdot Y$. Friedman would contend that these results reflect the long-run tendency of measured income to equal permanent income. The estimated long-run aggregate consumption function is simply a weighted sum of individual (permanent) consumption functions [Equation (5.41)].

Numerous hypotheses have proposed that Keynes' short-run consumption function is the empirically "true" relationship. These hypotheses suggest that the long-run data simply represent points on different short-run consumption functions and that variables other than income have induced shifts in the short-run consumption function over time. Many alternative independent variables have been added to try to explain these shifts in order to improve the fit of the short-run Keynesian relation with longer run time series data. (For example, in the Ando–Modigliani estimate (5.37) if nonhuman wealth a increases, the function shifts upward.) Among the variables empirically tested have been various measures of household assets, the composition of the population, the size of the household and its composition, and prices.

Income has been measured in a multitude of ways; for example, lagged income, per capita income, income relative to a prior peak level of income (relative income), money income, and net income. As a consequence, these approaches and comparisons between them tend to be cumbersome. They result in macroeconomic models that contain a large number of variables and that do not perform much better than simpler models at predicting the level of income.

In contrast, Friedman's consumption theory does not add new variables.[9] It reconciles the short-run empirical estimates of the consumption function with the long-run estimates by showing that the observed short-run relationship does indeed shift upward over time. However, it carries out this reconciliation as well as the reconciliation between neoclassical and Keynesian theories of consumption within a traditional neoclassical apparatus.

While empirical studies of consumption behavior are interesting and important, what most interests us is Friedman's and Ando and Modigliani's explicit emphasis on the role of wealth and the interest rate in the theory of consumption. These treatments have their antecedents in neoclassical (Austrian) capital theory of Boehm–Bawerk, as amplified by Irving Fisher and others. They constitute a body of theoretical and empirical evidence which suggests that consumption and saving behavior cannot be explained in a satisfying and empirically relevant way without reference to wealth and interest rate variables. They explain the observed data as well as, if not better than, theories of consumption that simply add variables, and yet they have the weight of decades of intellectual labor on their side. Therefore, in the macroeconomic models of later chapters both wealth and the interest rate (as well as the level of current income) will explicitly influence aggregate consumption (saving) behavior. Thus a more sophisticated consumption function in linear form can be written:

$$C = a + bY_d + vW + ei$$

where $a > 0$, $0 < b < 1$, $0 < v < 1$, and $e < 0$.

Using the budget identity $Y_d \equiv C + S$, this may be written as the saving relation:

$$S = -a + sY_d - vW - ei$$

---

[9]Friedman's permanent income is a proxy for wealth. Claims that wealth does not have a strong or even statistically significant empirical effect on current consumption are sometimes made. Nevertheless, many of the variables that are usually statistically significant in estimates of the consumption function are in fact proxies for wealth such as lagged income and equities.

where $s \equiv (1 - b)$.[10] In later chapters we shall employ these basic relations extensively.

Investment Expenditures

In the elementary model of income–expenditures determination developed earlier in this chapter, investment expenditures were assumed given and autonomous of any other variable in that model. In more realistic models this assumption is not retained. Investment expenditures may realistically be viewed as depending on a number of variables. Perhaps the most important of these is the interest rate. In what follows we shall present the theory that investment expenditures vary inversely with the market rate of interest.

Aggregate net investment expenditures are defined as the change in the capital stock of the economy. Capital is an input into the firm's production process. Therefore, in order to develop the theory of investment, one must start with the theory of production of the firm.

We assume that for a profit maximizing firm units of some factor X are a variable productive input and that other inputs Z are conceptually held constant. The model may be specified as follows:

$$\pi \equiv R - C \qquad \text{definition of profit} \qquad (5.43)$$
$$R \equiv PQ \qquad \text{definition of revenue} \qquad (5.44)$$
$$C \equiv P_x X + c \qquad \text{definition of cost} \qquad (5.45)$$
$$\pi \equiv PQ - P_x X - c \qquad (5.46)$$
$$Q \equiv f(X,Z) \qquad \text{production function} \qquad (5.47)$$

where π = profit
  R = revenue
  C = cost
  P = the price of output
  Q = the quantity of output
  P_x = the price of a unit of input X
  X = the quantity of X
  Z = other inputs
  c = the total cost of inputs other than X.

[10]These equations satisfy the conditions that, where transfer payments are assumed constant, the partial effects of a change in disposable income on saving s and consumption b must sum to unity, the partial effects of a change in the interest rate on saving $-e$ and consumption e must sum to zero, and the partial effects of a change in wealth on saving $-v$ and consumption v must sum to zero.

Equation (5.43) is the definition of profit as revenue less cost. Equation (5.44) is the definition of revenue as a product of the price of output and the quantity of output. Equation (5.45) is the definition of total cost as the product of the price and quantity of the variable input X plus the assumed fixed cost of other inputs. Equation (5.46) is the definition of profit after Equations (5.44) and (5.45) are substituted into (5.43). Equation (5.47) is the production function which is the behavioral relation between output Q and the variable input X and the fixed input Z.

To maximize profit units of X should be hired until the increment to profit is zero, that is, until the marginal cost of an additional unit is equal to the marginal revenue generated by employment of that unit. (We shall assume without examination that second-order conditions are satisfied.) Hiring a unit of X directly affects output through Equation (5.47):

$$\frac{\partial Q}{\partial X} = \frac{\partial (f(X,Z))}{\partial X}$$

where $\partial Q / \partial X$ is the marginal product of the input X which is assumed to be positive. It also affects cost in Equation (5.45):

$$\frac{dC}{dX} = \frac{d(P_x X)}{dX} = \frac{dP_x}{dX} X + P_x \frac{dX}{dX}$$

where dC/dX is the marginal factor cost of the input X. The increase in output directly affects revenue through Equation (5.44):

$$\frac{dR}{dQ} = \frac{d(PQ)}{dQ} = \frac{dP}{dQ} Q + \frac{dQ}{dQ} P$$

where dR/dQ is marginal revenue.

The effect on profit of hiring one unit of X is therefore

$$\frac{\partial \pi}{\partial X} = \frac{\partial R}{\partial X} - \frac{\partial C}{\partial X}$$

$$= \frac{dR}{dQ} \frac{\partial Q}{\partial X} - \frac{\partial C}{\partial X}$$

$$= \frac{\partial Q}{\partial X} \frac{dP}{dQ} Q + \frac{dQ}{\partial X} \frac{dQ}{dQ} P - \frac{dP_x}{dX} X - \frac{dX}{dX} P_x. \tag{5.48}$$

Setting this derivative equal to zero (the first-order condition) and collecting terms, we get[11]

$$\frac{\partial Q}{\partial X} \left(\frac{dP}{dQ} Q + \frac{dQ}{dQ} P \right) = \left(\frac{dP_x}{dX} X + \frac{dX}{dX} P_x \right)$$

$$\frac{\partial Q}{\partial X} \left(P + \frac{dP}{dQ} Q \right) = \left(P_x + \frac{dP_x}{dX} X \right)$$

$$\frac{\partial Q}{\partial X} \left[P \left(1 + \frac{1}{\epsilon_d} \right) \right] = P_x \left(1 + \frac{1}{\epsilon_s} \right)^{11} \tag{5.49}$$

where $\epsilon_d = PdQ/QdP$, the elasticity of demand, the percentage change in quantity of output divided by the percentage change in price of output; and $\epsilon_s = P_x dX/XdP_x$, the elasticity of factor supply, the percentage change in quantity of input divided by the percentage change in the input's price. This (first-order) condition for a profit maximum says that the marginal physical product $(\partial Q/\partial X)$ times marginal revenue $P(1 + 1/\epsilon_d)$ equals the marginal factor cost, $P_x(1 + 1/\epsilon_s)$. Under circumstances of pure competition in product and factor markets, both elasticities approach infinity and the profit maximizing condition is

$$\frac{\partial Q}{\partial X} \cdot P = P_x. \tag{5.50}$$

This indicates that X is hired until its marginal physical product times the price at which output is sold is equal to the price of a unit of X.

Now if X is units of *capital*, this profit maximizing condition will determine how much capital the firm will hire, only if it is recognized that capital, by definition, has a useful life that goes beyond the current period n years into the future. Therefore, the left-hand side of Equation (5.49) must be written as a discounted present value:[12]

$$PV = \sum_{j=1}^{n} \frac{\left(\frac{\partial Q}{\partial X} \right)_j \left[P_j \left(1 + \frac{1}{\epsilon_d} \right) \right]}{(1 + i)^j} = P_x \left(1 + \frac{1}{\epsilon_s} \right). \tag{5.51}$$

[11]This gives the familiar relationship between marginal revenue and marginal factor cost and their respective elasticities. Where demand is perfectly elastic ($\epsilon_d \rightarrow -\infty$), marginal revenue, the term within the square bracket on the left-hand side, is equal to the price of output because $(1/\epsilon_d) \rightarrow 0$. Where factor supply is infinitely elastic ($\epsilon_s \rightarrow \infty$), marginal factor cost, the term on the right-hand side, is equal to the price of the factor input because $(1/\epsilon_s) \rightarrow 0$.

[12]The notion of present value was discussed earlier in the theory of consumption; a more detailed discussion appears in Chapter 3.

where the interest rate is assumed fixed. Under circumstances of pure competition in both markets Equation (5.51) is written as

$$PV = \sum_{j=1}^{n} \frac{\left(\frac{\partial Q}{\partial X}\right)_j P_j}{(1 + i)^j} = P_x. \tag{5.52}$$

Let $(\partial Q/\partial X)_j P_j$, representing the expected marginal revenue product of capital in the jth year, be expressed as Y_j. Because of the assumption of diminishing marginal productivity of capital, Y_j is positive but decreases as additional units of capital are employed. Equation (5.52) simplifies to

$$PV = \sum_{j=1}^{n} \frac{Y_j}{(1 + i)^j} = P_x. \tag{5.53}$$

The market rate of interest i at which the expected income stream Y_j is discounted represents the "cost" of capital funds at which the firm must borrow. If it is financing its projects externally, this is the rate at which the firm must borrow in capital markets. If the firm is financing internally, it is the rate at which its funds could earn if invested in financial assets of comparable risk and durability. The profit maximizing condition generates the following decision rule for the firm: *hire units of capital until the present value of the last unit hired is just equal to its dollar cost.* This indicates that, as long as the actual capital stock is less than the desired capital stock given by this decision rule, the firm will add to its physical capital stock until $PV = P_x$. This is reflected in Figure 5.10. The firm's net investment I is the change in its capital stock.

Each locus in Figure 5.10 slopes downward and to the right because, given any market rate of interest, as the quantity of capital goods

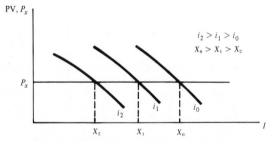

Figure 5.10.   The present value criterion for the investment decision.

hired (X) increases, the marginal physical product of capital $(\partial Q/\partial X)_j$ declines over the expected life of the unit of capital. This means that the marginal revenue product of capital $(\partial Q/\partial X)_j P_j$ also declines. Therefore at a given market rate of interest the present value PV declines as shown.

If we relax the assumption of pure competition in the output market, each locus in Figure 5.10 would decline more rapidly, because as the quantity of capital goods hired X increases, the quantity of output would rise. This increase in output would reduce marginal revenue [the term within the square brackets on the left-hand side of Equation (5.51)] because of a decrease in price in the product market associated with higher output. This would cause the marginal revenue product of capital, the numerator on the left-hand side of Equation (5.51), to decline for two reasons, diminishing marginal product and decreasing marginal revenue.

If we relax the assumption of pure competition in the market for capital goods, any purchase of capital goods would tend to put upward pressure on the price of these goods. Therefore, the P_x locus would be replaced by an upward sloping marginal factor cost line representing the right-hand side of Equation (5.51). In this case, units of capital would be hired until this upward sloping marginal factor cost locus intersected the present value locus in Figure 5.10. In both cases it can readily be seen that there would be less investment and less production if markets were not competitive in structure.

The example in Table 5.1 will elucidate the relationships described above. Assume that there is pure competition in product and factor markets so that Equations (5.52) and (5.53) apply. Column 4 shows that all output can be sold at the going market price of $100. Column 8 shows that all capital units can be purchased at the going market price of $7,000. Columns 2 and 3 depict the diminishing marginal physical product of capital. Column 5 shows the decreasing marginal revenue product of capital. If we assume for simplicity that this marginal revenue stream is constant for each unit of capital, and that each unit is infinitely lived, then in Equation (5.53) present value reduces to the simple perpetuity form discussed in Chapter 3:

$$PV = \frac{Y_j}{i} = P_x. \tag{5.54}$$

Using the given market rate of interest in column 6, we may thereby derive the present value of each unit of capital in column 7. In order to

Table 5.1. Present Value and the Marginal Expected Internal Rate of Return

1 Units of Capital	2 Output Q	3 Marginal Physical Product of Capital $\partial Q/\partial X$	4 Price of Output P	5 Marginal Revenue Product of Capital $(\partial Q/\partial X)P = Y_j$	6 Market Rate of Interest i	7 Present Value PV	8 Price of a Unit of Capital P_z	9 Marginal Expected Internal Rate of Return
0	10	—	$100	$ 0				
1	20	10	$100	$1000	10%	$10,000	$7,000	14.3%
2	29	9	$100	$ 900	10%	$ 9,000	$7,000	12.6%
3	37	8	$100	$ 800	10%	$ 8,000	$7,000	11.4%
4	44	7	$100	$ 700	10%	$ 7,000	$7,000	10.0%
5	50	6	$100	$ 600	10%	$ 6,000	$7,000	8.6%
6	55	5	$100	$ 500	10%	$ 5,000	$7,000	7.1%

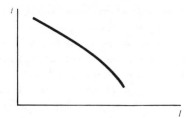

Figure 5.11. The aggregate investment relation.

maximize profit, capital is hired until this present value equals the price of a unit of capital. This occurs when four units are hired.

Table 5.1 and Equation (5.54) can be used to show an alternative to the present value decision rule. Rather than solve for the present value, let us ignore the market rate of interest and, dividing the expected income stream Y_j by the price of a unit of capital P_x, solve for the marginal expected internal rate of return, or marginal efficiency of capital. The marginal efficiency of capital is the rate of return that sets the present value, the left-hand side of Equation (5.54), equal to the price of capital, the right-hand side. Each unit of capital in Table 5.1 will then have a unique expected internal rate of return or marginal efficiency starting with $1,000/$7,000 = 14.3\%$ of the first unit, $900/$7,000 = 12.6\%$ on the second, 11.4% on the third, and so on. Profit is maximized where this rate, given in column 9, is just equal to the market rate of interest of 10%, or at four units of capital.[13]

For the economy as a whole net investment is defined as the change in the capital stock ($I \equiv \Delta X$). Given the desired capital stock X as derived above, if the actual capital stock of the economy is less than its desired level, the level of net investment expenditures in the economy is positive. As the interest rate increases, the desired capital stock, and hence the level of investment, decreases. This is evident in Figure 5.10; the relationship between the interest rate and aggregate investment is shown in Figure 5.11.

[13]These two criteria will not always generate the same decisions. The present value criterion would have the first use the market rate of interest in ordering or ranking investment projects. The marginal efficiency criterion does not use this information in ranking investment projects. Thus it could generate incorrect decisions in some cases. For example, a project with a higher internal rate of return than another project might actually have a smaller present value if its returns were relatively great in the distant future and the market rate at which future returns are discounted were quite high. In other cases the internal rate of return decision rule may be impracticable because Equation (5.53) may not yield a unique solution for i.

There is, of course, a good deal more to the analysis of the theory of investment.[14] Nevertheless, for our purposes it is sufficient to note that for the firm as well as the economy as a whole, there will be an inverse relationship between the market rate of interest and the level of investment. In the macroeconomic models that follow we express the relation between the market rate of interest and the level of investment expenditures in linear, slope-intercept form:

$$I = a' + hi$$

where $h < 0$, $a' > 0$.

Concluding Comments

This chapter has developed a basic overview of elementary macroeconomic theory. We began with the basic Keynesian theory of consumption and the related model of income determination. This theory is far from a satisfactory explanation of real-world behavior, and alternative, more realistic versions of its basic behavioral relations, the consumption and investment relations, were explored. Generally these more sophisticated functions entailed the introduction of an interest rate variable and (in the case of the consumption relation) a wealth variable. With these relations we may now proceed to the development of more realistic models of income (and interest rate) determination.

QUESTIONS

1. Explain the autonomous expenditures multiplier principle in words. Why is Keynes' MPC so important?
2. What would be the effect on consumption of a once-and-for-all reduction in autonomous taxation according to the permanent income theory of consumption as compared to the Keynesian theory of consumption?
3. Show that a businessman who chooses investment projects according to their expected internal rate of return may not be behaving rationally.
4. Consider the following model of the income-expenditure sector:

[14]See Robert Solow, *Capital Theory and the Rate of Return* (Chicago: Rand McNally, 1964); John Meyer and Edward Kuh, *The Investment Decision* (Cambridge: Harvard University Press, 1957); Jack Hirschliefer, *Investment, Interest and Capital* (Englewood Cliffs, NJ: Prentice-Hall, 1970), chapters 2–4; and Dale W. Jorgenson, "The Theory of Investment Behavior," in *Determinants of Investment Behavior*, Robert Ferber, ed. (New York: Columbia, 1967).

$C = 100 + .8Y_d$
$I = 200$
$G = 360$
$T = 200$
$C + I + G = Y$
$Y_d \equiv Y - T$

What is autonomous consumption? What is the marginal propensity to consume? The marginal propensity to save? What is the government deficit? What is the average propensity to consume at the equilibrium level of income? What is the value of the autonomous expenditures multiplier?

5. Explain in words why an individual's saving varies positively with the market rate of interest.

6. Explain in words why an individual's saving varies negatively with his wealth.

BIBLIOGRAPHY

ANDO, ALBERT, and FRANCO MODIGLIANI, "The 'Life Cycle' Hypothesis of Saving: Aggregate Implications and Tests," *American Economic Review* (March 1963).

BAILEY, M., "Formal Criteria for Investment Decisions," *Journal of Political Economy*, vol. 62 (October 1959), 476–488.

BOEHM-BAWERK, EUGEN VON, *Positive Theory of Capital* (New York: Stechert, 1923).

BRANSON, WILLIAM H., *Macroeconomic Theory and Policy* (New York: Harper and Row, 1972), ch. 11.

DE LEEUW, FRANK, and EDWARD M. GRAMLICH, "The Channels of Monetary Policy," *Federal Reserve Bulletin*, no. 55 (1969).*

DEUSENBERRY, JAMES, *Income, Saving and the Theory on Consumer Behavior* (Cambridge: Harvard University Press, 1949).

EVANS, MICHAEL K., *Macroeconomic Activity: Theory, Forecasting and Control* (New York: Harper and Row, 1967).

FISHER, IRVING, *The Theory of Interest* (New York: Macmillan, 1930).

FRIEDMAN, MILTON, *A Theory of the Consumption Function* (Princeton, NJ: Princeton University Press, 1957).

HIRSCHLIEFER, J., *Investment, Interest and Capital* (Englewood Cliffs, NJ: Prentice-Hall, 1970), chs. 2–4.

JORGENSON, D. W., "The Theory of Investment Behavior," in *Determinants of Investment Behavior*, R. Ferber, ed. (New York: Columbia, 1967).

LERNER, A. P., *The Economics of Control* (New York: Macmillan, 1944).

*Reprinted in THOMAS M. HAVRILESKY and JOHN T. BOORMAN, *Current Issues in Monetary Theory and Policy* (Arlington Heights, IL.: AHM Publishing Corporation, 1980).

MEYER, JOHN, and EDWARD KUH, *The Investment Decision* (Cambridge: Harvard University Press), 1957.

OTT, DAVID J., ATTIAT F. OTT, and JANG H. YOO, *Macroeconomic Theory* (New York: McGraw-Hill, 1975).

SOLOW, ROBERT, *Capital Theory and the Rate of Return* (Chicago: Rand McNally, 1964).

SPENCER, ROGER W., "Channels of Monetary Influence: A Survey," *Review*, Federal Reserve Bank of St. Louis (November 1974).*

VON FURSTENBERG, GEORGE M., and BURTON G. MALKIEL, "The Government and Capital Formation: A Survey of Recent Issues," *Journal of Economic Literature*, vol. 15 (September 1977), 835–878.

*Reprinted in THOMAS M. HAVRILESKY and JOHN T. BOORMAN, *Current Issues in Monetary Theory and Policy* (Arlington Heights, IL.: AHM Publishing Corporation, 1980).

SIX
Aggregate Demand

Introduction

In the previous chapter a simplistic model of the income–expenditures sector of the economy was developed. Earlier chapters examined money demand and money supply relations in some detail. The present chapter is our first attempt to integrate the income–expenditures and monetary sectors of the economy. We will develop a model which simultaneously determines equilibrium in the flow of income and expenditures as well as in the stock of money supplied and demanded.[1] Unlike previous chapters, the rate of interest will not be assumed given outside the model. Instead the interest rate—more specifically the long-term rate—is treated as a variable whose equilibrium value is determined simultaneously with that of the level of income.[2]

[1] The ideas capsuled here originate in Alvin H. Hansen's *A Guide to Keynes* (New York: McGraw-Hill, 1953) and in Sir John R. Hicks' "Mr. Keynes and the 'Classics,' A Suggested Interpretation," *Econometrica*, vol. 5 (1937), 147–159. Among the early mathematical treatments is Lawrence Klein's *The Keynesian Revolution* (New York: Macmillan, 1947). As a teaching device, this piece draws inspiration from Edward C. Budd's "Note on Money, Interest, and Income" (unpublished).

[2] As indicated in the early chapters of this book, there are many interest rates in the real world which are closely interrelated. For simplicity we focus only on the long-term rate as it may be most relevant for the investment decision. See the reading by Burton Malkiel which appears in the readings that follow Chapter 4 for a survey of the theory of the term structure of interest rates.

Despite this improvement, several aspects of the model developed in this chapter remain rather unrealistic. It is assumed that nominal wage and price levels are constant, so that all quantities are expressed in dollars of constant purchasing power. Government expenditures, taxation, and transfers are assumed to be zero. Relationships between expenditures, financing, and wealth will not be considered in detail. The next chapter will handle these elements in a more realistic manner.

The IS (Income–Expenditures Equilibrium) Curve

In the preceding chapter we saw that planned saving and planned consumption vary directly with the level of income, and that the level of planned investment varies inversely with the market rate of interest. We defined saving as current income not allocated to the purchase of consumption goods and services. These propositions, together with the familiar condition that planned saving must equal planned investment in equilibrium, suggest equilibrium combinations of the four variables (income, saving or consumption, investment, and interest rate).

The set of equilibrium relationships between the interest rate and the level of spending (consumption and investment expenditures) is called the *IS* curve. The *IS* curve shows, for a given interest rate, the level of income that will generate planned saving equal to planned investment. Some economists call this relationship the income–expenditures equilibrium curve, since for any level of production (or income), it shows the interest rate required to generate total aggregate expenditures (investment expenditures plus consumption expenditures) sufficient to absorb this output (or real income). In other words, with *given* commodity prices, there are unique combinations of interest rates and income levels which would clear the relevant markets without excess demand or supply, and hence without unplanned inventory change or unplanned saving.

The *IS* curve is derived from the investment and consumption functions and the condition that the economy must be in equilibrium. Figure 6.1 demonstrates the derivation of this relationship (where *positive* quantities are measured along all axes).

Saving is an increasing function of the level of income (quadrant 4 of Figure 6.1). For purposes of construction, the saving function replaces the consumption function (it will be recalled from the budget identity of the previous chapter that they can be used interchange-

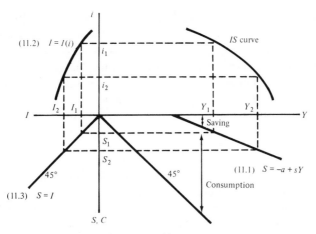

Figure 6.1.   Income–expenditures equilibria.

ably). The saving function is assumed to be linear in Figure 6.1 and may be represented as follows:

$$S = -a + sY \tag{6.1}$$

where s is the marginal propensity to save, $0 < s < 1$, and $-a$ is the level of dissaving or negative saving that occurs autonomously of the level of income; this negative autonomous saving is constant at all levels of income, $a > 0$. Consumption expenditures—equivalent to the volume of income that is not saved—are measured as the directed distance between the 45° line and the saving function. For the present we overlook the influence of the interest rate and the level of wealth on saving. These variables will be introduced into the saving function in the next chapter.

On the assumptions of profit maximizing behavior of business firms and diminishing returns in production, investment expenditures are a decreasing function of the rate of interest (quadrant 2 of Figure 6.1) as expressed in Equation (6.2). This is consistent with the theory discussed in the previous chapter. The principle of diminishing returns means that as a business firm acquires more units of a newly produced capital good, *ceteris paribus*, the discounted expected present value of successive units of that good declines.[3] In order to maximize profits, a

---

[3] At the margin of production, each newly produced capital good in the economy will have a successively smaller expected future income stream. Thus as the flow of

business firm will invest in desired units of capital until the discounted expected present value of the last capital good acquired is equal to the incremental cost of that capital good. Since the present value varies inversely with the rate at which expected future income is discounted (the market rate of interest), the lower the market rate, the greater the desired stock of newly produced capital goods.[4]

The investment function can, therefore, be expressed in general notation as

$$I = I(i). \qquad (6.2)$$

In Figure 6.1 the investment demand curve is drawn with a negative slope (the level of investment expenditures varies inversely with the market rate of interest) and concave to the origin. (Remember all axes measure positive quantities.) We present the equation more simply in our model by writing this function as the linear relationship:

$$I = a' + hi \qquad (6.2')$$

where h and a' are parameters and $h < 0$ and $a' < 0$.

The condition for equilibrium in the income–expenditures (flow) sector of the economy is that planned (or intended) saving equals planned (or intended) investment (quadrant 3 of Figure 6.1):

$$S = I. \qquad (6.3)$$

To determine a point on the IS curve, assume an arbitrary level of income (say Y_1) and from Equation (6.1) derive the amount of planned saving S_1 concomitant with that income level. From Equation (6.3) determine the amount of planned investment I_1 that necessarily must equal planned saving S_1 in order to maintain income–expenditures equilibrium. The line drawn in Figure 6.1 to represent Equation (6.2)

---

future income to the marginal investment good declines, its present value declines. The relationship between the future income stream from a capital good and its present value is discussed in the final section of Chapter 5.

[4]It should be pointed out that investment expenditures will be positive provided the stock of capital goods that is desired at the going market rate of interest exceeds the actual capital stock. Otherwise gross investment will be negative and equal to depreciation (capital consumption allowances) until the actual capital stock falls below the desired capital stock, *ceteris paribus*.

It should also be noted that in the present chapter we ignore the fact that the *financing* of investment expenditures by the business sector must increase the *wealth* of the private sector, and that increases in private wealth will have effects on both consumption expenditures (as seen in Chapter 5) and the demand for money (as discussed in Chapters 2 and 4).

discloses that this amount of investment will result only if the rate of interest is i_1. Hence i_1 and Y_1 represent a point of income–expenditures equilibrium which must lie on the IS curve and is therefore consistent with all three equations. Other points, such as i_2 and Y_2, are similarly derived.

The IS curve depicts a crucial macroeconomic relationship between the interest rate and the level of income in the income–expenditures sector of the economy. As the interest rate declines, planned investment spending increases [Equation (6.2)]. As investment spending increases, the level of income will rise; the rise in the level of income will generate sufficient planned saving [Equation (6.1)] such that the flow of planned saving will equal the flow of planned investment and the income–expenditures sector of the economy will be in equilibrium [Equation (6.3)].[5] The IS curve is not a demand or a supply curve but an income–expenditures equilibrium curve.

Substituting Equations (6.1) and (6.2′) into Equation (6.3), we may solve for the level of income Y in terms of all parameters and the rate of interest i. Because Equation (6.2′) indicates that the level of investment I is a linear function of the market rate of interest i, the income–expenditures equilibrium curve will be linear; its slope being constant and equal to h/s:

$$Y = \frac{a + a'}{s} + \frac{h}{s} \cdot i. \tag{6.4}$$

The LM (Money Market Equilibrium) Curve

In the previous section we used three linear equations to develop the income–expenditures equilibrium curve for the economy. Yet within this system there are four unknowns: investment I, saving S, the interest rate i, and the level of income Y. Clearly, unless one of the variables is given in a fourth equation (say the interest rate, $i = i_0$), one cannot find the equilibrium level of income, saving, or investment for the economy. We must add n equations in $n - 1$ unknowns in order to make a formal solution for this model possible.

Nevertheless, it would be unrealistic in the extreme to assume that the interest rate is given by dictate of the monetary authority. In the more general case, let us assume that the monetary authority at-

[5]As elementary macroeconomic theory teaches, the presence of equilibrium in a Keynesian model does not necessarily indicate a *full-employment* equilibrium.

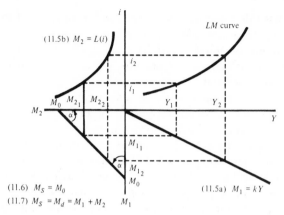

Figure 6.2. Money market equilibria.

tempts to control the nominal supply of money in existence.[6] Indeed, the interest rate, instead of being dictated, is the "price" which equates the stock of money supplied (so determined) to the stock of money demanded. The demand for money is, in turn, an increasing function of the level of income as well as a decreasing function of the interest rate.

In short, three additional behavioral equations (money supply, money demand, and the money market equilibrium condition) may be specified for the monetary sector of the economy. It is then possible to derive an equilibrium curve that combines these three equations and relates, for any given level of income, the rate of interest necessary to equate the demand for and supply of money. This curve, the "money market equilibrium curve," is denoted by LM and, in conjunction with the IS curve, expresses a complete general equilibrium model of aggregate demand in six equations and six unknowns. The LM curve as shown in Figure 6.2 is derived from these three basic monetary relations.

The total demand for money is considered to be a function of the level of income and the interest rate. The demand-for-money function used in this model derives from the analysis presented in Chapters 2 and 3. It is treated as consisting of two separate components. The first

---

[6]It is important to keep in mind that we assume that the general price level is constant in this model so that the monetary authority appears to be able to control the *real* stock of money. This is, of course, quite unrealistic. In fact, the Federal Reserve can control only the *nominal* stock of money. This restriction will be made explicit in subsequent chapters.

component of the demand for money is a function of the level of income and is drawn in quadrant 4 of Figure 6.2. This demand for "active" money balances is identified with the transactions motive for holding money. A high interest rate has been shown to bring about an economization of transactions balances. Accordingly, as discussed in Chapter 2, it is reasonable to indicate that the transactions demand will vary inversely with the interest rate and will vary less than in proportion to Y. Nevertheless, for the time being and in the interest of analytical simplicity the interest rate variable will be ignored in this portion of the total demand function for money, and the quantity of transactions balances demanded will be represented as varying in direct proportion to the level of current income:

$$M_1 = kY \qquad (6.5a)$$

where k is a parameter and the reciprocal of the income velocity of "active" money balances. As the price level is assumed constant, this represents a demand for real money balances. (In this discussion the precautionary motive for holding money is not explicitly related to any variable but, as mentioned in Chapter 2, may be assumed in all cases to be related to the same variables as the transactions motive.)

The second component of the demand for money M_2 is a function of the interest rate and is shown in quadrant 2 of Figure 6.2, where again all axes measure positive quantities. This portion of the total demand is identified with the speculative motive for holding money (or the "asset" demand for money). It is sometimes called the demand for "idle" balances and, as discussed in Chapter 3, is inversely related to the rate of interest. The liquidity preference function representing this relationship is shown in quadrant 2 of Figure 6.2. The function is negatively sloped and is convex to the origin. For simplicity's sake the equation of the liquidity preference curve can be expressed in general notation as

$$M_2 = L(i). \qquad (6.5b')$$

The reasons for the negative slope of the liquidity preference curve, as drawn in Figure 6.2 and described above, were examined in Chapter 3. In Tobin's analysis, for example, a larger percentage of financial wealth is held in the form of money as the interest rate declines, because a lower interest rate makes less attractive the risk of holding bonds. Later in this discussion it will be useful to write this portion of the total demand for money M_2 as the linear function

$$M_2 = m + ui \tag{6.5b'}$$

where u and m are, respectively, slope and intercept parameters, and where $u < 0$ and $m > 0$.

The nominal quantity of money supplied M_s is assumed to be determined by the monetary authority as M_0. In the present analysis we shall assume that this consists entirely of the noninterest bearing debt of government.[7]

$$M_s = M_0. \tag{6.6}$$

In quadrant 3 of Figure 6.2 the quantity of money supplied is measured as both the directed distance M_0 on the M_1 (vertical) axis and the directed distance M_0 on the M_2 (horizontal) axis. By geometry it may be seen that where the angle α equals the angle α' in the third quadrant, that portion of the money supply *not* held as transactions balances on the M_1 axis must be held as speculative balances on the M_2 axis. For instance, the directed distance on the M_1 axis, $M_{1_1}M_0$, is equal to the directed distance on the M_2 axis, $0M_{2_1}$, and the directed distance on the M_1 axis, $M_{1_2}M_0$, is equal to the directed distance on the M_2 axis, $0M_{2_2}$. Thus the third quadrant of Figure 6.2 depicts the condition that the supply of money M_0 must equal the quantity of money demanded $(M_1 + M_2)$:

$$M_s = M_1 + M_2 = M_d. \tag{6.7}$$

To determine a point on the *LM* curve, assume an arbitrary level of income (say Y_1) and derive from Equation (6.5a) the amount of M_1 (that is, M_{1_1}) concomitant with that level of income; the quantity that is necessary to satisfy the transactions demand for money or to "finance" the level of income Y_1. If M_{1_1} is desired as transactions balances and M_0 is the fixed money supply, by geometry it may be seen that only the amount M_{2_1} is available to satisfy the speculative demand for money. Given the liquidity preference function (6.5b), the interest rate i_1 is required to ration the supply of idle balances M_{2_1} among asset holders. Therefore i_1 is necessary to equate the demand for money $(M_{1_1} + M_{2_1})$ and the supply of money M_0 at the assumed income level of Y_1. The point i_1, Y_1 represents a point of money market equilibrium which must

---

[7]The interest bearing debt of government and all other forms of wealth, indeed the balance sheet identity, are not considered in the present chapter. Therefore, we overlook the influence of wealth on the demand for money and consumption, even though in previous chapters these variables played important roles.

lie on the *LM* curve and is therefore consistent with all three equations. Other points, for example, i_2, Y_2, are similarly derived.

The *LM* curve then is a set of equilibrium points for the monetary sector of the economy. Each point is consistent with the demand for money [Equations (6.5a) and (6.5b)], the supply of money [Equation (6.6)] and money market equilibriun [Equation (6.7)].

The *LM* curve depicts a crucial macroeconomic relationship between the interest rate and the level of income in the monetary sector of the economy. As the level of income Y rises, the quantity of transactions balances desired M_1 rises [Equation (6.5a)]. Given a fixed money supply M_0 [Equation (6.6)], individuals who desire more transactions balances must acquire them from those who hold idle balances M_2, that is, they must sell "bonds" to holders of idle balances. Holders of idle balances will only relinquish these money holdings for bonds when "bribed" by a higher interest rate, that is, a lower bond price [Equation (6.5b)]. Therefore, as the level of income rises, the interest rate must rise in order to maintain equilibrium between the supply of and the demand for money [Equation (6.7)], and the monetary sector of the economy will be in equilibrium. The *LM* curve is not a supply or demand curve but rather it is a money market equilibrium curve.

Substituting Equations (6.5a), (6.5b'), and (6.6) into (6.7), we may solve for the level of income Y in terms of all parameters and the market rate of interest i. Because Equation (6.5b') shows the quantity of speculative balances demanded M_2 as a linear function of the market rate of interest i, the money market equilibrium curve will be linear and its slope will be constant and equal to $-u/k$:

$$Y = \frac{M_0 - m}{k} - \frac{u}{k} \cdot i. \tag{6.8}$$

The unique equilibrium level of income and the equilibrium rate of interest can be determined by the intersection of the *IS* and the *LM* curves when both are plotted on the same graph in Figure 6.3. At this point both the monetary and the income–expenditures sectors of the economy are in equilibrium. Every point on *LM* represents a position of money market equilibrium; every point on *IS* represents a position of income–expenditures equilibrium. Where the two curves intersect, both sectors, and hence the entire model of aggregate demand, are in equilibrium.

Where Equations (6.2) and (6.5b) are linear, as Equations (6.2') and (6.5b'), the solution for the equilibrium level of income is derived from

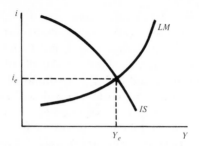

Figure 6.3. Aggregate equilibrium: the *LM* and *IS* curves.

six equations in six unknowns (Y, i, M_d, M_s, S, I) by rearranging both Equations (6.4) and (6.8) with the interest rate on the left-hand side:

$$i = \frac{M_0 - m}{u} - \frac{k}{u} Y \tag{6.8'}$$

$$i = \frac{-(a + a')}{h} + \frac{s}{h} Y. \tag{6.4'}$$

Setting the above expressions for the interest rate equal to each other and rearranging terms,

$$Y \left(\frac{s}{h} + \frac{k}{u} \right) = \frac{M_0 - m}{u} + \frac{a + a'}{h} .$$

Solving for the equilibrium level of income,

$$Y_e = \frac{\dfrac{M_0 - m}{u} + \dfrac{a + a'}{h}}{\dfrac{s}{h} + \dfrac{k}{u}}$$

$$= \left(\frac{M_0 - m}{u} + \frac{a + a'}{h} \right) \cdot \frac{hu}{su + hk}$$

$$= \frac{u(a + a') + h(M_0 - m)}{su + hk} \tag{6.9}$$

How Autonomous Expenditures Influence the *IS* Curve

As in the elementary macroeconomic theory presented in Chapter 5, autonomous expenditures may be treated as autonomous aggregate demand, the sum of autonomous investment expenditures and auton-

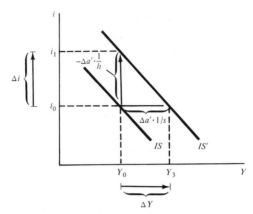

Figure 6.4. A change in income-expenditures equilibrium.

omous consumption expenditures.[8] Hence, an increase in autonomous expenditures can be reflected in Figure 6.1 either by moving the investment schedule horizontally to the left, or by shifting the saving schedule upward (an increase in autonomous consumption is identical to a decrease in autonomous saving). Thus at each point along the old *IS* curve there will be an excess aggregate demand for newly produced goods and services. In fact, in Figure 6.4 the entire region to the left of the new curve *IS'* is a region of excess aggregate demand for goods and services. From any point in this region, a specific rise in the level of income (or a specific rise in the interest rate) is necessary to increase output (or reduce aggregate demand) sufficiently to keep the income–expenditures sector in equilibrium.

In terms of saving and investment, at any point to the left of *IS'* in Figure 6.4 saving is less than investment. Either the level of income must rise (stimulating saving) or the rate of interest must rise (reducing investment) to bring the income–expenditures sector into equilibrium. At any point to the right of *IS'* saving exceeds investment. Either the level of income must fall (reducing saving) or the rate of interest must fall (stimulating investment) in order to bring the income–expenditures sector into equilibrium.

Therefore, starting from an initial position of equilibrium at any

[8]A government sector, which includes autonomous government expenditures and their financing by taxation or the issuance of debt and therefore involves fiscal policy, is discussed in the reading by Laurence H. Meyer which follows Chapter 7.

point on *IS* in Figure 6.4, an increase in autonomous expenditures will shift the curve to the right to *IS'*. Measured horizontally the *IS* curve shifts by the amount of the increase in autonomous aggregate demand times $1/s$. The rationale for this is quite clear. Take any level of income on the initial *IS* curve,

$$Y_0 = \frac{a + a'}{s} + \frac{h}{s} \cdot i_0. \tag{6.4}$$

Now change autonomous expenditures and observe the new level of income Y_1 which keeps the income–expenditures sector in equilibrium when the interest rate is held constant at i_0:

$$Y_1 = Y_0 + \Delta Y = \frac{a + a' + \Delta a'}{s} + \frac{h}{s} \cdot i_0.$$

Only if income increases by ΔY,

$$\Delta Y = Y_1 - Y_0 = \Delta a' \frac{1}{s}$$

at a fixed interest rate will sufficient saving ΔS be generated to equal the increase in autonomous investment $\Delta a'$ (or the decrease in autonomous saving),

$$\Delta a' = \Delta S = \Delta Y \cdot s$$

thus keeping the income–expenditures sector in equilibrium on the new curve *IS'* and satisfying Equation (6.3).

$$S + \Delta S = I + \Delta a'.$$

Similarly, measured vertically in Figure 6.4 the shift in the *IS* curve is $-\Delta a'(1/h)$. This may be readily seen. Rewrite Equation (6.4) with the interest rate on the left-hand side and take any interest rate on the initial *IS* curve:

$$i_0 = \frac{-(a + a')}{h} + \frac{s}{h} \cdot Y_0. \tag{6.4'}$$

Now change autonomous expenditures and observe the new level of the interest rate i_1 which keeps the income–expenditures sector in equilibrium if the level of income is held constant at Y_0:

$$i_1 = i_0 + \Delta i = \frac{-(a + a' + \Delta a')}{h} + \frac{s}{h} \cdot Y_0.$$

Only when the interest rate rises by Δi,

$$\Delta i = i_1 - i_0 = -\Delta a' \, \frac{1}{h}$$

at a fixed income level will investment spending by *reduced* sufficiently,

$$\Delta i \cdot h = -\Delta I$$

to offset the initial increase in autonomous investment $\Delta a'$ (or decrease in autonomous saving), thus keeping the income–expenditures sector in equilibrium and satisfying Equation (6.3) on the new curve IS',

$$S = I + \Delta a' - \Delta I.$$

So far we have only discussed the effect of a change in autonomous aggregate demand upon the entire income–expenditures equilibrium curve. The effect on the unique level of income and interest rate which keep *both* the income–expenditures and monetary sectors in equilibrium is discussed later in this chapter. Only when we consider the effect of changes in autonomous aggregate demand on both sectors can we develop a more sophisticated version of the autonomous expenditures multiplier principle of elementary macroeconomic theory.

How Money Influences the *LM* Curve

Because money is a stock and not part of the flow of spending and income and because in the present model it does not enter the saving and investment relations directly, monetary policy does not affect the *IS* curve. Rather it influences the *LM* curve. An increase in the quantity of money supplied will be shown as an increase in the length of the legs of the triangle in quadrant 3 of Figure 6.2. Thus at each point along the old *LM* curve there will be an excess supply of money (which will be used by individuals to acquire bonds).[9] In fact, the entire region to the left of *LM'* is a region of an excess supply of money. From any point in that region a specific rise in the level of income or specific decline in the interest rate is necessary to stimulate the demand for money suffi-

[9]Because money is a stock and the consumption of goods and services is a flow, there can never be a situation where money is used to acquire consumer goods and services directly; only bonds or capital goods (defined to include consumer *durables*) can be acquired. By the balance sheet identity, where the capital stock is assumed to be zero and where the supplies of money and bonds are assumed to be given, an excess supply of money is synonomous with an excess demand for bonds.

ciently to keep the money market in equilibrium. Any point to the right of LM' is one of an excess demand for money. A specific fall in the level of income or a specific rise in the interest rate is necessary to reduce the demand for money sufficiently to keep the money market in equilibrium. Thus, given an increase in the money supply only a specific lowering of the interest rate and/or a specific raising of the level of income will cause the increased money supply to be absorbed into transactions balances M_1 and/or speculative balances M_2 and keep the money market in equilibrium.

An increase in the money supply will, therefore, shift the LM curve to the right to LM' in Figure 6.5 by the amount of the increase in the money supply ΔM_s times $1/k$. This may be seen as follows. Take any level of income on the initial LM curve, Y_0,

$$Y_0 = \frac{M_0 - m}{k} - \frac{u}{k} \cdot i. \tag{6.8}$$

Now increase the money supply ΔM_s and observe the effect on the level of income which keeps the money market in equilibrium where the interest rate is held constant at i_0:

$$Y_1 = Y_0 + \Delta Y = \frac{M_0 - m + \Delta M_s}{k} - \frac{u}{k} \cdot i_0.$$

We see that only if income increases by ΔY,

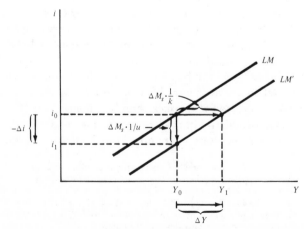

Figure 6.5. A change in money market equilibrium.

$$\Delta Y = Y_1 - Y_0 = \Delta M_s \frac{1}{k}$$

at an unchanged interest rate will the increased money supply be absorbed into transactions balances, thus keeping the money market in equilibrium on the new curve LM',

$$\Delta Y \cdot k = \Delta M_d = \Delta M_s.$$

Similarly, we may measure vertically the shift from LM to LM' in Figure 6.5 by $\Delta M_s(1/u)$. Rewrite Equation (6.8) with the interest rate on the left-hand side and take any interest rate on the LM curve, i_0,

$$i_0 = \frac{M_0 - m}{u} - \frac{k}{u} \cdot Y_0. \qquad (6.8')$$

Now increase the money supply ΔM_s and observe the new interest rate i_1 which keeps the money market in equilibrium if the level of income is held constant at Y_0:

$$i_1 = i_0 - \Delta i = \frac{M_0 - m + \Delta M_s}{u} - \frac{k}{u} \cdot Y_0.$$

Only if the interest rate falls by $-\Delta i$,

$$-\Delta i = i_1 - i_0 = \Delta M_s \frac{1}{u}$$

at an unchanged level of income, will the increased money supply be absorbed in speculative balances, thus keeping the money market in equilibrium on the new curve LM',

$$-\Delta i \cdot u = \Delta M_d = \Delta M_s.$$

Thus far we have discussed only how an increase in the money supply affects the entire money market equilibrium curve. The effect on the *unique* level of income and the interest rate which keep *both* the money market and the income expenditures sector in equilibrium is discussed later in this chapter.[10]

[10]Because money is assumed to consist entirely of the debt of government (outside money), money created by banks (inside money) is not considered. Thus this analysis overlooks the process by which total reserves (and/or the monetary base) are increased and results in a variable money supply expansion depending on the portfolio behavior of the banks and the public. (The reader may want to study Chapter 1 which elaborates on these factors in the money supply expansion process.) In short, for the immediate purposes of this analysis, the effects in the monetary sector of a simple, discrete expansion of the money supply are illustrated in Figure 6.5.

Multipliers and the Slopes of the Basic Functions: An Increase in Autonomous Expenditures

The two previous sections examined how changes in the autonomous expenditures and money supply parameters of our model disturbed the equilibrium in the money and income–expenditures sectors *separately* and shifted the *IS* and *LM* curves. Now let us examine how they affect overall, aggregate demand equilibrium. A good deal of theoretical and empirical controversy centers around hypotheses about the manner in which the interest rate and a measure of income affect the demand for money. Now we shall see the crucial influence of these hypotheses on the strength of the multipliers in this macroeconomic model. We shall assume in all cases that sufficient time passes in order for the multipliers to reach their (comparative static) equilibrium values.[11]

The inclusion of money market behavior and the rate of interest in this model modifies the form of the autonomous expenditures multiplier of elementary macroeconomic theory. The solution for income in the linear model was

$$Y_e = \frac{u(a + a') + h(M_0 - m)}{su + hk} . \tag{6.9}$$

The autonomous expenditures multiplier shows the change in income caused by a change in "autonomous" expenditures a, which shifts the *IS* curve. In Figure 6.6 the new equilibrium level of income Y'_e will be

$$Y'_e = Y_e + \Delta Y = \frac{u(a + a' + \Delta a) + h(M_0 - m)}{su + hk} .$$

Therefore, the change in income is

$$\Delta Y = \frac{u(\Delta a)}{su + hk}$$

[11]Permanent income explains more of the variation in the demand for money than current income. It was shown in Chapter 5 that the use of permanent income, as a weighted average of past and present levels of measured income, does not remove current income from the money demand and consumption functions, but rather adds a *lagged* value of income as a new explanatory variable in these relations. This modification of the basic model of this chapter simply means that while changes in the money supply or autonomous expenditures still affect income in the same direction, they would not *immediately* work their full multiplier effect. Instead, since past changes in income would also affect current income, any monetary or expenditures stimulus would take *time* to develop the full multiplier effect on income.

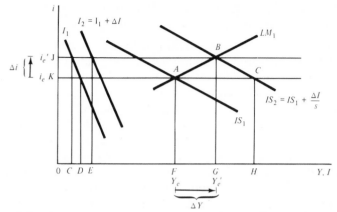

Figure 6.6. An increase in autonomous expenditures affects aggregate general equilibrium.

and the autonomous expenditures multiplier is a function of the slopes of the basic functions,

$$\frac{\Delta Y}{\Delta a} = \frac{u}{su + hk} .$$ (6.10)

In the previous chapter the model, which considered only the income–expenditures sector and assumed a constant interest rate, had an autonomous expenditures multiplier of $1/s$. This is considerably larger than the present autonomous expenditures multiplier, a multiplier that is derived from a more general equilibrium model which contains a money market as well as an income–expenditures sector and does not assume a constant interest rate. [12]

The effect of monetary phenomena on the autonomous expenditures multiplier is illustrated in Figure 6.6. The IS curve is drawn on the assumption that $a = 0$ and $0 < s < 1$. The marginal efficiency of investment schedule is located in the same quadrant as is the IS curve. The initial equilibrium position is at A, where equilibrium income Y_e is equal to OF; investment OD; consumption DF; and the rate of

---

[12]Those contemporary economists who believe that the effectiveness of fiscal policy has been overrated sometimes contend that the proponents of fiscal policy overlook this salient point. See, for example, David Fand, "Some Issues in Monetary Economics: Fiscal Policy Assumptions and Related Multipliers," *Review*, Federal Reserve Bank of St. Louis (January 1970), 23–27.

interest OK. If the investment schedule shifts to the right by an amount ΔI ($= CE$) and if the rate of interest were fixed at OK, the equilibrium level of income would rise by $FH = (1/s\ CE)$ to OH. However, the increase in aggregate income will induce an increase in the transactions demand for money and force the rate of increase up to OJ. The new equilibrium level of income Y'_e will be OG, and the increase in the level of income ΔY will only be FG rather than FH. The increase in the rate of interest has reduced the level of induced investment spending by CD and hence the level of income by $GH = (1/s) \cdot (CD)$. This occurs because, as the level of income increases, the demand for transactions balances M_1 increases and can only be satisfied, given a fixed money supply M_0, if speculative balances M_2 are relinquished. Speculative balances will only be relinquished and bonds accepted if the rate of interest rises. Because of the rise in the rate of interest, the level of investment spending falls by CD and the level of income will only rise to G.

Clearly, the rise in the interest rate reduces the size of the autonomous expenditures multiplier. The size of the multiplier depends upon the slopes of the basic functions from which it is derived. The slope of the saving schedule, Equation (6.1), is s and reflects the increase in saving, given a unit increase in the level of income. The slope of the investment schedule in linear form, Equation (6.2'), is h and reflects the amount by which investment must fall, given a unit increase in the interest rate, that is, $h = dI/di$.

The slope of the transactions demand for money schedule, Equation (6.5a), is k and reflects the increase in transactions balances demanded, given a unit increase in the level of income. The slope of the liquidity preference curve in linear form, Equation (6.5b'), is u and reflects the amount by which the quantity of speculative balances demanded must decrease, given a unit increase in the rate of interest, that is, $u = dM_2/di$. Hence, the effect of the interest rate and the level of income on the demand for money greatly influences the results brought about by a change in autonomous expenditures.

In reality, these slopes may not be constant for all points in the schedules (the functions may not be linear), although we assumed they are linear for purposes of deriving, most simply, the solution for the level of income. As explained for the more general case in Equations (6.2) and (6.5b), the absolute value of h falls as we move down along the investment schedule, and the absolute value of u rises as we move down along the liquidity preference schedule.[13] As discussed in Chapter 2, where the transactions demand is less than proportional, for example, under Baumol's square root rule, the interest rate will not be "bid up" much as income increases (the *LM* curve will be flatter), and, as can be seen in Equation (6.10), the autonomous expenditures multiplier will be greater in magnitude.

Within the more convenient linear framework the slope of the *IS* curve is equal to h/s and the slope of the *LM* curve is then equal to $-u/k$. This may be verified by examining the mathematical expressions for the *IS* and *LM* curves, Equations (6.4) and (6.8). (Remember $u, h < 0$ and $1 > k, s > 0$.)

In order to compare the new *LM–IS* autonomous expenditures multiplier to the simple autonomous expenditures multiplier of the elementary model of the previous chapter, $1/s$, it is instructive to rewrite it as

$$\frac{\Delta Y}{\Delta a} = \frac{1}{s + \dfrac{hk}{u}}. \tag{6.10}$$

If $dM_2/di = u = -\infty$ (a perfectly interest elastic liquidity preference schedule and hence *a horizontal LM curve*), or if $dI/di = h = 0$ (a completely interest inelastic investment schedule, and hence *a vertical IS curve*), then Equation (6.10) reduces to the simple autonomous expenditures multiplier. Aggregate demand would not be "choked off" by a rise in interest rates as income rose, either because the interest rate would not bid upward ($u = -\infty$), or because the rise in the rate would not affect spending ($h = 0$).

On the other hand, if $dM_2/di = u = 0$ (a completely interest inelastic speculative demand schedule, and hence *a vertical LM curve*), or if $dI/di = h = -\infty$ (a completely interest elastic investment schedule and *hence a horiztonal IS curve*), any increase in autonomous expenditures would *not* affect the level of income because the rise in the interest rate would "choke off" all the increased aggregate demand,

---

[13]To the extent that low interest rates are associated with massive unemployment, this model suggests that fiscal policy is a more reasonable stabilization tool during periods of unemployment (and monetary policy is more reasonable during periods of nearly full employment). See Phillip Cagan, "Current Issues in the Theory of Monetary Policy," in *Patterns of Market Behavior: Essays in Honor of Philip Taft*, Michael J. Brennan, ed. (Providence, RI: Brown University Press, 1965), 135–154.

that is, the autonomous expenditures multiplier would be zero, either because the rise in the interest rate would be immense as idle balances were sought to "finance" increased expenditures ($u = 0$), or because any rise in the rate would completely "choke off" spending ($h = -\infty$). In this case only an increase in the quantity of money, effecting a horizontal shift in the LM curve, could cause the level of income to rise.

The existence of a very interest inelastic demand curve for money ($u \to 0$) or a very interest elastic investment demand schedule ($h \to -\infty$) makes the change in the level of income following from a change in autonomous expenditure insignificant. This may be seen from Equation (6.10). Therefore, when the liquidity preference schedule is relatively interest inelastic or when investment spending is very interest sensitive, government policies to affect autonomous expenditures are considered to have a relatively less powerful effect on income.

Conversely, when the speculative demand for money schedule is very interest elastic ($u \to -\infty$) or when investment demand is very interest elastic ($h \to 0$) as can be seen in Equation (6.10), the change in the level of income following from a change in autonomous expenditures approaches the value of the simple multiplier $1/s$ of elementary models without a monetary sector. Therefore, when investment spending is very interest insensitive or when the liquidity preference schedule is relatively interest elastic, government policies to affect autonomous expenditures are considered to have a relatively more powerful effect on income.

Thus, we see that the order of magnitude of the autonomous expenditures multiplier is related to the orders of magnitude of the four slope parameters of our model, h, u, s, and k. The greater the absolute value of u, reflecting greater sensitivity of the public's holdings of speculative money balances to changes in the interest rate, the greater the magnitude of the autonomous expenditures multiplier in Equation (6.10). This is illustrated in Figure 6.7 which compares the orders of magnitude of the increases in income which follow from an increase in autonomous expenditures (shown as a shift in the IS curve from IS_1 to IS'_1) given two alternative LM curves. The steeper LM curve (LM_1) reflects a lesser absolute value of u, a less interest sensitive demand for money function; the less steep LM curve (LM_0) represents a more interest sensitive demand for money function. The curve

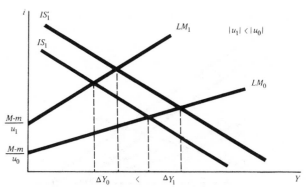

Figure 6.7. The greater the interest sensitivity of the demand for money, the greater the autonomous expenditures multiplier.

with a greater absolute value of u (LM_0) will give a larger change in the equilibrium level of income ΔY_0.

The less the absolute value of h, reflecting less sensitivity of investors to fluctuations in the interest rate, the greater the size of the autonomous expenditures multiplier in Equation (6.10). This is illustrated in Figure 6.8, which compares the orders of magnitude of the increases in income which follow from an increase in autonomous expenditures shown alternatively as a shift in the IS curve either from IS_0 to IS'_0 or from IS_1 to IS'_1 with a given LM curve. The steeper pair of IS curves (IS_1, IS'_1) reflect a lesser absolute value of h, a less interest sensitive investment spending function; the less steep pair of IS curves (IS'_0, IS'_0) represents a more interest sensitive investment function. The steeper IS curves, the ones with a lesser absolute value of h, will give a larger change in the equilibrium level of income ΔY_1.

Note that Figure 6.7 is constructed so as to hold all parameters constant except for u and autonomous expenditures a; Figure 6.8 is constructed so as to hold all parameters constant except for h and autonomous expenditures a. As seen in Figure 6.8, the magnitude of the horizontal shift in the IS curve is identical for IS_0, IS'_0 and for IS_1, IS'_1. Note also that, as in the case of the autonomous expenditures multiplier of elementary macroeconomics, the smaller the marginal propensity to save s, the larger the multiplier in Equation (6.10).[14]

[14]In more complex models additional leakages such as induced taxation, induced business saving (retained earnings), and induced imports may further reduce the magnitude of the multiplier.

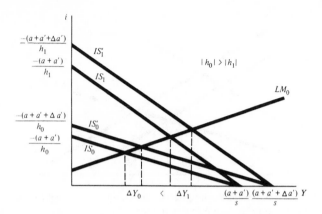

Figure 6.8. The less the interest sensitivity of the investment demand, the greater the autonomous expenditures multiplier.

Finally, the smaller the proportionality factor in the transactions demand for money k, the larger is the autonomous expenditures multiplier in Equation (6.10).[15]

Multipliers and the Slopes of the Basic Functions: An Increase in the Money Supply

The multiplier concept applies also to a shift in the LM curve caused by a change in the quantity of money supplied or a shift in the money demand function. In Figure 6.9 the new equilibrium level of income Y'', caused by a change in the quantity of money supplied ΔM is,

$$Y''_e = Y_e + \Delta Y = \frac{u(a + a') + h(M_0 - m + \Delta M)}{su + hk} .$$

Therefore the change in income is

$$\Delta Y = \frac{h\Delta M}{su + hk}$$

and the multiplier is a function of the slopes of the basic functions, or

$$\frac{\Delta Y}{\Delta M} = \frac{h}{su + hk}$$

[15]A decrease in the order of magnitude of either s or k increases *both* multipliers.

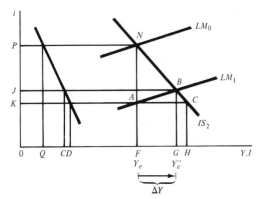

Figure 6.9. An increase in the money supply affects aggregate general equilibrium.

which may be written in a form which can be compared with previous multiplier expressions,

$$\frac{\Delta Y}{\Delta M} = \frac{h}{u} \left(\frac{1}{s + hk/u} \right) . \tag{6.11}$$

The difference between Equations (6.10) and (6.11) lies only in the term h/u. An increase in autonomous expenditures, as depicted by Equation (6.10), raises aggregate income by the multiple $[1/(s + hk/u)]$. The autonomous expenditures multiplier portion of Equation (6.11), the term in brackets, is the same as Equation (6.10). But an increase in M, as depicted by Equation (6.11), increases the level of income only insofar as it reduces the market rate of interest i and increases the level of investment spending I. The reduction in the market rate depends on the size of u (the fall in i with respect to an increase in M_s). The rise in investment spending depends on the size of h (the rise in I with respect to a fall in i). By calculus

$$\frac{dY}{dM} = \frac{di}{dM} \cdot \frac{dI}{di} \cdot \frac{dY}{dI} .$$

The existence of a very interest inelastic investment demand schedule ($h \rightarrow 0$) makes the change in the level of income following from a change in the quantity of money supplied ΔM insignificant. This can be seen from Equation (6.11). Even though a change in the money supply affects the interest rate, the rate has little effect on investment.

Therefore if investment is interest insensitive, as it may well be in many sectors of the economy, policies that affect the money supply are relatively less powerful.[16]

Also, the existence of a very interest elastic speculative demand schedule ($u \rightarrow -\infty$) makes the change in the level of income following from a change in the quantity of money supplied ΔM insignificant. This can be seen from Equation (6.11). Even if investment is interest sensitive, under these circumstances the money supply may be increased without much effect on the rate of interest, as individuals can be "induced" to hold additional speculative money balances without much decline in the interest rate. Therefore, when the speculative demand schedule is relatively interest elastic, policies that affect the money supply are less powerful.[17]

The effect of change in the money supply on the level of income, as shown in Equation (6.11), is illustrated in Figure 6.9. The initial equilibrium at N is disturbed by an increase in the quantity of money supplied ΔM. As discussed earlier, the LM curve shifts horizontally to the right by an amount equal to $\Delta M / k$. At the initial equilibrium level of income OF, the rate of interest will fall by $PK(= (1/u)\Delta M)$, that is, as excess money balances are used to acquire "bonds," the price of bonds rises and the market interest rate falls. At the lower interest rate, investment is stimulated by $QD(= (h/u)\Delta M)$. If the interest rate were fixed at OK, the simple multiplier process would move the economy to C, and the level of income would rise by FH. However, as discussed earlier in this section and illustrated in Figure 6.6, an increase in the level of income will force the interest rate back up to OJ as transactions balances must be obtained at the expense of speculative balances. The increase in the level of income will be limited to FG and the increase in the level of investment will be limited to QC.

Thus we see that the size of this multiplier is related to the orders of magnitude of the four slope parameters of our model, h, u, s, and k. The greater the absolute value of h, the greater the size of the monetary policy multiplier in Equation (6.11). This is illustrated in Figure 6.10 which compares the orders of magnitude of the increases in income which follow from an increase in the money supply (shown as a shift in the LM curve from LM_0 to LM_0') given two alternative IS

---

[16]See, for example, Phillip Cagan, *op. cit.*

[17]Estimated interest elasticities of the demand for money are reported in Tables 1 and 2 of the survey of empirical tests of the money demand function by John Boorman which follows Chapter 4.

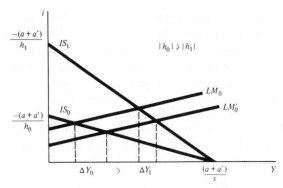

Figure 6.10. The greater the interest sensitivity of the investment demand function, the greater the monetary policy multiplier.

curves. The steeper IS curve (IS_1) reflects a lesser absolute value of h, a less interest sensitive investment demand function; the less steep IS curve (IS_0) represents a more interest sensitive investment function. The IS curve with a greater absolute value of h (IS_0) will give a larger change in the equilibrium level of income ΔY_0.

The less the absolute value of u, the greater the size of the monetary policy multiplier in Equation (6.11). This is illustrated in Figure 6.11 which compares the orders of magnitude of the increases in income which follow from an increase in the money supply, shown alternatively as a shift in the LM curve either from LM_0 to LM_0' or from LM_1 to LM_1' with a given IS curve. The steeper pair of LM curves

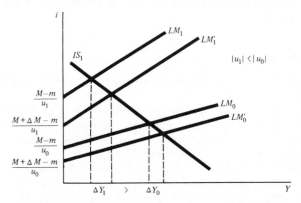

Figure 6.11. The less the interest sensitivity of the demand for money, the greater the monetary policy multiplier.

(LM_1, LM_1') reflect a lesser absolute value of u, a less interest sensitive demand for money function; the less steep pair of LM curves (LM_0, LM_0') represent a more interest sensitive demand for money function. The steeper LM curves, the ones with a lesser absolute value of u, will give a larger change in the equilibrium level of income ΔY_1.

Figure 6.10 is constructed so as to hold all parameters constant except for h and the supply of money; Figure 6.11 is constructed so as to hold all parameters constant except for u and the supply of money. The magnitude of the horizontal shift in the LM curves is identical for LM_0, LM_0' and LM_1, LM_1'.

Summary

This chapter has developed a framework within which the level of aggregate income and the rate of interest are simultaneously determined as part of a general equilibrium model of aggregate demand. Economists often analyze real-world problems with this paradigm in mind. However, the theory has its limitations. Government cannot be introduced into this model in any realistic way because it pays insufficient attention to the relationship between the flow of expenditures, the stock of wealth, and financing. Moreover, nominal wage and price levels were assumed given in the present model. This makes it an inadequate tool for analyzing inflation and related phenomena. While the chapters which follow will modify and extend the present model to correct these deficiences, it nevertheless represents an important advance over its predecessors and is a key building block in the repertoire of the economist.

QUESTIONS

1. Describe the economics of movements along the LM curve and along the IS curve.
2. Draw an LM curve. Why is the entire region to the right of the curve a region of excess demand (for money)? Starting from a point somewhere in this region, how must either real income or the interest rate change to bring about money market equilibrium?
3. Draw an IS curve. Why is the entire region to the left of the curve a region of excess aggregate demand? Starting from a point somewhere in this region, how must either the level of income or interest rate change to bring about equilibrium in the income–expenditures sector? Explain the assumed behavior which will bring about these changes.

4. Assume the Council of Economic Advisors (CEA) announces that the marginal propensity to save has fallen. Using the *LM–IS* model of this chapter, what would be the effect on the multipliers discussed in this chapter?

5. Assume the CEA announces that the amount of transactions balances held as a proportion of income has risen. What would be the effect on the multipliers discussed in this chapter?

6. Assume the CEA announces that the interest elasticity of investment demand has increased. Again, what would be the effect on the multipliers?

7. Explain completely (without the aid of graphs) why the size of the autonomous expenditures multiplier depends upon the interest sensitivity of the demand for money function.

8. Explain (without the aid of graphs) why a change in autonomous expenditures may be totally ineffective in changing the level of income in the economy if the demand for money function is interest insensitive.

9. Suppose all expenditures demand functions in the economy were completely unresponsive to changes in the rate of interest. What would the basic *LM–IS* graphical portrayal of this model look like? What would be the relative efficacy of monetary policy in such an economy? Explain.

10. Explain why the autonomous expenditures multiplier derived from the model of the income-expenditures sector which assumes a constant interest rate is generally larger than the autonomous expenditures multiplier derived from a more general equilibrium model which contains a money market and does not assume a constant interest rate.

11. Construct a graph similar to Figure 6.7 in this chapter, which shows the effect of a change in autonomous expenditures where all parameters except *k*, the proportionality factor in the transactions demand for money, are held constant. Then construct a graph similar to Figure 6.8, which shows the effect of a change in autonomous expenditures where all parameters except *s*, the marginal propensity to save, are held constant.

BIBLIOGRAPHY

ANDERSEN, LEONALL C., and KEITH M. CARLSON, "St. Louis Model Revisited," *International Economic Review*, vol. 15, no. 2 (June 1974), 305–327.*

ANDO, A., and STEPHEN GOLDFELD, "An Econometric Model for Evaluating Stabilization Policies," *Studies in Economic Stabilization*, Albert Ando, Edgar C. Brown, and Ann Friedlander, eds. (Washington, DC: The Brookings Institution, 1968), 215–287.

*Reprinted in THOMAS M. HAVRILESKY and JOHN T. BOORMAN, *Current Issues in Monetary Theory and Policy* (Arlington Heights, IL.: AHM Publishing Corporation, 1980).

BECHTER, DAN M., "Money and Inflation," Federal Reserve Bank of Kansas City, *Monthly Review* (July/August 1973), 3-6.*

BRUNNER, KARL, "The Role of Money and Monetary Policy," *Review*, Federal Reserve Bank of St. Louis, vol. 50 (July 1968), 9-24.

BUDD, EDWARD C., "Note on Money, Interest, and Income" (unpublished).

CAGAN, PHILLIP, "Current Issues in the Theory of Monetary Policy," in *Patterns of Market Behavior: Essays in Honor of Philip Taft*, Michael J. Brennan, ed. (Providence, RI: Brown University Press, 1965), 135-154.

CHOW, GREGORY, "Multiplier, Accelerator and Liquidity Preference in the Determination of the National Income of the United States," *Review of Economics and Statistics* (February 1967), 1-15.

DE LEEUW, FRANK, and EDWARD M. GRAMLICH, "The Channels of Monetary Policy: A Further Report on the Federal Reserve MIT Model," *Journal of Finance*, vol. 24, no. 2 (May 1966), 265-290.*

FAND, DAVID, "Some Issues in Monetary Economics: Fiscal Policy Assumptions and Related Multipliers," *Review*, Federal Reserve Bank of St. Louis (January 1970), 23-27.*

FRIEDMAN, MILTON, "The Lag Effect in Monetary Policy," *Journal of Political Economy* (October 1961), 447-466.

———, "The Role of Monetary Policy," *American Economic Review*, vol. 58 (March 1968), 1-17.

———, "Statement on the Conduct of Monetary Policy," *Second Meeting on the Conduct of Monetary Policy*, Hearings before the Committee on Banking, Housing, and Urban Affairs, U.S. Senate, 94th Congress, 1st Session (1975), 42-55.*

———, "A Theoretical Framework for Monetary Analysis," *Journal of Political Economy*, vol. 78 (March/April 1970).

FRIEDMAN, MILTON, and ANNA SCHWARTZ, "Money and Business Cycles," Conference on the State of Monetary Economics, *Review of Economics and Statistics*, Supplement (February 1963).

HAMBURGER, MICHAEL J., "The Lag Effect in Monetary Policy: A Survey of the Recent Literature," *Monetary Aggregates and Monetary Policy*, Federal Reserve Bank of New York (1974).*

HANSEN, ALVIN H., *A Guide to Keynes* (New York: McGraw-Hill, 1953).

HICKS, JOHN R. "Mr. Keynes and the Classics; A Suggested Interpretation," *Econometrica*, vol. 5 (1937), 147-159.

KLEIN, LAWRENCE, *The Keynesian Revolution* (New York: Macmillan, 1947)

LEIJONHUFVUD, AXEL, *On Keynesian Economics and the Economics of Keynes* (New York: Oxford University Press, 1968).

LOMBRA, RAYMOND E., and RAYMOND G. TORTO, "Measuring the Impact of Monetary and Fiscal Actions: A New Look at the Specific Problem," *Review of Economics and Statistics*, vol. 56, no. 1 (February 1974), 104-107.*

MAYER, THOMAS, "A Money Stock Target," *Monetary Policy Oversight*, Hearings before the Committee on Banking, Housing and Urban Affairs, U.S. Senate, 94th Congress, 1st Session (1975), 179-186.*

RITTER, LAWRENCE, "The Role of Money in Keynesian Theory," in *Banking and Monetary Studies*, Deane Carson, ed. (Homewood, IL: Richard D. Irwin, 1963), 134-150.

SAMUELSON, PAUL A., "Statement on the Conduct of Monetary Policy," *Second Meeting on the Conduct of Monetary Policy*, Hearings before the Committee on Banking, Housing, and Urban Affairs, U.S. Senate, 94th Congress, 1st Session (1975), 42-55.*

SCOTT, ROBERT H., "Estimates of Hicksian *IS* and *LM* Curves for the United States," *Journal of Finance*, vol. 21 (September 1966), 479-487.

*Reprinted in THOMAS M. HAVRILESKY and JOHN T. BOORMAN, *Current Issues in Monetary Theory and Policy* (Arlington Heights, IL.: AHM Publishing Corporation, 1980).

SEVEN
Aggregate Supply and Aggregate Demand

Introduction

In Chapter 6 we introduced a basic LM–IS analysis of the Keynesian model of aggregate demand. In that model the income–expenditures sector was represented by three linear equations, a saving function, an investment function and an equilibrium condition. Three linear equations also served to describe the monetary sector: a money demand function, a money supply equation and a market equilibrium condition. The aggregate economy was said to be in equilibrium when these six equations were solved simultaneously for the values of all of the variables, including income and the interest rate, which would satisfy the equilibrium conditions in both sectors.

Two crucial assumptions were made in the development of that model. First, the price level was assumed to be constant, so that changes in nominal values were also changes in real values. Second, equilibrium in aggregate demand (that is, in the income–expenditures sector and the monetary sector simultaneously) was referred to as equilibrium for the aggregate economy as a whole. No explicit reference was made to the supply (production and labor market) sector of the economy.

In this chapter we expand that analysis of the aggregate economy. To accomplish this four major modifications are made in the traditional **370** LM–IS model presented in Chapter 6. First, the money supply is made an endogenous variable, as suggested in Chapter 1, second, the influence of the interest rate on saving, first discussed in Chapter 5, is included; third, the price level and the level of nominal wages are introduced as explicit variables in the analysis; and fourth, a supply (labor market) sector is added.

In the next three chapters the order of presentation is based on the historical development of the theories attempting to explain the operation of the aggregate economy. We begin in the present chapter with a neoclassical model from which the quantity theory conclusions are derived. Keynesian factors such as wage rigidity, the liquidity trap and interest insensitive investment demand will be introduced later in the chapter.

Aggregate Demand[1]

The Income—Expenditures Sector

All behavioral relations in the income–expenditures sector of our model are specified to be relations between *real variables*, that is, neither households nor business firms suffer from money illusion. Money illusion refers to the notion that an equiproportionate change in both the nominal money stock and the prices of all commodities, even though it leaves all relative prices, real wealth, and the real value of money balances M/P unchanged, will nonetheless cause a change in some *real* aspect of an individual's economic behavior. As Don Patinkin notes ". . . if the initial paper-money endowment of an *illusion-free* individual were suddenly increased and he were simultaneously confronted in the market by new money prices, all of which had increased in the same proportion, he would once again have *no reason* for changing the amount demanded of any commodity."[2] (Italics added.) An

---

[1]The development of this model relates to the following works: Martin Bailey, *National Income and the Price Level* (New York: McGraw-Hill, 1962), chs. 2 and 3; Boris Pesek and Thomas Saving, *Money, Wealth, and Economic Theory* (New York: Macmillan, 1967), chs. 1 and 2; Robert Rasche, "A Comparative Static Analysis of Some Monetarist Propositions," *Review*, Federal Reserve Bank of St. Louis (December 1973), 15–23; Warren Smith, "A Graphical Exposition of the Complete Keynesian System," *The Southern Economic Journal*, vol. 23, no. 3 (October 1956), 115–125. The latter two articles are reprinted in Thomas Havrilesky and John Boorman, *Current Issues in Monetary Theory and Policy, op. cit.*

[2]Don Patinkin, *Money, Interest and Prices*, 2nd ed. (New York: Harper and Row, 1965), 22.

individual whose demand for or supply of some commodity *would change* in these circumstances would be said to be suffering from money illusion.

We assume that the investment decision depends on the interest rate and that the saving decision depends on the level of income and the interest rate. (The effect of wealth on consumption is ignored and for the time being government spending and taxation are also ignored.) The absence of money illusion implies that at given levels of real income and the interest rate, individuals will have the same amount of real saving and real investment regardless of the prevailing price level.[3] The relations embodying these assumptions may be written as follows:[4]

$$\frac{S}{P} = S\left(\frac{Y}{P}, i\right) = -\frac{a}{P} + s \cdot \frac{Y}{P} + \frac{e}{P} \cdot i. \qquad (7.1)$$

where $0 < s < 1$ and $a, e > 0$ and

$$\frac{I}{P} = I(i) = \frac{a'}{P} + \frac{h}{P} \cdot i \qquad (7.2)$$

[3]This is most easily rationalized if we assume unitary elasticity of price expectations. This implies that people expect the current price level to prevail in the future; but if prices change (unexpectedly), the public will then expect the new price level to prevail, that is, they would expect neither a return to the old price level nor a continuation of the rate of price change in its current direction. This concept was introduced by J. R. Hicks, in *Value and Capital* (Oxford: Clarendon Press, 1939), 205. As he states: "If the elasticity of expectations is unity, a change in current prices will change expected prices in the same direction and in the same proportion; if prices were previously expected to be constant at the old level, they are now expected to be constant at the new level; changes in prices are expected to be permanent."

[4]The following symbols are employed in this chapter:

P an index of the average price level in the economy
S aggregate saving in nominal dollars
Y aggregate income (national income) in nominal dollars
i an index of relevant interest rates in the economy
I aggregate investment expenditures in nominal dollars
M_s the money supply
M_d the demand for money
N_s the supply of labor
N_d the demand for labor
w the nominal wage rate
O the volume of real output (or measure of production)
K the capital stock
DD aggregate demand
SS aggregate supply

where $h < 0$ and $a' > 0$. These relations were derived from first principles in Chapter 5.

All variables other than the price level P and the interest rate i and all parameters other than the marginal propensity to save s are stated in nominal dollar terms, but are deflated by the index of the average price level to yield real values. Thus the terms a/P, a'/P, Y/P, etc., represent real values as implied by the assumed absence of any money illusion. This assumption further implies that if the price level should double, a, a', Y and the other nominal values would have to double in order to maintain a/P, a'/P, Y/P and the other real variables at constant real levels. This makes the linear saving and investment demand equations homogeneous of degree zero in nominal values and prices.[5]

By expressing the behavioral relations in this form and by assuming unitary elasticity of price expectations the average price level P is eliminated as a separate variable in these equations for the income–expenditures sector. Regardless of changes in the price level, real decisions remain unchanged. Consequently, the unknowns in these equations are specified as S/P, I/P, Y/P and i.

When these two behavioral relations are combined with the equilibrium condition for the income expenditures sector (for a closed economy where government expenditures and taxation are both assumed to be zero),

$$\frac{S}{P} = \frac{I}{P} \tag{7.3}$$

we derive a three-equation model in *four* unknowns. This linear system cannot be solved for equilibrium values of all four variables but it can, through substitution, be reduced to one equation in two unknowns.

Substituting Equations (7.1) and (7.2) into (7.3) yields

$$-\frac{a}{P} + s \cdot \frac{Y}{P} + \frac{e}{P} \cdot i = \frac{a'}{P} + \frac{h}{P} \cdot i$$

$$\frac{Y}{P} = \frac{a/P + a'/P}{s} + \frac{-e/P + h/P}{s} \cdot i. \tag{7.4}$$

---

[5]We shall not consider certain distributional effects of a changing price level in this discussion. Instead, we assume that when the average price level P changes, the prices of all goods and services in the economy change in the same proportion.

This linear form is very similar to the IS curve developed earlier, Equation (5.4). The intercept term is $(a/P + a'/P)/s$ which is identical to that of the IS curve of Chapter 5. The slope of the present IS curve is somewhat larger in absolute value (more interest sensitive) than that of the earlier IS curve:

$$\left| \frac{-e/P + h/P}{s} \right| > \left| \frac{h/P}{s} \right|$$

because of the inclusion in the numerator of $-e$, the (negative of the) slope of the saving function with respect to the interest rate. The marginal propensity to save out of real income is positive but less than unity; h/P is negative; while e/P can be expected to be positive; therefore, $(-e/P + h/P) < 0$. As a result, the slope of this equation, which represents all combinations of real income Y/P and the interest rate i which bring equilibrium to the income–expenditures sector (that is, combinations which equate planned saving and planned investment), will be negative. This equation is graphed in Figure 7.1.

Recalling the assumption about the absence of money illusion, examination of Equation (7.4) indicates that the *position of this curve is independent of the price level.* If the price level should increase, all nominal values would increase in the same proportion and the slope and intercept terms in Equation (7.4) would remain unchanged.

The Monetary Sector

The analysis of the monetary sector begins with the assumption that the *nominal* stock of money supplied to the economy is an increasing function of the interest rate. As already seen in Chapter 1 institutional and legal conditions establish the framework within which the public, depository institutions and the monetary authority interact to determine the actual nominal money supply. For example the monetary authority sets the reserve requirements which determine the vol-

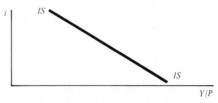

Figure 7.1.   Income–expenditures equilibrium curve IS.

ume of legal reserves that member banks must hold against their demand and time deposit liabilities. Also, the monetary authority has the power to control the size of the monetary base. The public, on the other hand, determines its preferred asset ratios, which influence the allocation of the monetary base among its alternative uses either as reserves against demand deposits, reserves against time deposits or as currency holdings of the public (see Chapter 1).

Given these factors, private behavior generates the final volume of money that will be created. Bank borrowing from the central bank can increase reserve holdings and expand the deposit creating capabilities of the banks. Holding reserve balances in excess of requirements tends to absorb legal reserves and to decrease the money creating abilities of banks. In this way the money stock depends on the behavior of banks relating to their desired holdings of excess and borrowed reserves.

As discussed in Chapter 1, one of the important factors affecting this aspect of bank behavior is the market interest rate. If the market rate is relatively high, banks will be induced to hold a relatively small volume of reserves in excess of legal requirements, since the interest rate represents the alternative cost of holding those reserves. But the lower the volume of desired excess legal reserves, the greater the volume of loans banks will extend and the larger the volume of deposit liabilities they will have outstanding for a given monetary base. Therefore, as holdings of excess legal reserves vary inversely with the market interest rate, the money stock can be expected to vary directly with variations in that rate.[6]

Similarly, banks will increase their borrowing from the Federal Reserve when the differential between the market rate and the discount rate increases. As a result, for a given discount rate, the higher the market rate, the greater the volume of bank borrowing and the larger the stock of liabilities created by the commercial banks.

---

[6]A money supply model that incorporates this relation in a structural equation is presented in Chapter 1. Note that having the money supply depend on the (endogenous) interest rate causes the money stock *to be affected* by economic activity as well as *to affect* that activity. It is this point that lies at the center of much of the so-called "reverse causation" controversy over the econometric models which purport that the money supply is a statistically exogenous variable. Compare, for example, David I. Fand, "Some Issues in Monetary Economics: Fiscal Policy Assumptions and Related Multipliers," *Review*, Federal Reserve Bank of St. Louis (January 1970), 23-27, and Raymond Lombra and Raymond Torto, "Measuring the Impact of Monetary and Fiscal Actions: A New Look at the Specification Problem," *Review of Economics and Statistics*, vol. 56, no. 1 (February 1974), 104-107. Keynesian and Monetarist econometric models are featured in a reading by Joseph M. Crews which follows this chapter.

Therefore, given the monetary base, the required reserve ratios set by the authorities and the preferred asset ratios of the public, the nominal money supply can be expected to vary directly with the rate of interest, that is,

$$M_s = \gamma(i) \qquad \frac{\partial M_s}{\partial i} > 0. \tag{7.5}$$

This relationship is shown in Figure 7.2. The position of this curve is assumed to depend on all the factors listed above. For example, if the monetary authority increases the monetary base, the curve will shift from M_s to $M_s{}'$. The slope of the curve will depend on the marginal responses of desired excess and borrowed reserve levels of commercial bankers to changes in the interest rate.

On the demand side of the money market we assume that the desire for money balances on the part of the public stems from two sources: first, a desire for real transactions balances to facilitate a real volume of output and second, a desire to maintain some proportion of real financial wealth in the form of real money balances.[7] In other words, the public demands a stock of *real* money balances, both to facilitate transactions and to hold as speculative (asset) balances. Following the discussion in Chapters 2–4 we express the transactions demand for real money balances as an increasing function of the level of real income Y/P and the speculative demand for real money balances as a decreasing function of the market rate of interest i; the public's behavior is again assumed free of money illusion. The effect of the level of wealth on the demand for money is ignored.[8]

$$(M/P)_d = L(Y/P, i), \qquad \frac{\partial (M/P)_d}{\partial (Y/P)} > 0, \qquad \frac{\partial (M/P)_d}{\partial i} < 0. \tag{7.6}$$

Equilibrium in the money market requires that the *real* value of the nominal quantity of money in circulation be just sufficient to satisfy the public's demand for real money balances:

$$\frac{M_s}{P} = \left(\frac{M}{P} \right)_d. \tag{7.7}$$

[7]See Alfred Marshall, *Money, Credit and Commerce* (London: Macmillan, 1923).

[8]Differing demand for money hypotheses lead to the same *general* functional form for the money demand relation. Our structural analysis is completely compatible with these alternative formulations. It is the *a priori* restrictions placed on the partial derivatives of these forms and the empirical specification of these equations that we would expect to differ under varying formulations of the theory of money demand. See Chapters 2–4 for a detailed analysis of the alternative hypotheses that yield these specifications.

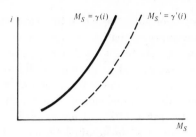

Figure 7.2. Supply of money function.

To make Equation (7.5) consistent with the equilibrium condition, we divide both sides of that equation by the price level P. Substitution of Equations (7.5) and (7.6) into (7.7) then yields the money market equilibrium equation:

$$\frac{1}{P} \cdot \gamma(i) = L(Y/P, i). \tag{7.8}$$

In order to solve this system of equations for equilibrium solutions in terms of the exogenous variables and the parameters of the model, let us assume linear functional forms to represent the relations between the nominal stock of money supplied and the interest rate and between the stock of real money balances demanded and real income and the interest rate. Thus,[9]

$$M_s = \gamma(i) = j + d \cdot i \tag{7.9}$$

and

$$\left(\frac{M}{P} \right)_d = L(Y/P, i) = \frac{m}{P} + k \frac{Y}{P} + \frac{u}{P} i. \tag{7.10}$$

Then, in equilibrium,

$$\frac{1}{P} \cdot M_s = \left(\frac{M}{P} \right)_d$$

$$\frac{1}{P} \cdot (j + di) = \frac{m}{P} + k \frac{Y}{P} + \frac{u}{P} i$$

$$\frac{Y}{P} = \frac{1}{k} \left[\left(\frac{1}{P} \cdot j - \frac{m}{P} \right) + \left(\frac{1}{P} \cdot d - \frac{u}{P} \right) i \right]. \tag{7.11}$$

[9]Compare this formulation to the linear functional forms [Equations (1.20) and (1.36) of Chapter 1]. Here the monetary base may be assumed to be incorporated in the intercept term j. This explains how the monetary base could appear as an exogenous variable in reduced form equations such as Equation (7.11).

It is extremely important to note that the parameters j and d from the (nominal) money supply equation *do not* react to price changes in the same way as the parameters m and u from the (real) money demand relation. The assumption of no money illusion on the part of individuals who demand real money balances implies that when the price level P changes, the nominal values m and u change by the same proportion, leaving the ratios m/P and u/P unchanged. The supply of money, however, is specified in nominal terms. It follows then that there is no reason for the parameters j and d to change when the price level changes. Consequently, in the money market equilibrium equation (7.11) there are three unknowns, real income Y/P, the interest rate i and the price level P. The presence of the price level as a distinct variable in this equation reflects our assumption that the behavior of the public, the banks and the monetary authority determines the *nominal* money stock.

The equilibrium condition in this market can be depicted as a family of market equilibrium curves. The graphical derivation of these *LM* curves is shown in Figure 7.3.

In Figure 7.3A real money balances M/P are measured along the horizontal axis. Since the demand for money depends upon both the level of real income and the interest rate, a family of money demand curves appears in the real money balances–interest rate plane. Each curve shows the volume of real money balances demanded at every level of the interest rate for a given level of real income. For example, $(M/P)_d Y_1/P_1$ shows how the demand for real money balances varies with the interest rate when real income is assumed to be Y_1/P_1. For any given level of the interest rate, real money balances demanded will be greater

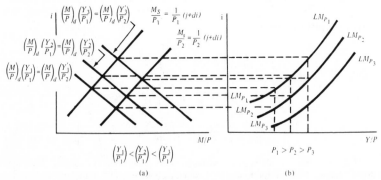

Figure 7.3. Monetary sector equilibrium curves *LM*.

the greater the level of real income. As a result $(M/P)_d Y_2/P_1$, representing the demand for real money balances at income level, $Y_2/P_1 >$ Y_1/P_1, lies to the right of $(M/P)_d Y_1/P_1$.

A given real income level Y_1/P_1 represents any one of an infinite number of nominal income–price level combinations. For example, if nominal income is Y_1 and the price level is P_1, real income will be Y_1/P_1. But this same real income level would also result from a nominal income level of $2Y_1$ and a price level of $2P_1$, that is, $2Y_1/2P_1 = Y_1/P_1$.

Let us assume an initial price level of P_1. If $Y_1 < Y_2 < Y_3$, then $Y_1/P_1 < Y_2/P_1 < Y_3/P_1$. Three curves showing how the demand for real money balances varies with the interest rate at these real income levels are drawn in Figure 7.3A.

Since the money supply relation is expressed in nominal terms, it must be modified to depict the real values reflected in our diagram. This is done simply by dividing the nominal money supply function by the average price level. Thus for an assumed initial price level P_1 the money supply relation $M_s/P_1 = (1/P_1)(j + di)$ is shown in Figure 7.3A as an upward sloping line.

Given the price level, the intersection point of the single money supply curve with the family of money demand curves yields combinations of the interest rate and the level of real income which equate the supply of and demand for real money balances. These points may be used to locate the money market equilibrium curve LM_{P_1} in Figure 7.3B.

As shown by Equation (7.11) for a given price level, the LM curve has an intercept of $(j/P - m/P)/k$ and a slope of $(d/P - u/P)/k$. This makes it quite similar to the LM curve of Equation (6.8). The slope of the present LM curve is somewhat flatter (more interest sensitive) than that of the earlier LM curve, $(d/P - u/P)/k > (-u/P)/k$, because of the inclusion of d/P, the slope of the money supply relation in the numerator.

What happens to the money demand curve if the price level should change? Suppose, for example, that the price level falls to $P_2 <$ P_1. There is some nominal income level $Y_1' < Y_1$ such that $Y_1'/P_2 = $ Y_1/P_1. Therefore, the money demand curve $(M/P)_d(Y_1'/P_2)$ coincides with $(M/P)_d(Y_1/P_1)$, both curves showing the relation between real money balances demanded and the interest rate at a given level of real income. But what happens to the money supply curve if the price level should change? Since the money supply function is specified in nominal terms, when the price level falls, the same volume of nominal balances supplied by the monetary system will represent a greater real volume of money balances. Therefore, at each interest rate $M_s/P_2 = 1/P_2(j + di)$ lies to the right of $M_s/P_1 = 1/P_1(j + di)$.

The new money supply curve together with the family of money demand curves generate a new money market equilibrium curve LM_{P_2}. The new curve lies to the right of LM_{P_1}, indicating that in money market equilibrium at the lower price level P_2 each interest rate level will now be associated with a higher level of real income and each real income level will now be associated with a lower interest rate. Along the new money market equilibrium curve LM_{P_2}, nominal money balances supplied to the economy at each interest rate represent a larger real stock of balances at the lower price level. Therefore, at unchanged interest rate levels only a higher level of real income can cause the nonbank public to demand these additional real money balances (for transactions purposes), thereby bringing the money market into equilibrium. As a consequence, at each interest rate level the new money market equilibrium curve LM_{P_2} lies *to the right* of the old money market equilibrium curve LM_{P_1}.

As another way of looking at this, at unchanged real income levels only a lower interest rate can cause the nonbank public to demand the additional real money balances (for speculative purposes), thereby bringing the money market into equilibrium. As a consequence, at each real income level the new money market equilibrium curve LM_{P_2} lies *below* the old money market equilibrium curve LM_{P_1}. (The simple analytics of a shift in the *LM* curve are discussed in more detail in Chapter 6.)

Proceeding in this manner, we can derive a family of money market equilibrium curves, one for each possible price level. For example, in Figure 7.3B the curve LM_{P_3} represents money market equilibrium for a still lower level of prices than the curve LM_{P_2}.

Aggregate Demand Equilibrium

Now consider the equilibrium curve for the monetary sector [Equation (7.11)] together with the equilibrium curve for the income–expenditures [Equation (7.4)]. If, as in Chapters 5 and 6 we assume that the price level is constant we are restricted to just one of the family of money market equilibrium curves. In Figure 7.4, where the two curves intersect, there is equilibrium in both the income–expenditures sector and the monetary sector.

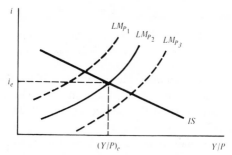

Figure 7.4. Expenditures and money market equilibrium at fixed prices.

Analytically this equivalent to solving Equations (7.4) and (7.11) simultaneously for the level of income and the interest rate at an assumed (constant) level of prices. This solution is presented below for an assumed price level P_2:

$$\frac{Y}{P_2} = \frac{a/P_2 + a'/P_2}{s} + \frac{-e/P_2 + h/P_2}{s} \cdot i \tag{7.4}$$

$$\frac{Y}{P_2} = \frac{1}{k}\left[\left(\frac{1}{P_2}\cdot j - \frac{m}{P_2} \right) + \left(\frac{1}{P_2}\cdot d - \frac{u}{P_2} \right)\cdot i \right] . \tag{7.11}$$

Solving each of these equations for the interest rate i yields

$$i = \frac{s}{-e/P_2 + h/P_2} \cdot \frac{Y}{P_2} - \frac{a/P_2 + a'/P_2}{-e/P_2 + h/P_2} \tag{7.4'}$$

and

$$i = \frac{-k}{[(-1/P_2)\cdot d + u/P_2]} \cdot \frac{Y}{P_2} + \frac{[(1/P_2)\cdot j - m/P_2]}{[(-1/P_2)\cdot d + u/P_2]} . \tag{7.11'}$$

Substitution then yields the solution (in terms of the parameters of the model) for the equilibrium level of income:

$$\frac{Y}{P_2}\left(\frac{s}{-e/P_2 + h/P_2} + \frac{k}{[(-1/P_2)\cdot d + u/P_2]} \right) =$$

$$\frac{a/P_2 + a'/P_2}{-e/P_2 + h/P_2} + \frac{[(1/P_2)\cdot j - m/P_2]}{[(-1/P_2)\cdot d + u/P_2]}$$

$$\frac{Y}{P_2} = \frac{\left[\dfrac{a/P_2 + a'/P_2}{-e/P_2 + h/P_2} + \dfrac{[(1/P_2)\cdot j - m/P_2]}{[(-1/P_2)\cdot d + u/P_2]} \right]}{\left[\dfrac{s}{-e/P_2 + h/P_2} + \dfrac{k}{[(-1/P_2)\cdot d + u/P_2]} \right]} .$$

Collecting terms,

$$\frac{Y}{P_2} = \frac{(a/P_2 + a'/P_2)[(-1/P_2)\cdot d + u/P_2] + [(1/P_2)\cdot j - m/P_2](-e/P_2 + h/P_2)}{s[(-1/P_2)\cdot d + u/P_2] + k(-e/P_2 + h/P_2)}$$

This equation is directly comparable to Equation (6.9). It differs only in its explicit inclusion of price level P_2 and in the inclusion of the new behavioral parameter e from the saving function.[10] The solution processes are identical.

Implicit in the analysis so far has been the assumption that the response of aggregate supply to changes in the level of aggregate demand consists exclusively of a quantity (real output) adjustment. This is implied by our earlier assumption of a constant, exogenously determined, general price level. In contrast, if we assume instead that the response of aggregate supply to changes in aggregate demand is not constrained to a pure quantity adjustment, then the general price level becomes a variable endogenous to our model.

With a variable price level, no single LM curve can be isolated to represent the locus of money market equilibrium values for the level of real income and the level of the interest rate and no unique solution for these variables can be found in the LM–IS quadrant. This is illustrated in Figure 7.4. In other words, the aggregate demand sector LM and IS

---

[10]The effects of a change in some component of autonomous expenditures may be seen in this equation. For example, assume that the volume of autonomous investment spending, a'/P, increases and shifts the IS curve:

$$\frac{\partial(Y/P_2)}{\partial(a'/P_2)} = \frac{(-1/P_2)\cdot d + u/P_2}{s[(-1/P_2)\cdot d + u/P_2] + k(-e/P_2 + h/P_2)}$$

$$= \frac{1}{s + \dfrac{k(-e/P_2 + h/P_2)}{(-1/P_2)\cdot d + u/P_2}} \ .$$

This derivative indicates the order of magnitude of the change in real income caused by an increase in autonomous investment expenditures. It may be employed in a strictly qualitative way to determine the direction of the effect of an increase in autonomous investment expenditures on the level of income. Since $1 > s > 0$, $1 > k > 0$, $(-e/P_2 + h/P_2) < 0$, $u/P_2 < 0$, and $1/P_2 \cdot d > 0$, the last term in the denominator

$$\frac{k(-e/P_2 + h/P_2)}{(-1/P_2)\cdot d + u/P_2}$$

will be positive. As a result, the derivative is seen to be *positive* and an *increase* in autonomous investment expenditures will *increase* the level of income. This result is directly comparable to Equation (6.10).

curves are not sufficient by themselves to provide a determinate solution for our model because we will have added to our aggregate demand sector a new variable, the general price level, but no new equations. Therefore, in order to be able to discuss the determination of the general price level jointly with the determination of the level of real income, the interest rate and all the other variables of the model, we now add a set of behavioral relations describing the aggregate supply (production and labor market) sector of the economy.

Aggregate Supply

We first explicitly introduce the labor market and aggregate production function into this model and examine its comparative-static characteristics under the neoclassical assumptions of perfect flexibility of the price level and the nominal wage level and no money illusion on either side of the labor market. Pure competition is assumed in all markets; the quantity of labor N is measured as a number of homogeneous man-hours.

The supply of labor   Assume that individuals attempt to balance the marginal disutility of labor against the marginal utility of income. Since the utility to be derived from money income depends on its real value or purchasing power, the quantity of labor supplied will depend primarily on the real return from offering labor services—the real wage rate w/P. Under the joint assumptions of diminishing marginal utility of consumption (out of earned income) and increasing marginal disutility of work, the labor supply function will have a positive slope indicating that laborers will only supply more labor at higher real wage rates. We may express this as follows:

$$N_s = N_s(w/P), \qquad \frac{\partial N_s}{\partial(w/P)} > 0. \tag{7.12}$$

The demand for labor.   On the demand side of the market, the profit maximizing condition indicates that under conditions of pure competition in all markets firms hire workers up to the point where the real wage they must pay is equal to the marginal productivity of labor.[11] Assume a simple aggregate production function,

[11]For the individual firm, given its production function, the demand curve for its product, and the labor supply curve it faces, profit may be defined as $\pi = P \cdot O - w \cdot N$

384 **Macroeconomic Models**

$$O = Y/P = l(N,K) \tag{7.13}$$

where O is the real volume of output from production and K is the capital stock used in the production process. Then

$$\frac{w}{P} = \frac{\partial O}{\partial N} = l'(N,K) \tag{7.14}$$

where $l'(N,K)$ is the first derivative of the aggregate production function with respect to labor input. Diminishing marginal productivity of labor (derived from the aggregate production function under the assumption that the stock of capital K and the level of technology are held constant and that the function increases monotonically over the relevant domain) implies a downward sloping demand for labor curve. These relations are represented graphically in Figure 7.5.

If we assume perfect flexibility of the nominal wage and price levels and perfectly competitive conditions in the labor market, the nominal wage rate will be bid to a level which, together with the current price level, will establish a real wage that equates the supply of and demand for labor. This is the position of intersection shown in Figure 7.5A. Since everyone who is willing to offer his labor services at this wage rate will be employed, this position is defined as full employment. When this level of employment is substituted into the production function (in Figure 7.5B), the full employment level of real output $(Y/P)_f$ is determined.[12]

$- c$, where c represents constant capital costs. The first-order condition for profit maximization requires

$$\frac{\partial \pi}{\partial N} = \left[\frac{dP}{dO} \cdot O + P \right] \frac{\partial O}{\partial N} - \left[\frac{\partial w}{\partial N} \cdot N + w \right] = 0$$

which simplifies to the general proposition that the profit maximizing firm will hire labor until its marginal revenue product equals its marginal factor cost,

$$\frac{\partial O}{\partial N} \left[P \left(1 + \frac{O}{P} \cdot \frac{dP}{dO} \right) \right] = w \left(1 + \frac{N}{w} \cdot \frac{\partial w}{\partial N} \right).$$

The reciprocals of the product terms in the brackets on either side of the equation represent the price elasticity of product demand and the wage elasticity of labor supply, respectively. In pure competition, these terms are equal to zero and the expression simplifies to the condition that the profit maximizing firm will hire labor until its marginal physical product is equal to the real wage, $\delta O/\delta N = w/P$. For further elaboration on the theory of the input decision of the profit maximizing firm see the last section of Chapter 5.

[12]The reader will note that we have associated full employment with the equilibrium solution in the labor market. Likewise, in the present model, which presents labor

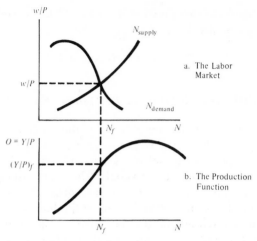

Figure 7.5. (a) Labor market. (b) Production function.

This may be shown symbolically. We may represent the aggregate supply sector as a system of four equations—labor supply, labor demand, the equilibrium condition and the production function—in four unknowns—N_s, N_d, Y/P and w/P. These relations are

$$N_s = N_s(w/P) \qquad (7.12)$$

$$N_d = N_d(w/P) \qquad (7.14')$$

$$N_s = N_d \qquad (7.15)$$

$$Y/P = l(N,K) \qquad (7.13)$$

where K, the capital stock, is assumed fixed. By substitution we can solve Equations (7.12), (7.14') and (7.15) for the level of employment N:

$$N_f = N(w/P).$$

supply and labor demand as functions of the real wage, involuntary unemployment will be associated with disequilibrium or with points off the supply curve of labor. In discussing these definitions Don Patinkin notes: "The norm of reference to be used in defining involuntary unemployment is the supply curve of labor, for this curve shows the amount of employment which the workers of the economy want to obtain in the light of the money wage, price level, and budget restraints with which they are confronted. Hence as long as workers are 'on their supply curve'—that is, as long as they succeed in selling all the labor they want to at the prevailing real wage rate—a state of full employment will be said to exist in the economy. . . . Thus, by definition, the extent of involuntary unemployment is identical with the extent of the excess supply of labor which exists at the prevailing wage rate." Don Patinkin, *Money, Interest and Prices*, 314–315.

Then from the production function [Equation (7.13)] we may solve for the full employment volume of output (Y/P):

$$(Y/P)_f = l(N(w/P), K) = \phi(w/P). \tag{7.16}$$

The Equilibrium Solution for All Three Markets

The solution for the equilibrium values of all the variables in our model may be viewed as follows. The labor market represents a fully determinate (that is, separable) subset of the global model. There are four equations (labor demand, labor supply, the equilibrium condition, and the production function) and four unknowns $(N_s, N_d, w/P,$ and $Y/P)$. This subset is sufficient to determine the level of employment, the volume of real output and the real wage rate (as shown in Figure 7.5). The substitution of this solution for the volume of real output into the income–expenditures equilibrium equation [Equation (7.4)] determines the rate of interest (that rate which will equate real planned saving S/P and real planned investment I/P at the full employment level of output).

The subsequent substitution of these solution values for Y/P and i into the monetary sector equilibrium equation [Equation (7.11)] determines the price level. Prices will be at that level sufficient to equate the *real* value of the *nominal* supply of money balances provided through the monetary system with the volume of real money balances demanded at the levels of Y/P and i determined in the labor market and the income–expenditures sector, respectively. Finally, the nominal wage rate w will be set at that level which, together with the absolute price level determined in the monetary sector, will equal the real wage w/P determined in the labor market. This model is presented graphically in Figure 7.6.[13]

Let us examine some of the characteristics of this model.

[13]This model is said to be solved *recursively*. One subset of the model, the labor market, is isolated and solved for the equilibrium values of the variables that enter the equations of that subset. One of these variables, real income Y/P, may then be treated as predetermined or "known" in another subset of the global model, the income–expenditures sector. Solution values for the remaining variables in the equations of that subset may now be determined. Again, one of the variables from that subset, the interest rate i, together with the level of real income may be treated as predetermined or "known" in the money market equations and those equations may be solved for the equilibrium values of the remaining variables—the price level, the real quantity of money demanded and the real value of the stock of nominal money balances supplied.

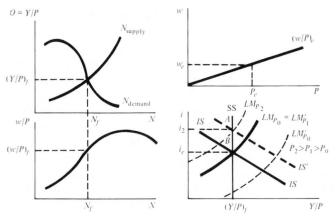

Figure 7.6. Aggregate general equilibrium.

(1) The levels of employment N, real output Y/P and the real wage rate w/P are determined in the labor market (in conjunction with the production function).

(2) The interest rate i is a "real" phenomenon determined in the income–expenditures sector by the intersection of the IS curve (IS) with the vertical line SS constructed over the full employment level of output $(Y/P)_f$ in Figure 7.6. It is that rate which is just sufficient to equate the real supply of saving with the real volume of investment demand at full employment.

(3) The absolute price level is determined in the monetary sector. Prices will adjust to that level necessary to make the real value of the quantity of nominal money balances supplied equal to the quantity of real money balances demanded at the level of real income and interest rate determined in the labor market and the income–expenditures sector, respectively. Graphically the determination of the absolute price level isolates LM_{P_0} from the entire family of monetary sector equilibrium curves (as shown in Figure 7.6).

(4) The nominal wage rate w will adjust to that level which together with the absolute price level P determines the equilibrium real wage rate w/P.

These conclusions reflect the neoclassical tenets that the interest rate is a real variable determined by *productivity* (investment) and *thrift* (saving) and that the quantity theory of money is a theory of the value of money (the absolute price level) rather than a theory of income determination or employment (see Chapter 4). In this neoclassical model the monetary variables (the absolute price level, the nominal wage rate and the money stock) are determined solely by the monetary relations in the model. Thus the equilibrium values of the real variables are independent of both the supply of and the demand for money.[14] In this way the neoclassical economists indicated that monetary forces determined not the value of real variables in the economy but rather only the absolute price level, that is, the value of money.[15]

Let us demonstrate these quantity theory results by examining the effects of an increase in the money supply. For example, assume the initial equilibrium exists at B in Figure 7.6. Suppose there is an exogenous increase in the monetary base which causes a shift in the money supply curve from $M_s = \gamma(i)$ to $M_s' = \gamma_2(i)$.

Now assume further that at each interest rate the nominal stock of money which would be supplied by the banking system is exactly twice as large as before. At each and every interest rate–real income level combination along the old money market equilibrium curve there exists an excess supply of money. The family of money market equilibrium curves shifts to the right since some combination of a higher level of real income or a lower interest rate is necessary to generate an increase in the demand for money to absorb the increase in supply, thereby maintaining money market equilibrium. As a result, in Figure 7.6, LM_{P_0} shifts out to LM_{P_0}'.

In terms of economic behavior, the increased monetary base at existing price and interest rate levels will provide banks with undesired excess reserves. As banks expand loans and increase their deposit liabilities, the nonbank public finds itself with excess real money bal-

[14]This may be seen from the recursive nature of our equation system. Since the equilibrium values of all real variables are in a sense "predetermined" in the production and expenditures sectors, if we change either the supply of or demand for money, *only* those variables determined in the monetary subset (P and w) will be affected. All variables predetermined in the production and expenditures subsets remain unchanged (in equilibrium).

[15]The equilibrium solution of this neoclassical model may be contrasted to that of a crude neoclassical model. In the crude neoclassical model the equations are the same as above except that the level of real income does not enter the saving-investment equations and the interest rate does not enter the money market equations. This results in the labor market determining the real wage, employment and real income as above; the saving-investment sector determining real saving, real investment and the interest rate; and the monetary sector (given the level of real income determined in the labor market) determining the equilibrium money stock and the general price level.

ances. As mentioned above, the excess supply of money can only be absorbed if there occurs some combination of an increase in real income or a decline in the interest rate.

However, in the present model real income cannot increase because the economy is at a full employment capacity level. Therefore, as individuals use their excess real money balances either (1) to purchase investment and consumer durable goods or (2) to purchase financial assets, only the general price level can rise. If the excess supply of money is spent directly on investment and consumer durable goods, there will be an immediate excess demand for these goods. If the excess supply of money is spent on financial assets, there will be a temporary increase in the price of those assets and a decrease in the market rate of interest, which also stimulates an increase in the demand for investment goods and consumer durables. Either way, there then occurs an excess demand for all goods and services which will exert upward pressure on the general price level. This will cease only when the price level has *exactly doubled* so as to restore real money balances to their previous equilibrium level. Finally, with real money balances restored to their former level, the LM curve in Figure 7.6 LM'_{P_1} is back at its original position but with prices and all niminal values exactly doubled. At the new equilibrium point B all real variables will have the same values they had prior to the increase in the money supply. The levels of employment, output, the interest rate and the real wage are unchanged. They will have been "neutral" to this increase in the money stock.[16]

With the interest rate at its original level i_0, the nominal money stock will be exactly twice as high as before $(M_s' = \gamma_2(i))$. Therefore, if prices exactly double, real money balances will be the same as in the initial equilibrium,

$$\frac{2M_s}{2P} = \frac{M_s}{P} \; .$$

The economy adjusts to a higher nominal money stock simply by reducing the value of that money stock to the equilibrium real value M/P. This adjustment requires a change in the price level but no change in any real variables.

We should note explicitly that the interest rate (and other real

---

[16]"Monetary neutrality" defines a situation in which the equilibrium values of the real variables are independent of changes in the money supply.

variables) may diverge from its equilibrium value during the period of changing prices, while the economy is adjusting to the new higher stock of money. Although the equilibrium rate of interest is determined by real factors (productivity and thrift), during transition periods[17] (the period during which the economy is adjusting to a new monetary equilibrium) the interest rate may be influenced by monetary forces. In the final equilibrium in this static model, however, the interest rate will have returned to its previous value.

Let us now relax the assumption that there is no government sector and consider the effect on an increase in government deficit spending. We shall treat the increase as being analogous to an increase in autonomous expenditures. Of course, this is not a completely accurate analogy because it overlooks the fact that government deficits must be financed. Nevertheless, we shall temporarily ignore the financing of the government's deficit.

Consider the equilibrium at point B of Figure 7.6. Under these assumptions an increased government deficit is depicted as a rightward shift in the IS curve from IS to IS'. Since we ignore the financing of this deficit, there is no further effect on IS and no effect on LM. The new IS curve intersects the old LM curve LM_P to the right of the full employment level of income. As real income is constrained to the full employment level, to the right of $(Y/P)_f$ there is excess aggregate demand.

Since real income is unchanged, the excess of expenditures requires a reallocation of saving and investment such that total expenditures remain unchanged. This can only occur if the market rate of interest rises to i_2 (as pointed out earlier, the rate of interest is a real phenomenon determined by the intersection of the IS curve and the SS curve).

With real income unchanged at a higher real market rate of interest, there exists an excess supply of money. As described above, an excess supply of money causes the price level to rise. As the price level increases, the money market equilibrium curve shifts leftward to LM_{P_2}. A new position of aggregate demand equilibrium is established at A. Thus the new higher price level is caused by the excess supply of money—the quantity theory of money holds.

Thus the increase in government deficit spending causes the real

[17]See Irving Fisher, *The Purchasing Power of Money* (New York: Augustus M. Kelly, Bookseller, Reprints of Economic Classics, 1963), ch. 4. Transition periods and dynamics were discussed in Chapter 4.

market rate of interest to rise. It has no effect on any other real variables. Employment, output, and the real wage are unchanged as shown in Figure 7.6. (The real wage is unchanged because the nominal wage and price levels change equiproportionately.) The autonomous expenditures multiplier is zero in this neoclassical model.

At A on the IS curve in the income–expenditures sector the level of real income is equal to the level of real expenditures. Compared to the previous equilibrium position B government expenditures have increased. Since real income has not increased, this implies that private expenditures must have fallen in an amount equal to the rise in government expenditures. In essence, greater government expenditures result in lower private expenditures. The government deficit causes the real interest rate to increase and this makes private consumption and private investment expenditures decline. Thus under these assumptions there is a *complete crowding out* of private expenditures by government expenditures.[18]

Aggregate Supply and Aggregate Demand: An Alternative Approach

We have seen that in this model with perfect price–wage flexibility the economy tends toward full employment through the competitive bidding for labor and jobs in the labor market; the interest rate is a real phenomenon determined by productivity and thrift; and the absolute price level P will be proportional to the nominal money stock (the quantity theory obtains).

This analysis may be presented by means of an alternative technique—a technique that makes the determination of the equilibrium price level more explicit. Let us consider first the aggregate demand subset (the income–expenditures sector and the monetary sector) of our global model.

For the aggregate demand subset [Equations (7.1)–(7.4), and (7.9)–(7.11)], Figure 7.7 shows how the family of LM curves (reproduced from Figure 7.3) may be combined with the IS curve to yield a single aggregate demand curve DD in the P, Y/P plane. This curve shows the level of aggregate demand for real output at various price levels. For example, for the nominal money stock which would be

---

[18]This should be contrasted to the reading by Laurence H. Meyer which follows this chapter in which under a regime of rigid nominal wages and prices complete crowding out takes place under rather extreme assumptions.

supplied at interest rate i_1 to be sufficient to induce a level of aggregate demand equal to $(Y/P)_1$, the price level would have to be P_1. At any *lower* price level fewer *nominal* transactions balances would be required and more real money balances would be available for asset holding purposes by the public, leading to a lower interest rate, higher investment demand and a higher level of real aggregate demand. Thus, the *DD* curve slopes downward to the right.[19]

Let us derive the equation for this aggregate demand curve in the P, Y/P plane. For analytical simplicity assume that the nominal money stock is fixed by the monetary authority: $M_s = M_0$. Continue to assume a linear demand for money function:

$$\left(\frac{M}{P} \right)_d = \frac{m}{P} + k \cdot \frac{Y}{P} + \frac{u}{P} \cdot i.$$

In equilibrium,

$$\frac{1}{P} \cdot M_s = \left(\frac{M}{P} \right)_d.$$

Substituting

$$\frac{1}{P} \cdot M_0 = \frac{m}{P} + k \frac{Y}{P} + \frac{u}{P} \cdot i$$

$$\frac{Y}{P} = \frac{1}{k} \left[\frac{1}{P} \cdot M_0 - \frac{m}{P} - \frac{u}{P} \cdot i. \right]. \tag{7.17}$$

Solving Equation (7.4), the equilibrium equation for the income-expenditures sector, for the interest rate yields

$$i = \frac{s}{-e/P + h/P} \cdot \frac{Y}{P} - \frac{a/P + a'/P}{-e/P + h/P}. \tag{7.4'}$$

Substitution of this result into Equation (7.17) yields

$$\frac{Y}{P} = \frac{1}{k} \left(\frac{1}{P} \cdot M_0 - \frac{m}{P} \right) - \frac{1}{k} \cdot \frac{u}{P} \left[\frac{s}{-e/P + h/P} \cdot \frac{Y}{P} - \frac{a/P + a'/P}{-e/P + h/P} \right]$$

$$\frac{Y}{P} \left[k + \frac{u}{P} \left(\frac{s}{-e/P + h/P} \right) \right] = \left(\frac{1}{P} \cdot M_0 - \frac{m}{P} \right) + \frac{u}{P} \left(\frac{a/P + a'/P}{-e/P + h/P} \right)$$

$$\frac{Y}{P} = \frac{(-e/P + h/P)[(1/P)M_0 - m/P] + u/P(a/P + a'/P)}{s(u/P) + k(-e/P + h/P)}. \tag{7.18}$$

[19]The *DD* curve is drawn concave to the origin to maintain consistency with the graphs presented later when nonlinearities are introduced into the basic relationships. This does not influence our essential conclusions in any way.

This equation is represented by the *DD* curve in Figure 7.7. It is similar to the solution for aggregate demand derived earlier in this chapter and only slightly more complicated than Equation (6.9).

In accord with our initial assumptions, when the price level P changes, all the nominal values, a, a', m, etc., change in equal proportion, leaving the *real* values a/P, a'/P, m/P, etc., unchanged. However, M_0 is determined by the monetary authority. Therefore, when P increases (decreases), M_0/P will decrease (increase) causing a decrease (increase) in Y/P; in other words in Equation (7.18):

$$\frac{\partial(Y/P)}{\partial P} = \frac{-M_0(1/P^2)(-e/P + h/P)}{s(u/P) + k(-e/P + h/P)} < 0.$$

There are two unknowns, Y/P and P, in Equation 7.18. We may solve for equilibrium values of these variables by reintroducing the aggregate supply sector.

First, we shall rewrite the labor market and production relations. The basic differences with the earlier development will be to treat the price level as a separate variable in the labor market and to write the labor demand and supply relations with the nominal wage as the dependent variable. The supply function is

$$w_s = f(N,P) \tag{7.12'}$$

where

$$\delta w_s/\delta N > 0 \text{ and } \delta w_s/\delta P > 0$$

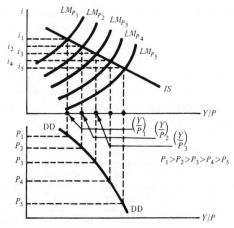

Figure 7.7.   Derivation of the aggregate demand curve.

the demand function is

$$w_d = g(N,P) \tag{7.14'}$$

where

$$\delta w_d/\delta N < 0 \text{ and } \delta w_d/\delta P > 0.$$

Equation (7.12') indicates that the nominal supply price of labor (the nominal wage asked by labor) varies directly with the quantity of labor supplied and directly with the general price level. This means that at a given price level labor suppliers will require an ever higher nominal wage as the quantity of labor hours they supply increases. It implies that, at a given level of employment, as the price level increases, labor suppliers shall ask for a higher nominal wage. If *money illusion* is completely absent, as the price level increases workers shall ask for a *proportionately* higher nominal wage. In this case Equation (7.12') is the equivalent of Equation (7.12) introduced earlier.[20]

Equation (7.14') indicates that the nominal demand price of labor, the nominal wage bid by employers, varies inversely with the quantity of labor demanded and directly with the general price level. This means that at a given price level labor demanders will be willing to pay an ever lower nominal wage as the quantity of labor demanded increases. It means that at a given level of employment employers will pay a higher nominal wage as the price level increases. If *money illusion* is completely absent, employers shall pay a *proportionately* higher money wage and Equation (7.14') will be the equivalent of Equation (7.14) introduced earlier.

The equilibrium condition is expressed as an equality between the nominal supply price and the nominal demand price of labor,

$$w_s = w_d. \tag{7.15'}$$

This relation is simply another way of viewing labor market equilibrium. If the market is in equilibrium, quantity demanded equals quantity supplied [Equation (7.15)] *and* supply price equals demand price [Equation (7.15')].

---

[20]There are *income* and *substitution* effects here. The real wage is the opportunity cost of leisure. As the real wage rises, leisure is more expensive, so the labor supplier substitutes labor for leisure, and the quantity of labor hours supplied increases. Conversely, as the real wage rises, real income rises, and more of all goods are "purchased," including leisure, and the quantity of labor hours supplied decreases. We shall assume that the substitution effect dominates the income effect and that there is an unambiguous positive relationship between the real wage and the quality of labor hours supplied.

The aggregate production function is unchanged from the earlier analysis

$$Y/P = l(N,K). \tag{7.13}$$

The present model is essentially very similar to the previous analysis of the labor market. It merely allows us to break out the general price level and the nominal wage as separate variables in the labor market.

The preceding four equations are represented graphically in Figure 7.8 on the next page.

Now consider the effect of an increase in the general price level

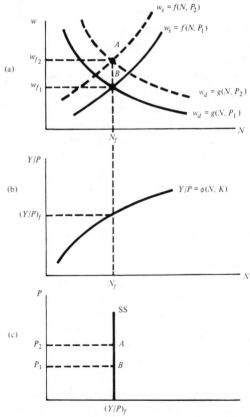

Figure 7.8. Labor market and production sector with nominal wage and price level as separate variables.

from P_1 to P_2. Under the assumption that $\delta w_s/\delta P = \delta w_d/\delta P$, the increase in the price level shifts the labor supply curve to the left by the same amount that it shifts the labor demand curve to the right. If neither labor suppliers nor employers have *money illusion*, that is, if both are equally aware that an increase in the price level decreases the real wage, the magnitude of the shifts will be equal. As a result the nominal wage will rise in the same proportion that the price level increased and the equilibrium quantity of labor hours will be unchanged. As labor input is unchanged, the level of output in Equation (7.13) is unchanged. The aggregate supply curve is the vertical line in Figure 7.8.

As discussed in the previous section, in the aggregate supply subset [Equations (7.12′)–(7.15′)], if prices and nominal wages are *perfectly flexible* and if there is no *money illusion*, the nominal wage rate will always adjust to assure full employment, regardless of the absolute price level. Therefore, regardless of the price level, the full employment volume of output $(Y/P)_f$ will be supplied and the aggregate supply curve will appear as SS in Figure 7.9. Thus aggregate supply SS and aggregate demand DD together determine the equilibrium price level. More correctly, conditions in the money market determine the price level *given* the interest rate and the volume of output supplied. Equilibrium occurs at point A in Figure 7.9. This represents the solution value obtained by substituting the full employment level of output determined in Equation (7.16),

$$(Y/P)_f = \phi(w/P)$$

into Equation (7.18) and solving for the price level P. The four characteristics of the equilibrium solution discussed in the previous section continue to apply for this alternative formulation.

Consider a decrease in aggregate demand caused by a drop in autonomous investment expenditures. In the neoclassical model this causes the interest rate to decline sufficiently to restore aggregate demand to its full employment level. This in turn causes the price level to decline. The fall in the price level causes the nominal wage level to decrease in the same proportion such that the real wage and the level of employment are unchanged.

We employ Figures 7.6, 7.8 and 7.9 to describe these effects. In Figure 7.9 a decrease in aggregate demand causes a downward shift in the DD curve to DD'. Full employment equilibrium would be restored

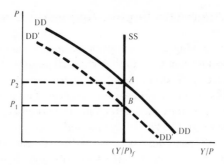

Figure 7.9. Determination of price level.

at P_1. In Figure 7.6 the aggregate demand sector is in equilibrium at A with IS' and LM_{P_2}, the relevant curves. A decrease in autonomous expenditures causes a shift from IS' to IS, which causes the market rate of interest to decline to i_e. With real income unchanged the lower interest rate creates an excess demand for money and an excess aggregate supply of output at the initial price level P_2. As described earlier, this condition creates downward pressure on the general price level. The decline in the price level to P_1 increases the real value of money balances such that money market equilibrium is restored at B in Figure 7.6.

As the price level declines from P_2 to P_1 in the labor market, depicted in Figure 7.8 on the previous page, demand shifts leftward and supply shifts rightward by the same amount. This causes the nominal wage to decline from w_{f_2} to w_{f_1} which is proportionate to the decrease in the price level. Therefore the real wage is unchanged, $w_2/P_2 = w_1/P_1$, at the full employment level.

In this situation there are no restraints on the nominal wage, the price level or the interest rate. As a result, given any decrease in aggregate demand, all three can adjust sufficiently to induce a volume of aggregate demand necessary to equal the full employment volume of aggregate supply. For example, if for some reason the market rate of interest did not immediately adjust when autonomous expenditures decreased, excess aggregate supply at P_2 in Figure 7.9 would cause the general price level to decline and real balances to increase. This would, in turn, lead to a decrease in the interest rate and stimulate induced investment spending so as to restore aggregate demand at the full employment level.

A General, Aggregate Supply-Aggregate Demand Model

We begin by modifying the assumption of perfect nominal wage flexibility of the previous analysis. Rather we shall assume that the nominal wage is imperfectly flexible. This may occur for two reasons. One reason is that laborers may suffer from a degree of money illusion in the labor market; that is, they may determine the volume of labor they are going to supply on the basis of the *nominal* wage rate rather than the *real* wage rate. Alternatively, because of the contract structure in the labor market or because of imperfect information regarding available job openings and prevailing rates,[21] nominal wages may be rigid. In either case the assumption of imperfect flexibility of the nominal wage rate will modify the conclusions of our model.

To demonstrate this we return to the basic model and impose special conditions on the labor supply equation:

$$w_s = f(N,P) \tag{7.12'}$$

where $\delta w_s/\delta N \to 0$ and $\delta w_s/\delta P \to 0$,

$$w_d = g(N,P) \tag{7.14'}$$

where $\delta w_d/\delta N < 0$ and $\delta w_d/\delta P > 0$, and

$$w_s = w_d \tag{7.15'}$$

$$Y/P = l(N,K). \tag{7.13}$$

In this case, not only is there money illusion on the supply side of the labor market but there is also rigidity of the nominal wage rate. The supply price of labor in the short run not only fails to respond to price level changes $(\delta w_s/\delta P \to 0)$ but it is also invariant with respect to the quantity of labor supplied $(\delta w_s/\delta N \to 0)$. This is depicted by the labor supply and aggregate supply curves in Figure 7.10. Assume that the price level decreases from P_f to P_1. Labor demanders, employers, decrease their demand for labor because they will now sell their output

---

[21]This is the basis of cases I and II in the model which follows. For further reading in this area, see Edmund S. Phelps, *Microeconomic Foundations of Employment and Inflation Theory* (New York: Norton, 1970). Another exposition of this approach is Robert Rasche, "A Comparative Static Analysis of Some Monetarist Propositions," *Review*, Federal Reserve Bank of St. Louis (December 1973), 15–22. This is reprinted in Havrilesky and Boorman, *Current Issues in Monetary Theory and Policy* (Arlington Heights, IL.: AHM Publishing Corporation, 1980). For a comparison of Keynesian and Monetarist econometric models see the reading by Joseph M. Crews which follows this chapter.

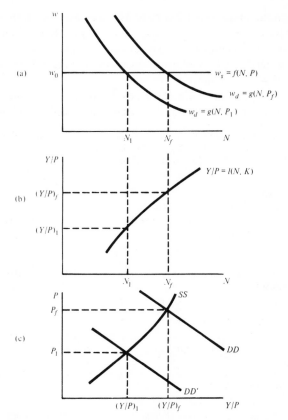

Figure 7.10. Derivation of the aggregate supply curve with nominal wage rigidity and money illusion on the supply side of the labor market.

at lower prices, that is, the marginal revenue product of labor has decreased. Employers have no money illusion.

In contrast, labor suppliers not only do not offer to work for lower nominal wages as the price level falls (they have money illusion, $\delta w_s / \delta P \to 0$), but also they do not offer lower nominal wages as employment decreases. Workers not only fail to realize that as the price level falls their real wage is rising and they can afford to reduce their nominal wage but they also fail to learn that they can obtain more employment by cutting their nominal wage offer.

Therefore in Figure 7.10, as the equilibrium quantity of labor hours decreases from N_f to N_1, output falls from $(Y/P)_f$ to $(Y/P)_1$; the decrease in the price level from P_f to P_1 is consistent with the decrease in output from $(Y/P)_f$ to $(Y/P)_1$.[22] Figure 7.10 shows that with a less than perfectly vertical aggregate supply curve, decreases in aggregate demand from DD to DD' will cause decreases in both the general price level and the level of output.

It is now possible to demonstrate the proposition that a key difference between Keynesian and neoclassical models is the wage and

[22]The slope of the aggregate supply curve depends on the slope of the production function and, implicitly, on the slope of the demand for labor curve. Assuming the money wage rate fixed at w_0, Equation (7.16) becomes

$$(Y/P) = \phi(w_0/P)$$

where $\delta(Y/P)/\delta P > 0$.

This can be simply proven. Assume $w = w_0$. Profit maximization by employers, under conditions or pure competition, yields the condition that the real wage equals the marginal physical product of labor,

$$w_0/P = l'(N,\overline{K}).$$

Rearranging terms and recalling that pure competition in the goods market means that price equals marginal cost,

$$P = MC = w_0/l'(N,\overline{K}).$$

Then the slope of the aggregate supply curve SS is

$$\frac{\partial P}{\partial(Y/P)} = \frac{\partial P}{\partial l'(N,K)} \cdot \frac{\partial l'(N,K)}{\partial N} \cdot \frac{\partial N}{\partial Y/P} \ .$$

Since a decline in the marginal physical product causes an increase in marginal cost and hence the price of output,

$$\frac{\partial P}{\partial l'(N,K)} < 0$$

since an increase in labor input causes a decrease in its marginal physical product,

$$\frac{\partial l'(N,K)}{\partial N} < 0$$

and since output varies directly with labor input,

$$\frac{\partial N}{\partial(Y/P)} > 0.$$

Therefore,

$$\frac{\partial P}{\partial(Y/P)} > 0.$$

Here, as assumed in the discussion of aggregate supply in the previous chapter, the production function increases monotonically over the relevant domain.

The presence of a fixed nominal wage implies that the labor market is not automatically at full employment equilibrium and that the above relation $Y/P = \phi(w_0/P)$ will not always represent a full employment solution.

price sensitivity of the labor supply relation. In Figure 7.11A there are three kinds of labor supply curves.

Case I   is the Keynesian case in which the nominal supply price of labor w_s is perfectly insensitive to the quantity of labor

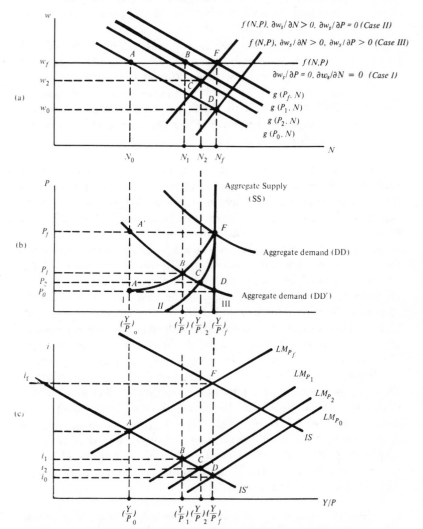

Figure 7.11.   Global aggregate model under Keynesian, "intermediate," and neoclassical conditions on the supply side of the labor market.

hours supplied, $\delta w_s/\delta N \to 0$ and perfectly insensitive to the general price level, $\delta w_s/\delta P \to 0$; that is, the nominal wage is fixed.

Case II   is the "intermediate" case in which the supply price of labor responds positively to changes in the quantity of labor hours supplied, $\delta w_s/\delta N > 0$ but does *not* respond to the general price level, $\delta w_s/\delta P \to 0$.

Case III   is the neoclassical case in which the supply price of labor responds positively to changes in quantity supplied, $\delta w_s/\delta N > 0$ and responds positively to changes in the general price level, $\delta w_s/\delta P > 0$. As in the previous chapter, we shall assume that the latter response is of the same magnitude as the response of the labor demand curve to the general price level, $\delta w_s/\delta P = \delta w_d/\delta P$.

In Figure 7.11B there are three aggregate supply curves, one for each of the Cases discussed above. Figure 7.11C shows the source of the movements in aggregate demand in Figure 7.11B. The *shift* in the aggregate demand curve in Figure 7.11B is caused by the shift in the *IS* curve in Figure 7.11C. The movements *along* the aggregate demand curve in Figure 7.11B are caused by shifts in the *LM* curves (induced by changes in the general price level, P_j) in Figure 7.11C.

Starting out from an assumed full employment equilibrium at F, all markets on the aggregate supply side clear, all markets on the aggregate demand side clear and there is no involuntary unemployment or excess capacity. Now assume a decrease in real autonomous expenditures $\Delta a/P$. This causes a shift in the *IS* curve in Figure 7.11C. The change in Y/P which will keep the income–expenditures sector in equilibrium is a multiple of the change in autonomous expenditures. There is an autonomous expenditures multiplier effect at work that causes real output to fall by the directed distance $(Y/P)_f-(Y/P)_0$ as shown in Figures 7.11B and 7.11C. With the price level unchanged at P_f the aggregate demand sector goes to points labeled A' in these graphs. At A' the aggregate demand sector is in equilibrium. However, the economy is only partially in equilibrium; the aggregate supply sector is not in equilibrium at A'.[23]

[23]Points A' represent aggregate demand equilibrium; the labor market nevertheless is not in equilibrium. As the price level (as well as the nominal wage) is assumed unchanged, at points A' we are off the labor demand and aggregate supply curves; there is *involuntary unemployment* in the labor market.

The excess supply of output, $(Y/P)_f-(Y/P)_0$, causes the general price level to decline. The decrease in the general price level from P_f to P_0 causes the demand for labor to shift to the left to $g(P_0, N)$. At the higher real wage w_f/P_0 less labor is demanded. Assuming Case I is applicable, the supply price of labor is not responsive to changes in P or to the reduction in employment. The aggregate supply sector is in equilibrium at points A in Figures 7.11A and 7.11B but the aggregate demand sector is not.

The decrease in the price level affects real aggregate demand by causing the stock of real money balances to increase, thereby causing the LM curve to shift rightward. In Figure 7.11C this is reflected as a movement downward along the IS' curve; in Figure 7.11B it is reflected as a movement downward along the aggregate demand curve. As real aggregate demand increases, real output increases.

Now switching to the aggregate supply sector, as output rises from $(Y/P)_0$ to $(Y/P)_1$ in Figure 7.11B the price level rises from P_0 to P_1. The rise in the price level causes the demand for labor to increase to $g(P_1, N)$ in Figure 7.11A. The upward movement along the aggregate supply curve in Figure 7.11B is a concomitant of the upward shift in the demand curve for labor in Figure 7.11A because the rise in the price level from P_0 to P_1, at a fixed nominal wage w_f, lowers the real wage to w_f/P_1. The lower real wage, in equilibrium, is consistent with the decrease in the marginal productivity of labor caused by the rise in output.

Switching back to the aggregate demand sector, at price level P_1 the relevant LM curve is LM_{P_1}, which gives a level of real aggregate demand of $(Y/P)_1$ in Figures 7.11B and 7.11C. Points B in all three graphs are positions of full quasi-equilibrium—"full" because aggregate demand and aggregate supply sectors are in equilibrium (that is, all markets clear) and "quasi" because there is still involuntary unemployment and excess capacity in the economy.[24]

[24]At this point a traditional policy prescription was to promote once and for all nominal wage cuts which would shift the cost and supply curves of business firms (and hence SS in Figure 7.11B) downward. Whether the concomitant reduction in the price level would stimulate aggregate demand is a moot point. In the case of DD in Figure 7.11B, a downward shift of SS would stimulate aggregate demand along DD. Real output and employment would rise. Consistent with the increase in output and employment and decrease in the marginal product of labor, the real wage rate would fall. With the increase in output there is therefore some upward pressure on marginal costs and prices and therefore the decrease in nominal wages exceeds the decrease in prices. For reasons developed in the final section of this chapter aggregate demand may not be price sensi-

Now assume that labor suppliers respond to the reduced level of demand for labor by lowering their nominal wage requests. The nominal wage is no longer perfectly rigid, $\delta w_s/\delta N > 0$. This means that Case II is applicable in Figure 7.11A and 7.11B. The aggregate supply curve in Figure 7.11B now reflects a greater sensitivity of the price level to changes in output. Compared to Case I the decline in nominal wage offers causes costs and, hence, supply prices to decline at all levels of output. As above, in the aggregate demand sector the decline in the general price level shifts the LM curve to the right. The new position of full quasi-equilibrium occurs with a lower general price level P_2, a lower nominal wage w_2 and a higher level of real income Y/P_2. The lower price level shifts the demand for labor leftward to $g(P_2, N)$. Points C in all three figures are positions of full quasi-equilibrium.

Now assume that labor suppliers also respond positively to the lower price level (they realize that with a lower price level *real* wages are higher). This means that Case III is applicable in Figure 7.11A and 7.11B. At a lower price level the supply curve of labor shifts rightward in Figure 7.11A to $f(N,P)$ where $\delta w_s/\delta P > 0$. As the price level declines in Figure 7.11B and 7.11C, aggregate demand is stimulated. The increase in aggregate demand associated with a lower price level in Figure 7.11B and 7.11C causes output to rise. The increase in output lowers the marginal productivity of labor and therefore the real wage.

Points D represent a position of full equilibrium in the macroeconomy. Compared to points C output has increased from $(Y/P)_2$ to $(Y/P)_f$, and the price level has fallen from P_2 to P_0. However the nominal wage level has fallen from w_2 to w_0 such that the real wage has fallen from w_2/P_2 to w_0/P_0. The new lower price level causes the demand for labor to shift leftward to $g(P_0, N)$.

Notice that if we had assumed a Case III (neoclassical) world at the outset, given the decrease in real aggregate demand, prices, nominal wages and the interest rate would have adjusted downward to maintain full employment output $(Y/P)_f$ at an unchanged real wage, $w_0/P_0 = w_f/P_f$. All four neoclassical implications discussed previously would obtain.

It should be noted that for Cases I and II final equilibrium values of the real variables in the model (N, Y/P, I/P, S/P, etc.) are no longer

---

tive; in fact it may be perfectly price inelastic. In this case if nominal wages fall, output does not increase, prices fall proportionately and the system remains unchanged in real terms. Such an aggregate demand function in the P, Y/P plane would be a vertical line through B.

independent of the absolute level of money wages and prices as they are in Case III, which assumed perfect price and wage flexibility. In contrast to the neoclassical model there are, in the solution of the Keynesian system, no separable subsets of the global model which may be solved recursively. All (labor market, income-expenditures and monetary sector) equations are solved simultaneously.

The influence of monetary conditions on the final Keynesian equilibrium can also be seen in Figure 7.11B. Since a change in the nominal money supply causes a shift in the family of LM curves and thereby a shift in the aggregate demand curve DD', this purely monetary change will affect the intersection of DD' and SS and, thereby, change the equilibrium values of real income and employment in Cases I and II. In short, money is no longer neutral. Modigliani stated this nicely:

> Systems with rigid wages share the common property that the equilibrium value of the "real" variables is determined essentially by monetary conditions rather than by "real" factors. . . . The monetary conditions are sufficient to determine money income and, under fixed (money) wages and given technical conditions, to each money income there corresponds a definite equilibrium level of employment. This equilibrium level does not tend to coincide with full employment except by mere chance.[25]

The preceding analysis demonstrates the importance of nominal wage rigidity and money illusion in the labor market for the implications of the global model. The greater the nominal wage rigidity and the greater the degree of money illusion on the supply side of the labor market, the less steep is the aggregate supply curve and the greater the extent of quantity adjustments (changes in output and employment) rather than price level adjustments to change in aggregate demand.

The policy implications of this analysis are quite interesting. If labor suppliers and labor demanders respond quickly to price and wage information there is a good deal less likelihood that changes in aggregate demand can have serious impact on output and employment. Most of the effect of changes in demand will be felt on the price and nominal wage levels. This, in turn, suggests that less credence be placed in the notion that inflation-causing increases in aggregate de-

[25]Franco Modigliani, "Liquidity Preference and the Theory of Interest and Money," *Econometrica* (January 1944). Reprinted in *Readings in Monetary Theory*, Friedrich A. Lutz and Lloyd W. Mints, eds. (Homewood, IL: Richard D. Irwin, 1951), 211.

mand can reduce unemployment other than temporarily, the idea of the Phillips curve.[26]

This can be succinctly seen by substituting Equations (7.12′) and (7.14′) into (7.15) and taking the total differential:

$$\frac{\partial w_s}{\partial N} \, dN + \frac{\partial w_s}{\partial P} \, dP = \frac{\partial w_d}{\partial N} \, dN + \frac{\partial w_d}{\partial P} \, dP.$$

Rearranging and multiplying by $\delta(Y/P)/\delta N$ (the marginal product of labor), the slope of the aggregate supply curve is

$$\frac{d(Y/P)}{dP} = \frac{\partial(Y/P)}{\partial N} \frac{dN}{dP} = \frac{\partial(Y/P)}{\partial N} \left(\frac{\partial w_d/\partial P - \partial w_s/\partial P}{\partial w_s/\ \partial N - \partial w_d/\partial N} \right).$$

The above expression shows that the greater the degree of nominal wage rigidity, the smaller is $\delta w_s/\delta N$ and, as $-\delta w_d/\delta N$ is positive, the greater is $\delta(Y/P)/\delta P$ and the flatter is the "slope" of the aggregate supply curve. It also indicates that the more prevalent is money illusion among labor suppliers, the flatter is the aggregate supply curve; that is, as $\delta w_s/\delta P$ decreases, $\delta(Y/P)/\delta P$ increases. In the neoclassical case where money illusion is absent, $\delta w_s/\delta P = \delta w_d/\delta P$, there is no wage rigidity and the aggregate supply curve is vertical, $\delta(Y/P)/\delta P = 0$.

One may view Keynesian and neoclassical models as lying on a spectrum in terms of the magnitude of quantity adjustments to changes in aggregate demand, that is, the magnitude of the basic autonomous expenditures multiplier. At the Keynesian extreme of this spectrum, in models without interest rate variations and with constant price and nominal wage levels, the autonomous expenditures multiplier is quite sizable; this essentially was the autonomous expenditures multiplier of Chapter 5. When money is introduced, changes in autonomous expenditures generate increases in the rate of interest, thereby choking off some expenditures—but the price and nominal wage levels are still held constant and the autonomous expenditures multiplier is somewhat smaller in magnitude; this basically was the multiplier of Chapter 6. When the interest rate *and* the price level are allowed to vary, but the nominal wage is still held constant (Case I in Figure 7.11), quantity adjustments to changes in aggregate demand are even smaller. When the interest rate, the price level and the nominal wage level are all

---

[26]In footnote 22 the tradeoff between the increase in the price level and employment is captured in the slope of the aggregate supply curve. If there is no money illusion among labor suppliers, the aggregate supply curve is vertical.

variable, quantity adjustments to changes in aggregate demand become very small, depending on the degree of money illusion on the supply side of the labor market. This is reflected in Case II in Figure 7.11. Finally, in a model of complete interest, wage and price flexibility and no money illusion, quantity adjustments are zero and the neoclassical implications prevail.

The processes discussed above can be viewed in a dynamic context. In the short run the price level and the nominal wage are rigid; in the long run they are perfectly flexible. In Figure 7.11 the economy may traverse over time a path from F to A' to B to C to D. Given a decrease in aggregate demand, the economy first responds in a Keynesian fashion, points A', and then works its way to a neoclassical position, points D. [27] Of course, the analysis can serve equally well in the other direction. The movement to points F *from* points D in Figure 7.11 because of an *increase* in aggregate demand can also be regarded as a dynamic process.

In the next section we illustrate this process. For simplicity we shall confine the analysis to the labor market. Keep in mind that now we will be talking about an *increase* in aggregate demand, not a decrease as in Figure 7.11.

Phillips Curve Analysis and the Rational Expectations Hypothesis[28]

A slight modification will allow the effect of money illusion in the labor market to be expressed in terms of a Phillips curve. Assume no nominal wage rigidity. We have already seen that an increase in the price level will normally stimulate employment if there is more money illusion

---

[27]Actually, in the most extreme Keynesian case, the quantity adjustment that occurs in a world of complete nominal wage, price level *and* interest rate rigidity, the world of the simple minded 1/1-MPC autonomous expenditures multiplier, is not even shown in Figure 7.11. It is measured as the horizontal displacement of the *IS* curve at an unchanged interest rate in Figure 7.11(c). That quasi-equilibrium would occur where the new *IS* curve *IS'* intersects the horizontal dotted line $i_f - F$ in Figure 7.11(c). Given a decrease in aggregate demand, with *all* prices including interest rates rigid, the economy might first tend to respond in this extreme Keynesian fashion. As interest rates begin to adjust downward, the movement would be to points A' in Figure 7.11; then, as the price level begins to adjust, the movement would be to points B; increasing the degree of nominal wage flexibility would subsequently carry the economy to points C and D.

[28]For further discussion of the Phillips Curve and the rational expectations hypothesis, see the reading by Thomas M. Humphrey that follows this chapter.

among labor suppliers than among labor demanders. Now assume that whatever change occurs in the flow of real aggregate expenditures, so as to cause the general price level to increase, this rate of increase will persist over time. This means that the resulting increase in the price level will itself persist over time and may, therefore, be expressed as a *rate* of inflation $\dot{P}$.[29] If this rate of price inflation is *not* fully anticipated by labor suppliers and *is* fully anticipated by labor demanders, the level of employment will temporarily rise and the rate of change of the nominal wage $\dot{w}$ will rise at a rate less than the rate of inflation.

This effect, seen in Figure 7.12, is a dynamic analog of the preceding static treatment of the labor market with money illusion on the supply side. At the initial level of full employment, D, labor suppliers and labor demanders both perfectly anticipate the prevailing rate of price increase $\dot{P}_0$. This is reflected in a rate of nominal wage increase $\dot{w}_0$ that equals the rate of increase in the price level. Then because of a (persistent) increase in aggregate demand (associated, for example, with a persistent increase in the rate of money supply growth), the rate of price inflation rises from $\dot{P}_0$ to $\dot{P}_f$. As in the previous static analysis, if we assume that labor demanders have less money illusion than labor suppliers, employers will (more completely) anticipate the rise in the rate of inflation and the demand for labor will rise. Employers anticipate that their marginal revenue product will rise because they expect to sell their output at higher prices. The rate of increase of the nominal wage rises from $\dot{w}_0$ to $\dot{w}_1$.

This increase in demand raises the level of employment from N_f to N_1 (point E in Figure 7.12). Individuals who were previously searching for new jobs now accept employment more readily. They choose to reduce the amount of time they would normally spend unemployed because they perceive a higher opportunity cost of being unemployed. They perceive a new higher rate of increase of the nominal wage without perceiving the new higher rate of price inflation, that is, they mistakenly believe that the real wage is increasing.

The response of labor suppliers to a perceived higher real wage may be viewed in terms of income and substitution effects. The substitution effect is the substitution of labor for leisure as the opportunity cost of leisure, the *perceived* real wage, increases. The income effect is the "purchase" of more noninferior goods, including leisure time, as

---

[29]The rate of inflation is the derivative of the price level with respect to time, expressed as a percentage $(dP/dt)/P = \dot{P}$.

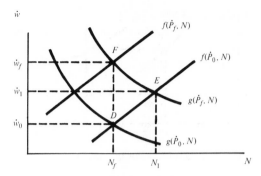

Figure 7.12. Labor market expressed in terms of rates of nominal wage and price level changes.

the real wage rises. On the assumption that the substitution effect dominates the income effect, the quantity of labor hours supplied will vary positively with a perceived increase in the real wage.

After a lag, labor suppliers will learn about the new rate of price inflation $\dot{P}_f$ and ask for a proportionately higher rate of increase in their nominal wage $\dot{w}_f$. In Figure 7.12 the supply curve shifts leftward and employment falls back to N_f. The market clears at point F. Individuals who are in the process of searching for new jobs are now aware that the real wage is not increasing, and they spend as much time searching for jobs as they did before the rate of inflation accelerated. The fiscal and monetary authorities can now increase employment (reduce unemployment among those searching for jobs) only by accelerating the rate of price inflation even further.

All of this can be translated into Phillips curve analysis. Assuming a fixed labor force, the level of unemployment U is defined as the difference between the labor force L and the level of employment N. In Figure 7.13 at point D there is an initial full employment level of output; the number of workers temporarily between jobs is $L - N_f = U_f$. This represents a "natural" level of unemployment; at this level of unemployment the rate of price inflation $\dot{P}_0$ is equal to the rate of increase of the nominal wage $\dot{w}_0$. The real wage is not changing. It may be said that all unemployment here is "frictional employment."

Assuming a persistent increase in the level of real aggregate demand, the rate of price inflation rises from $\dot{P}_0$ to $\dot{P}_1$, and as employment rises to N_1 in Figure 7.12, the level of unemployment initially falls to $U_1(= L - N_1)$ in Figure 7.13. In Figure 7.12 when the rate of increase

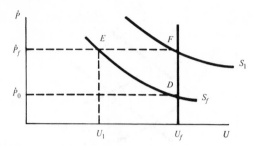

Figure 7.13.   Short- and Long-run Phillips curves.

of nominal wages rises from $\dot{w}_0$ to $\dot{w}_1$, labor suppliers believe that the real wage is rising because they do not yet perceive the rise in the rate of inflation. Consequently, those in the process of searching for new jobs will expedite the searching process as they now believe it more costly to remain unemployed. The relevant point is E in Figure 7.13.

This decline in unemployment is only temporary as workers' wage requests come to reflect the new anticipated rate of price inflation. The Phillips curve shifts rightward from S_f to S_1 as this new rate of price inflation $\dot{P}_f$ becomes fully anticipated. Those workers that are temporarily searching for jobs will no longer be induced to hasten the process because of the (false) perception of a higher real wage (the opportunity cost of being unemployed). We go to point F in Figure 7.13. Except for improvements in the job search process in the labor market, the only way in which unemployment can be reduced would be for government once again to accelerate the rate of price inflation such that it is unanticipated by labor suppliers, thereby inducing temporary movements along the short-run Phillips curve S_1.

The vertical line above U_f represents the long-run Phillips curve. The economy can be at a full employment equilibrium at any fully anticipated rate of price inflation. Only unexpected acceleration and deceleration of the rate of inflation can induce (temporary) changes in employment and production. The vertical, long-run Phillips curve is a dynamic analog of the vertical aggregate supply curve in Figure 7.11B.

On the one hand a sizable number of economists accept this view of the short-run Phillips curve but insist that some money illusion remains among labor suppliers in the long run because price expectations are based on past experience and are adjusted with a lag (the *adaptive expectations hypothesis*). Under this hypothesis, with a steadily rising inflation labor suppliers always expect inflation to be less than it actually is. This will produce a downward sloping (nonvertical) *long-run* Phillips curve. This implies that labor suppliers will tend to accept (some) reductions in real wages if they are accomplished by inflation.[30]

On the other hand many economists contend that it is unrealistic to believe that price expectations adapt only with a lag to historical price data. They argue that expectations are likely formed from all sorts of contemporaneous information. If individuals develop expectations rationally, they should be able to anticipate price inflation by getting information about its cause, the rate of increase of aggregate demand. Thus in a world of *rational expectations* changes in monetary and fiscal policy can affect output and employment only to the extent that such changes are unanticipated. According to the *rational expectations hypothesis* monetary and fiscal policy actions can successfully affect output and unemployment only to the extent that they are unpredictable.[31]

Other Sources of Inconsistency in the Aggregate Model

The likelihood of a rigid nominal wage structure or money illusion in modern industrialized economies was not the only problem posed by Keynes in his criticism of the market economy for its failure to maintain full employment. In fact, even under a regime of perfect price–wage flexibility, certain conditions may preclude the economy from automatically attaining a full employment level of output. Consequently, although the assumption of imperfect flexibility in the nominal wage rate may be realistic when analyzing the short-run behavior of the aggregate economy, let us restore our original assumption of perfect price–wage flexibility and examine some of the problems that may arise even under these circumstances.

Keynes suggested two possible features that could lead to unem-

---

[30]For further discussion of the Phillips Curve controversy, see Thomas M. Humphrey, "Some Recent Developments in Phillips Curve Analysis," *Economic Review*, Federal Reserve Bank of Richmond (January/February 1978), 15–23; reprinted in the readings which follow this chapter.

[31]See Thomas J. Sargent and Neil Wallace, "Rational Expectations and the Theory of Economic Policy," *Journal of Monetary Economics* (April 1976). This has suggested to some analysts that incumbent politicians have an incentive to stimulate the economy in order to produce temporarily lower unemployment rates prior to elections and then to switch to recession-causing, anti-inflationary policy after elections. William D. Nordhaus, "The Political Business Cycle," *Review of Economic Studies*, vol. 42 (April 1975), 169–189.

ployment within the framework of our static model, even though wages and prices were perfectly flexible. One of these is the liquidity trap and the other is a special case of interest insensitive aggregate demand. Each of these possibilities involves a situation in which the full employment level of saving is greater than the level of investment which could be induced at *any attainable* interest rate. In short, aggregate demand at full employment is less than aggregate supply at all attainable interest rates.

In the case of the liquidity trap money demand becomes perfectly elastic at some positive interest rate. For example, when conditions are such that virtually everyone expects bond prices to fall, people will prefer money to bonds. They will absorb any increase in the money stock into asset balances without requiring a reduction in the interest rate (see Chapter 3). Therefore, regardless of how large the supply of money may be, the market rate cannot fall below the level determined by money demand. Hence, even if sufficient investment could be induced to offset full employment saving at some low rate of interest, the actual market rate can never attain that low level and investment will remain insufficient at the attainable rate.

In the case of interest insensitive aggregate demand (with no liquidity trap) investment and consumption expenditures may be so unresponsive to changes in the interest rate that even at a near zero rate of interest sufficient investment cannot be generated to match full employment saving.

Graphically, we may present these two cases in terms of our original *LM*–*IS* curves. Note that in the case of the liquidity trap full employment equilibrium could be attained if the money market equilibrium curve could be shifted down so as to intersect the income-expenditures and full employment curves at point *B* [Figure 7.14A]. However, because of the liquidity trap, there is a floor in the level of the interest rate at i_1 and hence sufficient investment spending is not forthcoming at that rate to match full employment saving. Thus at point *A* aggregate demand is below aggregate supply and prices will continually fall. Though decreasing prices shift the upward-sloping portion of the monetary sector equilibrium curve out to the right (as shown by the dashed *LM* curves), they leave the horizontal section of the curve around point *A* unaffected. Hence, as the model is constructed, falling prices are not sufficient to restore equilibrium in a liquidity trap situation.

In the case of interest inelastic aggregate demand (Figure 7.14B),

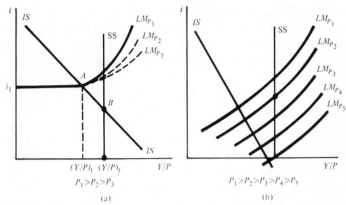

Figure 7.14. Inconsistent aggregate models with flexible prices. (a) Liquidity trap. (b) Inelastic demand.

the interest rate can be reduced as prices fall. Price deflation shifts the money market curve so that it intersects the income-expenditures curve at consecutively lower interest rates. Nevertheless, even if the interest rate is reduced to near zero, investment will be insufficient to match full employment saving. Again we have a situation in which prices will fall continually and yet are not capable of reducing the interest rate to the level necessary to restore full employment.

These two cases are demonstrated in terms of aggregate supply and demand relations in Figure 7.15. Since we are assuming complete price–wage flexibility, the aggregate supply curve is again a vertical line at the full employment level of income. However, at some price level the aggregate demand curve becomes vertical at a level of aggre-

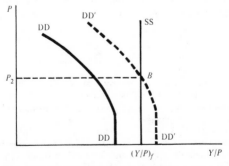

Figure 7.15. Liquidity trap and interest insensitive investment demand in terms of aggregate supply and demand curves.

gate demand for real output which is short of the full employment level. Because of the liquidity trap and interest inelastic expenditures, aggregate demand does not respond to price changes; it is relatively price inelastic over some range.[32] In our original model a fall in prices was always sufficient to free some money balances from use in transactions and make them available for asset-holding (speculative) purposes. Price level reductions were always sufficient to lower the interest rate and thereby stimulate additional investment expenditures and consumption expenditures and increase aggregate demand. As a result the aggregate demand curve DD sloped downward to the right over its entire range. In the present models, however, there is some price level (P_1 in the liquidity trap case, Figure 7.14A and P_5 in the interest insensitive expenditures case, Figure 7.14B) below which further price declines have no effect on the interest rate and, therefore, cannot induce additional spending in order to increase aggregate demand. Consequently, in Figure 7.15 the DD curve would become vertical at those price levels.[33]

The policy implications of these cases are very important. Since monetary policy (changes in the stock of money) works through shifts in the monetary sector equilibrium curve, monetary policy is no longer effective in restoring full employment. (This was previously demonstrated.) Therefore, only a policy that can bring about a positive shift in the income–expenditures sector curve (and, thus, the aggregate demand curve DD') can restore full employment. Since government expenditures are a part of aggregate demand and government taxation policy can affect aggregate demand indirectly through its influence on

---

[32]This may be seen in terms of Equation (7.18). That equation represents the aggregate demand relation depicted by the DD curve in Figure 7.15. As in Equation (7.18),

$$\frac{\partial(Y/P)}{\partial P} = \frac{-(-e/P + h/P)M_0 \, (1/P^2)}{k(-e/P + h/P) + s(u/P)} \, .$$

In the case of the liquidity trap, the interest rate coefficient in the money demand relation u/P becomes infinite (the public demonstrates an unlimited preference for liquidity). Consequently, as $u/P \to \infty$, $\delta(Y/P)/\delta P \to 0$ and changes in the price level become ineffective as a force for changes in aggregate demand.

In the case of perfectly interest insensitive expenditure demand functions, h/P, the interest rate coefficient in the investment demand equation, goes to zero. If saving is also perfectly interest inelastic, $e/P = 0$, and $\delta(Y/P)/\delta P = 0$. Again, price level changes cannot induce an increase in aggregate demand. Under these conditions the DD curve becomes vertical over some range as depicted in Figure 7.15.

[33]The survey of empirical tests of the money demand function which follows Chapter 4 shows little evidence of the liquidity trap.

private expenditures decisions, government fiscal policy alone may be sufficient to stimulate the volume of expenditures necessary to generate full employment. In the case above, for example (Figure 7.15), an increase in aggregate demand brought about by fiscal policy would shift *DD* to *DD'* and would restore full employment at price level P_2 (point B).[34]

Therefore, even with complete nominal wage–price flexibility certain cases may arise which prevent the economy from automatically reaching full employment equilibrium. Furthermore, in these cases it is possible to restore full employment *only* by the positive intervention of the government through fiscal policy.

The destruction of the assumed automaticity of the market economy (even under the assumption of price–wage flexibility) together with the summoning of governmental fiscal intervention into the economy to maintain full employment were serious blows both to the foundations of neoclassical analysis and to free market ideals. It is not surprising, therefore, that attempts have been made to restore the automaticity of the neoclassical model of the aggregate economy as an engine of analysis and a basis for economic policy recommendations.

Some Applications of the Neoclassical Model

Cost Push Inflation and the Neoclassical Model

It is often contended that individual money prices are determined by costs and that exogenous cost increases can raise the general price

---

[34]We may again employ the aggregate demand relation to demonstrate this point. Government fiscal policy (an increase in government expenditures, for example) affects our model through its impact on the autonomous expenditures parameters a/P and a'/P. As in Equation (7.18),

$$\frac{\partial(Y/P)}{\partial(a/P)} = \frac{\partial(Y/P)}{\partial(a'/P)} = \frac{u/P}{k(-e/P + h/P) + s(u/P)} > 0.$$

Thus an increase in autonomous expenditures will increase aggregate demand. The relative response in aggregate demand to a given change in autonomous expenditures will be determined by the parameters in the preceding equation. Most importantly, the numerically larger is u/P, the interest rate coefficient in the money demand function and a determinant of the interest elasticity of the demand for money balances, the greater will be the change in aggregate demand. Likewise, the smaller the sum of the interest coefficients in the expenditures demand equations ($-e/P + h/P$), the less will induced expenditures be cut back as the interest rate rises in response to the increase in autonomous demand and the greater will be the net increase in aggregate demand in the economy. These principles were discussed in Chapter 6.

level. In its extreme form, this view leads to the belief that unions and oligopolists unilaterally cause inflation. If so, it often is alleged that price inflation can be curbed exclusively by some form of wage and price controls, guidelines, or jawboning.

This outlook is inconsistent with the fact that in the history of the western world there has never been a period of sustained price inflation that has not been preceded by and directly associated with a sustained increase in the growth of the money supply. If unions in some sector of the economy ask for higher nominal wages and/or if oligopolists unilaterally raise their prices, elementary microeconomic theory indicates that costs and prices in that sector will indeed rise, thus exerting upward pressure on the price level in general, especially where wages and prices in other industries are not perfectly flexible downward. However, as the price level rises, the value of real money balance declines. The real balance model developed earlier indicates that the pressure of excess capacity and unemployed resources generated by the decline in aggregate demand will eventually reverse the price level increase and cause full employment equilibrium to be restored.

In Figure 7.16 the economy is in full employment equilibrium at point D at a price level of P_0. If unions raise the nominal wage in excess of productivity gains, prices are "pushed" up.[35] This causes the LM curve in Figure 7.16 to shift from LM_{P_0} to LM_{P_2}. The shift in LM occurs because of the reduction in the stock of real money balances as the nominal wage and hence the price level increase. If a real balance effect were not operative, aggregate equilibrium would occur at point C; if a real-balance effect were operative, aggregate equilibrium would be at E because the IS curve would shift to IS'_{P_2}, reflecting the decrease in consumption expenditures induced by the rise in the price level. At either C or E, however, there is excess capacity and unemployment in the economy. The price level must return to P_0 in order to restore equilibrium.

Monetary and fiscal authorities may believe, as discussed in the previous section, that as a matter of political convenience the process of

---

[35]This process can be seen in detail in Figure 7.11. Suppose the economy were at a full employment equilibrium such as D. A rise in the nominal wage requests of a union is reflected as an upward shift in the labor supply curve. This establishes a position of temporary underemployment equilibrium at C. The move from LM_{P_0} to LM_{P_2} in Figure 7.16 is consistent with the movement *along DD'* in Figure 7.11B from D to C; the move from LM_{P_2} to LM_{P_2} in Figure 7.16 would be consistent with a *shift* in DD' in Figure 7.11B such that it intersects SS at P_2.

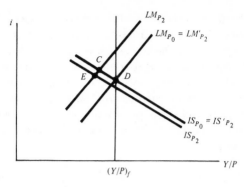

Figure 7.16. Cost push inflation and the real-balance model.

deflation would take too long to restore full employment. Such a belief might lead the Federal Reserve to increase the money supply, causing the LM curve to shift to LM'_{P_2} so that full employment is sustained at the new higher price level P_2. If the real balance effect were operative, IS would shift back to IS'_{P_2} as real balances are restored to their original level. In this fashion the Federal Reserve would ratify or validate the wage–price spiral.[36]

Anticipated Inflation in the Neoclassical Model

Throughout Chapters 5, 6, and 7 we did not distinguish between nominal and real rates of interest. And yet in Chapter 4 we saw that changes in the rate of inflation do affect interest rates. For example, if a lender is to receive a $100 interest income on a $1000 loan, the nominal rate of interest i is 10 percent. Nevertheless, if by the date of maturity of the loan, the price level has risen by 7 percent, the real rate of interest on the loan r is approximately 3 percent. This relationship may be approximated, *ex post*, as

$$i = r + \frac{\Delta P}{P} \qquad (7.9)$$

[36]A similar analysis applies to price level increases seemingly caused by an increase in the price of strategic imported raw materials such as petroleum. Where the demand for these goods is inelastic, a rise in their prices should shift purchasing power away from other goods and services whose prices should fall. Where these other prices are rigid downward, the price index will rise and real balances will decline as in the preceding analysis. Once again, the pressure on the monetary authority to validate the price spiral is significant.

where $\Delta P/P$ stands for the percentage rate of change of the price level. More precisely, $\Delta P/P$ is the discrete equivalent of $(dP/dt)/P$, or $\dot{P}$ for short, the derivative of the general price level with respect to time, expressed as a percentage. If there are uniform price expectations on the part of debtors and creditors regarding an increase in the future rate of inflation, then the current *nominal* rate of interest will rise. In Chapter 4 this was called the price inflation expectations effect.[37] The impact of price expectations on the nominal interest rate may be expressed, *ex ante*, as

$$i = r + \dot{P}_e. \tag{7.20}$$

where $\dot{P}_e$ is the expected rate of price inflation.

Let us examine the effect of inflationary expectations on our flexible price model. Initially we will assume that there is no real balance effect at work on expenditures. The real rate of interest and the general price level are at equilibrium levels and real income is at the full employment level. At this initial equilibrium the actual rate of price inflation is zero and individuals expect a zero rate of inflation.

Now, for a reason that we shall soon make explicit, assume that everyone suddenly expects the price level to rise in the future by a certain percentage rate each year. Given this expectation, we shall see how the nominal rate of interest rises by the amount of the expected rate of inflation as indicated by Equation (7.20). The nominal rate of interest will exceed the real rate of interest by an amount equal to the expected rate of inflation.

If an increase is expected in the rate of inflation from $\dot{P}_{e_0}$ to $\dot{P}_{e_1}$ in Figure 7.17 investment and consumption expenditures will increase as business firms and households accelerate their spending plans at the old nominal interest rate i_0. This is reflected in the shift in the IS curve from IS_0 to IS_1. As discussed in Chapter 5, the decision to invest in newly produced capital goods depends on the market rate of interest. When the nominal value of future returns rises because the flow of

---

[37]If we can assume that historical rates of inflation are predictors of future rates of inflation, a series for $\dot{P}_e$ can be constructed and the real rate of interest can be derived from the observed nominal rate. There are several studies of the effect of price expectations on interest rates. For example, William P. Yohe and Denis Karnosky, "Interest Rates and Price Level Changes, 1952–1969," *Review*, Federal Reserve Bank of St. Louis (December 1969), 18–38; William E. Gibson, "Interest Rates and Inflationary Expectations," *American Economic Review* (December 1972), 854–865; and Thomas Sargent, "Anticipated Inflation and the Nominal Rate of Interest," *Quarterly Journal of Economics* (May 1972), 212–225.

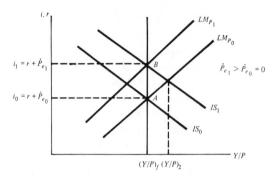

Figure 7.17. Price expectations in the price-flexible $LM-IS$ model.

future output is expected to be sold at higher prices, the present value of this future income stream rises and the demand for capital goods increases at the unchanged nominal market rate of interest which is used to discount this future income stream. At the unchanged nominal rate of interest with higher expected inflation, the real rate of interest, by definition is lower until the business firms also may realize that if the price of capital goods is expected to rise by, say, 5 percent during the forthcoming period, in order to obtain the same quantity of capital goods by the end of the period, they presently have to increase their nominal investment expenditures by 5 percent. Households also realize that at an unchanged nominal rate of interest, with a higher expected rate of inflation the real rate of interest is lower. Therefore, they increase their present real consumption. As a result of this increase in real investment and consumption demand, the nominal interest rate then rises in an amount equal to expected future price inflation. Assuming an equiproportionate increase in all individual prices, this leaves real investment and real consumption expenditures unchanged. At the new equilibrium (B) it also leaves the real rate of interest unchanged at r. In Figure 7.17 the levels of real investment and real consumption expenditures is the same at B as it is at A.[38]

Now consider the effect of a rise in the nominal rate of interest on the demand for money. As discussed in Chapter 4, the demand for real

[38]In reality, observed nominal rates of interest may not rise in an amount equal to anticipated inflation (that is, *real* rates of interest may fall). This may occur because real investment expenditures (private capital formation) may actually decline in response to the uncertainty (of future returns) that businessmen associate with high levels of inflation. There may also be modest increases in real saving as inflation erodes real financial wealth and creates consumer pessimism. This too would cause real rates of interest to decline.

money balances varies inversely with the *nominal* rate of interest because the nominal rate is the opportunity cost of tying up financial wealth in a noninterest earning form. With real income unchanged the increase in investment expenditures can only drive up the nominal rate of interest to i_1. At this higher equilibrium interest rate at an unchanged level of real income, there will be an excess supply of money. In Figure 7.17 IS_1 and LM_{P_0} intersect at $(Y/P)_2 > (Y/P)_f$. As discussed earlier the fact that real income cannot rise above $(Y/P)_f$ ensures that the excess supply of money will cause the general price level to rise.

As the general price level rises from P_0 to P_1, the real stock of money declines and the *LM* curve shifts leftward to LM_{P_1}. (If a real balance effect were at work on the expenditures side of the model, the *IS* curve would also shift leftward.) The new equilibrium level of the nominal rate of interest is $i_1 = r + \dot{P}_{e_1}$.

Thus the expectation of inflation causes an increase in the price level and the expectation is self-fulfilling. If expected inflation persists at $\dot{P}_e$, but the money supply is not increased, no further price level increases can occur. When individuals realize that the price level has stopped increasing, the expected rate of inflation will return to zero. The *IS* curve will shift leftward to IS_0 as business firms no longer desire to maintain the same flow of investment expenditures at the nominal rate of interest i_1. A reduced expected rate of inflation will cause investors to reevaluate downward the expected future income stream associated with investment projects. Decreases in the market rate of interest and the general price level will take place.

Now the leftward shift in the *IS* curve may cause a temporary decline in the level of output and employment. Realizing this and (as discussed in the preceding section) not desiring to wait for the market economy to correct itself, monetary policymakers may choose to increase the growth rate of the money supply. In fact, the only way $\dot{P}_{e_1}$ can be sustained in equilibrium in Figure 7.17 is for the Federal Reserve to continuously increase the nominal supply of (outside) money at the rate equal to the expected rate of inflation $\dot{P}_{e_1}$, *ceteris paribus*. Only then will expectations be continuously realized. The *price expectations effect* will be validated. Taken together, an initial rise in the price level caused by an expectation of inflation *plus* the continuous rate of price increase caused by continuous money supply expansion cause the nominal rate of interest to rise from i_0 to i_1 and result in a reduction in the stock of real money balances demanded. Individuals simply choose to hold fewer real money balances at a higher rate of interest.

The Effect of an Increase in the Nominal Money Supply on the Nominal Interest Rate

Now let us examine once more the effects of an increase in the money supply on the nominal interest rate. If in our price-flexible LM–IS model we were to hold both the price level and the level of real income constant and if price inflation were not anticipated, then the initial effect of an increase in the nominal supply of money would be to reduce the nominal rate of interest. In Chapter 4 this was called the *liquidity effect*.

We begin from a position of static full employment equilibrium at point A in Figure 7.18. Assume that the rate of money supply growth and the rate of inflation here are zero. Now assume a once and for all increase in the supply of money. As LM shifts to LM'_{P_0} the *liquidity effect* drives the interest rate down from i_0 to i_1 (from A to B) in Figure 7.18.

In Chapter 6 we saw that in an economy where the price (and nominal wage) level is assumed fixed an increase in the money supply will cause real income to rise. If real income *could* rise from $(Y/P)_f$ to $(Y/P)_2$, there would be upward pressure on the interest rate; it would rise from i_1 to i_2 (at point D in Figure 15.7). This is the *income effect* of money on interest discussed in Chapter 4.[39] The combined *liquidity and income effects* of an increase in the money supply would cause a net decline in the market rate of interest from i_0 to i_2 as long as there is a fixed nominal wage and price level. The decrease in the market rate is, of course, consistent with the rise in real income of the Keynesian models discussed in Chapter 6.

In the flexible-price model of the present chapter real income is constrained not to rise above the full employment level. Excess aggregate demand (an excess of actual over desired real money balances) causes the general price level to rise from P_0 to P_1.[40] After the initial rightward shift to LM'_{P_0} caused by the initial increase in the money stock, the LM curve shifts leftward back to LM'_{P_1} and full-employment

---

[39]In the reading by Laurence H. Meyer which follows this chapter the combined liquidity effect and income effect of an increase in money on real income was called the "liquidity *impact*" multiplier. Here we refer to the liquidity *effect* of money on the interest rate. The two labels should not be confused.

[40]The only way in which any additional output can be generated, to the right of Y/P_f at D in Figure 7.18 and B in Figure 7.19, is through money illusion in the labor market, whereby labor demanders anticipate an increase in the price and labor suppliers do not.

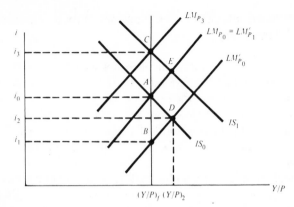

Figure 7.18. Liquidity, income and price expectations effects of an increase in the money supply.

equilibrium is restored at a price level and a level of nominal income that have risen proportionately with the increase in the nominal stock of money. In this case after an initial decline from the liquidity effect the market rate of interest returns to its original level i_0 at point A in Figure 7.18. The *nominal income effect* just offsets the *liquidity effect* and the equilibrium interest rate does not change.

As discussed earlier the expectation of future increases in prices may cause an increase in expenditures. This is reflected as a shift in the *IS* curve to IS_1 in Figure 7.18.[41] As the price level is driven upward by this increase in aggregate demand, the *LM* curve shifts leftward to LM_{P_3}. Thus the *price inflation expectations effect* on the nominal rate of interest is $i_3 - i_0$.[43] The new point of equilibrium is C in Figure 7.18. The new higher price level and interest rate will be sustained only if the money supply, which was initially assumed not to be growing, now increases at a rate equal to the expected rate of price inflation. If it does

[41]Once again, the only way in which additional output can be generated, to the right of $(Y/P)_f$ at E in Figure 7.18 and D in Figure 7.19, is through money illusion in the labor market, whereby labor demanders anticipate an increase in the *rate* of price inflation and labor suppliers do not.

[42]For further discussion of nominal versus real rates in a dynamic context see the survey article by Yung Chul Park, *op. cit.*, which follows this chapter, as well as Milton Friedman, "Factors Affecting the Level of Interest Rates," *1968 Conference Proceedings, Savings and Residential Financing* (Chicago: U.S. Savings and Loan League, 1969), 10–27 which follows Chapter 4.

not, the rate of price inflation must decline and the nominal rate of interest will return to i_0.

We have not yet shown how price expectations effects develop. We have simply assumed a sudden appearance of inflationary expectations. However, it is reasonable to assume that such expectations are formed either on the basis of recent inflationary experiences (adaptive expectations) or other experiences, including the pattern of recent monetary and fiscal policy actions. Essentially, if the price *level* has recently been rising in a fairly consistent manner, individuals may come to expect it to continue to rise. Thus a fairly constant *rate* of price inflation may be anticipated.[43] Moreover, since a sustained rise in the price level can result only from a continual increase in the supply of money, inflationary expectations may arise from individuals learning about the way in which the money supply is handled by the monetary authority.

For instance, the monetary authority may be attempting to control the nominal rate of interest. It can be seen from our model that if the Federal Reserve attempts to set the nominal rate of interest at any level other than the one which is equal to the equilibrium real rate of interest, it must result in either inflation or deflation.

Consider a case where the Federal Reserve is trying to keep the interest rate lower than the equilibrium real rate, perhaps because of concern in certain sectors of the economy with an interest rate that is "too high" or because of the belief that a lower interest rate can permanently stimulate real income and employment.

For example, assume that the economy is initially in equilibrium at point A' of Figure 7.19. Assume further that at this point the rate of inflation and the rate of money supply growth are both zero. Now consider an increase in the government deficit. (For simplicity we ignore the financing of the deficit.) This is represented by the shift in the IS curve from IS_0 to IS_1. This drives the real rate of interest up so that the nominal rate rises to i_3. At nominal interest rate i_3 the excess supply of money exerts upward pressure on the price level which

---

[43]There are two main theories of the formation of anticipations, *adaptive expectations* and *rational expectations*. Both, however, may use data from the past to predict the future. For further detail, see G. E. D. Box and G. M. Jenkins, *Time Series Analysis: Forecasting and Control* (San Francisco: Holden-Day, 1970); J. F. Muth, "Rational Expectations and the Theory of Price Movements," *Econometrica* (July 1961); and Thomas J. Sargent and Neil Wallace, "Rational Expectations and the Dynamics of Hyperinflation," *International Economic Review* (June 1973).

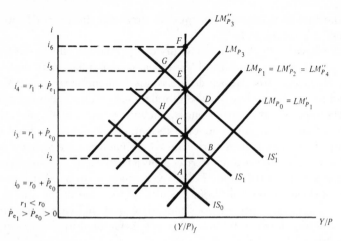

Figure 7.19. Effect of the monetary authority's attempt to control the interest rate.

causes LM to shift to LM_{P_1} such that the new equilibrium is at point C. If i_3 is popularly considered "too high" an interest rate, pressure may be brought on the monetary authority to "do something" about the high interest rate and it may therefore increase the supply of money.

This will cause the LM curve to shift rightward to LM'_{P_1}. As we have seen, an initial liquidity effect may succeed temporarily in keeping the rate of interest down to i_0. Nevertheless, A is no longer an equilibrium position and the rise in the price level from P_1 to P_2 will cause LM to shift to LM'_{P_2}. The nominal income effect will drive the interest rate back to i_3.

If whenever the interest rate rises above i_0 the money supply increases, the *rate* of money supply growth will eventually increase and the price level will begin to rise, period after period, so that a positive *rate* of inflation is established. As this rate of inflation comes to be expected $\dot{P}_{e_1}$, expenditures will increase in anticipation of inflation, and, as described earlier, the IS curve will shift to IS'_1. The price inflation expectations effect will then drive the nominal rate of interest even higher to i_4. If the money supply continues to grow at the rate that established this expectation, the equilibrium stock of real money balances must fall to a level that is consistent with the now higher opportunity cost of holding real money, i_4. This is depicted as a leftward shift of LM to LM_{P_3}. A new equilibrium position consistent with the new positive rate of money supply growth and fully anticipated rate of inflation is established at E in Figure 7.19.[44]

Now assume that the public grows weary of inflation. The Federal Reserve reduces the rate of money supply growth back to zero. In short-run, single period, analysis a constant nominal money stock combined with an increase in the price level, created by continued inflation, causes the LM curve to shift leftward to LM''_{P_3} in Figure 7.19. This initial liquidity effect causes a rise in the interest rate from i_4 to i_6 at point F. The graph simplistically shows that with a positive rate of inflation a cutback in money supply growth will result in a shortage of liquidity. Under conditions of subsequent wage–price stickiness or money illusion in the labor market this liquidity shortage could bring about a temporary reduction in real income and the economy will gravitate toward point G and the interest rate will decline to i_5.[45]

In a regime of flexible wages and prices the rate of price inflation declines rather quickly toward zero, consistent with the zero growth rate of the money supply. As this occurs, the liquidity shortage will be less severe. The LM curve may be depicted as shifting less further leftward than LM''_{P_3} in short-run, single period, analysis. If the price inflation goes immediately to zero, the income effect of zero inflation completely offsets the liquidity effect of zero money supply growth and the LM curve may be depicted as not shifting beyond LM_{P_3}.

As the new lower rate of money supply growth persists, the demise of inflationary expectations will shift the IS curve leftward to IS_1. The price inflation expectations effect generates a decline in the nominal rate of interest. With an unchanged nominal money supply the resulting increased demand for real money balances can only be satisfied if the price level declines. The decrease in the price level causes the LM curve to shift to LM''_{P_4}. Equilibrium is restored at point C in Figure 7.19 with the market rate of interest being i_3.

Thus despite the machinations of the monetary authority, the nominal rate of interest returns (whence it began) to equality with the

---

[44]Therefore the curve LM_{P_3} reflects an equilibrium stock of real money balances that has been determined by an equilibrium *rate* of price inflation that is consistent with the positive growth *rate* of the nominal money supply that established the expectation of that inflation. The term P_3 in LM_{P_3} does not refer to a price *level*.

[45]Because of money illusion in the labor market, there may be a temporary decline in output and employment at point G in Figure 7.19. This can be depicted as a movement to the right of the natural rate of unemployment along a short-run Phillips curve.

real long-run equilibrium rate of interest, *ceteris paribus*. By attempting to keep the interest rate below this level, the monetary authority accelerated the money supply growth rate which, to the extent that it generated unanticipated inflation, caused real income, output and employment to exceed *temporarily* their full employment levels such as at points B and D in Figure 7.19. As a result of inflation the nominal rate of interest rose. Public concern over inflation then induced the monetary authority to restrict the growth of the money supply and the market interest rate reached an even higher level. This caused real income and output to fall temporarily below their full employment levels at points G and H in Figure 7.19. In the long run given the initial increased government deficit, a no inflation, full employment equilibrium is attainable only at C.

This model suggests that in an otherwise stable economy, a process of boom and bust, inflation and recession, can result from the destabilizing policies of a monetary authority. In this particular case unstable patterns of money supply behavior arose from attempts to maintain a low interest rate in the face of an increased government deficit. Other stimuli for an unstable monetary environment might include a systematic pattern of "excessive" union wage settlements (discussed earlier in this chapter), increases in the prices of important raw material imports and periodic crop failures. In these instances, the monetary authority might increase the growth rate of the money supply, thereby "validating" these price increases, in order to forestall any temporary recessionary effects. In addition, it has been argued that even political considerations such as upcoming elections provide elected officials with an incentive to stimulate the economy in order to produce temporarily lower levels of unemployment.[46] Because variations in government deficits and these other factors will cause the *IS* and *LM* curves to shift, a policy of trying to compensate for the effect of these shifts on the market rate of interest and real income may be more destabilizing than a policy of sustaining stable money supply growth. For example, when the *IS* curve shifted from IS_0 to IS_1 in Figure 7.18, there would have been a good deal less instability had the monetary

[46]The political business cycle was discussed briefly in footnote 31.

A satisfactory theory of monetary instability would have to explain why the monetary authority is wont to validate inflationary pressures, monetize deficits, and purposely stimulate the economy at some times but not at others. See Thomas Havrilesky, "A Theory of Monetary Instability," Lombra, Kaufman and Dooley (eds.), *The Political Economy of Policymaking* (New York: Sage Publications, 1980) and Thomas Havrilesky, "The Discordance-Inequality Tradeoff," *Public Choice* (December, 1980).

authority not responded and simply let the system gravitate toward C.

It can further be argued that the unstable monetary environment discussed in the preceding paragraphs can generate inelastic price, wage and interest rate expectations and that these in turn generate even *more* instability, inefficiency and unemployment in the economy than described above. These are all important problems which cannot be explored further here. They are a proper subject for an entire book in the theory and practice of monetary policy.

In a regime where the monetary authority systematically attempts to keep money supply growth rates in line with prearranged *target* rates of growth, market participants will respond to deviations of actual money growth from target growth. A positive deviation may be viewed as a precursor of slower money supply growth and temporarily higher interest rates in the future. A negative deviation may be seen as a harbinger of faster money supply growth and temporarily lower interest rates in the future. In this sort of a policy environment the immediate liquidity and income effects described above may disappear and price inflation expectations effects will primarily be associated with target money supply growth rates. Short run interest rate movements are likely to be less volatile than under the less stable monetary policy regime portrayed in the preceding paragraphs and, aside from temporary "monetary policy anticipation effects," may more closely reflect movements in the underlying real rate of interest caused by shifts in saving, investment and government deficits.

QUESTIONS

1. What is the effect of an increase in government deficit spending in the neoclassical model? Does this effect differ for a "crude" neoclassical model (see footnote 15)?
2. a. Derive the *LM* curve for the "crude" neoclassical model (footnote 15).
   b. Derive the *IS* curve for the "crude" neoclassical model.
   c. What is the effect of introducing liquidity preference into 2(a)?
   d. What is the effect of introducing a Keynesian consumption function into 2(b)?
3. Prove that the aggregate demand relation slopes downward in $Y/P,P$ space. Prove that for a crude neoclassical model this relation has an elasticity of -1.
4. Derive the neoclassical aggregate supply curve.
5. Incorporate a neoclassical aggregate supply sector with a Keynesian aggregate demand sector. Are the implications Keynesian or neoclassical?

6. Assume that in the long run the structure of the economy assumes neoclassical properties. What are the long run implications for private expenditures in a world of escalating government expenditures?

7. Evaluate: Given a position of employment, a once and for all cut in nominal wages will increase real output and employment because lower prices will
   a. Lower directly the real interest rate.
   b. Increase real income and hence real consumption.
   c. Increase real money balances and hence lower the interest rate.
   d. Lower real wages and hence the quantity of labor supplied will decrease.
   e. Cause anticipations of further price declines.

8. Rank the following Keynesian propositions in the order of their importance to the result of underemployment equilibrium.
   a. A high interest elasticity of the speculative demand for money.
   b. The absence of an international sector in many models.
   c. Rigid nominal wages.
   d. The concept of income induced consumption spending.
   e. A low interest elasticity of investment demand.
   f. Rigid prices.

9. Why does the following reduce the magnitude of the autonomous expenditures multiplier?
   a. A variable interest rate.
   b. A flexible price level with a rigid nominal wage.
   c. Flexible price and nominal wage levels with money illusion on the part of labor suppliers.

10. Can a little (acceleration in) inflation be a good thing?

11. Using the Phillips curve model show that an "inflationary recession" is not a theoretical economic enigma.

12. What is meant when it is said that neoclassical economies has a flow theory of interest while Keynesian economies has a stock theory of interest?

13. "Monetary and fiscal policy can affect output and employment only to the extent that policy changes are unpredicted." Evaluate.

14. Analyze the effect of an increase in the price of imported oil in terms of the *LM–IS* real balances model. Now do the same with the complete aggregate demand-aggregate supply model.

15. Would the ability of government to tax by inflation be modified if interest were paid on all money balances?

16. How are the price expectations discussed in this chapter formed? Is it true that the price level must rise if it is *expected* to rise? Does this falsify the quantity theory of money?

17. Can the rate of interest or the real stock of money be determined by the monetary authority? Why or why not?

18. The unstable behavior of the money supply arises from dissatisfaction

within the economy and between economies over the distribution of income. This generates pressures for large and growing government deficits and pressures for rapid increases in nominal wages; the Federal Reserve must yield to these pressures. Thus, the degree of monetary instability is related to the extent of discord in the economy. Evaluate.

19. Consider chronic bond-financed government deficits. Assume a politically grounded Federal Reserve sensitivity to "high" interest rates. Develop the consequences.

20. When money supply growth accelerates above its long-run trend, nominal interest rates may fall for a short time (the liquidity effect), then they will begin to rise (the income effect). If acceleration continues, expectations of higher inflation will be formed (the price expectations effect). If a new money growth trend is established, interest rates will surely rise and bond and stock prices will fall, as the Federal Reserve validates the price expectations effect.

Conversely, when money growth rates decelerate below trend, interest rates will temporarily rise (the liquidity effect). When the economy cools off they will begin to fall (the income effect). If deceleration continues, expectations of lower price inflation will be formed (the price expectations effect). If a new trend line is established, they will shortly decline as the Federal Reserve validates the price expectations effect.

Using the present value formula of Chapter 3, describe how you would use this theory to develop a strategy for speculation in the stock and bond markets.

21. Explain why the real rate of interest temporarily falls when the rate of inflation accelerates and temporarily rises when the rate of inflation decelerates.

BIBLIOGRAPHY

ALCHIAN, ARMEN, "Information Costs, Pricing and Resource Unemployment," *Western Economic Journal* (June 1969).

ANDERSEN, LEONALL C., and KEITH M. CARLSON, "St. Louis Model Revisited," *International Economic Review*, vol. 15, no. 2 (June 1974), 305–327.*

BAILEY, MARTIN J., "The Welfare Costs of Inflationary Finance," *Journal of Political Economy* (June 1956).

BAILEY, MARTIN, *National Income and the Price Level* (New York: McGraw-Hill, 1971), chs. 2 and 3.

BARRO, ROBERT, and HERSCHEL GROSSMAN, *Money, Employment and Inflation* (New York: Cambridge University Press, 1976).

*Reprinted in THOMAS M. HAVRILESKY and JOHN T. BOORMAN, *Current Issues in Monetary Theory and Policy* (Arlington Heights, IL.: AHM Publishing Corporation, 1980).

BRANSON, WILLIAM, *Macroeconomic Theory and Policy* (New York: Harper and Row, 1972).

BOX, G. E. D., and G. M. JENKINS, *Time Series Analysis: Forecasting and Control* (San Francisco: Holden-Day, 1970).

CLOWER, ROBERT W., "A Reconsideration of Microfoundations of Monetary Theory," *Western Economic Journal*, vol. 6 (1967).

_____, "The Keynesian Counterrevolution: A Theoretical Appraisal" in *The Theory of Interest Rates*, F. H. Hahn and F. Brechling, eds. (New York: Macmillan, 1965).

FAND, DAVID I., "Some Issues in Monetary Economics: Fiscal Policy Assumptions and Related Multipliers," *Review*, Federal Reserve Bank of St. Louis (January 1970), 23–27.*

FISHER, IRVING, *The Purchasing Power of Money* (New York: Augustus M. Kelly, Bookseller, Reprints of Economic Classics, 1963).

FRIEDMAN, MILTON, "Factors Affecting the Level of Interest Rates," *1968 Conference Proceedings, Savings and Residential Financing* (Chicago: U.S. Savings and Loan League, 1969), 10–27.*

_____, "The Role of Monetary Policy," *American Economic Review*, vol. 58 (March 1968), 1–17.

FRIEDMAN, MILTON, and ANNA J. SCHWARTZ, "The Definition of Money," *Journal of Money, Credit and Banking*, vol. 1 (February 1969), 1–14.

GIBSON, WILLIAM E., "Interest Rates and Inflationary Expectations," *American Economic Review* (December 1972), 854–865.

HABERLER, GOTTFRIED, *Prosperity and Depression*, 3rd ed. (Geneva: The League of Nations, 1941), 491–503.

HAVRILESKY, THOMAS M. "A Theory of Monetary Instability," *The Political Economy of Policymaking*, Lombra, Kaufman and Dooley, eds. (New York: Sage Publications, 1979).

HICKS, J. R., in *Value and Capital* (Oxford: Clarendon Press, 1939), 205.

_____, "Mr. Keynes and the Classics: A Suggested Interpretation," in American Economic Association, *Readings in the Theory of Income Distribution* (New York: McGraw-Hill-Blakiston, 1946), 461–472.

HINES, A. G., *On the Reappraisal of the Economics of Keynes* (London: Martin Robertson, 1971).*

HUMPHREY, THOMAS M., "Changing Views of the Phillips Curve," *Monthly Review*, Federal Reserve Bank of Richmond (July 1973), 2–13.*

JOHNSON, HARRY G., Monetary Theory and Keynesian Economics, *Pakistan Economic Journal*, vol. 8 (June 1958), 56–70. Reprinted in Warren Smith and Ronald Teigen, *Readings in Money, National Income, and Stabilization Policy* (Homewood, IL: Richard D. Irwin, 1965), 32–43.

_____, "Inside Money, Outside Money, Income, Wealth and Welfare in Monetary Theory," *Journal of Money, Credit and Banking*, vol. 1 (February 1969), 30–45.

KEYNES, J. M., *The General Theory of Employment, Interest and Money* (London: Macmillan, 1936).

LANGE, OSCAR, "Say's Law: Restatement and Criticism," in *Studies in Mathematical Economics and Econometrics* (Chicago: University of Chicago Press, 1942).

LEIJONHUFVUD, AXEL, *Keynesian Economics and the Economics of Keynes* (New York: Oxford University Press, 1968).

LEONTIEF, WASSILY, "Postulates: Keynes' General Theory and the Classicists," in *The New Economics*, Seymour E. Harris, ed. (New York: Alfred A. Knopf, 1947), 232–242.

LOMBRA, RAYMOND, and RAYMOND TORTO, "Measuring the Impact of Monetary and Fiscal Actions: A New Look at the Specification Problem," *Review of Economics and Statistics*, vol. 56, no. 1 (February 1974), 104–107.*

MARSHALL, ALFRED, *Money, Credit and Commerce* (London: Macmillan, 1923).

MARTY, ALVIN, "Inside Money, Outside Money, and the Wealth Effect: A Review Essay," *Journal of Money, Credit and Banking*, vol. 1 (February 1969), 101–111.

MAYER, THOMAS, "The Empirical Significance of the Real Balance Effect," *Quarterly Journal of Economics*, vol. 73 (May 1959), 275–291.

METZLER, LLOYD A., "Wealth, Saving and the Rate of Interest," *Journal of Political Economy*, vol. 59 (April 1951), 93–116.

MODIGLIANI, FRANCO, "Liquidity Preference and the Theory of Interest and Money," in American Economic Association, *Readings in Monetary Theory* (New York: McGraw-Hill Blakiston, 1951), ch. 11.

———, "The Monetary Mechanism and Its Interaction with Real Phenomena," *Review of Economics and Statistics*, vol. 45 (February 1963), 79–107.

MUTH, J. F., "Rational Expectations and the Theory of Price Movements," *Econometrica* (July 1961).

NORDHAUS, WILLIAM D., "The Political Business Cycle," *Review of Economic Studies*, vol. 42 (April 1975), 169–189.

PARK, YUNG CHUL, "Some Current Issues in the Transmission Process of Monetary Policy," *Staff Papers, International Monetary Fund* (March 1972), 1–45.*

PATINKIN, DON, "Price Flexibility and Full Employment," *American Economic Review*, vol. 38 (September 1948), 543–564.

———, "Money and Wealth: A Review Article," *Journal of Economic Literature*, vol. 7 (December 1969), 1140–1160.

*Reprinted in THOMAS M. HAVRILESKY and JOHN T. BOORMAN, *Current Issues in Monetary Theory and Policy, op. cit.*

————, *Money, Interest and Prices*, 2nd ed. (New York: Harper and Row, 1965).

PESEK, BORIS, and THOMAS SAVING, *Money, Wealth, and Economic Theory* (New York: Macmillan, 1967), chs. 1–3.

PHELPS, EDMUND S., *Microeconomic Foundations of Employment and Inflation Theory* (New York: Norton, 1970).

PIGOU, A. C., "The Classical Stationary State," *Economic Journal*, vol. 53 (1943), 343–351.

————, "Economic Progress in a Stable Environment," *Econometrica*, vol. 14 (1947), 180–190.

RASCHE, ROBERT, "A Comparative Static Analysis of Some Monetarist Propositions," *Review*, Federal Reserve Bank of St. Louis (December 1973), 15–22.*

SAMUELSON, PAUL, "Money, Interest Rates and Economic Activity," *Proceedings of a Symposium of Money, Interest Rates and Economic Activity* (New York: American Bankers Association, 1967), 45–57.

SARGENT, THOMAS, "Anticipated Inflation and the Nominal Rate of Interest," *Quarterly Journal of Economics* (May 1972), 212–225.

SARGENT, T. J., and N. WALLACE, "Rational Expectations and the Dynamics of Hyperinflation," *International Economic Review* (June 1973).

SARGENT, THOMAS J., and NEIL WALLACE, "Rational Expectations and the Theory of Economic Policy," *Journal of Monetary Economics* (April 1976).

SCHOTTA, CHARLES R., "The Real Balance Effect in the United States, 1947–1963," *Journal of Finance*, vol. 19 (December 1964), 619–630.

SMITH, WARREN L., "A Graphical Exposition of the Complete Keynesian System," *The Southern Economic Journal*, vol. 23 (October 1956), 115–125.*

————, "A Neo-Keynesian View of Monetary Policy," *Proceedings of a Monetary Conference of the Federal Reserve Bank of Boston* (June 1969), 105–126.

SPENCER, ROGER W., "Channels of Monetary Influence," *Review*, Federal Reserve Bank of St. Louis (January 1973), 16–21.

TIMBERLAKE, RICHARD HENRY, "Patinkin and the Pigou Effect: A Comment," *Review of Economics and Statistics*, vol. 39 (August 1957), 346–348.

TOBIN, JAMES, "Money Wage Rates and Employment," in *The New Economics*, Seymour E. Harris, ed. (New York: Alfred A. Knopf, 1947), 572–587.

TUCKER, DONALD P., "Macroeconomic Models and the Demand for Money under Market Disequilibrium," *Journal of Money, Credit and Banking*, vol. 3 (February 1971), 57–83.

TYDALL, H. F., "Savings and Wealth," *Australian Economic Papers*, vol. 2 (December 1963), 228–250.

WOOD, JOHN H., "Money and Output: Keynes and Friedman in Historical

Perspective," *Business Review*, Federal Reserve Bank of Philadelphia (September 1972).*

YOHE, WILLIAM P., and DENIS KARNOSKY, "Interest Rates and Price Level Changes, 1952–1969," *Review*, Federal Reserve Bank of St. Louis (December 1969), 18–38.

Introduction to Readings / Part III

The three chapters of this section developed Keynesian and Neoclassical theories of the economy as a whole. These theories incorporated theories of the supply of and demand for money presented in Parts I and II.

The LM–IS, or Keynesian, model of the economy presented in Chapter 6 has been most often applied to analyzing monetary and fiscal policy. Yet this model has come under attack in recent years because it ignores the fact that all fiscal policy deficits have to be financed and that the financing of deficits could have important effects on the size and composition of aggregate private wealth and thereby second-order effects on the LM–IS model and its multipliers. The first article in this readings section, by Laurence H. Meyer, presents a framework for analyzing fiscal policy that incorporates these interactions.

As pointed out in Chapter 7, another important source of criticism of the Keynesian model has been that it claims that fiscal and monetary policy are capable of influencing output and employment. Some economists now argue that economic stabilization policies are capable of such an influence only under very special conditions. One school of thought, associated with the hypothesis which claims that there exists a natural rate of unemployment, contends that monetary and fiscal policy can affect output and employment only if there are wage and price expectational errors in certain markets, especially labor markets. Another school, not necessarily exclusive of the former, holds that systematic monetary and fiscal policy, by virtue of their predictability by rational economic agents, cannot possibly generate such errors and hence cannot affect output and employment. This rational expectations school conjectures that economic agents (households, firms, etc.) will exploit all pertinent information when making forecasts, including wage and price forecasts. The article by Thomas M. Humphrey presents an excellent survey of both the natural rate hypothesis and the rational expectations hypothesis.

Chapter 7 stressed the distinctions between the Keynesian and Neoclassical theories of the aggregate economy. There are many important distinctions between the ways in which Keynesians and

*Monetarists regard the way in which monetary impulses may be trans-
mitted (through short-term interest rates, long-term interest rates,
wealth, etc.) to spending, production, and prices. The reading by Yung
Chul Park examines the major views of Monetarists and Keynesians
regarding the channels through which monetary policy works. It is an
invaluable extension of the more basic work presented in Chapter 7.*

*In each of the earlier two sections of this book, we presented a
survey of empirical estimates of the money supply and money demand
relations discussed in the preceding chapters. When it comes to empirical estimates of macroeconomic models as a whole, such a survey
would be impossible to develop in a few pages. Yet, the article of Joseph
Crews focuses on just two models that are somewhat representative of
the Keynesian and Monetarist views—the Federal Reserve Board–MIT
econometric model and the econometric model of the Federal Reserve
Bank of St. Louis. Crews chooses these two models because each features a well-developed monetary sector, each is fairly well seasoned as
econometric models go, and each is representative of a particular view
of the transmission mechanism (discussed in the preceding article by
Park).*

Financing Constraints and the Short-Run Response to Fiscal Policy

Laurence H. Meyer

Monetarists have long emphasized that the impact of an increase in
government expenditures depends on how the increase is financed. In
particular, they have suggested that a bond-financed increase in government expenditures has only minimal effects on aggregate demand
and income, because the government borrowing necessary to finance
the additional public expenditures may "crowd out" a roughly equivalent amount of private spending and borrowing. This view is summarized as follows:

> Fiscal policy provides additional spending in a world of sparse
> spending opportunities. But it does not provide a new source of finance in
> a world where spending is constrained by sources of finance. The gov-
> ernment expenditures are financed in debt markets in competition with
> private expenditures. The case least favorable to fiscal policy is that in

which the additional government borrowing simply crowds out of the market an equal (or conceivably even greater) volume of borrowing that would have financed private expenditures.[1]

This paper presents a framework for analyzing fiscal policy that incorporates the interaction between government and the private sector in their spending and borrowing decisions. It shows that ambiguity surrounding the income-multiplier for increased government expenditures results from the failure to model correctly the stock repercussions of changes in government spending and private investment. Specifically, the ambiguity is caused by failure to allow for changes in the supply of capital (or private financial securities issued to finance the capital stock) that arise in response to debt-financed fiscal policy. When the analysis is amended to correctly incorporate the financing of private and public expenditures and to develop the relationship among saving, the deficit, and crowding out, the *initial* impact of an increase in government expenditure on aggregate demand and income is unambiguously positive.

Four Models of the Short-Run Response to Fiscal Policy

Four models of the response to fiscal policy are analyzed in detail. Each model includes the equilibrium conditions in the commodity and money markets (which correspond to the IS and LM curves in standard income-expenditure analysis) and the definition of disposable income, as shown in Equations (1) through (3). The demand for output depends on income and the interest rate [Equation (1)]; the money supply is exogenous, and the demand for money depends on the interest rate, income, and end-of-period value of household wealth [Equation (2)].[2] Disposable income is simply national income minus taxes net of transfers [Equation (3)].

---

[1]John M. Culbertson, *Macroeconomic Theory and Stabilization Policy* (New York: McGraw-Hill, 1968), 463.

[2]The model includes a wealth effect in the money demand function but not in the consumption function. This was done primarily to simplify the analysis, since the major concern involves the portfolio effects of fiscal policy. In addition, the relevant wealth variable in a consumption function is beginning-of-period wealth, and this is predetermined in the subsequent analysis. The only way a wealth effect in the consumption function could affect the conclusions is through an interest-induced wealth effect. Including an interest-induced wealth effect would be equivalent to making consumption (saving) depend on the interest rate. Such a modification is discussed later in the analysis.

Models 1–4

Model I:
1–3
with $L_a = 0$

$$\left\{ \begin{array}{l} (1)\ X = C_y Y + I_r r + \bar{C} + \bar{I} + \bar{G} \\ (2)\ \bar{m} = \bar{L} + L_x X + L_r r + L_a a \\ (3)\ Y = X - \bar{T} \end{array} \right.$$

Model II:
1–3 + 4,5

$$\left\{ \begin{array}{l} (4)\ a = \bar{m} + b + \bar{K} \\ (5)\ \Delta b = D_{-1} + \Delta \bar{G} - \Delta \bar{T} - \Delta \bar{m} \end{array} \right.$$

Model III:
1–3, 5–7

$$\left. \begin{array}{l} (6)\ a = \bar{m} + b + d \\ (7)\ \Delta d = I_{-1} + \Delta I = I_{-1} + I_r \Delta r \end{array} \right.$$

Model IV:
1–3, 8, 9

$$\left\{ \begin{array}{l} (8)\ a = \bar{a} + S \\ (9)\ S = Y - C = Y - (\bar{C} + C_y Y) \end{array} \right.$$

Notation:
  X = output or national income
  Y = disposable income
  r = interest rate
  $\bar{m}$ = money supply
  a = end-of-period wealth of households
  T = net taxes (taxes net of transfers)
  b = end-of-period supply of government bonds
  D_{-1} = deficit inherited from the previous period
  d = end-of-period supply of private securities
  I_{-1} = (net) investment in the previous period
  $\bar{a}$ = beginning-of-period wealth of households
  S = saving
  $\bar{G}$ = government expenditures on goods and services
  $\bar{C}, \bar{I}$ = autonomous private expenditures on consumption and investment
  C_y, I_r, L_x, L_r, L_a = model parameters

Parameter restrictions:
  $1 > C_y > 0$
  $-\infty < I_r < 0$
  $L_x > 0$
  $-\infty < L_r < 0$
  $1 > L_a > 0$

Model I, the traditional textbook model associated with the income-expenditure view, assumes $L_a = 0$ and includes *only* Equations (1) through (3). It also corresponds, however, to Friedman's representation of a common framework that would be acceptable to both monetarists and nonmonetarists.[3]

[3]See, for example, Milton Friedman, "A Theoretical Framework for Monetary Analysis," *Journal of Political Economy* (March/April 1970), 193–238.

Alternative Approaches to Modeling Wealth Determination

Models 2 through 4 include the determination of household wealth, and it is the modeling of wealth that is critical to the analysis in this article. Two definitions of wealth can be used to complete the model: Both are equally correct and yield identical results when the definitions are specified properly. The *sum of the assets* measure defines wealth as the sum of the assets that are held in household portfolios. The *perpetual inventory* measure defines wealth as the sum of last period's wealth and saving, where saving is measured as the change in wealth between last period and this period.[4] The sum of the assets approach links wealth to the rest of the model by using financing constraints that link the supply of money and bonds to spending decisions of the government and private sectors. The perpetual inventory approach links wealth to the rest of the model by adding a saving equation to the model.

Model 2 is an extension of Model 1 and incorporates both a wealth effect in the demand for money $(0 < L_a < 1)$ and a government financing constraint [Equation (5)]. The government financing constraint (GFC) requires that government expenditures (G) be financed by some combination of taxes net of transfers (T) and issue of money and government bonds $(\Delta m$ and Δb, respectively).[5] Equation (5) rewrites this restriction in terms of the inherited deficit (D_{-1}) and changes in government expenditures and taxes (ΔG and ΔT, respectively). The inherited deficit plus any increase in government spending in the present period relative to the previous period must be financed by increases in tax revenue net of transfers or by issue of money or government bonds.

Wealth is defined, according to equation (4), as the sum of money, government bonds, and the capital stock.[6] Both money and the capital

---

[4]Peter E. Kennedy, "Direct Wealth Effects in Macroeconomics Models: The Saving vs. the Definitional Approach," *Journal of Money, Credit and Banking* (February 1978), 94–98.

[5]The integration of the government financing constraint into macroeconomic models was advanced by the work of Carl Christ. See, for example, Carl F. Christ, "A Simple Macroeconomic Model with a Government Budget Constraint," *Journal of Political Economy* (January/February 1968), 53–67.

[6]The author assumes throughout that government bonds are part of net wealth and this assumption presumes the absence of "tax discounting." The evidence on tax discounting is mixed. For a review of the theory and evidence on tax discounting, see Willem H. Buiter and James Tobin, "Debt Neutrality: A Brief Review of Doctrine and Evidence," Cowles Foundation Discussion Paper No. 497 (Yale University, September

stock are assumed to be constant, and the supply of government bonds is determined via the GFC. Since all four models assume an exogenous money supply, increases in government expenditures are financed by increasing the government debt. This common assumption allows us to focus on debt-financed fiscal policy.

The critical assumption in Model 2 is that the capital stock is also exogenous. Although this assumption is common in short-run models of income determination, it presents serious difficulties for modeling the portfolio repercussions of fiscal actions.[7]

Models 3 and 4 further refine the analysis of fiscal policy by relaxing the assumption that the capital stock is fixed. These models introduce properly specified but alternative definitions of wealth. Model 3 essentially retains the wealth definition used in Model 2 but endogenizes the capital stock by defining the end-of-period capital stock as the sum of the beginning-of-period capital stock and investment over the period. All capital is assumed to be held by firms and purchased with external funds acquired by selling securities to the household sector. Thus, households can be viewed as indirectly holding the capital stock via their holdings of private securities, and the net wealth of the household sector can be rewritten as the sum of money, government bonds, and private securities [Equation (6)], where the supply of private securities is determined via the investment financing constraint [Equation (7)].[8] The simple structure of the model can be maintained by assuming that government debt and private securities are perfect

---

15, 1978). For an empirical investigation which finds no evidence of tax discounting, see Jess B. Yawitz, and Laurence H. Meyer, "An Empirical Investigation of the Extent of Tax Discounting," *Journal of Money, Credit and Banking* (May 1976), 247–56.

[7]Models embodying the assumption of a fixed capital stock have been used to investigate the portfolio repercussions of fiscal policy by Silber, Meyer, and B. Friedman. See William L. Silber, "Fiscal Policy in IS-LM Analysis: A Correction," *Journal of Money, Credit and Banking* (November 1970), 461–472; Laurence H. Meyer, "The Balance Sheet Identity, the Government Financing Constraint, and the Crowding-Out Effect," *Journal of Monetary Economics* (January 1975), 65–78; and Benjamin Friedman, "Crowding-Out or Crowding-In: Economic Consequences of Financing Government Deficits," *Brookings Papers on Economic Activity* (1978:3), 593–641.

[8]Equations (4) and (6) correspond to two different ways of defining wealth: net private wealth and net wealth of households. Net private wealth equals the capital stock (the economy's tangible or real assets) plus outside financial assets of the private sector (outside money and government bonds). Net wealth of households includes only the outside financial assets of the household sector (assuming all capital assets are held by businesses). The two are identical, provided capital in net private wealth is valued at its market value as defined by the value of the financial claims to that capital stock held in household portfolios.

substitutes in household portfolios.[9] The supply of private securities is determined by the investment financing constraint (IFC), the private sector counterpart to the GFC. The IFC [Equation (7)] links changes in the supply of private securities directly to (net) investment (expressed as last period's investment plus the change in investment from last period to the current period) and thus links private spending and financial decisions.

Properties of the Framework

These four models have a common framework: They are fixed price/variable output, one-good, two-asset models of the short-run response to fiscal policy. Additionally, Models 3 and 4 employ an end-of-period specification of asset market equilibrium.

The fixed price/variable output framework is appropriate for studying the response of output to policy actions in a disequilibrium setting where price flexibility is insufficient to sustain continuous full equilibrium.[10] Its suitability, however, is confined to developing insights about the *short-run* response to fiscal actions.

The framework described in this article extends the one-good, two-asset IS/LM model that is widely used in macroeconomics. The two assets included in the models are money and bonds. Both government and private debt are included in Models 3 and 4 and, in order to retain the two-asset framework, they are assumed to be perfect substitutes in household portfolios. To further simplify the analysis, households are assumed to hold all the financial assets and, in Models 3 and 4, firms are assumed to finance all investment externally.

[9]Firms finance acquisition of capital via private bonds, equities, and internal funds. To maintain the model's simple structure and allow every possibility for substantial portfolio effects associated with government deficits, all investment is assumed to be financed externally by emitting a single financial instrument which is a perfect substitute for government bonds in wealth owners' portfolios. In principle, the models employed in this article should distinguish between private debt, equity, and government debt. But the approach used here only makes the portfolio effect of deficit financing larger and the conclusion that there is an unambiguous one-period multiplier more noteworthy. For a three-asset version that is otherwise similar to the approach taken in this paper, see James Tobin and Willem Buiter, "Fiscal and Monetary Policies, Capital Formation, and Economic Activity," in George von Furstenburg, ed., *The Government and Capital Formation* (Cambridge: Ballinger Publishing Co., 1980), 73–151.

[10]For a rationalization of this approach, see Robert J. Barro and Herschel I. Grossman, *Money, Employment, and Inflation* (Cambridge: Cambridge University Press, 1976).

The models are developed to yield one-period multipliers only. Models 2, 3, and 4 are intrinsically dynamic since the supply of bonds continues to increase as long as the government runs a deficit and, in Models 3 and 4, as long as saving and investment occur. The GFC, for example, requires that government expenditure increases be financed not only in the initial period but during all future periods as long as the deficit continues. The models, however, investigate the impact of the increase in government spending during the initial period only.

To model the financial repercussions of spending decisions in a one-period framework, an end-of-period (EOP) specification of asset market equilibrium is used in Models 3 and 4.[11] In discrete time models, the concept of simultaneous equilibrium in stock and flow markets is subtle. Since flows are defined as rates over the unit interval and stocks are defined at a point during the interval, there is no natural way of defining simultaneous equilibrium.[12] For the following analysis, it is convenient to define simultaneous equilibrium as corresponding to flow equilibrium over the period and to stock equilibrium at the end of the period. By defining stocks at the end of the interval used to define the flow variables, the financing of expenditure flows over the period is allowed to affect the supplies of bonds outstanding, thereby allowing the model to include both the effect of the increase in expenditures and the effect of the associated increase in the supply of bonds.

---

[11]For a discussion of the modeling of simultaneous stock and flow equilibria in period models, see Duncan K. Foley, "On Two Specifications of Asset Equilibrium in Macroeconomic Models," *The Journal of Political Economy* (April 1975), 303–324.

[12]One way to eliminate the ambiguity is to reduce the unit interval of the period analysis until the beginning and the end of the period converge. This results in a continuous analysis in which flows at instantaneous rates and stocks can both be measured simultaneously. However, since this analysis focuses on capturing the stock repercussions of flow decisions, the end-of-period, discrete framework is particularly appropriate. Most continuous models are used to solve for either instantaneous or steady-state values of multipliers. Discrete models, on the other hand, are the most convenient approach when the analysis is to be carried out over a discrete interval, short of the time required to achieve full steady-state equilibrium. For example, Turnovsky notes: "While many macroeconomic models are formulated using discrete time, much of macroeconomic theory is formulated using continuous time. Both kinds of models have their place, and the choice between them is often dictated by convenience. If one is interested in analyzing short-run effects, discrete time models tend to be more useful. On the other hand, for steady-state and stability analyses, continuous models are usually more practical." Stephen J. Turnovsky, *Macroeconomic Analysis and Stabilization Policies* (Cambridge: Cambridge University Press, 1977), 43.

Model 1.   The Textbook Multiplier and Hicksian Crowding Out

The textbook *IS–LM* multiplier identifies a single source of crowding out, labeled by Modigliani and Ando as "Hicksian crowding out."[13] Model 1 includes neither a wealth effect in the demand for money ($L_a = 0$) nor any financing constraints. It is generally associated with the income-expenditure approach and has been widely criticized by monetarists. The multiplier for an increase in government expenditures in this model is:

$$\frac{\Delta X}{\Delta G} = \frac{1}{1 - C_y + \underbrace{(L_x/L_r)I_r}_{\text{Hicksian crowding out}}} \tag{10}$$

This multiplier has several properties: (1) In the absence of extreme values of the parameters, the multiplier is unambiguously positive, confirming the income expenditure view about the response to fiscal policy. (2) The multiplier does not allow for any effect of government borrowing on the response of output to the fiscal operation. Since money and taxes are held constant, the multiplier implicitly corresponds to a bond-financed fiscal action. Despite the absence of any effect associated with the increase in government borrowing, partial crowding out occurs via the income-induced rise in the interest rate. As income increases, the demand for money increases relative to the fixed supply of money. The resulting excess demand for money (and excess supply of bonds) exerts upward pressure on the interest rate which, in turn, restricts the interest responsive portion of aggregate demand (investment, in this model). However, as long as $L_r < 0$ and $I_r > -\infty$, $\Delta X/\Delta G$ remains positive and investment declines by less than the increase in government expenditures. The magnitude of Hicksian crowding out (or negative feedback) is controlled by the last set of terms in the denominator of Equation (1).

Thus, although some investment is crowded out by government spending, the fiscal multiplier is nevertheless unambiguously positive.

[13]Franco Modigliani and Albert Ando, "Impacts of Fiscal Actions on Aggregate Income and the Monetarist Controversy: Theory and Evidence," in Jerome Stein, ed., *Monetarism* (Amsterdam: North-Holland), 1976, 17–42. The terminology, "Hicksian crowding-out, reflects the origins of the IS-LM framework in the writing of J. R. Hicks. See, for example, J. R. Hicks, "Mr. Keynes and the Classics: A Suggested Interpretation," *Econometrica* (April 1937), 145–159.

Of course, this does not guarantee that the multiplier is large. Monetarists have generally argued that, even in this framework, fiscal policy will have a minimal effect due to the actual magnitude of Hicksian crowding out resulting from the small absolute value of the L_r parameter and the large absolute value of the I_r parameter.[14]

Model 2. The GFC and the Wealth Effect: Portfolio Crowding Out and the Ambiguous Fiscal Multiplier

To generate an ambiguous sign on the fiscal multiplier in this framework, the financing of government spending via the increase in the supply of government bonds must affect the interest rate and income. This requires that a wealth effect be added to the demand for money $(1 > L_a > 0)$ and that both the definition of wealth given by Equation (4) and the GFC [Equation (5)] be included in the analysis. The resulting fiscal multiplier is:

$$\frac{\Delta X}{\Delta G} = \frac{1 - \overbrace{.(L_a/L_r)I_r}^{\substack{\text{portfolio} \\ \text{crowding out}}}}{Q} \tag{11}$$

where the denominator, Q, is the same as in the first multiplier. The fiscal operation now has two direct impacts, indicated by the two terms in the numerator of Equation (2): The increase in G directly increases aggregate demand (the *direct fiscal impact*, also operative in Model 1) and the accompanying increase in the supply of bonds exerts upward pressure on interest rates, thereby reducing aggregate demand (the *direct portfolio impact*). The net effect of these two direct impacts— and, hence, the multiplier—is ambiguous. Thus, while Hicksian crowding out can, at most, induce partial crowding out, "portfolio crowding out" can, at least in this model, induce complete or even more than complete crowding out, as suggested by the quote at the beginning of this article.

Note that if $L_a = 0$, the multiplier collapses to the multiplier derived for Model 1. Income-expenditure, macroeconometric models typically use a transactions-based model of the demand for money

---

[14]See, for example, Milton Friedman, "Comments on the Critics," *Journal of Political Economy* (September/October 1972), 906–950.

(where $L_a = 0$), while monetarists generally prefer portfolio models of the demand for money (where $L_a > 0$). If $L_a = 0$, wealth owners want to retain the entire increment in wealth in the form of bonds; in this case, the increase in the supply of bonds does not induce an excess supply of bonds and, therefore, does not exert upward pressure on the interest rate. On the other hand, if $L_a > 0$, wealth owners want to diversify their portfolios and, hence, to split any increase in wealth between increased holdings of money and bonds. In this case, an increase in the supply of bonds and wealth will increase the demand for bonds by less than the increase in the supply of bonds, resulting in an excess supply of bonds and upward pressure on the interest rate.

Model 3.   Adding the Investment Financing Constraint: Returning to an Unambiguous Multiplier

Models 1 and 2 are useful as simple models which yield income-expenditure and monetarist results, respectively, but both are incomplete. Models 3 and 4 refine the analysis presented in Models 1 and 2 in different but equivalent ways. Although each combines portfolio crowding out with Hicksian crowding out as did Model 2, they yield unambiguously positive fiscal multipliers as did Model 1.

In order to allow for portfolio crowding out, it is necessary to continue assuming that $1 > L_a > 0$. The problem with Model 2 is that it accounts for the financing of government spending but ignores the financial repercussions of private spending. Model 3, therefore, respecifies the definition of wealth to include private securities along with government debt, and the IFC is added in order to link investment to the supply of private securities. Thus, Model 3 includes *dual* financing constraints: End-of-period wealth is now the sum of end-of-period supplies of money and bonds, and the GFC and IFC are used to determine end-of-period supplies of government, and private securities, respectively.

By redefining wealth, Model 3 refines the definition given in Model 2, where the capital stock was treated as fixed even though net investment was occurring. Consequently, Model 2 failed to address the portfolio repercussions of investment. Increases in the capital stock associated with investment must be absorbed into private portfolios, just as increases in government debt associated with government deficits must be absorbed.

The multiplier for Model 3 is:

$$\frac{\Delta X}{\Delta G} = \frac{\overbrace{1}^{\substack{\text{direct}\\\text{fiscal}\\\text{impact}}} - \overbrace{[L_a/(L_r + L_a\,I_r)]\,I_r}^{\substack{\text{direct}\\\text{portfolio impact}}}}{Q'} \tag{12}$$

where $Q' = 1 - C_y + [L_x/(L_r + L_a\,I_r)]\,I_r$. The two terms in the numerator reflect the two direct impacts associated with the fiscal operation. The direct fiscal impact is the dollar-for-dollar increase in aggregate demand associated with the increased government expenditure. The direct portfolio impact is the effect on investment associated with the increase in the supply of government bonds. The multiplier has a form similar to that of Model 2: A positive direct fiscal impact and negative portfolio impact are contained in the numerator. However, in the case of Model 3, it can be demonstrated that the direct portfolio impact is unambiguously smaller than the direct fiscal impact so that the multiplier is unambiguously positive. The numerator is positive because the terms in the direct portfolio impact can be combined to form a ratio less than unity $[L_a I_r/(L_r + L_a I_r) < 1]$.

The multiplier given by Model 3 implies that, although investment declines in response to an increase in government spending, the decline in investment induced by the increase in supply of government bonds is less than the increase in government expenditures. The increase in government debt raises the interest rate because it results in an increase in the supply relative to the demand for bonds. If the decline in investment due to the rise in the interest rate were to exceed the increase in government spending, the decline in private bonds (associated with the decline in investment) would exceed the increase in the supply of government bonds so that the total supply of bonds would fall rather than rise.[15] This situation, of course,

[15]The statement that a decline in investment induces a decline in the supply of private bonds requires clarification. As long as net investment is positive, the supply of bonds will be increasing. The bond financing of government expenditures raises the interest rate, lowers investment, and *lowers the supply of bonds relative to what it would have been* in the absence of the policy action. The multiplier $\Delta X/\Delta G$, in turn, indicates how income differs from what it would have been in the absence of the policy action. The multiplier, therefore, has a different interpretation than the usual *comparative static* multipliers derived from IS/LM models without financing constraints. Such multipliers indicate the change in income between the old and the new equilibrium levels of income. One-period multipliers in models with financing constraints, in contrast, only

would be contradictory since investment declines only if the interest rate rises. Because the decline in investment slows the rise in the interest rate, the resulting portfolio crowding out can be only partial. Although Hicksian crowding out occurs in response to the rise in income, it cannot alter the conclusion that the fiscal policy multiplier is unambiguously positive.

Model 4.   A Simplified Solution with the Perpetual Inventory Definition of Wealth

Model 4 underlies Modigliani and Ando's conclusion that the short-run response to fiscal policy is positive: "Clearly r cannot rise unless a rises; but a cannot rise unless saving increases, which requires a rise in $X!$"[16] Model 4 uses a perpetual inventory definition of wealth [Equation (8)] that is equivalent but alternative to that employed in Model 3. End-of-period wealth is defined in this case as beginning-of-period wealth plus saving over the period.[17] The $\Delta X / \Delta G$ multiplier for this model is:

$$\frac{\Delta X}{\Delta G} = \frac{1}{1 - C_y + \underbrace{[(L_x + L_a (1 - C_y))/L_r] I_r}_{both \text{ Hicksian and portfolio crowding out}}} \tag{13}$$

This multiplier, like that for Models 2 and 3, includes both Hicksian and portfolio crowding out and it is identical to that in Model 3 even if it doesn't appear to be.[18] As in Model 3, portfolio crowding out can be only partial.

Multiplier 4 resembles multiplier 1 but it contains an additional term in the numerator of the fraction in the denominator of the multi-

---

indicate how income differs from what it would have been in the absence of the policy change.

[16]Modigliani and Ando, "Impacts of Fiscal Actions on Aggregate Income and the Monetarist Controversy," 17.

[17]Capital gains have been ignored in order to simplify the analysis.

[18]To show that Models 3 and 4 are identical, put the numerator of Equation (3) in terms of a common denominator, $L_r + L_a I_r$; then multiply the numerator and denominator by $L_r + L_a I_r$; then divide the numerator and denominator by L_r. The equivalence of Models 3 and 4 can also be seen by comparing the two definitions of wealth: Model 3 defines the change in wealth as the sum of the deficit and investment, and Model 4 defines the change in wealth as equal to saving. Since $S = I + D$ is an equilibrium condition, the multipliers for Models 3 and 4 will be identical.

plier. This term, $L_a(1 - C_y)$, represents the effect of the increase in wealth (via saving) on the demand for money. Since the money supply remains unchanged, all additional wealth is implicitly held in the form of bonds. To induce the private sector to increase its holdings of bonds relative to money, the Treasury must offer a higher interest rate. But, as Modigliani and Ando have noted, portfolio crowding out is activated by the increase in wealth that is associated with an increase in saving and, hence, income.[19] Therefore, portfolio crowding out can restrain but not reverse the increase in income associated with the increase in government spending.

Model 4 highlights the role of saving in the analysis of crowding out. The increase in government bonds can be absorbed into private portfolios either by an increase in wealth (i.e., *induced saving generated by the fiscal action*) or by *displacing (i.e., crowding out) private debt*. Saving can be defined as the sum of the deficit and investment; the deficit can be defined as the difference between saving and investment. Any increase in the deficit must be offset, therefore, by a combination of increased saving (allowing absorption of increased government bonds) or decreased investment (replacing private securities with government bonds).

Model 4 analyzes the response to fiscal actions without directly including either the GFC or the IFC. Models 2 and 3 include the financing constraint in order to determine the end-of-period supplies of government and private bonds. The bond market is the redundant market in the analysis, and the perpetual inventory definition of wealth does not use end-of-period supplies of bonds. Consequently, Model 4 does not explicitly contain the supply of bonds or require the financing constraints in order to solve for the response to fiscal actions.

Refinements and Complications

This section discusses the implications of relaxing some of the assumptions employed in Models 1 through 4. First, some considerations relevant to an analysis of the longer-run response to fiscal actions are discussed. Second, two modifications that introduce the possibility that

---

[19]The "increase in wealth" in the above statement refers to the increase in wealth relative to what it would have been in the absence of the policy action. As long as saving is positive, wealth will increase. The policy action induces an increase in wealth only if it induces an increase in saving.

bond-financed fiscal policy may "pull in" rather than crowd out investment are considered. Finally, a modification that allows for an ambiguous short-run fiscal multiplier in Models 3 and 4 is discussed.

Longer-Run Considerations: Price Flexibility and Cumulative Stock Effects

Models 1 through 4 yielded only one-period multipliers. The longer-run response to fiscal actions is affected also by price flexibility and the cumulative effects of financing continuing deficits associated with once-and-for-all changes in government expenditures.

The models employed above assumed prices were fixed and were justified as simple disequilibrium models along lines developed by Barro and Grossman. However, they apply only to the analysis of the short-run response to fiscal actions. In the long run, price flexibility insures a unique equilibrium level of the unemployment rate via the Phillips Curve. Although fiscal policy may temporarily increase output and employment, most models yield zero long-run multipliers for the response of output and employment to policy actions.[20]

Another factor that affects the longer-run response to fiscal actions is the continuing increase in the supply of bonds associated with a once-and-for-all increase in government expenditures. The implications of the continued financing of deficits associated with once-and-for-all increases in government expenditures for the long-run response of income have been investigated by Blinder and Solow.[21]

Pulling In: Income-Induced Investment and Multiple Assets

In each of the models developed above, an increase in government expenditures reduced investment. The question they addressed was whether investment fell by more or less than the increase in government expenditures. Two simple modifications introduce the possibility that bond-financed increases in government expenditures may encourage rather than discourage investment. These modifications include adding income as an argument in the investment function and allowing government debt and private securities to be imperfect substitutes.

[20]See, for example, Modigliani and Ando's discussion of policy simulations with the MPS model in "Impacts of Fiscal Actions on Aggregate Income and the Monetarist Controversy."

[21]Alan S. Blinder and Robert M. Solow, "Does Fiscal Policy Matter?" *Journal of Public Economics* (November 1973), 319–337.

If investment depends on the level of income, investment may rise even though the fiscal operation raises the interest rate. Hendershott has referred to this phenomenon as pulling in rather than crowding out investment. [22]

In the two-asset model employed above, increased supply of government debt restrains investment, in part, because government and private securities are assumed to be perfect substitutes. If the model is refined to allow for at least three assets—money, government debt, and, for example, equities—the portfolio response to the increase in the supply of government debt becomes ambiguous. Tobin and Tobin and Buiter have used three-asset models to study the response to policy actions. [23] In the two-asset model, an increase in government debt creates excess supply in the securities market and upward pressure on "the" interest rate. The three-asset model involves two rates: The rate on government bonds and the rate on equities. The models generally focus on the rate on government debt and the price of equities, and they designate investment as a positive function of the price of equities.

An increase in government debt increases the rate on government bonds thereby inducing substitution out of equities into government debt. This *substitution effect* reduces the demand for equities and depresses their price (thus raising their rate of return). Wealth is also increasing, and wealth owners may wish to diversify their portfolios and hold some of their increased wealth in equities. This *wealth effect* increases the demand for equities, as well as their price. The net impact of the substitution and wealth effects is ambiguous. Equity prices and, hence, investment may rise or fall. In this three-asset example, if $L_a = 0$, an increase in the supply of government debt unambiguously raises equity prices and stimulates investment.

Interest-Responsive Saving

There is one modification of the models that permits a negative short-run response to fiscal policy—making saving a positive function of the

[22]Patric H. Hendershott, "A Tax Cut in a Multiple Security Model: Crowding-Out, Pulling-In and the Term Structure of Interest Rates," *Journal of Finance* (September 1976), 1185–1199.

[23]James Tobin, "An Essay on Principles of Debt Management," in *Fiscal and Debt Management Policies*, Commission on Money and Credit (Englewood Cliffs, N.J.: Prentice-Hall), 1963, 143–218; and Tobin and Buiter, "Fiscal and Monetary Policies, Capital Formation, and Economic Activity."

interest rate (and consumption a negative function of the interest rate). This modification would not alter the qualitative results of Model 1, although it would, of course, increase Hicksian crowding out and reduce fiscal multipliers. In Models 3 and 4, however, it results in a theoretically ambiguous sign on the fiscal multiplier. The explanation of the effect of this modification will be most easily understood with respect to Model 4. In that model, the key to the unambiguous result is the positive relation between income and saving: The wealth effect in the demand for money is activated by an increase in wealth which in turn requires an increase in income. If saving depends on the interest rate as well as income, however, saving can increase even if income falls. Saving has generally been considered unresponsive to interest rates, but recent work by Boskin has revived the belief that saving may be significantly interest-responsive, although it remains likely that this effect is quantitatively small.[24]

Conclusion

Increased sales of government securities necessary to finance increased government expenditures can be purchased either from the increased saving that is generated by the fiscal action or by the crowding out of private security purchases. In order to fully model the response to fiscal policy, it is essential to capture the relationships among the deficit, saving, investment, government, and private debt. This paper has developed two alternative ways of analyzing these relationships, both of which utilize end-of-period specifications of asset market equilibrium. The first approach includes both government and private sector financing constraints in the model; the second approach relates changes in wealth to saving behavior in the model. Both approaches yield positive impacts of increased government expenditures on aggregate demand and income as the first-period fiscal effect. At least in the short run, fiscal policy actions matter because complete crowding out does not occur.

[24]See, for example, Michael J. Boskin, "Taxation, Saving and the Rate of Interest," *Journal of Political Economy* (April 1978), S3–S27.

Reprinted from *Review*, Federal Reserve Bank of St. Louis (June/July 1980), 24–25 by permission of the publisher and author.

Some Recent Developments in Phillips Curve Analysis

Thomas M. Humphrey

Economists' views of the Phillips curve concept have changed drastically in recent years. The original interpretation of the Phillips curve as a stable trade-off relationship between inflation and unemployment has given way to the view that no such trade-off exists for policymakers to exploit. As a result, some economists now argue that economic stabilization policies are incapable of influencing output and employment, even in the short run.

Instrumental to this change were several key developments in Phillips curve analysis, most notably the so-called *natural rate* and *rational expectations* hypotheses. The purpose of this article is to explain these developments and their policy implications and to show how they altered economists' perceptions of the Phillips curve. Accordingly, the first half of the article traces the evolution of Phillips curve analysis focusing particularly on the natural rate hypothesis. The second half concentrates on the rational expectations idea, currently the most hotly-debated aspect of Phillips curve analysis.

Early Versions of the Phillips Curve

Phillips curve analysis has evolved through at least five major stages since its inception in 1958. The first stage involved the formulation of a simple, stable trade-off relation between inflation and unemployment. The initial Phillips curve depicted a relationship between money wage changes and unemployment. But the assumption that product prices are set by applying a constant mark-up to unit labor costs permitted the Phillips relationship to be transformed into a price-change equation of the form[1]

$$p = ax \tag{1}$$

Reprinted from *Economic Review*, January/February 1978, 15–23, by permission of the Federal Reserve Bank of Richmond and the author.

[1]For simplicity, the additive constant term contained in most empirical Phillips curve equations is disregarded in Equation (1).

where p is the percentage rate of price inflation, x is overall excess demand in labor and hence product markets—this excess demand being proxied by the inverse of the unemployment rate—and a is a coefficient expressing the numerical value of the trade-off between inflation and excess demand.

This equation expresses the early view of the Phillips curve as a stable, enduring trade-off permitting the authorities to obtain permanently lower rates of unemployment in exchange for permanently higher rates of inflation or vice versa. Put differently, the equation was popularly interpreted as offering a menu of alternative inflation-unemployment combinations from which the authorities could choose. Being stable, the menu never changed.

Economists soon discovered, however, that the menu was not as stable as originally thought and that the Phillips curve had a tendency to shift over time.[2] Accordingly, the equation was augmented with additional variables to account for such movements.

Introduction of Shift Variables

The addition of shift variables to the trade-off equation marked the second stage of Phillips curve analysis. The inclusion of these variables meant that the Phillips equation could now be written as

$$p = ax + z \tag{2}$$

where z is a vector of variables—productivity, profits, trade union effects, unemployment dispersion and the like—capable of shifting the inflation-excess demand trade-off. Absent at this stage were variables representing price expectations. Although the past rate of price change was sometimes used as a shift variable, it was rarely interpreted as a proxy for anticipated inflation. Not until the late 1960s were expectational variables fully incorporated into Phillips curve equations. By then, of course, inflationary expectations had become too prominent to ignore and many analysts were perceiving them as the dominant cause of observed shifts in the Phillips curve.

---

[2]Indeed, Phillips himself in his 1958 article had recognized the possibility of such shifts.

The Expectations-Augmented Phillips Curve and the Adaptive-Expectations Mechanism

Three innovations ushered in the next stage of Phillips curve analysis. The first was the respecification of the excess demand variable. Originally defined as the inverse of the unemployment rate, excess demand was redefined as the discrepancy between actual and normal capacity real output or, equivalently, as the gap between the actual and the natural rates of unemployment. The natural rate of unemployment itself was defined as the rate that, given the frictions and structural characteristics of the economy, is just consistent with demand-supply equilibrium in labor and product markets. This innovation effectively identified full-employment equilibrium (i.e., zero excess demand) with normal capacity output and the natural rate of unemployment.

The second innovation was the introduction of price anticipations into Phillips curve analysis resulting in the expectations-augmented equation

$$p = ax + p^e \tag{3}$$

where p is the price expectations variable representing the anticipated rate of inflation. This expectations variable entered the equation with a coefficient of unity, reflecting the assumption that price expectations are completely incorporated in actual price changes. The unit expectations coefficient implies the absence of money illusion, i.e., it implies that sellers are concerned with the expected real purchasing power of the prices they receive and so take anticipated inflation into account. As will be shown later, the unit expectations coefficient also implies the complete absence of a trade-off between inflation and unemployment in the long run when expectations are fully realized. Note also that the expectations variable is the sole shift variable in the equation. All other shift variables have been omitted, reflecting the view, prevalent in the early 1970s, that changing price expectations were the predominant cause of observed shifts in the Phillips curve.

The third innovation was the incorporation of an expectations-generating mechanism into Phillips curve analysis to explain how the price expectations variable itself is determined. Generally a simple *adaptive expectations* or *error-learning* mechanism was used. According to this mechanism, expectations are adjusted (adapted) by some fraction of the error that occurs when inflation turns out to be different than expected. In symbols

$$\dot{p}^e = B(p - p^e) \tag{4}$$

where the dot over the expectations variable indicates the rate of change (time derivative) of that variable, $p - p^e$ is the expectations error (i.e., the difference between actual and expected price inflation), and b is the adjustment fraction. Assuming, for example, an adjustment fraction of ½, Equation (4) says that if the actual and expected rates of inflation are 10 percent and 4 percent, respectively—i.e., the expectational error is 6 percent—then the expected rate of inflation will be revised upward by an amount equal to half the error, or 3 percent. Such revision will continue until the expectational error is eliminated. It can also be shown that Equation (4) is equivalent to the proposition that expected inflation is a geometrically-weighted average of all past rates of inflation with the weights summing to one. Therefore, the error-learning mechanism can also be expressed as

$$p^e = \Sigma \, w_i p_{-i} \tag{5}$$

where Σ indicates the operation of summing the weighted past rates of inflation, i represents past time periods, and w_i stands for the weights attached to past rates of inflation. These weights decline geometrically as time recedes, i.e., people are assumed to give more attention to recent than to older price experience when forming expectations. How fast the weights fall depends on the strength of people's memories of inflationary history. Rapidly declining weights indicate that people have short memories so that price expectations depend primarily on recent price experience. By contrast, slowly declining weights imply long memories so that expectations are influenced significantly by inflation rates of the most distant past. Both versions of the adaptive expectations mechanism (i.e., Equations (4) and (5)) were combined with the expectations-augmented Phillips equation to explain the mutual interaction of actual inflation, expected inflation, and excess demand.

The Natural Rate Hypothesis

These three innovations—the redefined excess demand variable, the expectations-augmented trade-off, and the adaptive-expectations mechanism—formed the basis of the so-called natural rate and accelerationist hypotheses that radically altered economists' views of the Phillips curve. According to the natural rate hypothesis, there exists no permanent trade-off between unemployment and inflation since real economic variables tend to be independent of nominal ones in long-run equilibrium. To be sure, trade-offs may exist in the short run. But they are inherently transitory phenomena that stem from unexpected inflation and that vanish when expectations adjust to inflationary experience. In the long run, when inflationary surprises disappear and expectations are realized, unemployment returns to its natural (equilibrium) rate. This rate is consistent with all fully-anticipated steady-state rates of inflation, implying that the long-run Phillips curve is a vertical line at the natural rate of unemployment.

Equation 3 embodies these conclusions. That equation, when rearranged to read $p - p^e = ax$, states that the trade-off is between *unexpected* inflation (the difference between actual and expected inflation $p - p^e$) and excess demand. The equation also says that the trade-off disappears when inflation is fully anticipated, i.e., when $p - p^e$ is zero. Moreover, if the equation is correct, excess demand must also be zero at this point, which implies that unemployment is at its natural rate. Zero excess demand and the natural rate of unemployment are therefore compatible with *any* rate of inflation provided it is fully anticipated. In short, Equation (3) asserts that if inflation is fully anticipated there will be no relationship between inflation and unemployment, contrary to the original Phillips hypothesis.

The Accelerationist Hypothesis

Equation (3), when combined with Equation (4), also yields the accelerationist hypothesis. The latter, a corollary of the natural rate hypothesis, states that since there exists no long-run trade-off between unemployment and inflation, attempts to peg the former variable below its natural (equilibrium) level must produce ever-accelerating inflation. Such acceleration will keep actual inflation always running ahead of expected inflation, thereby perpetuating the inflationary surprises that prevent unemployment from returning to its equilibrium level.

These conclusions are easily demonstrated. As previously mentioned, Equation (3) states that excess demand can differ from zero only as long as actual inflation deviates from expected inflation. But Equation (4) says that, by the very nature of the error-learning mechanism, such deviations cannot persist unless inflation is continually accelerated so that it always stays ahead of expected inflation. If inflation is not accelerated, but instead stays constant, then the gap between actual and expected inflation will eventually be closed. Therefore acceleration is required to keep the gap open if excess demand is to be maintained above its natural equilibrium level of zero. In other words, the long-run trade-off implied by the accelerationist hypothesis is between excess demand and the rate of acceleration of the inflation rate, in contrast to the conventional trade-off between excess demand and the inflation rate itself as implied by the original Phillips curve.[3]

Policy Implications of the Natural Rate and Accelerationist Hypotheses

Two policy implications stem from the natural rate and accelerationist propositions. First, the authorities can either peg unemployment or stabilize inflation but not both. If they peg unemployment, they will ultimately lose control of inflation since the latter eventually accelerates when unemployment is held below its natural level. Alternatively, if they stabilize the inflation rate, they will lose control of unemployment since the latter will return to its natural level at any steady rate of inflation. Thus, contrary to the original Phillips hypothesis, they cannot peg unemployment at any constant rate of inflation.

A second policy implication stemming from Equations (3) and (4) is that the authorities can choose from among alternative transitional adjustment paths to the desired steady-state rate of inflation. Suppose the authorities wish to move to a lower target inflation rate. To do so they must lower inflationary expectations, a major component of the inflation rate. But Equations (3) and (4) state that the only way to do this is to create slack capacity (excess supply) in the economy, thus causing the actual rate of inflation to fall below the expected rate, inducing a downward revision of the latter. The equations also indicate that the speed of adjustment depends on the amount of slack created. Much slack means fast adjustment and a relatively rapid attainment of

[3]The proof is simple. Equation (3) states a relationship among actual inflation, expected inflation, and excess demand. From that equation it follows that the relationship among the rates of change of those variables is given by the expression $\dot{p} = a\dot{x} + \dot{p}^e$ where the dots indicate rates of change (time derivatives) of the attached variables. Substituting Equation (4) into this expression yields $\dot{p} = a\dot{x} + b(p - p^e)$, which, by Equation (3)'s assertion that the expectational error $p - p^e$ is equal to ax, further simplifies to $\dot{p} = a\dot{x} + bax$. Finally, if excess demand is unchanging so that $\dot{x}$ is zero—as would be the case if the authorities were pegging x at some desired level—this last expression reduces to $\dot{p} = bax$ showing a trade-off relation between the rate of acceleration of inflation $\dot{p}$ and excess demand x.

the inflation target. Conversely, little slack means sluggish adjustment and relatively slow attainment of the inflation target. Thus the policy choice is between adjustment paths offering high unemployment for a short time or lower unemployment for a long time.

Statistical Tests of the Natural Rate Hypothesis

The fourth stage of Phillips curve analysis involved statistical testing of the natural rate hypothesis. These tests led to criticisms of the adaptive-expectations or error-learning model of inflationary expectations and thus helped prepare the way for the introduction of the alternative rational-expectations idea into Phillips curve analysis.

The tests themselves were mainly concerned with estimating the numerical value of the coefficient on the price-expectations variable in the expectations-augmented Phillips curve equation. If the coefficient is one, as in Equation (3), then the natural rate hypothesis is valid and no long-run inflation-unemployment trade-off exists for the policymakers to exploit. But if the coefficient is less than one, the natural rate hypothesis is refuted and a long-run trade-off exists. This can be seen by writing the expectations-augmented equation as

$$p = ax + \phi p^e \qquad (6)$$

where ϕ is the coefficient attached to the price expectations variable. In long-run equilibrium, of course, expected inflation equals actual inflation, i.e., $p^e = p$. Setting expected inflation equal to actual inflation as required for long-run equilibrium and solving for the actual rate of inflation yields

$$p(1 - \phi) = ax. \qquad (7)$$

This shows that a long-run trade-off exists only if the expectations coefficient is less than one. If the coefficient is one, however, the trade-off vanishes.

Many of the empirical tests estimated the coefficient to be less than unity and concluded that the natural rate hypothesis was invalid. But this conclusion was sharply challenged by economists who contended that the tests contained statistical bias that tended to work against the natural rate hypothesis. These critics pointed out that the tests invariably used adaptive-expectations schemes as empirical proxies for the unobservable price expectations variable. They further showed that if these proxies were inappropriate measures of expectations then estimates of the expectations coefficient could well be biased downward. If so, then estimated coefficients of less than one constituted no disproof of the natural rate hypothesis.

Finally, the critics argued that the adaptive-expectations scheme is a grossly inaccurate representation of how people formulate price expectations. They pointed out that it postulates naive expectational behavior, holding as it does that people form anticipations solely from a weighted average of past price experience with weights that are fixed and independent of economic conditions and policy actions. This implies that people look only at past price changes and ignore all other pertinent information—e.g., money growth rate changes, exchange rate movements, announced policy intentions and the like—that could be used to reduce expectational errors. It seems implausible that people would fail to exploit information that would improve expectational accuracy. In short, the critics contended that adaptive expectations are not wholly rational if other information besides past price changes can improve predictions.

Many economists have since pointed out that it is hard to accept the notion that individuals would form price anticipations from *any* scheme that is inconsistent with the way inflation is actually generated in the economy. Being different from the true inflation-generating mechanism, such schemes will produce expectations that are systematically wrong. If so, rational agents will cease to use them. For example, suppose inflation were actually accelerating or decelerating. According to Equation 4, the adaptive expectations model would systematically underestimate the inflation rate in the former case and overestimate it in the latter. Perceiving these persistent expectational mistakes, rational agents would quickly abandon the error-learning model for more accurate expectations-generating schemes. Once again, the adaptive-expectations mechanism is implausible because of its incompatibility with rational behavior.

From Adaptive Expectations to Rational Expectations

The shortcomings of the adaptive expectations approach to the modeling of expectations led to the incorporation of the so-called rational expectations approach into Phillips curve analysis. According to the rational expectations hypothesis, individuals will tend to exploit *all* the pertinent information about the inflationary process when making their price forecasts. If true, this means that forecasting errors ultimately could arise only from random (unforeseen) shocks occurring to the economy. At first, of course, forecasting errors could also arise because individuals initially possess limited or incomplete information about the inflationary mechanism. But it is unlikely that this latter condition would persist. For if the public is truly rational, it will quickly learn from these inflationary surprises and incorporate the new information into its forecasting procedures, i.e., the sources of forecasting mistakes will be swiftly perceived and systematically eradicated. As knowledge of the inflationary process improves, forecasting models will be continually revised to produce more accurate predictions. Eventually all systematic (predictable) elements influencing the rate of inflation will become known and fully understood, and indivdiuals' price expectations will constitute the most accurate (unbiased) forecast consistent with that knowledge.[4] When this happens people's price expectations will be the same as those implied by the actual inflation-generating mechanism. As incorporated in natural-rate Phillips curve models, the rational-expectations hypothesis implies that thereafter, except for unavoidable surprises due to purely random shocks, price expectations will always be correct and the economy will always be at its long-run steady-state equilibrium.

Policy Implications of Rational Expectations

The strict rational-expectations approach has some radical policy implications. It implies that systematic policies—i.e., those based on feedback control rules defining the authorities' response to changes in the economy—cannot influence real variables even in the short run, since people would have already anticipated what the policies are going to be and acted upon those anticipations. To have an impact on output and employment the authorities must be able to create a divergence between actual and expected inflation. This follows from the proposition that inflation influences real variables only when it is unanticipated. The authorities must be able to alter the actual rate of inflation without simultaneously causing an identical change in the expected future rate. This may be impossible if the public can predict policy actions.

Policy actions, to the extent they are systematic, are predictable.

---

[4]Put differently, rationality implies that current expectational errors are uncorrelated with past errors and all other known information, such correlations already having been perceived and eliminated in the process of improving price forecasts.

Systematic policies are simple rules or response functions relating policy variables to lagged values of other variables. These policy response functions can be estimated and incorporated into forecasters' price predictions. In other words, rational agents can use past observations on the behavior of the authorities to predict future policy moves. Then, on the basis of these predictions, they can correct for the effect of anticipated policies beforehand by making appropriate adjustments to nominal wages and prices. Consequently, when stabilization actions do occur, they will have no impact on real variables since they will have been discounted and neutralized in advance. The only conceivable way that policy can have even a short-run influence on real variables is for it to be unexpected, i.e., the policymakers must either act in an unpredictable random fashion or secretly change the policy reaction function. Apart from such tactics, which are incompatible with most notions of the proper conduct of public policy, there is no way the authorities can influence real variables. They can, however, influence a nominal variable, namely the inflation rate, and should concentrate their efforts on doing so if some particular rate is desired.

To summarize, the rationality hypothesis denies the existence of exploitable Phillips curve trade-offs in the short run as well as the long. In so doing it differs from the adaptive expectations version of natural-rate Phillips curve models. Under adaptive expectations, short-run trade-offs exist because expectations do not adjust instantaneously to policy-engineered changes in the inflation rate. With expectations adapting to actual inflation with a lag, monetary policy can generate unexpected inflation and consequently influence real variables in the short run. This cannot happen under rational expectations where both actual and expected inflation adjust identically and instantaneously to anticipated policy changes. In short, under rational expectations, systematic policy cannot induce the expectational errors that generate short-run Phillips curves.

A Simple Illustrative Model

The preceding arguments can be clarified with the aid of a simple illustrative model. The model contains five relationships including an expectations-augmented Phillips curve equation, an inflation-generating mechanism, a policy reaction function, a rational price expectations equation, and finally a rational money-growth expectations equation. Taken together, these equations show that deterministic policies, by virtue of their very predictability, cannot induce the expectational errors that generate short-run Phillips curves. Phillips curves may exist, to be sure. But they are entirely the result of unpredictable random shocks and cannot be exploited by policies based on rules. In sum, the model shows that, given expectational rationality and the natural rate hypothesis, systematic trade-offs are impossible in the short run as well as the long.[5]

Phillips Curve Equation

The first component of the model is the expectations-augmented Phillips curve equation

$$p - p^e = ax \qquad (8)$$

that expresses a trade-off relationship between unexpected inflation and real excess demand. In the rational expectations literature this equation is often treated as an aggregate supply function stating that firms produce the normal capacity level of output when actual and expected inflation are equal but produce in excess of that level when fooled by unexpected inflation. This view holds that firms mistake unanticipated general price increases for rises in the particular (relative) price of their own products. Surprised by inflation, they treat the price increase as special to themselves and so expand output.

An alternative interpretation of the equation treats it as a price-setting relation according to which businessmen raise their prices at the rate at which they expect other businessmen to be raising theirs and then adjust that rate upward if excess demand appears. Either interpretation yields the same result. Expectational errors cause real economic activity to deviate from its normal capacity level. The deviations disappear when the errors vanish.

Inflation-Generating Mechanism

The next relationship describes how inflation is generated in the model. Written as follows

[5]Note that the rational expectations hypothesis also rules out the accelerationist notion of a stable trade-off between excess demand and the rate of acceleration of the inflation rate. If expectations are formed consistent with the way inflation is actually generated, the authorities will not be able to fool people by accelerating inflation or by accelerating the rate of acceleration, etc. Indeed, no systematic policy will work if expectations are formed consistently with the way inflation is actually generated in the economy.

$$p = m + \epsilon \tag{9}$$

it expresses the rate of inflation as the sum of the growth rate of money m per unit of capacity real output and a random shock variable ϵ, the latter assumed to have a mean (expected) value of zero. The capacity-adjusted money growth rate is simply the difference between the respective growth rates of the nominal money stock and capacity real output, the latter variable serving as a proxy for the trend rate of growth of the real demand for money. In essence, Equation (9) says that while the rate of inflation is determined basically by the growth rate of money per unit of capacity output, it is also influenced by transitory disturbances unrelated to money growth. For convenience, it is assumed in what follows that the growth rate of capacity output is zero so that the capacity-adjusted money growth rate is identical to the growth of the nominal money stock itself.

Policy Reaction Function

The third ingredient of the model is a policy-reaction function stating how the monetary authorities respond to changes in the level of economic activity. Written as follows

$$m = m(x_{-1}) + u \tag{10}$$

it states that the current rate of money growth is a function of last period's excess demand x_{-1} and a random disturbance term u, the latter assumed to have a mean value of zero. The interpretation of the equation is straightforward. The authorities attempt to adjust money growth in the current period to correct real excess demand or supply occurring in the preceding period according to the feedback control rule $m = m(x_{-1})$. Money growth cannot be controlled perfectly by the feedback rule, however, and the slippage is represented by the random term u that causes money growth to deviate unpredictably from the path intended by the authorities. Note that the disturbance term u can also represent deliberate monetary surprises engineered by the policy authorities.

Price Expectations Equation

The fourth element of the model is a price-expectations equation describing how rational inflationary anticipations are formed. By definition, rational expectations are the same as the predictions yielded by the actual inflation-generating process, represented in the model by Equation (9). And since that equation states that the actual rate of inflation is equal to the actual money growth rate plus a random variable, it follows that the expected rate of inflation predicted by the equation is equal to the expected money growth rate plus the expected value of the random term. The latter, however, is zero and thus drops out, leaving anticipated inflation equal to expected money growth. In symbols

$$p^e = m^e. \tag{11}$$

Note that these symbols now have a dual interpretation. They represent anticipations formulated by the public. They also represent mathematical expectations—i.e., expected (mean) values of the stochastic inflation and money growth variables—calculated from a model that, in principle at least, is a true representation of the inflationary process. Here is the essence of the notion that people's expectations are rational when they are the same as those implied by the relevant economic model.[6]

Anticipated Money Growth Equation

Finally, rational expectations are employed to determine the anticipated rate of monetary growth. Here rational expectations are the same as the predictions of the actual money growth generating mechanism, represented in the model by Equation 10 (the policy-reaction function). Put differently, the expected value of the reaction function constitutes the rational expectation of money growth. And since the function contains a systematic (predictable) component whose expected value is simply itself and a random term with an expected value of zero, that expectation is

$$m^e = m(x_{-1}). \tag{12}$$

---

[6]Analysts often stress this point by expressing anticipated inflation formally as the mathematical expected value of the actual inflation rate, conditional on information available when the expectation was formed. Symbolically, $p^e = E(p/I)$ where E is the mathematical expectation and I is known information. Since this information includes the inflation-generating mechanism summarized by Equation (9), it follows that anticipated inflation will be equal to the mathematical expectation of that mechanism, i.e., to the sum of the expected values of the money growth rate and the random term, respectively.

In short, the anticipated rate of monetary growth is given by the predictable component of the policy-reaction function. Rational agents know everything in the policy-reaction function except the random element. They know the constant terms, the coefficients, and the predetermined variable. They use all this information in formulating expectations of the rate of monetary growth, expectations which are given by Equation (12).

The Reduced Form Equation

Equations (8) to (12) constitute the fundamental relationships of the rational-expectations model. The model can be condensed to a single reduced-form expression by substituting Equations (9) to (12) into Equation (8) to yield

$$\epsilon + u = ax \qquad (13)$$

which states that Phillips curve trade-offs result solely from inflationary surprises caused by random shocks. Note in particular that only that part of monetary growth arising from unpredictable random disturbances enters Equation (13). The systematic component is absent. This means that systematic monetary policy cannot affect real economic activity (as represented by excess demand x). Only unexpected money growth matters.

The foregoing implies that the authorities can influence economic activity in only two ways. First, they can pursue a random policy, altering monetary growth in a haphazard unpredictable manner. That is to say they can manipulate the disturbance term u in the policy reaction function in a totally unpredictable way. Second, they can secretly change the feedback control rule, thereby affecting output and employment during the time people are learning about the new rule. It is unlikely, however, that this latter policy would prove effective for very long since rational agents would learn to predict rule *changes* just as they predict the rule. This leaves random policy as the only way to affect economic activity. But randomness seems hardly a proper basis for public policy.

To summarize, the strict rational-expectations approach implies that expectational errors are the only source of departure from steady-state equilibrium, that such errors are short-lived and random, and that systematic policy rules will have no impact on real variables since those rules will already be fully embodied in rational price expectations. Thus, except for unpredictable random shocks, steady-state equilibrium always prevails and systematic monetary changes produce no surprises, no disappointed expectations, no transitory impacts on real economic activity. Trade-offs are totally adventitious phenomena that cannot be exploited by systematic policy even in the short run. In short, no role remains for counter-cyclical stabilization policy. The only thing such policy can influence is the rate of inflation, which adjusts immediately to expected changes in money growth. The full effect of anticipated policy actions will be on the inflation rate. It follows that the authorities should concentrate their efforts on controlling this variable if it is desirable to do so since they cannot systematically influence real variables.

Evaluation of Rational Expectations

The preceding paragraphs have shown what happens when rational expectations are incorporated into a model containing feedback policy rules, an inflation-generating mechanism, and an expectations-augmented Phillips curve or aggregate supply function embodying the natural rate hypothesis. An evaluation of the rational-expectations approach is now in order.

One advantage of the rational-expectations hypothesis is that it treats expectations formation as a part of optimizing behavior. By so doing, it brings the theory of price anticipations into accord with the rest of economic analysis. The latter assumes that people behave as rational optimizers in the production and purchase of goods, in the choice of jobs, and in making investment decisions. For consistency, it should assume the same regarding expectational behavior.

In this sense, the rational-expectations theory is superior to rival explanations, all of which imply that expectations are always consistently wrong. It is the only theory that denies that people make systematic expectation errors. Note that it does not claim that people possess perfect foresight or that their expectations are always accurate. What it does claim is that they perceive and eliminate *regularities* in their forecasting mistakes. In this way they discover the actual inflation-generating process and use it in forming price expectations. And with rational expectations the same as the mean value of the inflation-generating process, those expectations cannot be wrong on *average*. Any errors will be random, not systematic. The same cannot be said for other expectations schemes, however. Not being identical to the expected value of true inflation-generating process, those schemes will produce biased expectations that are systematically wrong.

Biased expectations schemes are difficult to justify theoretically. Systematic mistakes are harder to explain than is rational behavior. True, nobody really knows how expectations are actually formed. But a theory that says that forecasters don't continually make the same mistakes seems intuitively more plausible than theories that imply the opposite. Considering the profits to be made from improved forecasts, it seems inconceivable that systematic expectational errors would persist. Somebody would surely note the errors, correct them, and profit by the correction. Other forecasters would make similar corrections. Together, the profit motive and competition would reduce forecasting errors to randomness.

Criticism of the Rational-Expectations Approach

Despite its logic, the rational-expectations approach has many critics. Some still maintain that expectations are basically nonrational, i.e., that people are too stupid, naive, or uninformed to formulate unbiased price expectations. A variant of this argument is that expectational rationality will be attained only after a long learning period during which expectations will be nonrational.

Most of the criticism, however, is directed not at the rationality assumption per se but rather at three other assumptions underlying the rational-expectations approach, namely the assumptions of (1) costless information, (2) no policymaker information advantage, and (3) price flexibility. The first states that information used to form rational expectations can be obtained and processed costlessly. The second holds that private forecasters possess exactly the same information as the authorities regarding the inflationary process. The third assumption states that prices and the rate of inflation respond fully and immediately to anticipated changes in monetary growth and other events. In effect, this last assumption denies that prices are sticky and costly to adjust.

Critics maintain that all of these assumptions are implausible and that if any are violated then the strong conclusions of the rational-expectations approach cease to hold. In particular, if the assumptions are violated then activist policies can have systematic effects on real variables. Indeed, the critics have demonstrated as much by incorporating constraints representing information costs, policymaker informational advantages, and sluggish price adjustment into rational-expectations models similar to the one outlined above.

Proponents of the rational-expectations approach readily admit that such constraints can restore the potency of activist policies. But they still insist that such policies are inappropriate and that the proper role for policy is not to systematically influence real activity but rather to neutralize the constraints. Thus if people form baised price forecasts, then the policymakers should publish unbiased forecasts. If information is costly to collect and process, then a central authority should gather it and make it available. If the policy authorities have informational advantages over private individuals, they should make that information public rather than attempting to exploit the advantage. Finally, if prices are sticky and costly to adjust, then the authorities should minimize these price adjustment costs by following policies that stabilize the general price level.

In short, advocates of the rational expectations approach argue that feasibility alone constitutes insufficient justification for activist policies. Policies should also be *desirable*. Activist policies hardly satisfy this latter criterion since their effectiveness is based on deceiving people into making expectational errors. The proper role for policy is not to influence real activity via deception but rather to reduce information deficiencies and perhaps also to minimize the costs of adjusting prices.

Conclusion

This article has examined some recent developments in Phillips curve analysis. The chief conclusions can be stated succinctly. The Phillips curve concept has changed radically over the past 20 years as the notion of a stable enduring trade-off has given way to the view that no such trade-off exists for the policymakers to exploit. Instrumental to this change were the natural-rate and rational-expectations hypotheses, respectively. The former attributes trade-offs solely to expectational errors while the latter holds that systematic policies, by virtue of their very predictability, cannot possibly generate such errors. Taken together, the two hypotheses imply that systematic policies are incapable of influencing output and employment, contrary to the claims of policy activists. True, critics of the rational-expectations model have shown that relaxation of its more stringent assumptions restores the short-run potency of stabilization policy. But members of the rational-expectations school reply that activist policies are undesirable in any case since those policies must rely on deception. Whatever the verdict on the rational expectations approach, one must at least agree that it has posed a provocative challenge to proponents of activist stabilization policies.

BIBLIOGRAPHY

1. ARAK, M. "Rational Price Expectations: A Survey of the Evidence and Implications." Federal Reserve Bank of New York, Research Paper No. 7716, March 1977.
2. BARRO, R. J., and S. FISCHER. "Recent Developments in Monetary Theory." *Journal of Monetary Economics* 2 (April 1976), 155–164.
3. FRIEDMAN, M. "Unemployment versus Inflation: An Evaluation of the Phillips Curve." I. E. A. Occasional Paper 44, 11–30. London: The Institute of Economic Affairs, 1976.
4. FRISCH, H. "Inflation Theory 1963–1975: A Second Generation Survey." *Journal of Economic Literature* 15 (December 1977), 1290–1297, 1301–1302.
5. GORDON, R. J. "Recent Developments in the Theory of Inflation and Unemployment." *Journal of Monetary Economics* 2 (April 1976), 185–219.
6. ———. "The Theory of Domestic Inflation." *American Economic Review* 67 (February 1977), 128–134.
7. "How Expectations Defeat Economic Policy." *Business Week*, November 8, 1976, 74, 76.
8. LAIDLER, D. "Expectations and the Phillips Trade-Off: A Commentary." *Scottish Journal of Political Economy* 23 (February 1976), 55–72.
9. LEMGRUBER, A. C. *A Study of the Accelerationist Theory of Inflation.* Unpublished Ph.D. dissertation. University of Virginia, May 1974.
10. McCALLUM, B. T. "Rational Expectations and the Theory of Macroeconomic Stabilization Policy." The Thomas Jefferson Center for Political Economy at the University of Virginia. Non-Technical Report No. 107, June 6, 1977.
11. MILLER, P. "Epilogue." In *A Prescription for Monetary Policy: Proceedings from a Seminar Series*, 99–103. Minneapolis: Federal Reserve Bank of Minneapolis, December 1976.
12. ———, C. W. NELSON, and T. M. SUPEL. "The Rational Expectations Challenge to Policy Activism." In *A Prescription for Monetary Policy: Proceedings from a Seminar Series*, 51–63. Minneapolis: Federal Reserve Bank of Minneapolis, December 1976.
13. MULLINEAUX, D. J. "Money Growth, Jobs, and Expectations: Does a

Little Learning Ruin Everything?" Federal Reserve Bank of
Philadelphia. *Business Review*, November/December 1976, 3–10.

14. ———. "Inflation Expectations in the U.S.: A Brief Anatomy." Federal
Reserve Bank of Philadelphia. *Business Review*, July/August 1977,
3–12.

15. POOLE, W. "Rational Expectations in the Macro Model." *Brookings Papers on Economic Activity*, No. 2, 1976, 436–505.

16. SANTOMERO, A. M., and J. J. SEATER. "The Inflation-Unemployment
Trade-Off: A Critique of The Literature." Federal Reserve Bank of
Philadelphia. Research Paper No. 21, March 1977.

17. SARGENT, T. J. "Testing for Neutrality and Rationality. In *A Prescription
for Monetary Policy: Proceedings from a Seminar Series*, 65–85. Minneapolis: Federal Reserve Bank of Minneapolis, December 1976.

18. ———, and N. WALLACE. "Rational Expectations and the Theory of Economic Policy." *Journal of Monetary Economics* 2 (April 1976), 169–
184.

Some Current Issues on the Transmission Process of Monetary Policy

Yung Chul Park

There is widespread agreement that money is of some importance in
determining the course of economic events. There is, however, substantial disagreement concerning the extent to which money matters
(that is, the size of the money multiplier). Monetarists argue that
changes in the stock of money are a primary determinant of changes in
total spending. On the other hand, nonmonetarists, although they may
readily admit that money matters, also regard changes in the various
components of aggregate demand as having an important influence on
the level of economic activity; they, therefore, place as much emphasis
on fiscal policy as on monetary controls. In fact, a spectrum of views on
the importance of money ranges from "money matters little" at one
extreme to "money alone matters" at the other extreme. An important
question is the extent to which these differences in opinion may be
traced to differences in models of the monetary process (that is, the

Reprinted, with deletions, from the *Staff Papers*, International Monetary Fund
(March 1972), 1–43 by permission of the publisher and the author.

transmission mechanism explaining how monetary influences affect real output, employment, and the price level). The objective of this paper is to examine this question by reviewing critically the analytical bases for the different views among monetarists and nonmonetarists;[1] only casual reference will be made to the vast and growing empirical literature. Since the transmission process is an integral part of the entire operational structure of the economy, the survey cannot be carried out without discussing divergent views on how the economy in general operates. While this may lengthen the paper, it will help us to analyze the mechanism in a proper context. The review begins in Section I with a discussion of post-Keynesian developments, followed in Section II by an analysis of the nonmonetarist views of the neo-Keynesians and the neo-Fisherians. The monetarist view is elaborated in Section III, and a summary and concluding remarks comprise Section IV.

I. Post-Keynesian Analysis: The Wealth Effect, Credit Rationing, and Portfolio Balance

The Cost-of-Capital Channel

The main process by which monetary forces influence the real economy in Keynesian income/expenditure models is through the cost-of-capital channel. In a simple Keynesian framework, monetary policy operates through changes in the rate of interest. The change in the volume of money alters "the" rate of interest—a rate of interest usually approximated by the long-term government bond rate—so as to equate the demand for money with the supply. The change in the rate of interest affects investment and possibly consumption; the change in aggregate demand, in turn, has a multiple effect on equilibrium in-

---

[1]Readers are also referred to other excellent reviews on this topic and on recent developments in monetary economics: Maurice Mann, "How Does Monetary Policy Affect the Economy?" *Federal Reserve Bulletin*, Vol. 54 (1968), 803–814; Allan H. Meltzer, "Money, Intermediation, and Growth," *The Journal of Economic Literature*, Vol. VII (1969), 27–56; Harry G. Johnson, "Recent Developments in Monetary Theory—A Commentary," in *Money in Britain, 1959–1969*, ed. by David R. Croome and Harry G. Johnson (Oxford University Press, 1970), 83–114; Warren L. Smith, "On Some Current Issues in Monetary Economics: An Interpretation," *The Journal of Economic Literature*, Vol. VIII (1970), 767–782; Harry G. Johnson, "The Keynesian Revolution and the Monetarist Counter-Revolution," American Economic Association, *Papers and Proceedings of the Eighty-third Annual Meeting (The American Economic Review*, Vol. LXI, May 1971), 1–14.

come. Thus, the rate of interest is viewed as a measure of the cost of capital, as the indicator of the stance of monetary policy, and as the key linkage variable between the real and financial sectors.

In addition to the cost-of-capital channel, post-Keynesians also recognized two other channels, namely, the wealth effect on consumption expenditure and the credit rationing linkage between the financial and real sectors.

The Wealth Effect

The post-Keynesian view   One of the most significant post-Keynesian developments has been the emphasis on net private wealth as well as income as a factor influencing real flows of expenditures. The connection between net wealth of the private sector and consumption was first pointed out by Pigou[2] and Haberler,[3] and in a more rigorous manner by Patinkin,[4] in the form of real cash balance effect: changes in the real quantity of money could affect real aggregate demand even if they did not alter the rate of interest. The central feature of the real cash balance effect is the assumption that the stock of money is a component of the net wealth of the economy. However, the stock of money that these economists considered as part of net wealth was not the usually defined concept of narrow money (currency outside banks *plus* demand deposits) but rather the monetary base, or, in Gurley and Shaw's terminology, outside money alone.[5] The justification for excluding demand deposits (inside money) as part of wealth is that these deposits are claims of the public on the banking system that are counterbalanced by the debts of the public to the banking sector. Therefore, when the balance sheets of all economic units are consolidated, inside money disappears and, hence, should not be considered as part of wealth.

This justification, however, brings out immediately the question

[2]A. C. Pigou, "Economic Progress in a Stable Environment," *Economica*, New Series, Vol. XIV (1947), 180–188.

[3]Gottfried Haberler, *Prosperity and Depression* (New York, Third Edition, 1946), 242, 403, and 491–503.

[4]Don Patinkin, "Price Flexibility and Full Employment," in *Readings in Monetary Theory*, ed. by Friedrich A. Lutz and Lloyd W. Mints (New York, 1951), 252–283.

[5]Outside money is defined as the money that is backed by foreign or government securities or gold, or fiat money issued by the government, whereas inside money— commercial bank demand deposits—is based on private domestic securities. See John G. Gurley and Edward S. Shaw, *Money in a Theory of Finance*, The Brookings Institution (Washington, 1969), 363–364.

of why the same logic should not be applied to outside money, which is, after all, the noninterest-bearing debt of the government. If, indeed, outside money is government debt, as it has been treated in the post-Keynesian literature,[6] a consolidation of the balance sheet of the private and government sectors must result in the cancellation of outside money as an item of net wealth. It then follows that a change in outside money cannot exert a wealth effect, since the change cannot cause a simultaneous change in net wealth. To establish that the change in outside money does indeed have economic consequences, one has to provide an explanation other than that outside money is part of wealth. The explanation that has had widest support has been that the government, unlike other debtors, is unconcerned about the size of its debt and makes its economic decisions accordingly.[7] Thus, the only effect of the change in outside money is the effect of the increase in assets of the private sector. This explanation reduces the wealth effect of changes in outside money to a distribution effect of a wealth transfer between the private and government sectors. This explanation also suggests that the traditional distinction between inside and outside money is based not on a measure of wealth applicable to all types of assets but rather on asymmetric responses of various economic decision-making units to changes in assets and debts.[8]

Later developments have extended this wealth effect beyond money to other forms of wealth, such as the real market values of equities and interest-bearing government debt. It is fairly easy to appreciate the wealth effect or distribution effect associated with outside money. However, it is not evident whether the same argument could be applied to interest-bearing government debt. There is an important

[6]See James Tobin, "Money, Capital, and Other Stores of Value," American Economic Association, *Papers and Proceedings of the Seventy-third Annual Meeting* (*The American Economic Review*, Vol. LI, May 1961), 26–37; James Tobin, "Commercial Banks as Creators of 'Money,'" Chapter 1 in *Financial Markets and Economic Activity*, ed. by Donald D. Hester and James Tobin, Cowles Foundation, Monograph 21 (New York, 1967), 1–11, also included in *Banking and Monetary Studies*, ed. by Deane Carson (Homewood, Illinois, 1963); James Tobin, "Money and Economic Growth," *Econometrica*, Vol. 33 (1965), 671–684; Gurley and Shaw, *Money in a Theory of Finance* (cited in footnote 5); Don Patinkin, *Money, Interest, and Prices: An Integration of Monetary and Value Theory* (New York, Second Edition, 1965).

[7]The government, the argument claims, ignores the real value of its debt because it can pay its debts by issuing new debts; the government is able to do so since (1) it controls the supply of money and (2) it possesses the taxing power. See Harry G. Johnson, "Monetary Theory and Policy," in his *Essays in Monetary Economics* (Harvard University Press, 1967), 24.

[8]For a further elaboration on this point, see the following section.

difference between the two assets. Unlike outside money, the interest burden on interest-bearing government debt must be financed by future taxes. Hence, if the private sector discounts its future tax liablities in the same way in which it discounts future interest receipts, the existence of government bonds represents an asset as well as a liability to the public and will, therefore, not generate any net wealth effect.[9] However, if the public considers only a constant fraction of total interest-bearing government debt as a liablity, then an open market purchase of government bonds will increase net private wealth and thereby directly affect aggregate demand.

At the theoretical level, the link between the net wealth of consumers and real consumption has been refined as in the life cycle hypothesis of Ando, Brumberg, and Modigliani, which holds that consumers allocate consumption over their lifetime, given initial net worth, a rate of time preference, and expectations regarding labor income.[10]

The Keynesian approach uses the rate of interest on long-term bonds as the representative rate on all types of earning asset. "This implicitly assumes that equities, government bonds, and private debt are all perfect substitutes for one another."[11] As a result, the Keynesian analysis considers only substitution between money and bonds important but ignores entirely the substitutability between money and real assets or real expenditures. The intellectual importance of the real cash balance effect lies in the fact that it allowed the possibility of substitution between money, on the one hand, and real expenditures, on the other hand, in macroeconomic analysis.[12] This fact has, to a great extent, contributed to the explicit treatment of real capital goods in portfolio analysis and to a reemphasis on the role of money.

[9]Patinkin, *Money, Interest, and Prices* (cited in footnote 6), 289.

[10]Albert Ando and Franco Modigliani, "The 'Life Cycle' Hypothesis of Saving: Aggregate Implications and Tests," *The American Economic Review*, Vol. LIII (March 1963), 55-84; Franco Modigliani and Richard Brumberg, "Utility Analysis and the Consumption Function: An Interpretation of Cross-Section Data," in *Post Keynesian Economics*, ed. by Kenneth K. Kurihara (Rutgers University Press, 1954), 388-436; Franco Modigliani and Albert Ando, "The 'Permanent Income' and the 'Life Cycle' Hypothesis of Saving Behavior: Comparison and Tests," in *Consumption and Saving*, Vol. II, ed. by Irwin Friend and Robert Jones (Wharton School, University of Pennsylvania, 1960), 49-174.

[11]Tobin, "Money, Capital, and Other Stores of Value" (cited in footnote 6), 30.

[12]Milton Friedman, "Postwar Trends in Monetary Theory and Policy," in *Money and Finance: Readings in Theory, Policy, and Institutions*, ed. by Deane Carson (New York, 1966), 187.

The Pesek and Saving thesis In a recent book by Pesek and Saving,[13] the authors argue that commercial bank demand deposits (inside money) should also be treated as part of the net wealth of the economy, because demand deposits are an asset produced by banks and sold by them to the public in exchange for the latter's statements of indebtedness.[14] Demand deposits, unlike outside money, carry an "instant repurchase clause"—an obligation by the banks to repurchase them with outside money. But this characteristic, Pesek and Saving argue, does not affect the basic fact that demand deposits are part of net wealth.

If Pesek and Saving's thesis is valid, then their analysis will have important implications for the effects of monetary policy. Their analysis literally means that monetary authorities can directly create or destroy nominal private wealth at will through monetary policy. This, in turn, implies that monetary policy can affect aggregate demand *directly* and in theory can have strong effects on the level of economic activity. For instance, a central bank's open market purchase of government bills, given the money supply multiplier, will generate a multiple expansion of the initial increase in outside money. The increase in money supply should be considered an increase in nominal private wealth, which will, in turn, increase consumption expenditure. This means that the open market operation has a direct wealth effect in addition to the conventional liquidity effect[15] and the interest-rate-induced wealth effects (capital gains or losses on government bonds and equities) on total spending. For this reason, Pesek and Saving's argument deserves careful examination.

Pesek and Saving's view is based on the principle that the economically relevant measure of wealth is the capitalized value of a stream of net income. When this measure of wealth is applied to outside money, it is shown that outside money is a component of net wealth because it yields a net flow of services to the user—not because the government is unconcerned with its outstanding debt. The flow of services of outside money is the saving of time in barter transactions, which stems from the role of money as a medium of exchange. The saving of time may be used either for leisure or for the production of capital goods. Hence, outside money generates a positive stream of

[13]Boris P. Pesek and Thomas R. Saving, *Money, Wealth, and Economic Theory* (New York, 1967).
[14]*Ibid.*, Chapter 4, "Bank Money as Wealth," 79–102.
[15]The liquidity effect, or the substitution effect, refers to changes in interest rates that are brought about by changes in money supply via a liquidity preference relation.

income; the capitalized value of this income is then an addition to the net wealth of the economy. The same reasoning applies to demand deposits, the basic difference between government fiat money and demand deposits being one of institutional arrangements. The arrangement is that government fiat money is produced by the government, whereas demand deposits are produced by the government agents, namely, commercial banks that have received the monopoly right of producing money. From this point of view, there is no difference between outside money and demand deposits. To put it differently, inside money also represents a stream of net income, since demand deposits, as a medium of exchange, yield a flow of services that banks have agreed to provide. For inside money, however, the net income takes the form of the earnings of the banks through the process of money creation or intermediation. The capitalized value of the earnings is then an increase in the net wealth of the economy.[16]

To elaborate further on this point, let us assume that a commercial bank received $5,000 of demand deposits and that the bank is subject to a reserve requirement of 20 percent. The bank then retains $1,000 in cash reserves and creates demand deposits amounting to $4,000 by lending this amount to the private nonfinancial sector of the economy. Suppose that there is a single rate of interest, say, 5 percent, in this economy. This means that, *ceteris paribus*, the bank is earning an additional $200. The present value of this interest earning, given the 5 percent interest rate, is $4,000, which is exactly equal to the increase in demand deposits held by the public. This present value represents an increase in the net worth of the bank. Since the bank is a private one, the increase should be reflected also in the balance sheets of its stockholders; *ceteris paribus*, the increase in the net worth of the bank will be reflected in an increase in the market value of the bank's stocks, which is equivalent to an increase in the public's wealth.

The argument so far is based on the assumption that the costs of producing (or servicing) demand deposits are negligible. However, in reality the commercial banking industry has operating costs just like

[16]Reviewing the book by Pesek and Saving, Patinkin points out that the true origin of the net worth of the banking sector lies not in the production of demand deposits per se but in the monopoly right of producing demand deposits, which this sector has received from the government. See Don Patinkin, "Money and Wealth: A Review Article," *The Journal of Economic Literature*, Vol. VII (1969), 1140–1160. See also the reviews by Meltzer, "Money, Intermediation, and Growth" (cited in footnote 1), 32–36, and Smith, "On Some Current Issues in Monetary Economics: An Interpretation" (cited in footnote 1), 769–770.

any other industry and is fairly competitive. To the extent that there are operating costs connected with demand deposits (or outside money, for that matter), the whole value of demand deposits is not necessarily part of the net wealth of the economy. In the extreme case where the banking industry is fully competitive and is not subject to government controls and regulations, Patinkin shows that the capitalized value of the banks' operating costs (the sum of the present values of the current operating costs and of the imputed annual interest charge on the fixed assets) is equal to the value of demand deposits and that, consequently, demand deposits should be excluded from net national wealth.[17] The implication of the perfect competition case is, of course, that the true origin of the net worth of the banking sector is in its monopoly right of creating demand deposits.

However, if the assumption of zero costs of managing demand deposits is unrealistic, so is the assumption of perfect competition in the banking sector. A reasonable assumption would then be that, since entry into the banking industry is restricted by the necessity of obtaining a license, the present value of the income from creating demand deposits should be regarded, in part, as a component of net private wealth. This conclusion, in turn, raises an important question as to whether the conventional specification of the economically relevant wealth equation for theoretical as well as empirical studies is a proper one, and if it is not, how it should be modified.[18]

Net private (nonhuman) wealth (W) is generally defined as the sum of outside money and the market values of interest-bearing government debt and of the existing stock of physical capital:

$$W = PK + M_0 + B$$

where P = price level; K = real stock of capital; M_0 = outside money; B = supply of government bonds.[19]

The market value of real assets or equities (V) has been defined, for instance, as

---

[17]Patinkin, "Money and Wealth" (cited in footnote 16), 1147–1154.

[18]Once the monopoly is broken and perfect competition is restored in the banking sector, the monopoly profits (earnings) of banks will be transferred to the owners of demand deposits in the form of nonpecuniary services. See Meltzer, "Money, Intermediation, and Growth" (cited in footnote 1), 34.

[19]See, for example, Franco Modigliani, "The Monetary Mechanism and Its Interaction with Real Phenomena," *The Review of Economics and Statistics*, Vol. XLV (Supplement, February 1963), 80.

$$V = 100 \left(\frac{Y_{cd}}{R_d} \right)$$

where Y_{cd} = corporate dividend payments; R_d = dividend/price ratio on common stock (percentage).[20] On the other hand, Pesek and Saving define real nonhuman wealth for the purpose of general analysis as

$$W = \frac{M}{P} + \frac{y_n}{r_n} + \frac{g}{r_g}$$

where M = nominal quantity of money (narrow definition of currency *plus* demand deposits); P = price level; y_n = real nonhuman income; g = real nonhuman income yielded by government securities; r_n = capitalization rate applicable to real nonhuman income; r_g = capitalization rate applicable to real government interest payments.[21]

Brunner and Meltzer, following Pesek and Saving's reasoning, also explicitly introduce the net worth of the commercial banking sector into their definition of nonhuman wealth:

$$W = PK + B + (1 + \sigma)M_0$$

where σ = the banking system's net worth multiplier; σM_0 = the net worth contribution of the banking sector, or the capitalized value of net earnings of the banking system.[22]

The basic difference between the definition of Pesek and Saving (or of Brunner and Meltzer) and the conventional one is, of course, that the former includes demand deposits (in whole or in part) as a component of net private wealth whereas the latter does not. At first sight, it may appear that the appropriate definition of wealth is the specification of either Pesek and Saving or Brunner and Meltzer. But that is not so. It was pointed out that any increase in the net worth of the banking sector would, *ceteris paribus*, lead to a corresponding increase in the net worth of the nonbanking private sector in the form of an increase in the market value of bank stocks. This means that the value of demand deposits in Pesek and Saving's definition, or the net worth contribution

---

[20]Frank de Leeuw and Edward M. Gramlich, "The Channels of Monetary Policy," *Federal Reserve Bulletin*, Vol. 55 (1969), 481.

[21]Pesek and Saving, *Money, Wealth, and Economic Theory* (cited in footnote 13), 289–290.

[22]Karl Brunner and Allan H. Meltzer, "Fiscal and Monetary Policy in a Non-Keynesian World" (unpublished paper, 1970).

of the banking sector (σM_0) in Brunner and Metlzer's, is already included in the market value of equities $(PK, V,$ or $Y_n/r_n)$ to the extent that demand deposits (in whole or in part) are part of net wealth; adding the net worth of the banking sector to the market value of equities amounts to a double counting of the market value of commercial bank stocks. For this reason, the wealth definitions of Pesek and Saving and of Brunner and Meltzer should probably be rejected. One might then conclude that the conventional definition of net wealth is economically appropriate regardless of the validity of Pesek and Saving's thesis and that the direct wealth effect of monetary policy implied by their analysis has been accounted for in traditional analysis without being explicitly recognized.

Credit Rationing

Keynesian income/expenditure models assume a well-functioning competitive capital market in which desired investments are equilibrated to desired savings through the mechanism of the interest rate. In these models there exists a single short-run equilibrium rate of interest that simultaneously measures the rate of return to lenders, the cost of borrowings, the internal marginal rate of return from investments, and the opportunity cost of holding money. No one would question that the assumption of perfectly competitive capital markets is unrealistic; in reality, capital markets are not well functioning, and the price allocation mechanism may not work. It is, however, the proposition of the credit rationing channel that the Keynesian view of the transmission process of monetary policy and its consequences may have to be modified when market imperfections in capital markets are properly taken into consideration.

The most widely accepted view of the credit rationing channel appears to be the following proposition: under imperfect capital markets interest rates charged to borrowers by financial intermediaries, including commercial banks, are controlled by institutional forces, not by market forces, and tend not to change even when there is a change in the demand for funds, so that lenders ration the available supply of credit (by various nonprice terms). Accordingly, the demand for credit is limited "not by the borrowers' willingness to borrow at the given rate but by the lenders' willingness to lend—or, more precisely, by the funds available to them to be rationed out among the would-be borrowers."[23] Under these circumstances the single short-run equilibrium rate of interest in the perfect capital market framework is replaced by a plurality of rates—one for the lending units (depositors) and another for the rationed borrowers. This proposition implies that monetary policy could affect total expenditures directly by changing the degree of credit rationing and consequently the volume of lending, even if monetary controls did not change interest rates appreciably or if aggregate demand was interest inelastic. It also implies that insofar as "sticky" lending rates prevail, monetary policy would be less effective if it were geared to control the power of banks to create money rather than the actual money supply.[24]

While the credit rationing phenomenon has been well known, it has proved to be rather difficult to deal with effectively in macroeconomic analyses. One difficulty is that what is observed as credit availability is actually only a temporary disequilibrium situation in the capital market, one that may cause changes in interest rates in other parts of the capital market to levels that will eventually clear the market. Another difficulty is the empirical problem of measuring and identifying the degree of credit rationing. In most cases the specific details of credit rationing are not observable or recorded, so that indirect—often unsatisfactory—means must be used to represent credit rationing.

Portfolio Balance Approach

A more fundamental and basic development in monetary theory subsequent to Keynes' liquidity preference theory has been the capital theoretic formulation of the demand for money. This analysis emphasizes money as an asset that can be compared with other real as well as financial assets; its emphasis is on what is called portfolio balance. The analysis of portfolio and balance sheet adjustments has been extended beyond the Keynesian two-asset (money and bonds) models to include various financial and real assets other than bonds and has been integrated with varying degrees of complexity into the Keynesian income/expenditure framework.

The portfolio approach to monetary theory involves a new view of

[23]Modigliani, "The Monetary Mechanism and Its Interaction with Real Phenomena" (cited in footnote 19), 98.
[24]*Ibid.*, 100.

how the influence of monetary policy is transmitted to the real economy. The general view that has been emerging from the writings of both neo-Keynesians and monetarists stresses the impact of monetary policy changes on the composition of assets held by the public and the influence of these changes on interest rates on these assets and ultimately on the rate of return from investing in the production of new physical assets. In the portfolio view the impact on the real sector of an initial monetary disturbance is the result of changing relative prices among a wide array of financial and real assets. An increase in the supply of money, following an open market purchase of government securities, results in excessive holdings of money relative to other forms of wealth. Holders of wealth will be induced to exchange these excessive balances for other assets, which will in turn raise asset prices and lower rates of return across the board. As a result, an increase in the supply of money may eventually stimulate new investment in many directions.

This broad description of the transmission mechanism appears to be acceptable to both monetarists and nonmonetarists. There is, however, considerable disagreement as to the major variables and interest rates that must be defined in order to take account of all the ways in which monetary policy works out its effects. In what follows, focusing on this aspect, we will review and compare the views of nonmonetarists and monetarists on the transmission process of monetary policy.

II. The Nonmonetarist View

Neo-Keynesian Analysis: The Yale School View

It is always misleading to classify economists, who do not necessarily have common views about the subject matter concerned, under a single label as we do in this paper. It should be understood that the nomenclature is introduced solely for the convenience and clarity of exposition. Some economists whom we consider neo-Keynesians could take substantially different positions on particular issues. With this risk in mind, we summarize what appear to be the major arguments and findings of neo-Keynesians, or the Yale school.

(1) Neo-Keynesians consider that the stock of money, conventionally defined, is not an exogenous variable completely controlled by the monetary authorities but is partly an endogenous quantity that reflects

the economic behavior of financial intermediaries and nonfinancial private economic units.[25]

(2) The sharp traditional distinctions between money and other assets and between commercial banks and other financial intermediaries are not warranted. Instead, monetary analysis should

> focus on demands for supplies of the whole spectrum of assets rather than on the quantity and velocity of "money"; and to regard the structure of interest rates, asset yields, and credit availability rather than the quantity of money [or the rate of interest] as the linkage between monetary and financial institutions and policies on the one hand and the real economy on the other.[26]

This argument has been known as the New View, a view that clearly is related to, if not similar to, the Radcliffe Committee's position some years ago. In fact, Johnson claims that the Yale school has provided the intellectual foundations of the Radcliffe position on monetary theory and policy.[27]

(3) Proposition (2) implies that the crucial distinction in a neo-Keynesian framework is between the financial sector and the real sector rather than between the banking system and the rest of the economy or between liquid and illiquid assets. The construction of the financial sector reflects the theory of portfolio management by economic units. The theory takes as its subject matter stocks of assets and debts, and their framework is the balance sheet; the decision variables in this sector are stocks.[28] The real sector deals with flows of income, saving, expenditures, and the production of goods and services. Its accounting framework is the income statement, and the decision variables are flows. The two sectors are linked by "accounting identities—e.g., increase in net worth equals saving plus capital appreci-

---

[25]*Financial Markets and Economic Activity* (cited in footnote 6), "Foreword," viii. See also Lyle E. Gramley and Samuel B. Chase, Jr., "Time Deposits in Monetary Analysis," *Federal Reserve Bulletin*, Vol. 51 (1965), 1380-1406; John H. Kareken, "Commercial Banks and the Supply of Money: A Market-Determined Demand Deposit Rate," *Federal Reserve Bulletin*, Vol. 53 (1967), 1699-1712; J. A. Cacy, "Alternative Approaches to the Analysis of the Financial Structure," Federal Reserve Bank of Kansas City, *Monthly Review* (March 1968), 3-9; Richard G. Davis, "The Role of the Money Supply in Business Cycles," Federal Reserve Bank of New York, *Monthly Review* (April 1968), 63-73.

[26]Tobin, "Commercial Banks as Creators of 'Money'" (cited in footnote 6), 3.

[27]Johnson, "Recent Developments in Monetary Theory—A Commentary" (cited in footnote 1), 101.

[28]*Financial Markets and Economic Activity* (cited in footnote 6), "Foreword," v-vi.

ation—and by technological and financial stock-flow relations."[29] This, together with proposition (2), implies a rather complicated relationship between the two sectors in the linkage sequence. Some attempts have been made to synthesize the two sectors with varying degrees of simplification, but none of them seems satisfactory. Considering the emphasis on and the amount of attention paid to the building and analyzing of the interactions within the financial sector, it is indeed surprising to find that there has been no satisfactory attempt to bridge the gap. In our discussion we will consider perhaps the most widely accepted of these attempts, the synthesis developed by Brainard and Tobin.[30]

(4) While there is still considerable debate on the link between the real and financial sectors, there appears to be a consensus among neo-Keynesians that monetary policy operates through changes in the market price of equities that represent claims on existing real assets, such as plant and equipment.[31] The prime indicator of stance and the proper target of monetary policy is thus "the required rate of return on capital," or the equity yield. "Nothing else, whether it is the quantity of 'money' or some financial interest rate, can be more than an imperfect and derivative indicator of the effective thrust of monetary events and policies."[32] In a neo-Keynesian framework an expansionary monetary policy, for example, raises the price of equities (that is, reduces the yield on equities), thereby generating a positive discrepancy between the valuation of real assets on these markets (the price of equities) and their costs of production. The discrepancy provides an· incentive to expand production of these capital goods. Suppose that the existing plant and equipment of a corporation that could be reproduced for $1 million is valued at $2 million in the stock market. This margin between the market valuation and the cost of reproducing the existing capital goods will then stimulate new investment in these goods.[33] On

---

[29]Tobin, "Money, Capital, and Other Stores of Value" (cited in footnote 6), 28.

[30]William C. Brainard and James Tobin, "Pitfalls in Financial Model Building," American Economic Association, *Papers and Proceedings of the Eightieth Annual Meeting* (*The American Economic Review*, Vol. LVIII, May 1968), 99–122.

[31]Neo-Keynesians assume that capital goods have two separate market prices: the prices of existing (secondhand) capital goods represented by the price of equities and the output prices of these goods (or the prices of newly produced capital goods).

[32]Brainard and Tobin, "Pitfalls in Financial Model Building" (cited in footnote 30), 104.

[33]For further discussion on this investment behavior, see Brainard and Tobin, "Pitfalls in Financial Model Building" (cited in footnote 30), 112; Hyman P. Minsky, "Private Sector Asset Management and the Effectiveness of Monetary Policy: Theory

this reasoning, the stock market plays a significant role in influencing economic activity, and indeed changes in the Dow-Jones averages give some measure of the stance of monetary policy.[34]

The most serious criticism that may be made of the neo-Keynesian analysis is that despite the very complex financial sector, incorporating detailed specifications of asset preferences, its transmission mechanism remains naïve and simple. The synthesis by Brainard and Tobin assumes that the equity rate is the major link between money and the level of economic activity. Compared with the Keynesian transmission process, this simply involves replacing the rates of interest on financial assets by the equity yield—a yield that is now taken to represent the influence of monetary forces. Also, neo-Keynesians appear to ignore the relative importance of borrowing costs and, hence, the importance of debt financing in business firms.

The Neo-Fisherian View

All of the major empirical studies have found that the demand for money and velocity are responsive to interest rates, although the choice of rates between short-term and long-term is not clear cut. However, neither Keynes' speculative motive of holding money nor Tobin's portfolio selection theory provides a rational explanation of the nonzero interest elasticity of the demand for money in an economy where there exist short-term securities—such as time deposits, savings and loan shares, treasury bills, high-grade commercial papers and negotiable certificates of deposit for large investors—that dominate money. When these assets are readily available, the public—faced, for example, with a low current rate of interest and an expectation of capital losses owing to an expected rise in the current rate of interest—will be induced to shift from long-term to short-term securities, but not to money. This is so because these short-term assets

and Practice," *The Journal of Finance*, Vol. XXIV (1969), 229; W. L. Smith, "A Neo-Keynesian View of Monetary Policy," in *Controlling Monetary Aggregates* (Proceedings of a monetary conference in Massachusetts), Federal Reserve Bank of Boston (June 1969), 106; Ralph Turvey, *Interest Rates and Asset Prices* (London, 1960); James Tobin, "An Essay on Principles of Debt Management," in *Fiscal and Debt Management Policies*, Commission on Money and Credit (Englewood Cliffs, New Jersey, 1963), 150; James Tobin, "Monetary Semantics," in *Targets and Indicators of Monetary Policy*, ed. by Karl Brunner (San Francisco, 1969), 173–174.

[34]Tobin, "Monetary Semantics" (cited in footnote 33), 174. See the Appendix for a systematic discussion on the neo-Keynesian transmission process of monetary policy.

possess the same properties as money—near perfect liquidity and no risk of default—while yielding a positive rate of return.[35]

Given these short-term securities, changes in the current rate of interest and expectation of capital gains or losses no longer explain the substitution between long-term securities and money but the substitution between long-term and short-term securities.[36] Therefore, the only plausible theory of the demand for money that is consistent with the existing empirical evidence seems to be the transactions cost approach of the demand for money, developed by Baumol and Tobin.[37] The basic hypothesis of this approach, which has been labeled as neo-Fisherian, is that "the demand for money is basically related to the flow of transactions and arises from a lack of synchronization between receipts and payments, coupled with the transactions costs involved in exchanging money for short-term assets."[38] This hypothesis implies that (i) the wealth variable does not appear in the demand for money function, since money is held primarily to facilitate transactions and that (ii) the demand for money is sensitive to short-term interest rates.

The financial sector of the Federal Reserve–MIT economic model embodies the neo-Fisherian hypothesis.[39] In the financial sector of the model the reciprocal of velocity (the Cambridge k) is related to the rates of interest on short-term assets relative to transactions costs. Assuming no significant variation in transactions costs, the demand for money is then expressed as $M^d = k(i)Y$, where i = a set of available rates of return on short-term assets, Y = nominal gross national product (GNP), and M is narrow money.[40]

---

[35]See Smith, "On Some Current Issues in Monetary Economics: An Interpretation" (cited in footnote 1), 774–775.

[36]The Keynesian speculative demand for money ceases to be an explanation of holding money but becomes the basis for an expectational theory of the term structure of interest rates.

[37]William J. Baumol, "The Transactions Demand for Cash: An Inventory Theoretic Approach," *The Quarterly Journal of Economics*, Vol. LXVI (1952), 545–556; James Tobin, "The Interest-Elasticity of Transactions Demand for Cash," *The Review of Economics and Statistics*, Vol. XXXVIII (1956), 241–247.

[38]Franco Modigliani, Robert Rasche, and J. Philip Cooper, "Central Bank Policy, the Money Supply, and the Short-Term Rate of Interest," *Journal of Money, Credit and Banking*, Vol. II (1970), 167. The neo-Fisherian model of the demand for money developed by these authors is basically the one in the Federal Reserve–MIT econometric model.

[39]Robert H. Rasche and Harold T. Shapiro, "The F.R.B.–M.I.T. Econometric Model: Its Special Features," American Economic Association, *Papers and Proceedings of the Eightieth Annual Meeting* (*The American Economic Review*, Vol. LVIII, May 1968), 123–149.

[40]*Ibid.*, 137.

Within the neo-Fisherian framework, changes in the quantity of money have their direct impact on short-term interest rates.[41] Through the process of portfolio substitutions, changes in short-term interest rates affect, in turn, the long-term interest rates, equity yields, and possibly other rates of return on real assets.[42] Changes in these variables then influence aggregate demand for goods and services. This transmission process indicates that the full effect of monetary policy is subject to a considerable lag, because it takes time for changes in monetary policy to be reflected in long-term interest rates and equity yields and also requires additional delay for this rate change to be reflected in various components of aggregate demand.[43]

III. The Monetarist View

The theoretical framework used by nonmonetarists to explain how monetary and fiscal policies affect economic activity is a variant of the Keynesian income/expenditure model. While nonmonetarists are rather explicit in their theoretical argument, monetarists have not been very precise in providing a convincing explanation of how money affects the economy and how changes in the supply of money could have markedly more potent and direct effects than changes in fiscal variables. Instead, their argument seems to be based on several kinds of empirical evidence, the most widely publicized being the findings of the reduced form equation studies. These studies relate changes in

[41]However, if the monetary authorities dealt in the long-term bond market, changes in the quantity of money resulting from open market operations would affect the long-term interest rate directly.

[42]The process through which changes in short-term interest rates affect long-term interest rates may be explained directly by an equation from the term structure of interest rates based on the expectations hypothesis. This approach allows us to omit the equations of supply and demand for many financial assets. The Federal Reserve–MIT model follows this approach, relying on the term structure hypothesis developed by Franco Modigliani and Richard Sutch, "Innovations in Interest Rate Policy," American Economic Association, *Papers and Proceedings of the Seventy-eighth Annual Meeting* (*The American Economic Review*, Vol. LVI, May 1966), 178–197.

[43]In the Federal Reserve–MIT model the costs of capital are defined to be linear combinations of various long-term interest rates and the dividend/price ratio. The effect of monetary policy is felt immediately in the short-term interest rates. Through the term structure equation, changes in short-term rates affect the long-term rates with a time lag. The long-term rate in turn affects the cost of capital directly as one of its components and indirectly through the dividend/price ratio. The cost of capital influences the demand functions for final output with an additional time lag. See Rasche and Shapiro, "The F.R.B.–M.I.T. Econometric Model" (cited in footnote 39), 146. See also de Leeuw and Gramlich, "The Channels of Monetary Policy" (cited in footnote 20), 485–490. Editor's Note: The FRB-MIT model is surveyed in the next reading.

GNP to the simultaneous and lagged changes in the supply of money and a budget variable or autonomous expenditures.

In this section we will discuss the views of Friedman, Brunner, and Meltzer, and other monetarists. The general view that emerges from the writings of these monetarists is that "changes in the money stock are a primary determinant of changes in total spending, and should thereby be given major emphasis in economic stabilization programs."[44] In addition to this, monetarists emphasize the following three points: (1) The monetary authorities can dominate movements in the stock of money over time and over business cycles. (2) Movements in the quantity of money are the most reliable measure of the thrust of monetary impulses. (3) Monetary impulses are transmitted to the real economy through a relative price process (portfolio adjustment process), which operates on a vast array of financial and real assets.[45]

Friedman: The Monetary Theory of Nominal Income

Professor Milton Friedman, as the chief architect of the monetarist view, is responsible for the intellectual revival of the quantity theory in the postwar period—a revival that has for some years provoked a good deal of commentary and critical interpretation. Much of this controversy has been attributed to his failure to make explicit the theoretical framework that encompasses his views on the role of money. In two recent articles,[46] he has responded to this criticism, but it is not clear to what extent he has succeeded in answering his critics.[47]

[44]Leonall C. Andersen and Keith M. Carlson, "A Monetarist Model for Economic Stabilization," Federal Reserve Bank of St. Louis, *Review*, Vol. 52 (April 1970), 7. An important qualification of this is Friedman's view that, notwithstanding the importance of money, monetary policy—because it operates with a long and variable lag—should not be used for short-run stabilization. Instead, money should be allowed to grow at a constant rate over time. Editor's Note: The St. Louis model is surveyed in the next reading.

On the general view of monetarists, see Milton Friedman, *The Counter-Revolution in Monetary Theory*, first Wincott Memorial Lecture, delivered at the Senate House, University of London, September 16, 1970, Occasional Paper 33, Institute of Economic Affairs (London, 1970); Karl Brunner, "The 'Monetarist Revolution' in Monetary Theory," *Weltwirtschaftliches Archiv*, Band 105, Heft 1 (1970), 1–30.

[45]Karl Brunner, "The Role of Money and Monetary Policy," Federal Reserve Bank of St. Louis, *Review*, Vol. 50 (July 1968), 9, 18, and 24.

[46]Milton Friedman, "A Theoretical Framework for Monetary Analysis," *Journal of Political Economy*, Vol. 78 (March/April 1970), 193–238; "A Monetary Theory of Nominal Income," *Journal of Political Economy*, Vol. 79 (March/April 1971), 323–337.

[47]Prior to this, Patinkin had shown conclusively that Friedman's reformulation of the quantity theory was an elegant exposition of the modern portfolio approach to the demand for money. (See Don Patinkin, "The Chicago Tradition, the Quan-

Friedman's theoretical framework in the most recent expression of his views is a Keynesian income/expenditure model, which, he claims, is acceptable to both monetarists and nonmonetarists.[48]

The model is given as follows:

$$\frac{C}{P} = f\left(\frac{Y}{P}, r\right) \tag{1}$$

$$\frac{I}{P} = g(r) \tag{2}$$

$$\frac{Y}{P} = \frac{C}{P} + \frac{I}{P} \tag{3}$$

$$M^d = P L\left(\frac{Y}{P}, r\right) \tag{4}$$

$$M^s = h(r) \tag{5}$$

$$M^d = M^s \tag{6}$$

where Y = money income; C = consumption; I = investment; r = the rate of interest; P = the price level; M^s = supply of money; M^d = demand for money.

Equations (1)–(3) describe the real sector of the economy, while Equations (4)–(6) outline the monetary sector. In this model, real consumption expenditure is explained by real income and the interest rate (Equation 1) and real investment is explained by the interest rate (Equation 2). Equation (3) is the equilibrium condition in the commodity market, or the income identity. Real money balances are a function of real income and the rate of interest (Equation 4), while the nominal supply of money is assumed to be an increasing function of the interest rate (Equation 5). The equilibrium condition in the money market is given by Equation (6).

The model consists of six independent equations with seven endogenous variables (C, I, Y, P, M^d, M^s, r), so that the system of equations cannot determine simultaneously the solution values of these

---

tity Theory, and Friedman," *Journal of Money, Credit and Banking*, Vol. I, 1969, 46–70.) In recent writings, Friedman himself has acknowledged that his reformulation was much influenced by the Keynesian liquidity analysis. (See Friedman, "Postwar Trends in Monetary Theory and Policy" (cited in footnote 12), 188. See also Milton Friedman, "Money: Quantity Theory," *International Encyclopedia of the Social Sciences*, Vol. 10 (New York, 1968), 432–447.

[48]See Friedman, "A Theoretical Framework for Monetary Analysis" (cited in footnote 46), 217–218.

variables. One of these variables must be determined exogenously by relationships outside the system. Friedman discusses three different ways of solving the system that correspond to three different macroeconomic theories. The first two methods are well known in the literature; they are the income/expenditure theory and the quantity theory approach. The difference between the two theories is the condition that is added to make the model determine the solution values of the seven endogenous variables. The Keynesian income/expenditure theory assumes that the general level of prices is determined outside the system—the Keynesian assumption of price or wage rigidity ($P = P_0$). Given this assumption, the system of equations determines simultaneously the solution for the level of income and the rate of interest, as usually described in the familiar Hicksian IS/LM apparatus.[49] The quantity theory approach, on the other hand, assumes that real income is determined outside the system—the classical assumption of full employment. This assumption allows a dichotomy of the system into the real and monetary sectors, with the result that the demand for and supply of money functions determine the price level.[50] Friedman takes the view that the quantity theory model is valid for long-run equilibrium, so that, in the long run, variations in the rate of change in the quantity of money will change only the rate of inflation and not growth of real output.[51]

According to Friedman, neither the quantity theory nor the income/expenditure theory model is satisfactory as a framework for short-run analysis. This is so, Friedman claims, mainly because neither theory can explain "(a) the short-run division of a change in nominal income between prices and output, (b) the short-run adjustment of

---

[49]The price rigidity assumption, $P = P_0$, allows Equations (1)–(3) to define one relation between r and real income (IS curve) and Equations (4)–(6) to define a second such relation (LM curve). Their simultaneous solution gives the rate of interest and real income.

[50]Given the level of real income, $Y/P = y$, Equations (1)–(3) determine the rate of interest. Equations (4)–(6) then yield an equation relating the price level to the quantity of money.

[51]In conditions where the rate of growth of real output is determined independently by real forces in the economy, conditions that are assumed to prevail in the long run, changes in the money supply will dominate only changes in the price level, notwithstanding the fact that the demand for money is interest sensitive. Specifically, Friedman argues that in the long run monetary policy cannot control real variables—the real rate of interest, the level of unemployment, and real income—but can control only nominal quantities—the price level, money rate of interest, and nominal income. See Milton Friedman, "The Role of Monetary Policy," in his *The Optimum Quantity of Money and Other Essays* (Chicago, 1969), 105.

nominal income to a change in autonomous variables, and (c) the transition between this short-run situation and a long-run equilibrium described essentially by the quantity-theory model."[52]

The third alternative way to determine the system of equations is given by the monetary theory of nominal income—a theory that, Friedman claims, is superior to either the income/expenditure or the quantity theory as an approach to closing the system for the purpose of analyzing short-period changes. This third approach synthesizes Irving Fisher's ideas on the nominal and real interest rates and Keynes' view that the current market rate of interest (long-term) is determined largely by the rate that is expected to prevail over a long period. The Keynes and Fisher synthesis is then integrated into a quantity theory model together with the empirical assumption (i) that the real income elasticity of the demand for money is unity and (ii) that a difference between the anticipated real interest rate and the anticipated growth rate of real income is determined outside the system.[53] The result is a monetary model in which current income is related to current and prior nominal quantities of money.

The monetary model may be described as follows:[54]

The monetary sector   Given the assumption of unitary real income elasticity of the demand for money, Equation (4) can be rewritten as

$$M^d = F(r)Y. \qquad (4')$$

In order to simplify the exposition of the model, let us assume that the supply of money is determined exogenously:

$$M^s = M. \qquad (5')$$

Critics of Friedman have frequently pointed out that his extreme view of the role of money is valid only if the demand for money is insensitive to interest rates, implying a close linkage between the stock of money and income. In the light of the above discussion and his recent reformulation on the demand for money, this kind of criticism seems no longer valid. See also Milton Friedman, "Interest Rates and the Demand for Money" in his *The Optimum Quantity of Money and Other Essays*, 141–155.

[52]Friedman, "A Theoretical Framework for Monetary Analysis" (cited in footnote 46), 223. Both theories analyze short-run adjustments in terms of shifts from one static equilibrium position to another without explaining a dynamic adjustment process involved in such a change in equilibrium positions.

[53]This assumption is the counterpart of the third approach of the full employment and rigid-price assumptions of the quantity theory and income/expenditure theory.

[54]See Friedman, "A Monetary Theory of Nominal Income" (cited in footnote 46), 325–332.

Then Equations (4'), (5'), and equilibrium conditions (6) yield

$$M = F(r)Y. \tag{7}$$

Equation (7) can be written as

$$Y = \frac{1}{F(r)} M = H(r)M. \tag{8}$$

The Fisherian distinction between the nominal and real rate of interest is given by the following identity:[55]

$$r = q + \left(\frac{1}{P} \frac{dP}{dt} \right) \tag{9}$$

where q = the real rate of interest; $(1/P \, dP/dt)$ = the rate of change of the price level.

From Equation (9), it also follows that

$$r^* = q^* + \left(\frac{1}{P} \frac{dP}{dt} \right)^* \tag{10}$$

where the variables with an asterisk refer to anticipated (or expected) values.

Following Keynes' argument that market rates of interest are determined largely by speculators with firmly held expectations, Friedman assumes that[56]

$$r = r^* \tag{11}$$

From the identity, $Y = yP$, it follows that

$$\left(\frac{1}{P} \frac{dP}{dt} \right)^* = \left(\frac{1}{Y} \frac{dY}{dt} \right)^* - \left(\frac{1}{y} \frac{dy}{dt} \right)^* . \tag{12}$$

---

[55]Notice that both the simple quantity and income/expenditure theories assume a stable price level; hence, real and nominal rates of interest are the same.

[56]Suppose that a substantial number of asset owners have the same expectation on the future rate of interest and hold the expectation firmly, then the demand for money will become perfectly elastic at the current rate of interest that is equal to the expected rate of interest, namely, when $r = r^*$. Money and other earning assets (bonds in the Keynesian analysis) would become perfect substitutes; the demand for money has a liquidity trap at $r = r^*$. In this situation, the monetary authorities would not be able to change the rate of interest by changing the quantity of money; no matter what the monetary authorities do with the supply of money, asset owners will force the current rate of interest into conformity with their expectations on the future rate of interest. Friedman argues that this is the basic idea behind the Keynes' short-run liquidity trap. See Friedman, "A Theoretical Framework for Monetary Analysis" (cited in footnote 46), 214.

Combining Equations (10), (11), and (12) we obtain

$$r = q^* - g^* + \left(\frac{1}{Y} \frac{dY}{dt} \right)^* \tag{13}$$

where $g^* = (1/y \; dy/dt)^* = $ the anticipated rate of growth of real income.

Substitution of Equation (13) into (8) yields

$$Y = H \left[q^* - g^* + \left(\frac{1}{Y} \frac{dY}{dt} \right)^* \right] M. \tag{14}$$

Equation (14) states that the level of income Y is determined by q^*, g^*, $(1/Y \; dY/dt)^*$, and M. Friedman assumes that the difference between q^* and g^* is a constant. In a static framework, the expected rate of growth of nominal income $(1/Y \; dY/dt)^*$ may be treated as a predetermined variable. Then Equation (14) determines the level of nominal income for a given supply of money without any reference to the real sector of the model.[57] In a dynamic framework, however, it would be natural to regard $(1/Y \; dY/dt)^*$ as determined by the past history of nominal income. Since the past history of nominal income is

---

[57]Once we make the distinction between the nominal and real rate of interest, the rate of interest relevant to the consumption and investment functions is the real rate of interest, q. Hence, the equations describing the real sector of the model are modified as

$$\frac{C}{P} = f \left(\frac{Y}{P}, q \right) \tag{1'}$$

$$\frac{I}{P} = g(q) \tag{2'}$$

$$\frac{Y}{P} = \frac{C}{P} + \frac{I}{P}. \tag{3}$$

Assume that the realized real rate of interest q is constant,

$$q = q^* = q_0. \tag{15}$$

Then Equations (1')–(3) become a self-contained system of three equations with three unknowns: C/P, I/P, and Y/P. The price level would then be determined by substituting Y/P obtained from the real sector and Y from the monetary sector into the following identity, $Y = y \cdot P$.

Friedman considers this way of combining the monetary and real sectors as highly unsatisfactory for two reasons: the assumption of a constant real rate of interest is likely to introduce serious errors, particularly through the real sector, and the consumption function (1) ignores several important arguments, such as wealth and expected rate of inflation. See Friedman, "A Monetary Theory of Nominal Income" (cited in footnote 46), 330.

in turn a function of the past history of money as implied by Equation (8) for earlier dates, Equation (14) becomes a relation between the level of nominal income at each point in time and the past history of the quantity of money.

This dynamic character of the model may be better understood by analyzing an example given by Friedman. Take the logarithm of Equation (14) and differentiate with respect to time.

This gives

$$\frac{1}{Y}\frac{dY}{dt} = s \cdot \frac{d}{dt}\left(\frac{1}{Y}\frac{dY}{dt}\right)^{*} + \frac{1}{M}\frac{dM}{dt} \tag{15}$$

where $s = 1/H \; dH/dr =$ the slope of the regression of $\log H$ on the rate of interest.

Suppose that the expected rate of growth of nominal income is determined by an adaptive expectation process:[58]

$$\frac{d}{dt}\left(\frac{1}{Y}\frac{dY}{dt}\right)^{*} = \beta\left[\frac{1}{Y}\frac{dY}{dt} - \left(\frac{1}{Y}\frac{dY}{dt}\right)^{*}\right]. \tag{16}$$

Substituting Equation (16) into Equation (15) and solving for $(1/Y \; dY/dt)$, we have

$$\frac{1}{Y}\frac{dY}{dt} = \left(\frac{1}{Y}\frac{dY}{dt}\right)^{*} + \frac{1}{(1-\beta s)}\left[\frac{1}{M}\frac{dM}{dt} - \left(\frac{1}{Y}\frac{dY}{dt}\right)^{*}\right]. \tag{17}$$

When $(1/Y \; dY/dt)^{*} = 1/M \; dM/dt$, Equation (17) gives the quantity theory result that nominal income changes at the same rate as money supply.

Friedman states that his monetary model of nominal income corresponds to the broader framework implicit in much of the theoretical

[58]Equation (16) is analogous to

$$\left(\frac{1}{Y}\frac{dY}{dt}\right)^{*}_{T} = \int_{-\infty}^{T} e^{\beta(t-T)}\left(\frac{1}{Y}\frac{dY}{dt}\right)_{t} dt,$$

which means that the expected rate of growth of nominal income at T is a weighted average of past growth rates of nominal income, the weights ($e^{\beta(t-T)}$) declining exponentially where t is the time of the observation weighted. See Edgar L. Feige, "Expectations and Adjustments in the Monetary Sector," American Economic Association, *Papers and Proceedings of the Seventy-ninth Annual Meeting* (*The American Economic Review*, Vol. LVII, May 1967), 463–467.

and empirical work that he and others have done in analyzing monetary experience in the short run and is consistent with many of their empirical findings.[59]

However, Friedman's model sheds little light on his view concerning the precise mechanism through which changes in the quantity of money affect income. This is so because the model is designed primarily for empirical analysis of the relation between money and income. What this model reflects is rather his view on the appropriate empirical approach to evaluating the role of money—a view that is in sharp contrast to the more common one held by nonmonetarists. Contrary to the impression that one might gather from his model—possibly a rigid and mechanical connection between money and income—his view on the transmission mechanism in a conceptual framework is a complicated portfolio adjustment process that involves many uncertain channels and impinges on a wide array of assets and expenditures. The process[60] following an exogenous change in the supply of money begins with changes in the prices and yields of financial assets and spreads to nonfinancial assets. These changes in the prices of financial and nonfinancial assets influence spending to produce new assets and spending on current services. At the same time, these changes alter wealth of the public relative to income and thereby affect consumption. This is, in a simple fashion, the way in which the initial impulse is diffused from the financial markets to the markets for goods and services. The exposition stresses portfolio adjustment and is strikingly similar to that described by many economists.

The transmission process is also essentially consistent with the Keynesian liquidity preference doctrine as to how money affects income. As in the income/expenditure theory, interest rates play a key role. This being so, it has been pointed out that Friedman cannot be saying anything different from Keynes[61] and that there is no clear reason why one should look at money supply as a target as Friedman

[59]Friedman, "A Monetary Theory of Nominal Income" (cited in footnote 46), 324 and 334.

[60]Milton Friedman and Anna J. Schwartz, "Money and Business Cycles," *The Review of Economics and Statistics*, Vol. XLV (Supplement, February 1963), 59–63; Milton Friedman and David Meiselman, "The Relative Stability of Monetary Velocity and the Investment Multiplier in the United States, 1877–1958," *Stabilization Policies*, Commission on Money and Credit (Englewood Cliffs, New Jersey, 1963), 217–222; Milton Friedman, "The Role of Monetary Policy," in his *The Optimum Quantity of Money and Other Essays* (cited in footnote 51), 100, and *The Counter-Revolution in Monetary Theory* (cited in footnote 44), 24–25.

[61]Nicholas Kaldor, "The New Monetarism," *Lloyd's Bank Review* (July 1970), 9.

insists rather than at interest rates directly.[62] However, these criticisms miss the fundamental points of Friedman's view. The difference between Friedman and the nonmonetarists concerning the transmission process is not whether changes in the supply of money operate through interest rates but rather (i) the range of interest rates considered and (ii) the empirical approach to estimating the actual influence of monetary policy. Friedman argues that the impact of monetary policy is likely to be understated in magnitude and narrowed in scope in the Keynesian income/expenditure theory. One reason is that, since monetary policy impinges on a broad range of capital assets and a correspondingly broad range of associated expenditures, the Keynesian practice of looking only at recorded market interest rates, which are only part of a much broader spectrum of rates, makes one underestimate the actual impact of monetary policy. The rates of interest that influence investment decisions are for the most part implicit yields and hence not observable, so that one cannot hope to obtain useful results by looking at relations between market interest rates and the categories of spending associated with these rates. Also, recorded market interest rates may not provide an appropriate measure of the cost of capital, since these interest rates are not real rates of interest that reflect the basic forces of productivity but nominal rates that are influenced by the expected rate of inflation. Moreover, monetary influences may work through channels that we have not been able to identify. In fact, it may not be possible to trace through any particular channel, as monetary policy operates through an extremely complicated process of portfolio adjustments.

For all these reasons, Friedman considers that even the most complex structure of a general equilibrium model cannot be expected to capture actual monetary influences adequately. A more reliable empirical approach would be to pursue the methodology of positive economics, the essence of which is to select the crucial and simple theoretical relationships that allow one to predict something large (such as GNP) from something small (for instance, the supply of money), regardless of the intervening chain of causation. One such relationship is claimed to be the velocity function relating income to money, which is the essence of the quantity theory; another is the

[62]H. C. Wallich, "Quantity Theory and Quantity Policy," ch. 10 in *Ten Economic Studies in the Tradition of Irving Fisher* (New York, 1967), 260.

multiplier relationship relating income to autonomous expenditure, which is the essence of the income/expenditure theory.[63]

Friedman argues that the velocity function (that is, the relationship between money and nominal income) has been shown, on average, to be more stable and less affected by institutional and historical change than the multiplier relationship and that, consequently, the velocity function may be the key relationship in understanding macroeconomic developments.[64] It then follows that a much more promising approach to the question of evaluating the affects of monetary policy on the economy is to try to relate changes in income directly to changes in the quantity of money. Friedman's monetary model of nominal income seems to reflect this point of view.

Friedman's view, however, raises two important issues. One issue is concerned with the conditions under which one could derive a simple relationship between income and money. It has been argued frequently that Friedman's view is valid only if the demand for money is not significantly influenced by the rate of interest. As indicated earlier, Friedman now states clearly and repeatedly that the rate of interest is an important determinant of the demand for money. If indeed the demand for money depends on the rate of interest, then one cannot—critics of Friedman argue—hope to find such a simple relationship between money and income, unless one specifies an independent theory of the determination of the rate of interest.

The Keynes and Fisher synthesis that Friedman incorporates into his monetary model appears to be one such independent theory. It is an independent theory in the sense that the determination of the nominal rate of interest depends on relationships outside the system of six equations. According to Friedman's monetary model, the rate of interest is determined solely by the anticipated rate of growth of money income $(1/Y \; dY/dt)^*$, given the assumptions that $r = r^*$ and that $q^* - g^* = k_0$. While these assumptions are crucial to a model that allows one to relate current money income directly to current and prior quantities of money, it should be realized that they are also responsible for sev-

[63]This is Johnson's interpretation of Friedman's view. See Johnson, "Recent Developments in Monetary Theory—A Commentary" (cited in footnote 1), 86–87; see also Johnson, "The Keynesian Revolution and the Monetarist Counter-Revolution" (cited in footnote 1), 9.

[64]See Friedman and Meiselman, "The Relative Stability of Monetary Velocity and the Investment Multiplier in the United States, 1877–1958" (cited in footnote 60).

eral defects of the model. One serious defect is that the model rules out liquidity or substitution effects of a change in the quantity of money on the interest rate.

In Friedman's monetary model, a change in the rate of change of money supply ($1/M \ dM/dt$) directly affects the rate of growth of nominal income ($1/Y \ dY/dt$) (see Equation 17) with little direct effect on change in the interest rates, that is, the change does not initially produce the liquidity effect but immediately produces an income effect. The change in ($1/Y \ dY/dt$) then causes a change in the expected rate of growth of nominal income ($1/Y \ dY/dt$)* (Equation 16), which, in turn, influences the nominal rate of interest (Equation 13). In other words, the change in the rate of change in money supply affects market rates of interest only as it influences the courses of current and expected nominal income and, in consequence, the expected rate of inflation. This process does not appear to be supported by the existing empirical evidence on the effects of changes in money supply on the interest rates and income.[65] Nor does it seem to be consistent with Friedman's own earlier exposition on the transmission mechanism of monetary policy, in which he argues that a change in the supply of money has its first impact on the financial markets and much later on the market for goods and services.[66]

However, the failure of the model to explain the liquidity effect is clearly not a point of disagreement with Friedman, for he admits that the model neglects the effects of changes in the nominal quantity of money on interest rates.[67] Yet, it is not clear to what extent he ap-

---

[65]In examining the relationship between changes in the rate of change in money supply and changes in the commercial paper rates, Cagan found that an increase in the monetary growth rate initially exerts a negative liquidity effect on the interest rate. The negative effect is then offset by positive income and price effects within about one year, following the increase in the monetary growth rate. See Phillip Cagan, "The Channels of Monetary Effects on Interest Rates" (mimeographed, National Bureau of Economic Research, 1966).

Friedman himself acknowledges that change in the rate of change in the quantity of money will have no appreciable effect on the rate of change in money income for six months to nine months, on average, in the United States. See Friedman, "A Monetary Theory of Nominal Income" (cited in footnote 46), 335.

In a recent study by Gibson, however, the initial liquidity effects are shown to be fully offset by positive effects only after a period of three or five months, depending on which definition of money one uses. See William E. Gibson, "Interest Rates and Monetary Policy," *Journal of Political Economy*, Vol. 78 (May/June 1970), 431–455.

[66]See footnote 60.

[67]See Friedman, "A Monetary Theory of Nominal Income" (cited in footnote 46), 333. He also states that the model cannot explain satisfactorily the movements of inter-

preciates the analytical significance of relaxing either of his two critical assumptions to permit a strong liquidity effect in the model. Relaxation of these assumptions would mean that Friedman's model would be modified in such a way that the rate of interest is determined within the model through the interaction of demand for and supply of money together with other behavioral relationships in the real sector of the economy. Such a modification would then suggest that one may not utilize velocity to derive a simple relation between money income and the quantity of money.

The other issue that Friedman's monetary model raises is whether the methodology of positive economics embodied in the model is a scientifically acceptable method. The general consensus seems to be that the methodology is seriously inadequate. We shall return to this topic in some detail in the final section of this paper.

Brunner and Meltzer

The transmission process described by Brunner and Meltzer is basically a process of portfolio (balance sheet) adjustment, which is, on a general level of discussion, shared by both neo-Keynesians and other monetarists.[68] The difference between Brunner and Meltzer and other economists, if any, may be found in the different degrees of emphasis on the importance of real capital in the mechanism. Brunner and Meltzer point out that the analysis of portfolio balance reveals that changes in the level of output emerge fundamentally from this balance sheet adjustment, particularly in response to the public's decision to adjust its real capital holdings. In order, then, to capture the total effects of monetary policy changes, it is necessary to specify the appropriate

---

ests and velocity in the first 9 months or so after a distinct change in the rate of monetary growth. (*Ibid.*, 335.)

[68]For a more detailed discussion, see Karl Brunner, "The Report of the Commission on Money and Credit," *The Journal of Political Economy*, Vol. LXIX (December 1961), 605–620; Karl Brunner, "Some Major Problems in Monetary Theory," American Economic Association, *Papers and Proceedings of the Seventy-third Annual Meeting* (*The American Economic Review*, Vol. LI, May 1961), 47–56; Karl Brunner and Allan H. Meltzer. "The Place of Financial Intermediaries in the Transmission of Monetary Policy," American Economic Association, *Papers and Proceedings of the Seventy-fifth Annual Meeting* (*The American Economic Review*, Vol. LIII, May 1963), 372–382; Karl Brunner, "The Relative Price Theory of Money, Output, and Employment" (unpublished based on a paper presented at the Midwestern Economic Association Meetings, April 1967); Brunner and Meltzer, "Fiscal and Monetary Policy in a Non-Keynesian World" (cited in footnote 22).

stock-flow relationship centered on real capital goods, since changes in the asset price of real capital relative to its output price form a crucial linkage in the transmission process. Accordingly, they distinguish four classes of output—output for real consumption and for Types I, II, and III of capital goods—and also consider various financial assets together with the stocks of real capital disaggregated into the three types.

Type I capital goods are those that have separate market prices for equity claims on existing stock and for new output. (Examples under this category would be machinery, plant, and equipment.)[69] Type II capital goods have a single price for existing assets and new output of comparable quality (housing and automobiles); Type III has a price for new output only, and there is no market for existing assets or claims to them (consumer durables, such as washing machines). Corresponding to these different types of capital goods are different paths through which monetary policy can affect the real economy. An increase in the supply of money, for example, will, through portfolio substitutions, lead to an overall increase in the asset prices of all these types of real capital goods. The increase in the equity price for Type I real capital relative to its output price accelerates the actual rate of accumulation of this type of capital goods.[70] The increase in the asset price of Type II capital, *ceteris paribus*, stimulates the production of Type II capital goods. Furthermore, the rise in the asset prices of real capital and the fall in the rates of return on financial assets result in an increase in the market value of public wealth, which, in turn, raises the desired stock of Type III capital and consumption expenditure. The total effects of the expansionary monetary policy will then be the sum of these influences.[71]

The income/expenditure theory as represented by the conventional *IS–LM* framework, in Brunner and Meltzer's view, fails to accommodate the public's stock-flow behavior bearing on its real capital position, which they consider crucial in the transmission process. Because of this failure, Brunner and Meltzer argue that the Keynesian approach of relating investment expenditure to interest rates in some

---

[69]The transmission mechanism identified in the analysis of the neo-Keynesian portion centers around Type I capital goods.

[70]This process is analogous to the one described and emphasized by neo-Keynesians.

[71]Brunner and Meltzer, "The Place of Financial Intermediaries in the Transmission of Monetary Policy" (cited in footnote 68), 374–377. Brunner and Meltzer do not emphasize the interest rate effect on the desired stock of Type II capital but only the wealth effect.

financial assets as a measure of the costs of borrowing—supplemented by the wealth effect—can hardly capture the actual impact of monetary policy and that, thus, the Keynesian approach should be rejected. A more satisfactory approach that would be consistent with Brunner and Meltzer's view would require a structural model of general equilibrium—a model that specifies the whole spectrum of real and financial assets and the explicit relations between the production of new real capital goods and the existing ones. In a recent unpublished paper,[72] Brunner and Meltzer attempt to construct such a model. However, in formulating the model they choose to ignore entirely the markets for Types II and III of real capital goods and focus on the market for Type I real capital, the equity market. The result of this modification, or simplification, of their view is a model that is, in all important aspects, analogous to the neo-Keynesian model discussed in the Appendix.*

Therefore, the model suggests that Brunner and Meltzer—contrary to their claim—accept the Keynesian view on the nature of the transmission process; what they seem to reject is the heuristic simplification of reality with regard to the range of assets considered in the Keynesian income/expenditure theory . . .

IV. Concluding Remarks

The main purpose of this paper has been to review divergent views on the transmission process of monetary policy. The review indicates that at the level of general description there appear to be no significant differences in the transmission process of monetary influences among a variety of monetary economists. Both monetarists and nonmonetarists appear to support some version of the portfolio adjustment process as a framework to describe the effects of monetary policy on the real economy. The disagreement between them on this process centers on the range of assets and interest rates that should be considered and the technical relationships involving the stocks of real assets and the flows of real expenditure corresponding to these assets. The range of assets and interest rates considered by nonmonetarists is rather limited, whereas monetarists stress a broad range of assets and the expenditures asso-

---

[72]Brunner and Meltzer, "Fiscal and Monetary Policy in a Non-Keynesian World" (cited in footnote 22).
*The Appendix to this article is not reprinted here.—Ed.

ciated with these assets. Also, both monetarists and nonmonetarists emphasize the wealth effect channel and, in various forms, the credit rationing channel.

From these observations one might conclude that the question of the relative effectiveness of monetary and fiscal policy is essentially an empirical issue, not a theoretical one. Although the issue has evoked a great deal of empirical study in recent years, the controversy still is far from being settled. The evidence from several of the large-scale econometric models—the estimation method favored by nonmonetarists—is that monetary variables are, in general, less important than fiscal variables in influencing aggregate expenditures.[73]

On the other hand, monetarists have produced an imposing volume of empirical evidence of several kinds in support of their central proposition. One kind of evidence draws on historical case studies, such as the one by Friedman and Schwartz,[74] and the experience of a number of countries with easy-money policies that led to inflation after World War II. A second type of evidence is the "statistical stability" of the demand function for money in several industrial countries, notably in the United States. Some monetarists view the demand function for money as the crucial relationship in the understanding of macroeconomic developments. The stability of this function is then presented as evidence in favor of the traditional quantity theory as opposed to the income/expenditure theory, and the function is then used to explain and to predict the level of money income.[75] The demand function for money may well be of central importance to economic activity. However, insofar as the money demand is sensitive to interest rates, evidence for which has been demonstrated beyond any reasonable doubt in all of the major empirical studies on the demand function for money, one has to provide a theory of the determination of interest rates along with its interrelationship with a theory of income determination to prove that money indeed matters. A third type of empirical evidence bearing on this question is the reduced form equation studies, which invariably

[73]A notable exception is the Federal Reserve–MIT quarterly econometric model for the United States. It shows that monetary policy has a powerful effect, although less powerful than suggested by monetarists. See de Leeuw and Gramlich, "The Channels of Monetary Policy" (cited in footnote 20).

[74]Milton Friedman and Anna Jacobson Schwartz, *Monetary History of the United States, 1867–1960*, National Bureau of Economic Research, Studies in Business Cycles, No. 12 (Princeton University Press, 1963).

[75]See Karl Brunner and Allan H. Meltzer, "Predicting Velocity: Implications for Theory and Policy," *The Journal of Finance*, Vol. XVIII (1963), pp. 319–54.

show that the quantity of money is far more significant than various exogenous components of aggregate demand in explaining the movements in money income.

The debate on the reduced form approach, or the direct estimation method, also reflects a sharp disagreement between nonmonetarists and monetarists on the methodological questions of how best to estimate the effects of monetary and fiscal actions on the level of economic activity. As noted above, nonmonetarists favor estimation through large-scale econometric models. Monetarists, however, argue that the channels through which monetary policy operates are so diverse and complicated that it is inherently impossible to identify and to measure them with structural equation models, no matter how detailed they may be. Basically, for this reason, they contend that a more reliable method would be the direct estimation technique whereby final demand variables, such as money GNP, are regressed upon monetary and fiscal variables.

No one would deny the complexity involved in the channels of monetary policy; however, the important questions are whether this complexity justifies the use of the reduced form approach and, if it does, whether the approach is a scientifically acceptable method. Judging by the prevailing standards of academic economics, indeed, the direct estimation approach is seriously inadequate as an empirical methodology.[76]

One of the most serious weaknesses of the approach is that the structural model from which a reduced form equation is derived may not be consistent internally. The direct estimation approach completely ignores a priori restrictions on the coefficients of the independent variables of the equation, for example, the restrictions that are built into general equilibrium models through identities, lags, omitting variables, etc. Because of the absence of these restrictions, there is no way of knowing whether the structural model is consistent internally.[77] If it

[76]Johnson, "The Keynesian Revolution and the Monetarist Counter-Revolution" (cited in footnote 1), p. 12.

[77]A good example of the internal inconsistency of a reduced form equation may be found in the recent study by Leonall C. Andersen and J. Jordan, "Monetary and Fiscal Actions: A Test of Their Relative Importance in Economic Stabilization," Federal Reserve Bank of St.Louis, *Review*, Vol. L (November 1968), 11–24. They show that the impact coefficient of government expenditure on the level of money income is less than unity. Given that money income should rise by at least the same amount as the increase in government expenditure, Andersen and Jordan's finding means that some private endogenous spending is falling by a larger amount as a consequence of the government expenditure. Since they do not specify the structural model of their reduced form equation, one cannot determine what expenditure is falling and why. One possible

is not, the reduced form equation is no more than a linear equation relating an "alleged" endogenous variable, such as money GNP, to a set of "alleged" exogenous variables with no meaningful economic causations between the endogenous and exogenous variables.

Another equally damaging weakness is the problem of selecting exogenous monetary and fiscal variables. Depending upon which variable one assumes to be exogenous—monetary base, free reserves, narrow money, or broad money on the monetary side and the various definitions of autonomous expenditures on the fiscal side—one can take a "money mostly" stance, a "fiscal policy mostly" stance, or a "both matter" stance.[78]

In response to the first defect, some monetarists have begun to extend their efforts in specifying the details of the structural models that underlie the various reduced form equations that they estimate. These models are invariably some version of Keynesian income/expenditure models.[79] Therefore, the response may be an open admission that monetarists are increasingly compromising with the Keynesian income/expenditure theory, which they had set out to question. The response also suggests that monetarists are, in compromising with nonmonetarists, burdening themselves with another difficult task, namely, giving a convincing explanation as to why such a great divergence exists in empirical evidence between the reduced form and structural model approaches. A satisfactory answer has yet to come.

In view of these assessments of the monetarist view, it appears that one cannot read too much into the results of various reduced form equation studies. These assessments also suggest that a more promising road toward the settlement of the controversy concerning the relative strengths of fiscal and monetary actions lies in further development and refinement of existing econometric models. In this regard, the monetarist view suggests a number of factors that have been inadequately treated in existing models and that may account partly for the sluggish response of monetary influences in these models.

---

reason for such a low impact coefficient may be that the structural model is not consistent internally. See Edward M. Gramlich, "The Usefulness of Monetary and Fiscal Policy as Discretionary Stabilization Tools," *Journal of Money, Credit and Banking*, Vol. III (1971), 514.

[78]*Ibid.*, 523–524.

[79]This type of response can be found in a series of unpublished articles by Andersen in which he develops a Keynesian income/expenditure model and then derives from the model a reduced form equation. See Leonall C. Andersen, "Influence of Monetary and Fiscal Actions in a Financially Constrained Economy" (unpublished paper, May 1971).

We may point out two such factors relevant to our subject matter. One possible factor is the failure of existing econometric models to include implicit rates of return on real capital and consumer durables. The other is the failure to distinguish between nominal and real interest rates in some of these models. The rates of interest used in these models are nominal rates that are affected by the expectation on future prices. However, interest rates that are relevant to the consumption and investment functions are clearly the real rates of interest that are relatively unaffected by changes in the level of prices. It has been shown empirically that high nominal interest rates are accompanied by a high rate of increase in money supply—an easy stance of monetary policy—and vice versa.[80] This is so because a high growth rate of money supply causes a rise in current prices and then the expectation of future inflation, which ultimately leads to a higher nominal rate of interest. It is, therefore, questionable whether nominal interest rates are meaningful indicators of the monetary posture, except perhaps in the very short run.

When these and other factors[81] are properly taken into consideration, it is quite possible that econometric models may turn up a much sharper and more rapid response of monetary influence than has been shown in the past.

Econometric Models: The Monetarist and Non-Monetarist Views Compared

Joseph M. Crews

The Non-Monetarist View

Two fundamentally different views of the role of money in economic activity underlie current econometric models. The Monetarist view is

---

[80]See, for example, William P. Yohe and Denis S. Karnosky, "Interest Rates and Price Level Changes, 1952-69," Federal Reserve Bank of St. Louis, *Review*, Vol. 51 (December 1969), 18–38; William E. Gibson, "Price Expectations Effects on Interest Rates," *The Journal of Finance*, Vol. XXV (1970), 19–34; Gibson, "Interest Rates and Monetary Policy" (cited in footnote 65).

[81]For other factors, see David I. Fand, "The Monetary Theory of Nine Recent Quarterly Econometric Models of the United States: A Comment," *Journal of Money, Credit and Banking*, Vol. III (1971), 450–460.

Reprinted with deletions from the Federal Reserve Bank of Richmond, *Monthly Review* (February 1973), 3–12, by permission of the publisher and the author. The footnotes have been renumbered to follow the abridged article.

formulated as an econometric model by the Federal Reserve Bank of St. Louis. The non-Monetarist view, based largely on a disaggregated Keynesian approach to monetary analysis, has given rise to several large-scale econometric models containing up to several hundred equations. The approach is illustrated in this article by the so-called FRB-MIT model.[1]

The Historical Setting

Prior to the Depression of the 1930s, conventional economic theory considered the economy basically stable over the long run and tending toward full employment. The main theme of theoretical analysis was toward long-run equilibrium relationships, with little attention devoted to the short-run process through which long-run equilibrium was atained. In this context, the quantity of money, together with the level of output, was viewed as determining the level of prices, but having little to do with long-run real productive growth. This *quantity theory* was brought into serious question as a result of the Depression. The development of an alternative theory of money, interest, and output was initiated by the British economist John Maynard Keynes.

Neo-Keynesian Theory

The approach to macroeconomics developed by Keynes and those who refined his work is known as the income-expenditure approach. Its basic characteristics may be summarized briefly. First, the economy is viewed as consisting of a number of sectors, e.g., the consumption, investment, and government sectors. Demand in each sector is determined by factors peculiar to the sector. Then, all sectoral demands are added together to determine aggregate demand, measured by gross national product, GNP. This process is illustrated in Exhibit 1, where Equations 1 and 2 determine consumption and investment demand; government demand is exogenous. Aggregate demand is added together in Equation 4. With larger, more complex models, each of these

---

[1]Frank de Leeuw and Edward M. Gramlich, "The Channels of Monetary Policy: A Further Report on the Federal Reserve–MIT Model," *Journal of Finance,* 24 (May 1969), 265–290; and Leonall C. Andersen and Keith M. Carlson, "A Monetarist Model for Economic Stabilization," *Review,* Federal Reserve Bank of St. Louis, 52 (April 1970), 7–25. [The De Leeuw-Gramlich article and a more recent update of the Andersen-Carlson article are reprinted in this book. Ed.]

(1) $C_t = a_0 + a_1 Y_t + a_2 C_{t-1}$

(2) $I_t = b_0 + b_1 P_t + b_2 K_{t-1}$

(3) $W_t = c_0 + c_1 Y_t + c_2 t$

(4) $Y_t = C_t + I_t + G_t$

(5) $P_t = Y_t - W_t$

(6) $K_t = K_{t-1} + I_t$

where C = consumption

   Y = income

   W = wage income

   P = nonwage income

   I = net investment

   K = capital stock at end of period

   G = government expenditures on goods and services

   t = time

Exhibit 1. An Illustrative Model

Source: Adapted from a similar model presented in M. Liebenberg, A. Hirsch, and J. Popkin, "A Quarterly Econometric Model of the United States: A Progress Report," *Survey of Current Business*, 46 (May 1966), 13-16.

major components of aggregate demand is disaggregated. Consumption may be divided into expenditures for durables, nondurables, and services; in some cases, automobile demand is explained separately. Investment may be broken down into expenditures for producers' equipment, producers' structures, residential construction, and inventory changes. Government spending may be classified as Federal or state and local, with Federal expenditures further subdivided as defense or nondefense. This disaggregation procedure can be carried to any practical degree of detail, limited, of course, by the availability of appropriate data.

A second characteristic of neo-Keynesian models is a built-in policy transmission mechanism that deemphasizes the role of money. For the most part, this mechanism involves the *indirect* linkage of money with aggregate demand *via* interest rates. In its simplest form, it may be stated symbolically as:

$$\text{OMO} \rightarrow R \rightarrow M \rightarrow i \rightarrow I \rightarrow \text{GNP}.$$

An open market purchase of Government securities by the Federal Reserve, OMO, increases commercial bank reserves, R, and raises the banks' reserves-earning assets ratio. Banks operate to restore their desired ratios by extending new loans or by expanding bank credit in other ways. New loans create new demand deposits, thereby increasing the money supply, M. Given the public's liquidity preferences, a rising money supply causes the general level of interest rates, i, to decline. Given businessmen's "expected profits," expressed by Keynes as the *marginal efficiency of investment*, falling interest rates, i.e., reduced capital costs, induce expanded investment expenditures, I. Finally, increased investment spending causes successive rounds of new final demand spending, causing GNP to rise by a multiple of the initial change in investment.[2]

A number of refinements to this process have been made by later economists. For example, this transmission process involves Keynes's liquidity preference trade-off of money and financial assets. In more sophisticated versions, this trade-off is generalized to better approximate a real world of "numerous financial assets, hence numerous interest rates on . . . different securities. Different types of investment spending are most sensitive to particular interest rates, e.g., plant and equipment investment to the corporate bond rate, residential construction to the mortgage rate, and inventory investment to the bank-loan rate."[3] Policy-induced changes in bank reserves cause portfolio adjustments over a wide range of financial and real assets, eventually influencing the components of final demand spending.

In further refinement of the Keynesian theory, a number of writers now argue that changes in the money supply have direct wealth effects on consumption spending, in addition to the indirect wealth effects operating via interest rate changes, described above.

Two other characteristics of neo-Keynesian models are important as points of comparison with Monetarist models. First, the money supply, in the process described above, is an endogenous variable,

---

[2]William L. Silber, "Monetary Channels and the Relative Importance of Money Supply and Bank Porfolios," *Journal of Finance*, 24 (March 1969), 81–82.
[3]*Ibid.*, 84–85.

whereas Monetarists consider it exogenous. Second, the basic Keynesian model treats the price level as independent of monetary forces. Large-scale neo-Keynesian econometric models, which generally encompass nonmonetary theories of price level determination, are consistent with this treatment. These two points will be clarified at appropriate points in the discussion below.

The FRB–MIT Model

The generalized neo-Keynesian approach to model building may be illustrated by the FRB–MIT model, which is a large-scale model of the U.S. economy constructed by the Board of Governors of the Federal Reserve System and the Economics Department of the Massachusetts Institute of Technology. Its stated purpose is to quantify the monetary policy process and its impact on the economy.[4] The model consists of 10 sectors, the most important of which are the financial, investment, and consumption/inventory sectors. The financial sector is displayed in Exhibit 2 and the real sector in Exhibit 3.

The financial sector The purpose of the financial sector is to establish the linkage between the instruments of monetary policy and the financial variables that are important in the real sector of the economy. Several types of variables appear in this sector. First, the instruments of monetary policy are nonborrowed reserves and the Federal Reserve discount rate. Nonborrowed reserves serve as a proxy for open market operations. Second, demands for short-term financial assets are explained. These assets include free reserves, demand deposits, currency, commercial loans, and time deposits held by banks, savings and loan associations, and mutual savings banks. Supply, i.e., rate-setting, equations explain interest rates on Treasury bills, commercial loans, commercial paper, mortgages, industrial bonds, and state and local bonds. Other rate-setting equations determine the stock market yield and rates on time deposits held by banks, savings and loan associations, and mutual savings banks. A term-structure equation relates the corporate bond rate to the commercial paper rate.

The workings of the financial sector may be illustrated by tracing the effects of a Federal Reserve purchase of Government securities, represented in the model as an increase in nonborrowed reserves, RU.

---

[4]See de Leeuw and Gramlich, *op cit.*, 266.

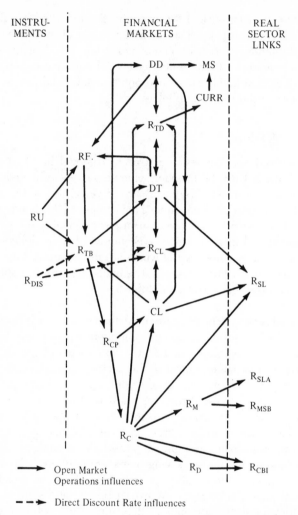

| INSTRU-MENTS | FINANCIAL MARKETS | REAL SECTOR LINKS |

Open Market
Operations influences

- - → Direct Discount Rate influences

Exhibit 2. The monetary policy process of the FRB–MIT Model

As shown in Exhibit 2, this purchase causes a rise in free reserves, RF, and a rise in the price of Treasury bills, represented by a fall in the bill rate, RTB. Commercial banks are assumed to have, under given market conditions, a desired proportion of earning to nonearning assets (reserves). An increase in nonborrowed reserves lowers the proportion of earning assets in the banks' portfolios below the desired level. In attempting to restore this ratio, banks attempt to purchase similar fixed coupon, short-term financial assets, increase their loan offerings, and increase their demands for commercial paper. The declining Treasury bill rate represents not only a decline in the yield on short-term Government securities but also a decline in short rates generally, for which RTB is a proxy. Other short rates, the commercial paper rate, RCP, and the rate on commercial loans, RCL, follow RTB downward. There follows a complex adjustment process serving to restore portfolio balance to the commercial banking market. This process is expressed primarily in the equations that determine the time deposit rate and the commercial loan rate.[5]

Part of the adjustment involves acquisition of longer-term financial assets, represented by a term-structure relationship linking the commercial paper rate and the corporate bond rate, RC. The corporate bond rate influences other long-term rates, the mortgage rate, RM, and the stock market yield, RD. These rates pass the monetary stimulus to the real sector by way of the industrial bond rate, RCBI; the state and local government bond rate, RSL; and the deposit rates of nonbank savings institutions, RSLA and RMSB.

The financial-real sector linkage   Monetary effects spread through the economy by way of three separate channels: the cost of capital, the net worth of households, and the availability of credit to the household sector. Continuing the above illustration, the impact of lower interest rates may be traced in Exhibit 3. The cost-of-capital channel captures the effect of three long-term interest rates—the corporate bond rate, the mortgage rate, and the stock market yield—on investment expenditures for plant and equipment, expenditures for consumer durables, expenditures for single- and multiple-family housing, and state and local Government construction spending.[6]

---

[5]This process is simplified in two ways for presentation in Exhibit 2. First, the portfolio balance terms are commercial loan-to-deposit ratios, which serve as measures of portfolio composition in determining each financial institution's desired deposit or loan rate. The actual market rate is a function of the discrepancy between the lagged actual rate and the desired rate. For simplicity, in Exhibit 2 each separate component of these ratios is shown rather than the full ratio. For example, rather than showing the ratio: CL/DD + DT, each component—commercial loans, CL; demand deposits, DD; and time deposits, DT—is shown separately. Second, in order to simplify the chart and to emphasize financial market interaction, no real sector feedback variables appear. These variables, such as GNP or net worth, enter the several asset demand equations as transactions or scaling variables. For further discussion of these points, see de Leeuw and Gramlich, *op. cit.*, 267–80.

[6]For a more detailed description of the cost-of-capital channel, see de Leeuw and Gramlich, *loc. cit.*

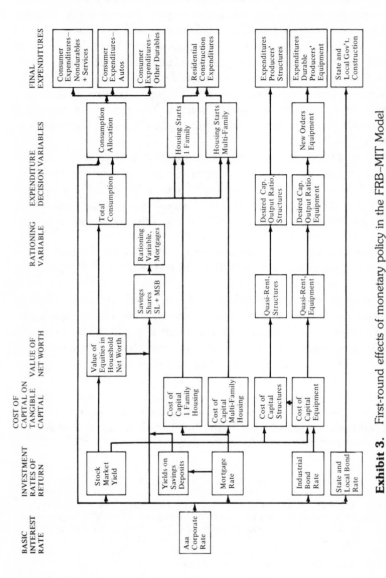

Exhibit 3. First-round effects of monetary policy in the FRB–MIT Model

Source: Frank de Leeuw and Edward M. Gramlich, "The Channels of Monetary Policy," *Journal of Finance*, 24 (May 1969).

The net worth channel passes the effect of changing rates of return on bonds to the stock yield, to equity values in the net worth of households, and to consumption expenditures.

Finally, credit rationing, the third channel, is found to be important in the housing sector. Savings institutions experience large fluctuations in their deposit flows, because of the sluggishness of their lending and deposit rates. In addition, their portfolios usually include a high proportion of long-term, low turnover mortgages. In times of rising interest rates, these institutions are forced to restrict mortgage lending. This nonprice rationing of credit influences the residential construction component of final demand.

The FRB–MIT model thus illustrates two basic characteristics of neo-Keynesian models: (1) a highly detailed sector-by-sector buildup of aggregate demand and (2) a detailed specification of the portfolio adjustment process that attaches a central role to interest rates as an indirect link between monetary policy and final demand.

As a point of comparison with Monetarist models, one further characteristic of the FRB–MIT model should be mentioned. Prices are determined in this model by real sector forces, that is, by a variable markup over wage costs.[7] Factors influencing the size of this markup include a productivity trend variable, which allows producers to maintain profit shares even though wages rise faster than prices. Demand shifts and nonlabor cost-push forces are other factors involved in this essentially nonmonetary theory of the price level.

The Monetarist View

Although the quantity theory was in eclipse during the period of neo-Keynesian preeminence, a group of economists, led by Professor Milton Friedman at the University of Chicago, continued to develop the Monetarist approach, restructuring the theory and gathering supporting statistical evidence. With the problems of increasing inflation in the late 1960s and the questionable effectiveness of the 1968 tax surcharge in dampening inflationary pressures, the policy prescriptions and forecasts of neo-Keynesian economists became increasingly subject to question.[8] The Monetarist view gained increased respect among academic economists and policymakers.

[7]See de Leeuw and Gramlich, *op cit.*, Appendix, A15–16.
[8]There is some debate concerning the effectiveness of the 1968 tax surcharge. See, for example, Robert Eisner, "Fiscal and Monetary Policy Reconsidered," *American*

Monetarist Theory

Modern Monetarists consider the economy basically stable, with most elements of instability the product of faulty monetary arrangements or improper policy. The reasoning behind this may be briefly summarized. First, there is a stable, but not precise, relationship between the growth rates of money and nominal, i.e., current dollar, national income or GNP. If money balances grow more rapidly in relation to income than people wish, they will attempt to spend the excess, causing prices to rise. On the other hand, if money grows too slowly in relation to income, people will try to build up their cash balances by reducing spending, which would result in a slowing of income growth and rising unemployment.[9] Changes in money and income do not occur simultaneously. On the average, a change in monetary growth will result in a change in real output growth 6 to 9 months later, followed by changes in prices in another six to nine months, according to Friedman's estimates.[10]

Carrying this logic further, the Monetarists consider fiscal policy, when not accompanied by changes in the money supply, to be an unlikely source of economic change. For example, increased Government spending, if not accompanied by monetary expansion, will tend to "crowd out" some private spending and have minimal impact on aggregate demand.[11] Fiscal policy distributes income between the private and public sectors but has little impact on price level changes.[12] Thus, short-run variations in prices, output, and employment are thought to be dominated by movements in a policy-determined money supply.[13]

Long-run real economic growth, on the other hand, is thought to be independent of monetary change, being determined by basic

---

Economic Review, 59 (December 1969), 897–905; and the subsequent comments and reply in *American Economic Review*, 61 (June 1971), 444–461. See also, Milton Friedman, "The Counter-Revolution in Monetary Theory," *Occasional Paper No. 33* (London: The Institute of Economic Affairs, 1970), 19–20, and Arthur M. Okun, "The Personal Tax Surcharge and Consumer Demand, 1968–70." *Brookings Papers on Economic Activity* (January 1971), 167–213.

[9] William N. Cox, III, "The Money Supply Controversy," *Monthly Review*, Federal Reserve Bank of Atlanta, 54 (June 1969), 73.

[10] Friedman, *op. cit.*, 22.

[11] Andersen and Carlson, *op. cit.*, 8.

[12] Friedman, *op. cit.*, 24.

[13] Ronald L. Teigen, "A Critical Look at Monetarist Economics," *Review*, Federal Reserve Bank of St. Louis, 54 (January 1972), 13.

growth factors such as expanding productive capacity, population growth, advancing technology, and natural resources. In the long run, monetary change affects only the price level. Accordingly, the basic objective of monetary policy is to "prevent money itself from being a major source of economic disturbance."[14] It follows that stabilization policy should seek a growth rate of money that closely approximates the long-term rate of growth of real productive capacity.

The Monetarist view of the role of interest rates in the policy transmission process may be summarized in the following way:

> Monetary impulses are . . . transmitted by the play of interest rates over a vast array of assets. Variations in interest rates change relative prices of existing assets, relative to both yields and the supply prices of new production. Acceleration or deceleration of monetary impulses are thus converted by the variation of relative prices, or interest rates, into increased or reduced production, and subsequent revisions in supply prices of current output.[15]

Further, while interest rates serve to facilitate real and financial asset adjustments, "the impact of changes in money on any specific interest rate is both too brief and too weak to be either captured statistically or identified as a strategic variable in the transmission process."[16] Therefore, the Monetarists view the *money supply as the strategic variable*, affecting income directly. This view may be represented schematically as:

$$OMO \rightarrow M \rightarrow SPENDING \rightarrow GNP.$$

A comparison of this description with the generalized neo-Keynesian portfolio adjustment process, as illustrated by the FRB–MIT model, focuses on two crucial points at issue: the range of assets involved in the adjustment process and the response patterns of interest rates and prices. Concerning the former, Friedman argues that the spectrum of assets and rates of return influenced by monetary action is extremely broad, including many implicit rates, which are not recorded.[17]

[14]Milton Friedman, "The Role of Monetary Policy," *American Economic Review*, 58 (March 1968), 12.

[15]Karl Brunner, "The Role of Money and Monetary Policy," *Review*, Federal Reserve Bank of St. Louis, 50 (July 1969), 18.

[16]W. E. Gibson and G. C. Kaufman, "The Relative Impact of Money and Income on Interest Rates: An Empirical Investigation," *Staff Economic Studies* (Washington, D.C.: Board of Governors of the Federal Reserve System, 1966), 3.

[17]Friedman, *Occasional Paper No. 33*, 25.

Friedman further argues that recorded rates do not reflect the real cost of capital but rather include anticipated rates of inflation. Moreover, monetary policy may be routed through as yet undiscovered channels. In short, the transmission process is too complicated to be captured by statistical models. The standard practice of using recorded interest rates both underestimates the full impact of monetary actions and narrows the scope of the transmission process to only a relatively few channels. Therefore, Friedman concludes, even the most complex econometric model cannot adequately represent the monetary process.[18]

Monetarists also question the response patterns of interest rates and prices in neo-Keynesian models. They regard the fall in interest rates in response to monetary expansion as a temporary effect. In a longer view, monetary expansion, whether via interest rate effects or direct spending effects, causes rising income and expenditures. The Monetarists are careful to distinguish nominal from real changes. When the economy is operating below the full-employment level, changes in nominal money may significantly affect real economic variables—output and employment—rather than rising prices. As the economy approaches full employment, however, quantities become less responsive, and prices begin to rise. The real value of money balances grows more slowly, or declines, causing a reversal of the initial interest rate effect.[19] Thus, changes in interest rates may be only a result of the adjustment process, rather than a crucial link; and may be directly, rather than inversely, related to changes in money.

Prices, in this process, are a function of "demand pressure"—determined by how close to full employment the economy is operating. In addition, an accumulation of price changes over time tends to generate "price expectations," which serve as a separate influence in future price movements. Thus, the long-run insensitivity of real variables to changes in the money supply and the predominant short-run influence of money on real output and employment are consistent.

[18]Yung C. Park, "Some Current Issues on the Transmission Process of Monetary Policy," *IMF Staff Papers*, 19 (March 1972), 24–26.

[19]For similar, but more detailed, expositions see Friedman, "The Role of Monetary Policy," *American Economic Review*, 58 (March 1968), 6; and David I. Fand, "A Monetarist Model of the Monetary Process," *Journal of Finance*, 25 (May 1970), 279–283.

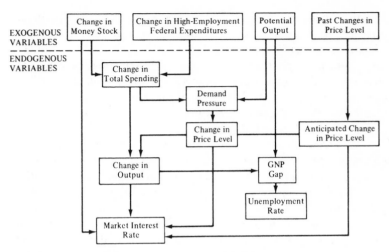

Exhibit 4. Flow diagram of the St. Louis Model.

Source: Leonall G. Andersen and Keith M. Carlson, "A Monetarist Model for Economic Stabilization," *Review,* Federal Reserve Bank of St. Louis, 52 (April 1970), 10.

The St. Louis Model

The process described above has recently been incorporated into an econometric model by the Federal Reserve Bank of St. Louis.[20] The model makes no attempt to specify the structure of the economy; rather, it explains such broad measures as total spending, prices, and unemployment in terms of changes in money, Government expenditures, potential output, and price expectations.

The process by which monetary action predominates short-run changes in total spending can be seen by tracing through the flow chart, Exhibit 4. The responses in the actual model accumulate over a number of periods, but no lags except price changes appear in the chart. Total spending, measured by GNP, responds more strongly to money supply changes than to changes in the full-employment budget. The latter actually has a negative impact after three quarters, reflecting the Monetarists' "crowding-out" hypothesis.

Potential output is determined by underlying factors such as

[20]For a more detailed development, see Andersen and Carlson, *op. cit.,* 8–11.

growth of natural resources, technology, labor force, and productive capacity. Total spending and potential output together determine the amount of "demand pressure" existing in the economy in the short run. Demand pressure, a measure of short-run market conditions, combines with long-run price expectations to determine the current change in the price level. Price expectations, measured by a five-quarter weighted average of past price level changes, enter price determination as a separate influence.

The model thus determines changes in total spending and prices separately. Short-run changes in real output are then calculated as a residual by subtracting the price factor from changes in total spending.

Changes in output are subtracted from changes in potential output to determine the GNP gap, a measure of productive slack in the economy. The unemployment rate is directly related to current and past levels of the GNP gap. Changes in output combine with changes in money supply, current and past changes in price levels, and price expectations to determine the level of interest rates. Market interest rates are a result of market interaction, not a crucial link in the transmission process as in the Keynesian view.

In sum, the St. Louis model is a direct formulation of the Monetarist view that monetary changes predominate short-run changes in the real economy, while in the long run money affects only nominal quantities. The model also reflects the contention that the full transmission mechanism cannot be captured by econometric models. The stable relationship found between money and total spending becomes the basis for a small, simple model that explains changes in broad economic aggregates in terms of changes in the money supply.

Summary

This article has examined the econometric implications of two alternative theories of the monetary process. Both the neo-Keynesians and the Monetarists see a general portfolio balance mechanism at work in the economy, but agreement seems to stop there. Their divergent views concerning the importance of interest rates, the direction of effect of money on interest rates, the nature of price determination, and the feasibility of representing the adjustment process econometrically have been discussed above.

Although the two models presented here are representative of current thinking, some preliminary movement toward synthesis is evident. Recent analytical work has introduced prices into Keynesian models as endogenous variables.[21] Later unpublished versions of the FRB-MIT model are structured so that either the money supply or reserves may be used as a policy variable.[22] Recent unpublished Monetarist work specifies structural detail more than in the past.[23] The problem of implicit interest rates remains unresolved. The resolution of this problem and the thrust of current research point in the direction of larger, more detailed econometric models.

[21]Arthur Benavie, "Prices and Wages in the Complete Keynesian Model," *Southern Economic Journal*, 38 (April 1972), 468–477; Teigen, *op. cit.*, 15 and footnote 27.

[22]"FRB-MIT-PENN Econometric Model," unpublished staff paper, Federal Reserve Board of Governors, July 13, 1971.

[23]Leonall C. Andersen, "Influence of Monetary and Financial Actions in a Financially Constrained Economy," unpublished paper, May 1971, 40.

Subject Index

Author Index

〵−〵